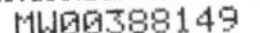

COM+ Programming from the Ground Up

Mark Michaelis

Osborne/**McGraw-Hill**

Berkeley New York St. Louis San Francisco
Auckland Bogotá Hamburg London Madrid
Mexico City Milan Montreal New Delhi Panama City
Paris São Paulo Singapore Sydney
Tokyo Toronto

Osborne/**McGraw-Hill**
2600 Tenth Street
Berkeley, California 94710
U.S.A.

For information on translations or book distributors outside the U.S.A., or to arrange bulk purchase discounts for sales promotions, premiums, or fund-raisers, please contact Osborne/**McGraw-Hill** at the above address.

COM+ Programming from the Ground Up

1234567890 AGM AGM 019876543210

ISBN 0-07-212045-2

Publisher
Brandon A. Nordin

Vice President and Associate Publisher
Scott Rogers

Acquisitions Editor
Wendy Rinaldi

Associate Acquisitions Editor
Ann Sellers

Project Editors
Madhu Prasher and Lisa Theobald

Acquisitions Coordinator
Monika Faltiss

Technical Editor
Paul Garland

Contributing Writers
Steve Yolleck and Philip Spokas

Copy Editor
Judith Brown

Proofreader
Simon Rossoff

Indexer
Valerie Robbins

Computer Designers
Roberta Steele and Dick Schwartz

Illustrator
Michael Mueller

Series Design
Peter Hancik

Cover Design
Greg Scott

This book was composed with Corel VENTURA™ Publisher.

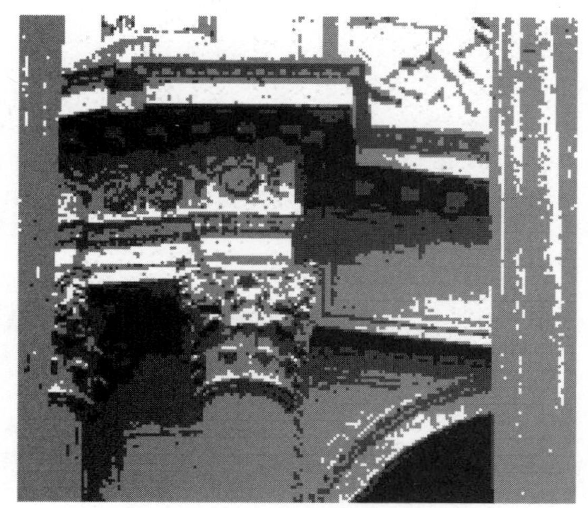

Contents

About the Author ...

Mark Michaelis lives in Glen Ellyn, Illinois. He is a senior software engineer at Real World Technology, which specializes in software for the manufacturing industry. He holds a BA in philosophy from the University of Illinois and has a Masters of Computer Science from the Illinois Institute of Technology. Mark also is Microsoft Certified Solution Developer (MCSD) certified. When not bonding with his computer, Mark enjoys traveling the globe and has a particular affection for Africa. Mark is actively involved with his church, is an enthusiastic amateur musician, and loves the outdoors. As a Microsoft MVP, Mark can often be found lurking at the Microsoft.public newsgroups—particularly the COM and ATL groups. He can be contacted at mark@michaelis.net.

About the Editor ...

Herbert Schildt is a leading authority on C and C++ and was a member of the ANSI/ISO committees that standardized C and C++. His programming books have sold more than 2.5 million copies worldwide and have been translated into all major foreign languages. He is the author of numerous bestsellers, including *C: The Complete Reference*, *C++: The Complete Reference*, *C++ Programming from the Ground Up*, *Windows 2000 Programming from the Ground Up*, and *Java 2: The Complete Reference*. Herb holds a master's degree in computer science from the University of Illinois.

Foreword by Herbert Schildt

For years I have tried to find the time to write a book about COM programming. Having written extensively about C, C++, Java, and Windows, a book on COM always seemed like the logical next step. Unfortunately, my busy writing schedule never did clear sufficiently for me to write that book. But things have a way of working out in the end. With the advent of COM+, the latest version of COM, I have been able to team up with a real COM expert: Mark Michaelis.

One of the joys that I have in life is helping new authors get started. I first met Mark when I was editing another Osborne book: *C/C++ Programming Annotated Archives*, to which Mark contributed a chapter. Because of our work together on that project I learned of Mark's expertise in COM. One thing led to another, and after a bit of coaxing on my part, I convinced him to write a book about COM+.

Mark and I worked together as author and editor. Mark wrote the majority of the book. I edited it, offering tips, suggestions, and a paragraph or two here and there. But the credit goes to Mark. It is his central vision and expertise that are reflected herein.

One thing that I think you will like most about this book is the depth of its coverage. Not content to settle for standard descriptions and stock explanations, Mark dug deep into header files, obscure example code, and lengthy technical notes to see what is really going on. Because of Mark's hard-driving approach, you will find tips and techniques in this book that you won't get elsewhere. So, in addition to covering all the fundamentals and essentials, Mark has gone the extra distance, putting that additional knowledge and insight into this book. I am sure that you will be pleased with the result.

Herbert Schildt

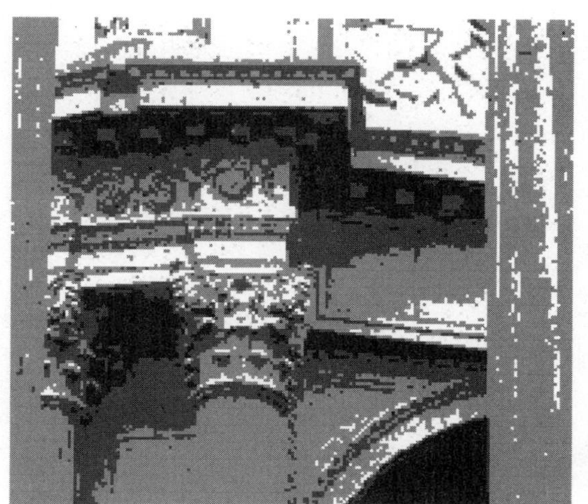

Acknowledgments

Special thanks go to SteveYolleck and Philip Spokas for their contributions to this work. Steve wrote the initial draft of Chapter 11, which covers ActiveX controls. In this chapter he explains the majority of the code and serves as the ActiveX expert for the book.

Philip contributed major portions of the COM+ material found in Chapters 14 and 15. He also programmed substantial parts of the final COM+ system and served as a valuable resource, especially in regard to COM+ transactions.

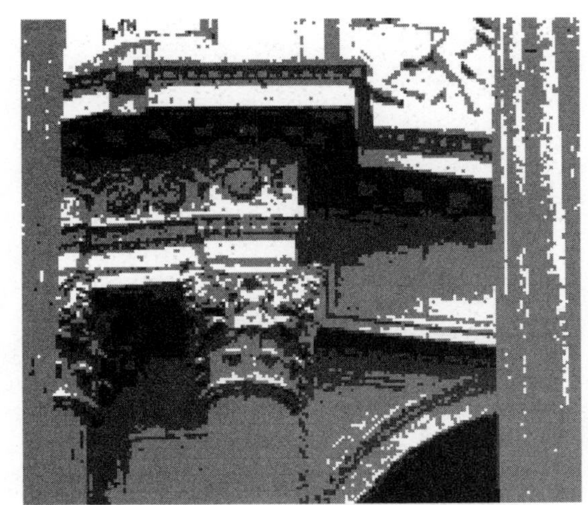

Introduction

COM+ is the latest version of Microsoft's COM technology. It is the union of COM, Microsoft Transaction Server, and several new services. As most readers will know, COM stands for Component Object Model. As described inside, COM defines a standard way of building software components. The "+" part enhances and streamlines the process. While the preceding description of COM+ is accurate, it does not capture the magnitude of the impact that COM+ is having on computing.

COM+ is important because it is driving forward the software component revolution, which is reshaping the way programs are written. No longer are programs bound by the traditional, monolithic model in which all functionality is contained within one file and is fixed at compile time. Instead, a component-based architecture uses free-standing components that can be used as needed, changed if necessary, and enhanced when possible, all without altering the core application code. Software components provide a flexible, resilient, yet manageable way of organizing large software systems.

It is not an overstatement to say that the software component revolution is redefining the very nature of programs and the way we think of them.

This book assumes no previous knowledge or experience in COM. Thus, it teaches COM+ programming "from the ground up." It starts by introducing the essential concepts behind COM, such as interfaces, vtables, and **IUnknown**. It then advances step-by-step through all of the COM fundamentals, including the interface definition language, events, smart pointers, connection points, and use of the Active Template Library. The book concludes by examining new COM features added by COM+, such as Component Services, transactions, and queued components. By the time you finish this book, you will have a solid, well-rounded understanding of COM+.

Programming Skills You Must Have

Make no mistake about it, by any measure COM+ is a challenging topic. You must already be an experienced C++ programmer with a firm understanding of such things as virtual functions, templates, and abstract classes. You must also know how to program Windows and be able to handle its central concepts, such as message loops, callback functions, and threading. Frankly, to fully master COM+ will require the use of all your programming skills. Although challenging, COM+ is also one of the most important disciplines that a professional programmer can master. You will be rewarded several times over for your efforts.

Software You Will Need

To try all the examples in this book you will need Windows 2000 and a modern, Windows-based C++ compiler. Most of the early examples in the book will also work with Windows 98 and Windows NT 4, but the COM+-specific ones (Chapters 14 and 15) require Windows 2000. The compiler used to test the examples in this book was Visual C++ 6.0 with Service Pack 3.

Don't Forget: Code on the Web

Remember, the source code for all of the programs in this book is available free of charge on the Web at **http://www.osborne.com**. Downloading this code saves you the work of typing in the examples.

Special Thanks

No book can be published by the author alone, and many people participated in making the publication of this one possible.

In addition to reading each chapter and checking for technical accuracy, Paul Garland, the technical editor, spent many hours compiling and testing the code to make sure that it was correct. Judith Brown provided copyedit assistance, which is a role I admire, as it is something I not only don't have expertise in, but even lack the patience to try. This is the second time I have worked with Madhu Prasher, who masterfully coordinated routing the manuscript to the appropriate places. Along with Lisa Theobald and Monika Faltiss, Madhu handled the multitude of details involved with publishing a book. Thanks to each of them.

Aside from my family, I most of all want to thank Ann Sellers and Herb Schildt. They each provided valuable encouragement throughout the project and were the ones who were most involved in the day-to-day decisions about the content and schedule of the book. They both believed in me and my abilities. Herb's expertise was obviously indispensable as he transformed rough technical notes into the appropriate format for a book. Thank you!

Real World Technology, the company I work for, has been extremely gracious in allowing me to take time off to write this book. This often occurred during extremely hectic release schedules, resulting in other team members working even longer hours than usual. I am especially grateful to Philip Spokas, as he bore the brunt of the additional stress and went out of his way to help relieve me of my workload. Others, such as Jeff Piell, Vlad Vayngart, and John Michaelis, also assisted in reading through some of the early chapters. Thanks so much.

Lastly, I am greatly indebted to my wife, Elisabeth, for supporting me throughout this project. She was pregnant with our son Benjamin while I was writing most of the book, and her ability to cope with all the transitions during the past year without help from me was truly tremendous. I know this became especially difficult as each deadline was missed, but she continued to do all she could to enable me to write. She made many sacrifices in order to allow me to finish. It is a wonderful blessing to be married to such an amazing woman.

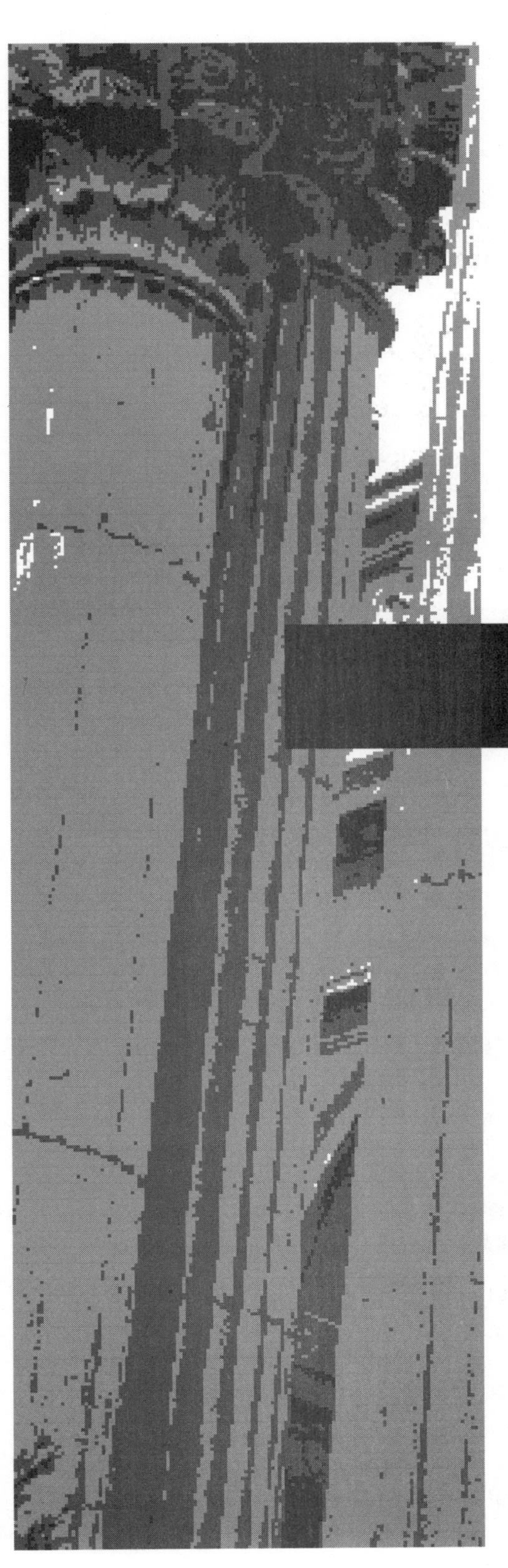

CHAPTER 1

Introducing COM+

COM+ is the latest version of Microsoft's COM system. COM stands for *Component Object Model*, which defines a set of rules that you must follow in order to build a component. The + signifies the addition of several new features and services that improve and, in some cases, simplify certain COM-related tasks. In the very near future, to be a professional programmer will imply the ability to write COM-compliant software components. Programmers without the ability to handle COM will be left behind. To put it bluntly, COM is in nearly every programmer's future.

This book is first and foremost a practical guide to COM+ programming. As such, it will not spend an inordinate amount of space on the theoretical aspects of COM+ except as they relate directly to programming. Our goal is to provide a hands-on approach that will have you utilizing the power of COM+ as soon as possible. That said, to effectively use COM+ to create software components requires that you understand the forces that drove its creation, its basic design philosophy, and several foundational concepts. You will also need to be familiar with several new terms and elements.

Since COM+ *is* COM, unless we are referring specifically to a feature unique to COM+, we will simply use the term COM throughout this book.

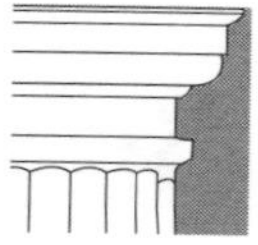

NOTE: This book assumes that you are fluent in C++ and have written Windows programs. If you are weak in either of these areas, you will need to fortify your skills before you can advance to COM+ programming.

The Component Revolution

We, the programmers of the world, are in the midst of a revolution that is changing the way programs are written. This is a strong statement but one that is not altogether rare in the software profession because we have already lived through many "revolutions." For example, the C language replaced FORTRAN, C++ catalyzed the move to object-oriented programming, and Java energized the Web. But the revolution at hand is especially significant because it is reshaping in fundamental ways the structure and architecture of programs. Furthermore, these changes affect a broad spectrum of applications and are changing the computing landscape itself. The revolution to which we refer is the move to *component software*. It can be stated with certainty that the component software revolution will produce profound and lasting effects.

Before beginning our examination of COM, it is helpful to understand in a general way why software components are important and how they change the architecture of a program. As you will see, components are not just another way to program; they are a better way to program.

Two Goals

The component revolution seeks to attain two of programming's most elemental goals:

- To manage increasingly complex programs
- To reuse code

Let's examine each of these goals.

Program Complexity

Complexity is the single greatest challenge faced by programmers. Beginners learn early in their programming careers that the longer the program, the longer the debugging time. As program size grows, so usually does its complexity, and there is a limit to the amount of complexity we, as humans, can manage. From a purely combinatoric standpoint, the more individual lines of code there are, the greater the chance for side effects and unwanted interactions. As most programmers today know, programs are growing exceedingly complex.

Software components help us manage complexity by allowing us to "divide and conquer." By applying component techniques, we can reduce an application to constituent parts. Each part can be coded and maintained separately, as an independent unit. It is also possible to use off-the-shelf components provided by third parties. By compartmentalizing units of functionality into autonomous resources, the programmer can reduce the complexity of a large program.

Reusable Code

From the dawn of computing, programmers have sought the ability to reuse their code. Since development and debugging is a costly process, code reuse is highly desirable. In the early days, code reuse was achieved by cuttingand pasting source code from one program to another, and, of course, this approach is still used today. One advance took the form of reusable function libraries, such as those provided by C. This was soon followed by standardized class libraries, such as those specified by C++.

Software components take code reuse a giant leap forward because they allow self-contained, binary modules to be created by independent developers. But unlike class or function libraries, which are compile-time modules, components are "plugged into" applications at runtime. Furthermore, any application that needs such a component can use it. Thus, once a component has been written, it can be used by an unlimited number of applications.

Software components extend reuse in another way. A component can be written in any computer language that supports the creation of components. It can then be used by any application that is component enabled, no matter what language was used to create that application. Thus, code created in one language can be used by a program written in another language. This enables an application to consist of several independent modules, each created using the most appropriate tool.

The Monolith vs. the Component Model

The architecture of a component-based application is fundamentally different from that of a traditional, monolithic program. To understand the differences, let's compare the same application as implemented by each approach.

The Monolith Model

To begin, imagine that you work for a software company as a product manager in charge of developing software for the manufacturing industry. The software is to run on computers that sit on the shop floor and track the production of a large variety of products, from airplanes to bottle caps. The application must also track engineering diagrams that describe how to perform a particular step in creating a part. The software will store information regarding production resources so that improvements can be made in the manufacturing process and will interface with business systems that have the orders for the parts that need to be produced. In addition, your system will interact with the machinery on the shop floor, starting and stopping it and responding to various events such as bottlenecks or breakdowns.

The traditional way to write this manufacturing software would be to create one large monolithic application. This application would consist of several thousand lines of code and require a large team of in-house programmers to maintain it. It would be developed in one language, such as C++. Even if certain aspects of the application could be more conveniently coded in another language, you would be reluctant to do so because of the problems associated with mixing two or more different languages.

The monolithic solution provides fixed functionality. In other words, there are few possibilities for customization for or by each customer. If customers dislike a particular part of the system, they will have to request a change and hope that the suggestion is implemented in the next version. Each different manufacturer will require a custom implementation. Every new customer will spawn a new development cycle. Upgrades in the field are difficult because the application comprises a single large executable file. The monolithic approach also prevents (or severely restricts) third-party add-ons or enhancements. Because all of the code is contained in the monolith, it is difficult to attach new functionality to the compiled code.

The Component Model

Now consider the same manufacturing system as implemented using software components. A component-based solution is designed around a set of free-standing components that provide the required functionality. For example, the portion of code that controls some piece of equipment on the shop floor (such as a packing machine) becomes an independent component. The core application communicates with that component in a well-defined, immutable manner. The component-based approach offers several advantages. First, the complexity of the entire application is reduced. Complexity tends to increase exponentially rather than linearly with respect to the amount of code within any one module. Developers using the monolithic approach must have intimate knowledge of not only their own code, but also all the code with which they wish to interact. In the monolithic approach, a small change in one part of the code could have significant side effects in other parts. When using the component-based approach, each module is independent. Thus, each programmer need manage the complexity of only the component on which he or she is working. Since each component is independent, the internals of one have no effect on the internals of another. Through divide-and-conquer techniques, the complexity of the application is reduced.

Because each component is independent, it is possible to write a component in whatever language seems appropriate. As long as the components maintain binary compatibility, the language is irrelevant. This enables each developer to use the best tool for the job.

The component-based approach provides a convenient way to customize or add functionality to the application. For example, if the user replaces one type of labeling machine with another, it is an easy matter to substitute the labeling component that handles the new machine. As long as the new component is "plug compatible" with the old component, the new component can provide whatever additional functionality is required. Furthermore, the new labeling component need not be supplied by the developer of the application. It can be supplied by the company that produced the new labeling machine, for example, or any other third party. Thus, the functionality of the application can be altered or expanded in ways unanticipated by the developer.

The Creation of COM

In the late 1980s and early 1990s Microsoft was bumping up against the limits of the monolithic model. For them, the system was Microsoft Office. They wanted to be able to have documents of one type, such as Microsoft Excel spreadsheets, embedded into documents of a second type, such as Microsoft Word documents. It was not satisfactory, however, to simply display the spreadsheet within the word processing document. In addition, they wanted to expose all the functionality of the spreadsheet from inside the word processing document as though it were built into the word processor. To address this problem, in 1991, Microsoft developed and released to the public a technology called *Object Linking and Embedding* (OLE). OLE was created to allow a document of one type to be linked or embedded into a document of a second type. The underlying technology used for OLE 1.0 was *Dynamic Data Exchange* (DDE), and although it worked, it was extremely complicated. Faced with these complications, Microsoft took a quantum leap forward when it created OLE 2. The single most important new feature of OLE 2 was the definition of the Component Object Model. Microsoft used COM to replace the DDE architecture of OLE.

By 1995, it was clear that COM, rather than OLE, was the key technology. OLE was just a small subset of the possible uses for COM. The result was a switch in focus from OLE, which allowed two different document types to communicate, to COM, which allowed any COM module to communicate with any other COM module. This became the solution for both the Microsoft Office dilemma and for other system developers who wanted to write complex systems consisting of many binary modules.

At first, many programmers were slow to embrace COM because it was new and seemed complicated. This, of course, changed because the power of COM was too significant to ignore. As you will see as you advance through this book, COM is not hard to use, and modern programming tools make it even easier.

What Is COM?

As stated at the start of this chapter, the Component Object Model defines a set of rules that you must follow when building a component. Thus, COM is not a specific type of application but a generalized model that you can use to build components for any type of application. Both ActiveX and OLE *use* COM, for example, but neither *is* COM.

COM defines a standard way of building components.

COM is important because it defines a *standard way* of building components. This is a key point and one that warrants some elaboration. In theory, anyone can define a component architecture. The trouble is that one person's approach would differ from the next person's, and their components would be incompatible. Software components are valuable only when we agree to use the same specification. Doing so enables one programmer's component to be used by a second programmer. As long as both programmers are following the same standard, their components will work together.

COM specifies a binary standard.

Perhaps the single most important feature of COM is that it specifies a *binary standard*. That is, it defines what a component will look like in its compiled form. COM does not dictate how the source code to a component is written. It specifies only the layout of the binary object. This makes COM a powerful, yet flexible component architecture.

COM defines an object-oriented way to create components. This is not surprising since COM stands for Component *Object* Model. While COM objects are somewhat different from the C++-style objects with which you are familiar, COM objects do adhere to the major tenets of OOP.

COM Attributes

The following attributes characterize the Component Object Model:

- Object-oriented programming
- Loose coupling
- Stable version transitioning
- Location transparency
- Language neutrality

Each is examined in turn.

Object-Oriented Programming

COM supports the three principles of object-oriented programming: encapsulation, polymorphism, and inheritance.

For the same reasons that encapsulation is important to object-oriented programming, it is important to COM components: It provides a way to bind together code and data, keeping both safe from outside interference or misuse.

Through encapsulation, the user of a component need know only how to interact with the component, not how it works. It is not necessary for the user of a component to know the format and layout of the data within the component and its algorithms. Nor is it important for the user to know in what language the module was written. Only the proper method of interfacing with the component needs to be understood.

Polymorphism, which is characterized by the phrase "one interface, multiple methods," is the attribute that allows one interface to control access to a general class of actions. As it applies to COM, polymorphism is the attribute that enables programmers to describe the general nature of some component while allowing each developer the freedom to implement the component as he or she sees fit. Thus, you can specify *what* a component does but let others decide *how* it does it.

Inheritance is the property that allows one component to inherit the capabilities of another. As you will see, COM supports inheritance a little differently than C++. This requires a slight paradigm shift on the part of the developer, but nevertheless, inheritance plays a pivotal role in the way COM works.

Loose Coupling

Each component is *loosely coupled*. This allows one component to be replaced by another at will. For example, if the compression component from one vendor proves insufficient, you want the flexibility to switch to another vendor with minimal impact on your application. As long as the new compression component is accessed in the same way as the original (that is, if it continues to support the same binary standard), then it can be substituted for the original.

Stable Version Transitioning

As components are upgraded from one version to the next, previously existing modules that interact with the new components should not break. This allows for the upgrade of each component without breaking existing applications that use the component. This is especially important considering that users of your software may install other applications on their systems, and these applications may supply versions of certain components that are newer than those used by your application. With COM, *version transitioning* is stable, allowing a smooth transition from one release to the next.

Location Transparency

Location transparency is another key COM attribute. Moving components from one computer to another merely involves reconfiguration, not a large development project. This provides the flexibility to distribute the load in a networked environment. Location transparency also applies to the context within which the component runs. It is possible for the component to run within the same process as your application or within a separate process.

IN DEPTH

Why Traditional DLLs Are Insufficient as a Component Model

It may have occurred to you that several aspects of COM are also attributes of a traditional Dynamic Link Library (DLL). For example, the DLL is also a binary standard, and it provides for a limited form of encapsulation. These similarities naturally give rise to the following question: Why can't DLLs be the model for software components? The problem is that the specification for a DLL does not address certain key concerns. For example, when using a compression module from a third party, where does the responsibility for allocating memory lie? If a pointer of the compression module is passed to another module, who is responsible for unloading the module, and how would he or she know when it was safe to unload it? Furthermore, which mechanism ensures that the interface supplied by one compression module matches that of another? A traditional DLL cannot answer these questions. There needs to be a standard that determines precisely what it means to be a component and how those components interact. This is, of course, the purpose of COM.

One last point: Although traditional DLLs by themselves are insufficient to fully specify a component standard, they are used to support COM. For example, often a COM component will be stored in a DLL. Therefore, DLLs are convenient for delivering COM components, as they provide the binding and loading mechanisms. With the addition of COM to the DLL, the drawbacks to the plain DLL mechanism are removed.

Language Neutrality

Because COM defines a binary standard, COM is *language neutral*. In other words, the computer language in which a component is written is not significant. For example, the fact that a compression component is developed in C++ by one vendor and in assembler by another does not prevent you from switching from one vendor to the second and back again. In addition, within your own application you can use different languages for different components. If it is easier to develop the user interface in Visual Basic and the machine communication module in C++, then do so. As it relates to COM, this is not a problem.

Component Objects

A component object is any binary object that complies with the COM standard.

Until now we have used the word "component" rather loosely to mean some type of "binary blob." Now is the time to define it precisely. In the context of COM, these binary blobs are called COM component objects or simply component objects. A *component object* is any binary object that supports the COM standard and provides a COM service. By definition a component object must support methods that enable it to be referenced by other COM objects and to destroy itself when all references are removed. Throughout the rest of the book the term *component* means a component object, unless stated otherwise.

Servers and Clients

A server is a component that supplies a service.

A client is an object that uses a server.

There are two sides to the COM equation: the *COM server* and the *COM client*. The server is a component that supplies a service to a client. Thus, the client uses the server to perform some task. In Figure 1-1 the server is implemented by the **FCAComp** component and is used by the **Email.exe** document.

Imagine that you have created the Fantabulous Compression Algorithm (FCA). This algorithm can compress files up to 200 percent, even if some other algorithm has already compressed them! To make your algorithm available to others, you compile it into a COM server. This exposes the functionality of the algorithm to others so that they can take advantage of the FCA. The applications written by your customers are COM clients. For example, as shown in Figure 1-1, an e-mail program can call your component in order to compress files before sending them over the Internet.

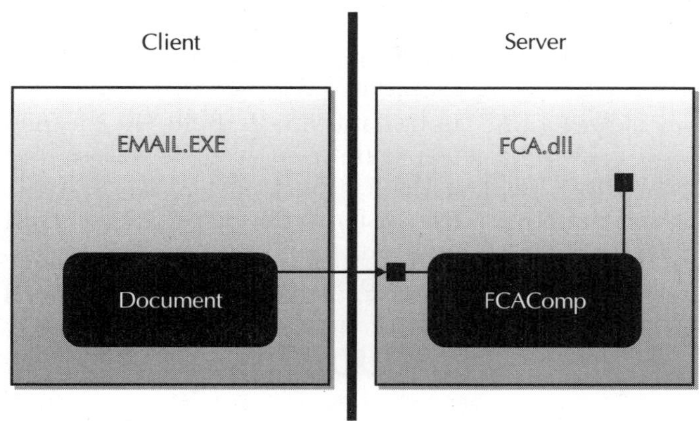

COM client attached to a COM server
Figure 1-1.

Although Figure 1-1 shows the client as an executable and the server as a DLL, both can be implemented as either DLLs or executables. When a component is implemented as a DLL, it is an *in-process server*. This means that it executes in the same process as its client. When it is compiled as an EXE, it is an *out-of-process server*, which means that it runs in a process separate from the client. Both types have their advantages and uses, which are discussed later in this book. For now it doesn't matter what form a component takes.

It is important to understand that a COM server can also act as a client when it uses the services of another component. The distinction between client and server is primarily one of "who is using whom" at that moment.

How COM Works: Interfaces and Vtables

Clients and servers communicate with each other through *interfaces*. It is through one or more interfaces that a component exposes its functionality to a client. It is not possible for a COM client to see the component object itself. Instead, only an interface can be viewed. Interfaces are the essence of COM. In fact, the COM standard is a description of standard interfaces and the protocols required to use them. In a component, an interface is implemented as a virtual function table, or *vtable*, for short. Since these two items are critical to understanding COM, we will examine them in detail.

Interfaces

An interface exposes the functionality of a component.

A COM interface defines the functionality of a component object. It is a description of the services that an object will provide and the mechanism by which a client learns the capabilities of a server. The interface defines a contract between the client and the server. Both must abide by its provisions in order for the client to utilize the server.

A CoClass is a class that supports a component object.

When implementing an interface in C++, you will normally use a class. In the language of COM, such a class is called a component class or *CoClass*. Thus, a CoClass is a class that implements the functions of a COM object and supports one or more COM interfaces.

COM interfaces are analogous to interfaces found in the real world. Consider the simple type of power supply that replaces batteries for various electronic appliances, such as a portable CD player. This power supply comes with a plug. Any device that has a socket that will fit that plug can be powered by the supply. The interaction between the power supply and the electronic appliance is analogous to that of a COM server and its client. The power supply is the server, and it comes equipped with a standard plug (interface). The electronic gadget is the client, and as long as it has the appropriate socket, the components can be connected. Once the connection is established, communication (in the form of electricity) can occur.

Earlier we defined a COM component as a binary object that supports the COM standard. Again consider the FCA component shown in Figure 1-1. It has one component that is designed to expose the FCA compression algorithm. The easiest way to make this function available is to expose a **Compress( )** function. The implementation of this function is defined within the CoClass **FCAComp**. The problem is that we cannot expose a CoClass directly to a COM client. Remember, COM defines a binary standard for components—not a source code standard. The only way to expose a function via COM is through an interface.

An interface is similar to a C++ abstract base class.

To define an interface, you must specify the functions that make up the interface. This includes the function names, return types, and parameters. In C++ terminology, an interface is similar to an abstract base class. In the language of COM, functions are often called *methods*, and we will use both terms in this book. An interface does not expose data, however. All data is accessed through the methods defined by the interface. In the language of COM, a data element that is of interest to users of a component object is called a *property*.

1

A component can support more than one interface. In fact, all useful components will implement at least two interfaces. Multiple interfaces can be used to add functionality or to provide a graceful means of transitioning from one version of a component to the next. You will notice that when drawing a component, as in Figure 1-2, small handles emerge from the top and side of the component box. These handles are the interfaces that the component supports.

To publish an interface is to make it publicly available.

Once it has been released to the public (that is, *published*), the interface should not be modified. To understand why interfaces cannot be changed, let's return to the analogy of the power supply. If you made the plug slightly larger or some shape other than round, that power supply would no longer work for the same electronic gadgets as it did before. With this in mind, consider changing the power supply by adding a plug with twice the voltage output as the original. This feature expands the uses to which the power supply can be put, but you need to be careful. An electronic gadget expecting the lower voltage will be damaged if you attach it to the high-voltage plug. This problem, however, does not prevent the enhancement to the power supply. Instead, you must simply use a different sized or shaped plug with which the low-voltage devices are not compatible. With this approach, high-voltage electronic gadgets can use the power supply without the risk of the power supply destroying low-voltage appliances. The lesson here is that once a plug has been defined, its function cannot be changed—at least not without potentially causing harm. Instead, an additional plug is added to support the higher voltage. Thus, the meaning of an existing plug must be immutable, but a new plug can be created.

In the same way that plugs and sockets are immutable, interfaces are fixed. To change a COM interface would render the component incompatible with clients that expected the original interface. Just as in the case of the power supply, if you want to provide new functionality or significantly change the

A component
Figure 1-2.

existing functionality of a component, it is necessary to add a new interface, keeping the existing interface as it is. Clients can be updated to support the new interface, but until that happens, they can continue to use the old interface. Without this discipline, clients using the old interface would fail.

In addition to providing access to functionality, interfaces perform a secondary function: They encapsulate the details of the implementation. Continuing with the power supply analogy, if you wanted to power a portable CD player in your car, you could easily remove the power supply and replace it with an automotive cord that connects into the cigarette lighter. In the case of the wall power supply, the transformer has to convert the AC power into DC power in order to run the CD player. But in the car, this is not necessary because the car electricity is already DC. The details of the electric current are remarkably hidden behind the interface. You do not need to worry about AC versus DC power when plugging in the CD player. Simply finding the correct plug is sufficient to access the correct power source. Here you see what is meant when we describe the functionality of the server as encapsulated behind the interface, hidden from the client. In the same manner, implementation is hidden between COM servers and COM clients.

In COM, there is no contractual unit smaller than an interface.

Interfaces are not unique to a particular component object. Many components can expose the same interface. This is the polymorphic aspect of COM: Any component can provide its own implementation of any interface. However, if a component implements an interface, it must *fully* implement it. As stated, an interface defines a contract between the client and server. Part of the contract requires that a component fully implement any interface it supports. By publishing a particular interface, a component is stating that it will abide by the terms of the interface contract and will expose *all* the functions within that interface. This is important because a client will call a function through an interface, expecting the function to be there. If it is not, trouble will follow. In some cases, it is possible to use placeholder code for the implementation of some function, but in all cases, your component is required to include that function in the interface map for a component. There are no contractual units smaller than an interface. Supporting an interface is an all-or-nothing proposition.

The rule that COM interfaces are immutable and fully implemented fulfills the version-transitioning requirement mentioned earlier. To add functionality to a component it is necessary to define new interfaces. Published interfaces cannot be altered.

1

IN DEPTH

Interface Not Fully Supported?

In COM programming, you will sometimes see a statement to the effect that an "interface is not fully supported." If interfaces always need to be fully supported, then how can this be allowed? The reason for the ambiguity is that sometimes a group of interfaces together is considered an interface. For example, a component may be said to support the OLE/DB interface or ActiveX control interface. Interfaces, therefore, can be combined into a set that makes up a new interface. In this context, the term interface is used to represent a set of individual interfaces, not just one. However, the fundamental rule that COM interfaces must be fully implemented still stands.

COM interface names begin with the letter *I*.

COM defines a large number of standard interfaces. All of the COM standard interfaces have names that begin with *I*. Here are some examples:

IClassFactory	IMalloc	IMoniker	IMarshal	IUnknown

Although you are not required to follow this convention for your own interfaces, most programmers do.

Without question, the most important COM interface is **IUnknown**, because it is the one interface that all components must implement. We will look more closely at **IUnknown** later in this chapter.

Vtables

A vtable is an array of virtual function pointers.

In COM, an interface is structured as a vtable. As mentioned earlier, this is short for virtual function table, and it is simply an array of function pointers that point to the functions that the interface exposes. Vtables are laid out in a standard way so that COM clients can access them. It is the immutability of the vtable layout that enables COM to define a binary standard. As long as a component supports this binary vtable standard, it can operate with other components that also support the standard.

To implement an interface on some object means to build the necessary vtable for that object. A COM vtable is identical to that used in C++ when calling a virtual function. Thus, C++ is fully compatible with COM.

A client never has direct access to the memory or methods of a server. Instead, all access is gained through a pointer to the vtable for the interface. Once a client has a pointer to a component's vtable, it can call methods defined by that component. For example, consider Figure 1-3. Here, the client **Email.exe** calls **Compress( )** via two pointers. The first is the pointer to **FCA**'s vtable. The second is the vtable pointer to **Compress( )** itself. Thus, double indirection is employed when calling any method in a component.

You might ask why clients can't simply call methods directly through their pointers in the client vtable rather than going through a second vtable pointer on the server. The vtable pointer is necessary when the server can be moved into a different process or even onto another computer. This helps fulfill the location transparency requirement. The client does not know in which context the server is actually running.

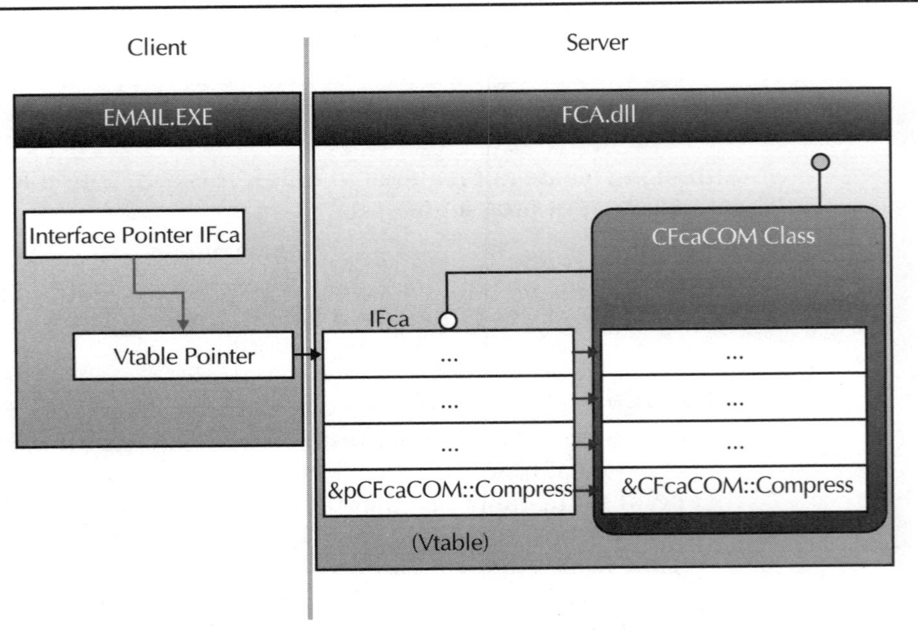

Client-to-vtable pointers

Figure 1-3.

1

IUnknown

IUnknown is the one interface that all components must implement.

The most important interface defined by COM is **IUnknown**. It is the one interface that must be implemented by all COM objects. Notice that whenever a COM object is drawn, it not only shows interfaces emerging from the side, but an interface also appears on the top (see Figure 1-1). This interface is **IUnknown**, and by convention it always appears at the top to indicate that the component is a COM object.

IUnknown defines three methods: **QueryInterface( )**, **AddRef( )**, and **Release( )**. **QueryInterface( )** is the method that your program will call to determine whether a component supports a particular interface. **AddRef( )** and **Release( )** manage reference counting, which is the mechanism that determines when a component is still being used by a client. Let's take a closer look at each of these methods.

QueryInterface( )

QueryInterface( ) performs two important functions. First, it determines whether a component implements a specific interface. Second, if the interface is supported, **QueryInterface( )** returns a pointer to that interface. Therefore, if you want to call a function in some interface, first call **QueryInterface( )** to obtain a pointer to that interface's vtable; then call the function through that pointer. If the interface is not supported, **QueryInterface( )** returns the error code **E_NOINTERFACE**.

Reference Counting with AddRef( ) and Release( )

A component object must keep track of how many objects are referring to it. When there are no references to the component, the component can destroy itself. To implement this successfully, the objects that connect to the component must notify the component that they have a reference to that component and then notify the component when that reference is removed. To achieve this, **IUnknown** defines the **AddRef( )** and **Release( )** methods. When **AddRef( )** is called, the component's reference count is incremented by one. When **Release( )** is called, the reference count is decremented by one. When the reference count reaches zero, the object can destroy itself.

At first glance it may not be clear why reference counting is important, because in the simplest case reference counting is not an issue. In a simple situation, a client creates a component, calls one or more methods on that component, and then deletes the component. Unfortunately, this simple scenario is the exception rather than the rule. Consider this possibility: The COM client instantiates a component, stores a reference to the component, and also passes that reference along to another object. Imagine now that the first object goes out of scope and its destructor is called. Should this first object, which created the component, now destroy it? If it does not destroy the component, who will be responsible for deleting the object, and when should this happen? Reference counting resolves this dilemma because the object itself determines when it can be destroyed.

IUnknown: Root of All COM Interfaces

IUnknown is at the root of all COM interfaces.

IUnknown is at the root of all COM interfaces. If an interface does not derive from **IUnknown**, either directly or indirectly, it is not a COM interface. Interface inheritance should not be understood in the traditional sense of object inheritance, where the implementation is inherited in a subclass along with the function header. Rather, interface inheritance means that the vtable structure for the first part of a derived class is exactly the same as the vtable structure of the base class. Therefore, all interfaces need to begin with the vtable structure defined by **IUnknown**, as shown in Figure 1-4. In this context the base class should be viewed as an abstract class, thereby declaring which functions need to be implemented but not actually implementing them.

In Figure 1-4, **IFca** is derived from **IUnknown**. Therefore, its vtable begins with the set of pointers to the function defined by **IUnknown**. Imagine that **Email** has a pointer to the **IUnknown** interface for a **CFcaCOM** object. In order for it to call **Compress( )**, **Email** would first call **QueryInterface( )** and request the **IFca** interface. Once this was obtained, **Email** would call the **Compress( )** function. If at some point **Email** once again needed a pointer to **IUnknown**, it would call **QueryInterface( )** on the **IFca** interface and request a pointer for **IUnknown**. If a CoClass A supports a set of interfaces {X}, then given any interface in {X}, it is possible to obtain any other interface within {X}. In other words, given interface **IA** in CoClass A, you can retrieve any other interface on CoClass A. The set of interfaces, {X}, supported by CoClass A cannot change at runtime.

1

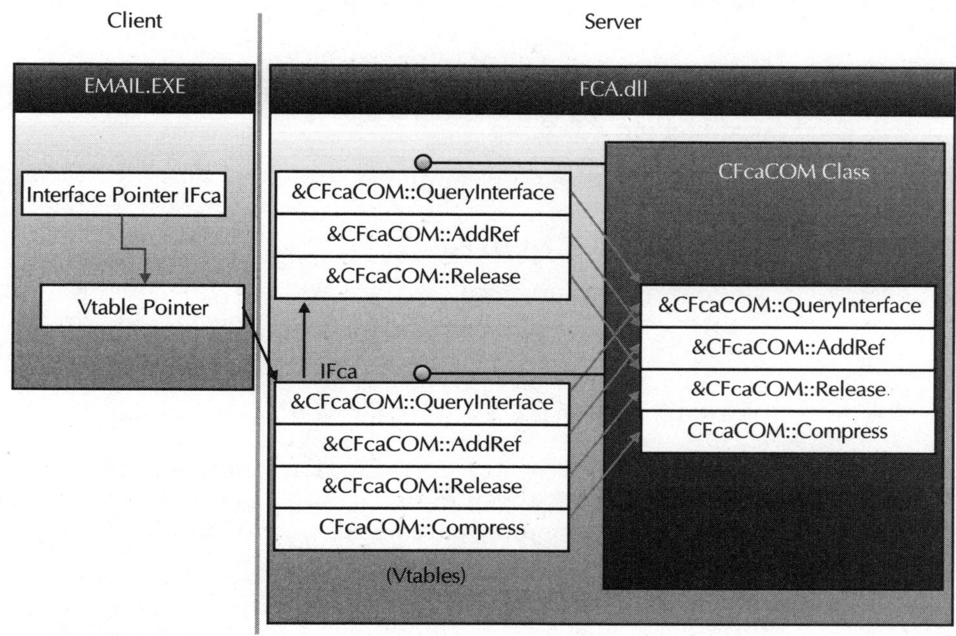

IFca derived from **IUnknown**
Figure 1-4.

The Interface Definition Language and Type Libraries

Interfaces are specified using IDL.

A specific language, called the *Interface Definition Language*, or IDL, has been created to define COM interfaces. It is usually stored in a file with the IDL suffix and is compiled, at least within Visual Studio, by **MIDL.exe** (Microsoft IDL compiler). Be aware that applications created using the Visual C++ MFC Application Wizard will create an ODL (Object Definition Language) file rather than an IDL file. ODL was the precursor to IDL and was compiled by **mktyplib.exe**. Both IDL and ODL files, however, are now supported by the MIDL compiler that generates the type libraries for the component being compiled.

An IDL file compiles into a type library.

An IDL file is compiled into a type library. To expose an interface to clients it is necessary to describe the interface. This description is stored within the type library of the component. The type library is packaged as part of the DLL or executable file that contains the component, or it can be distributed separately in a TLB file.

In the chapters that follow, we will look more closely at IDL and type libraries.

Globally Unique IDs

When programming for COM, you will not use names to refer to components or interfaces. Instead, you will use *globally unique identifiers* (GUIDs). Here is an example:

```
106E7900-1851-11D3-A47F-0000861C844E
```

GUID stands for globally unique identifier.

Other GUIDs will have a similar format, but the numbers will differ. Ugly as they may seem, this is of little consequence when programming because GUIDs are, for the most part, handled automatically by the compiler.

GUIDs are crucial to the interoperability of component objects, allowing them to be used on any system without the possibility of name conflicts. Within one system, such as the manufacturing system discussed at the beginning of the chapter, it is trivial to define a unique user-friendly name for each component within the system. A problem, however, arises when interfacing not only with your own components but also with those created by other vendors. A name conflict is inevitable sooner or later, given the number of components and the ease with which they can be created. For example, if two parties both create a component called **Timer** and you install both **Timer** components onto your system, which one gets invoked when **Timer** is requested? Even on one computer you may create a component called **test**, and then a week later create a new component with the same name. The solution to the ambiguity is to assign globally unique IDs to each of the components.

Name ambiguity is not limited to the components themselves, however. The same ambiguity potentially exists for each interface and each type library. Therefore, these are also assigned GUIDs.

GUIDs are generated using an algorithm created by the Open Systems Foundation's (OSF) Distributed Computing Environment (DCE). Each value generated is a 16-byte (128-bit) universally unique identifier (UUID). UUID was the original term used by the OSF, but since GUID has emerged, the two terms are used interchangeably. The algorithm used to generate the UUID uses the 48-bit network adapter ID and the current date and time within the nearest 100-nanosecond interval starting from midnight on the morning of October 15, 1582. This approach makes the chances of two GUIDs being the same exceedingly low.

The COM API

The Component Object Model is supported by its own API. In the COM API, "Co" prefixes several of the functions. As expected, Co stands for component object. This API is responsible for initializing the COM subsystem, locating and instantiating components, allocating memory, and managing remote procedure calls. Aside from these necessary operations, the COM API stays out of the way. Thus, once the connection between client and server has been established, communication between the two is lightweight (makes minimal use of system resources).

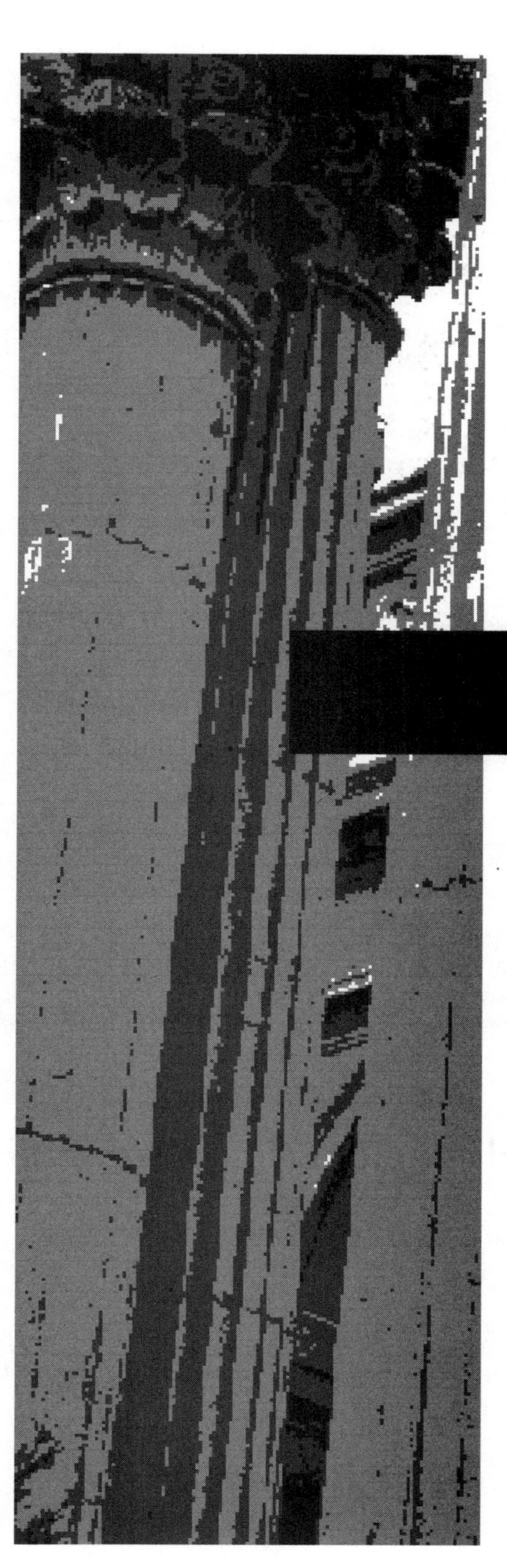

CHAPTER 2

COM Fundamentals: Building a Simple Component and Client

All COM components share a common architecture, or infrastructure as it is sometimes called. In this chapter we will examine the elements that make up this infrastructure. We will do this by developing a COM component and a client that uses that component. The component will implement a "stopwatch" that can be used to time program execution. For example, you can use the stopwatch to find the length of time a function call takes.

Today, many (perhaps most) programmers use a class library, such as the ATL or MFC, when creating COM components. Because of the overhead associated with a typical COM project, the use of these development tools is understandable. In fact, most of the examples in the remainder of this book will use the ATL. However, in this chapter we will develop a COM component using only C++ and the Windows API because it is the approach that most clearly shows the underlying architecture of a COM component.

The COM details are important. Without understanding them, you would find it difficult to debug your code when problems arise. Often COM problems will manifest themselves as program crashes in areas apparently unrelated to COM, and a clear understanding of the COM architecture is essential in helping you locate the bug. A solid knowledge of the details is also required if you want to optimize a component. Finally, fundamental COM skills have become more important with COM+, which adds even greater complexity to the base COM architecture. Frankly, to be a top-notch COM programmer implies a thorough understanding of COM's fundamental building blocks.

Since COM is fully compatible with the C++ language, it is possible to build a COM server and its client using standard C++. Remember, COM does not define a new language but rather a standard by which component sharing can take place regardless of the language. Therefore, you can build a COM solution from the ground up using just C++ and the Windows API, without the use of a specialized template library or tools. In this chapter we will do exactly that.

How We Will Proceed

To clearly illustrate each piece of COM, we will use an incremental approach. We will begin by building a non-COM, C++-style DLL that will be accessed from a client using the standard load library technique. Thus, this first version will not use COM. This initial implementation establishes a starting point that we will slowly transition to full COM compliance. By using this approach, we will start in territory familiar to most C++ programmers and then add each element of COM, one step at a time. The advantage of this approach is that the purpose and effect of each COM feature is readily apparent.

Although several steps will be needed to convert a non-COM DLL into a COM-based component, no single step is difficult to understand. By the time you finish this chapter you will have a thorough understanding of the essential ingredients found in all COM solutions. Here are the steps we will follow in order to build the complete COM solution:

1. Build a traditional C++ Win32 DLL and client (without COM).
2. Add the **IUnknown** interface.
3. Implement **QueryInterface( )**.
4. Manage reference counting.
5. Build a class factory.
6. Use the COM API.

After completing step 6, we will have created a fully COM-compliant component. In the process, the various details, issues, and concepts common to all COM objects will have been discussed.

Remember, this chapter will not use any class libraries, such as the ATL. This way you can have a clear view of the COM infrastructure without being distracted by the additional complexities that these libraries introduce. After you have a firm foundation of the underlying COM architecture, later chapters will investigate how the ATL enhances the architecture.

One other thing: The compilation instructions in this chapter and throughout this book are for Visual C++. This is the compiler that is most commonly used when creating COM objects. If you are using a different compiler, simply generalize to your own environment.

A Traditional Stopwatch Implementation

As stated, we will begin by creating a traditional C++/API implementation of a stopwatch. Remember, this first implementation is not COM compliant. Its purpose is to serve as a starting point, to which we will add the COM functionality. As you look at the code, however, you will notice that various COM conventions are used early on. For example, many functions return the **HRESULT** data type, which is the COM function return type. We will also use COM-like function names. This is not a trick to hide COM underneath the covers but simply a way of putting some conventions in place at the beginning so that fewer changes will be needed as we transition into a fully COM-compliant system. It also helps you to start thinking in terms of COM.

The Initial Stopwatch Design

Figure 2-1 shows an overview of the initial design of the stopwatch component. The stopwatch component is contained in the **Timers.dll** Dynamic Link Library. The client is found in **StopwatchClient.exe**, which will call **LoadLibrary( )** to load **Timers.dll**. In the final COM-based implementation, **LoadLibrary( )** will not be used because COM supplies its own API functions to handle the loading of a component. It is used only by the non-COM implementation. Once loaded, the stopwatch can be used.

The stopwatch is supported by two classes. The first is **IStopwatch**, which is an abstract class. The second is **CStopwatch**, which is a concrete class that implements **IStopwatch**. Although **IStopwatch** does not use the usual *C* prefix naming convention, it is a normal C++ abstract class. The name is prefixed with *I* because this is the convention used by COM for all interfaces, which is what **IStopwatch** is called in COM terminology.

To use the stopwatch, the client will call **DllGetClassObject( )** to create a new stopwatch object. This function returns a pointer to an object of type **IStopwatch**. The **IStopwatch** pointer can then be used by **StopwatchClient.exe** to time a portion of program execution. In the example shown later, the overhead of a function call is timed.

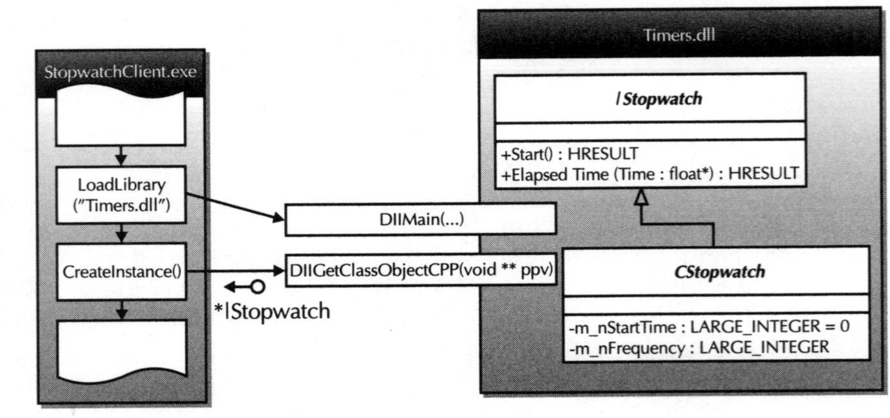

The traditional, non-COM DLL design of the stopwatch and its client
Figure 2-1.

Building the Timers.dll Library

During this first stage we will build the server DLL, **Timers.dll.** This is the module that contains the stopwatch component.

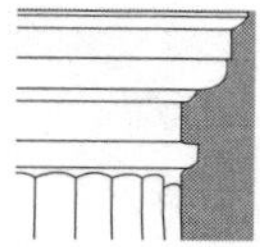

REMEMBER: All the code in this book is available free, online at **www.osborne.com**. Although you can enter the examples by hand, it is easier to use the download code.

Creating a Win32 DLL Project

Use the following steps to create a new Win32 DLL project:

1. From the Visual C++ IDE, select File | New. At the New dialog, select the Projects tab, and then select the Win32 Dynamic-Link Library project, as shown in Figure 2-2.

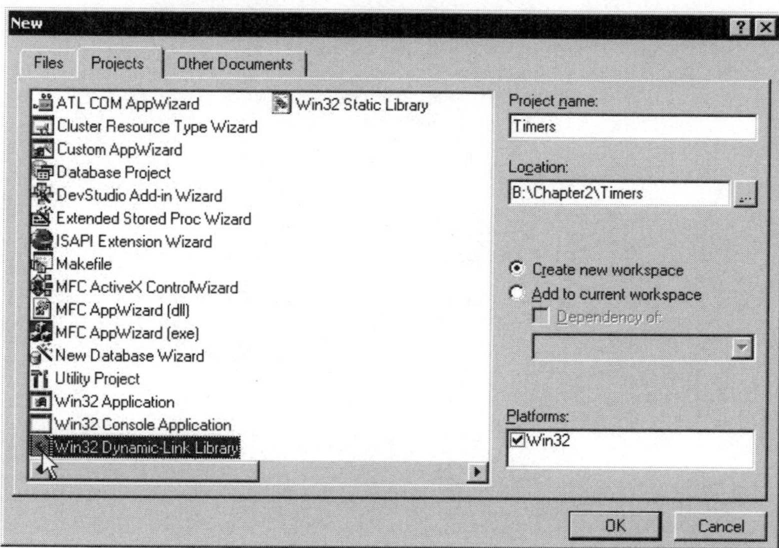

Starting a new DLL project

Figure 2-2.

2. For the name of the project, enter **Timers**, and then enter the name of the directory in which you want to store the project.
3. After clicking the OK button, you will be prompted with an option for what kind of DLL you would like to create. Select An Empty DLL project, and then click Finish.

This will set up an empty project (that is, without any source files) with the options set to compile into a DLL.

Coding the Classes

The next step in the process is to define the **CStopwatch** and **IStopwatch** classes.

1. From the Insert menu, select New Class.
2. For the class name, enter **CStopwatch**, and then click OK.

This will add two new files, **Stopwatch.cpp** and **Stopwatch.h**, to the project. Open **Stopwatch.h** and enter the text shown here:

```
// Stopwatch.h: interface for the CStopwatch class.
//
//////////////////////////////////////////////////////////////////////

#if !defined(STOPWATCH_H)
#define STOPWATCH_H

#if _MSC_VER > 1000
#pragma once
#endif // _MSC_VER > 1000

#include <windows.h>

class IStopwatch
{
public:
  // Utility functions
  virtual unsigned long __stdcall Release() = 0;

  // IStopwatch specific functions
  virtual HRESULT __stdcall Start() = 0;
  virtual HRESULT __stdcall ElapsedTime(float *Time) = 0;
};
```

```
class CStopwatch : public IStopwatch
{
public:
  CStopwatch();
  virtual ~CStopwatch();

private:
  // The frequency of the counter
  // returned by QueryPerformanceCounter()
  LARGE_INTEGER m_nFrequency;

  // The counter value when the start method was last called.
  LARGE_INTEGER m_nStartTime;

public:
  // Utility functions
  unsigned long __stdcall Release();

  // IStopwatch specific functions
  HRESULT __stdcall Start();
  HRESULT __stdcall ElapsedTime(float *Time);

};
#endif // !defined(STOPWATCH_H)
```

Notice near the top of the code that **windows.h** is included. As with most Windows programs, this header (and the subordinate headers that it includes) defines several data types as well as the API functions we will use to make the time measurements. One key COM data type defined by including **windows.h** is **HRESULT**. It is a **typedef** for **LONG**, as shown here:

```
typedef LONG HRESULT;
```

Next comes the declaration of the **IStopwatch** class. The first method, **Release( )**, will call the destructor when the client is finished with the class. You will notice that **Release( )** is the same name that COM defines in the **IUnknown** interface. Eventually this function will be part of that interface implementation.

The other methods in the class are **Start( )** and **ElapsedTime( )**, which are declared like this:

```
  virtual HRESULT __stdcall Start() = 0;
  virtual HRESULT __stdcall ElapsedTime(float *Time) = 0;
```

Start( ) is called to start the timer. **ElapsedTime( )** is called to return the quantity of time elapsed since **Start( )** was last called. The elapsed time is returned via the **Time** parameter, which is passed by reference.

You will notice that all the functions are declared as pure virtual functions, beginning with the keyword **virtual** and ending with **= 0**. The virtual declaration forces vtables to be created—a necessary requirement for COM. Because **IStopwatch** contains pure virtual functions, it is an *abstract class*. This means that all classes that inherit **IStopwatch** must implement the functions found in the interface. You will recall from Chapter 1 that when implementing an interface, *all* the functions of the interface must be implemented. Since each function in the interface is declared as a pure virtual function, each class derived from **IStopwatch** must implement all of **IStopwatch**'s functions, thus enforcing the "fully implemented" rule.

HRESULT is the return type used by most COM functions.

Notice also that both the **Start( )** and **ElapsedTime( )** methods return **HRESULT** values that indicate whether they completed successfully or failed. Since external modules will access these methods, C++-style exception handling cannot be used. Instead, results are passed back to the calling functions via an **HRESULT** value. In general, a return value of **S_OK** indicates that "all is well," whereas **E_FAIL** indicates that something failed. Later on when we look at error handling in detail, you will see that several more **HRESULT** values can be returned and interpreted as success or failure. Because of the variety of **HRESULT** values, you should always use the **SUCCEEDED(HRESULT hr)** and **FAILED(HRESULT hr)** macros when checking status return codes.

The next class is **CStopwatch**, which is inherited from **IStopwatch**. Aside from the two member variables, **CStopwatch** is exactly the same as **IStopwatch**. The two variables, **m_nStartTime** and **m_nFrequency**, are used to store the return values from the QueryPerformance API timing functions.

Here is the skeleton code of the **CStopwatch** implementation. Enter it now. In the next section we will be filling in the details. Now is a good time to try compiling the project, just to make sure you have everything set up correctly.

```
// Stopwatch.cpp: implementation of the CStopwatch class.
//
//////////////////////////////////////////////////////////////////////

#include "Stopwatch.h"
```

```
//////////////////////////////////////////////////////////////////////
// Construction/Destruction
//////////////////////////////////////////////////////////////////////

CStopwatch::CStopwatch()
{
}

CStopwatch::~CStopwatch()
{
}

//////////////////////////////////////////////////////////////////////
// Utility Functions
//////////////////////////////////////////////////////////////////////

unsigned long __stdcall CStopwatch::Release()
{
  delete this;
  return 0;
}

//////////////////////////////////////////////////////////////////////
// Stopwatch Function Implementation
//////////////////////////////////////////////////////////////////////

// IStopwatch specific functions
HRESULT __stdcall CStopwatch::Start()
{
  return S_OK;
}

HRESULT __stdcall CStopwatch::ElapsedTime(float *Time)
{
  return S_OK;
}
```

Adding the Timing Code

We are now going to add the timing code to **CStopwatch**. The additions to the code are highlighted in boldface type.

1. At the top of the **Stopwatch.cpp** file, insert the **mmsystem.h** header file. This file supplies the declaration for the high-resolution timers.

```
// Stopwatch.cpp: implementation of the CStopwatch class.
//
//////////////////////////////////////////////////////////////////////

#include "Stopwatch.h"
#include <mmsystem.h> // Multimedia timers
```

IN DEPTH

Timing Using High-Resolution Performance Counters

The API timing function that the stopwatch component uses is **QueryPerformanceCounter( )**, which returns the value of the high-resolution performance counter. This is one of the multimedia performance counters, and it can measure time in microseconds (10^{-6}). This makes it quite accurate. Its prototype is shown here:

```
BOOL QueryPerformanceCounter(LARGE_INTEGER *lpCount);
```

After the call, the variable pointed to by *lpCount* will contain the current counter value. **LARGE_INTEGER** is a structure that holds a 64-bit integer. The function returns nonzero if successful and zero otherwise.

The exact resolution of the **QueryPerformanceCounter( )** is system dependent, however, so it is necessary to query the system to get the frequency of the ticks that **QueryPerformanceCounter( )** returns. **QueryPerformanceFrequency( )** provides this value, returning the number of ticks per second. Its prototype is shown here:

```
BOOL QueryPerformanceFrequency(LARGE_INTEGER *lpFreq);
```

After the call, the variable pointed to by *lpFreq* will contain the frequency. The function returns nonzero if successful and zero otherwise.

The exact time calculation is made by calling the timing function **QueryPerformanceCounter( )** to start and a second time to stop. Subtracting the stop counter from the start counter returns the number of ticks that occurred during the period between start and stop. Dividing the difference by the frequency of ticks will return the number of seconds between start and stop. Because the timing functions themselves consume a small amount of time, a small overhead should be subtracted. The timing formula is shown here:

$$ElapsedTime = \frac{StopCounter - StartCounter}{Frequency} - Overhead$$

2

IN DEPTH
CONTINUED

In this chapter the overhead will be ignored. Later, in Chapter 4, we will take the overhead into consideration when we add a COM property.

QueryPerformanceCounter( ) is not available on all computers. If the time returned is 0, the hardware does not support this call. Instead, use **timeGetSystemTime( )**. This function is not quite as accurate as **QueryPerformanceCounter( )**, but it should otherwise work without a problem. In **timeGetSystemTime( )**, values are measured in milliseconds (10^{-3}). In order to make the stopwatch work on all machines, consider adding an **if** condition around all calls to **QueryPerformanceCounter( )**.

2. Now add the implementation of the constructor.

```
//////////////////////////////////////////////////////////////////////
// Construction/Destruction
//////////////////////////////////////////////////////////////////////

CStopwatch::CStopwatch()
{

  // Initialize the member variables
  m_nStartTime.QuadPart = 0;

  // Save the frequency of the performance counters
  QueryPerformanceFrequency ((LARGE_INTEGER*) &m_nFrequency);

}
```

This code initializes the member variables. **m_nFrequency** is initialized with a call to **QueryPerformanceFrequency( )**, which returns the frequency of the ticks counted by **QueryPerformanceCounter( )**, as explained in the In-Depth box.

3. Next, add each of the properties and methods. In the **Start( )** function, add a call to save the start time returned from **QueryPerformanceCounter( )** into **m_nStartTime**.

```
//////////////////////////////////////////////////////////////////////
// Function Implementation
//////////////////////////////////////////////////////////////////////
```

```
// IStopwatch specific functions
HRESULT __stdcall CStopwatch::Start()
{
  if ( QueryPerformanceCounter( (LARGE_INTEGER*) &m_nStartTime) )
    return S_OK;
  else
    return E_FAIL;
}
```

4. In the **ElapsedTime( )** function you need to set **nStopTime**. In addition, **ElapsedTime( )** needs to calculate the elapsed time so that it can be returned to the client.

```
HRESULT __stdcall CStopwatch::ElapsedTime(float *Time)
{
  HRESULT hr;
  LARGE_INTEGER nStopTime;

  // Set the stop time immediately so that a minimum
  // amount of timer code is executed between the start
  // and stop times
  if ( !QueryPerformanceCounter( (LARGE_INTEGER*) &nStopTime )
    || (m_nStartTime.QuadPart == 0)
   )
  {
    // Either QPC failed or
    // start was not called before stop
    hr = E_FAIL;
  }
  else
  {
    *Time = (float) (nStopTime.QuadPart - m_nStartTime.QuadPart);
    *Time = (*Time / m_nFrequency.QuadPart);
    hr = S_OK;
  }

  return hr;
}
```

At this point the coding for the classes is complete. Compile the code to make sure no errors have been introduced.

Defining the Export Functions

The next step is to implement the entry point functions for the DLL. These are the functions that will be exposed to external modules so that they can call into the DLL.

1. From the File menu again, select New.
2. At the Files tab, select C++ Source File, enter **Timers.cpp** for the filename, and click OK.

We will export only two functions from **Timers.dll**: **DLLMain( )** and **DllGetClassObject( )**. **DLLMain( )** is a function that is called when the DLL is loaded and again when it is unloaded. This function is standard to all Windows DLLs regardless of whether they are COM related or not. **DllMain( )** is roughly equivalent to **main( )** in a standard C++ executable except that **main( )** is called only once. In contrast, **DllMain( )** is called whenever threads using the DLL are terminated, or when **LoadLibrary( )** or **FreeLibrary( )** is called. **DllMain( )** is shown here:

```
// Timers.cpp : Implementation of DLL Exports.

#include <windows.h>
#include "Stopwatch.h"

////////////////////////////////////////////////////////////////////
// DLL Entry Point

extern "C"
BOOL __stdcall DllMain(HINSTANCE hInstance, DWORD dwReason,
  LPVOID /*lpReserved*/)
{
  return TRUE;  // All is well
}
```

Interestingly, the implementation of **DllMain( )** is optional. However, since we will be using it later to implement some initialization, we will include **DllMain( )** now.

The last function, **DllGetClassObject( )**, is shown next. This function is defined by COM but implemented by you. For now we will use this function to create an object of a specified class and return an interface pointer to that object. In this case, the function is used by the client to request a pointer to an **IStopwatch** object. Later in the chapter, this will change as we fully implement COM.

```
////////////////////////////////////////////////////////////////////
// Returns IStopwatch back to the caller

extern "C"
HRESULT __stdcall DllGetClassObject(
  REFCLSID rclsid,
  REFIID riid,
  LPVOID* ppv)
{
```

```
  *ppv = static_cast<IStopwatch*>(new CStopwatch);

  return S_OK;
}
```

Notice that this version of **DllGetClassObject( )** does not use the **riid** or **rclsid** parameters. They are not needed at this time because we are currently building a non-COM component. By including the additional parameters now, we save a little work later on.

Notice that in order to pass back an **IStopwatch** pointer instead of a **CStopwatch** pointer, a C++ **static_cast** is used. Recall that **static_cast** provides a compile-time cast in which no runtime type checking is performed. Thus, it is essentially the same as the traditional cast operator. In this case, the cast changes the type of the pointer so that it is pointing to the expected type. Since a **static_cast** performs no runtime checking of the conversion, it is the programmer's responsibility to ensure that the conversion is valid.

The last step required before we move to the **StopwatchClient** is to declare the names of the functions that will be exported. To do this, insert a new "text file" called **Timers.def** and enter the following code:

```
; Timers.def : Declares the module parameters.

LIBRARY     "Timers.DLL"

EXPORTS
  DllGetClassObject   @1 PRIVATE
```

As you may know, it is also possible to export a function by using a **_ _declspec(dllexport)** statement. However, since the ATL project wizard currently uses DEF files, we will adopt that convention from the start.

Compile the project again to make sure everything has been entered correctly.

Now we have completed the entire **Timers.dll**, so we are ready to move on and create a client that will test it.

Building the StopwatchClient.exe

The purpose of **StopwatchClient** is to test the **Timers.dll** library. Therefore, it is relatively simple and far less involved than the **Timers.dll**. For this task we will use a console-based application rather than a full-blown

GUI program. Of course, as far as using the stopwatch component is concerned, the same techniques will work in either a console or GUI program.

Creating a Win32 Console Application Project

To begin, create a new Win32 console application project. For the name of the project, enter **StopwatchClient**, and again select the directory in which you want to put the project. When prompted by the wizard, select the "An empty project" option. After you click the Finish button, the **StopwatchClient** project will be created with no files in it, but the compiler options will have been set properly.

Writing the StopwatchClient

Add a new C++ source file to the **StopwatchClient** project called **StopwatchClient.cpp**. We will now gradually add each section of the **StopwatchClient** code, explaining it as we go.

To begin, add the include files and declarations shown here:

```
// StopwatchClient.cpp :
//   Defines the entry point for the console application.
//

// std::out etc.
#include <iostream>

#include "..\Timers\Stopwatch.h"

// NOTE:  The following line will vary depending on
// where the Timers.dll is located.
#define TIMERSDLL "..\\Timers\\Timers.dll"

typedef HRESULT (__stdcall *DLLGETCLASSOBJECT) (REFCLSID rclsid,
  REFIID riid, LPVOID* ppv);
```

The **Stopwatch.h** file is included because it contains the definition of **IStopwatch,** which is the class that is returned from **Timers.dll** and will be used to handle the timing. Next, **TIMERSDLL** is set to be the path to the location of **Timers.dll**. If you have put the **Timers** project into a different location, you will have to change this. Be sure, however, to use two backslashes for a folder rather than one, or your code will not compile.

Next comes a **typedef** for the **DllGetClassObject( )** function that is located in the **Timers.dll**. Declaring this **typedef** makes it easier to call the function through a pointer. It also provides one location at which to change the function declaration.

The **CreateInstance( )** function shown next encapsulates the code necessary to retrieve the **IStopwatch** object from the **Timers.dll**.

```
// Instantiates a stopwatch object and returns it by reference
HRESULT CreateInstance(void** ppv)
{
  HRESULT hr = E_FAIL;
  HINSTANCE hinstDll;
  DLLGETCLASSOBJECT DllGetClassObject;
  GUID guid;

  hinstDll = LoadLibrary(TIMERSDLL);
  if (hinstDll == NULL)
    std::cout << "Unable to load \"" TIMERSDLL "\"" << std::endl;
  else
  {
    DllGetClassObject =
      (DLLGETCLASSOBJECT) GetProcAddress(hinstDll,
        "DllGetClassObject");
    if (DllGetClassObject != NULL)
      hr = DllGetClassObject(guid, guid, ppv);
  }
  return hr;
}
```

Using the **LoadLibrary( )** API function, **CreateInstance( )** first loads **Timers.dll** into the address space of **StopwatchClient.exe**. If the load is successful, it proceeds to retrieve a function pointer to the **DllGetClassObject( )** function using the **GetProcAddress( )** API. Finally, **DllGetClassObject( )** is called using the function pointer, and the **IStopwatch** pointer is returned to **main( )**, from which **CreateInstance( )** was called, via **ppv**. At this time the first two parameters of **DllGetClassObject( )**, **rclsid** and **riid**, are not used, so a null GUID is passed.

Here is the code for **main( )**:

```
int main(int argc, char* argv[])
{
```

```
  float nElapsedTime;
  HRESULT hr;
  IStopwatch* pStopwatch = NULL;

  hr = CreateInstance((void**) &pStopwatch);

  if ( !SUCCEEDED(hr) )
    std::cout << "ERROR: Unable to create Stopwatch!!";

  else
  {
    pStopwatch->Start();
    pStopwatch->ElapsedTime( &nElapsedTime );

    std::cout << "The overhead time is "
      << nElapsedTime << std::endl;

    pStopwatch->Release();

    pStopwatch = NULL;

  }

  return 0;
}
```

2

The code inside **main( )** is straightforward. First **CreateInstance( )** is called to retrieve a pointer to **IStopwatch**. If this is successful, the stopwatch is started and stopped, producing a measurement for the overhead of calling the stopwatch. Once timing is complete, the **IStopwatch** object is released. As you will recall, calling **Release( )** causes the stopwatch to be deleted.

Now the coding is complete. Compile **StopwatchClient.exe** and run it to see that everything is working. The output should look something like Figure 2-3.

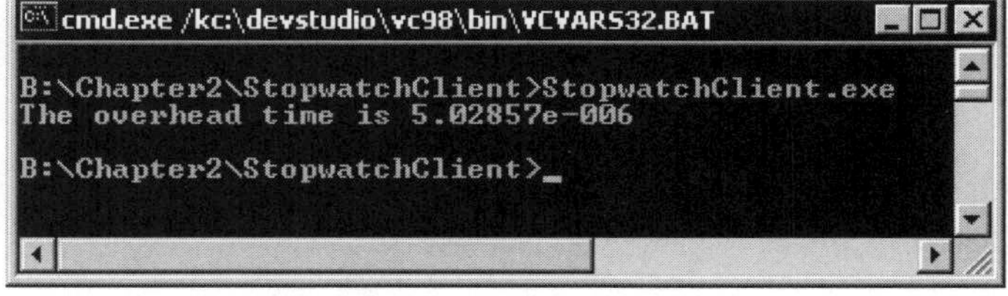

StopwatchClient output using **LoadLibrary( )**
Figure 2-3.

Reviewing the Starting Point

At this point, we have created a fully functional, but non-COM-based, stopwatch component. To use the component, the client will load its DLL, create a stopwatch object, and then call the appropriate functions. This implementation contains all the essential elements of a component, but without the COM methodology. The remainder of this chapter will transform the implementation into a COM-compliant component.

Adding IUnknown

> The first three function pointers in an interface vtable must be the **IUnknown** methods.

The first step in converting **IStopwatch** into a COM component is to add the **IUnknown** interface. As we have already discussed in Chapter 1, **IUnknown** must be at the root of all COM interfaces. This means that the first three pointers in an interface vtable must point to the three methods of **IUnknown**.

Before beginning, let's review two important terms: interface and CoClass. An interface defines and exposes the functionality of a component object. It is a description of the services that an object will provide and the mechanism by which a client learns the capabilities of a server. In C++, interfaces are created using an abstract class. Therefore, **IStopwatch** defines the interface to the **CStopwatch** class. A CoClass is the class that is responsible for implementing the functions of a COM object and supports one or more COM interfaces. Thus, **CStopwatch** is the CoClass that implements **IStopwatch**.

The declaration for **IUnknown** is shown here. As expected, each method is a pure virtual function.

```
struct IUnknown
{
  virtual HRESULT __stdcall QueryInterface(
    REFIID riid,
    void **ppvObject) = 0;
  virtual unsigned long __stdcall AddRef() = 0;
  virtual unsigned long __stdcall Release() = 0;
};
```

One interesting thing to note about this definition is that **IUnknown** has two of the rare instances in which an **HRESULT** value is not returned from a COM function. A second item of interest is that **IUnknown** is not declared using **class** but rather **struct**. Interestingly, this is true of all interfaces that are declared using the MIDL compiler, as you will see later in this book. Although both **class** and **struct** work when declaring COM interfaces,

struct offers the added advantage of having all its methods defined as public by default. Since the purpose of an interface is to be called externally, there seems little point in defining one with private or even protected functions. Since **struct** and **class** are otherwise equivalent (for instance, both create identical vtable structures), it doesn't matter which keyword is used. For example, we could use **struct** to declare **IStopwatch**, as shown here, and everything will continue to function as before.


```
struct IStopwatch
{
public:
  // Utility functions
  virtual unsigned long __stdcall Release() = 0;

  // IStopwatch specific functions
  virtual HRESULT __stdcall Start() = 0;
  virtual HRESULT __stdcall ElapsedTime(float *Time) = 0;
};
```

Although we will continue to use **class** when defining interfaces, which is in keeping with traditional C++ coding practices, you are free to use **struct** if you like.

Two Ways to Implement IUnknown

There are two methods for implementing **IUnknown** as the root of an interface. The first is by manually redeclaring each member of **IUnknown**. The second is through the use of C++-style inheritance. Each approach is examined here.

IUnknown Functions Redeclared

One way to put **IUnknown** at the root of an interface is to redeclare each of the **IUnknown** methods at the top of the interface. The result of doing this for **IStopwatch** is shown here:

```
class IStopwatch
{
public:
  // IUnknown methods
  virtual HRESULT __stdcall QueryInterface(
```

```
    REFIID riid,
    void **ppvObject) = 0;
  virtual unsigned long __stdcall AddRef() = 0;
  virtual unsigned long __stdcall Release() = 0;

  // IStopwatch specific methods
  virtual HRESULT __stdcall Start() = 0;
  virtual HRESULT __stdcall ElapsedTime(float *Time) = 0;
};
```

Although this method works properly, the disadvantage is that the same code has to be duplicated for every interface. Although this is unlikely to increase the code size of the compiled module, there is little point in doing it when C++ offers a better option.

IUnknown Inherited

To implement **IUnknown** using inheritance, an interface inherits **IUnknown** as a base class. Therefore, to add **IUnknown** to **IStopwatch**, you could specify **IUnknown** as a base class, as shown here:

```
class IStopwatch : public IUnknown
{
public:
  // Stopwatch specific functions
  virtual HRESULT __stdcall Start() = 0;
  virtual HRESULT __stdcall ElapsedTime(float *Time) = 0;
};
```

Since **IUnknown** is defined for you by including **windows.h**, you can simply inherit it. As you can see, this approach offers the advantage of more compact code while reducing the possibility of error.

When using inheritance to add **IUnknown**, you need to be careful about one point: Avoid inheriting two or more bases classes at the same time. Although multiple base classes can be utilized at the level of the CoClass, such as **CStopwatch**, it is important for interfaces that multiple inheritance is not used. The reason for this is that there is no standard that defines the order in which an inherited class will appear in the vtable. Therefore, if **IStopwatch** inherits from two other interfaces—**IUnknown** and **ISomethingElse**, for example—there is no guarantee that **IUnknown** will be first (which it must be).

IUnknown Must Be Fully Implemented

IUnknown must be fully supported by all COM objects. Therefore, whenever a client requests the **IUnknown** interface, the component object should return a pointer to an **IUnknown** object. Figure 2-4 shows both the **IUnknown** requirements. Furthermore, in the previous section we already created one of the required methods of **IUnknown**: **Release( )**. The other two methods that need to be added are **QueryInterface( )** and **AddRef( )**. These are required to fully implement **IUnknown**.

2

Add IUnknown

Now we will add the **IUnknown** interface to the **Stopwatch** component both as a stand-alone interface and as the root of the **IStopwatch** interface.

Open **Stopwatch.h** and change the **IStopwatch** interface to inherit from **IUnknown**. Since the **Release( )** method is already declared in **IUnknown**, this can be removed altogether from **IStopwatch**. In addition to changing **IStopwatch**, add the necessary **AddRef( )** and **QueryInterface( )** declarations to the **CStopwatch** class. Remember, each interface function is a pure virtual function, which forces derived classes to implement all the methods of the abstract class. Interfaces only declare the methods, they do

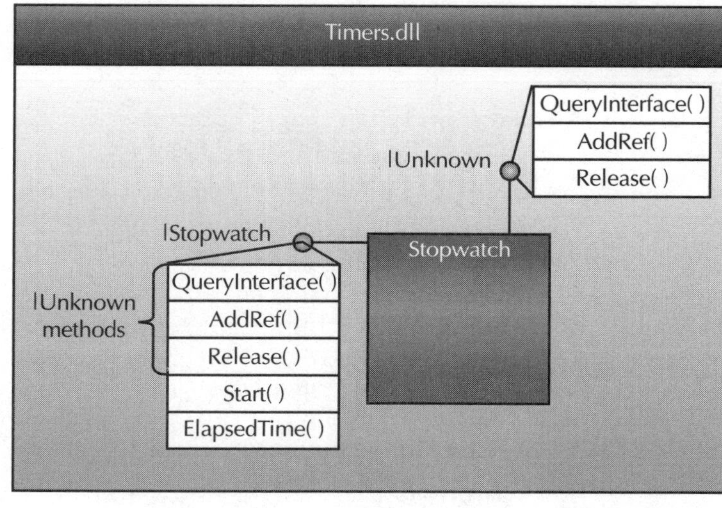

The **Stopwatch** component with **IUnknown** fully supported
Figure 2-4.

not implement them. The CoClass, which inherits the interfaces, is responsible for implementing them. Here is the updated version of **IStopwatch** and **CStopwatch**. The changes are highlighted.

```
#include <windows.h>

class IStopwatch : IUnknown
{
  public:
  // Stopwatch specific functions
  virtual HRESULT __stdcall Start() = 0;
  virtual HRESULT __stdcall ElapsedTime(float *Time) = 0;
};

class CStopwatch : public IStopwatch
{
public:
  CStopwatch();
  virtual ~CStopwatch();

private:
  // The frequency of the counter
  // returned by QueryPerformanceCounter()
  LARGE_INTEGER m_nFrequency;

  // The counter value when the start method was last called.
  LARGE_INTEGER m_nStartTime;

public:
  // IUnknown methods
  HRESULT __stdcall QueryInterface(
    REFIID riid,
    void **ppvObject);
  unsigned long __stdcall AddRef();
  unsigned long __stdcall Release();

  // IStopwatch specific functions
  HRESULT __stdcall Start();
  HRESULT __stdcall ElapsedTime(float *Time);

};
```

Note that **IUnknown** is not explicitly defined in **Stopwatch.h**; instead the declaration is found in the headers included by **windows.h**.

After declaring the **QueryInterface( )** and **AddRef( )** methods in **CStopwatch**, we now need to provide their implementation.

Implementing QueryInterface( )

The **QueryInterface( )** implementation supports multiple interfaces on one component object. When the client has a pointer to one interface, it can call **QueryInterface( )** on that interface and request a different interface. This is why all interfaces must have **IUnknown** as their root within the vtable. If they did not, there would be no consistent way of requesting a different interface.

QueryInterface( ) Rules

There are three fundamental rules for using the **QueryInterface( )** function, as follows:

1. The set of interfaces {X} supported by a component object cannot change at runtime.
2. Given any interface in the set of interfaces {X} supported by a component object, a client can successfully request any interface in {X}.
3. If a request for interface IX returns successfully, a second request for the same interface, IX, on the same component object must return the same pointer.

The first two rules mean that if a client successfully requests an interface, the client will be able to successfully retrieve that same interface again during the lifetime of the component. On the other hand, if the first request for an interface fails, any subsequent requests will also fail.

From the first two rules, three general principles can be derived:

- Symmetry: Given interface IA, you can successfully request interface IA.
- Reflexivity: Given interface IA, if you successfully query for interface IB, then you can successfully request interface IA from IB.
- Transitivity: Given interface IA, if the client successfully queries for IB from IA and then successfully queries for IC from IB, then the client will be able to successfully query for IA from IC.

Figure 2-5 shows the state transition diagram for a component object that supports three interfaces. Each circle represents a client having a pointer to the specified interface. It shows that given a pointer to any interface, it is

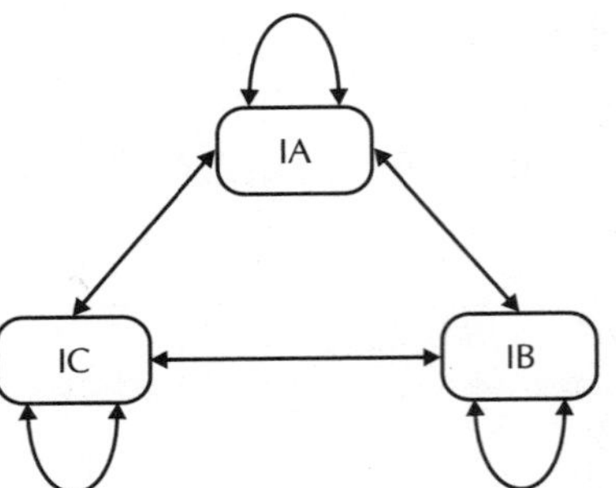

State transitions for three interfaces

Figure 2-5.

possible to directly call **QueryInterface( )** and successfully retrieve the pointer to any other interface.

COM does not provide a means by which a client can request a list of interfaces supported by a component.

Note that there is no means for requesting a list of all the interfaces supported by the component object. The client must know which interface to request before it can request it.

Rule 3 is required specifically because multiple inheritance is supported in the CoClass. Often a CoClass is derived from multiple base classes, as shown in Figure 2-6. The problem with this is that in order to return the **IUnknown** interface on **CCoClassObject1**, there has to be a decision as to which **IUnknown** inheritance branch to use. Rule 3 states that it does not matter which one is chosen as long as the same one is chosen every time within the lifetime of the component.

As we have already seen, the declaration for **QueryInterface( )** is

```
HRESULT __stdcall CStopwatch::QueryInterface(
  REFIID riid,
  void **ppvObject)
```

The first parameter, **riid**, is the GUID of the interface being requested. The second parameter, **ppvObject**, is a **void **** pass-by-reference pointer that will be used to return the interface pointer to the client.

Each interface needs to be assigned a unique GUID.

In spite of the fact that for any given interface, the **QueryInterface( )** method can return only a limited number of interfaces, the value passed in to identify the interface is globally unique rather than simply unique to the component object. This is important because a component object can support the same interface that another component object supports. Without these globally

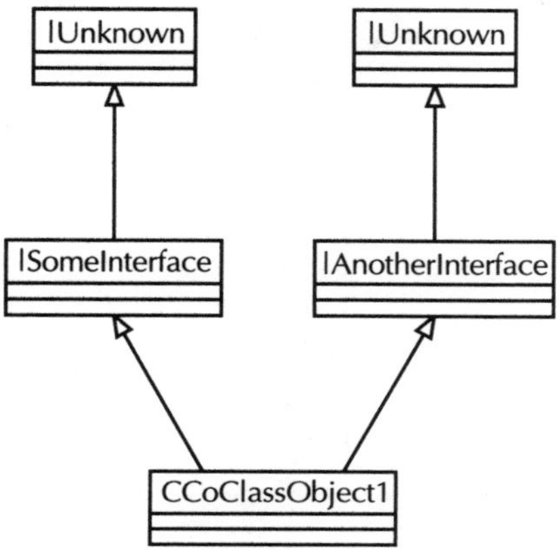

Multiple inheritance in the CoClass
Figure 2-6.

unique values, this would not be possible. Therefore, before **QueryInterface( )** can be implemented it is necessary to provide a means for uniquely identifying each interface. Since GUIDs are unique identifiers, they are obviously the candidates to be used and the choice implemented by COM.

Generating a GUID

Visual Studio 6.0 supplies two utilities for generating GUIDs. The first is a command prompt program called **Uuidgen.exe**, and the second is called **Guidgen.exe**. The latter is found in the Common\Tools directory of your Visual Studio installation (usually c:\Program Files\Microsoft Visual Studio\Common\Tools). Alternatively, you can run the utility from Projects | Add To Project | Components and Controls. At the dialog, select the Visual C++ Components directory, and then select the GUID Generator, as shown in Figure 2-7.

The result will be the Create GUID dialog shown in Figure 2-8. Select the third option, the **const** declaration format, and then click the Copy button. This will place a newly generated GUID into the paste buffer. It can now be used in a constant declaration for each of the interfaces.

The standard naming convention for interface GUIDs is to prefix them with IID_. Although the GUID declarations could be placed in any of the header files, we will create a new file called **Timers_i.c**. This will be the location for all GUID identifiers. As you shall see later, the MIDL compiler

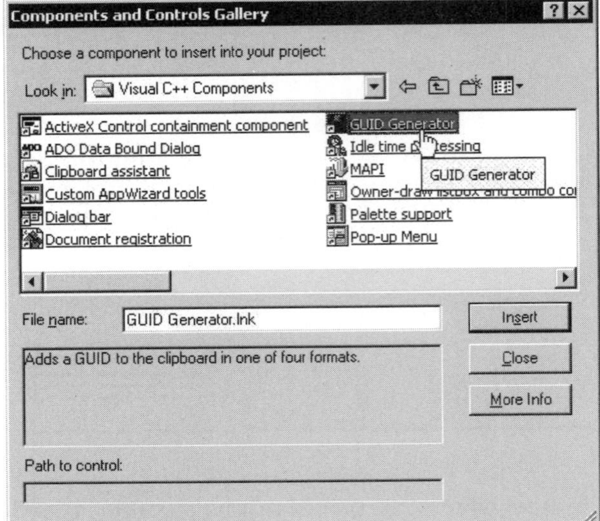

Components and Controls Gallery dialog used to run the GUID Generator

Figure 2-7.

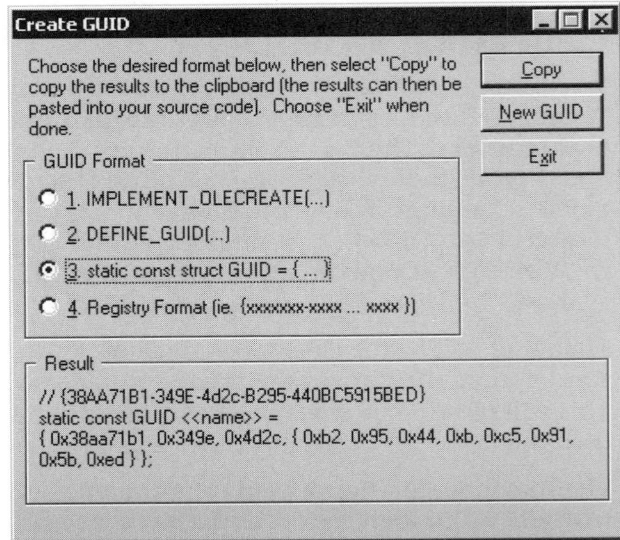

Guidgen.exe is used to generate GUIDs

Figure 2-8.

automatically generates this file to declare all the GUIDs supported by the component server.

Enter the following code into **Timers_i.c**. Although the GUID generator is not required, you can use it to create your own values. Whether you use the GUIDs below or you generate your own, be sure that you consistently use the same set of GUIDs throughout the chapter.


```
#ifndef TIMERS_I_C
#define TIMERS_I_C

#include <windows.h>

// {EEBF6D1E-8EF1-4acf-9E5F-4D95E01D698A}
const IID IID_IStopwatch =
  { 0xeebf6d1e, 0x8ef1, 0x4acf,
    { 0x9e, 0x5f, 0x4d, 0x95, 0xe0, 0x1d, 0x69, 0x8a } };

// {83DC3C46-1259-4f95-A2D1-CD11A8819E2E}
const CLSID CLSID_Stopwatch =
  { 0x83dc3c46, 0x1259, 0x4f95,
    { 0xa2, 0xd1, 0xcd, 0x11, 0xa8, 0x81, 0x9e, 0x2e } };

#endif //TIMERS_I_C
```

All component objects must have unique CLSIDs associated with them.

Notice that there are two GUIDs. The first, **IID_IStopwatch**, is for the **IStopwatch** interface, and the second, **CLSID_Stopwatch**, is for the **Stopwatch** component object's class ID. COM requires that all component objects also have their own GUIDs, called class IDs (CLSIDs). The CLSID is used because one component server can provide multiple types of component objects. The client will use **CLSID_Stopwatch** when it calls **DllGetClassObject( )** to request a particular component object.

The one item missing from **Timer_i.c** is the IID for **IUnknown**. This is because **IUnknown** is a published GUID and already defined. Using the registry (canonical) format, the GUID for **IUnknown** is {00000000-0000-0000-C000-000000000046}.

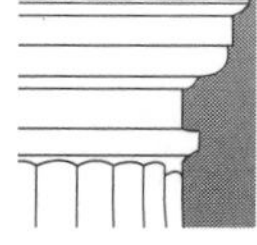

NOTE: The interface ID for **IUnknown** *is always* {00000000-0000-0000-C000-000000000046}.

Add QueryInterface( )

We are now ready to implement **QueryInterface( )**. Open **Stopwatch.cpp** and add the code for **QueryInterface( )** shown here:

```
HRESULT __stdcall CStopwatch::QueryInterface(
  REFIID riid,
  void **ppvObject)
{
  HRESULT hr = S_OK;

  if (riid == IID_IUnknown)
    *ppvObject = static_cast<IUnknown*>(
      static_cast<IStopwatch*>(this));
  else if (riid == IID_IStopwatch)
    *ppvObject = static_cast<IStopwatch*>(this);
  else
  {
    ppvObject = NULL;
    hr = E_NOINTERFACE;
  }

  if (SUCCEEDED(hr))
    (static_cast<IUnknown*>(*ppvObject))->AddRef();

  return hr;
}
```

There are two things to note about this code. The first is the **static_cast** of **this** to **IStopwatch** and then again to **IUnknown**. Since **CStopwatch** is derived from only **IStopwatch**, none of the multiple-inheritance ambiguities described above occur. In spite of this, it is a good practice to explicitly convert to **IUnknown** so that if a second interface base class is added later, no trouble will result. This is why a double cast is used here. There is also a second solution to the multiple-inheritance cast. Instead of casting **this** to **IStopwatch** and then again to **IUnknown**, we could simply cast to **IStopwatch**:

```
    *ppvObject = static_cast<IStopwatch*>(this);
```

This may seem a strange approach since **IUnknown** was requested. It works, however, because in C++ a base-class pointer can point to an object derived

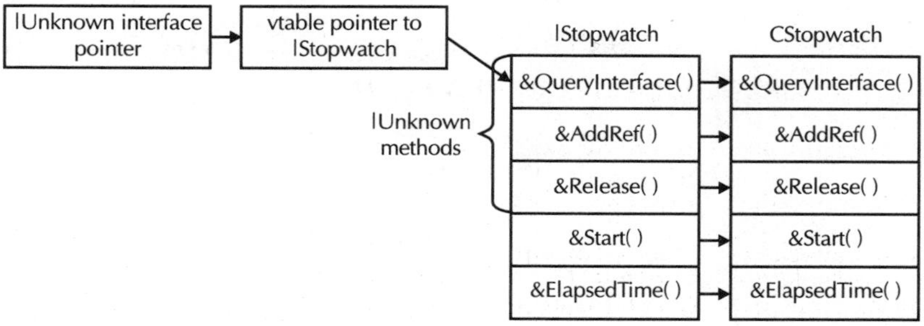

IUnknown methods called through **IStopwatch**

Figure 2-9.

from that base. Since **IUnknown** is at the root of all interfaces, including **IStopwatch**, calls to the **IUnknown** functions can be made through the **IStopwatch** pointer (just as though the pointer was to **IUnknown**). As Figure 2-9 shows, however, the vtable structure for **IUnknown** is a subset of **IStopwatch**, and all function calls will simply utilize the **IUnknown** implementation on **IStopwatch**.

Multiple inheritance is not allowed for any interface.

The next item in the **QueryInterface( )** implementation is the call to **AddRef( )**. (**AddRef( )** is implemented in the next section.) Notice that in this call there is no explicit cast from the type of object to which **ppvObject** points. It may seem obvious that this is not necessary, since there is no inheritance level between **IStopwatch** and **IUnknown**, but there is a more subtle reason. Even if an additional level existed between **IUnknown** and the object type pointed to by **ppvObject**, multiple inheritance is not allowed at the interface level, so no ambiguity can occur.

One last point concerning **QueryInterface( )** is that whenever the requested interface is not available, **E_NOINTERFACE** should be returned, and **ppvObject** must be set to **NULL**.

Calling QueryInterface( )

Now that we have implemented **QueryInterface( )**, let's change **DllGetClassObject( )** to use it. Since we now have the CLSIDs and IIDs, we can use them so that the client can request which component object to instantiate (we support only one at the moment) and which interface on that component to return. The code changes for **DllGetClassObject( )** are shown here:

```
///////////////////////////////////////////////////////////////////////////////
// Returns a component object to the caller

extern "C"
HRESULT __stdcall DllGetClassObject(
  REFCLSID rclsid,
  REFIID riid,
  LPVOID* ppv)
{
  HRESULT hr;
  if (rclsid == CLSID_Stopwatch)
  {
    CStopwatch* stopwatch = new CStopwatch;
    hr = stopwatch->QueryInterface(riid, ppv);
  }
  else
    hr = CLASS_E_CLASSNOTAVAILABLE;

  return hr;
}
```

DllGetClassObject( ) checks for which component object is being requested via **rclsid**. If the component is the stopwatch, it instantiates the CoClass and then calls **QueryInterface( )** to retrieve the correct interface to pass back to the client.

Before we can compile and test, we need to implement the **AddRef( )** function that is being called by **QueryInterface( )**. We will also need to modify the client to use the new **QueryInterface( )** mechanism. Up to this point we have not explained why **AddRef( )** is called, however. We will now begin to investigate it in detail as we add the next piece to the COM puzzle: reference counting. (For those who wish to check that your code compiles correctly at this point, simply edit the **Stopwatch.h** header file and add an empty implementation to **AddRef( )** by removing the semicolon and replacing it with "{ return 0; }". Be sure to undo the change after compiling, as we will soon be adding the real implementation to **Stopwatch.cpp.**)

Reference Counting

So far, when we created a stopwatch component and then accessed it via a **LoadLibrary( )** call, we were able to avoid any reference counting issues. Such issues arise when multiple references exist for the same component.

Reference counting is used to control a component object's lifetime.

Reference counting is the method for controlling a component object's lifetime. The goal is to ensure that when there is a reference to a component, that object stays in memory, and when there is no longer a reference to a component, that object is released from memory.

For example, imagine that when a user logs on to the computer, the system makes a call to **Stopwatch.Start( )** to start the timer. The system then passes the stopwatch instance to various monitor programs so that they can call **Stopwatch.ElapsedTime( )** to determine how long the user has been logged on. A problem arises when the user logs out. Which component is responsible for calling **Stopwatch.Release( )**? Even if you decided that the client that created the stopwatch—in this case the system—should be responsible for calling **Release( )**, when and how would it know that it was safe to do so? That is, how would the system know when all the clients no longer needed the stopwatch? Furthermore, if the system called **Release( )** when the user logged out, what would happen if one of the monitor programs was running as an NT/2000 service and decided to call into **Stopwatch.ElapsedTime( )** again? Even with our simple client, serious trouble would occur if we had one pointer to **IUnknown** and a second to **IStopwatch** and then, after calling **IUnknown.Release( )**, we called **IStopwatch.Start( )**.

One solution to the preceding problems is to set up a reference counting mechanism that tracks how many clients have a reference to the component object. Once the reference count drops to zero, the component object can be destroyed. This is, of course, the solution used by COM.

Implementing Reference Counting

The implementation of reference counting is relatively simple. It consists of incrementing a counter variable each time a pointer refers to an interface, and decrementing it when that reference is removed. Once the reference count reaches zero, the object deletes itself. Although it would be possible to have a separate "component manager" implement reference counting, the method chosen by COM is to have each interface (implementation) be responsible for keeping the reference count and handling the increments and decrements. This is, of course, accomplished by calling **AddRef( )** and **Release( )**, which were introduced in Chapter 1. Now we will look at them in greater detail.

There are at least two options for implementing reference counting: Either the component can have a separate reference count variable for each interface, or the component can simply have one reference count that is shared by all the interfaces it supports. COM allows either possibility. In the former case, once all the interface reference counts drop to zero, the component can delete itself. In the latter case, when the shared reference count reaches zero, the object can be removed. The advantage to the single reference count is simplicity. Each interface vtable points to the same **AddRef( )** and **Release( )** methods, which have to be implemented only once. Here is the single reference counting approach that we will use:

```
unsigned long __stdcall CStopwatch::AddRef()
{
  return InterlockedIncrement( &m_nReferenceCount );
}

unsigned long __stdcall CStopwatch::Release()
{
  if (InterlockedDecrement( &m_nReferenceCount ) == 0)
  {
    delete this;
    return 0;
  }
  return m_nReferenceCount;
}
```

Notice the use of the API functions **InterlockedIncrement( )** and **InterlockedDecrement( )** in place of C++ increment and decrement operators **++** and --. These API functions prevent more than one thread from simultaneously accessing the variable—in this case **m_nReferenceCount**—and throwing off the count. This is important because a component object might be accessed by multiple threads.

In the **Release( )** function, when **m_nReferenceCount** is zero, a hard-coded 0 value is returned. Since **m_nReferenceCount** is zero at this point, it may seem strange to return the constant 0 rather than just letting execution continue to the **return m_nReferenceCount** statement. The reason is that when **delete this** is called, the **m_nReferenceCount** variable will be destroyed along with the object, so it will no longer exist. Any attempt to access it after it has been destroyed may result in an error.

As mentioned earlier, you could implement a reference count for each interface. One advantage to this method is that you can easily locate an imbalanced number of **AddRef( )** and **Release( )** calls for a particular interface. As we shall see shortly, there is no way to force the client to use the reference counting mechanisms correctly, and this can often lead to an extra **Release( )** or **AddRef( )** call; so the ability to see the count on each interface could be very helpful in debugging. You can also take advantage of this method when a particular interface uses a significant number of resources that other interfaces on a component object do not require: If the reference counting is per interface, you can release these resources when the reference count for the heavyweight interface drops to zero, and reallocate them when the interface is requested. This optimizes the resource utilization for the component.

To finish off the reference counting code in **Timers.dll**, make two more changes. First, add the highlighted line to **Stopwatch.h**:

```
public:
    CStopwatch();
    virtual ~CStopwatch();

private:
  // Reference counting
  long m_nReferenceCount;
...
```

Finally, change **Stopwatch.cpp** as shown here:

```
  // Initialize the member variables
  m_nStartTime.QuadPart = 0;
  m_nReferenceCount = 0;
```

Using COM Reference Counting

*For every **AddRef( )** call on an interface there must be a matching **Release( )** call on the same interface.*

Reference counting for the component object is relatively simple. The hard part is writing the client so that it always uses the reference counting mechanisms correctly. The goal is that **AddRef( )** and **Release( )** need to be called in pairs. In other words, whenever **AddRef( )** is called, **Release( )** needs to be called later.

Although it is possible that the component object has only one reference counter for the entire component, it is not safe for the client to assume this. Therefore, the client cannot call **AddRef( )** on one interface and then call **Release( )** on a different interface and assume that the reference counting will be handled correctly. Although this may work in situations where the reference counting variable is the same for all interfaces, you cannot assume

It is the client's responsibility to count references properly.

this to be true. Instead, the **AddRef( )** and **Release( )** pairs must always match on the same interface.

In general, give **AddRef( )** and **Release( )** the same attention that you give to **new** and **delete**. Keep in mind, however, that **new** and **delete** are called only once for each instance of an object; **AddRef( )** and **Release( )** are called for each *reference* or *pointer* to an *interface*.

Two principles determine when to call **AddRef( )** and when to call **Release( )**:

- Whenever an interface pointer is assigned an interface, **AddRef( )** should be called on that interface.
- **Release( )** should be called before a non-null interface pointer goes out of scope or is reassigned a new value.

Let's look at a few examples.

First, consider a situation in which a new interface pointer is returned to the client. We have already seen this example at work in **CStopwatch::QueryInterface( )**, shown in the previous section. In this case, when **QueryInterface( )** is called, the client passes in a null interface pointer. The component object then assigns the address of an interface to the pointer and calls **AddRef( )**. Thus, the server calls **AddRef( )**, but the client is responsible for calling **Release( )**. This complicates matters because it is very easy to forget to call **Release( )**. When checking reference counting calls on the client, be sure that you match all **QueryInterface( )** and **CoCreateInstance( )** (to be discussed later) calls with **Release( )** calls. (It is interesting to note that although **CStopwatch::QueryInterface( )** calls **AddRef( )** on the **IUnknown** interface, the client should assume that **AddRef( )** on the requested interface was called. Since only one interface reference counter is being used, it is irrelevant on which interface **AddRef( )** is called in this case. For the sake of simplicity, **IUnknown** was chosen.)

Next, consider a case in which an interface pointer is copied to a new location. In this situation, both principles could apply. First, the client must check that the current value of the interface pointer being assigned is **NULL**. If it is not, then **Release( )** should be called on the interface first. Second, after the assignment is made, **AddRef( )** should be called. Thus, the following sequence must be executed:

```
if (pI2 != NULL)
  pI2->Release( );
pI2 = pI1;
pI2->AddRef( );
```

For the next example, assume that a non-null interface pointer goes out of scope. Before the variable does go out of scope, however, it should be checked to see whether it is pointing to an interface. If it is, **Release( )** should be called.

```
{
  IUnknown pIUnk = NULL;
...
  if (pIUnk != NULL)
    pIUnk->Release( );
}
```

For the last example, imagine that a call into a function passes an interface that is then changed to a new interface. In other words, a pointer to interface IX on component object A is passed into the function using pass-by-reference. The function then changes the pointer to point to interface IX on component object B. This example is simply a combination of the first two examples. Here is the code:

```
HRESULT Refresh(IUnknown* pIUnk)
{
  if (pIUnk != NULL)
    pIUnk->Release( );
...
  pIUnk = m_pIUnk;
  pIUnk->AddRef( );
}
```

In the code above, the interface is **IUnknown**. Before the function changes the pointer to point to the same interface on a different component object, it first checks that **pIUnk** is not **NULL** so that it knows to call **Release( )**. After that, it assigns the pointer to a different component and calls **AddRef( )** on the interface of the new component.

The principles described above are waived in two places due to a third principle:

- Special knowledge about interface lifetime can be used to eliminate reference counting calls.

In other words, if you know that an object will not be released during the lifetime of a new interface assignment, then **AddRef( )** and **Release( )** can be eliminated for this new interface pointer. You will see an example of this type of optimization in the implementation of the stopwatch client that follows.

Here is the updated **StopwatchClient.cpp** that implements reference counting. It also incorporates the changes related to the **QueryInterface( )** implementation described in the previous section.

```
// StopwatchClient.cpp :
//   Defines the entry point for the console application.
//

// std::out etc
#include <iostream>

#include "..\Timers\timers_i.c"
#include "..\Timers\Stopwatch.h"

// NOTE:  The following line will vary depending on
// where the Timers.dll is located.
#define TIMERSDLL "..\\Timers\\Timers.dll"

typedef HRESULT (__stdcall *DLLGETCLASSOBJECT)(REFCLSID rclsid,
  REFIID riid, LPVOID* ppv);

// Instantiates a stopwatch object and returns it by reference.
HRESULT CreateInstance(REFCLSID rclsid, REFIID riid, void** ppv)
{
  HRESULT hr = E_FAIL;
  HINSTANCE hinstDll;
  DLLGETCLASSOBJECT DllGetClassObject;

  hinstDll = LoadLibrary(TIMERSDLL);
  if (hinstDll == NULL)
    std::cout << "Unable to load \"" TIMERSDLL "\"" << std::endl;
  else
  {
    DllGetClassObject =
      (DLLGETCLASSOBJECT) GetProcAddress(hinstDll,
        "DllGetClassObject");
    if (DllGetClassObject != NULL)
      hr = DllGetClassObject(rclsid, riid, ppv);
  }
  return hr;
}

void UseStopwatch(IStopwatch* const pStopwatch)
{
  float nElapsedTime;
```

```
  pStopwatch->Start();
  pStopwatch->ElapsedTime( &nElapsedTime );

  std::cout << "The overhead time is "
   << nElapsedTime << std::endl;
}

int main(int argc, char* argv[])
{
  HRESULT hr;
  IUnknown* pIUnknown      = NULL;
  IUnknown* pIUnknown2     = NULL;
  IStopwatch* pStopwatch  = NULL;

  hr = CreateInstance(
    CLSID_Stopwatch, IID_IUnknown, (void**) &pIUnknown);

  if ( !SUCCEEDED(hr) )
    std::cout << "ERROR: Unable to create Stopwatch!!";

  else
  {
    pIUnknown2 = pIUnknown;
    // AddRef() not called because lifetime of pIUnknown wraps
    // pIUnknown2...

    hr = pIUnknown2->QueryInterface(
      IID_IStopwatch, (void**) &pStopwatch);

    if ( !SUCCEEDED(hr) )
      std::cout << "ERROR: Unable to retrieve Stopwatch interface!!";
    else
    {

      UseStopwatch(pStopwatch);

      pStopwatch->Release();

      pStopwatch = NULL;
    }

    pIUnknown->Release();
  }

  return 0;
}
```

In two situations in the **Stopwatch.cpp** code above, the reference counting calls are eliminated. The first is in the call to **UseStopwatch( )**. Here, a copy constructor is called, which copies the pointer of **pStopwatch** located in **main( )** to **pStopwatch** located in **UseStopwatch( )**. Since this is a copy, principle one should apply, and yet no **AddRef( )** or **Release( )** is called. The reason is that we can be sure that the **pStopwatch** located in **main( )** will keep the **IStopwatch** interface in memory during the lifetime of the call to **UseStopwatch( )**, so the need for reference counting in this scenario can be disregarded. In general, you do not have to worry about reference counting in situations when an interface pointer is passed *by value* to a function. It is important to realize, however, that this applies only when the interface pointer is required to pass a pointer to the function, not when the function needs to change the pointer. In fact, to safeguard against this, it is a good practice for you to include the **const** operator as demonstrated previously when you have control over the function header.

The third principle is also the reason why no reference counting methods are called when assigning **pIUnknown2** in **main( )**. In this case, since **pIUnknown2** is finished using the interface before **pIUnknown** calls **Release( )**, it is safe for **pIUnknown2** to skip any reference counting. Please note: Although this will work, you need to be very careful because it is easy to forget that you did it (or not notice when someone else did it) and mistakenly call **pIUnknown->Release( )** before **pIUknown2** is finished. In general, use this optimization only when performance is of the utmost importance and the code is executed frequently. Also, if you do skip reference counting, clearly document it in the comments so that it will be flagged for the next programmer. Lastly, do not count on a global interface pointer to keep an interface in memory. In multithreaded environments, **Release( )** on the global pointer may be called, causing the assumption to fail.

At this point, **IUnknown** has been fully implemented and the client modified to accommodate the changes. Compile and test the code. There are, however, still a few more steps to take toward full COM compliance. The next one we will examine is the class factory.

Building a Class Factory

A class factory creates component objects of one type only.

Throughout the chapter, we have used **DllGetClassObject( )** to instantiate a COM object and then return that object's interface to the client. However, in reality, COM handles this slightly differently. Instead of returning a pointer to the component object's interface, COM returns a component factory that can create objects of the type identified by the CLSID requested by the client. In other words, instead of returning the requested object, the function

DllGetClassObject( ) returns an object whose sole responsibility is to create objects of the requested type. The component object returned by **DllGetClassObject( )** is known as the *class factory*, and it is used to create objects of a particular type and that type only.

The class factory needs to support only two interfaces. The first is **IUnknown** and the second is **IClassFactory** or its more recent incarnation, **IClassFactory2**. **IClassFactory2** supports permissions so that the client is required to have appropriate privileges to instantiate a component object. For now, **IClassFactory** is sufficient. **IClassFactory** is defined like this:

```
IClassFactory : public IUnknown
{
public:
    virtual HRESULT __stdcall CreateInstance(
        IUnknown *pUnkOuter,
        REFIID riid,
        void **ppvObject) = 0;

    virtual HRESULT __stdcall LockServer(
        BOOL fLock) = 0;
```

IClassFactory is derived from **IUnknown**. Therefore, **IClassFactory** is obviously a COM interface supporting the standard **QueryInterface( )** and reference counting functions.

The first function listed is **CreateInstance( )**. The declaration of this function is similar to the **DllGetClassObject( )** function we have already looked at. There are, however, two differences. The first is that there is no parameter specified for the CLSID. Since the class factory can create only one type of COM object, there is no need for this parameter. The second difference is the first parameter of type **IUnknown**. This parameter is used when an interface is aggregated. We will look at this parameter in more detail in a later chapter, but for now we shall simply ignore it since we are not using aggregation in our project. **CreateInstance( )** is used to request a new instance of an object and obtain a pointer to the interface requested in the **REFIID** parameter. This function, therefore, fulfills the main purpose of the class factory—that of manufacturing objects of a specific type.

The purpose of the next function, **LockServer( )**, is a little more subtle. This function is used to keep the entire DLL in memory and prevent it from being unloaded. The **fLock** parameter in **LockServer( )**, therefore, either locks the

DLL in memory or releases it so that it can be unloaded when it's no longer required. Since the **IClassFactory** interface supports reference counting, via **IUnknown**, you may be surprised at the need for the **LockServer( )** function. The problem is that **IUnknown** counts the references on a particular component instance, but there is no method that tracks references on the DLL, indicating when the DLL can be unloaded. The **LockServer( )** function is responsible for incrementing and decrementing a count, which then tracks whether or not the DLL should stay loaded. **LockServer( )**, therefore, is used so that rather than loading the DLL every time when going from zero instantiated objects to one instantiated object, the DLL is loaded only the first time. Future transitions from zero to one component object will not require reloading the DLL if **LockServer( )** is called.

In the same way that **AddRef( )** and **Release( )** need to be called in pairs, **LockServer(TRUE)** and **LockServer(FALSE)** also need to be called in pairs. The difference, however, is that the same instance of a class factory is not required to be used for each call. Therefore, you can call **DllGetClassObject( )** to retrieve one instance of the class factory, call **LockServer(TRUE)**, and then release the class factory instance. At a later time, another call to **DllGetClassObject( )** can retrieve a different instance of a class factory and call **LockServer(FALSE)** on this later instance, thereby freeing up the DLL to be released once no other object instances exist. The way **LockServer( )** works is to keep a global counter variable that is incremented each time **LockServer(TRUE)** is called and decremented with **LockServer(FALSE)**.

The declaration for **StopwatchClassFactory**, which is in **StopwatchClass-Factory.h**, is shown next.

```
// StopwatchClassFactory.h: interface for the
//   CStopwatchClassFactory class.
//////////////////////////////////////////////////////////////////////

#if !defined(StopwatchClassFactory_H)
#define StopwatchClassFactory_H

#if _MSC_VER > 1000
#pragma once
#endif // _MSC_VER > 1000

#include <windows.h>
#include "timers_i.c"
```

```
class CStopwatchClassFactory : public IClassFactory
{
public:
    CStopwatchClassFactory();
    virtual ~CStopwatchClassFactory();

private:
    // Reference counting
  long m_nReferenceCount;

public:
  // IUnknown methods
  HRESULT __stdcall QueryInterface(
    REFIID riid,
    void **ppvObject);
  unsigned long __stdcall AddRef();
  unsigned long __stdcall Release();

  // IClassFactory
  HRESULT __stdcall CreateInstance(
    IUnknown *pUnkOuter,
    REFIID riid,
    void **ppvObject);

  HRESULT __stdcall LockServer(
    BOOL fLock);

};

#endif // !defined(StopwatchClassFactory_H)
```

The full **CStopwatchClassFactory** implementation, which is in the file **StopwatchClassFactory.cpp**, is shown here:

```
// StopwatchClassFactory.cpp: implementation of the
//   CStopwatchClassFactory class.
//
//////////////////////////////////////////////////////////////////////

#include "StopwatchClassFactory.h"
#include "Stopwatch.h"

extern long g_nServerLockCount;
```

```
//////////////////////////////////////////////////////////////////////
// Construction/Destruction
//////////////////////////////////////////////////////////////////////

CStopwatchClassFactory::CStopwatchClassFactory()
{
  m_nReferenceCount = 0;
}

CStopwatchClassFactory::~CStopwatchClassFactory()
{
}

/////////////////////////////////////////////////////////////////////
// IUnknown Functions
/////////////////////////////////////////////////////////////////////

HRESULT __stdcall CStopwatchClassFactory::QueryInterface(
  REFIID riid,
  void **ppvObject)
{
  HRESULT hr = S_OK;

  if (riid == IID_IUnknown)
    *ppvObject = static_cast<IUnknown*>(
      static_cast<IClassFactory*>(this));
  else if (riid == IID_IClassFactory)
    *ppvObject = static_cast<IClassFactory*>(this);
  else
  {
    ppvObject = NULL;
    hr = E_NOINTERFACE;
  }

  if (SUCCEEDED(hr))
    (static_cast<IUnknown*>(*ppvObject))->AddRef();

  return hr;
}

unsigned long __stdcall CStopwatchClassFactory::AddRef()
{
  if(InterlockedIncrement( &m_nReferenceCount ) == 1)
    InterlockedIncrement( &g_nServerLockCount );
  return m_nReferenceCount;
```

```
}

unsigned long __stdcall CStopwatchClassFactory::Release()
{
  if (InterlockedDecrement( &m_nReferenceCount ) == 0)
  {
    delete this;
    InterlockedDecrement( &g_nServerLockCount );
    return 0;
  }
  return m_nReferenceCount;
}

////////////////////////////////////////////////////////////////////
// CStopwatchClassFactory Function Implementation
////////////////////////////////////////////////////////////////////

HRESULT __stdcall CStopwatchClassFactory::CreateInstance(
  IUnknown *pUnkOuter, REFIID riid, void **ppvObject )
{
  HRESULT hr;
  CStopwatch* pStopwatch = new CStopwatch;

  hr = pStopwatch->QueryInterface(riid, ppvObject);
  if (FAILED(hr))
    delete pStopwatch;

  return hr;
}

HRESULT __stdcall CStopwatchClassFactory::LockServer( BOOL fLock )
{
  if (fLock)
    InterlockedIncrement( &g_nServerLockCount );
  else
    InterlockedDecrement( &g_nServerLockCount );
  return S_OK;
}
```

There are two things to notice about the **StopwatchClassFactory** files. First, because **LockServer( )** is responsible for the entire DLL, the counter variable **g_nServerLockCount** is not local to the class factory but instead global to the entire DLL. It is, therefore, declared using **extern** with the actual declaration in **Timers.cpp**. Second, **AddRef( )** and **Release( )**

have been modified slightly to lock the server using the newly added **g_nServerLockCount** variable. This is necessary because any instance of an object should cause the DLL to stay in memory. Previously, **AddRef( )** and **Release( )** were used to indicate only when a component instance could be deleted; now they are also used to indicate when there are no more component objects instantiated, thereby allowing the entire DLL to be deleted.

It is also necessary to make the same modifications to **CStopwatch**, as shown here:

```
unsigned long __stdcall CStopwatch::AddRef()
{
  if(InterlockedIncrement( &m_nReferenceCount ) == 1)
    InterlockedIncrement( &g_nServerLockCount );
  return m_nReferenceCount;
}

unsigned long __stdcall CStopwatch::Release()
{
  if (InterlockedDecrement( &m_nReferenceCount ) == 0)
  {
    delete this;
    InterlockedDecrement( &g_nServerLockCount );
    return 0;
  }
  return m_nReferenceCount;
}
```

Since the code for **IUnknown** in **CStopwatchClassFactory** and **CStopwatch** is almost identical, it is a prime candidate for either a subclass or template implementation, which is exactly how the ATL implements it.

Another file that needs to be updated now that we have the class factory is **Timers.cpp**, which is shown next.

```
// Timers.cpp : Implementation of DLL Exports.

#include <windows.h>
#include "StopwatchClassFactory.h"
#include "timers_i.c"

// Global lock counter used by IClassFactory::LockServer()
long g_nServerLockCount = 0;
```

```
///////////////////////////////////////////////////////////////////
// DLL Entry Point

extern "C"
BOOL __stdcall DllMain(HINSTANCE hInstance, DWORD dwReason,
  LPVOID /*lpReserved*/)
{
  return TRUE;  // All is well
}

///////////////////////////////////////////////////////////////////
// Determines whether the DLL can be unloaded yet
extern "C"
HRESULT __stdcall DllCanUnloadNow(void)
{
    return (g_nServerLockCount == 0 ) ? S_OK : S_FALSE;
}

///////////////////////////////////////////////////////////////////
// Returns a component object class factory back to the caller

extern "C"
HRESULT __stdcall DllGetClassObject(
  REFCLSID rclsid,
  REFIID riid,
  LPVOID* ppv)
{
  HRESULT hr;
  if (rclsid == CLSID_Stopwatch)
  {
    CStopwatchClassFactory* pStopwatchClassFactory =
      new CStopwatchClassFactory;
    hr = pStopwatchClassFactory->QueryInterface(riid, ppv);
    if(FAILED(hr))
    {
      delete pStopwatchClassFactory;
    }
  }
  else
    hr = CLASS_E_CLASSNOTAVAILABLE;

  return hr;
}
```

There is one function added to **Timers.cpp** that we have not covered yet: **DllCanUnloadNow( )**. This function is defined by COM, but created by you. It is added so that the client can determine whether the server is ready to be unloaded. Periodically, COM will try to unload DLLs that are no longer needed. In order to do this safely, without unloading a DLL that is still in use, COM calls **DllCanUnloadNow( )** to check whether the server is still being used. **DllCanUnloadNow( )** simply checks the **g_nServerLockCount** variable, and if it is zero, it returns **S_OK**, meaning that it is okay to unload the DLL; or else it returns **S_FALSE**. Notice that because **IUnknown**'s **AddRef( )** and **Release( )** are also incrementing **g_nServerLockCount**, only one variable is needed to determine whether to keep the DLL loaded.

Since **DllCanUnloadNow( )** is called from the client, it also needs to be exported. Therefore, one last change needs to be made to **Timers.def**, as shown here:

```
; Timers.def : Declares the module parameters.

LIBRARY      "Timers.DLL"

EXPORTS
  DllGetClassObject   @1 PRIVATE
  DllCanUnloadNow     @2 PRIVATE
```

Update the Client and Test

The component server is now complete. And after a few registry adjustments, it will be possible to call the **Timers.dll** using the COM API. Before we do this, however, let's test the class factory and the **DllCanUnloadNow( )** function using the **StopwatchClient.exe**. The updated client code is shown here, with the changes highlighted.

```
// StopwatchClient.cpp :
//   Defines the entry point for the console application.
//

// std::out etc
#include <iostream>

#include "..\Timers\timers_i.c"
#include "..\Timers\Stopwatch.h"
#include "..\Timers\StopwatchClassFactory.h"


// NOTE:  The following line will vary depending on
```

```
// where the Timers.dll is located.
#define TIMERSDLL "..\\Timers\\Timers.dll"

typedef HRESULT (__stdcall *DLLGETCLASSOBJECT)(REFCLSID rclsid,
  REFIID riid, LPVOID* ppv);

typedef HRESULT (__stdcall *DLLCANUNLOADNOW)(void);

// A handle to the Timers DLL
HINSTANCE hinstDll;


// Instantiates a stopwatch object and returns it by reference.
HRESULT CreateInstance(REFCLSID rclsid, REFIID riid, void** ppv)
{
  HRESULT hr = E_FAIL;
  DLLGETCLASSOBJECT DllGetClassObject;
  IClassFactory* pClassFactory;

  hinstDll = LoadLibrary(TIMERSDLL);
  if (hinstDll == NULL)
    std::cout << "Unable to load \"" TIMERSDLL "\"" << std::endl;
  else
  {
    DllGetClassObject =
      (DLLGETCLASSOBJECT) GetProcAddress(hinstDll,
        "DllGetClassObject");
    if (DllGetClassObject != NULL)
    {
      // Request the Stopwatch Class Factory
      hr = DllGetClassObject(rclsid, IID_IClassFactory,
        (void**) &pClassFactory);

      if(SUCCEEDED(hr))
      {
        hr = pClassFactory->CreateInstance( NULL, riid, ppv );
        pClassFactory->Release();
      }
      pClassFactory = NULL;
    }

  }
  return hr;
}
```

2

```
void UnloadDLL()
{
  DLLCANUNLOADNOW DllCanUnloadNow;
  DllCanUnloadNow = (DLLCANUNLOADNOW) GetProcAddress(hinstDll,
    "DllCanUnloadNow");
  if (DllCanUnloadNow != NULL)
  {
    // Request the Stopwatch Class Factory
    if ( (DllCanUnloadNow()) == S_OK )
      FreeLibrary(hinstDll);
       }
}

void UseStopwatch(IStopwatch* const pStopwatch)
{
  float nElapsedTime;

  pStopwatch->Start();
  pStopwatch->ElapsedTime( &nElapsedTime );

  std::cout << "The overhead time is "
    << nElapsedTime << std::endl;
}

int main(int argc, char* argv[])
{
  HRESULT hr;
  IUnknown* pIUnknown      = NULL;
  IUnknown* pIUnknown2     = NULL;
  IStopwatch* pStopwatch   = NULL;

  hr = CreateInstance(
    CLSID_Stopwatch, IID_IUnknown, (void**) &pIUnknown);

  if ( !SUCCEEDED(hr) )
    std::cout << "ERROR: Unable to create Stopwatch!!";

  else
  {
    pIUnknown2 = pIUnknown;
    // AddRef() not called because lifetime of pIUnknown wraps
    // pIUnknown2...

    hr = pIUnknown2->QueryInterface(
      IID_IStopwatch, (void**) &pStopwatch);
```

```
    if ( !SUCCEEDED(hr) )
      std::cout << "ERROR: Unable to retrieve Stopwatch interface!!";
    else
    {

      UseStopwatch(pStopwatch);

      pStopwatch->Release();

      pStopwatch = NULL;
    }

    pIUnknown->Release();
  }

  UnloadDLL();
  return 0;
}
```


Notice that now the client calls **FreeLibrary( )** after checking that it is safe to unload the DLL. You will want to compile and test all of the code to confirm that you entered everything correctly before moving on.

Using the COM API

Since the **Timers.dll** is complete and fully COM compliant, it is now possible to change the client to use the COM API rather than the traditional **LoadLibrary( )** and **FreeLibrary( )** API functions. In addition, the COM API can be used to return component objects to the client without having to implement the **CreateInstance( )** function by hand. Before we can use the COM API, there is one last step that the client will need.

Registering the Server

Registering the component sets up an entry in the Windows registry that indicates where the component is stored.

One significant drawback in the current system is that the path to **Timers.dll** is hard-coded into the client. The result is that if the **Timers.dll** is not stored in the correct directory relative to the directory of the client, the call to **LoadLibrary( )** will fail. To avoid this problem, COM stores the location of the component server in the registry so that when the client tries to access the server, it can look up where the server is located.

Most of today's COM components are self-registering. To do this requires that the server export the **DllRegisterServer( )** and **DllUnregisterServer( )**

functions (which we will examine later in this book). Since there is only one registry key to add for this server, rather than implement these functions, we will simply add the required registry entries by hand in this chapter. To do this, run the registry editor, **Regedit.exe**. All the COM-related keys are found in the "My Computer\HKEY_CLASSES_ROOT" key, with the CLSIDs located in "My Computer\HKEY_CLASSES_ROOT\CLSID." Right-click on this key, and then select New | Key, as shown in Figure 2-10.

For the key name, enter the CLSID for the stopwatch, which is

```
{83DC3C46-1259-4f95-A2D1-CD11A8819E2E}
```

(Remember to use your own GUID values if you generated different ones back when you implemented **QueryInterface( )**.) Instead of the format used in **Timers_i.c**, use the registry format. This is the same format used in the comment when declaring the CLSID. Now add a child key to the CLSID key you created above. This key should be called "InprocServer32" to signify that the server is an in-process DLL. The full key name would be "My Computer\HKEY_CLASSES_ROOT\CLSID\{83DC3C46-1259-4f95-A2D1-CD11A8819E2E}\InprocServer32." After adding this last key, you need to set the key value to the full path of the **Timers.dll**. Double-click on the (Default) item, and set the Value data to the **Timers.dll** path, as shown in Figure 2-11. We are now ready to change the client to use the COM subsystem.

Initializing and Uninitializing COM

Each thread that uses COM must make a call to **CoInitialize( )/CoInitializeEx( )** and **CoUninitialize( )**.

Before any of the COM API can be called, it is necessary to initialize the COM subsystem on each thread that will use COM. This is done with a call to **CoInitialize( )** or its successor **CoInitializeEx( )**. If you choose to use **CoInitializeEx( )**, it is also necessary to define **_WIN32_DCOM**. The advantage of the "Ex" function is that it provides the ability to specify the

Adding the **Stopwatch** CLSID key to the registry

Figure 2-10.

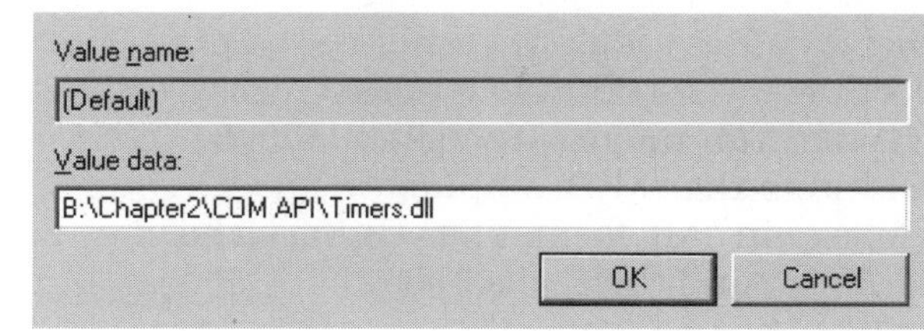

Editing the data value for the InprocServer32 value

Figure 2-11.

2

threading model. For now we don't need to worry about thread models and will simply call **CoInitialize( )**. Its prototype is shown here:

```
HRESULT CoInitialize(LPVOID *NotUsed);
```

Here, *NotUsed* is reserved and must be **NULL**.

Not only is it necessary to initialize COM, but it must also be uninitialized when no longer needed. The call to do this is **CoUninitialize( )**. A call to **CoUninitialize( )** checks to see whether there are any more references on the DLL, and then unloads the COM library and frees the COM server DLLs that were loaded on the thread accordingly. Its prototype is shown here:

```
void CoUninitialize( );
```

Instantiating Component Objects with CoCreateInstance( )

Previously in this chapter, we created a function called **CreateInstance( )** that was responsible for instantiating the component object with a call to **DllGetClassObject( )**. When using the COM library, it is no longer necessary to implement **CreateInstance( )** because COM has an equivalent function called **CoCreateInstance( )**, which is declared as

```
HRESULT __stdcall CoCreateInstance(
    REFCLSID rclsid,     // CLSID of the requested component
    LPUNKNOWN pUnkOuter, // IUnknown of controlling component
    DWORD dwClsContext,  // Execution context of component server
    REFIID riid,  // Requested interface of the component
    LPVOID * ppv);   // Address by which to return the component interface
```

This function is similar to the **CreateInstance( )** function we declared except that it has two additional parameters, *pUnkOuter* and *dwClsContext*. The first parameter is used in aggregation, and we will examine it further in a later chapter. The second parameter indicates the *context* in which the component server is running. This parameter specifies the type of server that contains the requested component. The possible values are as follows:

CLSCTX_INPROC_SERVER	Indicates that the component runs in the same process as the client. Therefore, the component server is a DLL. If the component server is on a remote machine, a surrogate server or proxy will be invoked locally.
CLSCTX_INPROC_HANDLER	Indicates that the component is probably remote but that there is a local, client-side implementation of the class structures.
CLSCTX_LOCAL_SERVER	The component server is a local executable and, therefore, runs in a separate process.
CLSCTX_REMOTE_SERVER	The component server is running on a different machine, which is where the component is then created and managed.

In addition, these values can be combined to indicate that multiple contexts are acceptable. There are two defined constants that are combinations of the above values:

CLSCTX_SERVER	Same as CLSCTX_INPROC_SERVER | CLSCTX_LOCAL_SERVER | CLSCTX_REMOTE_SERVER
CLSCTX_ALL	Same as CLSCTX_INPROC_HANDLER | CLSCTX_SERVER

Since we know that the server is a local DLL, we will use the value **CLSCTX_INPROC_SERVER**.

Here is the final listing of the client code:

```
// StopwatchClient.cpp :
//   Defines the entry point for the console application.
//
```

```
// std::out etc
#include <iostream>
#include <windows.h>

#include "..\Timers\timers_i.c"
#include "..\Timers\Stopwatch.h"

void UseStopwatch(IStopwatch* const pStopwatch)
{
  float nElapsedTime;

  pStopwatch->Start();
  pStopwatch->ElapsedTime( &nElapsedTime );

  std::cout << "The overhead time is "
    << nElapsedTime << std::endl;
}

int main(int argc, char* argv[])
{
  HRESULT hr;
  IStopwatch* pStopwatch  = NULL;

  CoInitialize( NULL );

  hr = CoCreateInstance(
    CLSID_Stopwatch,
    NULL,
    CLSCTX_INPROC_SERVER,
    IID_IStopwatch,
    (void**) &pStopwatch);

  if ( !SUCCEEDED(hr) )
  {
    std::cout << "ERROR: Unable to create Stopwatch!!\n";
    switch(hr)
    {
    case REGDB_E_CLASSNOTREG:
      std::cout << "     Class not registered.\n";
      break;
    case E_NOINTERFACE :
      std::cout << "     No such interface implemented.\n";
      break;
    case CLASS_E_NOAGGREGATION   :
      std::cout << "     No aggregation.\n";
```

```
        break;
      default:
        std::cout << "      Unexpected error.\n";
        break;
      }
  }

  else
  {
    UseStopwatch(pStopwatch);

    pStopwatch->Release();

    pStopwatch = NULL;
  }

  CoUninitialize();
  return 0;
}
```

At this point, all the code has been completed. Both the component server and the client are COM compliant, and the server can be called using the COM API. In the next chapter we will use the Visual C++ wizard to create the same component using ATL.

Reviewing the Key Elements of a COM Component

We have covered a lot of ground since the start of this chapter. Before moving on, let's review the key elements that must be present in order for a component to comply with COM.

First, every interface must implement **IUnknown** at the top of the vtable. In other words, the first three functions on all interfaces must be **QueryInterface( )**, **AddRef( )**, and **Release( )**.

Second, every component must support the **IUnknown** interface, meaning that if **QueryInterface( )** is called on any of the component interfaces and **IUnknown** is requested, the call should complete successfully, returning a pointer to the **IUnknown** interface on the component.

Third, each component must implement the COM reference counting mechanism using **AddRef( )** and **Release( )**. This can be done for each individual interface or else once for the entire component.

Fourth, you must create a class factory for your component. A class factory is used to instantiate a particular type of COM object.

Fifth, you must register the component.

Last, from the client you must call the COM API to initialize and uninitialize the COM system and to create an instance of your component. Thus, you will call **CoInitialize( )** to initialize the COM system, **CoCreateInstance( )** to instantiate a component, and **CoUninitialize( )** to shut down the COM system and release the component DLL.

Although this chapter has described and illustrated the fundamental elements of COM, we have only scratched the surface. We purposely used a simple situation: one in which an executable called into a DLL running in the same process as the executable. More complex situations, of course, exist, such as calling across boundaries or working with a component running on a separate machine. Fortunately, COM is able to handle many of these complexities without requiring any code changes on your part. In the next chapter we will dive into the details of the ATL wizard and see how quickly we can generate component objects without having to labor over so many of the COM details.

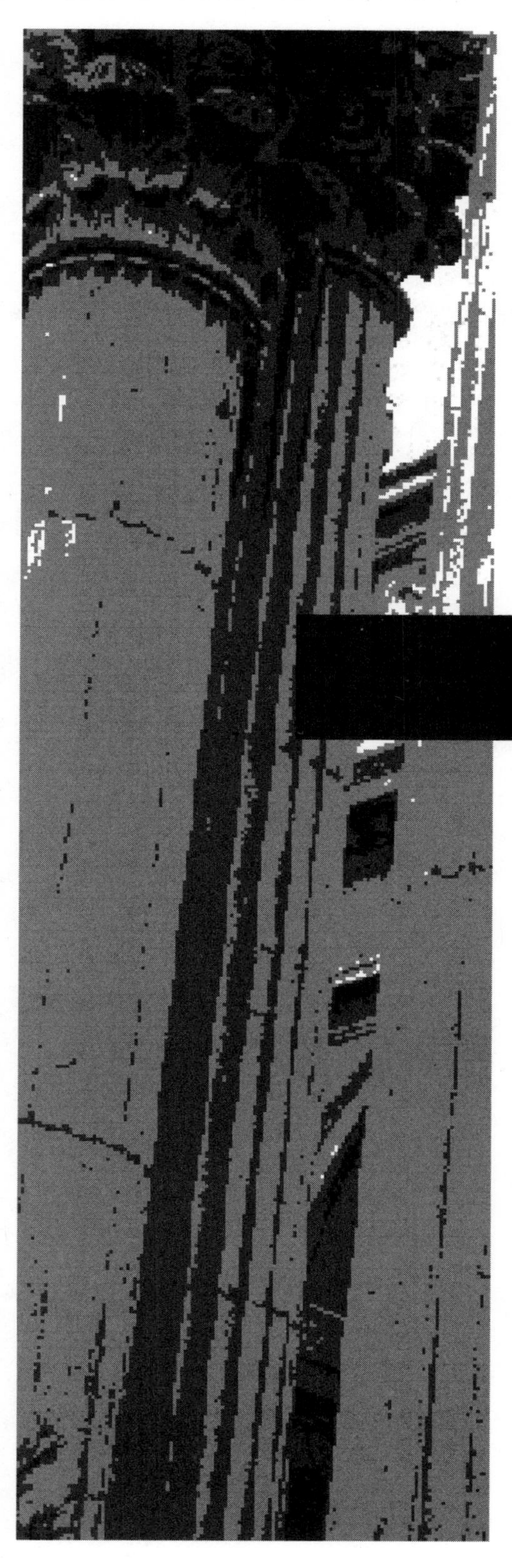

CHAPTER 3

Introducing the ATL

Although it is certainly acceptable to create COM components by hand, as shown in Chapter 2, doing so is the exception rather than the rule. There are several reasons for this, but perhaps the most important is that coding COM solutions manually involves a lot of tedious, sometimes repetitious work because you must reimplement the **IUnknown** functionality yourself. In response to this (and other issues), Microsoft created the ATL, which stands for Active Template Library. The ATL is a class library designed expressly for the purpose of creating COM objects. It provides built-in support for several interfaces, including **IUnknown** and **IClassFactory**. It also supports the creation of ActiveX controls, which are some of the most commonly created COM objects. Finally, the ATL is supported in Visual C++ by the ATL Application Wizard, which allows you to automate the creation of COM components. Because of these advantages, the rest of this book will use the ATL.

We will begin our examination of the ATL by developing the same stopwatch COM server created in Chapter 2, except that this time we will use the ATL AppWizard to generate the initial skeletal code. Most of the chapter, therefore, will discuss the process for creating an ATL project using the wizard. Along the way, we will also introduce several new COM concepts and features, such as the **IDispatch** interface, marshalling, apartments, and aggregation. However, we will defer an in-depth look at the ATL class architecture until later. We will finish by using the stopwatch client we created in Chapter 2 to test the new ATL-based stopwatch server.

Creating a COM Server Using the ATL AppWizard

The **Stopwatch** component that we will create in this chapter will offer the same functionality as the stopwatch timer we created in Chapter 2. In fact, from the client's perspective the stopwatch will be exactly the same. The main difference is that the ATL will be used internally for the implementation, but this change will be invisible to the client. Figure 3-1 shows the design of this component.

The box that appears below the **IStopwatch** interface is the interface design for **IStopwatch**. Notice that the **IUnknown** interface methods—**QueryInterface( )**, **AddRef( )**, and **Release( )**—are not explicitly shown in the diagram because they are assumed to be supported by all interfaces.

Running the ATL AppWizard

To create an ATL version of the stopwatch, we will use the ATL AppWizard provided by Visual C++. To run the ATL AppWizard, go to the File menu and

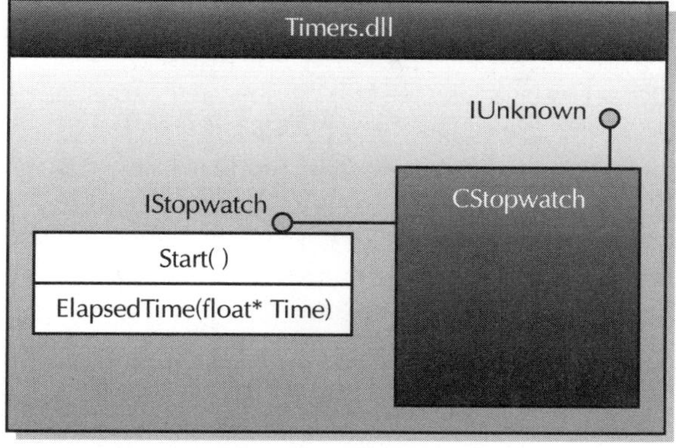

The **Timers.dll** with COM class and interfaces
Figure 3-1.

select New. When the New dialog appears, be sure to select the Projects tab, and then choose the ATL COM AppWizard project. Enter a project name and click the OK button. There is only one step for this wizard, and the dialog for this step is shown in Figure 3-2. As you can see, the dialog box includes several options. Each is examined in turn.

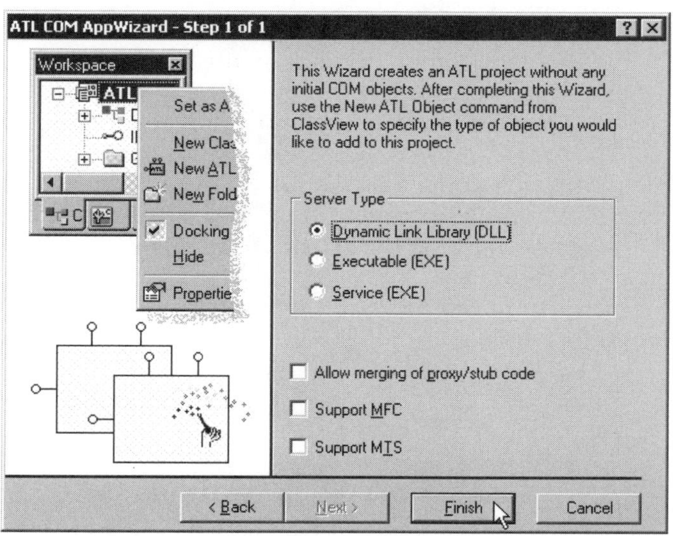

ATL COM AppWizard, step 1 of 1
Figure 3-2.

Server Type

The Server Type group box allows you to choose the form of the executable component. Let's look at each option.

Dynamic Link Library When compiled as a Dynamic Link Library (DLL), a component can run within the same process as the calling client. The result is that usually no context switching will need to take place between calls. (The details of when a context switch is necessary and when it can be avoided are discussed in a later chapter.) This provides for the fastest access because direct vtable pointers can be used between the COM client and the COM server. One of the disadvantages of a DLL, however, is that it cannot run on its own. In other words, it requires a separate executable to instantiate it. Of course, for many applications of COM, this is not an issue. ActiveX controls are typically created as DLLs, for example, because they are always hosted within another application and provide no useful functionality when used alone.

Executable Many applications are compiled as executables because they are designed to run on their own. An e-mail program is designed to run as a stand-alone program, for example, so that users can interact with it, writing and sending e-mails through the user interface. In many situations, however, it would be nice to add e-mail functionality to another program. For example, imagine a second program that monitors the temperature at a remote site. When the temperature reaches a critical level, the program sends an e-mail letting you know. In order to allow the monitoring program to send the e-mail, the e-mail program must support a COM interface that allows the monitor program to programmatically send an e-mail rather than using the user interface. The advantage, therefore, of an executable server is that the program can be run in a stand-alone mode or be called from another program. The disadvantage of this method is that the executable server cannot be run within the same process space as the calling program. The result is a slight delay in each function call as parameters are packaged and sent (marshalled) across the process boundaries from one executable to the next.

Service A service executable has the same disadvantages and advantages as a normal executable with one addition. A service can run without any user interaction. In fact, it is required that a service be able to run without user interaction. This means that a service cannot display any modal dialogs (while running as a service) because there would not be a user to close the dialogs, and the application would freeze as a result. A service can be set to start automatically when the computer starts, without waiting for a user to sign on. An application server is a prime candidate for a service. The monitoring program described in the previous section would be a good choice for running as a service because it should run when the computer starts and continue to run even if no one logs on to the system.

Marshalling is the procedure for passing parameters between processes or machines.

A proxy is the piece of code that packages parameters for a remote procedure call.

A stub is the piece of code that unpacks the parameters in a remote procedure call.

Allow Merging of Proxy/Stub Code

To understand the "Allow merging of proxy/stub code" option, you need to understand *marshalling*. One of the areas in which the COM API is most involved is when instantiating COM objects that are run in a separate process or on a different computer. Marshalling is the procedure for passing function arguments across process and machine boundaries. Marshalling a parameter involves "piping" it through a byte stream across to another process running either locally or on another computer. As we discussed in the beginning of Chapter 1, one of the key requirements for the COM solution is that the location at which a component server is running should be transparent to the client. There should not be any changes required in the client in order to instantiate a COM object on another machine. Marshalling is the feature that achieves this.

Marshalling is implemented using *proxies* and *stubs*, as shown in Figure 3-3. A proxy is a piece of code that packages the parameters. A stub is the piece of code that unpacks the parameters.

The client talks to a proxy running in the context of the client process. This proxy behaves exactly as would a component running locally with

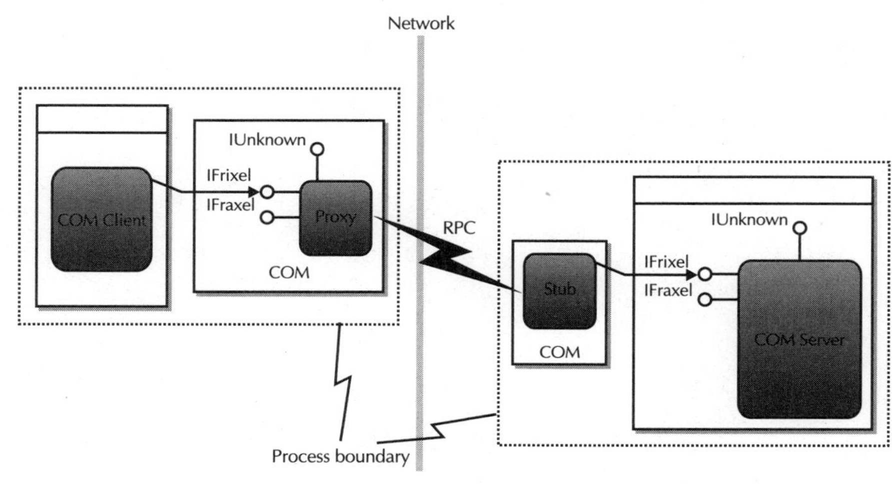

Marshalling across the network using a proxy
Figure 3-3.

the exception of some performance differences. The proxy then uses remote procedure calls (RPCs) to communicate with a stub that is running on the server machine. The stub passes parameters from the client to the server as though the client resided in the same process as the server. Marshalling enters into the process when parameters are passed back and forth between client and server. It is the marshalling code's responsibility to package the arguments so that they can be sent across the wire and then be unpacked on the server machine—even if the server is running a different operating system or is perhaps a different type of CPU.

The proxy can be distributed two ways. The first is to have it defined within a separate DLL. The second method is to merge the proxy stub into the server DLL so that both the server and the proxy code are all combined within the same module, as shown in Figure 3-4.

The advantage of merging the proxy/stub code into the server DLL is that there are fewer files to manage and distribute. In addition, the installation for a distributed server is the same as the installation for the local server because the files are the same.

The disadvantage with this, however, is that the server DLL includes the implementation of the server functionality, so the DLL could be larger. This clearly depends on the amount of code within the server. In small projects the difference is negligible.

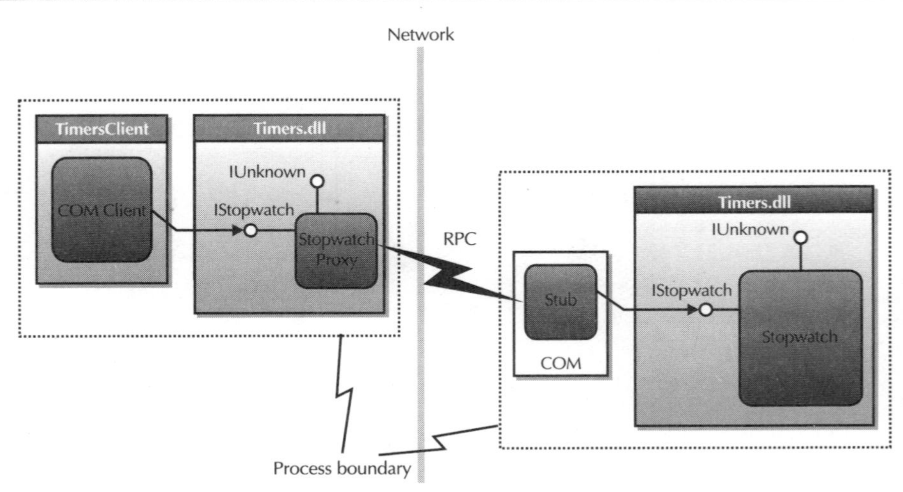

Client calling proxy/stub merged into server DLL
Figure 3-4.

Support MFC

MFC (Microsoft Foundation Classes) is a large library of C++ classes that wrap the Windows API functions. MFC is a powerful tool for programming Windows. Unfortunately, due to the expansive functionality of this library, it is necessary to distribute the MFC runtime DLL along with your component. This adds a burden that ATL was specifically designed to avoid. The advantage of adding MFC support, obviously, is that you get the additional functionality that MFC provides. This includes a significant amount of user interface functionality. It also includes the **CString** class that many Visual C++ programmers have come to appreciate. In general, MFC support should not be added simply to gain access to **CString**. There are other string classes, such as the standard C++ string class **string**, that do not carry the additional baggage of the MFC runtime DLL. Of course, if you know that you will need some of the other MFC classes, then feel free to request support for MFC. There are many useful classes, and they could save you considerable work.

If you choose not to add MFC support, you can add it at a later time simply by including the following lines at the top of the **stdafx.h** file:

```
#include <afxwin.h>
#include <afxdisp.h>
```

Support MTS

The last check box in the AppWizard involves Microsoft Transaction Server (MTS) support. Checking this option makes an addition to the build script, adding **MTX.lib** and **MTXGUID.lib**. **MTX.lib** defines the Component Services API. This enables you to make API calls in order to implement transaction support. **MTXGUID.lib** defines the GUIDs associated with various Component Services objects and interfaces. If you select this option and then do not make any calls to the **MTX.lib** file, a warning will appear during the link phase of a compile. The warning states, "LINK : warning LNK4199: /DELAYLOAD:mtxex.dll ignored; no imports found from mtxex.dll." This can be safely ignored.

Note that MTS support only applies to the NT 4.0 platform. Windows 2000 uses a newer version of this technology called Component Services that does not require MTS support.

As with MFC support, switching to add or remove this option in the future is simple. If you decide not to select this option up front and then want to add it later, simply open the Link tab of the Project Settings dialog, and add "mtx.lib mtxguid.lib delayimp.lib" to the Object/Library modules of the General category. Be sure that when you do this you have selected All

Configurations in the Settings For drop-down menu, or else you will be changing it for one particular build only. Removing these same library files will reverse the process.

Finishing the Wizard

For the component in this chapter, do not make any changes to the default settings shown in Figure 3-2: Dynamic Link Library (DLL) is selected, no proxy/stub code merging, no MFC support, and no MTS support. With the exception of the first option, these options will have little effect on the discussions within this chapter and the next. After you click the Finish button, the files listed in Table 3-1 should be generated. Notice that they are very similar to the same files we created by hand back in Chapter 2.

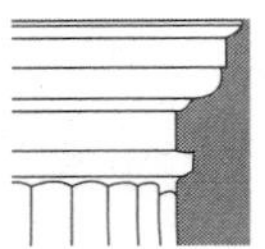

NOTE: If the "Allow merging of proxy/stub code" option is selected in the wizard, a **dlldatax.c** file will also be created. This file contains the code to merge the proxy/stub code into the server DLL.

Now compile the component to verify that everything is working correctly. This should create the **Timers.dll** and register it, but since there is not yet any functionality, nothing can be done with the component.

Files Created by the ATL AppWizard
Table 3-1.

Filename	Description
Timers.cpp	The bulk of the code within this file is concerned with registering the component so that the COM API knows how to instantiate it. In addition, this module defines the class factory code. Lastly, the DLL entry point, **DllMain( )**, is defined.
Timers.def	The definition file that tells the compiler which functions to export. Only the class factory and registration functions are exported by default.
Timers.idl	The IDL (interface definition language) file defines the interfaces that are going to be exposed through COM. No interfaces are defined initially because no COM classes have been added to the project yet.
Timers.rc	The project's resource file.
StdAfx.cpp, StdAfx.h	Standard precompiled header files.

A component self-registers by using the **regsvr32.exe** utility.

Figure 3-5 shows what we have created so far: a component skeleton without any functionality. If there is anything interesting about the component, it can be found in **Timers.cpp**. This file defines the entry points for the DLL as we saw in Chapter 2. Initially, these are all related to registration of the component within the Windows registry so that clients can locate them without requiring them to be in the path of the client application. In Chapter 2 we implemented this registration manually by editing the registry. In contrast, the ATL version is known as self-registering because it can be used by the registration utility, **regsvr32.exe**, to automatically add the appropriate items to the Windows registry.

A complete listing of **Timers.cpp** is shown here. Included are functions that register and unregister the components **DllRegisterServer( )** and **DllUnregisterServer( )**, respectively.

```
// Timers.cpp : Implementation of DLL Exports.


// Note: Proxy/Stub Information
//     To build a separate proxy/stub DLL,
//     run nmake -f Timersps.mk in the project directory.

#include "stdafx.h"
#include "resource.h"
#include <initguid.h>
#include "Timers.h"

#include "Timers_i.c"


CComModule _Module;
```

Timers.dll after running the Application Wizard
Figure 3-5.

```
BEGIN_OBJECT_MAP(ObjectMap)
END_OBJECT_MAP()

/////////////////////////////////////////////////////////////////////////////
// DLL Entry Point

extern "C"
BOOL WINAPI DllMain(
  HINSTANCE hInstance,
  DWORD dwReason,
  LPVOID /*lpReserved*/)
{
  if (dwReason == DLL_PROCESS_ATTACH)
  {
    _Module.Init(ObjectMap, hInstance, &LIBID_TIMERSLib);
    DisableThreadLibraryCalls(hInstance);
  }
  else if (dwReason == DLL_PROCESS_DETACH)
    _Module.Term();
  return TRUE;  // ok
}

/////////////////////////////////////////////////////////////////////////////
// Used to determine whether the DLL can be unloaded by OLE

STDAPI DllCanUnloadNow(void)
{
  return (_Module.GetLockCount()==0) ? S_OK : S_FALSE;
}

/////////////////////////////////////////////////////////////////////////////
// Returns a class factory to create an object of the requested type

STDAPI DllGetClassObject(REFCLSID rclsid, REFIID riid, LPVOID* ppv)
{
  return _Module.GetClassObject(rclsid, riid, ppv);
}

/////////////////////////////////////////////////////////////////////////////
// DllRegisterServer - Adds entries to the system registry

STDAPI DllRegisterServer(void)
{
  // registers object, typelib and all interfaces in typelib
  return _Module.RegisterServer(TRUE);
}
```

```
//////////////////////////////////////////////////////////////////////
// DllUnregisterServer - Removes entries from the system registry

STDAPI DllUnregisterServer(void)
{
  return _Module.UnregisterServer(TRUE);
}
```


The object map specifies the objects implemented by the component server.

We will delay a complete discussion of this code (and all of its implications) until later in this book, but a few words are in order now. To begin, notice the references to the **_Module** variable. This variable is a **CComModule** object, and it is declared at the top of the **Timers.cpp** file in the global scope. **CComModule** is the ATL class that supports servers. **_Module** is similar to "MyApp" for those of you familiar with MFC programming. If you look at each of the generated functions within **Timers.cpp**, you will notice that they all call functions on the **_Module** object.

Following the declaration of **_Module** is the *object map*. This specifies the objects in the module. That is, it is a list of the component objects implemented by the component server. At this point, the object map is empty, but we will soon be adding an object to it. Here, the **BEGIN_OBJECT_MAP** and **END_OBJECT_MAP** macros are used to simply open and then close the empty map.

Notice that the code inside **DllMain( )** differs from that written by hand in Chapter 2. ATL provides its own mechanism to instantiate an object and to terminate (release) it. When the DLL is loaded, **_Module.Init( )** initializes all data members. This is followed by a call to **DisableThreadLibraryCalls( )**. This turns off further notifications when additional threads from the same process connect to the same instance of the DLL. Therefore, after the first time one of the DLL's components have been instantiated by a call to **CoCreateInstance( )** or **CoCreateClassObject( )**, **DllMain( )** is no longer accessed by the same process until the DLL is to be unloaded. When the DLL is released, **_Module.Term ( )** is called.

DllCanUnloadNow( ) and **DllGetClassObject( )** also perform the same operations as those shown in Chapter 2, but the precise way in which they do it differs. In the case of **DllCanUnloadNow( )**, the ATL function **_Module.GetLockCount( )** is used to determine when it is safe to unload the DLL. It returns the lock count for the invoking object. For **DllGetClassObject( )**, the function **_Module.GetClassObject( )** is called, which creates the type of object specified by the class ID. Generally, this is the class factory for the object requested in the client's call to **CoCreateInstance( )**.

DllRegisterServer( ) and **DllUnregisterServer( )** also translate into calls to **CComModule** member functions. These are **RegisterServer( )** and **UnregisterServer( )**.

Adding a COM Object

The next step toward creating the **Stopwatch** component is to add the **Stopwatch** object to the server DLL. "Object" is really not the correct term. What is actually generated is a class, which is the template for an object—not the object itself. However, since this is the term used by the wizard, we will use it here too. This will create the **CStopwatch** class. After this step we should be able to instantiate the **Stopwatch**, but we will not yet have added any methods that can be called. We will also discuss the various wizard options associated with adding the COM object.

From the Insert menu, select New ATL Object. This menu selection can also be made from the Class View pane of the browser window by right-clicking on the project, as shown in Figure 3-6, to open the shortcut menu.

The ATL Object Wizard will appear, allowing you to select what kind of object to create. Most of the objects are variations of the "Simple Object," including

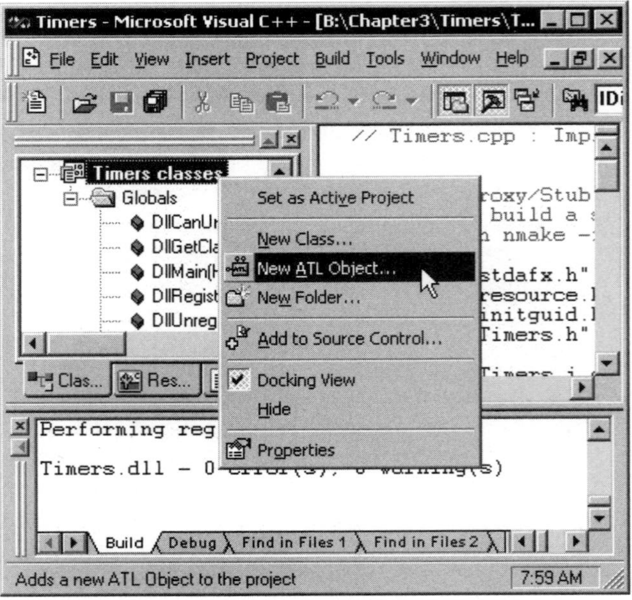

Adding an ATL object to the project

Figure 3-6.

some additional functionality mainly in the area of additional interfaces required by the type of object selected. From this dialog you can begin to get a feel for how extensively COM is used within the Windows platform. Everything from Microsoft Management Console applications and ActiveX controls to OLEDB data providers are utilizing COM. For the **Stopwatch** component we are creating in this chapter, we do not require any of these additional interfaces, so you should select Simple Object and click the Next button. At this point you will see the dialog shown in Figure 3-7.

Table 3-2 describes the text boxes in the Names tab.

Before clicking the OK button, take a look at the Attributes tab, shown in Figure 3-8. You are presented with a myriad of options, each of which will have significant impact on how your object will behave. We will briefly examine these options in the following sections.

Threading Model

A thread is a path of execution. Every process has at least one thread, called the *main thread*, but a process can create additional threads. For single-CPU machines, multiple threads are executed through a process known as *time slicing,* in which the operating system cycles through each of the threads in a very short time interval so that each thread appears to be executing simultaneously. (On systems that have two or more processors, threads run concurrently.) By creating two or more threads of execution, it is possible to

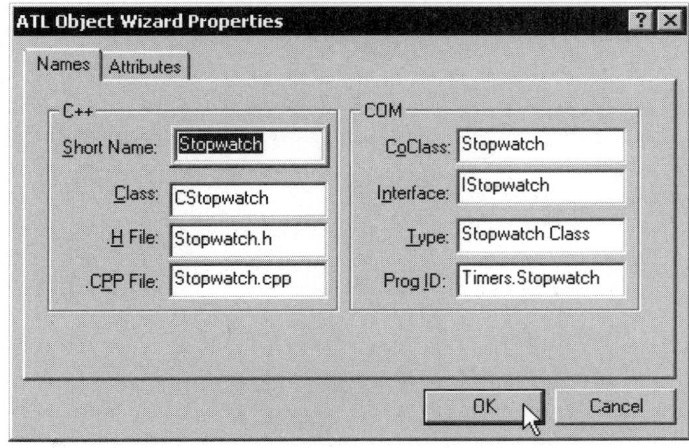

ATL Object Wizard Properties dialog with the Names tab selected

Figure 3-7.

Text Box	Description
Short Name	The name in this box sets the default name in all the other boxes.
Class	The name of the C++ class that will implement the functionality of the COM object we are creating.
.H File, .CPP File	The names of the files that will be created for this COM object.
CoClass	The name of the COM object being created. As mentioned in Chapter 1, this is called the CoClass.
Interface	All COM objects, by default, support the **IUnknown** interface. For a COM object to perform useful work, it needs to support an additional interface that will allow COM clients to call into it. The Interface box allows you to specify the name of the interface. By default, the interface name is the COM object name prefixed by an *I*.
Type	Type is used to enter a short description of the component. This will appear when adding the component to a client project. This comment allows you to give further insight into the purpose of a component beyond what the name provides. This field should be customized whenever the name is not sufficiently descriptive. However, it can easily be changed by editing the IDL file.
Prog ID	In Chapter 1 we discussed the fact that components are identified by a GUID called the CLSID. It is possible, however, to identify a component by a user-friendly name called the program ID. This value is not universally unique, so it should be used with caution when programming, but it is certainly an aid when trying to identify a component.

Text Boxes on the Names Tab of the ATL Object Wizard
Table 3-2.

write very efficient programs because CPU time need not be wasted waiting for a blocked thread to finish. Chapter 13 is devoted entirely to the topic of threading.

An apartment defines a logical execution context.

Before we look at the options provided by the wizard, you need to have a basic understanding of an *apartment*. An apartment refers to a logical context within which COM components execute. Each COM object (instance) runs in exactly one apartment. Methods and properties within the component can

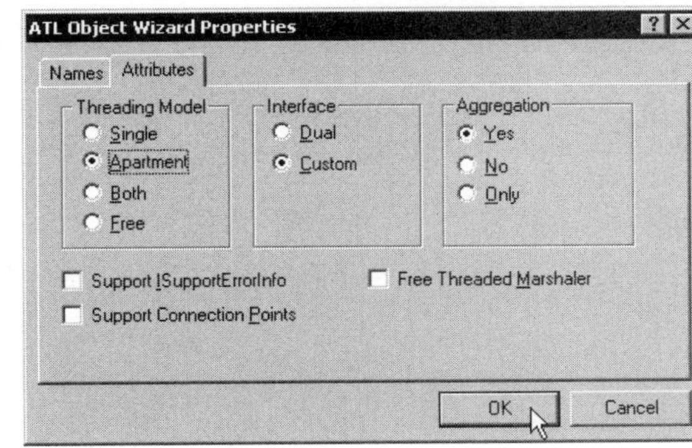

ATL Object Wizard Properties dialog with the Attributes tab selected
Figure 3-8.

be called (based on the COM standard) only by the thread or threads that belong to the apartment. Until Windows 2000 arrived, there were two types of apartments. The first is the Single Threaded Apartment (STA), in which exactly one thread is running. The second is the Multi-Threaded Apartment (MTA) that allows more than one thread per apartment.

Following are the threading model options presented in the ATL wizard. Here, we describe the effect of the threading model rather than discuss the details of how the threading model works.

Single

In the single threading model, COM forces all calls from all component object instances to be from the one main STA thread. All instances of the component run within the same apartment, known as the main STA. The effect of this is that calls into the CoClass code will all be serialized, and only one thread will be executing within any component at a time. Therefore, while one request is being processed *on any instance* of the component, other calls will wait until they can be executed by the same thread. The advantage of this is that the component developer need not worry about synchronizing access to any resources associated with the component, because COM will do this for the programmer.

If you choose the single threading option, you avoid the burden of having to synchronize access by multiple threads to shared resources because single threading causes all access to be serialized. Even items in the shared scope of the class do not need to be protected. This advantage, however, could be the source of a significant performance decrease. If all threads are serialized when entering the component, there will be no parallel execution within the component class. In the majority of circumstances, the single threading model is too restrictive and can cause a performance bottleneck. The single threading model should not be confused with the STA model, which is more common and often referred to simply as the "apartment model," described next.

Apartment

Apartment threading offers a level of parallel processing above single threading. In apartment threading, each instance of the component object can be accessed by only one thread at a time. However, two different requests into two different component objects can execute simultaneously because the components are allowed to run in single threaded apartments other than the main single threaded apartment. When in doubt as to which threading model to use, choosing Apartment is usually a good bet. As mentioned, the apartment model is sometimes referred to as the "Single Threaded Apartment" model because it dictates that each apartment with an apartment modeled component can have one and only one thread. Because each component instance can be accessed by a different thread simultaneously when placed into separate apartments, it is necessary to synchronize access to shared static data. Instance data (member variables), however, will be protected via COM.

Free

In the free model, multiple threads could be running within an apartment simultaneously. Therefore, each component runs within a multithreaded apartment. In the free model, the client can call into any method on any component without being queued by COM. This offers some advantages because of the level of parallelism that can occur, but you should not choose it without fully understanding the consequences.

First, the free model requires that the class can execute in only one MTA and can never execute in an STA. Therefore, if a client running in an STA tries to access a component running in the free model, the calls will all have to be proxied to the server component, thereby significantly decreasing the performance. Simply allowing multiple threads to access your component object simultaneously is not a guarantee of better performance.

Secondly, with the free model it is necessary that you take considerable care to synchronize access to all data within a component—in other words, COM does not handle any of the synchronization. You, the component writer, need to protect all access to data so that no deadlocks or race conditions can occur. All components assigned to the free threaded model run within the same MTA of which there is only one per process.

In spite of all the drawbacks, at times this model may be the right choice. For example, if your component has worker threads, you would probably not want it to execute within an STA because these worker threads would not be allowed to run within the STA.

Both

A component that is marked as Both has qualities of the apartment model and the free model. In the both model, how the code executes is dependent on the context of the client. If the client is running in an STA, the component will operate as though it were configured as Apartment, but if the client is running in an MTA, the component objects will execute in MTA. In the both model you are still faced with handling all your own synchronizations, but the advantage over the free model is that all calls from an STA client will not need to be proxied.

Free Threaded Marshaler

Before moving away from the discussion of threads entirely, let's look at one more check box that appears on the Attributes tab. The Free Threaded Marshaler check box is used so that even if an object is being called from outside its own apartment but within the same process, it will not be necessary for you to invoke a proxy/stub call. Instead, selecting this check box will cause your component to be aggregated from the free threaded marshaler. This will allow a call to be made directly into your component, often providing a performance enhancement. It enables efficient marshalling of interface pointers across threads within the same process. Therefore, if you do not have multiple threads within your apartment, this not required. Instead, it is intended for use with free threaded components.

The drawback to using the free threaded marshaler is that you need to be extra careful not to store any interface pointers which are passed as parameters across apartment boundaries. If you need to do this you will have to marshal them explicitly since the COM subsystem no longer takes care of the work for you. This provides a big opportunity for error and can result is some hard-to-find bugs if a mistake is made.

As with many of the items already discussed, if you wish to add the free threaded marshaler at a later time, you can do this without much difficulty. Do not check this option unless you know you need it. If at some later point you discover it will provide a performance enhancement and you have made your component thread safe, you can always add it. We will discuss how to add this support, along with other threading issues, in Chapter 12.

Interface

The ATL Simple Object Wizard offers two interface options: Dual and Custom. Each is examined here.

Dual

Selecting the Dual interface option will add **IDispatch** support to the component. The **IDispatch** interface is required by all scripting languages (Visual Basic Script, Java Script, etc.). Scripting languages are not strongly typed, and they require special handling in order to use COM. **IDispatch** is a standard interface that allows objects to couple loosely to a component object, calling a particular function at runtime without binding to the vtable at compile time. **IDispatch** exposes function IDs for all the functions supported by a particular component. Each function is assigned an ID that is unique to that component. At runtime the client then passes in a function name to the **IDispatch** interface and requests the function ID corresponding to the function name. Once the client has the dispatch ID (**DISPID**), it can call **IDispatch::Invoke( )** to access a particular method.

IDispatch supports late binding, which is the quality that allows a function call to be resolved at runtime.

The ability to call a class and bind only to the particular function at runtime is known as *late binding*. It presents some flexibility and ease of use when it comes to programming, but it introduces some drawbacks. First, as with any loosely coupled language, there is a greater chance that the code could fail at runtime and produce unexpected results owing to programming errors. Second, the time it takes to call a function is increased considerably over calling into the vtable directly (*early binding*). In spite of these drawbacks, it is a great convenience to be able to call a COM object from scripting languages. It is, therefore, a good practice to have COM objects support the **IDispatch** interface.

A dual interface supports both a custom interface and the **IDispatch** interface.

Fortunately, **IDispatch** support is not provided as an exclusive option. Since components can support multiple interfaces, a COM object can continue to support a custom interface so that direct vtable calls can be made into the component. The combination of supporting both custom interfaces and the **IDispatch** interface is known as a *dual interface*. Supporting the dual interface, therefore, is a superset of the custom interface option.

Custom

The distinction between a custom interface and supporting a dual interface is simply that the custom interface selection will not add **IDispatch** support to the object. Usually you will not choose this option. There is little cost to supporting the **IDispatch** interface, so you might as well support it by default. In other words, if a client always accesses the component through the custom interface, the fact that **IDispatch** is supported will add no overhead to the component. If, however, the client requires the **IDispatch** interface, it will be there.

One reason you may wish not to support **IDispatch** is if you are going to be accessing your component using custom marshalling because you are passing data types that are not supported by **IDispatch**. In this case, you would not want to publish support for **IDispatch** because it would not be supported correctly.

A second reason for not implementing the dual interface is if you are trying to duplicate an interface that has already been defined without **IDispatch**. This, in fact, is true for the **Stopwatch** component. Since we already defined the interface in the previous chapter, we should not have it support the **IDispatch** interface. Normally it would not be a problem simply to add another interface, except that the method used to implement **IDispatch** is inheritance. In other words, when **IDispatch** is supported, **IStopwatch** inherits **IDispatch**, which then inherits **IUnknown**. Using inheritance changes the vtable layout; so instead of the **Start( )** method of **IStopwatch** appearing immediately following the **Release( )** method of **IUnknown**, **Start( )** appears after all the **IDispatch** methods. The result is a change to the **IStopwatch** interface that will then break the compatibility of the previous **Stopwatch** component's clients.

Aggregation

Selecting to support aggregation allows a second component that wraps the inner component to be created in such a way as to expose the inner component's interfaces as though they were part of the outer component.

Aggregation is the process by which an outer object exposes the interfaces of an inner object.

Figure 3-9 shows how the outer component supports both **IInner** and **IOuter** interfaces. **OuterComp.dll**, however, does not contain any code that implements the **IInner** interface. Instead, when a client calls **QueryInterface( )** and requests **IInner**, **Outer** will call **Inner** and request **IInner**. The key here is delegation. **Outer** delegates the functionality of

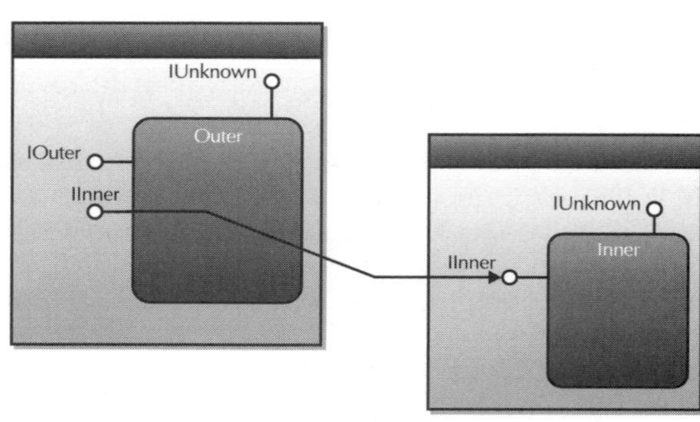

An outer component exposing an interface from an inner component
Figure 3-9.

IInner to **Inner**. Notice that the pointer to **IInner** returned from **Outer** is the same as the pointer returned by **IInner**.

Support ISupportErrorInfo

In Chapter 2 we saw that the return values of many COM functions are **HRESULT** values. As explained, an exception cannot be thrown from a COM function because exceptions are not supported across COM boundaries. Given this restriction, it would appear that the only way to send any error information back to a COM client would be via an error code that is embedded within an **HRESULT** value. This would be a rather serious limitation. How, for example, would you indicate which parameter was bad in a function call with multiple parameters? Or how could you pass back the name of a missing file? The solution is to create an interface that the client could query to retrieve this additional information. Rather than supplying your own proprietary interface, however, Microsoft has included a standard interface called **IErrorInfo**. By checking the **ISupportErrorInfo** option, you indicate that the object will support the standard **IErrorInfo** interface.

At first it may seem strange that you need to support the **ISupportErrorInfo** interface in order to indicate that your component supports the **IErrorInfo** interface. You need to do this because, while each COM object may support multiple interfaces, it will support only one of each type of interface. Therefore, a COM object supports only one **IErrorInfo** interface. Adding the **ISupportErrorInfo** interface, therefore, provides the capability to indicate which interfaces will support the **IErrorInfo** interface.

NOTE: If you are working with an MFC project, you will notice that it is possible to throw a COM exception (**COleDispatchException**). This is because MFC catches the exception and passes it back using the **IErrorInfo** mechanism.

3

Support Connection Points

So far all discussions relating to COM have been about a client initiating a request to a server and then the server processing that request and returning control to the client. There are, however, many times when the server may wish to notify the client of a particular event. Consider, for example, the temperature-monitoring application discussed earlier in this chapter in which the temperature has reached a critical level. Perhaps the easiest way to implement event notification is for the client to poll the server, watching for a change notification. The problem, of course, is that polling places a burden on the server and network even when no significant event occurred. That is, polling is inherently inefficient.

Now consider the advantage of the temperature monitor being able to notify the client of the event. In this case, the event would occur and the server would make one call to the client to notify it of the event. In this scenario, the client becomes the server and the server becomes the client. In order to achieve this *callback*, the client needs to support an interface for the server to call into. Microsoft has implemented a set of these interfaces that all fall into the category of "connection points." We will examine this in detail in Chapter 10.

Finishing the Wizard

The only change you need to make in the dialog shown in Figure 3-8, then, is to select the Custom interface rather than the Dual interface as we explained above. After clicking the Finish button, you will find that the three files listed in Table 3-3 have been added to your project.

In addition to the files shown in Table 3-3, two of the existing files were changed (this does not include **Timers.dsp**, the project file that keeps a list of all the files included in the project). The first is **Timers.cpp**. The changes made to this file were to include the **Stopwatch** object in the set of object map macros. These macros, starting with **BEGIN_OBJECT_MAP** and ending with **END_OBJECT_MAP**, define (among other things) the function pointers for the **CreateInstance( )** function for both the **Stopwatch** CoClass and its

Files Added when Inserting a Stopwatch Simple ATL Object into Your Project

Table 3-3.

Filename	Description
Stopwatch.h	This file contains the C++ declaration for the **Stopwatch** CoClass.
Stopwatch.cpp	This is the implementation file for most of the interfaces supported by the **Stopwatch** CoClass.
Stopwatch.rgs	This file stores the entries that need to be imported into the registry when the component is registered.

class factory. The **Stopwatch** client uses **CreateInstance( )** to instantiate the **Stopwatch** object.

```
#include "Timers_i.c"
#include "Stopwatch.h"


CComModule _Module;

BEGIN_OBJECT_MAP(ObjectMap)
OBJECT_ENTRY(CLSID_Stopwatch, CStopwatch)
END_OBJECT_MAP()
```

Since **Timers.dll** supports only one COM object, **Stopwatch**, there is only one entry in the object map.

The second file that was changed is the IDL file, **Timers.idl**. This file contains the interface definitions and determines which interfaces are supported by which components. As already mentioned in Chapter 1, the MIDL compiler compiles the IDL file into a type library that can be read by many of the development products. In addition, the MIDL compiler generates C/C++ header files that are then included automatically in your projects. Previously the **Timers.idl** file did not have any interfaces defined. The updated version is shown next. While we won't explore IDL files until Chapter 4, it is still useful to examine **Timers.idl** briefly now. You will see that two sections of code have been added. The first is the entry that declares the **IStopwatch** interface. It will contain each of the **IStopwatch** methods and properties. The second section declares all the custom interfaces that the component supports. The **[default]** attribute indicates that this is the default interface for the component.

```
// Timers.idl : IDL source for Timers.dll
//

// This file will be processed by the MIDL tool to
// produce the type library (Timers.tlb) and marshalling code.

import "oaidl.idl";
import "ocidl.idl";
  [
    object,
    uuid(D215B210-F0F3-455E-A6CB-A8D6308058B4),

    helpstring("IStopwatch Interface"),
    pointer_default(unique)
  ]
  interface IStopwatch : IUnknown
  {
  };

[
  uuid(BE5AA5BB-EE1A-49D3-8565-0BCD45F8C354),
  version(1.0),
  helpstring("Timers 1.0 Type Library")
]
library TIMERSLib
{
  importlib("stdole32.tlb");
  importlib("stdole2.tlb");

  [
    uuid(A4C682A2-3CCE-46E9-986D-54B5ACEBBBBE),
    helpstring("Stopwatch Class")
  ]
  coclass Stopwatch
  {
    [default] interface IStopwatch;
  };
};
```

At this point, the component is slightly more interesting than it first appeared back in Figure 3-5. Included in the component now, as you can see in Figure 3-10, is the **Stopwatch** CoClass.

Although the component supports the **IStopwatch** interface, no methods or properties have yet been added, so there is still little we can do with the

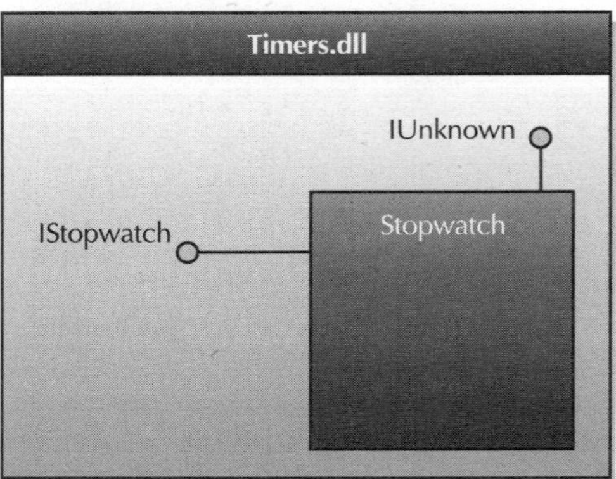

Timers.dll after adding the **Stopwatch** CoClass
Figure 3-10.

component. In fact, to say that the component supports **IStopwatch** is not quite accurate. At the moment, this is a different **IStopwatch** (from that defined in Chapter 2) because it does not support the properties and methods that were previously defined as being part of the **IStopwatch** interface.

Adding the Stopwatch Methods and Properties

The last step before our COM server is complete is to add the start and stop methods that provide the functionality of our component.

Declaring the Methods and Properties

First we will declare the functions. This can click be done by hand, but since Visual C++ has provided some quick menu items to do this for us, we will use them. Select the ClassView tab, and then right-click on the **IStopwatch** interface. Now select the Add Method menu item, as shown in Figure 3-11. The dialog in Figure 3-12 will appear.

Enter **Start** for the method name, and then click the Attributes button. The Edit Attributes dialog will be displayed, as shown in Figure 3-13. This dialog allows you to add attributes to the IDL. It is generally a good practice to provide as much information as is reasonable in the IDL, so enhancing the **[helpstring]** attribute is highly recommended. Many development environments, including all those within Visual Studio, read in the help

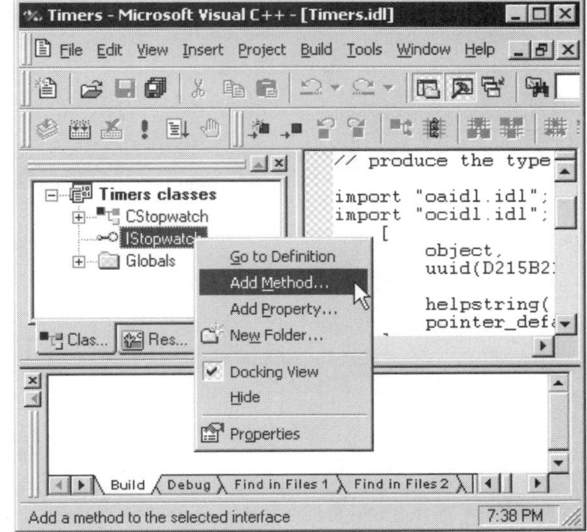

Adding the **Start( )** method to the Stopwatch

Figure 3-11.

strings and display them to the user of your component at design time. The more information you can provide, the more you will help those programmers using your component. Use a simple phrase that describes what the property or methods do or contain. Note that you are limited to 255 characters.

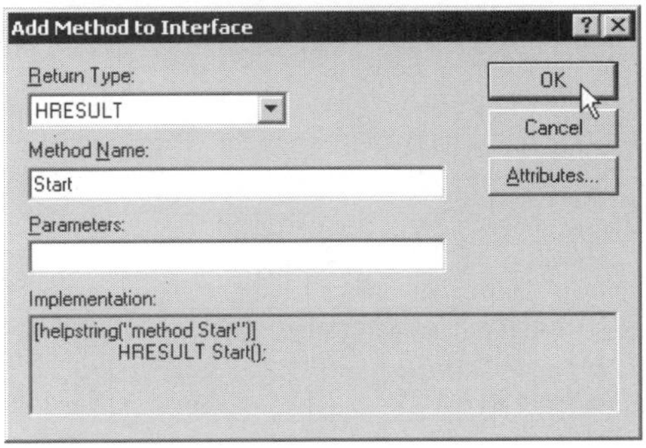

Add Method to Interface dialog

Figure 3-12.

Edit Attributes
Method Name:
Start
OK
Cancel
Attributes:
Name
Value
helpstring
"Starts the timer"

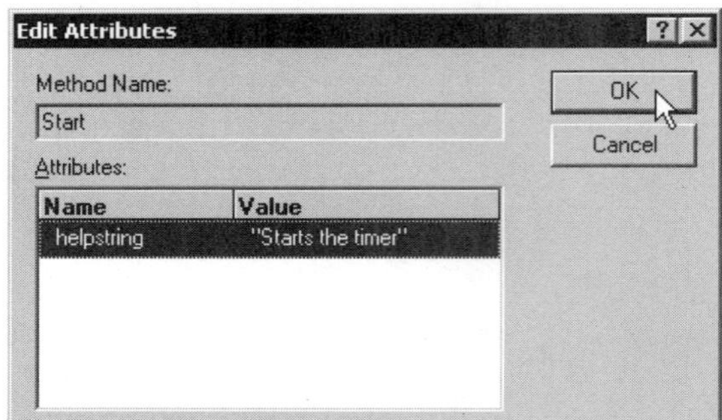

The Edit Attributes dialog for the **Start( )** method
Figure 3-13.

Even the simple message entered in Figure 3-13 is more helpful than the default, "method Start." One other point: You can also change the help string from the IDL file by editing the **[helpstring]** attribute.

Repeat the same procedure for the **ElapsedTime( )** method. Remember, however, that this method includes a return value indicating the elapsed time, as shown in Figure 3-14.

We will discuss the details of each of the attributes later. For now, simply notice that even though the **ElapsedTime( )** method returns **Time,** this

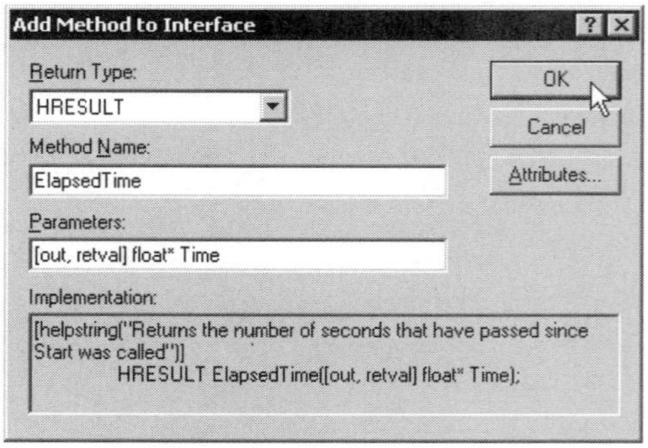

Add Method to Interface
Return Type:
HRESULT
OK
Cancel
Method Name:
ElapsedTime
Attributes...
Parameters:
[out, retval] float* Time
Implementation:
[helpstring("Returns the number of seconds that have passed since Start was called")]
HRESULT ElapsedTime([out, retval] float* Time);

Adding the **ElapsedTime( )** method to the IStopwatch interface
Figure 3-14.

is done using a pass-by-reference parameter so as not to break the guideline that only **HRESULT** values are returned from a COM function.

At this point the interface is completely defined, and all that is left is to fill in the code that actually does the timing. Before we do this, however, let's take a look at the IDL file that has been generated. It is shown here with the most recent changes highlighted:


```
// Timers.idl : IDL source for Timers.dll
//

// This file will be processed by the MIDL tool to
// produce the type library (Timers.tlb) and marshalling code.

import "oaidl.idl";
import "ocidl.idl";
  [
    object,
    uuid(D215B210-F0F3-455E-A6CB-A8D6308058B4),

    helpstring("IStopwatch Interface"),
    pointer_default(unique)
  ]
  interface IStopwatch : IUnknown
  {
    [helpstring("Starts the timer")]
      HRESULT Start();
    [helpstring("Returns the number of seconds that have \
                  passed since Start was called")]
      HRESULT ElapsedTime([out, retval] float* Time);
  };

[
  uuid(BE5AA5BB-EE1A-49D3-8565-0BCD45F8C354),
  version(1.0),
  helpstring("Timers 1.0 Type Library")
]
library TIMERSLib
{
  importlib("stdole32.tlb");
  importlib("stdole2.tlb");

  [
    uuid(A4C682A2-3CCE-46E9-986D-54B5ACEBBBBE),
```

```
    helpstring("Stopwatch Class")
  ]
  coclass Stopwatch
  {
    [default] interface IStopwatch;
  };
};
```

Notice how the **ElapsedTime( )** and **Start( )** functions are declared. Although the syntax is reminiscent of C++, it differs in several ways. For example, the **Time** parameter to **ElapsedTime( )** is preceded by **[out, retval]**, which indicates that the variable pointed to by **Time** will be modified by the function (out) and that this value also constitutes the "return value" (retval). Keep in mind that **ElapsedTime( )** actually returns an **HRESULT** value that indicates success or failure. However, it is the value assigned through **Time** that is, for all practical purposes, the value returned by **ElapsedTime( )**. As mentioned, we will look closely at the IDL in the next chapter.

NOTE: We have used the C++ line continuation format (the backslash) to fit the **helpstring** attribute onto the page. This, however, will not compile, so this line feed along with the backslash should be removed.

If you consider that so far none of the code within the project was written by hand, you will realize that although there is quite a bit of complexity to COM, much of it has been implemented by Microsoft. This leaves you free to focus on the functionality of your component rather than the infrastructure of COM itself.

Adding the Timing Code

We are now going to add the timing code. This code is almost exactly the same as that used in the previous chapter. The first step in adding the actual timing code is to edit the constructor to provide some initialization code. Normally initialization code is placed within the constructor, but because ATL does not create a vtable for the implementation class, initialization code is instead placed in a public function called **FinalConstruct( )**. While we are editing the header file, we will also add several member variables. Recall that each of the values returned from the performance API calls are

LARGE_INTEGERs. A full listing of **Stopwatch.h** with the changes highlighted is shown here:

```
// Stopwatch.h : Declaration of the CStopwatch

#ifndef __STOPWATCH_H_
#define __STOPWATCH_H_

#include "resource.h"       // main symbols

////////////////////////////////////////////////////////////////////
/
// CStopwatch
class ATL_NO_VTABLE CStopwatch :
  public CComObjectRootEx<CComSingleThreadModel>,
  public CComCoClass<CStopwatch, &CLSID_Stopwatch>,
  public IStopwatch
{
public:
  CStopwatch()
  {
  }

DECLARE_REGISTRY_RESOURCEID(IDR_STOPWATCH)

DECLARE_PROTECT_FINAL_CONSTRUCT()

BEGIN_COM_MAP(CStopwatch)
  COM_INTERFACE_ENTRY(IStopwatch)
END_COM_MAP()

// IStopwatch
public:
  STDMETHOD(ElapsedTime)(/*[out, retval]*/ float* Time);
  STDMETHOD(Start)();

  // Perform class initialization
  HRESULT FinalConstruct();

private:
  // The frequency of the counter returned
  // by QueryPerformanceCounter()
  LARGE_INTEGER m_nFrequency;

    // The counter value when the start
```

3

```
    // method was last called.
    LARGE_INTEGER m_nStartTime;

  };

  #endif //__STOPWATCH_H_
```

Notice one point about **Stopwatch.h**: The class **CStopwatch** is derived from **CComObjectRootEx** and **CComCoClass**. These classes are part of the ATL framework.

Since we have already seen most of the timing code in the last chapter, we will not go through detailed code changes again. A full listing of **Stopwatch.cpp** is shown here:

```
// Stopwatch.cpp : Implementation of CStopwatch
#include "stdafx.h"
#include "Timers.h"
#include "Stopwatch.h"

#include <mmsystem.h> // Multimedia timers

////////////////////////////////////////////////////////////////////////
// CStopwatch

HRESULT CStopwatch::FinalConstruct()
{
  // Initialize the remaining member variables
  m_nStartTime.QuadPart = 0;

  // Save the frequency of the performance counters
  QueryPerformanceFrequency ((LARGE_INTEGER*) &m_nFrequency);

  return S_OK;
}


STDMETHODIMP CStopwatch::Start()
{
  if ( QueryPerformanceCounter( (LARGE_INTEGER*) &m_nStartTime) )
    return S_OK;
  else
    return E_FAIL;
}

STDMETHODIMP CStopwatch::ElapsedTime(float *Time)
```

IN DEPTH

A Registration Shortcut

One shortcut that will make the registration of components easier is to associate all DLL and OCX files with the **regsvr32.exe** program. By default, these files have no program association. Double-click on one of them, and you will be prompted with the Open With dialog. Select the Other (Browse…) button, and then browse to and select the **regsvr32.exe** program. Be sure the "Always use this program to open these files" check box is checked, and then click OK. Now whenever you double-click on a DLL, it will automatically register itself. Note that not all DLLs are COM DLLs, so some may display an error indicating that they could not be registered. This error is for informational purposes only and will not have any negative impact on your system. Perform the same procedure for OCX files.


```
{
  HRESULT hr;
  LARGE_INTEGER nStopTime;

  // Set the stop time immediately so that a minimum
  // amount of timer code is executed between the start
  // and stop times
  if ( !QueryPerformanceCounter( (LARGE_INTEGER*) &nStopTime )
       || (m_nStartTime.QuadPart == 0)
     )
  {
    // Either QPC failed or
    // start was not called before stop
    hr = E_FAIL;
  }
  else
  {
    *Time = (float) (nStopTime.QuadPart - m_nStartTime.QuadPart);
    *Time = (*Time / m_nFrequency.QuadPart);
    hr = S_OK;
  }

  return hr;
}
```

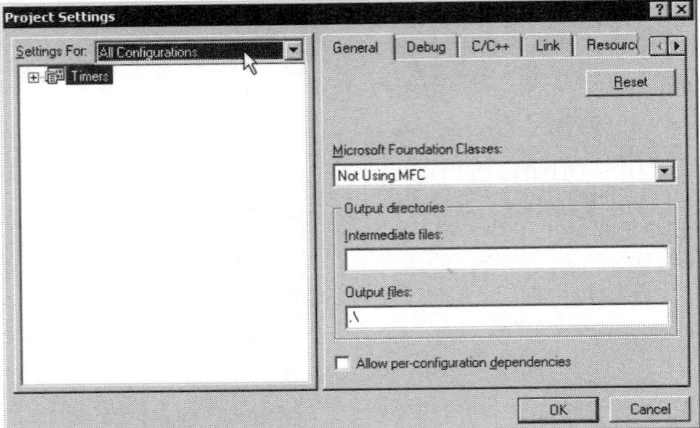

Changing the Output files directory for all configurations
Figure 3-15.

Before compiling, go to the Project Settings dialog (choose Project | Settings). Change the Settings For drop-down to All Configurations. Now change the output directories so that the Output files directory is ".\," as shown in Figure 3-15. This is done so that no matter which compile you choose—Debug, Unicode, or Release—your component will always be placed in the same directory as the rest of your source code. This makes it easier to reference the **Timers.dll** when you create the COM client that will access the **Stopwatch** component. Try compiling the **Timers** project.

Registering a Component

A self-registering component can automatically register itself in the system registry.

Whenever you build a component, Visual C++ automatically registers it for you. This is due to the "Custom Build" step that is added to the project and can be viewed from the Project Settings dialog. If you move the component to a different location or onto a different computer, you will need to register the component manually. As we saw in Chapter 2, registering the component sets up a reference in the Windows registry that indicates where the component is stored so that clients can access it. Another item specified by the registration mechanism, which we did not worry about in the previous chapter, is the threading model of the component.

In the previous chapter we registered the **Timers.dll** manually by editing the registry by hand. The **Timers.dll** created by the wizard, however, is self-registering. This means that it includes the required functions that allow it to automatically register itself in the registry when requested. To register a component manually, you use **regsvr32.exe**, which is located in the **winnt\system32** directory. Register the **Timers.dll** by entering

```
regsvr32.exe Timers.dll
```

at the command prompt. Note that you will need to be in the same directory as the **Timers.dll** or else provide the path.

Whenever an error occurs within a client indicating that a component cannot be found, one of the first things you should try is to (re-)register the particular component in question.

Accessing the Stopwatch Component from the Client

We are now ready to test the **Stopwatch** component. Since we have already developed a client for the **Timers.dll** in the previous chapter, only a small number of changes are needed in order to reuse the client. In fact, the only reason that the previous **StopwatchClient.exe** cannot be used in its current form is because new GUIDs were generated when the ATL wizard created the new project. Therefore, if you want to use the same **StopwatchClient.exe** to access the new **Stopwatch** component, you can do this by changing the GUIDs inside the new server to reflect the same GUIDs in the old server. It is important to note, however, that this can be done only because the interface definition for **IStopwatch** is exactly the same for both components. Second, if you have two different DLLs supporting the same component object with the same GUID, whichever one was registered last will be loaded by COM.

To change the new **Timers.dll** to support the same GUID as the previous DLL, you need to edit the component server's IDL file, since this is where the ATL wizard defines the GUIDs. The following listing shows the required changes. Note that if you used a different GUID in Chapter 2, you will need to use that same GUID here. Also note that in the IDL file, the GUID registry format is used.

```
// Timers.idl : IDL source for Timers.dll
//

// This file will be processed by the MIDL tool to
// produce the type library (Timers.tlb) and marshalling code.

import "oaidl.idl";
```

```
import "ocidl.idl";
  [
    object,
    uuid(EEBF6D1E-8EF1-4acf-9E5F-4D95E01D698A),

    helpstring("IStopwatch Interface"),
    pointer_default(unique)
  ]
  interface IStopwatch : IUnknown
  {
    [helpstring("Starts the timer")]
      HRESULT Start();
    [helpstring("Returns the number of seconds that have passed
since Start was called")]
      HRESULT ElapsedTime([out, retval] float* Time);
  };

[
  uuid(BE5AA5BB-EE1A-49D3-8565-0BCD45F8C354),
  version(1.0),
  helpstring("Timers 1.0 Type Library")
]
library TIMERSLib
{
  importlib("stdole32.tlb");
  importlib("stdole2.tlb");

  [
  uuid(83DC3C46-1259-4f95-A2D1-CD11A8819E2E),
  helpstring("Stopwatch Class")
  ]
  coclass Stopwatch
  {
    [default] interface IStopwatch;
  };
};
```

Unfortunately, there is one other place where the GUID is hard-coded. This is in the "REGISTRY" resource called **IDR_STOPWATCH**. This resource can be edited from the registry editor, but it is easier if you open the storage file, **Stopwatch.rgs**, directly.

```
HKCR
{
  Timers.Stopwatch.1 = s 'Stopwatch Class'
  {
    CLSID = s '{83DC3C46-1259-4f95-A2D1-CD11A8819E2E}'
  }
  Timers.Stopwatch = s 'Stopwatch Class'
  {
    CLSID = s '{83DC3C46-1259-4f95-A2D1-CD11A8819E2E}'
    CurVer = s 'Timers.Stopwatch.1'
  }
  NoRemove CLSID
  {
    ForceRemove {83DC3C46-1259-4f95-A2D1-CD11A8819E2E} =
                    s 'Stopwatch Class'
    {
      ProgID = s 'Timers.Stopwatch.1'
      VersionIndependentProgID = s 'Timers.Stopwatch'
      ForceRemove 'Programmable'
      InprocServer32 = s '%MODULE%'
      {
        val ThreadingModel = s 'Apartment'
      }
      'TypeLib' = s '{D7EBA784-2BF1-11D3-A48B-0000861C844E}'
    }
  }
}
```

After making the above changes and recompiling (and registering) the **Timers.dll**, you will be able to run the **StopwatchClient.exe** program discussed in the previous chapter and have it call into the new server.

We have now finished creating a component server using the ATL wizard. In the process, we have introduced several more COM elements, including **IDispatch**, apartments, aggregation, and marshalling. You have also seen how to register a COM component using **regsvr32.exe**. In the next chapter we will take a more detailed look into the IDL, interface properties, and methods. We will also look at the **#import** statement to see how the preprocessor is helping out.

CHAPTER 4

Introducing the IDL

In this chapter we will begin our exploration of the IDL (interface definition language). We will do so by examining the **Timers.idl** file, looking at how it defines the COM interface for the **Stopwatch** object. You will recall that an IDL file defines the interfaces supported by components. Generally, it also defines the type library for those interfaces. For the Timers project, the IDL file defines the **IStopwatch** interface and type library, which are used by the **Stopwatch** component object.

Output from the MIDL Compiler

An IDL file is compiled by the MIDL compiler. Before you look at the IDL itself, it will be useful for you to review the output files created by MIDL. First is the type library. This binary file contains information about the objects exposed by a COM server. The type library is loaded by development tools that read the interfaces of the component objects described by the type library. More importantly, the type library can be used by the standard COM marshaller to marshal across COM boundaries. As we saw in the previous chapter, the type library is not always a separate TLB file. Sometimes it is compiled as a resource into the DLL or executable with which it is associated.

Second, the MIDL compiler creates a C/C++ header file that can then be included in a C/C++ project. The IDL file, which is the input to the MIDL compiler, is not compatible with C/C++; so it is preprocessed by the MIDL compiler, which outputs C/C++ code in the form of a header file. For C++, the result is that classes can then be derived from the interfaces. Furthermore, the various enumerations, structures, and unions included in the IDL can be used within the C/C++ code. In the Timers project, the name of the file is **Timers.h**.

Next comes the interface UUID file that declares the GUIDs associated with each of the interfaces and classes within the IDL file. These can be used in your program. So, rather than coding a long GUID value, you can use a constant. For example, when you need to refer to the Stopwatch ID, you can use **CLSID_Stopwatch**.

Last, the IDL file is used to create proxy/stub source files that can then be compiled into a proxy DLL and used by COM clients to reach component objects that are running across the network.

IDL Basics

The interface definition language is the means through which you will define the interfaces that are supported by a COM object. IDL defines a number of keywords that constitute statements and attributes. Although not a programming language per se, the structure of the IDL will be familiar to all programmers. Although the exact contents of an IDL file vary, depending upon usage and need, an IDL file for a COM object will contain two main elements: interface declarations and a library statement.

As a vehicle for learning about the IDL, we will use the **Timers.idl** file that was generated in Chapter 3. It contains the essential ingredients found in all ATL-generated libraries. **Timers.idl** is shown here:


```
// Timers.idl : IDL source for Timers.dll
//

// This file will be processed by the MIDL tool to
// produce the type library (Timers.tlb) and marshalling code.

import "oaidl.idl";
import "ocidl.idl";
  [
    object,
    uuid(EEBF6D1E-8EF1-4acf-9E5F-4D95E01D698A),

    helpstring("IStopwatch Interface"),
    pointer_default(unique)
  ]
  interface IStopwatch : IUnknown
  {
    [helpstring("Starts the timer")]
      HRESULT Start();
    [helpstring("Returns the number of seconds that have \
        passed since Start was called")]
      HRESULT ElapsedTime([out, retval] float* Time);
  };

[
  uuid(BE5AA5BB-EE1A-49D3-8565-0BCD45F8C354),
  version(1.0),
  helpstring("Timers 1.0 Type Library")
]
library TIMERSLib
{
  importlib("stdole32.tlb");
  importlib("stdole2.tlb");

  [
    uuid(83DC3C46-1259-4f95-A2D1-CD11A8819E2E),
```

```
    helpstring("Stopwatch Class")
  ]
  coclass Stopwatch
  {
    [default] interface IStopwatch;
  };
};
```

The **import** keyword includes another file.

One of the first things to notice is that the IDL syntax is similar to C++ and that an IDL file is conceptually similar to a C++ header file. Also notice the **import** statement. This is used to specify another declaration file (header file, IDL, or ODL file) in a manner similar to C++'s **#include** statement. For example, in **Timers.idl** the **oaidl.idl** and **ocidl.idl** files are included using the **import** keyword. The files included here provide declarations for types such as **HRESULT** and **IUnknown**. Although **import** is the IDL method for including an external file within the IDL, **#include** is also supported.

Next in **Timers.idl** comes the interface definition for **IStopwatch**. This definition is used to generate a C/C++ header file that defines the **IStopwatch** class. In general, an IDL file will begin with one or more interface definitions.

Once all the interfaces are defined, the library is defined. The library is the set of all the interfaces and CoClasses supported by the DLL or executable. The information in the library is used to generate the type library file. Within the library, each CoClass is declared along with the interfaces supported by the CoClass.

In the sections that follow, we will look closely at the interface and library declarations that make up an IDL file.

Interfaces

Interfaces are a key part of a COM component, and you will spend a significant part of your development time designing the ones that ultimately get defined in the IDL code. An interface is defined by using the keyword **interface**. It has this general form:

[*header*]
interface *name* : *inherited-interface*
{
  interface definition
}

In IDL, interfaces are declared using the **interface** keyword.

An interface declaration consists of two main parts. The first part is the *header*, which comprises various attributes that affect the entire interface. The second part is the *interface definition*, or body of the interface. This is where the elements of the interface are declared. The name of the interface is specified by *name*. If the interface inherits another interface, the name of the inherited interface is specified by *inherited-interface*. Technically, the inherited interface is optional, but it is almost always specified. Most often, **IUnknown** or **IDispatch** are the inherited interfaces, although it is not uncommon to specify another interface, especially when a new interface version is being created.

Interface Header Attributes

The IDL defines several attributes, which modify various statements.

Associated with the elements of an IDL file are various *attributes*. These are the words that appear within square brackets (such as those used to delimit a header), and they provide additional information about the items (interfaces, methods, CoClasses, etc.) that they modify. Each attribute is an IDL keyword, and multiple attributes are each separated by a comma.

The header for the **IStopwatch** interface is shown here:

```
[
  object,
  uuid(EEBF6D1E-8EF1-4acf-9E5F-4D95E01D698A),

  helpstring("IStopwatch Interface"),
  pointer_default(unique)
]
```

The header attributes are **object**, **uuid( )**, **helpstring( )**, and **pointer_default( )**. Let's look at each of these in turn.

object

The **object** attribute is a means of specifying that the interface is a COM interface. If an interface is designated as **object**, it can be called remotely (via COM), and each method must return an **HRESULT**. One exception to this rule occurs when **object** is used in conjunction with the **local** attribute. The addition of the **local** designation signifies that this interface will not be called remotely, and therefore, no proxy code will be generated.

Without the **object** attribute, the interface is assumed to be a DCE RPC (Distributed Computing Environment Remote Procedure Call) interface.

All COM interfaces must have the **object** attribute.

Microsoft, therefore, added the **object** attribute as a modification to the original DCE RPC specifications in order to support COM. All the COM interfaces you define will have the **object** designation.

uuid

The next attribute is **uuid( )**. This assigns a GUID to the interface so that the interface can be identified uniquely amongst all interfaces, even if it has the same name as a second interface. You will notice that this attribute also has a parameter. Attribute parameters are specified in parentheses immediately following the attribute. For the **uuid( )** attribute the parameter is the GUID to be assigned to the interface. The GUID is specified using the registry format without the curly brackets, as shown here:

```
[
  uuid(83DC3C46-1259-4f95-A2D1-CD11A8819E2E),
  ...
]
```

helpstring

Next comes the **helpstring( )** attribute. We have already seen this attribute in the previous chapter when it was used on the **Start( )** and **ElapsedTime( )** methods. As before, this attribute is read in by the developer tools so that the programmer can get a little more information about an interface than is available from the interface name alone. The maximum **helpstring** length is 255 characters.

pointer_default

The last attribute is **pointer_default( )**. Remember that the server could be running in a different address space or even on a different computer than the client. This prevents the client from being able to directly access the memory of the server and vice versa. Therefore, when a pointer parameter is passed, a pointer address needs to be translated into the address space of the server. The **pointer_default( )** attribute dictates how this translation will occur and what values are allowable for the pointer.

When specifying a parameter as a pointer, several ambiguities need to be resolved as to how the pointer should be treated. For example, is it okay to change a **NULL** pointer to non-**NULL** (or vice versa) within the function call on the server? Alternatively, is it okay to expect new memory to be allocated on the client if a pointer changes from **NULL** to non-**NULL**? The

pointer_default( ) attribute specifies how pointers will be handled by default for all method parameters within an interface. Therefore, unless designated explicitly on the parameter, the **pointer_default( )** value will be applied to all pointer parameters within all methods and properties of the interface. The possible **pointer_default( )** values are **ref**, **unique**, and **ptr**. By default, the ATL wizard specifies **unique** for the **pointer_default( )**, which is appropriate for most situations. Even when circumstances for special pointer handling do occur, individual parameters can be qualified with **ref**, **unique**, or **ptr**, localizing the impact to the specific parameter rather than to an entire interface.

The **ref** attribute specifies that **NULL** is not a valid value for the pointer and that the pointer always contains a valid value. Furthermore, the pointer value is constant; the pointer must not be changed to a different location in memory. Lastly, you cannot change the size of the allocated memory structure that the pointer references.

The **unique** attribute allows a pointer to be **NULL**, and it can be changed from **NULL** to non-**NULL** and vice versa. In addition, memory on the client can be allocated to accommodate a change from **NULL** to non-**NULL**. In the reverse case, when a pointer goes from non-**NULL** to **NULL**, it is allowable for the server to orphan the memory referenced. Therefore, the client should always have a second pointer to this memory to avoid a memory leak. There are three other significant restrictions. First, because the pointer can be **NULL,** it is important that **unique** pointers never be used to specify the size of a memory structure such as an array. Such parameters should instead use the **ref** attribute if a pointer is passed. Second, you cannot specify an **out**-only parameter (discussed shortly) because then the server stub (when a remote call is used) does not have enough information to duplicate the **unique** pointer in the server's address space. Third, you cannot use aliasing for any of the pointer parameters within the same method. In other words, you cannot have two parameters within the same function that point to the same memory. The problem is that each pointer will be treated separately; so if **NULL** is passed in, the function will allocate memory for two pointers in separate locations rather than just one location.

The **ptr** attribute is also referred to as a *full pointer*. This is the least restrictive of the pointer options. Essentially, it is the same as the **unique** attribute except that the last restriction, regarding aliasing, no longer applies. This approach is expensive, and the occurrence of a situation where aliasing is required is rare. In general, there are low-cost alternatives that eliminate the need to select this attribute.

Interface Declaration

Aside from the attributes, the IDL syntax for an interface closely resembles a C++ class declaration. Of course, in place of the C++ keyword **class**, we find that the IDL **interface** keyword is used. The interface declaration for **IStopwatch** is shown here:

```
interface IStopwatch : IUnknown
{
  [helpstring("Starts the timer")]
    HRESULT Start();
  [helpstring("Returns the number of seconds that have \
      passed since Start was called")]
    HRESULT ElapsedTime([out, retval] float* Time);
};
```

When specifying inheritance, a colon is used to designate which interface to inherit. As we have already discussed, multiple inheritance is not supported, so you can specify only one base interface. If the interface you want to inherit has not yet been defined, you must declare its name so that it can be inherited. (This is called a *forward declaration*.) For example, if you want to derive an interface from **IBaseInterface** but you have not yet defined this interface, you can do the following:

```
interface IBaseInterface;
interface IDerivedInterface : IBaseInterface
{
  ...
}
```

Later on, you can define the **IBaseInterface**.

Just as we saw in Chapter 2, the **IStopwatch** interface is derived from **IUnknown**. Convention dictates that interfaces should be prefixed with an *I* and that each word within the interface name should begin with a capital letter. Underscores are not used between words.

In the body of the interface, you will specify the types, methods, and properties supported by the interface. For example, the body for **IStopwatch** specifies the **Start( )** and **ElapsedTime( )** methods. Before examining these elements, however, we will digress slightly at this point, looking at how an interface definition gets translated into a C++ class.

C++ Interface Definition

Although IDL is similar to C++, it is not the same as C++, and therefore, it cannot be included directly in a C++ program. Instead, the IDL file needs to be compiled by the MIDL compiler into a C++ header file. This file can then be included into a project so that any CoClasses that will support an interface can derive from the C++ interface definition. **Timers.h** is the name of the generated header file in the Timers project, and it is included at the top of both **Timers.cpp** and **Stopwatch.cpp**. Below is a listing of the C++ definition of the **IStopwatch** interface found inside **Timers.h**. The full **Timers.h** file is rather long, but the bulk of its length can be attributed to the fact that there are separate declarations for C and C++, where C++ is distinguished with the declaration of **__cplusplus**.


```
#if defined(__cplusplus) && !defined(CINTERFACE)

  MIDL_INTERFACE("EEBF6D1E-8EF1-4acf-9E5F-4D95E01D698A")
  IStopwatch : public IUnknown
  {
  public:
    virtual /* [helpstring][id] */
      HRESULT STDMETHODCALLTYPE Start( void) = 0;

    virtual /* [helpstring][id] */
      HRESULT STDMETHODCALLTYPE ElapsedTime(
        /* [retval][out] */ float __RPC_FAR *ElapsedTime
      ) = 0;

  };

#else     /* C style interface */

...

#ifndef __TIMERSLib_LIBRARY_DEFINED__
#define __TIMERSLib_LIBRARY_DEFINED__

/* library TIMERSLib */
/* [helpstring][version][uuid] */

EXTERN_C const IID LIBID_TIMERSLib;

EXTERN_C const CLSID CLSID_Stopwatch;
```

```
class DECLSPEC_UUID("83DC3C46-1259-4f95-A2D1-CD11A8819E2E")
Stopwatch;
```

Let's examine the key elements of this file.

MIDL_INTERFACE

The interface definition part of the file listed above begins with the **MIDL_INTERFACE** macro, which is defined as follows:

```
#define MIDL_INTERFACE(x) struct __declspec(uuid(x)) __declspec(novtable)
```

Notice that hidden within this macro is the **struct** keyword, thereby declaring the interface as a **struct** rather than a **class**, as we discussed in Chapter 2. Next come the Microsoft-specific compiler instructions. Essentially, **__declspec** is a means of communicating to the Visual C++ compiler that it is safe to make a storage optimization of some sort.

The first instruction is **__declspec(uuid(x))**, which causes the GUID to be branded to the interface so that later if you specify **__uuidof(*Interface*)**, the GUID associated with the interface will automatically be returned. The **__uuidof** designation can also be used on type names, pointers, references, specific array types, specialized templates, or a variable of a type assuming the **__declspec(uuid(x))** was used in the declaration of the type. This enables easy access to the GUID without ever having to enter it by hand.

For example, because the **__declspec(uuid( ))** was used before the **IStopwatch** declaration shown here

```
struct _declspec(uuid("EEBF6D1E-8EF1-4acf-9E5F-4D95E01D698A"))
  IStopwatch : public IUnknown
{
  ...
}
```

it is possible to use the code **__uuidof(IStopwatch)** wherever **IStopwatch** is defined. So when we want to call **CoCreateInstance( )** from a COM client we can use

```
  hr = CoCreateInstance(__uuidof(TIMERSLib::Stopwatch), NULL,
    CLSCTX_INPROC_SERVER,
```

```
    __uuidof(TIMERSLib::IStopwatch),
    (void**)&pStopwatch);
```

This will return the GUID associated with the interface. In addition, you could use **__uuidof(this)** anywhere inside the **CStopwatch** class since **__declspec(uuid( ))** is used before the **CStopwatch** declaration. Notice in the above code that the same principle is used to retrieve the class ID from the **Stopwatch** object.

The second **__declspec** macro, **__declspec(novtable)**, is a Microsoft-specific optimization that is used to prevent a vtable from being created. Essentially this optimization stops the compiler from generating code to initialize the virtual function pointers of the class, thereby removing the only references to the vtable. This optimization results in a reduction in code size because the vtable does not need to be created. One side effect of this optimization is that you are prevented from instantiating the class, effectively making it into an abstract class. Since interfaces in C++ are usually implemented as abstract classes anyway, this is an insignificant side effect for interfaces.

IStopwatch

After the **MIDL_INTERFACE** macro (back in **Timers.h**) comes the C++ declaration for the **IStopwatch** interface. Just as we saw in Chapter 2, the interface is derived from **IUnknown**. Each of the methods inside is declared with **STDMETHODCALLTYPE**, which is a macro for **__stdcall**. Notice too that each function ends with "= 0," making them pure virtual functions and **IStopwatch** an abstract class. We will look more closely at how methods are declared in a moment.

EXTERN_C

At the end of the **Timers.h** file you will notice two **typedef** declarations prefixed with **EXTERN_C**, which is defined like this:

```
#define EXTERN_C extern "C"
```

Therefore, each of the **EXTERN_C** declared constants in **Timers.h** has been defined elsewhere in another file.

MIDL-Generated UUID File

The file where the **EXTERN_C** declared constants are defined is the MIDL-generated UUID file. In the Timers project, this file is called **Timers_i.c**, and it is listed here:

```
/* this file contains the actual definitions of */
/* the IIDs and CLSIDs */

/* link this file in with the server and any clients */


/* File created by MIDL compiler version 5.01.0164 */
/* at Mon Oct 25 06:45:10 1999
 */
/* Compiler settings for B:\Chapter4\temp\Timers\Timers.idl:
    Oicf (OptLev=i2), W1, Zp8, env=Win32, ms_ext, c_ext
    error checks: allocation ref bounds_check enum stub_data
*/
//@@MIDL_FILE_HEADING(  )
#ifdef __cplusplus
extern "C"{
#endif


#ifndef __IID_DEFINED__
#define __IID_DEFINED__

typedef struct _IID
{
    unsigned long x;
    unsigned short s1;
    unsigned short s2;
    unsigned char  c[8];
} IID;

#endif // __IID_DEFINED__

#ifndef CLSID_DEFINED
#define CLSID_DEFINED
typedef IID CLSID;
#endif // CLSID_DEFINED

const IID IID_IStopwatch = {0xEEBF6D1E,0x8EF1,0x4acf,
                        {0x9E,0x5F,0x4D,0x95,0xE0,0x1D,0x69,0x8A}};
```

```
const IID LIBID_TIMERSLib = {0xD7EBA784,0x2BF1,0x11D3,
                           {0xA4,0x8B,0x00,0x00,0x86,0x1C,0x84,0x4E}};


const CLSID CLSID_Stopwatch = {0x83DC3C46,0x1259,0x4f95,
                           {0xA2,0xD1,0xCD,0x11,0xA8,0x81,0x9E,0x2E}};


#ifdef __cplusplus
}
#endif
```


Timers_i.c declares the GUIDs for each component in the project and each component's custom interfaces. This enables you to use friendly constant names such as **CLSID_Stopwatch** rather than the long GUIDs they represent. This provides a second mechanism for declaring the GUID. Therefore, there are two ways to get access to a GUID value. The first is the **__uuidof( )**, which we looked at earlier. The question, then, is which to use when? Since they both provide the same information, there is no hard-and-fast rule. When writing the client, however, many times you will not have a copy of the UUID file (**Timers_i.c**) because the control is provided by a third party. In this case you probably will need to use the **__uuidof( )** unless you defined the constants yourself. Note, however, that the **#import** preprocessor directive, which we will discuss in the next chapter, can generate the constant names for you if the **named_guids** option is chosen.

Methods

Let's now return to the **interface** declaration in the IDL file. The body of the interface declares all the methods supported by the interface. They each appear within the curly braces of the interface definition and have attributes of their own. COM methods take this general form:

> [*attributes*] HRESULT *name*(*param-list*);

In general, each definition begins with zero or more attributes. After that, the return value is specified and then the method name. When naming the method, use an uppercase letter at the beginning of each word. As with interface names, no underscores are used. For COM, each method returns an **HRESULT** indicating the success or failure of the call. Here is a simple example: the **Start( )** method from the **Timers.idl** file.

```
[helpstring("Starts the timer")] HRESULT Start();
```

The MIDL compiler converts each function to a C++ pure virtual function inside the header file (in this case **Timers.h** shown earlier); so, therefore, they are redeclared inside the CoClass header file (**Stopwatch.h**). The return values on the methods within **Stopwatch.h** are specified with the **STDMETHOD** method. This equates to "**HRESULT** __stdcall," as shown here:

```
#define STDMETHODCALLTYPE  __stdcall
#define STDMETHOD(method)  virtual HRESULT STDMETHODCALLTYPE method
```

Since **IStopwatch** is an abstract class, **CStopwatch** must implement each of the pure virtual functions defined in **IStopwatch**. Therefore, any changes to the IDL file need to be reflected in the function definitions within the CoClass and vice versa. Because the CoClass **CStopwatch** is derived from the interface **IStopwatch**, any in-process call into the component object is a direct vtable call.

Let's consider the entire **Start( )** method declaration from start to finish within the Timers project. First, the **IStopwatch** interface declares the **Start( )** method as part of its interface inside the **Timers.idl** file, as shown here:

```
  interface IStopwatch : IUnknown
  {
    [helpstring("Starts the timer")]
      HRESULT Start();
...
  };
```

Second, the MIDL compiler generates a C++ header file called **Timers.h**, which redeclares the interface in C++ and changes the IDL **Start( )** declaration to be C++ compatible. Here is the C++ version with all the macros expanded:

```
  struct declspec(uuid("EEBF6D1E-8EF1-4acf-9E5F-4D95E01D698A")),
    declspec(novtable)
  IStopwatch : public IUnknown
  {
  public:
    virtual __stdcall Start( void) = 0;
...
  };
```

Note again the use of the pure virtual function. Next, the **CStopwatch** class inherits **IStopwatch**, and, thereby, it is forced to implement the **Start( )** method.

```
class ATL_NO_VTABLE CStopwatch :
    public CComObjectRootEx<CComSingleThreadModel>,
    public CComCoClass<CStopwatch, &CLSID_Stopwatch>,
    public IStopwatch
{
…
public:
    STDMETHOD(Start)();
…
};
```


Finally, the function is implemented within **Stopwatch.cpp**.

```
STDMETHODIMP CStopwatch::Start()
{
...
}
```

If you were to add a method by hand, you would need to be sure to include all these steps. The only file that you should never have to change is the MIDL-generated header file (**Timers.h**). If this seems like something that could become rather tedious, you are in luck, because this is exactly what the ATL wizard can do. Whenever you use the wizard to add a method or property (by right-clicking on the interface in the browse pane), all the declarations are added for you. Unfortunately, this helps only at the time of initially generating the method. Once a method has been generated and then needs to be changed, you will need to go through by hand and change it in each place (again, with the exception of the MIDL-generated file).

Whenever the IDL and your implementation class get out of synchronization with one another, the compiler will show the following error:

```
c:\devstudio\vc98\atl\include\atlcom.h(1827) : error C2259:

  ... cannot instantiate abstract class due to following members:
  ...
```

This is not exactly a clear indication that the problem is a mismatched IDL-to-CoClass declaration. Furthermore, since the error occurs in **atlcom.h**, it is difficult to pinpoint the source. Essentially what the error is saying is that there is a mismatch between the interface definition within the IDL file and the overriding function declarations within your COM implementation class, which results in the pure virtual functions of the interfaces not being overridden correctly. The error occurs because there was a change made in the IDL, which affected how the CoClass function should be declared, or vice versa, a change in the coclass was not reflected in the IDL code. Knowing what caused the error is helpful, but unfortunately, it still does not identify where the problem is.

Information about where the problem is located is provided in the error that follows error C2259 and is shown here:

```
c:\devstudio\vc98\atl\include\atlcom.h(1827) : warning C4259:
   '... ::put_Total(long,long)': pure virtual function was not defined
```

The warning also refers to the **atlcom.h** file, but the text following the warning number refers to the function that is the source of the problem. Given the function name, you can identify which IDL function is mismatched with the C++ definition.

Method Attributes

Before we move on from the method declaration, we should briefly examine several attributes that apply to methods. Most of these are related to enabling help. There is one, however, that is especially important because of its ability to aid when versioning an interface. This attribute is **hidden**.

Among other things, the **hidden** attribute can be used to maintain compatibility with old interfaces. This attribute can be applied to a method, property, interface, CoClass, or entire library. Anything qualified with this attribute will no longer appear in any object browser that the development tool may support. For example, if you apply the **hidden** attribute to the **ElapsedTime( )** method, when coding the client, you will not see this method in the Visual C++ IntelliSense drop-down list displaying the **ElapsedTime( )** function. The function, however, is still supported, so that if you used it in the program, it would still compile. The **hidden** property discourages programmers from using the method in any new development while maintaining compatibility with existing application code.

We have already examined the **helpstring** attribute because it, like all the other help-related attributes, can be used on the interface declaration as well as on the individual function declarations. Here is a list of the help attributes:

Attribute	Purpose
helpfile(*filename*)	Specifies the name of the help file.
helpcontext(*numcontext*)	Sets the context within the help file. *numcontext* is a 32-bit context identifier that maps into the help file.
helpstring(*helpstring*)	Provides a 255-character or less help string, which is associated with the item **helpstring** modifies.
helpstringcontext(*contextid*)	Specifies a specific string context within the help file. *contextid* is a 32-bit context identifier.
helpstringdll(*dllname*)	Used in localization to specify the name of the DLL in order to perform a document string lookup.

4

Parameters

Now that you know how to declare the methods, it is time to turn our focus to the parameters within the methods. Not only can the entire method declaration have attributes, but so can the individual parameters of the methods. For example, the **ElapsedTime( )** method, shown here, has two attributes, **out** and **retval**, associated with the **Time** parameter:

```
[helpstring("Returns the number of seconds that have \
    passed since Start was called")]
  HRESULT ElapsedTime([out, retval] float* Time);
```

We will examine three parameter attributes: **in**, **out**, and **retval**. Of these, **in** and **out** are the most important. These attributes designate the direction in which a parameter is intended to pass data. The **retval** attribute is a way of conveniently returning data to the client as though the parameter it decorates were a function return value. Let's look at each of these a little more closely.

in

The **in** attribute designates the parameter as being passed from the client to the server. For example, consider a function called **SetOverhead( )** shown here:

```
[helpstring("Sets the number of seconds to be subtracted \
    from the ElapsedTime as overhead")]
  HRESULT SetOverhead([in] float NewOverhead);
```

The **in** attribute designates that a parameter is being passed into the server.

SetOverhead( ) is responsible for assigning an overhead to the **Stopwatch** object. This value will then be automatically subtracted from the actual elapsed time before it is returned to the client. **in** is used to indicate that the **NewOverhead** value is to be input but not returned to the client. Conceptually, **in** parameters should be viewed as pass-by-value parameters. Changes made to the parameter by the server do not affect the argument in the client.

Changes to an **in** parameter do not affect the value used in the call.

Let's look at one slightly more complicated example where the **in** parameter is a COM interface rather than a simple data type. The following function passes the **IStopwatch** interface:

```
[helpstring("Sets the stopwatch"]
  HRESULT SetStopwatch([in] IStopwatch* NewStopwatch);
```

In this example, the **IStopwatch** interface pointer is passed into the server, and the server can then call into various methods of the interface. The server cannot change the pointer reference, however. The server could not instantiate a new **Stopwatch**, for example, and change the address of the **IStopwatch** interface, thereby expecting the new object to be returned to the client.

out

An **out** parameter passes information to the client.

The **out** attribute indicates that the parameter is to be returned to the client but that no information is being passed from the client to the server. The server, therefore, should not expect that a parameter marked with this attribute will contain any valid data and should instead treat it as an uninitialized variable.

If the **out** parameter is a pointer (which it always should be), the server should set it to **NULL** if an error occurs, in order to prevent the client from accessing it as though it contained valid data.

Note that the **in** and **out** attributes can also be used concurrently, indicating that a particular parameter is intended to be passed from the client to the server and then back again after the server has had a chance to modify it.

retval

Often the **out** parameter is used in conjunction with the **retval** attribute, which indicates the return value of a function. It does not change how data is passed from the client to the server; it simply makes the client code more readable. You will notice that this attribute is part of the **ElapsedTime( )** function. In **StopwatchClient.exe** we are using "raw" interface calls, so this attribute has no effect. However, when using smart pointers, instead of passing in a pointer to a **float** as an **ElapsedTime( )** parameter, you simply assign the **ElapsedTime( )** return value to a **float** variable. So, rather than coding the **ElapsedTime( )** call as we did in **StopwatchClient.exe**, you can code it using smart pointers as shown here:

```
TIMERSLib::IStopwatchPtr pStopwatch;
float nElapsedTime = 0;
...
pStopwatch->Start();
nElapsedTime = pStopwatch->ElapsedTime();
```

We will defer the discussion of the declaration of **pStopwatch** until the next chapter when we look at smart pointers. For the moment, focus on the call to **ElapsedTime( )**. As you can see, there is no parameter passed as part of the function. This is because the interface definition uses the **retval** attribute, which specifies the **Time** parameter to be the "return value" of the **ElapsedTime( )** function. Therefore, instead of using the usual "pass-by-reference" syntax,

```
pStopwatch->ElapsedTime(&nElapsedTime);
```

you can simply assign the **ElapsedTime( )** result to **nElapsedTime**. Under the covers, the **IStopwatchPtr( )** class is still passing the **nElapsedTime** as a parameter, but this is hidden from the code using the smart pointer wrapper classes.

In Visual Basic, the same concept is used. In fact, a Visual Basic programmer must call **ElapsedTime( )** as shown here,

```
Dim oStopwatch as New Stopwatch
Dim nElapsedTime as float
oStopwatch.Start()
nElapsedTime = oStopwatch.ElapsedTime()
```

rather than calling **ElapsedTime( )** with a statement something like this:

```
oStopWatch.ElapsedTime(nElapsedTime)
```

Remember that the **retval** attribute does not change what or how data is sent, but rather it makes the client code more readable by changing how a function call is written.

Since the **retval** attribute is used to return data to the client, it must always be used in conjunction with the **out** attribute. Obviously, since there can be only one return value per function call, **retval** can be used on only one parameter per method. In addition, IDL syntax requires that if there are multiple parameters on a function, the **retval** parameter (if used) must always be on the last parameter of the function.

Properties

Properties are values stored within an object.

Now that you know how to define a method, let's look at how methods are used to define properties. *Properties* are values that are stored within an object. (That is, a property is a data member of an object.) Properties are accessed through an *accessor function*. The distinction between whether a function is a property or a method is sometimes rather subtle. In general, however, properties are nouns or adjectives, whereas methods are verbs. For example, the properties on a **Car** object may be **Make( )** and **Model( )**, whereas the methods may be **Turn( )**, **Brake( )**, and **Accelerate( )**.

A property is accessed via an accessor function.

Sometimes an item can be either a property or a method depending on the name and how it is used. For example, you could have a property called **Visible( )** that shows a window object when set to true and hides the window when set to false. Alternatively, you could define two methods, **Show( )** and **Hide( )**. In this example, a property would probably be more suitable because there may be times when you do not want to change a window's status but rather just obtain its current state. Checking the **Visible( )** property would make this easy, but determining the state from the **Show( )** or **Hide( )** methods would require a possible change in state that was not intended.

Properties are implemented via methods. Consider the property called **Total** declared below:

```
[propget] HRESULT Total([out, retval] long *pNewTotal);
[propput] HRESULT Total([in] long NewTotal);
```

Notice that the **Total** property consists of two methods with the same name, but with the **propget** and **propput** attributes added. Although a COM object browser would show this as being one property, it involves two functions in the interface. In this example, the first is used to obtain the property value, and the second is used to set it. The purpose of a property, therefore, is to make the client code more readable and the object interface easier to understand. So, for example, rather than providing two methods, **GetTotal( )** and **SetTotal( )**, a COM server will instead provide one property called **Total**.

The C++ implementation for properties is handled via functions. The two IDL property declarations are compiled into two function declarations in the C++ header file. In the C++ versions, the names are prefixed with "get_" or "set_" for **propget** or **propput**, respectively. Using the **Total( )** example above, the C++ declarations in the C++ headers file would be as follows:

```
virtual HRESULT __stdcall get_Total(
  long *pVal) = 0;

virtual HRESULT __stdcall put_Total(
  long newVal) = 0;
```

If you used the wizard to add the property, the COM object's C++ file would use the **STDMETHOD** macro, however, as shown:

```
STDMETHOD(get_Total)(/*[out, retval]*/ long * pNewTotal);
STDMETHOD(put_Total)(/*[in]*/ long NewTotal);
```

Property Attributes

Three IDL attributes unique to properties are **propget**, **propput,** and **putpropref**. For a single property, each attribute can be used only once. In other words, you cannot have two functions declared with **propget** if they are both for the same property. Each attribute is examined next.

propget

propget specifies a get accessor function.

The **propget** attribute specifies a property-accessor function that is called to retrieve the property value. Since the **propget** attribute implies that a value is being returned, obviously, one of the parameters of the accessor function must have an **out** attribute. It is also required that this same parameter have the **retval** attribute. Since the **retval** attribute is used, the return parameter must also be the last parameter in the parameter list.

propput

propput specifies a set accessor function.

The **propput** attribute is used to declare an accessor function as being the "set" function. Therefore, it indicates which method will be used to set the property value. As with the **propget** attribute, the value is passed using the last parameter in the function. In the case of the **propput** method, however, this parameter must have the **in** attribute to indicate that it is being passed to the server.

propputref

propputref specifies a set accessor function that uses a pointer or reference.

The difference between **propput** and **propputref** is that in the latter case a pointer or reference is passed rather than the value. For example, if you created an interface that had a property called **Stopwatch** that accessed an instance of **IStopwatch**, this property would be declared as follows:

```
[propputref] HRESULT Stopwatch([in] IStopwatch* NewStopWatch)
[propget] HRESULT Stopwatch([out, retval] IStopwatch** StopwatchValue)
```

Note that if a **propputref** attribute is used, then in the **propget** declaration, two levels of indirection are specified.

For those who are coding for Visual Basic clients, the **propputref** indicates to Visual Basic that the **Set** statement should be used for an assignment.

Read-Write Properties

In the **Total( )** property examples shown so far, both the *get* and the *put* functions are declared. This enables the property as read-write. It is possible to declare a property as read-only by removing the property *put* function. For example, if the **Total( )** property was a calculated value rather than a value that was set, you would probably want to make it read-only.

It is also possible to make a function write-only by removing the *get* accessor function, although this is not generally considered a good practice. Clients should be capable of checking a property value before setting it, but without the ability to retrieve the current property value, this checking is not possible.

Additional Parameters on Properties

Although it is more common that property functions have only a single parameter (which is the return parameter), properties can have additional parameters, too. Consider a property that returns an object that supports many interfaces—for example, a **HeadOfHousehold( )** property, which returns a person object. A person object could support many interfaces, such as **IPerson**, **IParent**, **IEmployee**, and **IHomeOwner**.

If, by default, the **HeadOfHousehold( )** property returned the **IPerson** interface, the client would be required to make a second round-trip call to **QueryInterface( )** to retrieve the **IHomeOwner** interface. However, the client will usually know ahead of time which interface it requires. Therefore, in the **HeadOfHousehold( )** property call, the client could pass the **REFIID** of the interface it requires, and the **HeadOfHousehold( )** property could return an **IUnknown****. The property declaration would be as follows:

```
[propget] HRESULT HeadOfHousehold(
  [in] REFIID riid, [out, retval] IUnknown** HeadOfHouseholdValue);
```

The call into this property from the client would look a little like a method call even when using smart pointers, as shown here:

```
pIHomeOwner = pIFamily->HeadOfHouseHold(_uuidof(IHomeOwner));
```

Interestingly enough, the **HeadOfHousehold( )** example, with its specification of the requested interface GUID being sent, is a case for the addition of a special IDL attribute.

Whenever you want to return an object and you do not know which interface will be requested by the client, you can use the **iid_is( )** attribute. This is a special way for the client to request a particular interface. In the above example, the server code would look as follows:

```
[propget] HRESULT HeadOfHousehold(
  [in] REFIID riid, [iid_is(riid), out, retval] IUnknown** HeadOfHouseholdValue);
```

Unfortunately, the **iid_is** parameter is not even included in the type library yet, and we are still waiting for some of the development tools (such as Visual Basic) to begin using it. It is a good idea to know about this attribute, however, because it is often used by some of the low-level interfaces and, with any luck, it will be supported more widely down the road.

Although the **HeadOfHousehold( )** example serves well to explain properties with additional parameters, there is one major drawback to the **HeadOfHousehold( )** property declarations shown previously. They each use a **REFFIID** data type, which is not one of the basic COM data types, and therefore is not supported by Visual Basic 6.0 or earlier. The result is that these functions cannot be called from Visual Basic. One work-around is to not use the **iid_is** attribute and, in addition, to pass the **riid** parameter as a string. More often, however, component servers simply return a specific interface and expect the client to call **QueryInterface( )** if it is not the one they want.

Defining the Type Library

Once all the interfaces have been defined, it is time to define the type library and each of the CoClasses that belong in the library. The interfaces and CoClasses defined in the library section of the IDL are going to be included in the type library that is generated using the MIDL compiler. Simply declaring the interfaces within the IDL but outside the library does not add them to the type library. They have to be declared within the library section.

The library is defined by using the keyword **library**. It has this general form:

```
[ header ]
library name
{
  library definition
}
```

A type library is specified by the **library** statement.

Like **interface**, the **library** statement is composed of two parts. The first part is the header that specifies various attributes that affect the entire library. One of these must be **uuid**. The second part is the library definition. The name of the library is specified by *name*.

The ATL wizard includes three library attributes. Two of these, **uuid** and **helpstring,** are the same as those used in the interface definition. The last one, **version**, is used to indicate the version of the type library.

The body of the library contains the declarations of the various interfaces and CoClasses supported by the library. To declare a particular interface, use the **interface** keyword. As long as the interface has already been declared elsewhere, the entire interface should not be redefined. For example, to add the **IStopwatch** interface to the library, use the following:

```
library TIMERSLib
{
   ...
   interface IStopwatch;
   ...
};
```


This declares the interface but does not associate it with any CoClass. Usually, the reason for doing this is because you want multiple objects to support the same interface, and each of these objects is not necessarily defined within the same IDL file or component server module.

Notice from the **Timer.idl** file that you can import into the library body a different type library that has been created previously. This is done using the **importlib** statement. Importing a type library makes any type definitions within other libraries available within the newly declared library.

If the interface that you want to include in the type library is going to be supported by a particular CoClass, there is no need to include the **interface** statement in the library statement, as shown above. Instead, declaring the CoClass as supporting the interface will automatically pull its definition into the type library. Let's look at the CoClass next. Notice that the CoClass definition occurs within the library section.

In Chapter 3, while running the ATL wizard, an option was presented for adding the type library to the DLL. The directive is at the bottom of the **Timers.rc** file in the line

```
1 TYPELIB "Timers.tlb"
```

This inserts the type library into the DLL resources. (Those of you who have created OLE documents using the older versions of the MFC wizard can use a similar line to insert the type library into your projects.)

Defining the CoClass

Just like the interface, the CoClass definition starts with attributes. The attributes created by the ATL wizard are the component object's GUID, the component's version number, and finally, a help string. The GUID and the help string are defined the same way as the interface, using the **uuid** and **helpstring** attributes.

As with each definition we have seen so far, the CoClass starts out with a listing of its attributes inside square brackets. We have already discussed both default attributes, **helpstring** and **uuid**. There is one attribute, however, that the ATL wizard did not add and yet is important to be aware of if you are going to be versioning your component objects. Just like with the library, CoClasses can each be branded with a version number using the **version** attribute.

The **version** attribute uniquely identifies a particular version of a CoClass. The **version** attribute takes one attribute—the version number of the CoClass. The version number is broken down into two parts, which are separated by a period character. The first part of the number is the major version, and the second is the minor version. Notice that the period character between the major version number and the minor version number is not a decimal point but rather a delimiter. Version 7.21, which represents a major version of 7 and a minor version of 21, is higher than version 7.3 but lower than version 7.30. Notice, therefore, that trailing zeros are significant.

Following a listing of each of the CoClass attributes, the CoClass itself is defined using the keyword **coclass**.

```
coclass Stopwatch
{
  [default] interface IStopwatch;
};
```

*The keyword **coclass** defines a CoClass.*

The definition is used to declare what interfaces the component object supports—in other words, what interfaces can successfully be requested via **QueryInterface( )**.

Within the **coclass** statement, each interface is listed using the keyword **interface** or **dispinterface**. The latter is used if the interface can be accessed through **IDispatch** only. We will encounter the **dispinterface** in Chapter 10 when we look at defining source interfaces.

Two significant attributes can be added to the interface declaration. The first is **default**. It indicates that the associated interface is the default interface to be accessed via scripting-based languages, including Visual Basic. When a variable is declared within Visual Basic, for example, it is usually declared as being of the CoClass type. For example, to declare a **Stopwatch** object, specify

```
Dim MyStopwatch As Stopwatch
```

This specifies that the CoClass is **Stopwatch**, but it is not clear what interface is to be used. This is where the **default** attribute applies. The interface used will be the interface that has the **default** attribute.

Surprisingly, each CoClass can have two default interfaces. One of them, however, must also have the **source** attribute. The **source** attribute designates an interface not as an interface supported by the CoClass specifically but rather as an interface for the client to support. It designates an interface as the one a CoClass can call into in order to notify the client of a particular event rather than having the client poll the server to find out when the event occurred. We will look at the event notification mechanism in more detail in Chapter 10.

Adding the Overhead Property to the Stopwatch

Before we end this chapter, let's add one property to the **Stopwatch** component: **Overhead**. This property will identify the overhead, in seconds, associated with calling **Start( )** and **ElapsedTime( )**, without executing any intervening code. That is, **Overhead** will contain the time it takes to call **Start( )** and **ElapsedTime( )**. When timing a code sequence, you will subtract **Overhead** from the total elapsed time. Doing so yields the elapsed time of the sequence itself, without the time associated with calling **Start( )** and **ElapsedTime( )**.

To begin, you need to add the property to the **Stopwatch** object. This is done on the Class View tab by selecting Add Property from the context menu of the interface, as shown in Figure 4-1.

Inside the Add Property to Interface dialog, enter **float** for the Property Type and then **Overhead** for the Property Name. Do not change the Function Type check boxes. The dialog is shown in Figure 4-2.

Now, compile the project. Following is a listing of the new IDL file that is produced, with the changes highlighted.

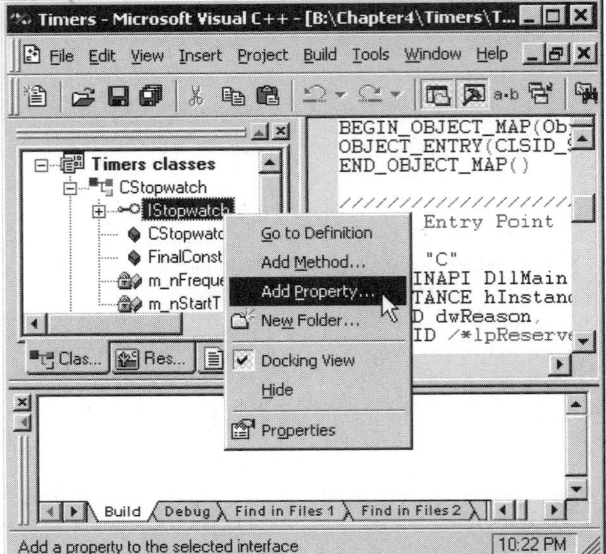

Adding a property with the context menu

Figure 4-1.

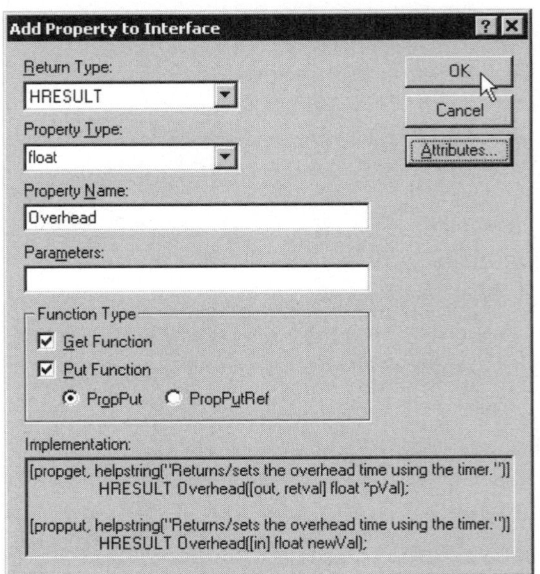

Add Property to Interface dialog

Figure 4-2.

```
// Timers.idl : IDL source for Timers.dll
//

// This file will be processed by the MIDL tool to
// produce the type library (Timers.tlb) and marshalling code.

import "oaidl.idl";
import "ocidl.idl";
  [
    object,
    uuid(EEBF6D1E-8EF1-4acf-9E5F-4D95E01D698A),
    helpstring("IStopwatch Interface"),
    pointer_default(unique)
  ]
  interface IStopwatch : IUnknown
  {
    [helpstring("Starts the timer")]
      HRESULT Start();
    [helpstring("Returns the number of seconds that have \
        passed since Start was called")]
      HRESULT ElapsedTime([out, retval] float* Time);
    [propget, helpstring("Returns/sets the overhead time \
        of the stopwatch.")]
      HRESULT Overhead([out, retval] float *pVal);
    [propput, helpstring("Returns/sets the overhead time \
        using the stopwatch.")]
      HRESULT Overhead([in] float newVal);
  };

[
  uuid(D7EBA784-2BF1-11D3-A48B-0000861C844E),
  version(1.0),
  helpstring("Timers 1.0 Type Library")
]
library TIMERSLib
{
  importlib("stdole32.tlb");
  importlib("stdole2.tlb");

  [
    uuid(83DC3C46-1259-4f95-A2D1-CD11A8819E2E),
    helpstring("Stopwatch Class")
  ]
  coclass Stopwatch
  {
```

```
    [default] interface IStopwatch;
  };
};
```

The **Stopwatch.h** header file was also changed by the wizard when the property was added. It is shown here:

```
// Stopwatch.h : Declaration of the CStopwatch

#ifndef __STOPWATCH_H_
#define __STOPWATCH_H_

#include "resource.h"       // main symbols

/////////////////////////////////////////////////////////////////////////////
// CStopwatch
class ATL_NO_VTABLE CStopwatch :
  public CComObjectRootEx<CComSingleThreadModel>,
  public CComCoClass<CStopwatch, &CLSID_Stopwatch>,
  public IStopwatch
{
public:
  CStopwatch()
  {
  }

DECLARE_REGISTRY_RESOURCEID(IDR_STOPWATCH)

DECLARE_PROTECT_FINAL_CONSTRUCT()

BEGIN_COM_MAP(CStopwatch)
  COM_INTERFACE_ENTRY(IStopwatch)
END_COM_MAP()

// IStopwatch
public:
  STDMETHOD(get_Overhead)(/*[out, retval]*/ float *pOverhead);
  STDMETHOD(put_Overhead)(/*[in]*/ float OverheadValue);
  STDMETHOD(ElapsedTime)(/*[out, retval]*/ float* Time);
  STDMETHOD(Start)();

  // Perform class initialization
  virtual HRESULT FinalConstruct();

private:
```

```
    // The frequency of the counter returned
    // by QueryPerformanceCounter()
    LARGE_INTEGER m_nFrequency;

    // The counter value when the start
    // method was last called.
    LARGE_INTEGER m_nStartTime;

    // Stores the overhead for calling
    // the start and stop without
    // executing any additional code.
    float m_nOverhead;
};

#endif //__STOPWATCH_H_
```

4

Included in the above listing is a manually added **m_nOverhead** variable to store the value of the **Overhead** property.

The last step in completing the **Stopwatch** component is to edit the **Stopwatch.cpp** file and enter the **Overhead** code. First, the **m_nOverhead** variable needs to be initialized. This is done by calling **Start( )** and **ElapsedTime( )** from inside **FinalConstruct( )**, as shown here:

```
HRESULT CStopwatch::FinalConstruct()
{

    // Save the frequency of the performance counters
    QueryPerformanceFrequency ((LARGE_INTEGER*) &m_nFrequency);

    Start();
    ElapsedTime( &m_nOverhead );

    // Initialize the remaining member variables
    m_nStartTime.QuadPart = 0;

    return S_OK;
}
```

By setting the **Overhead** this way, the expense of crossing the COM boundary is not included in the time measurement. The **Overhead** property is read-write, however, to allow a COM client to call **Start( )** and **ElapsedTime( )** from outside of the server and then set the **Overhead** value to include the cost of crossing the COM boundary. Note that the actual overhead is not guaranteed to remain the same throughout the server's lifetime. If the CPU was busy with other operations, it is possible that there will be some variation in what the "true" overhead is.

When the client uses the **Overhead** property, the server needs to store the new overhead value when the client sets it and to return it when the client requests it. A full listing of the code is shown here:

```
// Stopwatch.cpp : Implementation of CStopwatch
#include "stdafx.h"
#include "Timers.h"
#include "Stopwatch.h"

#include <mmsystem.h> // Multi-media timers

///////////////////////////////////////////////////////////////////////////
// CStopwatch

HRESULT CStopwatch::FinalConstruct()
{

  // Save the frequency of the performance counters
  QueryPerformanceFrequency ((LARGE_INTEGER*) &m_nFrequency);

  Start();
  ElapsedTime( &m_nOverhead );

  // Initialize the remaining member variables
  m_nStartTime.QuadPart = 0;

  return S_OK;
}


STDMETHODIMP CStopwatch::Start()
{
  if ( QueryPerformanceCounter( (LARGE_INTEGER*) &m_nStartTime) )
    return S_OK;
  else
    return E_FAIL;
}

STDMETHODIMP CStopwatch::ElapsedTime(float *Time)
{
  HRESULT hr;
```

```
  LARGE_INTEGER nStopTime;

  // Set the stop time immediately so that a minimum
  // amount of timer code is executed between the start
  // and stop times
  if ( !QueryPerformanceCounter( (LARGE_INTEGER*) &nStopTime )
       || (m_nStartTime.QuadPart == 0)
     )
  {
    // Either QPC failed or
    // start was not called before stop
    hr = E_FAIL;
  }
  else
  {
    *Time = (float) (nStopTime.QuadPart - m_nStartTime.QuadPart);
    *Time = (*Time / m_nFrequency.QuadPart);
    hr = S_OK;
  }

  return hr;
}

STDMETHODIMP CStopwatch::get_Overhead(float *pOverhead)
{
  *pOverhead = m_nOverhead;
  return S_OK;
}

STDMETHODIMP CStopwatch::put_Overhead(float OverheadValue)
{
  m_nOverhead = OverheadValue;
  return S_OK;
}
```

Now let's modify the client to use the **Overhead** property. Below is a listing of the new client code.

```
// StopwatchClient.cpp :
//   Defines the entry point for the console application.
//

// std::out etc
#include <iostream>
#include <windows.h>
```

```
#include "..\Timers\timers_i.c"
#include "..\Timers\Timers.h"

void UseStopwatch(IStopwatch* const pStopwatch)
{
  float nElapsedTime;
  float nOverhead;

  pStopwatch->get_Overhead(&nOverhead);

  std::cout << "The overhead time without going "
    "across the COM boundary is "
    << nOverhead << std::endl;

  pStopwatch->Start();
  pStopwatch->ElapsedTime(&nElapsedTime);

  std::cout << "The overhead time with the "
    "COM boundary is "
    << nElapsedTime << std::endl;

  std::cout << "The expense of using the "
    "COM boundary is "
    << (nElapsedTime - nOverhead) << std::endl;

  pStopwatch->put_Overhead(nElapsedTime);

}

int main(int argc, char* argv[])
{
  HRESULT hr;
  IStopwatch* pStopwatch  = NULL;

  CoInitialize( NULL );

  hr = CoCreateInstance(
    __uuidof(Stopwatch), //CLSID_Stopwatch,
    NULL,
    CLSCTX_INPROC_SERVER,
    __uuidof(IStopwatch), // IID_IStopwatch,
    (void**) &pStopwatch);

  if ( !SUCCEEDED(hr) )
  {
```

```
        std::cout << "ERROR: Unable to create Stopwatch!!\n";
        switch(hr)
        {
        case REGDB_E_CLASSNOTREG:
          std::cout << "     Class not registered.\n";
          break;
        case E_NOINTERFACE :
          std::cout << "     No such interface implemented.\n";
          break;
        case CLASS_E_NOAGGREGATION  :
          std::cout << "     No aggregation.\n";
          break;
        default:
          std::cout << "     Unexpected error.\n";
          break;
        }
      }

      else
      {
        UseStopwatch(pStopwatch);

        pStopwatch->Release();

        pStopwatch = NULL;
      }

      CoUninitialize();
      return 0;
    }
```


For those of you who run the code, you will notice that often the client outputs the expense of calling across the COM boundary as 0 or even negative. This is because the COM server is making direct vtable calls into the server, so it is not any slower than when called directly from the COM server. You will see the operation become more expensive, however, when the COM server is running out-of-process or across the network.

We are nearly finished with the **Stopwatch** component. The last piece we need to add is some error handling so that a client will be provided with a little more information when an error occurs. Before we do this, however, we will first look at a few more of the details associated with writing a COM client and consider some more complex data types than the **float**s we have used so far.

IN DEPTH

Changing an Interface

In a strict sense, adding the **Overhead** property to **IStopwatch** is a modification to an already defined interface. As we explained early on in this book, interfaces are not to be changed once they have been published. Thus, in a strict sense, we should not be altering **IStopwatch**, since its form was fully defined in Chapter 2. Of course, in the context of an evolving example in a book, this is not an issue. That is, the **IStopwatch** interface is not a "released" interface, but a textbook example, and changing it is not a problem. Furthermore, simply adding a method will not cause an existing client to fail, because the vtable will look unchanged to the client since the property was appended to the end of the vtable.

However, *if* **IStopwatch** had been a published interface, it would have been wrong to add the **Overhead** property to it. Once it was released we would, instead, consider creating a new interface called **IStopwatch2**, which is derived from **IStopwatch**. Such an interface would be declared as follows:

```
interface IStopwatch2 : IStopwatch
{
    [propget, helpstring("Returns/sets the overhead time \
       of the stopwatch.")]
     HRESULT Overhead([out, retval] float *pVal);
   [propput, helpstring("Returns/sets the overhead time \
       of the stopwatch.")]
     HRESULT Overhead([in] float newVal);
};
```

This new interface would ensure that no new client would attempt to call the **Overhead** property on the older **IStopwatch** interface.

The key point is that in the real world, once an interface is released, it must not be altered. This applies even in such a simple interface as **IStopwatch**.

If you make a change as significant as this, you will also want to change the version on the type library. Earlier in the chapter, you saw how to do this using the **version** attribute on the library statement. In addition, you should edit the various version-related resources such as the RGS file and the string tables.

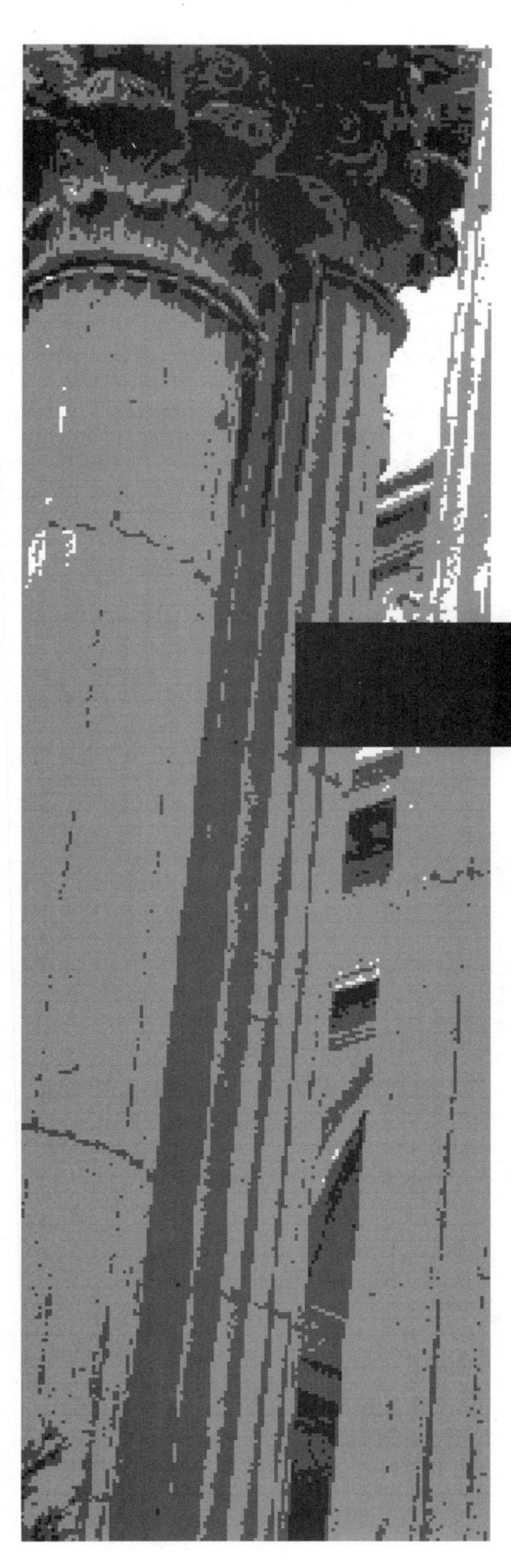

CHAPTER 5

The Client Side of COM and Using Smart Pointers

As you know, a COM client is a program that uses the features provided by a COM server. So far, we have been using very simple clients to demonstrate the COM servers that we have developed. In this chapter we are going to look more closely at the client. In the process, we will examine one of the most helpful C++ methods for working with COM servers—the **#import**-generated smart pointers. *Smart pointers* wrap much of the reference counting mechanism, thus reducing the burden placed on the client programmer. In addition, the smart pointer wrapper classes make it easier to use a COM object because, in contrast to the raw interfaces we have used so far, they are "aware" of many of the IDL attributes, which we examined in the previous chapter.

Client Overview

To use a server, a client must perform these three steps:

1. Initialize the COM subsystem.
2. Instantiate a COM object.
3. Call into that object (usually through a smart pointer).

In the following sections, each of these steps is discussed in detail as it relates to the client side of COM.

Initializing and Uninitializing the COM Subsystem

Before any client thread can make a call into a COM server, the thread needs to be initialized with a call to the COM subsystem. The COM API provides two functions to do this. The first is **CoInitialize( )**, and this is the function we used in **StopwatchClient.exe** in Chapter 3. Although **CoInitialize( )** is still perfectly valid and widely used, it has been superseded by **CoInitializeEx( )**. For new code, you should use **CoInitializeEx( )**. Its prototype is shown here:

HRESULT CoInitializeEx(void **pNotUsed*, DWORD *dwInitOptions*);

CoInitializeEx( ) is the currently recommended way of initializing COM.

The *pNotUsed* parameter is the same as the parameter to **CoInitialize( )** and must be **NULL**. The second parameter, *dwInitOptions*, determines what threading or *concurrency* model will be required for objects that are created on the thread. It specifies whether calls into the thread will have to wait for a previous call to complete. Essentially, **dwInitOptions** identifies the apartment model that the thread will be assigned to. In other words, *dwInitOptions* identifies the context in which other threads can make calls to the server instantiated by the client thread.

The possible values for *dwInitOptions* are defined by the following enumeration:

```
typedef enum tagCOINIT{
  COINIT_APARTMENTTHREADED = 0x2,
  COINIT_MULTITHREADED     = 0x0,
  COINIT_DISABLE_OLE1DDE   = 0x4.
  COINIT_SPEED_OVER_MEMORY = 0x8,
} COINIT;
```

The first two values, **COINIT_APARTMENTTHREADED** and **COINIT_MULTITHREADED**, relate directly to the concurrency model. With **COINIT_APARTMENTTHREADED**, all calls must be synchronized so that there is no simultaneous access to an object instance. **COINIT_APARTMENTTHREADED** creates a new STA. If **COINIT_MULTITHREADED** is specified, then no such synchronization occurs and the first MTA is created or the thread is assigned to the existing MTA.

COINIT_DISABLE_OLE1DDE disables Dynamic Data Exchange for OLE1. **COINIT_SPEED_OVER_MEMORY** optimizes execution speed rather than memory usage. All *dwInitOptions* values can be combined except **COINIT_APARTMENTTHREADED** and **COINIT_MULTITHREADED**, which are mutually exclusive.

Calling **CoInitialize( )** is the same as calling **CoInitializeEx( )** as follows:

```
CoInitializeEx(NULL, COINIT_APARTMENTTHREADED);
```

In spite of the fact that **CoInitializeEx( )** is the currently recommended function, you should be careful when choosing to use it since it is not supported on Windows 95 unless DCOM is installed. In fact, there is no declaration for **CoInitializeEx( )** unless you also define **_WIN32_DCOM** (as anything) or **_WIN32_WINNT** as 0x0400 or greater, as can be seen here in a code snippet from **objbase.h**:

```
#if (_WIN32_WINNT >= 0x0400 ) || defined(_WIN32_DCOM) // DCOM
WINOLEAPI  CoInitializeEx(LPVOID pvReserved, DWORD dwCoInit);
#endif // DCOM
```

Whether you initialize COM using **CoInitialize( )** or **CoInitializeEx( )**, uninitializing the COM subsystem is done by calling **CoUninitialize( )**.

One other point: There are times when a COM DLL module remains loaded even after all clients have stopped using it and there are no longer any instantiated objects within the module. If you want to force the COM subsystem to unload unused libraries, you can do this with a call to **CoFreeUnusedLibraries( )**. Note that calling **CoFreeUnusedLibraries( )** is not a substitution for clean reference counting because **CoFreeUnusedLibraries( )** will not unload your component unless there are no more references to it.

OleInitialize( ) and OleUninitialize( )

OleInitialize( ) and **OleUninitialize( )** are another pair of COM initialization and uninitialization API functions. These should be used in place of **CoInitialize( )** and **CoUninitialize( )** when the server application uses the clipboard, drag and drop, Object Linking and Embedding (OLE), or in-place activation. **OleInitialize( )** automatically initializes the concurrency model as Single Threaded Apartment (STA). This is important because the functions listed above are not thread safe; so using STA automatically prevents any concurrent access.

Instantiating COM Objects

In Chapter 2 we discussed the **CoCreateInstance( )** API function that is used to instantiate a COM object, and that discussion will not be repeated here. There are, however, other ways to instantiate a COM object. A few of these are examined here.

Creating Multiple Objects

There are times when you will want to create not just one object, but many objects of the same type. This can be done using the **CoCreateInstance( )** method, but there is another way that is more efficient. As we saw in Chapter 2, the call to **CoCreateInstance( )** calls into the server DLL through the **DllGetClassObject( )** function. In turn, this function returns a pointer to the class factory back to the COM subsystem. The COM subsystem then requests that the class factory instantiate an object. Once the object has been created, COM releases the class factory because it is no longer needed. When you are creating many COM objects, all from the same class factory, it is inefficient to reinstantiate the class factory each time you create a new COM object. To avoid this inefficiency, you can request a pointer to the class factory interface directly and then use the same class factory to instantiate all the components you want. The COM API for retrieving the class factory is **CoGetClassObject( )**, and its declaration is shown here:

STDAPI CoGetClassObject(REFCLSID *rclsid*, DWORD *dwContext*,
COSERVERINFO * *Server*, REFIID *riid*,
LPVOID * *ppv*);

CoGetClassObject( ) retrieves a class factory.

The first parameter, *rclsid*, is the class ID of the type of objects you wish to create. This is the same class ID that you would use if you were to call **CoCreateInstance( )**. *dwContext* identifies the context in which the object should be instantiated and is also the same as that used if **CoCreateInstance( )** were called. *Server* points to the machine where the object will be instantiated. This parameter is for instantiating objects on remote machines when using DCOM and can be **NULL**. *riid* is the interface ID of the class factory. This will be the ID of either **IClassFactory** or its cousin **IClassFactory2**. Note that this is not the ID of the interface on the class objects you wish to create. Lastly, a pointer for retrieving the class factory interface is required.

The code that uses a class factory pointer to instantiate objects would look something like this:

```
// CoGetClassObjectExample.cpp :
//   This example demonstrates how to use CoGetClassObject().
//

// std::out etc
#include <iostream>
#include <windows.h>

#include "..\Timers\timers_i.c"
#include "..\Timers\Timers.h"

int main(int argc, char* argv[])
{
  HRESULT hr;
  IClassFactory* pStopwatchClassFactory;
  IStopwatch* pIStopwatches[5];
  int i = 0;

  CoInitialize( NULL );

  hr = CoGetClassObject(
    __uuidof(Stopwatch),
    CLSCTX_INPROC_SERVER,
```

```
        NULL,
        __uuidof(IClassFactory),
        reinterpret_cast<void**> (&pStopwatchClassFactory) );

    if ( FAILED(hr) )
    {
        std::cout << "ERROR: Unable to create class factory."
          << std::endl;
    }

    else
    {
      while( (i<5) && (SUCCEEDED(hr)) )
      {
        hr = pStopwatchClassFactory->CreateInstance(
          NULL, __uuidof(IStopwatch),
          reinterpret_cast<void**> (&pIStopwatches[i]) );
        i++;
      }

      if( FAILED(hr) )
        std::cout << "ERROR: Failed to create all stopwatches."
           << std::endl;

      // Do something with the stopwatch object

      hr = S_OK;
      while( (i > 0) && (SUCCEEDED(hr)) )
      {
        i--;
        pIStopwatches[i]->Release();
      }

      pStopwatchClassFactory->Release();
    }

    CoUninitialize();
    return 0;
}
```

For those of you who want to try this program, simply use the wizard to generate a console application as we did in Chapter 2. Place the above code into the main file.

In the code, we declare the **IClassFactory** interface pointer as we would any other interface pointer. Next, we call **CoGetClassObject( )** to request that the COM subsystem call into the COM server module and instantiate a class factory. Assuming this is successful, the class factory is then assigned to **pStopwatchClassFactory**. Once the class factory interface has been returned, you can call **CreateInstance( )** on the interface to create each of the objects.

CoCreateInstanceEx( )

CoCreate-InstanceEx( ) instantiates an object over a network.

DCOM is the protocol that enables COM objects to communicate with each other over a network.

You should be aware of one more significant API function when instantiating objects. This is **CoCreateInstanceEx( )**. This function instantiates an object over the network and has it run on remote machines using the Distributed Component Object Model (DCOM). With **CoCreateInstanceEx( )** you can specify on which computer to instantiate the object. Because of the property of location independence, however, it is not required that you use the **CoCreateInstanceEx( )** API to use DCOM. Instead, it is possible to use an object on a remote system by simply configuring the client computer to redirect an instantiation call to a different computer using the **Dcomcnfg.exe** utility. Rather than getting distracted by the intricacies of DCOM now, we will investigate its details and the use of **CoCreateInstanceEx( )** in Chapter 12, which is devoted to the topic of DCOM. We mention it now to make you familiar with its existence and its distinction from **CoCreateInstance( )**.

Importing a COM Server Definition into the Client

One of the most useful tools for creating a COM client in C++ is the **#import** preprocessor directive. This directive tells the precompiler to open the type library of a COM server module and generate header files that wrap the functionality of the component. This is valuable when creating a client because it allows you to focus on the details of what you want the client to do rather than the details of reference counting and other COM intricacies. Essentially, **#import** adds several conveniences for writing COM clients.

Let's return to the Timer project and see what **#import** does to aid in the COM client development effort. Following is a listing of what the **StopwatchClient** code looks like with **Timers.dll** imported.

```
// StopwatchClient.cpp :
//   Defines the entry point for the console application.
//

// std::out etc
#include <iostream>

#import "..\Timers\Timers.dll" no_namespace

void UseStopwatch(IStopwatchPtr pStopwatch)
{

  float nElapsedTime;
  float nOverhead;

  nOverhead = pStopwatch->Overhead;

  std::cout << "The overhead time without going "
    "across the COM boundary is "
    << nOverhead << std::endl;

  pStopwatch->Start();
  nElapsedTime = pStopwatch->ElapsedTime();

  std::cout << "The overhead time with the "
    "COM boundary is "
    << nElapsedTime << std::endl;

  std::cout << "The expense of using the "
    "COM boundary is "
    << (nElapsedTime - nOverhead) << std::endl;

  pStopwatch->Overhead = nElapsedTime;

}

int main(int argc, char* argv[])
{

  CoInitialize( NULL );
  try
  {

    IStopwatchPtr pStopwatch(__uuidof(Stopwatch));
```

```
    UseStopwatch(pStopwatch);

  }
  catch(_com_error e)
  {

    std::cout << "ERROR: " << e.ErrorMessage() << std::endl;

  }

  CoUninitialize();
  return 0;
}
```


As you can see from the highlighted entries, several things in the client code above are different from the way we originally wrote it in Chapter 2. First, the **#include** of **Timers.h** and **Timers_i.c**

```
#include "..\Timers\timers_i.c"
#include "..\Timers\Timers.h"
```

has been replaced by the **#import** of the **Timers.dll**:

```
#import "..\Timers\Timers.dll" no_namespace
```

As briefly mentioned in the introduction, the **#import** statement automatically generates the required header files from the type library.

When we created the **Timers.dll**, one of the files generated by the IDL compiler was the **Timers.tlb** file—the type library. Although the type library can be distributed as a separate file, it is also possible to include it as a resource within the DLL so that it is not necessary to distribute it separately, as was discussed in Chapter 4.

The **#import** directive retrieves the embedded type library from the DLL and examines it in order to generate the required header files for using the server.

Importing the server DLL causes a TLH and a TLI file to be generated.

The result of the **#import** directive is the generation of a TLH and a TLI file. The TLH file is the header file for each of the COM objects supported in the type library. It is similar in functionality to the combined functionality of the **Timers.h** and **Timers_i.c** files that we included originally in the **StopwatchClient** project. At the bottom of the TLH file is a **#include** for the

TLI file. This file contains in-line implementations for each of the functions supported by the COM objects.

In the preceding example, the **#import** line included a **no_namespace** attribute. By default, all declarations imported by **#import** are assigned a namespace using the type library name. Therefore, since the type library name assigned in **Timers.idl** was **TIMERSLib** by default, all the declarations are within the **TIMERSLib** namespace. Since our project is small, a namespace conflict is unlikely; so the **no_namespace** attribute was added, which allows the **Stopwatch** declarations to remain in the current namespace. An alternative approach is to use a statement such as the following, which simply brings the **TIMERSLib** namespace into the global namespace:

```
using namespace TIMERSLib;
```

Several more attributes can be used with the **#import** directive. Table 5-1 lists some of the most common ones.

In addition to specifying the DLL for **#import**, you can use the type library directly. Type libraries can also be read from ActiveX controls compiled as OCXs or any other module from which the type library can be retrieved using the **LoadTypeLib( )** API function. For example, if you wanted to access the COM objects that are part of the Visual Studio build environment, you would use something similar to the following import. (The path may vary depending on where you installed Visual Studio.)

```
#import "c:\devstudio\common\msdev98\bin\ide\devbld.pkg"
```

As you can see, the Visual Studio team did not place the type library into a DLL or TLB file at all. Instead, they compiled it into a PKG file.

One thing to be aware of when changing the **#import** attributes is that sometimes Visual Studio fails to recognize the change until you do a "Rebuild all." This can also occur when you change the interface (during development), making the addition of new methods or properties unavailable to the client. Again, perform a "Rebuild all" to correct this problem.

Smart Pointers

As explained earlier in this book, each time a client instantiates an object, it must increment the reference count on that object by calling **AddRef( )**. When the client releases the object, it must decrement the reference count by

#import Attribute	Description
no_implementation	Adds a forward declaration for the wrapper classes but does not provide any implementation. This removes the **#include** of the TLI file from the generated TLH file. This is used mainly for precompiled header files to limit the changes to these files, thereby reducing the number of files that need to be compiled. **no_implementation** must be used with **implementation_only** later in the project. Failure to do so will cause linker errors.
implementation_only	Generates the TLI file, which contains the implementation of the wrapper files. It should be used in conjunction with the **no_implementation** attribute in another file.
named_guids	Adds a declaration for the GUIDs within the type library. This allows you to use the traditional **CLSID_<coclassname>** or **IID_<interfacename>** syntax rather than the newer **__uuidof** syntax when trying to access a particular GUID.
no_namespace	Causes imported declarations not to be put into a separate namespace.
rename_namespace	Renames the namespace to prevent namespace conflicts.

Common Attributes Used in the **#import** Statement
Table 5-1.

5

Smart pointers automate reference counting.

calling **Release( )**. Because of the potential for error and the tedious nature of reference counting, **#import** generates *smart pointers* that automate this process. They are one of **#import**'s most important features, and we will begin our exploration of them here.

The _com_ptr_t Template Class

All the interface smart pointers that are generated by **#import** are based on the **_com_ptr_t** template class. The **_com_ptr_t** class wraps the three **IUnknown** methods: **QueryInterface( )**, **AddRef( )**, and **Release( )**. It also provides several of its own member functions that perform various other operations, some of which we will look at in the course of this discussion.

The **#import** statement generates smart pointers for the interfaces defined by a component. If you look back at the new version of **StopwatchClient.cpp** shown earlier in this chapter, you will notice that rather than using the **CoCreateInstance( )** or **CoCreateInstanceEx( )** to instantiate the **Stopwatch** object, the following following line is used:

```
IStopwatchPtr pStopwatch(__uuidof(IStopwatch));
```

IStopwatchPtr is the **#import**-generated smart pointer wrapper class for the **IStopwatch** interface. The convention is to take the interface name, **IStopwatch**, and add "Ptr" to the end. This declares a smart pointer to the interface. **IStopwatchPtr** is defined inside **Timers.tlh**, which is listed here:

```
// Created by Microsoft (R) C/C++ Compiler
// Version 12.00.8447.0 (ef610348).
//
// Timers.tlh
//
// C++ source equivalent of Win32 type library ..\Timers\Timers.dll
// compiler-generated file created 12/31/99 at 15:48:12
// DO NOT EDIT!

#pragma once
#pragma pack(push, 8)

#include <comdef.h>

//
// Forward references and typedefs
//

struct /* coclass */ Stopwatch;
struct __declspec(uuid("eebf6d1e-8ef1-4acf-9e5f-4d95e01d698a"))
/* interface */ IStopwatch;

//
// Smart pointer typedef declarations
//

_COM_SMARTPTR_TYPEDEF(IStopwatch, __uuidof(IStopwatch));

//
// Type library items
//
```

```
struct __declspec(uuid("83dc3c46-1259-4f95-a2d1-cd11a8819e2e"))
Stopwatch;
    // [ default ] interface IStopwatch

struct __declspec(uuid("eebf6d1e-8ef1-4acf-9e5f-4d95e01d698a"))
IStopwatch : IUnknown
{
    //
    // Property data
    //

    __declspec(property(get=GetOverhead,put=PutOverhead))
    float Overhead;

    //
    // Wrapper methods for error-handling
    //

    HRESULT Start ( );
    float ElapsedTime ( );
    float GetOverhead ( );
    void PutOverhead (
        float pVal );

    //
    // Raw methods provided by interface
    //

    virtual HRESULT __stdcall raw_Start ( ) = 0;
    virtual HRESULT __stdcall raw_ElapsedTime (
        float * Time ) = 0;
    virtual HRESULT __stdcall get_Overhead (
        float * pVal ) = 0;
    virtual HRESULT __stdcall put_Overhead (
        float pVal ) = 0;
};

//
// Named GUID constants initializations
//

extern "C" const GUID __declspec(selectany) LIBID_TIMERSLib =
  {0xd7eba784,0x2bf1,0x11d3,
    {0xa4,0x8b,0x00,0x00,0x86,0x1c,0x84,0x4e}};
```

```
extern "C" const GUID __declspec(selectany) CLSID_Stopwatch =
  {0x83dc3c46,0x1259,0x4f95,
    {0xa2,0xd1,0xcd,0x11,0xa8,0x81,0x9e,0x2e}};
extern "C" const GUID __declspec(selectany) IID_IStopwatch =
  {0xeebf6d1e,0x8ef1,0x4acf,
    {0x9e,0x5f,0x4d,0x95,0xe0,0x1d,0x69,0x8a}};

//
// Wrapper method implementations
//

#include "Timers.tli"

#pragma pack(pop)
```

Notice that the declaration for **IStopwatchPtr** occurs in the following line:

```
_COM_SMARTPTR_TYPEDEF(IStopwatch, __uuidof(IStopwatch));
```

This creates a specialization of the **_com_ptr_t** template class explicitly for **IStopwatch**. In general, the **_COM_SMARTPTR_TYPEDEF** macro is used to create a smart pointer specialization.

If we drill into the **_COM_SMARTPTR_TYPEDEF** macro, we see that the actual declaration for **IStopwatchPtr** uses the **_com_ptr_t** template class, which is defined in **compip.h**. All the wrapper code for the **IStopwatch** interface is contained in **_com_ptr_t**. This is a complicated template class, which not only provides several new functions to the **IStopwatch** interface, but also overloads several operators to mask much of the reference counting details. This makes it easier to focus on object functionality rather than COM details. Notice, for example, that in all the preceding code not once is there an explicit call to **AddRef( )** or **Release( )**. This is not because **AddRef( )** and **Release( )** are not needed, but because such calls are being handled by the **_com_ptr_t** class so that you, as the client programmer, need not be so concerned with them.

Let's take a look at how **_com_ptr_t** works.

Construction

Let us first consider what takes place in the constructor for **IStopwatchPtr**. In **StopwatchClient.cpp** the parameter passed to the constructor is the GUID of the **Stopwatch** CoClass, as shown here:

```
IStopwatchPtr pStopwatch(__uuidof(Stopwatch));
```

This instructs the wrapper class to be initialized with a pointer to the **IStopwatch** interface on an instantiated **Stopwatch** object. Often, programmers make the mistake of specifying the interface (**IStopwatch**) for the **__uuidof** parameter. Since this also results in a GUID, the code will compile. When it runs, however, the object will fail to be instantiated and instead results in the error, "Class not Registered." To help prevent this error, consider why the CLSID is used rather than the IID. An interface can be supported by many objects of different kinds—with different CLSIDs. Because the **IStopwatch** interface can be supported by many COM objects, when you request to create an object and return a specific interface, you need to identify which object to instantiate. If you simply identified which interface, COM would not know from which object to return the requested interface. Furthermore, the interface pointer knows what IID it is associated with, so why would the **_com_ptr_t** require you to specify an interface ID?

The **_com_ptr_t** class defines several constructors. The one used by the preceding statement is shown here:

explicit _com_ptr_t(const CLSID &*ClassID*,
DWORD *dwContext* = CLSCTX_ALL) throw(_com_error);

Here, *ClassID* is the class ID of the CoClass being wrapped, and *dwContext* determines the context, which defaults to **CLSCTX_ALL**. This constructor automatically calls the **_com_ptr_t** member function **CreateInstance( )**, which creates an instance of the specified object.

If you don't want to instantiate the COM object at declaration time (which would not be feasible when used as a member variable), you can instead call the **CreateInstance( )** function on the smart pointer directly. **_com_ptr_t** defines three versions of **CreateInstance( )**. The one we are using is shown here:

HRESULT CreateInstance(const CLSID &*ClassID*,
IUNKNOWN **pOuterIUnkn* = NULL,
DWORD *dwContext* = CLSTX_ALL) throw( );

Be aware, however, that unlike the previous constructor, **_com_ptr_t::CreateInstance( )** does not throw a **_com_error** exception. Instead it returns an **HRESULT**, which will need to be checked. Below is some code that uses the **_com_ptr_t::CreateInstance( )** function and then issues its own exception using **_com_issue_error** (to be discussed shortly).

```
HRESULT hr;
if (SUCCEEDED( hr =
     pStopwatch.CreateInstance(__uuidof(Stopwatch))))
  UseStopwatch(pStopwatch);
else
  _com_issue_error(hr);
```

Destruction

The **_com_ptr_t** destructor automatically calls **Release( )**.

When a **_com_ptr_t** object is destroyed, **Release( )** is automatically called on the interface. This explains the next significant change within the **StopwatchClient.cpp** code. When an **IStopwatchPtr** variable goes out of scope, **Release( )** is not called explicitly by your code. Rather, it is called indirectly through **_com_ptr_t**'s destructor. Thus, in spite of the fact that we are using COM to access the **Stopwatch** object, we are able to write all the client code without having to worry as much about reference counting. In fact, although both **Release( )** and **AddRef( )** are available from the smart pointer, it is rarely necessary to call them explicitly.

The Member Selection Operator, ->

We are now ready to look at why **_com_ptr_t** is called a smart pointer. At first glance, you might look at the call to the **Start( )** function on the **pStopwatch** variable and think that **IStopwatchPtr** was somehow derived from **IStopwatch**. Surprisingly, however, this is not the case. Instead, **_com_ptr_t** overloads the member selection operator, **->**, and returns the **IStopwatch** interface. In effect, therefore, the code **pStopwatch->Start( )** first returns an **IStopwatch** pointer and then proceeds to call the **Start( )** method on this interface. If we were to rewrite the code fully expanded it might look something like this:

```
pStopwatch.m_pInterface->Start( );
```

The **m_pInterface** variable used above is a member variable that contains the interface pointer represented by the smart pointer class. In the **Stopwatch** case, it is an **IStopwatch***.

Let's take a look at how the member selection operator is overloaded. This code is found inside **comip.h**, where **_com_ptr_t** is defined.

```
// Allows this class to be used as the interface itself.
// Also provides simple error checking.
//
Interface* operator->() const throw(_com_error)
{
  if (m_pInterface == NULL) {
    _com_issue_error(E_POINTER);
  }

  return m_pInterface;
}
```

As you can see in the above code, the additional functionality that we did not provide in our expanded code is the check for **NULL** on the interface pointer.

Given the overloading of the member selection operator, you should remember that this member function call is made on the **IStopwatch** interface, not **IStopwatchPtr** as you would expect at first glance. However, if you look back at **StopwatchClient.cpp** and the way the **UseStopwatch**( ) function has changed, you will notice that **IStopwatch** does not appear to be the same as it was when we first used it back in Chapter 2. The next section explains why.

A New Kind of IStopwatch

Notice how the **IStopwatch** properties are accessed inside **UseStopwatch( )**. Previously, the code to set or get the **Overhead** property was via the **get_Overhead( )** and **set_Overhead( )** functions. However, with the **IStopwatchPtr**, you can access the property as though it were a member variable. This is why in the **StopwatchClient.cpp** code we see

```
float nElapsedTime;
float nOverhead;

nOverhead = pStopwatch->Overhead;
...
pStopwatch->Overhead = nElapsedTime;
```

Functions are also accessed differently. Without the smart pointer wrapper, the **ElapsedTime( )** function had to use pass-by-reference in order to return the elapsed time. With **IStopwatchPtr**, however, the value can be a function return value, as in

```
nElapsedTime = pStopwatch->ElapsedTime();
```

This is possible because the **#import** statement recognized that the **ElapsedTime( )** function had a **retval** attribute, and therefore it constructed the wrapper class accordingly.

As we already saw, strictly speaking, the methods and properties above are not called on the **IStopwatchPtr** class. Instead, the **_com_ptr_t** template overloads the member-selection operator and returns an **IStopwatch** interface pointer. The new functionality, therefore, is provided by the **IStopwatch** class.

Obviously, however, since the syntax for accessing the methods and properties is not the same as it was defined in the **Timers.idl** file, **IStopwatch** must be different from before. Below is the declaration of the generated **IStopwatch** interface as defined in **Timers.tlh**.

```
struct __declspec(uuid("eebf6d1e-8ef1-4acf-9e5f-4d95e01d698a"))
IStopwatch : IUnknown
{
    //
    // Property data
    //

    __declspec(property(get=GetOverhead,put=PutOverhead))
    float Overhead;

    //
    // Wrapper methods for error-handling
    //

    HRESULT Start ( );
    float ElapsedTime ( );
    float GetOverhead ( );
    void PutOverhead (
        float pVal );

    //
    // Raw methods provided by interface
    //

    virtual HRESULT __stdcall raw_Start ( ) = 0;
    virtual HRESULT __stdcall raw_ElapsedTime (
        float * Time ) = 0;
    virtual HRESULT __stdcall get_Overhead (
        float * pVal ) = 0;
    virtual HRESULT __stdcall put_Overhead (
```

```
        float pVal ) = 0;
};
```

Notice how not every method in the interface returns an **HRESULT**. Instead, previously defined **retval** parameters have become function returns.

As we mentioned before, the implementation of the wrapper functions is found inside **Timers.tli**, which is listed below.

```
// Created by Microsoft (R) C/C++ Compiler
// Version 12.00.8447.0 (ef610348).
//
// Timers.tli
//
// Wrapper implementations for Win32
// type library ..\Timers\Timers.dll
// compiler-generated file created 12/31/99 at 15:48:12
// DO NOT EDIT!

#pragma once

//
// interface IStopwatch wrapper method implementations
//

inline HRESULT IStopwatch::Start ( ) {
    HRESULT _hr = raw_Start();
    if (FAILED(_hr)) _com_issue_errorex(_hr, this, __uuidof(this));
    return _hr;
}

inline float IStopwatch::ElapsedTime ( ) {
    float _result;
    HRESULT _hr = raw_ElapsedTime(&_result);
    if (FAILED(_hr)) _com_issue_errorex(_hr, this, __uuidof(this));
    return _result;
}

inline float IStopwatch::GetOverhead ( ) {
    float _result;
    HRESULT _hr = get_Overhead(&_result);
    if (FAILED(_hr)) _com_issue_errorex(_hr, this, __uuidof(this));
    return _result;
}
```

```
inline void IStopwatch::PutOverhead ( float pVal ) {
    HRESULT _hr = put_Overhead(pVal);
    if (FAILED(_hr)) _com_issue_errorex(_hr, this, __uuidof(this));
}
```

Notice that within each of these functions an exception is thrown when an error occurs. This is important because it provides a mechanism for returning the **HRESULT** to the calling function, as we shall see in the next section. Also, you can see how each function makes a call back into the **IStopwatch** class' raw interface functions. These are the methods prefixed with "raw_" and the properties prefixed with "get_" and "put_". If you ever need to access the interface directly, you too can use these raw access methods on the interface declaration. The other difference in the way the new interface is defined is that each function shown above calls **_com_issue_errorex( )** whenever an error occurs. Let us consider this next.

Error Handling Using Exceptions

As long as no errors occur, it is a great benefit to have so many of the COM details hidden inside the interface wrapper classes. Unfortunately, errors do occur, and, therefore, the client must be able to respond to these errors by checking the **HRESULT** return values. However, these returned **HRESULT**s are not available in the same way as before because the properties and methods provided by the smart pointer wrappers return values through function returns instead. To provide access to the **HRESULT** whenever an error occurs (where **SUCCEEDED( )** would return false, or **FAILED( )** would return true), an exception of type **_com_error** is thrown. Embedded within the **_com_error** class is the **HRESULT** returned from COM in a function called **Error( )**. The exception is thrown using the **_com_issue_error( )** and **_com_issue_errorex( )** functions. The functions are used to throw exceptions of type **_com_error**.

```
void __stdcall
  _com_issue_error(HRESULT) throw(_com_error);
void __stdcall
  _com_issue_errorex(HRESULT, IUnknown*, REFIID) throw(_com_error);
```

This explains why there is a **try/catch** block around all the COM calls. Inside the **catch** block, you can check the returned **HRESULT** and respond appropriately.

```
try
{
  ...
}
catch(_com_error e)
{
  std::cout << "ERROR: " << e.ErrorMessage() << std::endl;
}
```

We will look into the details of **_com_error** in Chapter 9 when we take an in-depth look at error handling. For now it is sufficient that you understand how to use the class to report errors as shown in the preceding code. The **_com_error**.**ErrorMessage( )** function retrieves any system errors. **ErrorMessage( )** calls the **FormatMessage( )** API function and retrieves from the operating system the error string corresponding to the **HRESULT**. In Chapter 9 you will see how to return custom error messages to the client application using the **IErrorInfo**.

One drawback to using exception handling is that memory leaks often occur because not all necessary cleanup is performed inside the catch block. However, since we are using smart pointers, this is not an issue because the destructor automatically calls **Release( )** appropriately when **IStopwatchPtr** goes out of scope.

Throwing exceptions appears not only on the **#import** implementation of **IStopwatch**. Notice that **_com_ptr_t** provides these implementations of each of the **IUnknown** functions.

```
void AddRef( ) throw(_com_error);

void Release( ) throw(_com_error);

template<typename _InterfaceType> HRESULT QueryInterface(
                    const IID& iid,  _InterfaceType*& pIptr) throw ( );

template<typename _InterfaceType> HRESULT QueryInterface(
                    const IID& iid, _InterfaceType** pIptr) throw( );
```

Providing this functionality may be curious to some of you because each of these functions is already available from the **IStopwatch** interface. In other words, because **_com_ptr_t** has additional implementations of these functions, two methods exist for calling **AddRef( )**, **Release( )**, and **QueryInterface( )**. The first calls **AddRef( )** on the raw interface pointer returned from the **_com_ptr_t->** operator. The second calls **_com_ptr_t**'s **AddRef( )** member function directly.

```
IStopwatchPtr pStopwatch;

pStopwatch->AddRef(); // Calling AddRef() using raw Interface
pStopwatch.AddRef();  // Calling AddRef() using _com_ptr_t
```

In this code, the first call uses the raw interface version of **AddRef( )** because the -> operator returns the raw interface pointer. The second uses the **AddRef( )** member function from **_com_ptr_t**. What is the difference? If no **Stopwatch** object has been instantiated, then calling the first function will attempt to call a function on a null pointer to **IStopwatch***. In the second case, **_com_ptr_t** provides a wrapper to **AddRef( )**, which checks the pointer and throws an exception if **NULL** is encountered. Below is the **_com_ptr_t** code for **AddRef( )** as implemented in **comip.h**.

```
void AddRef() throw(_com_error)
{
  if (m_pInterface == NULL) {
    _com_issue_error(E_POINTER);
  }

  m_pInterface->AddRef();
}
```

The same functionality shown above also occurs in **_com_ptr_t::Release( )**.

Although **_com_ptr_t::AddRef( )** and **_com_ptr_t::Release( )** both throw **_com_error** exceptions if a problem occurs, this is not what happens with **QueryInterface( )**. Instead, **QueryInterface( )** returns an **HRESULT**, which needs to be checked. Although this is inconsistent, it makes sense, because many times the fact that a particular interface is not supported is not an error condition. For example, consider the two interfaces **IStopwatch** and **IStopwatch2**. The second interface is a newer version of the first, providing additional functionality. Before a client could call any of the properties and methods on the newer interface, it would have to retrieve it using **QueryInterface( )**, as shown here:

```
HRESULT hr;

IStopwatchPtr pIStopwatch(__uuidof(Stopwatch));
```

```
IStopwatch2Ptr pIStopwatch2;
hr = pIStopwatch.QueryInterface(__uuidof(IStopwatch2), pIStopwatch2);

if (SUCCEEDED(hr))
{
   ...
}
```

This raises the question, why have the **QueryInterface( )** function on the **_com_ptr_t** at all? The only difference in **_com_ptr_t**'s implementation is that you do not need to worry about explicitly casting the interface pointer to a **void**** before calling **QueryInterface( )**. If we were to call **QueryInterface( )** on the raw interface pointer, the code would look something like this:

5

```
IStopwatch* pIStopwatch;
IStopwatch2* pIStopwatch2;
pIStopwatch->QueryInterface(__uuidof(IStopwatch2),
                  reinterpret_cast<void**> (&pIStopwatch2) );
```

The difference between this and the **_com_ptr_t::QueryInterface( )** version is simply that in the latter you do not need to worry about the cast to **void**** because **_com_ptr_t** does this for you—not rocket science, but still a nice feature if you are calling **QueryInterface( )** multiple times. Although there will be times when you still may want to call the raw interface functions (using the **->** versions), our suggestion is that you stick with the smart pointer versions unless you have a specific reason not to.

One last point in this area. Earlier in this chapter we looked at the **_com_ptr_t::CreateInstance( )** function. Unlike the constructor for a **_com_ptr_t**, calling **CreateInstance( )** does not throw a **_com_error** exception. Instead, it returns an **HRESULT**, so be sure to check the return value before calling into the interface.

Mixing Smart Pointers with Raw Interfaces

In spite of the significant work that **_com_ptr_t** does to hide reference counting, you cannot become completely reckless in its use. Consider, for example, the automatic conversion from an **IStopwatchPtr** to an **IStopwatch*** using the assignment operator as shown:

```
IStopwatchPtr pStopwatchPtr1(__uuidof(Stopwatch))
IStopwatchPtr pStopwatchPtr2(__uuidof(Stopwatch))
```

```
IStopwatch* pIStopwatch = pStopwatchPtr1;
pIStopwatch->AddRef();
pStopwatchPtr1 = pStopwatchPtr2;
...
pIStopwatch->Release();
```

Such an assignment invokes the code shown below. This code is part of the **_com_ptr_t** implementation inside **comip.h**.

```
operator Interface*() const throw()
{
  return m_pInterface;
}
```

Notice that no **AddRef( )** takes place; so you need to call it explicitly after the assignment because a new reference to the object has been created.

Consider an assignment in the opposite direction, however:

```
IStopwatchPtr pStopwatchPtr1(__uuidof(Stopwatch));
IStopwatchPtr pStopwatchPtr2(__uuidof(Stopwatch))
IStopwatch* pIStopwatch = pStopwatchPtr1;  // No AddRef()
pIStopwatch->AddRef();
pStopwatchPtr2 = pIStopwatch;             // AddRef called.
pIStopwatch->Start()
...
pIStopwatch->Release();
```

The code above invokes the **_com_ptr_t** assignment operator shown below. As before, this code is found in **comip.h**.

```
_com_ptr_t& operator=(Interface* pInterface) throw()
{
  if (m_pInterface != pInterface) {
    Interface* pOldInterface = m_pInterface;

    m_pInterface = pInterface;

    _AddRef();

    if (pOldInterface != NULL) {
      pOldInterface->Release();
    }
```

```
  }

  return *this;
}
```

In this case, the smart pointer calls **AddRef( )** on the new value and then releases the pointer on the old value. The difference, obviously, is that **AddRef( )** is called.

Although the smart pointers are "smart," they have not removed the need to consider reference counting altogether. Such drawbacks and subtleties occur because both raw interfaces and smart pointer interfaces are mixed together within the same code. Therefore, we strongly encourage you to pick one of these two methods (presumably the smart pointers) and use it consistently throughout your code.

If, however, mixing raw interfaces with smart pointers is unavoidable, use the following two rules:

- When assigning a value (either a smart pointer or a raw interface pointer) to a raw interface pointer, follow the normal reference counting rules as previously discussed. (Always call **AddRef( )** and then **Release( )** when you are finished unless you are sure that another reference count will keep the object in memory during the lifetime of the interface pointer.)
- When assigning a value (either a smart pointer or a raw interface pointer) to a smart pointer, the smart pointer will take care of the reference counting appropriately.

Passing Interfaces Across COM Boundaries

If the reference counting taking place between raw interface pointers and smart interface pointers when an explicit assignment occurs is confusing, it is even more confusing in an implicit assignment! Such an assignment would occur when passing a smart pointer to a function that takes a raw interface pointer or vice versa, such as when passing an interface across COM boundaries. This is often one of the times you may find you cannot avoid having to mix raw interface pointers with smart pointers. In these cases, there are some helper functions within **_com_ptr_t**. Not only do these functions make the conversion more explicit, but they also aid by adding a few error checks. Lastly, they can be used to cut down on the overall number of reference counting calls when they are not explicitly needed. The catch, of course, is knowing when to use them.

Consider the following server interface definition for a fictitious **StopwatchStack** component:

```
interface IStopwatchStack : IUnknown
{
  HRESULT Push( [in] IStopwatch* NewStopwatch);
  HRESULT Pop( [out, retval] IStopwatch** StopwatchItem);
};
...
library STOPWATCHSTACKSVRLib
{
...
  coclass StopwatchStack
  {
    [default] interface IStopwatchStack;
  };
};
```

Such a component would keep a set of **Stopwatch** objects in a stack structure.

Now consider writing a client to access this interface. For example, you may create a loop that pushes five stopwatches onto the stack as follows:

```
void UseStack()
{
  long i;  IStopwatchStackPtr
  pStopwatchStack( __uuidof(StopwatchStack) );
  IStopwatchPtr pStopwatch;
  IStopwatch* pIStopwatch = NULL;
  for(; i<5; i++)
  {
    pStopwatch.CreateInstance(__uuidof(Stopwatch) );
    pIStopwatch = pStopwatch.Detach();
    pStopwatchStack->Push( pIStopwatch );
  }
}
```

The key function here is the highlighted **Detach( )** function, which is a member of **_com_ptr_t**. Its prototype is shown here:

Interface *Detach( ) throw( );

Detach( ) unencapsulates and returns an interface pointer. It releases **_com_ptr_t**'s internal interface reference and assigns it to another interface pointer.

The **Detach( )** function copies the interface stored in the smart pointer to the raw interface. The important difference between this assignment and simply assigning the smart pointer to the raw interface pointer directly is that **Detach( )** also sets the smart pointer's internal interface pointer (**m_pInterface**) to **NULL**. In effect, **Detach( )** assigns **_com_ptr_t**'s internal interface pointer to a different interface pointer, and then it sets its internal interface pointer to **NULL**. No **AddRef( )** takes place, however, because once **Detach( )** finishes, there are no additional references. Before calling **Detach( )**, **_com_ptr_t** had one reference to the interface. After calling **Detach( )**, the new assigned interface pointer has one reference, but the **_com_ptr_t** no longer has any; so the net reference count change is zero. Hence, no reference counting is performed.

The purpose of the **Detach( )** function is to release ownership of the interface pointer to a different pointer. Before calling **Detach( )**, the smart pointer maintained a reference to the interface. After calling **Detach( )**, however, the responsibility for the reference was shifted to the raw interface pointer.

5

Using the **Detach( )** method cuts down on the number of reference counting calls that need to be made. If, instead of using the **Detach( )** method, a straight assignment was made, this loop would end up making 10 extra calls to the server. Not a big deal when running in-process, but consider the expense if each of those calls were across the network. Fortunately in this case, even if you forget to use the **Detach( )** function,
the smart pointer will handle the reference counting appropriately.

By the way, the previous code can be simplified even more because of the automatic conversion of **_com_ptr_t** to raw interfaces. Instead, the code could be written as

```
for(; i<5; i++)
  {
    pStopwatch.CreateInstance(__uuidof(Stopwatch) );
    pStopwatchStack->Push( pStopwatch.Detach() );
  }
```

Attach( ) encapsulates an interface pointer.

Just as there is the need to release ownership of an interface, there is also the need to take ownership. This is done using the **_com_ptr_t::Attach( )** function. It has the two versions shown here:

void Attach(Interface **pIface*) throw( );

void Attach(Interface **pIface*, bool *CallAddRef*) throw( );

Here, *pIface* is a pointer to the interface being attached. In the second form, if *CallAddRef* is true, then **AddRef( )** is called on the interface; otherwise, **AddRef( )** is not called.

The second version of **Attach( )** is useful when you need to ensure that a call to **AddRef( )** will occur during the assignment. Consider the example below:

```
class Monitor
{
  void Initialize();
  IStopwatchPtr m_pStopwatch;
  ...
}

void Monitor::Initialize()
{
  IStopwatch* pStopwatch;

  m_pStopwatch.Attach(pStopwatch, true);
  pStopwatch->Start();
  pStopwatch->Release();
}
```

In this case, an **AddRef( )** was performed in the assignment to **m_pStopwatch**. (Remember, **AddRef( )** would not occur in an explicit assignment.) This is a good thing to do if you plan on continuing to use the raw interface pointer as is done in the example with a call to **Start( )**. On the other hand, if instead the assignment was made and no additional calls on the interface were made, no release would be necessary and the **fAddRef** parameter could simply default to false.

```
m_pStopwatch.Attach( pStopwatch );
m_pStopwatch->Start( );
```

In summary, the **Attach( )** and **Detach( )** functions are used to transfer ownership. If you wish to clear a smart pointer and pass its interface to another owner, use the **Detach( )** function. If you wish to take ownership either completely or in addition to the original owner, use the **Attach( )** function.

There is a lot of code in the **_com_ptr_t** class, and we have barely scratched the surface. It is well worth opening **comip.h** and examining the **_com_ptr_t** class to look at the details on your own to gain a fuller understanding.

Another COM Client Example

Before we finish the chapter, we are going to look at creating a new client project that uses many of the principles discussed above. This project uses the Microsoft Agent COM components. For those of you unfamiliar with this product, Microsoft Agent is the technology used for displaying the various Microsoft Office Assistants that lurk around your screen and try to provide valuable tips on how to use the Office products more efficiently. For running Windows 2000, the Microsoft Agent is included as part of the operating system. If you are not running Windows 2000, and you do not already have Microsoft Agent installed, you will have to download the Agent from Microsoft's Web site at **http://www.microsoft.com/msagent**.

In our example, we are going to use the same technology to animate the characters and have them read aloud a string that is specified on the command line. Below is a screen showing such an animation. Unfortunately, you will not be able to hear what the character says; so to assist, a balloon pops up with the words as well.

To create the Merlin project, create a new empty console application and insert a file called **Merlin.cpp** into the newly created project. Into this file add the following code:

```
// Merlin.cpp : Defines the entry point for the console application.
//

#define _WIN32_DCOM  // Needed in order to call CoInitializeEx()

#include<windows.h>
```

```
#include <iostream>

#include<TCHAR.h>

// Import the Microsoft Agent Control
#import "c:\winnt\msagent\agentsvr.exe" no_namespace

//  Exception declaration not yet standardized
#pragma warning(push)
#pragma warning( disable : 4290 )

const long PAUSE_AFTER_SPEAKING = 20000;
const BSTR DEFAULT_SPEECH =
  L"This is a test of the Emergency Broadcast System!!";

void SayIt(IAgentExPtr ptrAgent, _bstr_t message_text)
  throw (_com_error);

int main(int argc, char* argv[])
{

  HRESULT hr;
  int n_return = 0;

  try
  {
    int arg_count = 1;
    _bstr_t message_text;
    IAgentExPtr ptrAgent;

    // Initialize COM
    hr = CoInitializeEx(NULL, COINIT_APARTMENTTHREADED);
    if( FAILED( hr ))
      _com_issue_error(hr);

    // Figure out what to say
    if (argc > arg_count)
    {
```

```
      // The user specified the message text on the command line
      message_text = argv[arg_count];
    }
    else
    {
      message_text = DEFAULT_SPEECH;
    }

    hr = ptrAgent.CreateInstance(__uuidof(AgentServer));

    if( FAILED( hr ))
    {
      _com_issue_error(hr);
    }
    SayIt(ptrAgent, message_text);

  }
  catch(_com_error e)
  {
    std::cout < "ERROR(" < e.Error() < "):  ";
    if( e.Description().length() > 0)
      std::cout < (char*)e.Description() < std::endl;

    std::cout < e.ErrorMessage() < std::endl;
    n_return = 1;
  }

  // Uninitialize COM
  CoUninitialize();

  return n_return;

}


HRESULT CreateAgent( IAgentExPtr& ptrAgent,
  _bstr_t Machine,
  COAUTHIDENTITY AuthorId)
{
  HRESULT hr;
```

```
// CoCreateInstanceEx structures
COAUTHINFO author_info;
COSERVERINFO server_info;
MULTI_QI mqi[1];

if ( Machine.length() == 0 )
{
  hr = ptrAgent.CreateInstance(__uuidof(AgentServer));
  if( FAILED(hr) )
    _com_issue_error(hr);
}
else
{

  // Initialize COAUTHINFO
  ZeroMemory( &author_info, sizeof(author_info) );
  author_info.dwAuthnSvc = RPC_C_AUTHN_WINNT;
  author_info.dwAuthzSvc = RPC_C_AUTHZ_NONE;
  author_info.dwImpersonationLevel = RPC_C_IMP_LEVEL_IMPERSONATE;
  author_info.dwCapabilities = EOAC_NONE;
  author_info.pAuthIdentityData  = &AuthorId;

  ZeroMemory( &server_info, sizeof(server_info) );
  server_info.pwszName = Machine;
  server_info.pAuthInfo = &author_info;

  ZeroMemory( mqi, sizeof(mqi) );
  mqi[0].pIID = &__uuidof(IAgentEx);
  mqi[0].pItf = static_cast<IUnknown*>(ptrAgent);

  hr = CoCreateInstanceEx( __uuidof(AgentServer),
    NULL, CLSCTX_REMOTE_SERVER,
    &server_info, 1, mqi);

  if ( FAILED(hr) )
  {
    // The CreateFailed
  }
  else if( FAILED(mqi[0].hr) )
  {
```

```
        // QueryInterface failed
        hr = mqi[0].hr;
        ptrAgent = NULL;
      }
      else
        // Attach to the returned interface
        ptrAgent.Attach( reinterpret_cast<IAgentEx*> (mqi[0].pItf) );

  }

  return hr;
}


void SayIt(IAgentExPtr ptrAgent, _bstr_t message_text)
{
  HRESULT hr = E_FAIL;

  IAgentCharacterExPtr pCharacter;
  IDispatchPtr ptr_idisp_character;
  VARIANT var;
  VariantInit(&var);
  long nCharacterId;
  long nRequestId;

  // Load the character and retrieve it.
  ptrAgent->Load(var, &nCharacterId, &nRequestId);
  VariantClear(&var);
  ptrAgent->GetCharacter(nCharacterId, &ptr_idisp_character);
  pCharacter = ptr_idisp_character;
  ptr_idisp_character.Release();

  pCharacter->Show(false, &nRequestId);
  pCharacter->Speak( message_text, L"", &nRequestId );
  Sleep(PAUSE_AFTER_SPEAKING);
  pCharacter->Hide(1L, &nRequestId);
  pCharacter.Release();
  ptrAgent->Unload(nCharacterId);

}

#pragma warning(pop)
```

Before we dive into the code, many of you may be wondering how to find out about what interfaces are supported and how to use these interfaces. For most components, some interface documentation will accompany the COM server. In the case of the Microsoft Agent, help files are available from the same URL as the control itself. In some circumstances, there may not be such documentation. In these cases, you can use **oleview.exe** (distributed with Visual Studio) to open the type library and view all the methods, properties, and possibly even the various help strings. From these you may be able to figure out how to call into the COM server. If this fails, you will have to contact the COM server vendor and see if it can provide the necessary documentation.

For the most part, the preceding code is self-explanatory. To start out, we import the **agentsrv.exe**. This is located inside your WINNT directory in a folder called **msagent**. Next, the program obtains the text that was specified on the command line. This is the text that the Microsoft Agent will say. If no text was specified, then default text stored in **DEFAULT_SPEECH** is used. Next we instantiate the agent with a call to **CreateInstance( )**.

Given the Agent interface smart pointer we can call **SayIt( )**. Inside **SayIt( )**, the first thing is to load in the default character with a call to **ptrAgent->Load( )**. Once the character is loaded, we can retrieve an interface pointer to it by calling **ptrAgent->GetCharacter( )**. Unfortunately, **ptrAgent->GetCharacter( )** returns an **IDispatch** pointer so we need to convert it to an **IAgentCharacterEx** pointer using the implicit cast functionality in **_com_ptr_t**. Note that under the covers in this implicit cast, **_com_ptr_t** calls **QueryInterface( )** in the assignment **pCharacter = ptr_idisp_character**. To actually display the character and have it say something, calls to **Show( )** and **Speak( )** are made before releasing and unloading the character. Technically, explicit calls to **Release( )** are not required but invoking them as soon as an interface is no longer needed is a better use of resources than keeping them in memory until the function exits.

As you can see in this example, we have eliminated much of the need for reference counting. Although a significant number of interfaces are being passed back to the client, all the concern with when to release an interface has pretty much been eliminated via the use of **#import** and the wrapper classes it generates using **_com_ptr_t**. Later on when we look at DCOM, we will change this example to display characters on remote computers rather than simply on the local machine. This way you could have a character say something over the network to someone sitting in a different office or even over the Internet to someone in a different country.

We have not yet covered one item in this example. This relates to the use of the strings and the **_bstr_t** class. This will be discussed in detail in the following chapter. We have covered a lot of ground in this chapter. By now you should feel much more comfortable developing COM clients.

IN DEPTH

Providing Interface Descriptions

One of the questions most frequently asked by COM newcomers is this: "How do I know what interfaces are supported by third-party servers?" Since many of today's applications support COM interfaces, the only thing that stands in the way of using these interfaces is knowing what they are and what DLLs you need to include. Because of this, as a component developer it is key that you provide appropriate documentation for your servers. At a minimum, each method and property defined within your IDL should have the appropriate help strings to explain it. This way, a developer using your server will be able to open the type library (using OLE View or some other COM object viewer) and see how to use your component. Ideally, however, help strings are not sufficient, and you will also want to distribute help files and even sample code along with your component.

If, on the other hand, you specifically want to prevent people from coding against your component—for licensing reasons, for example—then add the **hidden** attribute to all the properties and methods of your IDL and distribute only the version of the TLB generated from this modified IDL. Remember, for your own development work, you will still want a version of the IDL without the **hidden** attribute.

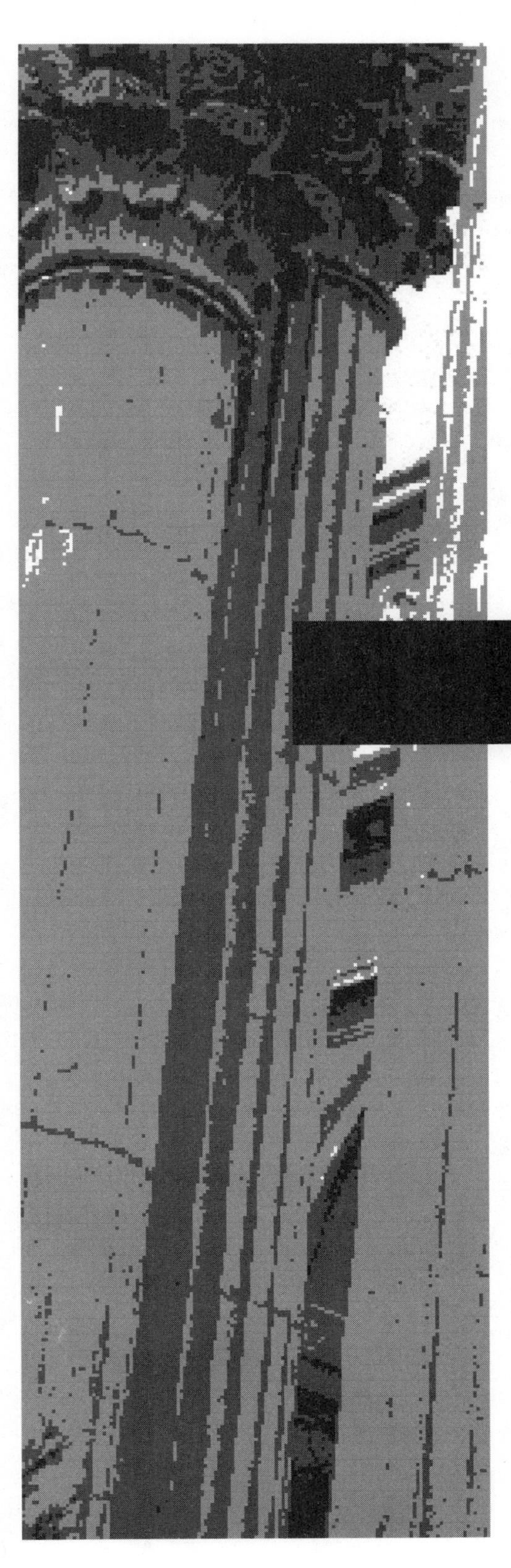

CHAPTER 6

Working with the COM String Known as BSTR

The preceding chapter ended with an example that used COM strings, but we postponed a discussion of those strings until we could devote an entire chapter to them. Here we are going to investigate them in detail. Many beginning COM programmers find that one of the most frustrating things about COM is working with the various string types. Specifically, there is confusion with **BSTR**, the fundamental COM string type, and how to convert it to and from other string types. Probably even less well understood are the intricacies of memory management. When is the client responsible for freeing an allocated string? When is the server responsible? It is not that COM strings are complicated, but sometimes their proper usage gets lost among the other details of working with COM. Frankly, many beginning programmers flounder in this area for a while. It is because of this that we are now going to dedicate an entire chapter to the topic.

This chapter explains how to handle strings both within your program and when passing them to a COM client or server. The chapter begins by looking at some problems associated with sharing strings between the COM client and the COM server in a language-neutral, location-independent manner. Next, we examine some of the API functions used to manipulate strings. Then we discuss two wrapper classes that are designed to make working with the COM string data type, **BSTR**, significantly less cumbersome.

COM String Fundamentals

COM designers were faced with several challenging questions when it came to deciding how strings were to be represented and how they were then to be passed across the COM boundaries. For instance, of the two predominant types of string character set, which should be used? Different languages represent strings differently. For example, Visual Basic strings differ from those supported by C++. What string format should be used? In addition, strings can be of varying lengths, so there needs to be a way to determine the length of a specific string when it crosses the COM boundary. Furthermore, sometimes strings require the allocation of memory; what are the rules that govern memory management in order to prevent memory leaks or references to unallocated memory blocks? The next few sections describe COM's answers to these questions.

Unicode vs. ANSI Data Types

Two character sets are widely used in computing: ANSI and Unicode. The size of the individual characters that make up each set is not the same. The ANSI character set uses 8-bit characters. Unicode uses 16-bit characters. This raises the obvious question: Which of these formats should COM use?

ANSI characters are 8 bits wide. Unicode characters are 16 bits wide.

Unfortunately, Unicode is not a compatible format—even across the Windows family of operating systems. The Windows 9X platforms, for example, have only rudimentary support for Unicode characters, and on the Windows 3.1 platform (the prevalent operating system during the time that COM was being developed), the support is even more limited. Even with the rudimentary Unicode support, all API function calls on the Windows 9X platform use the ANSI character set; so conversion between the two different formats becomes a frequent operation, making the code inefficient. On Unicode-compatible systems such as Windows NT/2000 and Windows CE the reverse problem occurs. Many API functions are Unicode; so if the ANSI character set is selected, conversion needs to take place in the opposite direction. Clearly, there were negatives no matter which character set was chosen, but this didn't eliminate the need to choose.

OLECHAR, LPOLESTR, and LPCOLESTR

The basic character data type for COM is **OLECHAR**.

Given the problem of choosing between ANSI and Unicode, the designers of COM opted for a third alternative: a platform-independent character representation. The character representation selected was **OLECHAR**. At the time of its creation, the underlying data type for **OLECHAR** varied from operating system to operating system. But this is something that the COM marshaller ended up handling automatically so that programmers did not need to be concerned about converting a string from one type to another when going between two different machines running two different operating systems. Today the most prevalent COM platforms are based on the Win32 API, and on these, **OLECHAR** is a **typedef** for a **wchar_t**. The *w* indicates that this is a wide (Unicode) character.

OLECHAR is defined as a **wchar_t** and, therefore, is a Unicode character.

When used to form a string, **OLECHAR**s are represented by an **LPOLESTR**, which is simply a **typedef** for an **OLECHAR***. Some form of **LPOLESTR**, therefore, is the data type that should be used to send strings across COM boundaries. **LPCOLESTR** is the **const** declaration of the same data type.

Working with LPOLESTRs

Although **OLECHAR** solved the ANSI versus Unicode dilemma, there is still another issue to consider: The basic C++ string is a null-terminated character array that is manipulated via pointers of type **char***. Therefore, if you attempt to assign a string literal to an **LPOLESTR**, you will receive a compile error. For example:

```
// Compile ERROR!!  Unable to convert
OLECHAR *olestr = "A string literal!";
```

Instead, you should prefix such a string with **L**, as shown here:

```
LPOLESTR szMyString = L"This is a Unicode string.";
```

This is especially important (but often missed) when using **printf( )** or even **ATLTRACE( )**. For example,

```
LPOLESTR szMyString = L" Hello, my name is Inigo Montoya.";
// ERROR: Literal ANSI strings should not be
// combined with LPOLESTRs
ATLTRACE("szMyString = '%s'", szMyString);
```

will compile and will even run. The result, however, in the trace window is

```
szMyString = 'T'
```

which is probably not what is intended. Instead you will need to use the **L** prefix or the **OLESTR( )** macro, as in

```
LPOLESTR szMyString = L"Hello, my name is Inigo Montoya.";
ATLTRACE(L"szMyString = '%s'", szMyString);
ATLTRACE(OLESTR("szMyString = '%s'"), szMyString);
```

You will want to keep a few more API functions in your bag of tricks for working with **LPOLESTR**s. Two functions are commonly used for copying strings. The first is the ANSI function, **wcscpy( )**, which is defined as follows:

wchar_t *wcscpy(wchar_t **target*, const wchar_t **source*);

The second is (as of this writing) an undocumented ATL function called **ocscpy( )**:

inline OLECHAR *ocscpy(LPOLESTR *target*, LPCOLESTR *source*);

To return the length of an **LPOLESTR**, you will want to use the ANSI **wcslen( )** or the ATL version, **ocslen( )**. To compare strings, use **wcscmp( )** for case-sensitive compares or **_wcsicmp( )** for case-insensitive compares.

To Unicode Compile or Not to Unicode Compile?

How a COM character will be represented is a decision that the COM designers made for us. The question that we as COM developers face is "In what character set should the code be compiled?" If a module is to run only on Windows NT or Windows CE where Unicode is supported, there is no reason to compile the code in an ANSI-compatible format. This would simply introduce unnecessary inefficiencies because of the conversion from one type to another. However, restricting a module to run only on a Unicode-compatible platform is a pretty severe restriction, and it should probably be reserved for NT services or the like unless you are confident that there is no need to run on the Windows 9X platform. As the Windows 9X generation of operating systems is phased out, however, this will become less of an issue.

The next option is, of course, to compile the code in an ANSI-compatible format. This makes it viable for the module to run on Windows 9X as well as the Unicode-compatible NT/2000 and CE platforms, but it introduces the need to convert Unicode to ANSI on the latter platforms. This results in a slight performance hit.

The last option is to have two different binary modules: one that will run on a Unicode-compatible platform and the other that can run on an ANSI-character-set-only platform. The good thing about this decision is that regardless of which option you select, as long as you code with care, changing your mind is a compile switch away. In fact, by default, the ATL wizard creates both an ANSI configuration and a Unicode configuration, allowing you to compile and release your component servers in either format or even in both. All you need to do is maintain the discipline of always using the **TCHAR** data type so that your code remains compatible with both character sets.

TCHAR

TCHAR is the generic character type.

The ability to switch between one character set and the next using a compile switch is provided via the generic text data type known as **TCHAR**, which is defined like this:

```
#ifdef  UNICODE
typedef WCHAR TCHAR, *PTCHAR;
#else   /* UNICODE */
typedef char TCHAR, *PTCHAR;
#endif /* UNICODE */
```

As you can see in the code above, how **TCHAR** is defined depends on whether or not **UNICODE** is defined. Consequently, to utilize the same source code for multiple character sets, the programmer's only responsibility is to be sure to use the character-set-neutral data type **TCHAR**. For example, instead of declaring a variable or parameter as **char**, you should use **TCHAR**, as shown here:

```
TCHAR c;
```

When working with literal character strings it is necessary to use a method similar to the **TCHAR** method. By default, C++ string literals are of type **char***. We have already seen how to designate these as wide characters by using the **L** prefix in front of the string. However, if you use the **TCHAR*** data type, the **L** prefix will not work in a non-Unicode compile unless you are explicitly setting it to a Unicode string. The fix is to use the **TEXT** macro or its abbreviation, **_T**. Since both of these macros are defined the same way, it does not matter which you choose. Although we have not made any official counts, the **_T** is probably the macro of choice for most programmers. The definitions of each of the macros are shown below:

```
#ifdef  UNICODE
#define __T(x)       L ## x
#else   /* not UNICODE */
#define __T(x)       x
#endif /* UNICODE */
#define _T(x)        __T(x)
#define _TEXT(x)     __T(x)
```

For example, to assign a string to a literal value in an ANSI/Unicode-compatible manner, you would do something like the following:

```
TCHAR *p_tchar = _T("The Dread Pirate Roberts takes no survivors!");
```

Handling Varying String Sizes with BSTR

The next problem with strings is that they do not have a fixed size. In one case, a string could be 30 characters, and in a second case, it could be 130. Therefore, whenever a string is passed as a parameter, the size of the string needs to be sent as well. There are several possible solutions to this problem. For example, an additional parameter could be used to indicate the size of the string being passed. The problem with this is that it makes the passing of what should be a simple data type into a complex process. Even in a simple method that requires only two string parameters, the method call becomes cumbersome.

A second solution would be to use a particular marker at the end of the string. For example, **LPOLESTR** always ends with a null character. Consequently, to figure out the length of a string, you could iterate through each character until the null character was found. This is certainly a viable solution, and it is sometimes used in interfaces. Strings of this type are not considered one of the intrinsic COM data types (often referred to as OLE Automation data types), however, and the MIDL compiler will issue a warning if you use it. The drawback with a marker is that it prevents the marker from being a part of the string. For example, if you use the null character as a separator between a list of names, as soon as the first name has been read, the null character will be encountered and the remaining names will be discarded, possibly resulting in a memory leak. The same principle applies if you send binary data using the **LPOLESTR** data type.

Because of these issues, the **BSTR** data type was introduced. **BSTR** is a pointer to an **OLECHAR** string just as the **LPOLESTR** is a pointer to an **OLECHAR** string. What distinguishes the **BSTR** is that the length of the string, not including the final null terminator, is specified in the four bytes preceding the string pointer, as shown in Figure 6-1.

Since this is a Unicode string, each character takes up two bytes. The length indicator appears in the address space immediately preceding the **OLECHAR** pointer and identifies the string to be 24 bytes. It is required that the **BSTR** be terminated with a null just as an **LPOLESTR** is terminated. This enables the **BSTR** to be used in the same locations that an **LPOLESTR** is used. The **BSTR** avoids the drawback of an **LPOLESTR**, however. Because the length of a **BSTR** is explicitly specified, null characters can be embedded within the **BSTR** as well. Therefore, **BSTR**s can be used to send binary data as well as simple strings. When a **BSTR** with binary data is sent via COM, the entire set of data will be sent because the length prefix determines how much data is to be passed.

A **BSTR** can be used to send binary data.

Because of the special structure of **BSTR**s, several special API functions have been added to assist in working with them. The need for such functions is especially apparent when it comes to creating and destroying strings that are passed across the COM boundary. This brings us to the next problem with strings. How are they allocated and freed, and who (the client or the server) is responsible for which operations?

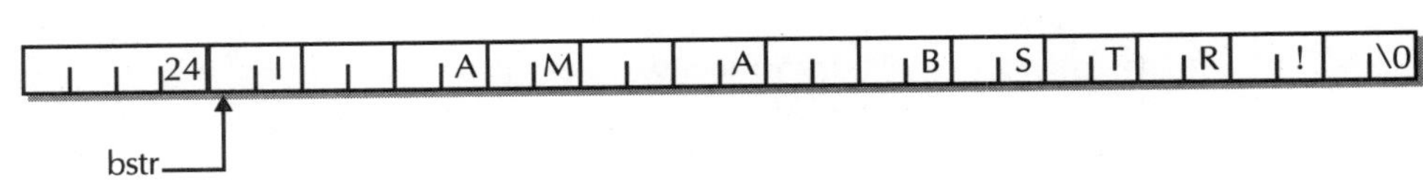

Address space of a **BSTR** data type

Figure 6-1.

Common API Functions for Handling BSTRs

Since **BSTR**s have a special structure, they should be allocated using the **BSTR** allocation functions, **SysAllocString( )** and **SysFreeString( )**. **SysAllocString( )** is declared as follows:

```
BSTR SysAllocString(const OLECHAR *szSource);
```

This function is used to copy the data stored in *szSource* into a **BSTR** data type. The function returns a pointer to the string or **NULL** on failure.

Since an **OLECHAR*** string is terminated with a null character, you cannot use **SysAllocString( )** to allocate a **BSTR** that contains binary data. Instead, you will want to use **SysAllocStringLen( )**, which allows you to specify the length of the resulting **BSTR** and is defined as follows:

```
BSTR SysAllocStringLen(const OLECHAR *szSource, unsigned int size);
```

SysAllocStringLen( ) can also be used to change the *szSource* string length. The second parameter, *size*, designates how many characters are to be copied regardless of any null character location, terminating or otherwise. **SysAllocStringLen( )** automatically appends a null character. If *size* is longer than the length of the *szSource* string, additional memory will still be allocated but not initialized, and the **BSTR** will end up with an embedded null. On the other hand, if *size* is less than the total length of *szSource*, the remaining characters will be left off the resulting **BSTR**.

NULL can be specified for the *szSource* value for both **SysAllocString( )** and **SysAllocStringLen( )**. In the latter case, the memory for the string will be allocated but not initialized.

There are several other string API functions, as shown in Table 6-1.

All **BSTR**s must be freed with **SysFreeString( )** in order to deallocate the memory previously allocated.

For every call to allocate a **BSTR**, there must be a corresponding call to **SysFreeString( )** to deallocate the memory. Memory deallocation needs to occur on assignment, when an existing **BSTR** is being reassigned as well as when an exception is thrown. In other words, before assigning a **BSTR** variable with a new value, you must first call **SysFreeString( )** or an equivalent. Any time you forget the call to **SysFreeString( )**, you will be introducing a memory leak just as you would by using the **new** operator but not calling **delete** when you were done with the allocated memory.

API Function	Description
BSTR SysAllocString (const OLECHAR **szSource*);	Allocates a **BSTR** from an **OLECHAR***. To avoid unexpected results do not use a **BSTR** as the *szSource* parameter unless you are certain it does not contain embedded null characters.
BSTR SysAllocStringByteLen(LPCSTR *pszSource*, unsigned int *len*);	Used for **BSTR**s that are to contain binary data rather than a true string. The input is an ANSI string pointer; however, since the purpose is to store binary data into the **BSTR**, it will not convert the ANSI characters to Unicode.
BSTR SysAllocStringLen(const OLECHAR **szSource*, unsigned int *len*);	Allocates a **BSTR** of length equal to *len*. If *szSource* is **NULL**, the memory will be allocated but the **BSTR** will be uninitialized.
VOID SysFreeString(BSTR *bstr*);	Frees the memory allocated to *bstr*.
INT SysReAllocString(BSTR FAR * *pbstr*, const OLECHAR FAR * *szSource*);	Reallocates a **BSTR** to the *szSource* string. *pbstr* will be freed automatically before it is reassigned the value in *szSource*. If the new string is of a different length, *pbstr* will be resized.
INT SysReAllocStringLen(BSTR FAR * *pbstr*, const OLECHAR FAR **szSource*, unsigned int *len*);	Reallocates *pbstr* to the size specified in *len*. *pbstr* is freed before making the new assignment. A maximum of *len* characters are copied into the new **BSTR** from *szSource*. If there are fewer than *len* characters in *szSource*, the remaining characters in *pbstr* will be uninitialized.

API Functions for Handling **BSTR**s
Table 6-1.

6

API Functions for Handling **BSTR**s *(continued)*
Table 6-1.

API Function	Description
UINT SysStringByteLen(BSTR *bstr*);	Returns the number of bytes allocated for *bstr* not including the terminating null character.
UINT SysStringLen(BSTR *bstr*);	Returns the number of characters in *bstr* not including the terminating null character.

String Memory Management Across COM Boundaries

You have seen that all **BSTR**s are allocated with **SysAllocString( )** or one of its cousins, and freed with **SysFreeString( )**. The rules for memory management with **BSTR**s across COM boundaries are slightly more complicated, however. Unlike interfaces, which use **IUnknown** reference counting, **BSTR** has no reference counting mechanism. What happens, for example, when the server returns a string via an **[out]** parameter? Should it destroy the memory allocated to the string, or should it expect the callee to be responsible for this?

To start with, we are going to look at the problem from the server perspective. What is the server's responsibility when passing strings? In this section we will be working with a COM object called **StringObjectUsingRawBstr** whose implementation can be found in **StringObjectUsingRawBstr.cpp**. We will show only the relevant portions of this code, however. For full details you can download the code from the Osborne web site. At the end of the section we will turn things around and examine the same issues from the perspective of a COM client.

A COM server should not maintain a reference to a variable passed across a COM boundary. Instead, a copy should be made.

The governing principle for a server passing **BSTR**s across COM boundaries is that the client is responsible for freeing the **BSTR**. This is true whether the **BSTR** is an **[in]** or an **[out]** parameter. The only time that a server should be freeing a string in regard to passing it to the client is before assigning a new value to an **[in, out]** parameter. In this case, the client passes in an allocated string, and the server frees it and then assigns the pointer to the location of a newly allocated string that the client will free. For the server, the governing principle is always to create a copy of incoming and outgoing **BSTR**s rather than adding another reference to an existing **BSTR**.

Consider the example of a member variable that is to be passed to a COM client as an **[out]** parameter and still referenced by the server. The IDL method declaration would be as follows:

```
HRESULT GetString([out] BSTR* ReturnString);
```

The implementation for this method cannot simply assign an internal member variable to the **ReturnString** parameter, as shown here:

```
STDMETHODIMP CStringObjectUsingRawBstr::get_Value(
  /*[out, retval]*/ BSTR *pReturnString)
{
  *pReturnString = m_str;     // CAREFUL!!...the client will
                              // free the BSTR when you
                              // don't expect it.
  return S_OK;
}
```

In this example, **GetString( )** is a function defined by a COM object called **CStringObjectUsingRawBstr**. Although there is nothing inherently wrong with the assignment, a problem arises due to the intention that the **m_str** value is an internal **BSTR** that will continue to be used by the server. By passing the value to an **[out]** parameter, you create an additional reference on the **BSTR**, which violates the principle that **BSTR**s passed across COM boundaries must not have more than one reference. Why is this a problem? At some point, the client will free the **BSTR** value. Doing this will deallocate the memory pointed to by **m_str**. Now, if the server nonetheless tries to use **m_str**, an error will result.

To correct the code, one of two things should occur. Either a copy of the **m_str** string should be created, or **m_str** should be set to **NULL** after the assignment. This way, there is only one reference to the allocated string. The code below demonstrates each possibility. (In this code, **m_str** is declared as a **BSTR** within the **CStringObjectUsingRawBstr** class.) Here is the first way:

```
STDMETHODIMP CStringObjectUsingRawBstr::get_Value(
  /*[out, retval]*/ BSTR *pValue)
{  // Client is responsible for passing a BSTR that is unallocated
  // so don't call SysFreeString().
  // Client is responsible for calling SysFreeString() on the
  // returned string.
  *pValue = SysAllocString( m_str );
  return S_OK;
}
```

Here is the second possibility:

```
STDMETHODIMP CStringObjectUsingRawBstr::get_Value(
  /*[out, retval]*/ BSTR *pValue)
{
  *pValue = m_str;
  m_str = NULL;  // Set to NULL because m_str no longer
                 // owns the string.
  return S_OK;
}
```

Make a copy of an incoming **BSTR** if you plan to access its data outside the context of the COM function call.

Now that you understand how to pass outgoing parameters, let's take a look at those that are incoming. For incoming **BSTR**s, you should consider the parameter data to be on loan for the time of the function call. Therefore, you can count on a **BSTR** being valid for the duration of the call; but if you wish to use the **BSTR** outside the context of the function call, you will need to make a copy of it. For example:

```
CStringObjectUsingRawBstr::CStringObjectUsingRawBstr()
{
  m_str = NULL;
}

STDMETHODIMP CStringObjectUsingRawBstr::put_Value(
  /*[in]*/ BSTR NewValue )
{
  // NewValue on loan from Client. Client responsible for
  // freeing NewValue at some point so make a copy of
  // the incoming value after clearing the previous value
  // in m_str.
  if( SysReAllocString(&m_str, NewValue) )
    return S_OK;
  else
    return E_OUTOFMEMORY;
}
```

When you use **[in] BSTR** parameters, it is a good idea to treat them as **const OLECHAR* const** parameters even though they are not declared as such. It is even possible to edit the IDL and function declaration to use **const BSTR const** in place of a mutable **BSTR**. If you do this, however, a 4114 warning, "same type qualifier used more than once," will be issued; so you may want to turn it off by using this:

```
#pragma warning( disable : 4114 )
```

Before we leave our discussion of how the server is to handle strings, let's consider two more function examples. The first is the **Swap( )** function, which takes an **[in, out]** parameter and is shown below:

```
// Swap m_str with pSwapValue
STDMETHODIMP CStringObjectUsingRawBstr::Swap(
  /*[in, out]*/ BSTR* pSwapValue)
{
  BSTR str = NULL;

  // Ownership transferred to str
  str =  *pSwapValue;

  // Set pSwapValue to own m_str
  *pSwapValue = m_str;

  // Set m_str to own str
  m_str = str;

  return S_OK;
}
```


In the above function, notice how ownership of the two strings moves from one variable to another. Normally, setting the previous owner to **NULL** should follow such a transfer in ownership. In this case, however, the owner is being assigned a new value immediately anyway, so there is no concern about having two owners by the time the function exits and crosses back over the COM boundaries.

The next function demonstrates how to append two strings:

```
STDMETHODIMP CStringObjectUsingRawBstr::Append(
  /*[in]*/ BSTR Suffix,
  /*[out, retval]*/ BSTR* pNewValue)
{
  HRESULT hr=S_OK;
  int nLength = SysStringLen( m_str );
  int nSuffixLength = SysStringLen(Suffix);

  // Resize m_str to include the length of sSuffix
  if (!SysReAllocStringLen(&m_str, m_str,
      nLength+nSuffixLength ))
  {
    pNewValue = NULL;
    hr = E_OUTOFMEMORY;
  }
```

```
  else
  {
    // Copy sSuffix to the end of m_str
    memcpy(m_str+nLength, Suffix,
      nSuffixLength*sizeof(OLECHAR));

    // Set pNewValue to return m_str to the client
    *pNewValue = SysAllocString( m_str );
  }

  return hr;
}
```

In this example, notice how **SysReAllocStringLen( )** allocates a string that is bigger than the **const OLECHAR*** source string being copied. The extra memory is uninitialized, but the **memcpy( )** function is used to set it to **Suffix**, the string to be appended.

Now that you understand the workings of strings from the server perspective, let us consider how to call the **CStringObjectUsingRawBstr** object, defined above, from the client. In this case, we will use the raw interfaces rather than the **_com_ptr_t** smart pointer classes discussed in the previous chapter because the smart pointer classes use the **_bstr_t** wrapper class, which masks the underlying string details. Consider the following:

```
BSTR str1 = NULL;
BSTR str2 = NULL;
BSTR str3 = NULL;
...
// [in] parameters must pass NULL or an allocated string
str1 = SysAllocString(L" Bye bye, boys! Have fun storming"
  " the castle!");
pIComString->put_Value(str1);
// Free the [out] parameter string
SysFreeString(str1);

// [out] parameters must pass unallocated strings or
// a memory leak will occur.
pIComString->get_Value(&str2);
SysReAllocString(&str2, L"Think it will work?");

str3 = SysAllocString(L"It would take a miracle.")
pIComString->Append( str3 );
SysFreeString(str3);
```

```
// Passing to an [in,out] function one must pass
// a valid string or NULL value
pIComString->Swap(&str2);
// Free the [out] parameter string
SysFreeString(str2);
```

To begin, **str1** is assigned a string literal. Be aware that you could easily make the mistake of assigning the literal string directly to the **BSTR**, but this would leave the length prefix portion of the **BSTR** uninitialized—not a good thing. Instead, **SysAllocString( )** is called. After calling the **put_Value( )** function and passing the string as an **[in]** parameter, the client frees the string. For **[out]** parameters, the client must be sure to initialize the string before passing it. This is why when declaring **str2**, the value is set to **NULL**. After calling **get_Value( )**, we use **SysReAllocString( )** to deallocate the previous string and then reallocate it to a new value. For the **Append( )** call, the same procedure as the previous **put_Value( )** call is followed. Lastly, even though **Swap( )** uses an **[in, out]** parameter, there is nothing different in what the client must do. As with all **[in]** parameters, the client must allocate the memory, as already done, in this case with a call to **SysReAllocString( )**. Afterwards, the client must free the allocated string.

One potential snag that we have so far only briefly mentioned is the use of embedded null characters within a **BSTR**. This is ironic since embedded nulls are considered an advantage over using **LPOLESTR**s because they can be used to pass binary streams of data. Nonetheless, embedded null characters can also cause unexpected results. The problem occurs when **BSTR**s are used as **LPOLESTR** parameters. **LPOLESTR**s use a null to signify the end of a string. Therefore, if a **BSTR** with embedded nulls is passed as a **LPOLESTR**, the conversion will truncate the string to the first null character and assume the end of the string has been reached. Although it is uncommon for **BSTR**s to be passed with embedded null characters, be careful when you make this assumption. When in doubt as to the existence of embedded nulls, you can test by comparing the length returned by **wcslen( )** with the length returned by **SysStringLen( )**, as shown here:

```
BSTR bstr;
...
if( wcslen((LPOLESTR) bstr) == SysStringLen(bstr) )
  std::cout << _T("No embedded NULLs in bstr") << std::endl;
...
SysFreeString(bstr);
```

Here are a few guiding principles for working with **BSTR**s:

- **[in]** parameters are owned by the *client*. Therefore, servers should create a copy if they wish to access the value after the function returns. The server should *not* free or change these parameters in any way.
- **[out]** parameters are freed by the *client*.
- The *client* must pass a **BSTR** that is **NULL** or unallocated into an **[out]** parameter on a server.
- The *server* should not free an **[out]** parameter before setting it.
- Inside a server, **[in, out]** parameters must be freed before being reassigned new **BSTR** values.
- Beware when using **SysAllocString( )** and **SysReAllocString( )** if the source parameter is a **BSTR** in place of an **LPOLESTR**. Even though a **BSTR** parameter will compile, there could be an embedded null character, which will produce unexpected results and quite probably a memory leak. If the source string is a **BSTR** and you are unsure whether there are any embedded nulls, use **SysReAllocStringLen( )** or **SysAllocStringLen( )**.
- Always use **SysStringLen( )** to get the length of a **BSTR**. Do not assume that if the beginning of a **BSTR** is a null character, the string is an empty string. Although this may be true generally, **BSTR**s can contain embedded nulls, which would make the assumption false.

Given the error-prone nature of manual memory management, there is clearly a need for a wrapper class when it comes to string manipulation. Fortunately, two of these are provided—**CComBSTR** and **_bstr_t**—which we will cover shortly.

String Conversion Functions

Before we leave the string handling functions, let's briefly examine some utilities for converting one string format to another. Table 6-2 lists the macros used for converting strings from one type to another.

A2BSTR	OLE2A	T2A	W2A
A2COLE	OLE2BSTR	T2BSTR	W2BSTR
A2CT	OLE2CA	T2CA	W2CA
A2CW	OLE2CT	T2COLE	W2COLE
A2OLE	OLE2CW	T2CW	W2CT
A2T	OLE2T	T2OLE	W2OLE
A2W	OLE2W	T2W	W2T

ATL String Conversion Macros

Table 6-2.

In Table 6-2 the "2" stands for "to," and the characters on the left and right of the 2 are the source and destination character set types, respectively. Here is what they stand for:

Code	Stands For
A	ANSI
OLE	OLECHAR
T	TCHAR
W	WCHAR
C	const

Before you use any of the macros, be sure to specify the **USES_CONVERSION** macro, or you will get a compile error such as this:

error C2065: '_lpw' : undeclared identifier

Here is a short example using the **W2A( )** macro:

```
USES_CONVERSION;
LPOLESTR szMyString = L"Truly, you have a dizzying intellect. Vizzini ";
ATLTRACE(OLESTR("szMyString = '%s'\n"), szMyString);
char *str;
str = W2A(szMyString);
ATLTRACE("str = '%s'... NOT!!\n", str);
```

All these macros are ATL based; so if you wish to use them in a non-ATL project, you will have to include the **atlconv.h** header.

Two other conversion functions are defined and automatically included by the **#import** directive. As yet, neither is documented, but when you're writing a client, they are probably easier to use than the above macros, which are more appropriate inside ATL projects. Both functions appear within **comutil.h** and belong to the **_com_util** namespace. The two functions are used for converting ANSI character strings to **BSTR**s and back again. Their declaration is shown here:

```
namespace _com_util
{
  BSTR __stdcall ConvertStringToBSTR(const char* szSource)
    throw(_com_error);
  char* __stdcall ConvertBSTRToString(BSTR source)
    throw(_com_error);
}
```

CComBSTR

Although it is certainly possible to work with COM strings using system calls, it can be frustrating especially when you need to write three or four lines to perform some simple string manipulation. More importantly, there is a high risk of a memory leak occurring because **SysFreeString**( ) is not called before a **BSTR** goes out of scope. Fortunately, several string wrapper classes make working with **BSTR**s significantly easier.

CComBSTR wraps BSTR.

The first **BSTR** wrapper class we will look at is **CComBSTR**. **CComBSTR** is defined within ATL's **atlbase.h**. Because of its definition within one of the ATL files, **CComBSTR** is used most commonly inside ATL projects, to pass strings back and forth from COM clients. This section focuses on such a situation. In the next section we will examine the **_bstr_t** class, which performs similarly but is generally used within a COM client because it is automatically included by the **#import** directive.

CComBSTR has only one data member—a public **BSTR** called **m_str**. The purpose of **CComBSTR** is to wrap the **BSTR** data type to assist with **BSTR** memory management. In addition, it includes various helper functions such as **LoadString( )**, which loads a resource string into the **CComBSTR**, and **ToUpper( )/ToLower( )**, which converts the string to a particular case. A **CComBSTR** can be constructed from an **int**, **LPOLESTR**, another **CComBSTR**, and even a **GUID**. (Under an ANSI compile, **LPCSTR** is also supported.) **CComBSTR** also supports a default constructor (no parameters). With the exception of the default constructor, which initializes **m_str** to **NULL**, all other constructors allocate memory for the internal **BSTR**. For example, one of the constructors takes both an integer and an **LPOLESTR** and is implemented as follows in **atlbase.h**:

```
CComBSTR(int size, LPCOLESTR szSource)
{
  m_str = ::SysAllocStringLen(szSource, size);
}
```

This constructor initializes the **CComBSTR** variable to be **size** long and to be initialized with whatever characters from **szSource** will fit into the allocated string, as we described the **SysAllocStringLen( )** function earlier.

Since **CComBSTR** allocates memory in the constructor, it inevitably needs to release it in the destructor too. This is done with a call to **SysFreeString( )**, as you would expect.

Memory management is key in assignment as well as during instantiation and deletion. Therefore, several functions aid in this effort. First, the assignment operator is overloaded so that you can assign strings of various types to a **CComBSTR**. You can assign either another **CComBSTR** variable to a **CComBSTR**, or you can assign an **LPOLESTR**. (**LPCSTR** is also available in an ANSI compile.) Unlike when assigning one raw **BSTR** to another, **CComBSTR** always allocates memory and copies the string, rather than simply changing the destination **BSTR** to point to the source **BSTR**. Below is the assignment operator code taken from Microsoft's **atlbase.h** header file:

```
CComBSTR& operator=(LPCOLESTR pSrc)
{
  ::SysFreeString(m_str);
  m_str = ::SysAllocString(pSrc);
  return *this;
}
```

The operator **+=** is also overloaded, allowing you to append another **BSTR**, **LPOLESTR**, or **CComBSTR**. This operator calls **AppendBSTR( )** and returns the resultant **CComBSTR**. Since **AppendBSTR( )** uses **SysAllocStringLen( )**, it is designed to handle embedded nulls. A third function, **Append( )**, achieves the same result, but unlike **AppendBSTR( )**, it requires use of the **CComBSTR** constructor, too, and does not account for embedded nulls.

In Chapter 5 we examined the **_com_ptr_t** and saw that it had two functions that aided the translation of raw interfaces to **_com_ptr_t** data types while minimizing the reference counting. The two functions were **Attach( )** and **Detach( )**. As with many of the wrapper classes and smart pointers we will discuss in this book, **CComBSTR** supports the same two functions. Rather than raw interfaces, **CComBSTR** uses **BSTR**. The **Attach( )** function is used to point a **CComBSTR** at an existing **BSTR** without calling **SysAllocString( )**. As before, the purpose is to transfer ownership. After calling **Attach( )**, you are no longer responsible for having to explicitly free the **BSTR** because the **CComBSTR** data type will take care of doing this instead.

One thing to note about **Attach( )** is that it is allowed only if the **CComBSTR** was not set before calling **Attach( )**—that is, the **m_str** member variable was **NULL**. Let's take a look at the implementation. Again, this is found in **atlbase.h**.

```
void Attach(BSTR src)
{
  ATLASSERT(m_str == NULL);
  m_str = src;
}
```

Just as the **Attach( )** function is used to take ownership of an existing **BSTR**, the **Detach( )** function is used to release ownership. The result of **Detach( )** is that a **BSTR** is assigned the value of **m_str** and then set to **NULL** so that when the **CComBSTR** destructor is called, **SysFreeString( )** will not be invoked. Below is the implementation code found in **atlbase.h**:

```
BSTR Detach()
{
  BSTR s = m_str;
  m_str = NULL;
  return s;
}
```

The last function related to memory allocation that we will discuss here is **Copy( )**. Since the assignment operator also copies a string, you might be somewhat surprised to learn that there is also an explicit **Copy( )** function. What is unique about the **Copy( )** function, however, is that it takes into consideration the length of the **BSTR**, thereby accounting for the possibility that there could be embedded nulls. For example, the **Copy( )** function defined in **atlbase.h**, shown below, uses **SysAllocStringLen( )** rather than **SysAllocString( )**, as we have seen in the other assignments so far.

```
BSTR Copy() const
{
  return ::SysAllocStringLen(m_str, ::SysStringLen(m_str));
}
```

Although currently absent from Microsoft's documentation, there is also a **CopyTo( )** function that takes a **BSTR*** as a parameter rather than returning it using a function return. The return value from the **CopyTo( )** function is an **HRESULT**. Below is the **CComBSTR**::**CopyTo( )** prototype:

HRESULT CopyTo(BSTR **pBSTR*);

6

CComBSTR supports a few functions relating to string manipulation rather than memory allocation—specifically, functions such as **Length( )**, **LoadString( )**, **ToUpper( )**, **ToLower( )**, along with **WriteToStream( )** and **ReadFromStream( )**. The declarations and descriptions of these and the most common **CComBSTR** functions are shown in Table 6-3. Note that for the entire table **LPCSTR** versions are available only for non-Unicode compiles. Also, note that included in Table 6-3 are the **ToUpper( )** and **ToLower( )** functions, which are, as of this writing, undocumented.

As we stated at the beginning of the section, in general **CComBSTR** is used within a COM server built with ATL. It is especially designed to work without requiring exception handling, decreasing the overall code size for the ATL project. Although it could be used from a COM client, this would require the addition of **atlbase.h** to the project, which is generally not necessary because there are some Microsoft standard types that can be used for this purpose instead. Following Table 6-3 is a listing of server code showing how the **CComBSTR** class is used to pass parameters from the server to the client depending on the **[in]** and/or **[out]** parameter of the IDL function declaration.

Function	Description
CComBSTR( ); CComBSTR(int *size*); CComBSTR(int *size*, LPCOLESTR *szSource*); CComBSTR(int *size*, LPCSTR *szSource*); CComBSTR(LPCOLESTR *pSource*); CComBSTR(LPCSTR *pSource*); CComBSTR(const CComBSTR &*source*);	A variety of constructors for **CComBSTR**. Each allocates memory that is destroyed by the destructor when the variable goes out of scope.
operator BSTR( ) const;	Converts **CComBSTR** to a **BSTR** by returning **m_str**.
BSTR *operator &( );	Returns the address of **m_str**.
CComBSTR &operator=(LPCOLESTR *pSource*); CComBSTR &operator=(LPCSTR *pSource*); CComBSTR &operator=(const CComBSTR &*source*);	Copies the **BSTR** specified by *pSource* or *source* into **m_str**.
BSTR Copy( ) const; HRESULT CopyTo(BSTR **pBSTR*);	Copies the **m_str** value to a **BSTR**. The **Copy( )/CopyTo( )** functions use **SysAllocStringLen( )**, which means they are capable of handling strings with embedded null characters.
void Attach(BSTR *bstr*);	Attaches the **CComBSTR** to the **BSTR** *bstr* parameter. After calling **Attach( )**, you no longer need to explicitly free the *bstr* variable because the **CComBSTR** destructor will do this for you.
BSTR Detach( );	Returns the value stored in **m_str** and sets **m_str** to **NULL**. Ownership now belongs to the returned **BSTR**.
void Empty( );	Frees **m_str** and sets it to **NULL**.

CComBSTR Functions; **m_str** Is the **CComBSTR** Member Variable

Table 6-3.

Function	Description

void Append(const CComBSTR &*bstr*);
void Append(LPCOLESTR *lpstr*);
void Append(LPCOLESTR *lpstr*, int *length*);
void Append(LPCSTR *lpstr*);
void AppendBSTR(BSTR *bstr*);
CComBSTR &operator+=(const CComBSTR &*bstr*);
	Appends strings of various kinds onto **m_str**. When appending an **LPCOLESTR**, you can specify the number of characters you wish to append using the *Length* parameter. Due to the variety of **CComBSTR** constructors, the operator **+=** can be used for each string type, but this will invoke a constructor before calling **AppendBSTR( )**.

bool LoadString(UINT *nID*); bool LoadString(HINSTANCE *hInstance*, UINT *nID*);	**LoadString( )** is used to load a string resource. Note that when using **LoadString(UINT nID)**, you must have a **CComModule** object called **_pModule**. This is created for you when you use the ATL wizard. If you did not do this, however, use the second version of **LoadString( )**. *nID* specifies which resource, and *hInstance* identifies the module containing the resource file.
unsigned int Length( ) const	Returns the length of the wrapped **BSTR** using **SysStringLen( )**.
HRESULT ReadFromStream(IStream **pStream*); HRESULT WriteToStream(IStream **pStream*);	Reads or writes an **m_str** to a stream interface, **IStream**.
bool operator !( );	Returns **true** if **m_str** is **NULL** and **false** otherwise.
HRESULT ToUpper( ); HRESULT ToLower( );	Converts **m_str** to be all uppercase or all lowercase.

CComBSTR Functions; **m_str** Is the **CComBSTR** Member Variable *(continued)*
Table 6-3.

6

Here is a listing of another COM component that uses **CComBSTR**. This code can be found in **StringObjectUsingCComBSTR.cpp**.

```
// StringObjectUsingCComBSTR.cpp : Implementation of
// CStringObjectUsingCComBSTR
#include "stdafx.h"
#include "Strings.h"
#include "StringObjectUsingCComBSTR.h"

#pragma warning( push )
#pragma warning( disable : 4114 )

///////////////////////////////////////////////////////////////////////////
// CStringObjectUsingCComBSTR


STDMETHODIMP CStringObjectUsingCComBSTR::put_Value(
  /*[in]*/ const BSTR const NewValue )
{
  m_str = NewValue;
  return S_OK;
}

STDMETHODIMP CStringObjectUsingCComBSTR::get_Value(
  /*[out, retval]*/ BSTR *pValue)
{
  *pValue = m_str.Copy();
  return S_OK;
}

// Swap m_str with pSwapValue
STDMETHODIMP CStringObjectUsingCComBSTR::Swap(
  /*[in, out]*/ BSTR* pSwapValue)
{
  CComBSTR str;

  // Ownership transferred to str
  str.Attach(*pSwapValue);
```

```
    // Set pSwapValue to own m_str
    *pSwapValue = m_str.Detach();

    // Set m_str to own str
    m_str = str.Detach();
    return S_OK;
}

STDMETHODIMP CStringObjectUsingCComBSTR::Append(
    /*[in]*/ const BSTR const  Suffix,
    /*[out, retval]*/ BSTR* pNewValue)
{
    m_str.AppendBSTR(Suffix);
    return S_OK;
}

#pragma warning( pop )
```


There is little more to say about the code than what we have already covered in this section. The listing, however, shows a complete picture of how to write **BSTR** parameters with **[in]**, **[out]**, and **[in, out]** attributes.

_bstr_t

_bstr_t keeps an internal reference count.

In Chapter 5 we worked with COM strings as part of the Merlin project. Because this was not an ATL project, we did not have access to **CComBSTR** without explicitly adding it. Instead, we used **_bstr_t** for manipulating **BSTR**s. **_bstr_t** was added automatically with the **#import** directive, which we used to import the Microsoft Agent control. What distinguishes **_bstr_t** most from **CComBSTR** is that **_bstr_t** keeps an internal reference count. In many cases this reference counting mechanism makes **_bstr_t** more efficient, because it reduces the number of times memory is allocated and deallocated. Another distinguishing characteristic is that **_bstr_t** requires exception handling, something that is not included in an ATL project by default.

For the reasons described above, **_bstr_t** is more suited for a COM client application, and this is the focus we will use in this section. The definition of **_bstr_t**, along with its implementation, is found in **comutil.h**.

The constructors for **_bstr_t** are similar to those found in **CComBSTR**. Each is shown below:

_bstr_t( ) throw( );
_bstr_t(const _bstr_t &*source*) throw( );
_bstr_t(const char **source*) throw(_com_error);
_bstr_t(const wchar_t **source*) throw(_com_error);
_bstr_t(const _variant_t &*var*) throw(_com_error);
_bstr_t(BSTR *bstr*, bool *bMakeCopy*) throw(_com_error);

A **_bstr_t** object can be constructed from a **BSTR**, a variant, a **wchar_t***, a **char***, and finally, another **_bstr_t**. (Don't worry if you are unfamiliar with the variant data type, as we will be discussing it in the next chapter.) Note that there is one additional parameter on the **BSTR** version of the constructor. Rather than simply passing a **BSTR**, the *bMakeCopy* parameter is used to indicate whether the **_bstr_t** should attach to *bstr*—thereby taking ownership and the responsibility to free it—or else be copied into the new **_bstr_t** variable. If *bMakeCopy* is **false**, **_bstr_t** attaches to *bstr* in a manner similar to the way **CComBSTR::Attach( )** worked. When this approach is used, *bstr* does not need to be freed explicitly. If *bMakeCopy* is **true**, a copy is made. Be careful however; if you call the **_bstr_t** constructor without specifying the *bMakeCopy* parameter, you will invoke the **wchar_t*** constructor. This will cause a copy of the source **BSTR** to be made, so you are still responsible for freeing the source. It's probably best to provide the *bMakeCopy* parameter explicitly so that you don't err in either direction. The second advantage in using this function is that it takes into consideration the possibility of embedded nulls.

Below is a list of the assignment operators that are overloaded in **_bstr_t**:

_bstr_t &operator=(const char **source*) throw(_com_error);
_bstr_t &operator=(const wchar_t **source*) throw(_com_error);
_bstr_t &operator=(const _bstr_t &*source*) throw( );
_bstr_t &operator=(const _variant_t &*var*) throw(_com_error);

This list shows that a **_bstr_t** can be assigned from either a **char*** or a **wchar_t***, making translation from a Unicode or ANSI string automatic. For most assignment functions, **SysAllocString( )** is called, essentially invoking a copy. Therefore, just like the constructors, if a **BSTR** is assigned, the destination **_bstr_t** does not take ownership, and it will still need to be freed. The one exception occurs for the constructor whose source is a **_bstr_t**. In this case the reference counting mechanism is invoked instead.

The fundamental structure of **_bstr_t** is different from the **CComBSTR** we saw before. Rather than having only a **BSTR** member variable, **_bstr_t** has a member variable declared as a private object of type **Data_t** called **m_Data**. **Data_t** is an internal class within **_bstr_t**, which has three member variables of its own. The first, a **wchar_t***, is actually used to store a **BSTR**. The second, a **char***, is used to convert a **BSTR** to a **char***. Finally, there is the reference counter, an **unsigned long**. Because **m_Data** is a private member, the **BSTR** value of **_bstr_t** cannot be accessed in the same manner as it was in **CComBSTR**, via the public member variable **m_str**. Instead, assigning the **_bstr_t** to another string type will automatically retrieve the internal **BSTR**. Below is a list of each of the pointer dereferencing operators:

```
operator const wchar_t*( ) const throw( );
operator wchar_t*( ) const throw( );
operator const char*( ) const throw(_com_error);
operator char*( ) const throw(_com_error);
```


As you can see, these allow you to assign the **_bstr_t** to either a Unicode or ANSI string, which is an operation not supported by **CComBSTR** without specifying an explicit cast. The important point to be aware of in these operators is that they do not make a copy. This is counter to the assignment operators we just examined. Therefore, if you use the operator for **wchar_t*** to assign a **_bstr_t** to **BSTR**, you should *not* free the **BSTR**, as it is still owned by the **_bstr_t**. Consider the sample code below:

```
BSTR bstr = SysAllocString(L"Have fun storming the castle!");
_bstr_t bstr_t;

bstr_t = bstr;

// ERROR: bstr must be free before being re-assigned.
bstr = bstr_t;

// ERROR: bstr_t still owns the string so it
//        is responsible for freeing it.
SysFreeString(bstr);
```

There are two errors in this sample, as noted in the comments. The first occurs when **bstr** is assigned the value of **bstr_t**. In the first assignment, "bstr_t = bstr," a copy of **bstr** was made. Therefore, **bstr** still owns its original string. If **bstr** is assigned a new value, however, a memory leak will result because there is no way to free the original value in **bstr**. Instead,

SysFreeString(bstr) should be called first. In the second error, the reverse happens. When **bstr_t** is assigned to **bstr**, **bstr_t** maintains ownership of the **BSTR** it created, and therefore, it will free this string within its destructor. The corrected sample code is shown below:

```
BSTR bstr = SysAllocString(L"Have fun storming the castle!");
_bstr_t bstr_t;

bstr_t = bstr;

// Free the bstr before assigning it a new value.
SysFreeString(bstr);

// Don't free bstr as bstr_t maintains ownership.
bstr = bstr_t;
```

Obviously, the opportunity for error is great. Similar to what you saw in the last chapter, the problem is the mixing of the raw type with a smart type—in this case, mixing **BSTR** with **_bstr_t**. The best solution to the problem is to avoid mixing the two. Once you begin using **_bstr_t**, use it consistently throughout your code. If you encounter a **BSTR** that cannot be avoided, assign it to a **_bstr_t** and free the original **BSTR** immediately. If you need to go the other way, converting a **BSTR** to a **_bstr_t**, use the **copy( )** function shown here:

BSTR copy( ) const throw(_com_error);

This creates a copy of the **_bstr_t**'s internal **BSTR**, leaving you to free the result.

The other reason for trying to avoid mixing raw **BSTR**s with **_bstr_t** is due to the reference counting. In order for reference counting to be more efficient, you need to use **_bstr_t** consistently throughout your code rather than oscillating between **_bstr_t** and the raw **BSTR**. Otherwise, a copy will be made rather than an increment in the reference count. Since the wrapper classes generated by the **#import** directive use the **_bstr_t** class by default, not mixing **BSTR** with **_bstr_t** is the natural tendency anyway.

As with **CComBSTR**, **_bstr_t** includes an append function that uses the += operator. In addition, **_bstr_t** includes a + operator and various friend functions for the same operator. These can be useful if you are trying to do many concatenation operations. Aside from a **length( )** function (used to obtain the length of the string), all the remaining functionality in **_bstr_t** is related to various relational operators. Table 6-4 lists all the **_bstr_t** functionality along with a brief description.

Function	Description

_bstr_t( ) throw( );
_bstr_t(const _bstr_t &*source*) throw( );
_bstr_t(const char **source*) throw(_com_error);
_bstr_t(const wchar_t **source*) throw(_com_error);
_bstr_t(BSTR *bstr*, bool *bMakeCopy*) throw (_com_error);
_bstr_t(const _variant_t &*var*) throw(_com_error);
	The constructors for **_bstr_t**. Each of the constructors calls **SysAllocString( )** (or **SysAllocStringLen( )**) to make a copy of the input string. However, if *bMakeCopy* is false, the new **_bstr_t** will simply take over ownership of *bstr*.

_bstr_t &operator=(const char **source*) throw(_com_error);
_bstr_t &operator=(const wchar_t **source*) throw(_com_error);
_bstr_t &operator=(const _variant_t &*var*) throw(_com_error);
_bstr_t &operator=(const _bstr_t &*source*) throw ( );
	The assignment operators for **_bstr_t** enable the automatic translation from both ANSI and Unicode strings to **_bstr_t**. Except for the last constructor, which takes a **_bstr_t**, all assignment operators create a copy of the *source* string.

operator const wchar_t*( ) const throw( );
operator wchar_t*( ) const throw( );
operator const char*( ) const throw(_com_error);
operator char*( ) const throw(_com_error);
	Various extractors that convert a **_bstr_t** to a different string type. Note that each of these does not perform a copy. This is especially important when using the **wchar_t** operator to assign a **_bstr_t** to a **BSTR** because you should not then free the resulting **BSTR**.

BSTR copy( ) const throw(_com_error);	Creates a copy of the internal **BSTR** string and returns it.

_bstr_t &operator+=(const _bstr_t &*suffix*) throw(_com_error);
_bstr_t operator+(const _bstr_t &*suffix*) const throw(_com_error);
friend _bstr_t operator+ (const char **prefix*, const _bstr_t &*suffix*);
friend _bstr_t operator+(const wchar_t **prefix*, const _bstr_t &*suffix);*
	These functions are used for concatenating strings of various types with a **_bstr_t** string.

The **_bstr_t** Functionality
Table 6-4.

Function	Description

bool operator!( ) const throw( );
bool operator==(const _bstr_t &*str*) const throw( );
bool operator!=(const _bstr_t &*str*) const throw( );
bool operator<(const _bstr_t &*str*) const throw( );
bool operator>(const _bstr_t &*str*) const throw( );
bool operator<=(const _bstr_t &*str*) const throw( );
bool operator>=(const _bstr_t &*str*) const throw( );
	Various string comparison operators. The NOT operator returns **true** if **_bstr_t** is **NULL**.

unsigned int length ( ) const throw( );	Returns the length of the string using **SysStringLen( )**.

The **_bstr_t** Functionality *(continued)*
Table 6-4.

One additional characteristic of **_bstr_t** is that whenever it is working with a **BSTR**, **_bstr_t** always uses **SysAllocStringByteLen( )** in combination with **SysStringByteLen( )** to avoid any of the problems discussed in the beginning of the chapter relating to embedded nulls. This does not mean that you cannot fool **_bstr_t**, though. For example, if you passed a **BSTR** into the **wchar_t*** constructor, rather than using one of the **BSTR**-specific functions, you cannot count on it working properly with embedded nulls.

For the most part, you can use a **_bstr_t** as though it were an intrinsic data type. However, when calling an interface with an **[out] BSTR*** parameter, you will need to convert a **_bstr_t** before calling into the interface. A full sample using a **_bstr_t** with **[in]**, **[out]**, and **[in,out] BSTR** function parameters is shown below:

```
try
  {

    _bstr_t str1;
    _bstr_t str2;

    IStringObjectPtr pIStringObject(
      __uuidof(StringObjectUsingCComBSTR) );
```

```
    // [in]
    // an _bstr_t type is automatically initialized for you
    str1 = L"Hello, my name is Inigo Montoya.";
    pIStringObject->Value = str1;

    // [out] parameters must pass unallocated strings or
    // a memory leak will occur. With _bstr_t you still
    // need to do this.
    str2 = pIStringObject->Value;
    str2 = L"Truly, you have a dizzying intellect.";

    // Passing to an [in,out] function one must pass
    // a valid string or NULL value
    BSTR bstr = str2;
    pIStringObject->Swap(&bstr);

  }
  catch(_com_error e)
  {
    std::cout << "ERROR: " << e.ErrorMessage() << std::endl;
  }
```


Because the preceding code is using the **#import** generated smart pointers, a **try/catch** block surrounds all the calls. Notice in this code that when calling the **Swap( )** function, **bstr** is assigned the value of **str2** using the assignment operator, but **SysFreeString( )** is not called explicitly. This is because after the assignment, **str2** continues to maintain ownership.

Choosing a String Wrapper

In this chapter we have gone into many of the intricacies of working with COM strings known as **BSTR**s. We have investigated the details of memory management and how to pass strings from a client to a server and back again. We discussed how to convert from one string type to another without too much difficulty. We also looked at two string wrappers that help significantly in hiding much of the tedium involved in working with COM strings, so that you can focus on the functionality of your program. Since there are two string wrappers, an obvious question may be which to use when. Many people simply choose the wrapper they are most comfortable with, which is often the one they learned first. Each wrapper has specific strengths, however, and each is better suited for certain situations than others. Here is one general guideline: The **_bstr_t** class should be used for COM clients and the **CComBSTR** should be used within ATL servers. Let us consider why.

IN DEPTH

CString

MFC's **CString** is probably the most familiar string class for Visual C++ programmers who have not used ATL before. Since this book uses ATL and not MFC, we will not examine in detail the **CString** class. We will, however, briefly discuss how to use it with **BSTR**s. **CString** has two **BSTR**-related functions. The first is

```
BSTR AllocSysString( ) const;
```

which appropriately allocates a **BSTR** and copies the **CString** value into it. This is often used when returning **BSTR**s in an **[out]** parameter. The second function,

```
BSTR SetSysString(BSTR *bstr) const;
```

is used to reallocate an existing **BSTR** with the value in **CString**. This is often used for changing an **[in,out]** parameter and assigning it a new value. **CString** supports an **LPOLESTR** assignment operator and constructor.

As mentioned in Chapter 3, to work with **CString**, you also need to distribute the MFC DLLs. This adds a significant burden to what could otherwise be a lightweight component server. Because of this, it is better to use one of the other wrapper classes whenever possible.

First, and most obviously, **CComBSTR** is an ATL wrapper, so it is always available in an ATL project. Second, it does not throw any exceptions, which enables it to be used without the C runtime library. In contrast, **_bstr_t** throws exceptions whenever an error occurs, thus forcing a dependency on the C runtime library and increasing the overall code size. Third, **_bstr_t** is included in a client project automatically whenever you use the **#import** directive. In fact, all interface definitions that require **BSTR**s are automatically declared with the **_bstr_t** data type by default.

Each wrapper provides some functionality that does not direct it more in either direction. **CComBSTR** does not have an explicit extractor for a **char*** string. However, these operations are easily accomplished within an ATL

project through the use of the conversion macros. Furthermore, when it comes to string concatenations, **_bstr_t** provides slightly more functionality.

Ultimately, either wrapper class will work in both a client and a server. In fact, sometimes a server will also be a client to a different COM server, blurring the lines even further.

Quite a bit of sample code in this chapter has not been shown within the context of an entire project. The project structure is identical to the Stopwatch and StopwatchClient projects we have covered so far in the book, however, so there is little point in rehashing this code. A full listing of all the code is available from the Osborne web site. Note that this code does not do any real work—in other words, there is no output. It is provided purely to demonstrate how to use a **BSTR** and its two wrapper classes **CComBSTR** and **_bstr_t**.

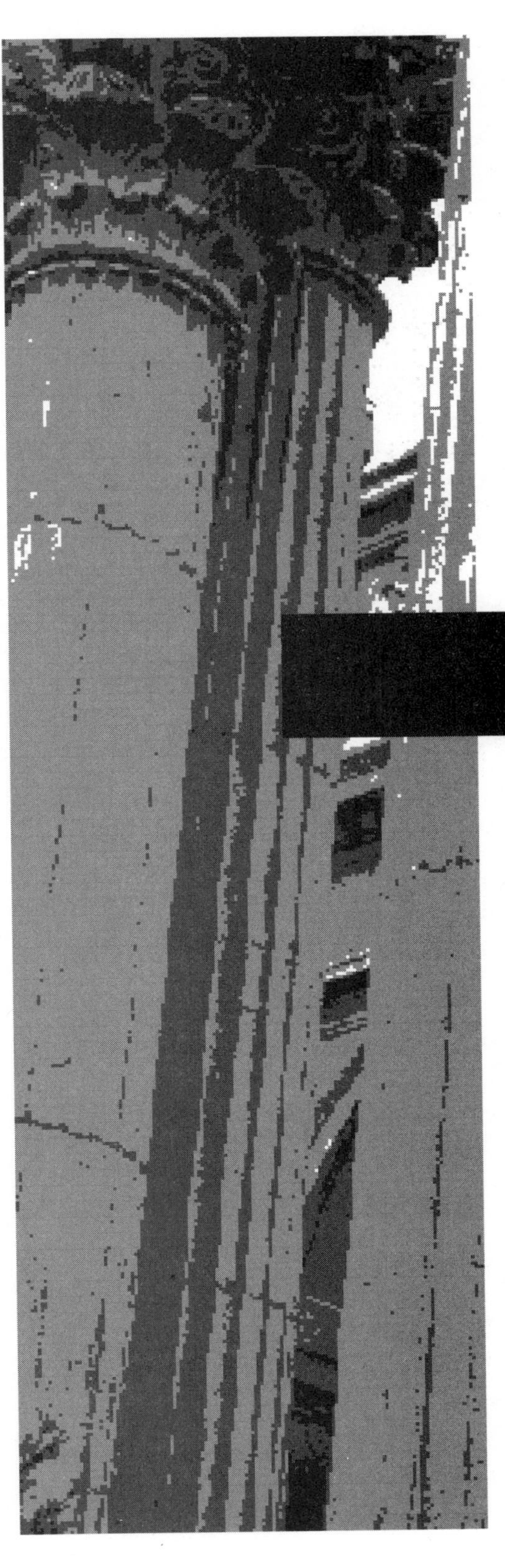

CHAPTER 7

More COM Data Types

In Chapter 6 we looked at one of COM's data types: **BSTR**. Here we will examine several others. As part of our coverage of the standard COM data types, we will also look at a few new IDL declarations and attributes.

Since COM is a language-independent architecture, not every data type in every language can intrinsically be passed across COM boundaries. You saw an example of this in Chapter 6, when strings were described. In this case, we did not simply pass a **char***, but instead we used the COM data type, **BSTR**. In theory, it would be possible to require that all COM clients be written in C++, allowing you to create servers that passed any C++ data type. In practice, this choice would severely limit the compatibility with COM clients written in other languages, thereby defeating one of the intrinsic values of COM: language independence. More importantly, the COM subsystem would not know how to marshal such data types in order to send them across the network when doing remote DCOM calls. This would force you to write custom marshalling code. COM resolves these problems by defining standard data types that can be passed between client and server.

Valid COM Data Types

Before looking at the standard COM data types, we will examine another IDL attribute: **oleautomation**. This attribute modifies an interface definition. For example, you can modify the **IStopwatch** interface as shown in the code sample below:

```
[
    object,
    oleautomation,
    uuid(EEBF6D1E-8EF1-4acf-9E5F-4D95E01D698A),
    helpstring("IStopwatch Interface"),
    pointer_default(unique)
  ]
  interface IStopwatch : IUnknown
  {
  ...
  };
```

The **oleautomation** attribute declares that the interface uses only standard COM data types. We recommend that you always use this attribute. In fact, any object that is declared as a **dual** interface (recall from Chapter 3 that such an interface is derived from **IDispatch** and decorated with the **dual** attribute) is automatically declared as supporting only those data types that are **oleautomation** compatible. Furthermore, **dual** interfaces are created by default by the ATL object wizard. The only reason we did not use the **oleautomation** attribute earlier was that it would have detracted from the topic at hand. However, we can add this attribute now because the interface will still be fully backward compatible with the previous version.

The data types supported by the **oleautomation** attribute are shown in Table 7-1. As you have already seen, pointers to each of these data types can also be passed.

Lest you think the list is restrictive, consider that the support for **IUnknown*** enables any COM interface to be passed. Since all interfaces are "derived" from **IUnknown**, a pointer to any COM interface is also a pointer to **IUnknown**. This allows you to pass complex data types of virtually any

Type Name	C++ Data Type	Size	Description
Byte	unsigned char or BYTE	8-bit	An unsigned character.
Boolean	VARIANT_BOOL	16-bit	Represents a Boolean value, where 0 is false and –1 is true. The representations of these values are **VARIANT_FALSE** and **VARIANT_TRUE**, respectively.
Double	double	64-bit	A floating point number.
Float	float	32-bit	A floating point number.
Integer	int	<platform dependent>	A platform-dependent integer. On a 32-bit platform an integer is 32 bits.
Long	long	32-bit	A signed integer.
Short	short	16-bit	A signed integer.
String	BSTR	pointer	A string pointer prefixed by the length.
Currency/fixed point decimal	CURRENCY or CY	8-byte	A fixed-point number with four decimal places.

COM Data Types
Table 7-1.

Type Name	C++ Data Type	Size	Description
Date	DATE	64-bit	The decimal portion of the date represents the number of days since 1899. The number following the decimal is the time.
Scode	SCODE	32-bit	Used to describe an error or warning.
Enumeration	*enum type*	32-bit	A user-defined enumeration type.
Variant	VARIANT		A variant structure for representing multiple data types.
Dispatch Interface	IDispatch*	pointer	An **IDispatch** interface pointer.
Unknown Interface	IUnknown*	pointer	An **IUnknown** interface pointer.

COM Data Types *(continued)*
Table 7-1.

type as long as you make them COM objects. Furthermore, the string data type, **BSTR**, can be used to pass binary data, although you should be careful because some languages may not be able to interpret this data even if they can access it. Finally, structures can also be passed in cases when defining an entire interface would be overkill.

As stated at the beginning of the chapter, although it is possible to specify other data types that are not intrinsically COM compatible, few common languages besides C/C++ can interpret them, and standard COM marshalling will not be able to transmit them. This defeats the purpose of COM being a language-neutral and location-transparent protocol; therefore, in general, non-COM data types should not be used unless you are implementing some custom marshalling.

Since most COM data types do not require any special discussion, we will not cover in depth each of the above types. Instead we will focus on a few of them that require special handling.

Boolean Values Using VARIANT_BOOL

When declaring a Boolean parameter, use VARIANT_BOOL.

Those of you who program in more than one language may have noticed that the physical value of a Boolean data type is not consistent among all languages. Consider, for example, that in Visual Basic the value of **True** is –1. In C++, however, **true** is equivalent to 1. Comparing a Visual Basic **True** value with a C++ **true** value, therefore, will not result in a valid comparison. This incompatibility provides an opportunity for subtle errors. Also, the size of a Boolean value varies between the two languages. Visual C++ defines a Boolean as an intrinsic data type of 1 byte. In contrast, Visual Basic uses a 32-bit value (at least on a Win32 platform). To avoid such discrepancies the COM developers defined a standard COM Boolean data type known as the **VARIANT_BOOL**.

The valid values for VARIANT_BOOL are VARIANT_TRUE (–1) and VARIANT_FALSE (0).

The valid values for a Boolean are **VARIANT_FALSE** and **VARIANT_TRUE**, where **VARIANT_FALSE** equals 0 and **VARIANT_TRUE** equals –1. This means that whenever you pass a Boolean value via COM it should always be one of these two values.

7

IN DEPTH

Handling True and False

In COM, true and false provide the opportunity for some subtle errors. In fact, Mark had a harsh reminder of the pitfalls surrounding true and false in a COM project while working with the Merlin project in Chapter 5, as he explains here:

"In the **IAgentCtl/ IAgentCtlEx** interface there is a **Connected** property that needs to be called before any other properties on the interface are accessed. This property is declared as type **VARIANT_BOOL**. In a slight haste to write the sample, I first assigned the **Connected** property the C++ value **true**. However, when I proceeded to use other properties in the interface, I was rewarded with an error informing me that the Microsoft Agent was not installed properly. Since Microsoft Agent is installed automatically with Windows 2000, I knew that its installation

IN DEPTH
CONTINUED

was unlikely to be the problem. As part of my debugging effort I ended up checking what the **Connected** property value was after assigning it **true**, and discovered my mistake when the returned value was still **false**. It was only after much hand wrenching that I eventually realized the mistake I had made and changed the assignment to **VARIANT_TRUE**. I share this rather embarrassing story to illustrate the importance of using the correct Boolean values, and also to suggest that when you write a server, you convert any non-false value to be **VARIANT_TRUE**."

Remember, when checking a value, do not simply check whether the value is equal to **VARIANT_TRUE**, but rather that it is not **VARIANT_FALSE**. If you are going to be storing the value, you should convert it to one of the **VARIANT_BOOL** types just to be sure. The code below shows such a conversion:

```
VARIANT_BOOL vBool;
bool b = 1;
vBool = b ? VARIANT_TRUE : VARIANT_FALSE;
```

This last point regarding how to check and convert a **VARIANT_BOOL** is not a COM requirement but rather a convenience that helps avoid the problem Mark had. Ultimately, Mark's problem occurred because **VARIANT_BOOL** is a 16-bit value, and automatic cast between integers and C++ Boolean data types provides the impression that the correct type is being passed even when it is not.

Variant Data Types

Another common data type that you will encounter is called the *variant*. The variant is used to pass data of an unknown type at design time. The variant is designed to contain any of the data types found in Table 7-1; therefore, they are used to store data of any valid COM (OLE automation) data type. In scripting languages, there is no strong data typing, and instead variants are used exclusively. Another place variants often appear is in optional function parameters, which we will discuss later in the chapter.

Essentially, variants allow you to pass loosely typed data. For many, this could be a controversial "feature," and yet, because COM does not inherently support function overloading, it can be quite useful. For example, consider a collection of items. A collection is a set of data items of the same type. A collection is the COM equivalent of an STL container in C++. In order to support random access into the collection of **Stopwatch** objects in C++, for example, by both a string key and an integer index value, you could provide two methods, as shown here:

HRESULT Item ([in] BSTR *Key*, [out, retval] IStopwatch** *Stopwatch*)

HRESULT Item ([in] long *Index*, [out, retval] IStopwatch** *Stopwatch*)

Function overloading like this is not available with COM interfaces. Instead, with the **VARIANT** data type, the same functionality can be achieved using one method, as shown here:

HRESULT Item([in] VARIANT *Key*, [out, retval] IStopwatch** *Stopwatch*)

The **VARIANT** *Key* parameter allows the client to specify either a string or a numeric value. Once the server receives the call, it checks what type of data was passed at runtime and then keys into the collection using that data type.

The VARIANT Structure

The following code shows the full **VARIANT** data structure as defined inside **oaidl.h**:

```
struct  tagVARIANT
  {
  union
    {
    struct  __tagVARIANT
      {
      VARTYPE vt;
      WORD wReserved1;
      WORD wReserved2;
      WORD wReserved3;
      union
        {
        LONG lVal;                              //  VT_I4
        BYTE bVal;                              //  VT_UI1
        SHORT iVal;                             //  VT_I2
        FLOAT fltVal;                           //  VT_R4
```

```
    DOUBLE dblVal;                          //  VT_R8
    VARIANT_BOOL boolVal;                   //  VT_BOOL
    _VARIANT_BOOL bool;
    SCODE scode;                            //  VT_ERROR
    CY cyVal;                               //  VT_CY
    DATE date;                              //  VT_DATE
    BSTR bstrVal;                           //  VT_BSTR
    IUnknown __RPC_FAR *punkVal;            //  VT_UNKNOWN
    IDispatch __RPC_FAR *pdispVal;          //  VT_DISPATCH
    SAFEARRAY __RPC_FAR *parray;            //  VT_ARRAY
    BYTE __RPC_FAR *pbVal;                  //  VT_BYREF|VT_UI1
    SHORT __RPC_FAR *piVal;                 //  VT_BYREF|VT_I2
    LONG __RPC_FAR *plVal;                  //  VT_BYREF|VT_I4
    FLOAT __RPC_FAR *pfltVal;               //  VT_BYREF|VT_R4
    DOUBLE __RPC_FAR *pdblVal;              //  VT_BYREF|VT_R8
    VARIANT_BOOL __RPC_FAR *pboolVal;       //  VT_BYREF|VT_BOOL
    _VARIANT_BOOL __RPC_FAR *pbool;
    SCODE __RPC_FAR *pscode;                //  VT_BYREF|VT_ERROR
    CY __RPC_FAR *pcyVal;                   //  VT_BYREF|VT_CY
    DATE __RPC_FAR *pdate;                  //  VT_BYREF|VT_DATE
    BSTR __RPC_FAR *pbstrVal;               //  VT_BYREF|VT_BSTR
    IUnknown __RPC_FAR *__RPC_FAR *ppunkVal;
                                            //  VT_BYREF|VT_UNKNOWN
    IDispatch __RPC_FAR *__RPC_FAR *ppdispVal;
                                            //  VT_BYREF|VT_DISPATCH
    SAFEARRAY __RPC_FAR *__RPC_FAR *pparray;
                                            //  VT_BYREF|VT_ARRAY
    VARIANT __RPC_FAR *pvarVal;             //  VT_BYREF|VT_VARIANT
    PVOID byref;                            //  VT_BYREF
    CHAR cVal;                              //  VT_I1
    USHORT uiVal;                           //  VT_UI2
    ULONG ulVal;                            //  VT_UI4
    INT intVal;                             //  VT_INT
    UINT uintVal;                           //  VT_UINT
    DECIMAL __RPC_FAR *pdecVal;             //  VT_BYREF|VT_DECIMAL
    CHAR __RPC_FAR *pcVal;                  //  VT_BYREF|VT_I1
    USHORT __RPC_FAR *puiVal;               //  VT_BYREF|VT_UI2
    ULONG __RPC_FAR *pulVal;                //  VT_BYREF|VT_UI4
    INT __RPC_FAR *pintVal;                 //  VT_BYREF|VT_INT
    UINT __RPC_FAR *puintVal;               //  VT_BYREF|VT_UINT
    struct  __tagBRECORD
    {
    PVOID pvRecord;
    IRecordInfo __RPC_FAR *pRecInfo;
    }   __VARIANT_NAME_4;
}       __VARIANT_NAME_3;
```

```
      }    __VARIANT_NAME_2;
    DECIMAL decVal;
    }      __VARIANT_NAME_1;
  };
typedef VARIANT __RPC_FAR *LPVARIANT;

typedef VARIANT VARIANTARG;

typedef VARIANT __RPC_FAR *LPVARIANTARG;
```

Interestingly enough, aside from one exception, this provides a complete list of all the **oleautomation**-compatible data types, which is also the list of all data types inherently supported by Visual Basic. The exception is the type **PVOID** member, which is a **void***. Not only is this not supported by Visual Basic, but there is no marshalling support for this data type, so even C++ cannot use it for out-of-process calls very easily. In general, we recommend you do not use **PVOID**, as it breaks the purpose behind having COM in the first place; create a new COM object instead.

Notice that included in the definition is a **typedef** for **VARIANTARG**. In C++, this is simply a **VARIANT** type. It is used in API functions to pass a variant that requires a reference mechanism.

Although the **VARIANT** structure is long, it is quite simple. The first item in the structure, **vt**, identifies which other data member within the structure is being used to store the actual data being passed. For example, if a string value is being passed, then **vt** would be **VT_BSTR**, and **bstrVal** would point to a **BSTR**. In the **VARIANT** listing above, each of the **VT_** comments indicates the **vt** value for the corresponding data member. To retrieve the data from a variant, therefore, you need to check the **vt** parameter and then remove the data from the appropriate data member, as shown here:

```
HRESULT CPotion::Add(VARIANT NewIngredient)
{
  BSTR Spell;
  switch (NewIngredient.vt)
  {
  case VT_BSTR:
    // Add string to potion
    break;
  case VT_BYREF|VT_UNKNOWN
    // Add COM object to potion
    break;
...
  }
}
```

Common Variant-Handling API Functions

Although it is possible to access the **VARIANT** structure directly, this can become quite tedious after a short time. For example, consider trying to retrieve a **long** from a **VARIANT**. There are at least six possible ways a valid **long** could be stored in a variant: **uiVal**, **ulVal**, **uintVal**, **iVal**, **lVal**, and **intVal**. To retrieve the value, therefore, you would have to write six different methods. Fortunately, several APIs can help in working with variants, as shown in Table 7-2.

API	Description
VOID VariantInit(VARIANTARG **pVariant*);	Initializes a variant. This function should be called on all **VARIANT** structures before they are accessed. The **vt** data member will be set to **VT_EMPTY** after calling **VariantInit( )**.
HRESULT VariantClear(VARIANTARG **pVariant*);	Empties the data referenced by the variant data structure. If the variant refers to an interface, **Release( )** will be called on the interface. **SysFreeString( )** will be called on any **BSTR** data. The **vt** data member will be set to **VT_EMPTY** after calling **VariantClear( )**.
HRESULT VariantCopy(VARIANTARG **pDestination*, VARIANTARG **pSource*);	Copies the data from one variant to another. Any data members that require reference counting will be incremented appropriately.
HRESULT VariantCopyInd(VARIANT **pDestination*, VARIANTARG **pSource*);	Copies the data from one variant to another, but clears the destination variant before performing the copy. Furthermore, any data items that are pointers to standard data types will be changed to be values rather than references. For example, if the source is a **VT_BYREF | VT_BSTR**, it will become **VT_BSTR** in the destination variant.

Common Variant-Handling API Functions
Table 7-2.

Common Variant-Handling API Functions *(continued)*
Table 7-2.

API	Description
HRESULT VariantChangeType(VARIANTARG **pDestination*, VARIANTARG **pSource*, unsigned short *wFlags*, VARTYPE *vt*);	Coerces one variant data type into a variant of a different type. *vt* specifies the type into which the source variant should be coerced.
HRESULT VariantChangeTypeEx(VARIANTARG **pDestination*, VARIANTARG **pSource*, LCID *lcid*, unsigned short *wFlags*, VARTYPE *vt*);	Performs the same operation as **VariantChangeType( )** except that the local ID is used. This may be important when changing from a **VT_DATE** to a **VT_BSTR**, for example.

In addition to those shown in the table, there are many more API functions for converting one specific **VARIANT** type into another. Given the **VariantChangeType( )/VariantChangeTypeEx( )** function, however, there seems little reason to use an API function that specifically handles a particular conversion.

Let's now go back and look at the implementation of the **Item( )** method on a collection, as discussed earlier. The IDL declaration would look like this:

HRESULT Item([in] VARIANT *Key*, [out, retval] VARIANT **SelectedItem*)

This method retrieves a particular variant from a collection of variants. Below is the implementation. Note that **CCollectionMap** is not a standard class but rather a fictitious class used in the sample code.

```
HRESULT CCollectionMap::Item(
  VARIANT Key,
  VARIANT* pSelectedItem )
{
  HRESULT hr;
  VARIANT SelectedVariant;

  if(pSelectedItem == NULL)
    return E_POINTER;
```

7

```
    VariantInit( &SelectedVariant );

    if(Key.vt == VT_BSTR)
    {
      hr = GetItem( (LPOLESTR)Key.bstrVal, &SelectedVariant );
    }
    else
    {
      // Convert the key into a long
      hr = VariantChangeType(&Key, &Key, NULL, VT_I4);
      if( SUCCEEDED(hr) )
        hr = GetItem( Key.lVal, &SelectedVariant );
    }

    // Check that the requested item was found
    if (SelectedVariant.vt != VT_EMPTY)
    {
      VariantCopy( pSelectedItem, &SelectedVariant );
    }
    else
      // Index doesn't exist in our collection
      hr = E_FAIL;

    VariantClear( SelectedVariant );
    return hr;
  }
```

As you can see in the function above, the data type of the key is examined by checking **Key.vt**. If **Key.vt** equals **VT_BSTR**, then **GetItem(LPOLESTR, VARIANT*)** is called to retrieve the requested item. **GetItem( )** is not shown, but you should assume that it uses **VariantCopy( )** to return the requested variant.

If the variant is not a **BSTR**, an attempt is made to coerce the variant value into a **long** by using the **VariantChangeType( )** function. Be sure to check the returned **HRESULT** after using **VariantChangeType( )** because the conversion may fail. In the code sample above, if the coercion to a **long** succeeds, then **GetItem(long, VARIANT*)** is called to return a pointer to the requested item, just as before.

To verify that the variant was retrieved successfully, a **SelectedVariant.vt** is checked for **VT_EMPTY**. Assuming the value was not **VT_EMPTY**, **VariantCopy( )** is called to copy the selected variant to the outgoing **VARIANT** pointer, **pSelectedItem**. As with **BSTR**s, **VARIANT** structures

Within a COM server, **VARIANTs** should be copied to and from out- and in-going parameters.

should always be copied into outgoing parameters. This is important because the copy operation correctly handles any reference counting that needs to occur due to an additional reference to a COM object pointed to by the new variant. The copy function is **VariantCopy( )**. The copy operation also correctly handles copying **BSTR** values. If you simply assign one **VARIANT** structure to a second **VARIANT** structure, none of the reference counting mechanisms will be used, and this could result in some hard-to-find reference counting errors.

To copy one variant to another variant, be sure to use **VariantCopy( )**. This will take care of any necessary reference counting on interfaces owned by the source variant.

The preceding code could be optimized somewhat by removing the call to **VariantCopy( )** and **VariantClear( )**. Instead, you could simply assign the **pSelectedItem** to the local variant, as shown below:

```
...
  // Check that the requested item was found
  if (SelectedVariant.vt != VT_EMPTY)
  {
    *pSelectedItem = SelectedVariant );
  }
  else
    // Index doesn't exist in our collection
    hr = E_FAIL;

  return hr;
...
```

7

It was not shown this way the first time, however, as this optimization does not apply in all cases and can be used here only because the **GetItem( )** functions were said to use **VariantCopy( )**.

As with the **BSTR**, the raw **VARIANT** also has two wrapper classes that can be used to take care of many of the variant operation details.

CComVariant

CComVariant is a variant wrapper class provided by ATL.

The first of the wrapper classes is the ATL **CComVariant**, which is defined along with **CComBSTR** in **atlbase.h**. With the exception of the **Clear( )** and **ChangeType( )** functions, **CComVariant** has a subset of the methods and properties found on **CComBSTR**. A list of each of these is shown in Table 7-3.

Function	Description
CComVariant( ); CComVariant(BYTE *byteSource*); CComVariant(bool *bSource*); CComVariant(double *nSource*); CComVariant(float *nSource*); CComVariant(int *nSource*); CComVariant(long *longSource*, VARTYPE *vtSource* = VT_I4); CComVariant(short *nSource*); CComVariant(LPCOLESTR *sz*); CComVariant(LPCSTR *sz*); CComVariant(BSTR *bstr*); CComVariant(CY *cySource*) CComVariant(const VARIANT&*Source*); CComVariant(IDispatch **pIDispatch*); CComVariant(IUnknown **pIUnknown*); CComVariant(const CComVariant &*Source*);	There are a variety of constructors for **CComVariant**. Each constructor calls **VariantInit( )**. *bSource* is coerced into either **VARIANT_FALSE** or **VARIANT_TRUE**, a convenience we discussed in the previous section. If a **long** is passed, you can also specify the variant type, *vtSource*; however, the only valid values for *vtSource* are **VT_I4** (the default) and **VT_ERROR**. Each of the string constructors will call **SysAllocString( )**, thereby making a copy of the source string. *Source* is always copied in the **VARIANT/CComVariant** constructor, leaving ownership of *Source* unchanged. **AddRef( )** is called on the interface constructors *pIDispatch* and *pIUnknown*. There is no **DATE** constructor. The destructor calls **VariantClear( )**.

Properties and Methods of **CComVariant**

Table 7-3.

Function	Description
CComVariant& operator=(BYTE *byteSource*); CComVariant& operator=(bool *bSource*); CComVariant& operator=(double *nSource*); CComVariant& operator=(float *nSource*); CComVariant& operator=(int *nSource*); CComVariant& operator=(long *longSource*); CComVariant& operator=(short *nSource*); CComVariant& operator=(LPCOLESTR *sz*); CComVariant& operator=(LPCSTR *sz*); CComVariant& operator=(BSTR *bstr*); CComVariant& operator=(CY *cySource*); CComVariant& operator=(const VARIANT& *Source*); CComVariant &operator=(IDispatch **pIDispatch*); CComVariant &operator=(IUnknown **pIUnknown*); CComVariant &operator=(const CComVariant &*Source*);	The assignment operator for **CComVariant** works the same way as the constructor and handles the same set of data types.
HRESULT Attach(VARIANT* *pSource*);	Attaches to *pSource* via a memory copy (not using **VariantCopy( )**). The destructor will call **VariantClear( )**, so to prevent *pSource* from being cleared again, **pSource->vt** is set to **VT_EMPTY**.

Properties and Methods of **CComVariant** *(continued)*
Table 7-3.

7

Function	Description
HRESULT Detach(VARIANT* *pSource*);	Clears *pSource* before assigning its encapsulated **VARIANT**. Once *pSource* has been set, the internal **VARIANT** of **CComVariant** is set to **VT_EMPTY**. Note that the caller is now responsible for calling **VariantClear( )** on *pSource*.
void Clear( );	Clears the encapsulated **VARIANT** by calling **VariantClear( )**. This call appropriately releases interfaces and **BSTR**s.
HRESULT Copy(const VARIANT **pSource*);	Copies *pSource* into the encapsulated **VARIANT** using **VariantCopy( )**.
HRESULT ChangeType(VARTYPE *vt*, const VARIANT **pSource* = NULL);	Converts the internal **VARIANT** to type *vt*. If *pSource* is **NULL**, the default, then the encapsulated **VARIANT** is converted. Otherwise, a converted *pSource* is assigned to the internal **VARIANT**.
HRESULT ReadFromStream(IStream **pStream*); HRESULT WriteToStream(IStream **pStream*);	Reads or writes a **VARIANT** to a stream interface, **IStream**.

bool operator==(const VARIANT &*Source*);
 	
bool operator!=(const VARIANT &*Source*);
 	
bool operator<(const VARIANT &*Source*);
 	
bool operator>(const VARIANT &*Source*);
	Various **VARIANT** comparison operators.

Properties and Methods of **CComVariant** *(continued)*
Table 7-3.

Many functions of **CComVariant** are similar to those we have already examined in the previous chapter when we looked at **CComBSTR**. What is remarkable about **CComVariant** is what it does not do. First, it does not have any explicit mechanism for handling a **DATE** except when writing or reading it from a stream. Second, no **VARIANT** with a pointer reference, where (**vt && VT_BYREF**) is true, is intrinsically handled. Third, there are no conversion operators that would, for example, convert a **CComVariant** to a **BSTR** or even to a **long**. Even the **Attach( )** and **Copy( )** functions work only with **VARIANT**s. Therefore, if you wish to assign a **CComVariant** to a particular OLE automation type, you will have to retrieve a copy of the variant, change its type, perform the assignment, and finally clear the retrieved variant. This is basically the same set of steps you would use for a raw **VARIANT**, so **CComVariant** provides little help in this area. Below is a code sample showing the procedure:

```
CComVariant comvariant(42);
VARIANT variant;
BSTR bstr;

VariantInit( &variant );
if( SUCCEEDED( VariantCopy(&variant, &comvariant) ) )
{
  if(
    SUCCEEDED( VariantChangeType(&variant, &variant, 0, VT_BSTR) )
    )
    bstr = SysAllocString( variant.bstrVal );
  VariantClear( &variant );
}
```

7

If you take a look at the **CComVariant** declaration, you will see that **CComVariant** is derived from **tagVARIANT**. **tagVARIANT** is simply a **typedef** for **VARIANT**, thus **CComVariant** is derived from **VARIANT**. Because of this derivation, **CComVariant** can be used in place of a **VARIANT**. This is why, in the above code, it is possible to specify **comvariant** as **VariantCopy( )**'s second parameter.

_variant_t

_variant_t is a Microsoft-specific, C++ wrapper class for **VARIANT.**

Just as the **BSTR** has both an ATL wrapper class and a Microsoft-specific C++ runtime wrapper class, so does a **VARIANT**. The latter wrapper class is **_variant_t**, and it has many of the same functions found in **CComVariant**. However, there are a few useful additions. A complete list is shown in Table 7-4.

_variant_t Class Members
Table 7-4.

Function	Description
_variant_t( ) throw( );	There are a variety of constructors for **_variant_t**. Each constructor calls **VariantInit( )**.
_variant_t(BYTE *byteSource*) throw( );	
_variant_t(bool *bSource*) throw( );	*bSource* is coerced into either **VARIANT_FALSE** or **VARIANT_TRUE**.
_variant_t(double *dblSource*, VARTYPE *vtdblSource* = VT_R8) throw(_com_error);	If a **double** is used in the constructor, then *vtdblSource* can be either **VT_R8** (the default) or **VT_DATE**.
_variant_t(float *nSource*) throw( );	
_variant_t(long *longSource*, VARTYPE *vtlongSource* = VT_I4) throw(_com_error);	If a **long** is passed, you can also specify the variant type *vtlongSource*. Valid values are **VT_I4** (the default), **VT_ERROR**, and **VT_BOOL**. In the latter case, coercion to **VARIANT_FALSE** or **VARIANT_TRUE** is performed on *longSource*.
_variant_t(short *shortSource*, VARTYPE *vtshortSource* = VT_I2) throw(_com_error);	If a **short** is the source, you can also specify the variant type *vtshortSource*. Valid values are **VT_I2** (the default) and **VT_BOOL**. In the latter case, coercion to **VARIANT_FALSE** or **VARIANT_TRUE** is performed on *shortSource*.
_variant_t(const wchar_t **wcsSource*) throw(_com_error);	
_variant_t(const char **sz*) throw(_com_error);	
_variant_t(const _bstr_t &*bstrSource*) throw(_com_error);	Each of the string constructors will call a version of **SysAllocString( )**. For *bstrSource*, **SysAllocStringByteLen( )** is used, making it safe for **BSTR**s with embedded **NULL**s.
_variant_t(const CY &*cySource*) throw( );	*Source* is always copied in the **VARIANT/_variant_t** constructor, leaving ownership of *Source* unchanged.
_variant_t(const DECIMAL &*decSource*) throw( );	
_variant_t(const VARIANT &*Source*) throw(_com_error);	**AddRef( )** is called on the interface constructors *pIDispatch* and *pIUnknown*. (**VariantClear( )** will call **Release( )**.)
_variant_t(const VARIANT **pSource*) throw(_com_error);	The destructor calls **VariantClear( )**.
_variant_t(VARIANT &*Source*, bool *bCopy*) throw(_com_error);	
_variant_t(IDispatch **pIDispatch*, bool *bAddRef* = true) throw( );	
_variant_t(IUnknown **pIUnknown*, bool *bAddRef* = true) throw( );	
_variant_t(const _variant_t &*Source*) throw(_com_error);	

Function	Description

_variant_t &operator=(BYTE *byteSource*) throw(_com_error);
 	
_variant_t &operator=(bool *bSource*) throw(_com_error);
 	
_variant_t &operator=(double *dblSource*) throw(_com_error);
 	
_variant_t &operator=(float *nSource*) throw(_com_error);
 	
_variant_t &operator=(long *longSource*) throw(_com_error);
 	
_variant_t &operator=(short *shortSource*) throw(_com_error);
 	
_variant_t &operator=(const wchar_t **wcsSource*) throw(_com_error);
 	
_variant_t &operator=(const char **sz*) throw(_com_error);
 	
_variant_t &operator=(const _bstr_t &*bstrSource*) throw(_com_error);
 	
_variant_t &operator=(const CY &*cySource*) throw(_com_error);
 	
_variant_t &operator=(const DECIMAL &*decSource*) throw( );
 	
_variant_t &operator=(const VARIANT &*Source*) throw(_com_error);
 	
_variant_t &operator=(const VARIANT **pSource*) throw(_com_error);
 	
_variant_t &operator=(IDispatch **pIDispatch*) throw(_com_error);
 	
_variant_t &operator=(IUnknown **pIUnknown*) throw(_com_error);
 	
_variant_t &operator=(const _variant_t &*Source*) throw(_com_error);
	The assignment operator for **_variant_t** works the same way as the constructor.

_variant_t Class Members *(continued)*
Table 7-4.

Function	Description

operator BYTE( ) const throw(_com_error);
operator bool( ) const throw(_com_error);
operator double( ) const throw(_com_error);
operator float( ) const throw(_com_error);
operator long( ) const throw(_com_error);
operator short( ) const throw(_com_error);
operator _bstr_t( ) const throw(_com_error);
operator CY( ) const throw(_com_error);
operator DECIMAL( ) const throw(_com_error);
operator IDispatch*( ) const throw(_com_error);
operator IUnknown*( ) const throw(_com_error);
	The conversion operators automatically convert to the specified type when necessary, using **VariantChangeType( )**.

Attach(VARIANT &*varSrc*) throw(_com_error);	Attaches to *varSrc* via a memory copy (not using **VariantCopy( )**). The destructor will call **VariantClear( )**, so to prevent *varSrc* from being cleared again, **pSource->vt** is set to **VT_EMPTY**.
VARIANT Detach( ) throw(_com_error);	Returns the encapsulated **VARIANT** and then sets it to **VT_EMPTY**. The caller is now responsible for calling **VariantClear( )** on the returned **VARIANT**.
void Clear( ) throw(_com_error);	Clears the encapsulated variant by calling **VariantClear( )**.
void ChangeType(VARTYPE *vt*, const _variant_t **pSource* = NULL) throw(_com_error);	Converts the internal **VARIANT** to type *vt*. If *pSource* is **NULL**, the default, then the encapsulated **VARIANT** is converted. Otherwise, a converted *pSource* is assigned to the encapsulated **VARIANT**.
void SetString(const char **sz*) throw(_com_error);	Uses **SysAllocString( )** to create a **BSTR** and assign it to **_variant_t**.

_variant_t Class Members *(continued)*

Table 7-4.

Function	Description
bool operator==(const VARIANT &*Source*) const throw(_com_error);	Various **VARIANT** comparison operators.
bool operator==(const VARIANT **pSource*) const throw(_com_error);	
bool operator!=(const VARIANT &*Source*) const throw(_com_error);	
bool operator!=(const VARIANT **pSource*) const throw(_com_error);	

_variant_t Class Members *(continued)*
Table 7-4.

7

The functionality that distinguishes **_variant_t** from **CComVariant** occurs mainly in its * operators. Whereas **CComVariant** could be assigned only to another **VARIANT** type, **_variant_t** has several * operators that enable automatic conversion to various OLE automation data types. For example, shown below are the two lines needed to convert a **VARIANT** of type **VT_BSTR** to a **short**:

```
_variant_t variant(L"42");
short n = variant;
```

Another characteristic of the **_variant_t** is that it can be initialized to a **VARIANT** of type **VT_DATE**. Using the **_variant_t(double dblSource, VARTYPE vtdblSource = VT_R8)** constructor, you can specify a *vtdblsSource* of type **VT_DATE** in order to create a **VT_DATE VARIANT**. One disadvantage of the **_variant_t** is that it does not have internal support for the less-than or greater-than comparison operators. This makes it more difficult to use in many of the STL containers.

Enumerations

Enumerations in the IDL are similar to enumerations in C++.

Enumerations are an important part of interface definitions, and have not been included in any of the **Stopwatch** IDL code so far. Just as they are in C++, enumerations are a way of defining a set of constant integer values that make code more readable. To define an enumeration inside an IDL file, use the following syntax:

```
typedef [<attributes>] enum <tag> {
  [<attributes>] enumlist
} <enumname>;
```

The possible attributes are **helpstring**, **helpcontext**, **hidden**, and **uuid**. With the exception of the attributes, the syntax is the same as the C++ syntax for **typedef** and **enum**. Here is an example:

```
typedef [uuid(39FB3AB1-DE17-4a10-A3DB-95236C055135),
  helpstring("Possible mental states when reading Chapter 7")]
  enum TmMentalState
{
  [helpstring("Time to take a break")] tmMentalStateExcited = 0,
  [helpstring("Everything is clear as mud")] tmMentalStateConfused,
  [helpstring("Need a compass")] tmMentalStateLost,
  [helpstring("Need a Mountain Dew")] tmMentalStateAsleep,
  [helpstring("Need a hamburger")] tmMentalStateHungry,
} TmMentalState;
```

Simply defining an enumeration within the IDL will not automatically add it to the type library. Instead, to make it available you either need to use it within a property/method or declare it specifically inside the type library.

For example, if you declare a function that uses **TmMentalState**, the enumeration will be added to the type library, and any IntelliSense drop-downs or object browser will have access to it. For example, if you have already added the enumeration above, you can define a method that uses this enumeration:

```
HRESULT SetMentalState([in] TmMentalState as CurrentMentalState);
```

Now, without any additional code, the **TmMentalState** enumeration will be available in the type library so that when you write code to call the method, the IntelliSense drop-down will automatically display a list of the possible values, as shown in Figure 7-1.

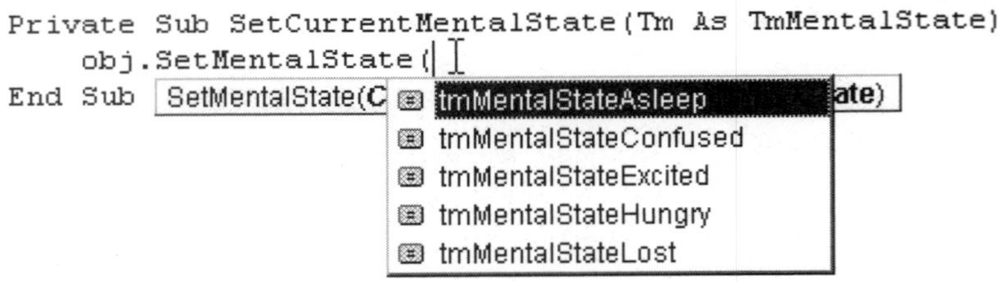

```
Private Sub SetCurrentMentalState(Tm As TmMentalState)
    obj.SetMentalState(
End Sub  SetMentalState(C  tmMentalStateAsleep  ate)
                          tmMentalStateConfused
                          tmMentalStateExcited
                          tmMentalStateHungry
                          tmMentalStateLost
```

IntelliSense drop-down in Visual Basic, using an enumeration
Figure 7-1.

Notice the naming conventions used in the enumeration definition. First, the tag and the enumeration name are the same. In addition, all the enumerations begin with a two- or three-letter application or product prefix: uppercase first letter and lowercase second letter. In the example in Figure 7-1, this is "Tm."

Also, note that in the enumeration list the values begin with the application prefix except that the first letter is lowercase. Following the application prefix, the enumeration name is used, "MentalState." It is important to include the enumeration name because often two enumerations can have similar values. For example, you could have a printer port enumeration default, **TmPrinterPortDefault**, and a paper tray default, **TmPaperTrayDefault**. Without these prefixes, obviously, the names "Default" would overlap, forcing the use of fully qualified names. As you will see in Chapter 9, enumeration constants are often used to define custom **HRESULT**s.

Optional Parameters

Now we turn our attention to another IDL attribute: **optional**. To begin, consider the example of **Define( )** method declared as follows within an IDL:

7

```
HRESULT Define([in] BSTR Word,
  [in, optional] VARIANT LocaleID,
  [out, retval] BSTR* Definition);
```

The first parameter, **Word**, is the word to be defined by the function. The next parameter, **LocaleID**, specifies the language of the incoming word. Lastly, **Definition** is used to return the **Word** parameter's definition.

The implementation of **Define( )** could be as follows:

```
STDMETHODIMP CComString::Define(
    /*[in]*/ BSTR Word,
    /*[in, optional]*/ VARIANTARG LocaleID,
    /*[out, retval]*/ BSTR* Definition)
{
  long localeid = 0;
  HRESULT hr = E_INVALIDARG;

  switch(LocaleID.vt)
  case VT_I4:
    localeid = LocaleID.iVal;
    hr = S_OK;
    break;
```

```
  case VT_EMPTY:
    localeid = GetUserDefaultLCID(NULL)
    hr = S_OK;
    break;
  ...
  }

  if (SUCCEEDED(hr))
  {
  // Set word return Definition
  }

  return hr;
}
```

The interesting thing about the **Define( )** method that we have not yet covered is the **optional** attribute on the **LocaleID** variant parameter. Using the **optional** attribute is another way of implementing pseudo function overloading. Whenever you use this attribute, COM will allow you to call into a function without specifying anything for the **optional** parameter. The one catch with this attribute is that it fully works only with **VARIANT** parameters. If you use **optional** with a parameter of a different type, such as a **BSTR** or a **long**, it will still operate as expected from Visual Basic, but C++ clients will ignore the attribute and require you to specify the parameter instead. In other words, **optional** does not work from C++ clients unless the parameter data type is a **VARIANT**. This C++ restriction is not surprising because it is consistent with the documentation. What *is* surprising is that it works with Visual Basic. It would be convenient if this restriction were removed altogether and Visual C++ were changed to support additional data types for the **optional** attribute, but so far this has not happened. Another documented restriction is that **optional** should not be used with the **retval** attribute.

Specifying Default Values

Another attribute similar to **optional** is **defaultvalue( )**, which enables you to specify a default value for the parameter to which the attribute is attached. For example, consider an **Add( )** function on a fictitious **CollectionArray** object. This function would enable the client to specify the location at which an item would be inserted. The declaration would look something like this:

```
HRESULT Add(
  [in] VARIANT Item,
  [in, defaultvalue(1)] long Position);
```

In this case, if the client did not specify the **Position** parameter, by default the item would be inserted as the first item in the array. This would not work with the **optional** attribute because **Position** would default to zero, which would not work in an array that starts its indexing at one. (Note that COM collections are usually one-based rather than zero-based collections. However, the consistency in this area is low, and you are sure to encounter both types.)

Unfortunately, Visual C++ clients do not fully support the **defaultvalue( )** attribute either. If you use the interface header file generated by the server, the **Add( )** function will be declared as follows:

```
virtual /* [helpstring][id] */ HRESULT STDMETHODCALLTYPE Add(
  /* [in] */ VARIANT Item,
  /* [defaultvalue] [in] */ long Position = 1) = 0;
```

In this case, the **defaultvalue( )** attribute works. If, however, you use the **#import** precompile functionality inside the client code, the generated header file will not include the default parameter, as shown here:

```
inline HRESULT ICollectionArray::Add (
  const _variant_t & Item,
  long Position) {
  HRESULT _hr = raw_Add(Item, Position);
  if (FAILED(_hr)) _com_issue_errorex(_hr, this, __uuidof(this));
  return _hr;
}
```


Clearly, the default value was ignored by the **#import**, and since this is the most probable way of declaring the COM object within your project, it makes the **defaultvalue( )** attribute difficult to use from C++. In spite of the C++ drawbacks, **defaultvalue( )** is still a useful feature for Visual Basic.

The **defaultvalue( )** can be used in combination with the **optional** attribute, and you might think that this would be a way of avoiding the C++ problem listed above. In other words, using the **optional** and **defaultvalue( )** attributes together would indicate that if the **optional** parameter were not specified, the default value would be used. However, one requirement for **defaultvalue( )** parameters is that it must be possible to specify a constant default value as an intrinsic data type such as 5 or "Fail." This is not possible with a **VARIANT** structure, so this is not a viable work-around.

Passing Arrays

One item we have not yet covered is how to pass arrays over COM boundaries. The data type for passing an array is **SAFEARRAY****. A safe array is a special array that can handle any of the standard COM data types, appropriately allocating and releasing memory through the use of the safe array API functions. A list of the most commonly used functions is shown in Table 7-5.

Function	Description
SAFEARRAY *SafeArrayCreate(VARTYPE *vt*, unsigned int *nDims*, SAFEARRAYBOUND **pBound*);	Creates a **SAFEARRAY** to contain data of type *vt* with the dimensions specified in *pBound*. *nDims* specifies the number of dimensions in the array. All data for the specified data type is initialized when **SafeArrayCreate( )** is called.
HRESULT SafeArrayPutElement(SAFEARRAY **pSafeArray*, long **pIndices*, void **pVoid*);	**SafeArrayPutElement( )** is used to set a specific item in the array to the value specified by *pVoid*. *pIndices* points to the specific element.
HRESULT SafeArrayGetElement(SAFEARRAY **pSafeArray*, long **pIndices*, void **pVoid*);	Retrieves the item from **SAFEARRAY** *pSafeArray* that is stored in the location pointed to by *pIndices*.
HRESULT SafeArrayCopy(SAFEARRAY **pSafeArray*, SAFEARRAY ***ppSafeArrayOut*);	Copies a **SAFEARRAY** *ppSafeArrayOut* into *pSafeArray*. Before calling **SafeArrayCopy( )**, *pSafeArray* should be created with a call to **SafeArrayCreate( )** or one of its alternatives.
HRESULT SafeArrayGetLBound(SAFEARRAY **pSafeArray*, unsigned int *nDim*, long **pnLowerBound*); HRESULT SafeArrayGetUBound(SAFEARRAY **pSafeArray*, unsigned int *nDim*, long **pnUpperBound*);	Retrieves the upper/lower bounds of the dimension specified with *nDim*.
HRESULT SafeArrayDestroy(SAFEARRAY **pSafeArray*);	Destroys an existing array along with all the data contained in the array, calling the appropriate deallocation functions as necessary.

Commonly Used **SAFEARRAY** API Functions
Table 7-5.

Commonly Used SAFEARRAY API Functions *(continued)* **Table 7-5.**

Function	Description
HRESULT SafeArrayRedim(SAFEARRAY *pSafeArray*, SAFEARRAYBOUND *pNewBounds*);	Redimensions an array to the new dimensions specified by *pNewBounds*. If the array becomes smaller, memory will be deallocated appropriately for the data that is removed. Items that still fit within the dimensions of the new array will remain.

The key to creating a safe array is to first set up the **SAFEARRAYBOUND**'s structure, which specifies the dimensions of the **SAFEARRAY** to be created. Let's again consider the safe array example found in the fictitious **CCollectionMap** object. The **CCollectionMap** object has a property called **Keys( )** that returns a **SAFEARRAY** containing all the keys used when adding items to the collection. Below is a listing of the **get_Keys( )** function, which creates and returns this list:


```
STDMETHODIMP CCollectionMap::get_Keys(
  /*[out, retval]*/ SAFEARRAY** ppKeys)
{

  HRESULT hr = S_OK;
  // Counts how many keys are actually added
  // to the array
  long keyCount=0;
  VariantCollectionIterator it;
  static const NDIMENSIONS = 1;
  SAFEARRAY* pSA = NULL;
  SAFEARRAYBOUND dimension[NDIMENSIONS];
  BSTR bstr = NULL;

  if(ppKeys==NULL)
    return E_POINTER;

  // Set the array dimensions
  // Set the lower bound
  dimension[0].lLbound = 0;
  // Set the number of elements
  dimension[0].cElements = m_Collection.size();

  pSA = SafeArrayCreate(VT_BSTR, NDIMENSIONS, dimension);
```

```
  if (pSA == NULL)
    hr = E_FAIL;

  // Add each key
  it = m_Collection.begin();
  while( SUCCEEDED(hr) &&
    (it != m_Collection.end()) )
  {
    hr = SysReAllocString(&bstr, it->first);

    if(SUCCEEDED(hr))
      hr = SafeArrayPutElement(pSA, &keyCount, bstr);

    keyCount++;

    it++;
  }

  // Free the bstr that was used to iterate
  // through the items.
  SysFreeString(bstr);

  if(SUCCEEDED(hr))
    *ppKeys = pSA;
  else
    SafeArrayDestroy(pSA);

  return S_OK;

}
```

To begin, **dimension** is declared as an array of one item. This defines the array as having one dimension only. Next, the lower bound of the array is set to 0 using the **lLbound** data member, while the number of elements is set in **cElements**. Now we are ready to create and initialize the **SAFEARRAY** structure with a call to **SafeArrayCreate( )**.

Once the array has been created and the data within the array initialized, all that is left is to copy in each item. This is done using **SafeArrayPutElement( )** for each element in the array. Assuming the entire process was successful, **pSA** is assigned to ***ppKeys** so that it can be returned to the client. However, if there was a failure, then **pSA** is deallocated via a call to **SafeArrayDestroy( )**.

Passing a Variable Number of Arguments

Now that you know how to pass arrays, you can use this knowledge to pass a variable number of parameters in a manner similar to how **main( )** in a C/C++ program works. The mechanism for doing this is to use a **SAFEARRAY** of variant data types in conjunction with the **vararg** IDL attribute. Here is a sample declaration:

```
[vararg] HRESULT Initialize([in] SAFEARRAY(VARIANT) psa);
```

The **vararg** attribute signifies that this method takes a variable number of arguments. Now you can simply work with *psa* as though it were a normal safe array. For example, you can call **SafeArrayGetUBound( )** to get the number of items in the array and then use **SafeArrayGetElement( )** to retrieve each value.

Passing COM Objects

As you have already learned, whenever you want to pass a COM object, you must pass the interface. For example, consider a Ferrari object. Such an object would support multiple interfaces: **IUnknown**, **IDispatch**, **ICar**, **IFerrari**, and **ITransportation**. If you were to write a server that returned the Ferrari object, you could do it as follows: 7

```
HRESULT BrandNewFerrari([out] IFerrari *NewFerrari);
```

The advantage of this method is that it is strongly typed, so it is easy to know exactly what kind of data type the **BrandNewFerrari( )** method returned, **IFerrari***. The disadvantage of such a method is that if, when calling the **BrandNewFerrari( )** method, the client actually wanted the **ICar** interface, then the client would be required to make a **QueryInterface( )** call in order to access the **ICar** interface.

The way to avoid this problem is to use the **iid_is** attribute on the interface parameter, as shown here:

```
HRESULT BrandNewFerrari([in] REFIID riid,
                        [out, iid_is(riid)] IUnknown **NewFerrari);
```

Using the **iid_is** attribute, the client can call into the function and request that an object, **Ferrari**, be returned via a specific interface. The required interface is specified by the client using the *riid* parameter. Using this method, the client can avoid making an extra call across the COM interface, which may involve marshalling across process or even machine boundaries.

There is one serious drawback to using the **iid_is( )** attribute. Visual Basic does not know anything about the **REFIID** data type, which prevents it from using the method. You could use the same mechanism and pass the interface ID using a **BSTR** or **LPCOLESTR**, but this will not be allowed with the **iid_is** attribute.

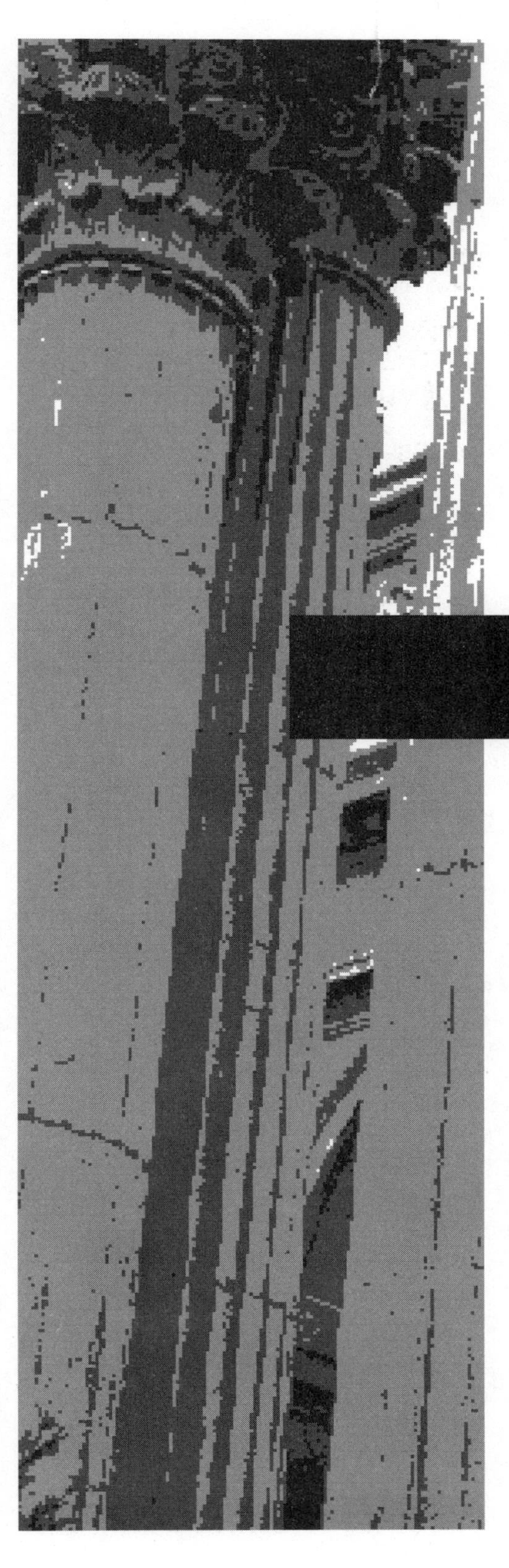

CHAPTER 8

Exploring IDispatch

IDispatch is arguably the second most commonly used interface in COM, after **IUnknown**. You will recall from Chapter 3 that an object that supports a dual interface is one that supports the **IDispatch** interface. In this chapter we are going to look at **IDispatch** in detail.

IDispatch is used to call the properties and methods on an object without identifying which properties and methods to call at compile time. For example, consider a method named **Item( )**. Rather than explicitly specifying a call to **Item( )**, you can specify a call to **IDispatch::Invoke( )**, passing in the name **Item** at runtime as a parameter. This allows you to determine at runtime which function to call. For C++ programmers who are used to a strongly typed language, there may seem little use for the **IDispatch** interface. However, scripting languages such as Visual Basic Script are not typed at all. Instead, all variables are automatically defined as **VARIANT**s, and the only way to call into a particular method or property on an object is via the **IDispatch** interface. Therefore, when writing your component objects, you probably want to support **IDispatch** in order to make your component available to as many COM clients as possible.

With late binding, the address of a method or property is resolved at runtime. In COM, this occurs through the use of **IDispatch.**

With early binding, the address of a method or property is resolved at compile time.

Calling a method by using the **IDispatch** interface is known as *late binding*, because the methods and properties to call are not specified until runtime. On the other hand, if you call into a COM object directly, as we have in the previous chapters (without using the **IDispatch** interface), it is known as *early binding*. Assuming there is no marshalling, early binding generally translates into a direct vtable call.

The binding for **IDispatch** is so loose that it is possible to write a client without any knowledge of the server. You would not even be required to know anything about any of the properties and methods because all this information could be gathered at runtime. For example, you could write a COM client that instantiated objects at random and called into an "Initialize" method if it determined that such a method existed. This is not particularly useful, but it demonstrates how loosely coupled the client and the server could be. Consider, for example, the times in C++ when you pass a function pointer. This is not something supported with COM, but the same functionality could be achieved using the **IDispatch** interface.

To begin, we will convert the **Stopwatch** object to support dual interfaces. Next, we will write a quick Visual Basic script to call the **Stopwatch** object. Finally, we will change **StopwatchClient.exe** to use the **IDispatch** support added to the **Stopwatch** object. Note that in general you will not want to use the **IDispatch** interface when there is a direct vtable interface that you can call, but for demonstration purposes, we use it here anyway.

Creating a Stopwatch Component that Supports a Dual Interface

To convert the **Stopwatch** component to support a dual interface, we need to add support for **IDispatch**. Usually, you will want to use the New ATL Object wizard to generate a dual interface. However, back in Chapter 3 we specifically turned this off by selecting Custom from the attributes dialog of the **Stopwatch** object, because we did not want to change the original **Stopwatch** interface. Now we will add dual-interface support manually. This approach provides an understanding of what the wizard does. We are not going to go into the details of how ATL implements **IDispatch**, as it is beyond the scope of this book. Fortunately, since ATL does such a good job of wrapping the functionality, it is only on rare occasions that you may need to change the default implementation.

Declaring a Dual Interface Inside the IDL

As mentioned, we could not make **IStopwatch** into a dual interface back in Chapter 3 because this would be changing the interface from the way it was defined in Chapter 2. Since this is still true, instead of changing **IStopwatch**, we are going to add a second interface. Often you will see that when a second interface is released, developers simply add "Ex" onto the end of the original interface name. This seems like an appropriate solution until it comes time for version three. What do you name the interface then, "I...ExEx"? Not exactly the ideal choice. Therefore, the recommended naming convention is to add a numeral to the end. That way, each time a modification to the original interface is required, you can simply increment the numeral. Following this convention, the new interface we are going to add in this chapter is **IStopwatch2**, and it will be a dual interface, derived from **IDispatch**. Below is the new **Timers.idl** file with the changes highlighted.

8

```
// Timers.idl : IDL source for Timers.dll
//

// This file will be processed by the MIDL tool to
// produce the type library (Timers.tlb) and marshalling code.

import "oaidl.idl";
import "ocidl.idl";
  [
    object,
    uuid(EEBF6D1E-8EF1-4acf-9E5F-4D95E01D698A),
```

```
    oleautomation,
    helpstring("IStopwatch Interface"),
    pointer_default(unique)
  ]
  interface IStopwatch : IUnknown
  {
    [helpstring("Starts the timer")]
      HRESULT Start();
    [helpstring("Returns the number of seconds that have passed \
      since Start was called")]
      HRESULT ElapsedTime([out, retval] float* Time);
  [propget, helpstring("Returns/sets the overhead time using \
      the timer.")]
      HRESULT Overhead([out, retval] float *pVal);
  [propput, helpstring("Returns/sets the overhead time using \
      the timer.")]
      HRESULT Overhead([in] float newVal);
  };

  [
    object,
    dual,
    oleautomation,
    uuid(C04E9202-BAFA-45e2-9F07-942D7CF76361),
    helpstring("IStopwatch2 Interface"),
    pointer_default(unique)
  ]
  interface IStopwatch2 : IDispatch
  {
    [id(1), helpstring("Starts the timer")]
      HRESULT Start();
    [id(DISPID_VALUE), helpstring("Returns the number of seconds \
      that have passed since Start was called")]
      HRESULT ElapsedTime([out, retval] float* Time);
    [id(2), propget, helpstring("Returns/sets the overhead time \
      using the timer.")]
      HRESULT Overhead([out, retval] float *pVal);
    [id(2), propput, helpstring("Returns/sets the overhead time \
      using the timer.")]
      HRESULT Overhead([in] float newVal);
  };

#define MAJORVERSION 2
#define MINORVERSION 0
#define VERSION MAJORVERSION.MINORVERSION
enum TmLibraryVersion
```

```
{
  tmLibraryVersionMajor = MAJORVERSION,
  tmLibraryVersionMinor = MINORVERSION
};

[
  uuid(D7EBA784-2BF1-11D3-A48B-0000861C844E),
  version(VERSION),
  helpstring("Timers 2.0 Type Library")
]
library TIMERSLib
{

   importlib("stdole32.tlb");
   importlib("stdole2.tlb");

   [
     uuid(83DC3C46-1259-4f95-A2D1-CD11A8819E2E),
     version(2.0),
     helpstring("Stopwatch Component")
   ]
   coclass Stopwatch
   {
     [default] dispinterface IStopwatch2;
     interface IStopwatch;
   };
};
```


Let's first take a look at the declaration of the new interface, **IStopwatch2**. There are several differences between **IStopwatch** and **IStopwatch2**. First, the **dual** attribute has been added to the **IStopwatch2** interface attribute list. This declares the interface as being a dual interface and, therefore, supporting **IDispatch**. Another added attribute is **oleautomation**. This attribute was discussed at the beginning of Chapter 7. Here, we have added it to the new interface to identify the interface as being OLE automation compatible.

Each method and property on a dispatch interface must have a unique ID associated with it. This is known as the dispatch ID.

Notice that at the beginning of each property and method an **id** attribute has been added. To be able to call into a dispatch interface, each property and method must have a *dispatch ID* associated with it. This is done using the **id** attribute.

Observe in the code that although all properties and methods are required to have unique dispatch IDs, because a property can have two functions, get and set, they use the same ID. In other words, if both a **get** and a **put/putref** declaration appear for a particular property, the same ID is used for both. This is why the **Overhead** property has 2 specified as the ID parameter twice.

In the **IStopwatch2** interface declaration, an explicit **id** attribute has been added for each function in the interface. It is not required that the **id** attribute be specified explicitly. You can leave off the attribute altogether, in which case the MIDL compiler will automatically generate IDs for you. These generated IDs, however, are not consecutive integers starting with 1 and going up. For example, if we changed the **IStopwatch2** interface so it no longer had any of the **id** attributes, the generated type library would look like this:

```
[
...
]
interface IStopwatch2 : IDispatch
{
     [id(0x60020000), helpstring("Starts the timer")]
       HRESULT Start();
     [id(00000000), helpstring("Returns the number of seconds
       that have passed since Start was called")]
       HRESULT ElapsedTime([out, retval] single* Time);
     [id(0x60020002), propget, helpstring("Returns/sets the overhead
       time using the timer.")]
       HRESULT Overhead([out, retval] single* pVal);
     [id(0x60020002), propput, helpstring("Returns/sets the overhead
       time using the timer.")]
       HRESULT Overhead([in] single pVal);
};
```

As you can see, in this case the IDs start at 0x60020000 and go up from there. Notice that the **ElapsedTime( )** method continues to use 0 as the dispatch ID. This is because this method was modified with the **id(DISPID_VALUE)** attribute.

Several dispatch IDs have been reserved for specific purposes. For example, 0, the value of **DISPID_VALUE**, designates the property or method as the “default” property. Although rarely used from C++ (because C++ programmers prefer to use the direct vtable calls, not **IDispatch** calls), it occurs quite commonly in Visual Basic code. Essentially, if no method is specified when calling an object, the default method is used. Take a quick look at the Visual Basic code shown below for an example:

```
Dim oStopwatch As New Stopwatch
oStopwatch.Start
MsgBox "The timer has begun. Push Ok to stop the timer", vbOKOnly
Debug.Print "The elapsed time was " & oStopwatch.ElapsedTime
Debug.Print "The elapsed time was " & oStopwatch
```

Although the Visual Basic code could call **oStopwatch.ElapsedTime( )** explicitly, as it did in the second-to-last line, it can also leave off the method name entirely, causing Visual Basic to call into the method on the dispatch interface whose ID was 0. There are several more of these reserved dispatch IDs within the collections interfaces. In addition, ActiveX controls also have several reserved dispatch IDs. For now, just be sure that all your dispatch IDs are greater than 1 and that they are unique since all the reserved values are less than 0.

Now that you know that each property and method has a unique ID, let's look at the final difference between **IStopwatch** and **IStopwatch2**—the fact that **IStopwatch2** is derived from **IDispatch**. It is this last difference that truly distinguishes **IStopwatch2** from **IStopwatch**, making it into a different interface. For example, no longer is **Start( )** at the head of the vtable. Instead, it has been bumped until later by **IDispatch**'s **GetTypeInfoCount( )**. Below is the listing for **IDispatch** as defined in **oaidl.h**:

```
MIDL_INTERFACE("00020400-0000-0000-C000-000000000046")
IDispatch : public IUnknown
{
public:
    virtual HRESULT STDMETHODCALLTYPE GetTypeInfoCount(
        /* [out] */ UINT __RPC_FAR *pctinfo) = 0;

    virtual HRESULT STDMETHODCALLTYPE GetTypeInfo(
        /* [in] */ UINT iTInfo,
        /* [in] */ LCID lcid,
        /* [out] */ ITypeInfo __RPC_FAR *__RPC_FAR *ppTInfo) = 0;

    virtual HRESULT STDMETHODCALLTYPE GetIDsOfNames(
        /* [in] */ REFIID riid,
        /* [size_is][in] */ LPOLESTR __RPC_FAR *rgszNames,
        /* [in] */ UINT cNames,
        /* [in] */ LCID lcid,
        /* [size_is][out] */ DISPID __RPC_FAR *rgDispId) = 0;

    virtual /* [local] */ HRESULT STDMETHODCALLTYPE Invoke(
        /* [in] */ DISPID dispIdMember,
        /* [in] */ REFIID riid,
        /* [in] */ LCID lcid,
        /* [in] */ WORD wFlags,
        /* [out][in] */ DISPPARAMS __RPC_FAR *pDispParams,
        /* [out] */ VARIANT __RPC_FAR *pVarResult,
        /* [out] */ EXCEPINFO __RPC_FAR *pExcepInfo,
        /* [out] */ UINT __RPC_FAR *puArgErr) = 0;

};
```

The way that **IDispatch** works is for the client to first ask the component whether it supports a particular method, and if so, what is its dispatch ID. Therefore, when the client wants to call the **Start( )** method on the component, it will first pass in the name of the method, "Start," to the **GetIDsOfNames( )** function. Assuming the component supports the method, it will then return the dispatch ID corresponding to the method. Once the dispatch ID for the method has been retrieved, you can then call into that method using **IDispatch**::**Invoke( )**. Take a look at Table 8-1 for a complete list of each of the methods on **IDispatch**. We will look further into the details of how to use the **IDispatch** interface when we look at coding the **StopwatchClient** project.

Now that we have defined the **IStopwatch2** interface, it is time to add it to the type library. Returning to the **Timers.idl** code, skip the code relating to the version and help string attributes. The only other change is that the **IStopwatch2** interface is set as being the **[default]** interface. The **IStopwatch** interface is still available but is no longer the **[default]** interface. Choosing to keep the old interface in the library statement depends on the level of compatibility you require. Components that have already been compiled will continue to work without a problem even if you remove **IStopwatch** as part of the library. This is because, as you will see shortly, **Stopwatch.cpp** continues to have **IStopwatch** within its **COM_MAP** macro. Therefore, when **QueryInterface( )** is called and a request for the **IStopwatch** interface is made, the call will return successfully.

IDispatch Function Descriptions
Table 8-1.

Function	Description
HRESULT GetIDsOfNames(REFIID *riidNotUsed*, OLECHAR FAR **szNames*, unsigned int *nNamesCount*, LCID *lcid*, DISPID FAR **nDispIds*);	**GetIDsOfNames( )** is used to query the component object to determine whether it supports the method identified by the first element in *szNames*. If the method is supported, the dispatch ID is returned in *nDispIds*. An array is used for both *szNames* and *nDispIds* to allow for identifying the additional parameters that may be part of the method call. *nNamesCount* identifies the total count of names passed. *lcid* identifies the localization constant associated with the names; in general this can be **LOCALE_SYSTEM_DEFAULT**.

Function	Description
HRESULT GetTypeInfo(unsigned int *iTypeInfo*, LCID *lcid*, ITypeInfo FAR* FAR **ppTypeInfo*);	Returns a pointer to the *ITypeInfo* interface specified by the *iTypeInfo* parameter. As before, *lcid* identifies the localization value.
HRESULT GetTypeInfoCount(unsigned int FAR **pTypeInfoCount*);	Returns a count of the number of type information interfaces supported by the object. Usually the returned value is either 1 or 0. By default, an ATL project uses 1. Setting the value to 0 indicates that the component does not provide runtime information, thereby hiding the object from various object browsers.
HRESULT Invoke(DISPID *nDispId*, REFIID *riidNotUsed*, LCID *lcid*, WORD *wFlags*, DISPPARAMS FAR **pParameters*, VARIANT FAR **pVarResult*, EXCEPINFO FAR **pExcepInfo*, unsigned int FAR **pnParameterError*);	This method is the one that is actually used to call into a component and execute a method. The method that you wish to call is identified by *nDispId*. The *wFlags* parameter is used to identify the type of method being called. Possible values are **DISPATCH_METHOD**, **DISPATCH_PROPERTYGET**, **DISPATCH_PROPERTYPUT**, and **DISPATCH_PROPERTYPUTREF**. The *pParameters* argument is used to pass in each of the arguments required by the method call. *pExcepInfo* is used to return any errors that may occur. The last parameter, *pnParameterError*, identifies which of the parameters is invalid.

IDispatch Function Descriptions *(continued)*
Table 8-1.

Where the incompatibility does occur is when you try to compile an older client project against the new type library. The code will not compile because the **IStopwatch** interface will not be declared in the new library. Therefore, the client application will either have to import the older type library or change **IStopwatch** data types to **IStopwatch2**. Making the last change would be little more than a search and replace, as all the functions and methods on **IStopwatch** are also supported by **IStopwatch2**. The reason for forcing this incompatibility is that new programs will be written only against the new interface because the older one will not be available. In the preceding code, we choose to make the **IStopwatch** interface available even for new programs, so we leave it in the library.

Interface Inheritance and IDispatch

Before leaving the **IDispatch** interface definition, it is worth taking a quick look at interface inheritance again and how **IDispatch** fits into the picture. From the **Timers.idl** you will have already picked up that there are three levels to the **Stopwatch** object interface hierarchy, as shown in Figure 8-1.

If, at some point after **IStopwatch2** has been released, you decide to "add" a method to **IStopwatch2**, you will probably want to do this by adding another layer. In other words, you would add an **IStopwatch3** interface, which derives from **IStopwatch2** and has the additional methods or properties. Figure 8-2 shows this new interface diagram.

One important thing to be aware of when doing this is that all dispatch IDs for both **IStopwatch2** and any of the interfaces derived from **IStopwatch2** must have unique dispatch IDs. If they don't, you will end up with the not-so-helpful message below:

```
error MIDL2020 : error generating type library :
  AddImplType failed : Stopwatch
```

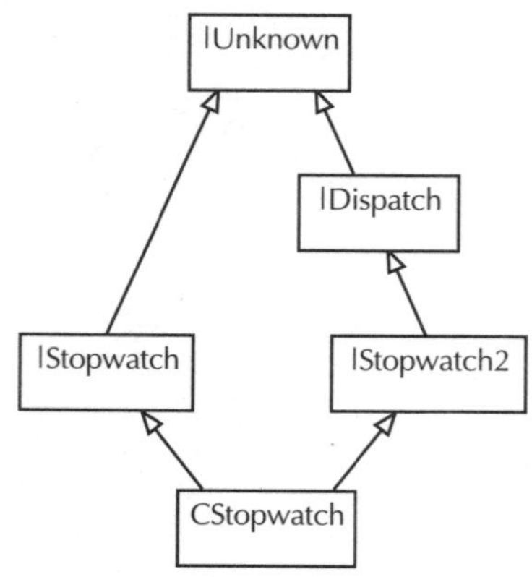

Interface diagram for **CStopwatch** as implemented

Figure 8-1.

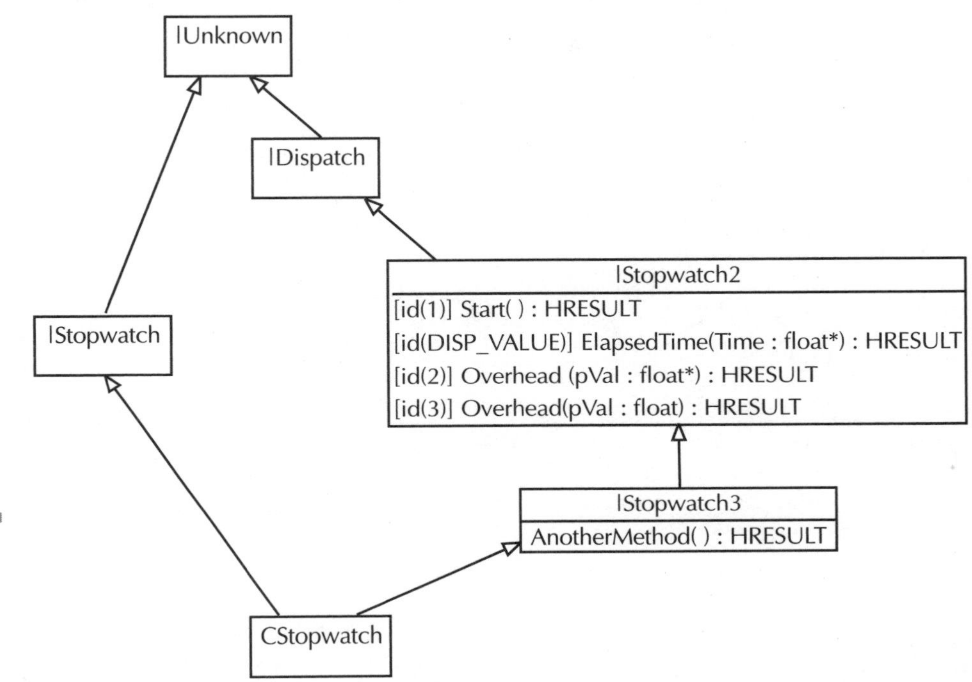

Deriving an interface from a dispatch interface
Figure 8-2.

As you can see, this error message not only does not indicate what the error was, but it also fails to inform you as to where the error is located.

To ensure that all your IDs on derived interfaces are unique, simply avoid using the interface IDs on the derived interface altogether, as shown in Figure 8-2. This way, the MIDL compiler will generate unique values for you. Another solution is to use an **enum** to define the last dispatch ID on the parent interface.

Implementing IDispatch Inside Your Component

Let's now take a look at how easy it is to implement **IDispatch** with ATL. In spite of the complexity associated with the **IDispatch** interface, only a simple change needs to be made inside your C++ code to support a dual interface on the **Stopwatch** component. The change is to add the

IDispatchImpl template class to the inheritance structure of **CStopwatch**. This is demonstrated in the code below:

```
///////////////////////////////////////////////////////////////////////
// CStopwatch
class ATL_NO_VTABLE CStopwatch :
  public CComObjectRootEx<CComSingleThreadModel>,
  public CComCoClass<CStopwatch, &CLSID_Stopwatch>,
  public IStopwatch,
  public IDispatchImpl<IStopwatch2, &IID_IStopwatch2,
    &LIBID_TIMERSLib, tmLibraryVersionMajor,
    tmLibraryVersionMinor>
{
   ...
}
```

By adding the highlighted lines, your object now implements the **IDispatch** interface methods. As you can see, there is essentially nothing to it. (Isn't ATL great!)

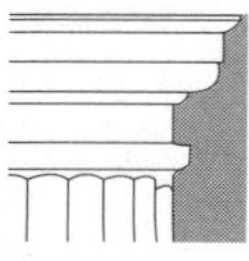

NOTE: To investigate further the intricacies of how **IDispatchImpl** works, examine its declaration in **atlcom.h.**

Updating the COM Map

The COM map in ATL identifies each of the additional interfaces that a component supports.

One more important change needs to be made to support newly declared interfaces. Any new interfaces must be added to the interface map, or *COM map*, of the object to which they are applied. The interface map contains a list of each interface that has been added so that when a client calls **QueryInterface( )** to request a particular interface, the **QueryInterface( )** implementation function will know that the interface exists. The updated code below shows the additional changes to **Stopwatch.h** that are required.

```
BEGIN_COM_MAP(CStopwatch)
      COM_INTERFACE_ENTRY(IStopwatch)
      COM_INTERFACE_ENTRY(IStopwatch2)
      COM_INTERFACE_ENTRY(IDispatch)
END_COM_MAP()
```

Note that in the preceding COM map, many interfaces supported by **Stopwatch** are not explicitly shown. The obvious one not seen is **IUnknown**, but interfaces like **ITypeLib** and **IErrorInfo** are also supported but not included in the COM map. The reason for this is that ATL implements quite a few interfaces for you implicitly, and therefore they do not need to be added to the COM map.

Versioning Your Component

When you change a type library, increase its version number.

Whenever you change the type library in a manner that is not compatible with the earlier version, you need to change the major version number. This way, when requesting a type library from your component, you can request the one specifically associated with the applicable version. Let's consider the previous version as published. Given this assumption, we now need to bump the version number to indicate a new type library.

As we shall see shortly, it is important that the same version numbers used in the type library statement also be used as parameters in the **IDispatchImpl< >** template. To do this, we need to define constants that are available to the MIDL precompiler and then placed into the C++ library header file. At first, you might think you could simply use a **#define** declarative. This, however, will not work because the precompiler will remove the **#define**s and replace them with their corresponding macro implementation code so that the MIDL compiler will not be aware that they even existed.

Another kind of MIDL statement, called **cpp_quote**, is used to put code into the header file—in our case, **Timers.h**. For example, you could use

```
cpp_quote("#define tmLibraryVersionMajor 2")
cpp_quote("#define tmLibraryVersionMinor 0")
```

The exact text that is placed within the **cpp_quote** string will then be inserted into the **Timers.h** file.

cpp_quote is very useful in many circumstances, but it too is not sufficient for what we are trying to do. The problem is that **cpp_quote** text is ignored by the MIDL compiler (except, of course, for purposes of placing it in the C++ header file). Therefore, you cannot use the **#define** macros within the type library version attribute. One solution to this dilemma is to use a **#define** in conjunction with the **enum** declaration, as shown again here:

```
#define MAJORVERSION 2
#define MINORVERSION 0
#define VERSION MAJORVERSION.MINORVERSION
```

```
enum TmLibraryVersion
{
  tmLibraryVersionMajor = MAJORVERSION,
  tmLibraryVersionMinor = MINORVERSION
};

[
  uuid(D7EBA784-2BF1-11D3-A48B-0000861C844E),
  version(VERSION),
...
};
```

Using this method, the version numbers are available in both the C++ header file and within the version attribute.

Now that you know how to declare the version numbers for both C++ code and the version attribute type library, let's see how these declarations are used in C++ again and why they are so important.

By default, when you use the ATL wizard to generate a class that supports a dual interface, the optional version parameters (which we saw earlier) are not included. Instead the declaration looks like this:

```
//////////////////////////////////////////////////////////////////////
// CStopwatch
class ATL_NO_VTABLE CStopwatch :
  public CComObjectRootEx<CComSingleThreadModel>,
  public CComCoClass<CStopwatch, &CLSID_Stopwatch>,
  public IStopwatch,
  public IDispatchImpl<IStopwatch2, &IID_IStopwatch2,
    &LIBID_TIMERSLib>
{
   ...
}
```

Without the version numbers, the default values 1 and 0 for the **IDispatchImpl** template declaration will be used, as shown below:

```
template< class T,
  const IID* piid,
  const GUID* plibid,
  WORD wMajor = 1, WORD wMinor = 0,
  class tihclass = CComTypeInfoHolder >
class IDispatchImpl : public T
```

For this template, the first parameter is the name of the interface that is to be the dual interface. The second parameter is the IID of the aforementioned interface. Next comes the GUID of the type library. The last three parameters are optional, beginning with the major and minor version numbers of the type library and ending with the class that will handle the type information.

The key parameters in our discussion are the version parameters. If we simply left the defaults, the project would still compile, but there would be an inconsistency with the way the type library is declared and registered and the way the **IDispatch** implementation expects it. The result is that the first time a client calls into the dispatch interface to request a dispatch ID, the call will fail and return an **HRESULT** of **TYPE_E_LIBNOTREGISTERED**. Thus, the **tmLibraryVersion** enumeration declaration of **tmLibraryVersionMajor** and **tmLibraryVersionMinor** inside the IDL must match the numbers used in the **IDispatchImpl** template. With the enumerations, we can override the default version numbers used for the **IDispatchImpl** template, as shown again here:

```
// CStopwatch
class ATL_NO_VTABLE CStopwatch :
...
  public IDispatchImpl<IStopwatch2, &IID_IStopwatch2,
    &LIBID_TIMERSLib, tmLibraryVersionMajor,
    tmLibraryVersionMinor>
{
...
}
```

Unfortunately, although the enumeration method helps keep the version numbers in sync for the **Stopwatch** component, you will still be forced to remember to edit the **IDispatchImpl** template parameters for any new components that you may add to the project.

Updating the File Version

Unfortunately, the type library is not the only place that has a version number associated with it. In addition, the compiled DLL has a version associated with it so that when you view the properties of the DLL from Explorer, you can see the version of the control. To update the file version numbers, go to the Resource View tab in the workspace window of Visual Studio. From there you will notice a Version folder, as shown in Figure 8-3. Within this folder is a **VS_VERSION_INFO** resource. Double-click on this

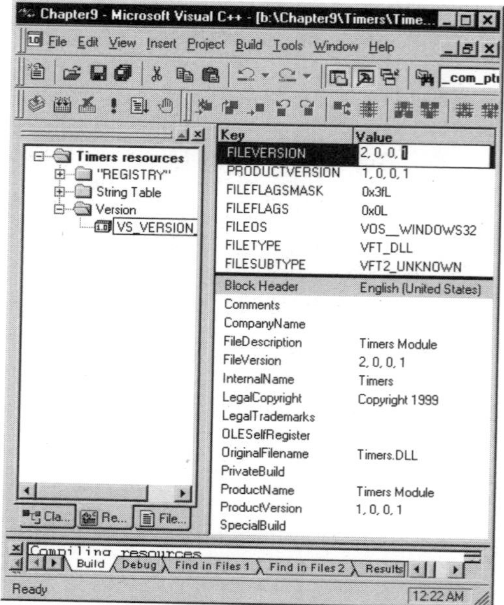

Setting the file version for **Timers.DLL**

Figure 8-3.

file and edit the file version. This can be a critical update because it allows users to distinguish between versions of your DLL without having to rely on things like exact file size or CRC checks. Given two DLLs, if you consistently update the version number, users can easily see which DLL is most current.

Updating the Registry for the New CLSID and Type Library Versions

The last item on the list of version changes is to reflect the IDL changes into the registry. This is done via an edit to the **Stopwatch.rgs** file, as we did before. The specific changes are shown in the highlighted lines below:

```
HKCR
{
  Timers.Stopwatch.1 = s 'Stopwatch Component 1.0'
  {
    CLSID = s '{83DC3C46-1259-4f95-A2D1-CD11A8819E2E}'
  }
  Timers.Stopwatch.2 = s 'Stopwatch Component 2.0'
```

```
  {
    CLSID = s '{83DC3C46-1259-4f95-A2D1-CD11A8819E2E}'
  }
  Timers.Stopwatch = s 'Stopwatch Component 2.0'
  {
    CLSID = s '{83DC3C46-1259-4f95-A2D1-CD11A8819E2E}'
    CurVer = s 'Timers.Stopwatch.2'
  }
  NoRemove CLSID
  {
    ForceRemove {83DC3C46-1259-4f95-A2D1-CD11A8819E2E} =
                 s 'Stopwatch Component 2.0'
    {
      ProgID = s 'Timers.Stopwatch.2'
      VersionIndependentProgID = s 'Timers.Stopwatch'
      Version = s '2.0'
      ForceRemove 'Programmable'
      InprocServer32 = s '%MODULE%'
      {
        val ThreadingModel = s 'Apartment'
      }
     'TypeLib' = s '{D7EBA784-2BF1-11D3-A48B-0000861C844E}'
    }
  }
}
```


Specifically, you will notice the addition of a **Timers.Stopwatch.2** key and the update of the **CurVer** and **VersionIndependentProgID** setting to now be **Timers.Stopwatch.2**. These changes reflect an update in the program ID. Previously, the version-neutral program ID, or ProgID, for the Stopwatch component was **Timers.Stopwatch**. There was, however, a specific ProgID for version 1.0, **Timers.Stopwatch.1**. Now that we have a version 2 of the component, we need to change the version-independent ProgID to point to the newly created version 2 ProgID, **Timers.Stopwatch.2**. In addition, an update to the Version key is made. Last, a cosmetic change is made to the name of the component as it appears in an object browser listing so that the version number is reflected in the name.

Testing the IDispatch Interface

The easiest way to verify that the **IDispatch** interface on a component is working correctly is to write a quick Visual Basic or Java Script program that will exercise your component. As we mentioned earlier, scripting languages require the **IDispatch** interface to access a component. Below is a listing of a Visual Basic Scripting (VBS) file, **StopwatchClient.vbs**, that tests version 2 of the **Stopwatch** component.

```
' Force all variables to be declared
Option Explicit

Const ApplicationName = "Stop Watch Tester"

' Call the TestStopwatch Function
TestStopwatch()

' TestStopwatch is used to test the
' Timers.Stopwatch component.
Private Sub TestStopwatch

    Dim oTimer ' As Stopwatch
    Dim nElapsedTime ' As Integer

    Set oTimer = CreateObject("Timers.Stopwatch")
    MsgBox "Select OK to start the stopwatch", _
      vbOKOnly, ApplicationName
    oTimer.Start
    MsgBox "Select OK to Stop the stopwatch", _
      vbOKOnly, ApplicationName
    nElapsedTime = oTimer.ElapsedTime()
    MsgBox "The elapsed time was " & nElapsedTime & " seconds.", _
  vbOkOnly, ApplicationName

End Sub
```

To instantiate the **Stopwatch** component, a call to **CreateObject( )** is made using the ProgID of the object to be instantiated. Next, a dialog appears prompting a user to start the stopwatch. This is followed by a call into the **Start( )** method of the **Stopwatch** component via the **IDispatch** interface. Following this, a second dialog is displayed, prompting the user to click the OK button to stop the stopwatch. Finally, after saving the elapsed time, the number of elapsed seconds between start and stop is displayed to the user.

Calling the IDispatch Interface from a C++ COM Client

Now that we have updated the server to support a dual interface, we are ready to update the **StopwatchClient.exe** project to see how to call into an **IDispatch** interface using C++. A listing of the updated

StopwatchClient.cpp file is shown below. Because it involves a complete rewrite of the **UseStopwatch( )** function, changes are not marked in the following listing as it would essentially be the entire file.

```
// StopwatchClient.cpp :
//   Defines the entry point for the console application.
//

// std::out etc
#include <iostream>

#import "..\Timers\Timers.dll" no_namespace


void UseStopwatch(IStopwatchPtr pStopwatch)
{
  float nElapsedTimeLateBound;
  float nElapsedTimeEarlyBound;
  float nDummy;

  // Declare an enumeration corresponding to the FunctionNames
  // array.
  enum StopwatchMethods
  {
    StopwatchMethodsStart,
    StopwatchMethodsElapsedTime,
    StopwatchMethodsOverhead,
    StopwatchMethodsTotal
  };
  // IDispatch stuff for calling the Stopwatch Object
  OLECHAR FAR* FunctionNames[StopwatchMethodsTotal]
    = {L"Start", L"ElapsedTime", L"Overhead"};
  DISPID DispIds[StopwatchMethodsTotal];
  _variant_t varElapsedTime;
  _variant_t varOverhead;
  // Create an array to store the method params. Since
  // we never have more than one param this array is for
  // one item only
  _variant_t varParms[1];
  DISPPARAMS dpParms = { NULL, NULL, 0, 0};

  HRESULT hr;

  // A vtable pointer to the Stopwatch object
  IStopwatch2Ptr pStopwatch2(__uuidof(Stopwatch));
```

8

```
// Create a new Stopwatch object which will be timed
IDispatchPtr pDispStopwatch;
// Get the dispatch interface
pStopwatch.QueryInterface( __uuidof(IDispatch), &pDispStopwatch );


//****** Scenario 1 ******//
// Start the stopwatch
pStopwatch->Start();

// Now do something using the vtable call
// Note that although we are calling stopwatch
// object this is simply what we are using as
// the thing to time. We don't actually care
// what the returned elapsed time is.
{
  pStopwatch2->Start();
  nDummy = pStopwatch2->ElapsedTime();
}

// Stop the stopwatch to see how long it
// took to do something
nElapsedTimeEarlyBound = pStopwatch->ElapsedTime();

std::cout << "The early bound elapsed time is "
  << nElapsedTimeEarlyBound << std::endl;

//****** Scenario 2 ******//
// Start Stopwatch
// Now we are going to time how long it takes to call IDispatch
// including doing the name lookup.
pStopwatch->Start();

// Time something that uses late binding
{
  if(FAILED(
    hr = pDispStopwatch->GetIDsOfNames(
      IID_NULL,
      &FunctionNames[StopwatchMethodsStart],
      1,
      LOCALE_SYSTEM_DEFAULT,
      &DispIds[StopwatchMethodsStart]
      )
  ))
    _com_raise_error(hr);
```

```
    if(FAILED(
      hr = pDispStopwatch->Invoke(
        DispIds[StopwatchMethodsStart],
        IID_NULL,
        LOCALE_SYSTEM_DEFAULT,
        DISPATCH_METHOD,
        &dpParms,
        &varElapsedTime,
        NULL,
        NULL)
    ))
      _com_raise_error(hr);

    if(FAILED(
      hr = pDispStopwatch->GetIDsOfNames(
        IID_NULL,
        &FunctionNames[StopwatchMethodsElapsedTime],
        1,
        LOCALE_SYSTEM_DEFAULT,
        &DispIds[StopwatchMethodsElapsedTime])
    ))
      _com_raise_error(hr);

    if(FAILED(
      hr = pDispStopwatch->Invoke(
        DispIds[StopwatchMethodsElapsedTime],
        IID_NULL,
        LOCALE_SYSTEM_DEFAULT,
        DISPATCH_METHOD,
        &dpParms,
        &varElapsedTime,
        NULL,
        NULL)
    ))
      _com_raise_error(hr);

  nDummy = varElapsedTime;
}

// Stop the stopwatch
nElapsedTimeLateBound = pStopwatch->ElapsedTime();

std::cout << "The late bound elapsed time "
  " including a query for disp ids is "
  << nElapsedTimeLateBound << std::endl;
```

```
std::cout << "The expense of using the "
  "IDispatch without dispid is "
  << (nElapsedTimeLateBound - nElapsedTimeEarlyBound)
  << std::endl;

//****** Scenario 3 ******//
// Start the stopwatch
pStopwatch->Start();

// One more time...this time without querying
// for the dispatch ids
{
  if(FAILED(
    hr = pDispStopwatch->Invoke(
      DispIds[StopwatchMethodsStart],
      IID_NULL,
      LOCALE_SYSTEM_DEFAULT,
      DISPATCH_METHOD,
      &dpParms,
      &varElapsedTime,
      NULL,
      NULL)
  ))
    _com_raise_error(hr);

  if(FAILED(
    hr = pDispStopwatch->Invoke(
      DispIds[StopwatchMethodsElapsedTime],
      IID_NULL,
      LOCALE_SYSTEM_DEFAULT,
      DISPATCH_METHOD,
      &dpParms,
      &varElapsedTime,
      NULL,
      NULL)
  ))
    _com_raise_error(hr);

  nDummy = varElapsedTime;
}

// Stop the stopwatch
nElapsedTimeLateBound = pStopwatch->ElapsedTime();
```

```
std::cout << "The late bound elapsed time "
  "given the disp ids is "
  << nElapsedTimeLateBound << std::endl;

std::cout << "The expense of using the "
  "IDispatch given the disp ids is "
  << (nElapsedTimeLateBound - nElapsedTimeEarlyBound)
  << std::endl;

//****** Scenario 4 ******//
// Call the overhead property
// just to show how to do it....
if(FAILED(
  hr = pDispStopwatch->GetIDsOfNames(
    IID_NULL,
    &FunctionNames[StopwatchMethodsOverhead],
    1,
    LOCALE_SYSTEM_DEFAULT,
    &DispIds[StopwatchMethodsOverhead]
    )
))
  _com_raise_error(hr);

// Set the first parameter
varOverhead = nElapsedTimeEarlyBound;
varParms[0] = varOverhead;

// Add the parameters to the dispatch
// parameter array
dpParms.rgvarg = &varParms[0];
// Set the number of parameters
dpParms.cArgs = 1;
dpParms.cNamedArgs = 1;
DISPID dispidPut = DISPID_PROPERTYPUT;
dpParms.rgdispidNamedArgs = &dispidPut;

// Set the overhead property using IDispatch
if(FAILED(
  hr = pDispStopwatch->GetIDsOfNames(
    IID_NULL,
    &FunctionNames[StopwatchMethodsOverhead],
    1,
    LOCALE_SYSTEM_DEFAULT,
    &DispIds[StopwatchMethodsOverhead])
```

```
  ))
    _com_raise_error(hr);

  if(FAILED(
    hr = pDispStopwatch->Invoke(
      DispIds[StopwatchMethodsOverhead],
      IID_NULL,
      LOCALE_SYSTEM_DEFAULT,
      DISPATCH_PROPERTYPUT,
      &dpParms,
      NULL,
      NULL,
      NULL)
  ))
    _com_raise_error(hr);

}

int main(int argc, char* argv[])
{

  CoInitialize( NULL );
  try
  {
    IStopwatchPtr pStopwatch(__uuidof(Stopwatch));
    UseStopwatch(pStopwatch);

  }
  catch(_com_error e)
  {
    std::cout << "ERROR: " << e.ErrorMessage() << std::endl;
  }

  CoUninitialize();
  return 0;
}
```

Although there is a lot of new code in the listing above, the overall structure of the **StopwatchClient** program has not changed. As before, we continue to pass an **IStopwatch** pointer to the **UseStopwatch( )** function. This emphasizes the fact that although we did make some significant changes to the **Stopwatch** component, it continues to function with the old interfaces. Furthermore, the compatibility is so complete that the final version of the **StopwatchClient.exe** from Chapter 2 will still work.

In the next example, we are going to time how long it takes to call **Start( )** and then **ElapsedTime( )** using three different methods. The first method is to use early binding, direct vtable calls, as we have in all chapters so far. Then in the second method, we will use the **IDispatch** interface, asking for the dispatch IDs and then using them to invoke a particular method. In the last scenario, we will still use the **IDispatch** interface, but we will time how long it takes to invoke methods without having to query for the dispatch IDs. At the end of **UseStopwatch( )**, we will call a property using the **IDispatch** interface.

Let's now begin to investigate the code. To call into the **IDispatch** interface, it is necessary to pass the name of the function we want to call. Therefore, an array containing the function name is declared, **FunctionNames**. In addition, an array to store each of the returned IDs is created, **DispIds**. To index into both of these arrays, the **StopwatchMethods** enumeration is declared.

The next significant declarations are the **pStopwatch2** and **pDispStopwatch** interface variables. Previously, we had instantiated only one **Stopwatch** object, and that was before we even entered the **UseStopwatch( )** function. However, because we are going to be timing calls to the same component type that we are going to use to retrieve elapsed times, a second instantiation of **Stopwatch** is made. The **IStopwatch** interface that is passed to **UseStopwatch( )**, **pStopwatch**, will be used to calculate the time it takes to call two functions on the second stopwatch instance, the one declared as **pStopwatch2**. In addition, **pDispStopwatch** will point to the **IDispatch** interface on the same component as **pStopwatch2**. Notice that **pDispStopwatch** is declared as **IDispatchPtr**, indicating that it is, in fact, an **_com_ptr_t** smart pointer declared by the **#import** of the **Timers.dll**.

8

In scenario one, we time how long it takes to call **Start( )** and **ElapsedTime( )** using the vtable call. First, we call **Start( )** on **pStopwatch** and then call **Start( )** and **ElapsedTime( )** on **pStopwatch2**. We then record the elapsed time into **nElapsedTimeEarlyBound** and send it to **std::cout**.

In scenario two, we time how long it takes to call **Start( )** and **ElapsedTime( )** using the **IDispatch** interface. To call into **IDispatch**, a client first needs to know the dispatch ID of the method to be called. To retrieve the ID, it is first necessary to call **GetIDsOfNames( )**, passing in the name of the method to be identified. In the first call, we wish to retrieve the dispatch ID of the **Start( )** method. This is stored as the first item in the **FunctionNames** array. The return value is then placed into the first item in the **DispIds** array. Once the dispatch ID has been retrieved, we are ready to call into the **Invoke( )** method. Notice how the fourth parameter of this call identifies the type of method. In our case, **Start( )** is a method, so **DISPATCH_METHOD** is used. Since the **Start( )** method does not have any return value, **NULL** is passed for the result variant. A similar procedure is followed for calling the **ElapsedTime( )** method, except this call does return a value. The value is returned into **varElapsedTime**.

In scenario three, we don't really do anything different from what we already did in scenario two except that this time, the elapsed time calculation does not include the time it takes to call **GetIDsOfNames( )**, so the overall time is faster.

In scenario four, we set the **Overhead** property. This is slightly different from the other examples we have seen so far because it involves sending a parameter. To start out, we simply retrieve the dispatch ID just as we did before. Next, we proceed to set up the parameters that are going to be passed in the **Invoke( )** call. **varOverhead** is assigned to **nElapsedTimeEarlyBound**. **varOverhead** is then entered as the first item in the **varParms** array. The code here shows a few extra steps, but this makes it easier to translate the code to pass multiple parameters rather than just one. Next, the **dpParams** structure is populated. **dpParams** is a **DISPPARAMS**. We have already been using this structure in previous calls, but because there were not any parameters to pass, we simply initialized it to be empty. Below is the **DISPPARAMS** definition found in **oadil.h**:

```
typedef struct  tagDISPPARAMS
    {
    /* [size_is] */ VARIANTARG __RPC_FAR *rgvarg;
    /* [size_is] */ DISPID __RPC_FAR *rgdispidNamedArgs;
    UINT cArgs;
    UINT cNamedArgs;
    }  DISPPARAMS;
```

The purpose of this structure is to encapsulate all the parameters that are passed to the invoke method. **rgvarg** contains the array of each of the parameters, all of which are **VARIANT**s. **rgdispidNamedArgs** contains the IDs of each of the parameters. Therefore, you do not need to pass all the parameters (assuming the parameters are optional), and in addition, they do not need to be passed in order. The last two items, **cArgs** and **cNamedArgs**, are used to indicate how many parameters are specified in **rgvarg** and **rgdispidNamedArgs**, respectively. In the property case, the named argument ID is simply set to **DISPID_PROPERTYPUT**, as we are calling the put property. In the more general case where multiple parameters are being sent, you need to call **GetIDsOfNames( )** with an array for the second and last parameters. In our example, however, there were no multiple parameters, so only a single item was sent. As it turns out, in C++, sending an array of one and sending a pointer to a single item is the same thing. Therefore, throughout our examples only a pointer to a single item was used.

The output from the **StopwatchClient.exe** is shown in Figure 8-4.

If you look at the times, you will see that although accessing methods and properties via the **IDispatch** interface always takes longer, the differences are not that great. Do not, however, take this data to be indicative of the expense of using **IDispatch**. Since the **Stopwatch** object has only three methods (with less than three parameters per method), the call to **GetIDsOfNames( )** is reasonably fast. This will not be true with larger interfaces. Estimates as to the performance degradation typically range from 10 to 100 times slower when using **IDispatch**.

CComDispatchDriver

Given the difficulty of calling into the **IDispatch** interface, you will be pleased to know that in addition to the **IDispatchPtr** class that was automatically provided because of the **#import** statement in the preceding code, there is also an ATL wrapper class specifically designed for working with **IDispatch**. The name of the class is **CComDispatchDriver**, and Table 8-2 lists the member functions. Note that **CComDispatchDriver** has a public member variable, **p**, which is a pointer to the encapsulated **IDispatch** interface.

Given the number of lines of code needed to call the **IDispatch** interface directly, there is certainly a need for a wrapper class. One of the nicest things about **CComDispatchDriver** is that you no longer need to call **IDispatch::GetIDsOfNames( )** before calling a function whose name you

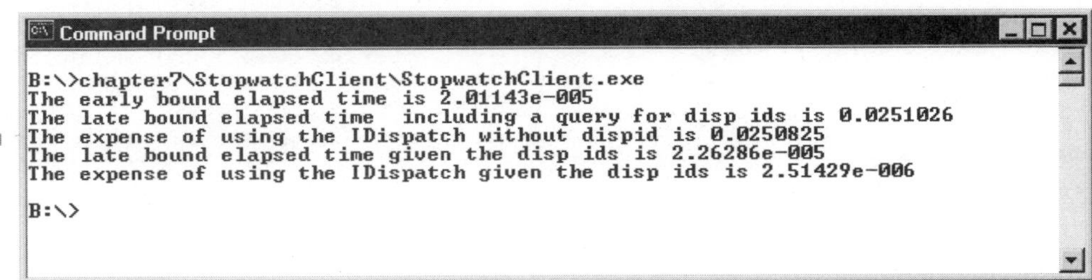

StopwatchClient.exe output

Figure 8-4.

Class Member	Description
CComDispatchDriver( ); CComDispatchDriver(IDispatch *pIDispatch); CComDispatchDriver(IUnknown *pIUnknown);	There are three constructors for **CComDispatchDriver**. In addition to the default constructor, you can also instantiate a **CComDispatchDriver** from an **IUnknown** or an **IDispatch** pointer, the former of which will call **QueryInterface( )** to retrieve the **IDispatch** pointer.
IDispatch *operator =(IDispatch *pIDispatch); IDispatch *operator =(IUnknown *lUnknown);	The assignment operator can take either an **IDispatch** pointer or an **IUnknown** pointer. If the **CComDispatchDriver** member variable **p** has already been initialized with a different **IDispatch** interface, **Release( )** will be called on that interface before the assignment is made.
operator IDispatch*( );	The **IDispatch*** extractor operator retrieves the **IDispatch** interface stored in **p**. Note that **Release( )** is not called, and when the **CComDispatchDriver** class goes out of scope, it will still call **Release( )**.
IDispatch *operator->( ); IDispatch **operator&( ); IDispatch &operator*( );	These various accessor operators retrieve **p** in various forms. First, the member-selection operator retrieves the **IDispatch** pointer in order for you to call properties and methods on the interface directly. The address operator returns the address of **p**, and the dereference operator returns the value at **p**.
HRESULT GetIDOfName(LPCOLESTR *lpsz*,DISPID **pdispid*);	**GetIDOfName( )** is an easier form of **IDispatch::GetIDsOfNames( )**. You simply specify the name and it returns the dispatch ID corresponding to the name.
HRESULT GetProperty(DISPID *dwDispID*, VARIANT **pVar*); HRESULT PutProperty(DISPID *dwDispID*, VARIANT **pVar*);	The **GetProperty( )** and **PutProperty( )** allow you to get and set properties given the dispatch ID.
HRESULT GetPropertyByName(LPCOLESTR *lpsz*, VARIANT **pVar*); HRESULT PutPropertyByName(LPCOLESTR *lpsz*, VARIANT **pVar*);	The **Get**- and **Put PropertyByName** functions perform the same purpose as the **Get**- and **PutProperty** functions above except you do not need to first retrieve the dispatch IDs. Simply pass the name of the property and the variant that you want to retrieve or set the property with.

CComDispatch-Driver Class Members
Table 8-2.

Class Member	Description
HRESULT Invoke0(DISPID *dispid*, VARIANT **pvarRet* = NULL); HRESULT Invoke0(LPCOLESTR *lpszName*, VARIANT *pvarRet = NULL); HRESULT Invoke1(DISPID *dispid*, VARIANT **pvarParam1*, VARIANT **pvarRet* = NULL); HRESULT Invoke1(LPCOLESTR *lpszName*, VARIANT **pvarParam1*, VARIANT **pvarRet* = NULL); HRESULT Invoke2(DISPID *dispid*, VARIANT **pvarParam1*, VARIANT **pvarParam2*, VARIANT **pvarRet* = NULL); HRESULT Invoke2(LPCOLESTR *lpszName*, VARIANT **pvarParam1*, VARIANT **pvarParam2*, VARIANT **pvarRet* = NULL); HRESULT InvokeN(DISPID *dispid*, VARIANT **pvarParams*, int *nParams*, VARIANT **pvarRet* = NULL); HRESULT InvokeN(LPCOLESTR lpszName, VARIANT *pvarParams, int nParams, VARIANT *pvarRet = NULL);	There are several Invoke functions in addition to the one accessible directly off the **IDispatch** interface. Each is prefixed by "Invoke" and followed by a number that indicates the number of parameters that are being passed. **InvokeN( )** allows for an array of parameters when there are more than two. Each Invoke function has two forms. The first form takes the dispatch ID in order to identify the function, and the second takes the function name.
BOOL operator!( )	The NOT operator returns **true** if the **p** is **NULL**, otherwise it returns **false**.

CComDispatchDriver Class Members *(continued)*

Table 8-2.

CComDispatch-Driver Class Members *(continued)*

Table 8-2.

Class Member	Description

static HRESULT GetProperty(IDispatch **pDisp*, DISPID *dwDispID*, VARIANT **pVar*);
 	
static HRESULT PutProperty(IDispatch **pDisp*, DISPID *dwDispID*, VARIANT **pVar*);
	Two more methods can be used for accessing properties. The difference with these two is that they are static, so you do not need to instantiate a **CComDispatchDriver** object. Instead, the **IDispatch** pointer is passed as a parameter.

have not already retrieved. This is because of the **GetPropertyByName( )** and **PutPropertyByName( )** functions, and the fact that the **Invoke( )** functions are overloaded to take a **LPCOLESTR** or a dispatch ID. The drawback of using the "ByName" calls, however, is that they are rather inefficient if you are calling the same function multiple times because they have to re-retrieve the ID each time, even though it was retrieved earlier. In these cases you should call **GetIDOfName( )** first, and then use one of the functions that uses the dispatch ID rather than the name. A second problem is that a raw variant is used whenever a parameter is passed. This forces you to create the variant first before using the function. In spite of these drawbacks, the class is still very useful if you ever get caught and have to call into the dispatch interface by hand. If you look closely at the documentation of **CComDispatchDriver**, you may notice that not all the above class members are listed. They can, however, be viewed if you open **atlcom.h**.

IN DEPTH

An ATL Shortcut

Since **CComDispatchDriver** is an ATL class, it is not available by default in a non-ATL-based project. Furthermore, you cannot simply include the **CComDispatchDriver** header file, **atlcom.h**, because there is a dependency. Instead you need to add ATL support to your program. Although you will not achieve full support, you can get reasonably close by including **atlbase.h** followed by a declaration of **_Module**, as shown below:

```
#include <atlbase.h>
CComModule _Module;
#include <atlcom.h>
```

Using this method, not all the classes in **atlcom.h** will have full functionality, but many of them will. If you want to use a particular class, you should check the class for references to **_Module**. Of course, the class could still have a reference to another class that is using the **_Module**, so a cursory look is not guaranteed to be sufficient. The MSDN Knowledge Base article Q175190 describes how to add full ATL support. (It does this as though you are within an MFC project, so a little translation will be needed.)

IN DEPTH

An ATL Shortcut

Since **CComDispatchDriver** is an ATL class, it is not available by default in a non-ATL-based project. Furthermore, you cannot simply include the **CComDispatchDriver** header file, **atlcom.h**, because there is a dependency. Instead you need to add ATL support to your program. Although you will not achieve full support, you can get reasonably close by including **atlbase.h** followed by a declaration of **_Module**, as shown below:

```
#include <atlbase.h>
CComModule _Module;
#include <atlcom.h>
```

Using this method, not all the classes in **atlcom.h** will have full functionality, but many of them will. If you want to use a particular class, you should check the class for references to **_Module**. Of course, the class could still have a reference to another class that is using the **_Module**, so a cursory look is not guaranteed to be sufficient. The MSDN Knowledge Base article Q175190 describes how to add full ATL support. (It does this as though you are within an MFC project, so a little translation will be needed.)

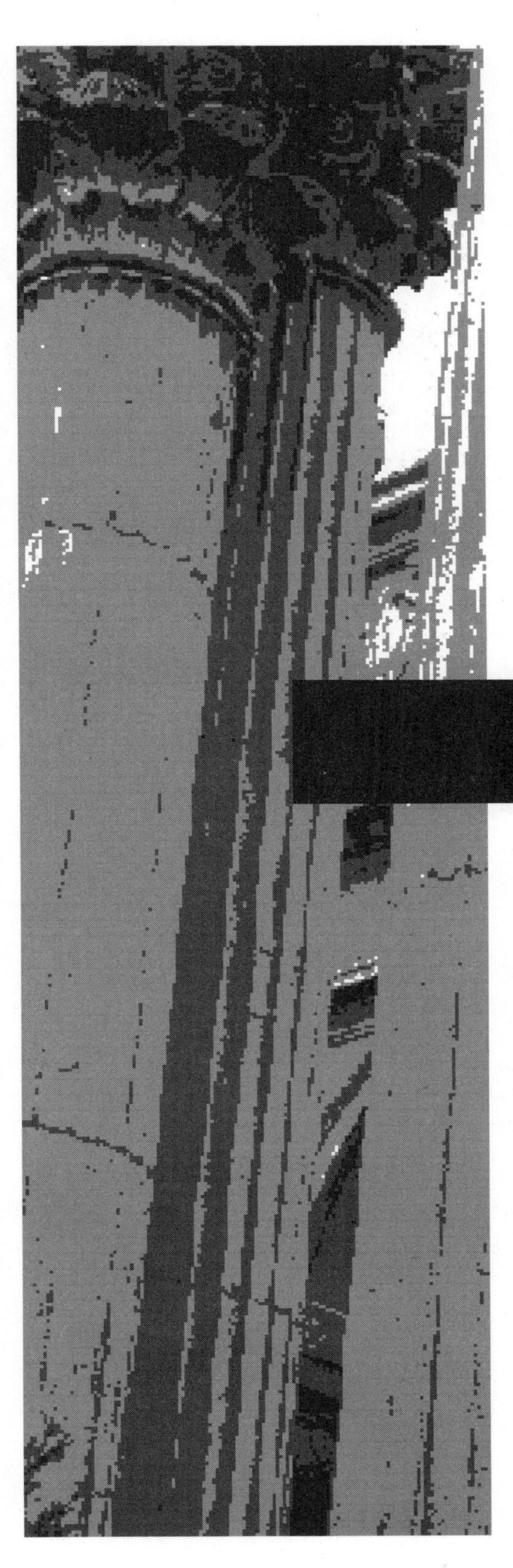

CHAPTER 9

Error Handling and Component Debugging

The proper reporting and handling of errors is an important part of successful COM programming. In the preceding chapters we briefly discussed the reporting of server-side errors back to the client. For example, you have seen that a client is notified of an error through the **HRESULT** value returned by the server. No information, however, as to what went wrong is provided in those examples. Here you will see how to add such information.

This chapter explores the standard COM error reporting mechanism. We will begin by examining the structure of **HRESULT**. Next, you will learn how to create your own custom error codes. Then, you will learn how to implement rich error handling, which includes such things as the passing of error strings and help file references. At the end of the chapter we will move beyond reporting errors to debugging errors. ATL provides some easy-to-implement trace facilities that you can use to check your code.

The HRESULT Structure

As you saw in Chapter 2, **HRESULT** is a **typedef** for a **long**. As explained, an **HRESULT** return value can be checked for success or failure using the **SUCCEEDED** and **FAILED** macros. These macros check whether the value of an **HRESULT** is zero or positive (success), or negative (failure). This simple test is based on the fact that the **HRESULT** can be broken down into sections, as shown in Figure 9-1.

The first bit in an **HRESULT** value indicates success or failure. When this bit is set, an **HRESULT** is negative and it indicates an error. The next few bits are reserved and can be ignored.

The facility code indicates the category of the error.

The next set of bits is known as the *facility code*, and it is used to group a set of **HRESULT**s into a particular category. Strangely enough, documentation on the exact reserved portion size and the facility code size is a little inconsistent, but an examination of the source code indicates that the facility code is 13 bits and, hence, the reserved portion is 2 bits. Fortunately, as you shall see at the end of the next section, there are macros that handle retrieval of the various portions of the structure. In almost all cases in which you return a custom error code, you will use **FACILITY_ITF** for the facility code value. This indicates that the error code at the end of the **HRESULT** is associated directly with the

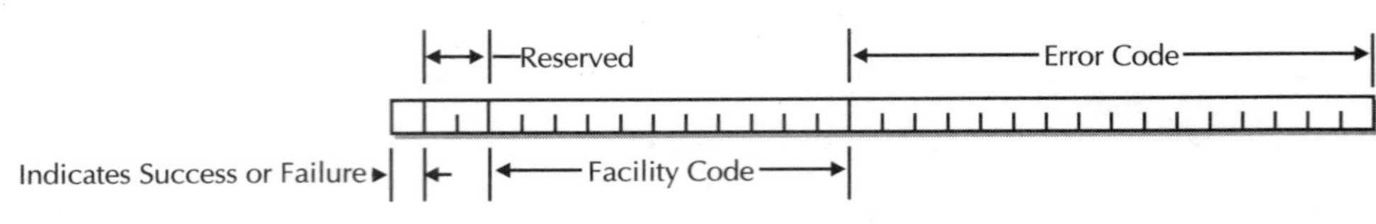

HRESULT structure
Figure 9-1.

interface that issued the error. Therefore, if two different interfaces returned an **HRESULT** with a facility code of **FACILITY_ITF** and the same error code, the errors could be entirely unrelated. As a COM client, you will encounter other facility codes, such as **FACILITY_WIN32** (API function errors), **FACILITY_DISPATCH** (**IDispatch**-related errors), and **FACILITY_RPC** (RPC/DCOM-related errors).

The last 16 bits contain the error value or *code*. This code is the part of the **HRESULT** that you are probably going to be most interested in once you have established that a failure occurred, because it describes what happened.

The code can also be used to return information when no error occurs—in other words, when the success/failure code is 0. For example, you could return **S_FALSE** to indicate that a property is false. Contrast this with returning **E_FAIL**, which doesn't tell a client anything about a particular property value, but rather indicates that an error occurred while trying to retrieve the property.

Error Handling with Custom HRESULTs

One way to enhance the error handling and reporting capabilities of your COM components is to create your own **HRESULT** error codes. By doing so you will be able to pass precise error information back to the client without incurring a large overhead.

Creating a Custom HRESULT

You can define your own custom error codes by using the **MAKE_HRESULT** macro, as shown here:

MAKE_HRESULT(SEVERITY_ERROR, FACILITY_ITF, *nCode*)

This produces an **HRESULT** indicating a failure on a custom interface with error value *nCode*. Since you will rarely use a different facility code, it can be helpful to simplify this macro into a second macro defined as follows:

```
#define MAKE_HRESULT_ERROR(nCode) \
    MAKE_HRESULT(SEVERITY_ERROR, FACILITY_ITF, nCode)
```

Note that **MAKE_HRESULT_ERROR** is not a standard macro but rather just a simplification of **MAKE_HRESULT**, which you will have to declare explicitly if you wish to use it.

In spite of the simplicity involved here, there is one other catch: There are several reserved **HRESULT** values. All values you specify must be between 0x200 and 0xffff.

Returning custom values to a COM client is valuable, but you also need to document the error corresponding with the value. This documentation can be provided in a help file, but a better way is to provide an enumeration corresponding to each error. This way, the interface errors are self-documenting. Furthermore, the client can use the enumerated values to compare against the **HRESULT**s returned. The added advantage that enumerations provide is that you can associate help strings with each value. Below is an update to the **Timers.idl** demonstrating the declaration of an error enumeration:

```
#include <winerror.h>
#define MAKE_HRESULT_ERROR(nCode) \
    MAKE_HRESULT(SEVERITY_ERROR, FACILITY_ITF, nCode)

  typedef [uuid(39FB3AB1-DE17-4a10-A3DB-95236C055135),
    helpstring("Possible error return codes")]
    enum TmError
  {
    [helpstring("The hardware does not support \
      the high performance counters")]
      tmErrorHighPerformanceTimersNotSupported =
      MAKE_HRESULT_ERROR(0xffff),
    [helpstring("Start needs to be called before ElapsedTime.")]
      tmErrorStartNotCalled,
    // Other error codes go here
  } TmError;
```

Notice that in order to use the **MAKE_HRESULT** macro inside your IDL code, you also need to include **winerror.h**. Alternatively, you could simply hard-code the values and not use the macro.

In the above code, 0xffff is for the first value, not 0x200. This is because the values are negative, so you want to start with the lowest negative value and use the enumeration to increase each entry by one.

To make these enumerations available to COM clients, the enumeration also needs to be declared in the **library** statement. Therefore, you will need to add one more line to your IDL, as follows:

```
library TIMERSLib
{
...
  enum TmError;
...
}
```

Let's now update the **Stopwatch.cpp** code to reflect the enumeration declaration, as shown below:

```
STDMETHODIMP CStopwatch::Start()
{
  if ( QueryPerformanceCounter( (LARGE_INTEGER*) &m_nStartTime) )
    return S_OK;
  else
    return tmErrorHighPerformanceTimersNotSupported;
}

STDMETHODIMP CStopwatch::ElapsedTime(float *Time)
{
  HRESULT hr;
  LARGE_INTEGER nStopTime;

  // Set the stop time immediately so that a minimum
  // amount of timer code is executed between the start
  // and stop times
  if ( !QueryPerformanceCounter( (LARGE_INTEGER*) &nStopTime ) )
  {
    hr = tmErrorHighPerformanceTimersNotSupported;
  }
  else if (m_nStartTime.QuadPart == 0)
  {
    hr = tmErrorStartNotCalled;
  }
else
  {
    *Time = (float) (nStopTime.QuadPart - m_nStartTime.QuadPart);
    *Time = (*Time / m_nFrequency.QuadPart);
    hr = S_OK;
  }

  return hr;
}
```

Now in the above code, rather than returning **E_FAIL** as we did before, we return a custom **HRESULT** value, providing more information to the client as to what went wrong.

Rather than having to define a custom error for every problem, you can use some errors that are predefined. Table 9-1 lists some of the most common ones. There are many more **HRESULT** values. For a more complete list, you can browse through **winerror.h**, where several of them are defined.

Standard HRESULT	Description
E_UNEXPECTED	An unexpected error occurred. By the way, the corresponding system error message for this is "Catastrophic failure," so use it with caution.
E_NOINTERFACE	The requested interface is not supported. This value is returned from a call to **QueryInterface( )** when the requested interface is not supported by the component.
E_NOTIMPL	This indicates that although a method has been defined on an interface, no implementation for the method or property has actually been provided.
E_OUTOFMEMORY	A memory allocation call failed.
E_ACCESSDENIED	Usually results from a problem with security and a user not having sufficient rights to perform the requested operation.
E_INVALIDARG	One of the arguments passed into a method was invalid.
E_POINTER	Similar to **E_INVALIDARG** but usually corresponds to a pointer containing **NULL** when it shouldn't, or vice versa.
E_FAIL	A generic message indicating that the call failed. Try to avoid this value because it essentially provides no information as to the cause of the error.

Common **HRESULT** Return Values
Table 9-1.

Many API functions also return their own **HRESULT**s. This is especially true with most of the COM API functions. In these cases, rather than always creating your own custom error, you can simply return the **HRESULT** that the API function returned. Furthermore, if you call one of the Win32 API functions and it returns a Win32 error (or you retrieve the error via a call to the **GetLastError( )** API function), you can return this error to the client by using the **HRESULT_FROM_WIN32** macro as follows:

```
}
...
  DWORD err = GetLastError( );
  return HRESULT_FROM_WIN32( err );
}
```

This is the same as calling

```
}
...
  DWORD err = GetLastError( );
  return MAKE_HRESULT(SEVERITY_ERROR, FACILITY_WIN32, err);
}
```

Before we end our discussion of **HRESULT**s, here are three macros that can be used by a client to retrieve the various parts of an **HRESULT**:

HRESULT_SEVERITY(*hr*):	Retrieves the severity code
HRESULT_CODE(*hr*):	Retrieves the error code
HRESULT_FACILITY(*hr*):	Retrieves the facility code

Rich Error Handling

Rich error handling provides extended error information.

Although returning an **HRESULT** error code is certainly the essential part of error handling, it is possible to provide a more detailed response. For example, it would be of significant value to return to the client a string describing the error along with a help file reference, which describes the error. Providing such additional information is referred to as *rich error handling*.

The IErrorInfo Interface

IErrorInfo is the interface that provides extended error information.

The COM designers decided to report extended error information to a client application by providing a standard error interface that is implemented by the COM server. The name of the standard interface is **IErrorInfo**. After returning an **HRESULT** indicating failure, the client calls into **IErrorInfo** to retrieve more information about the error. There are only five member functions in the **IErrorInfo** interface; each of them is listed in Table 9-2.

Using **IErrorInfo** is straightforward. After receiving a failed **HRESULT**, the client will check to see if **IErrorInfo** is supported. If it is, the client can then retrieve its pointer via a call to **QueryInterface( )** and then call **GetDescription( )** to obtain a string describing the message. If appropriate, this string can be displayed via a message box.

The ISupportErrorInfo Interface

There is one additional piece of complexity to the rich error handling mechanism. Once a client receives an **HRESULT** error, it cannot

Interface Member	Description
HRESULT GetDescription(BSTR *pBstrDescription*);	Returns a short string describing the error.
HRESULT GetSource(BSTR *pBstrSource*);	**GetSource( )** is used to identify the component on which the error occurred. If you have a section of code that uses multiple objects and is surrounded by a **try/catch** block, identifying which object type caused the error helps locate what happened. Generally the source will contain the ProgID of the component.
HRESULT GetGUID(GUID *pGUID*);	Indicates on which interface a particular error occurred. Since each object can support multiple interfaces, an error code is not unique to a particular object. The GUID adds the additional uniqueness identifier.
HRESULT GetHelpContext(DWORD *pdwHelpContext*);	Returns the help context ID related to the error.
HRESULT GetHelpFile(BSTR *pBstrHelpFile*);	Returns the help file path that contains documentation of the error.

Interface Members of **IErrorInfo**
Table 9-2.

ISupportErrorInfo is the interface that determines whether an object supports **IErrorInfo.**

immediately call into the **IErrorInfo** interface. It first needs to check that the interface that returned the error does actually support rich error handling. The reason for this is that although there is only one **IErrorInfo** interface on a particular component, not every interface supported by the component will necessarily have rich error handling information. For example, **IInterface1** may populate the rich error handling information, but **IInterface2**, which is supported by the same component, may not populate the **IErrorInfo** data. The client, therefore, needs to ask the component whether a particular interface supports **IErrorInfo**.

To do this, a client first needs to request the **ISupportErrorInfo** interface. The **ISupportErrorInfo** interface has only one method: **InterfaceSupportsErrorInfo( )**. This method takes a **REFIID** to the interface, returning an **HRESULT** of **S_OK** if the interface GUID corresponds to an interface that supports **IErrorInfo** and **S_FALSE** otherwise. The prototype for **InterfaceSupportsErrorInfo( )** is shown here:

```
HRESULT InterfaceSupportsErrorInfo(REFIID refID);
```

Figure 9-2 shows a diagram of the full process on the **Stopwatch** object.

Adding ISupportErrorInfo to the Stopwatch Project

You may recall from Chapter 3 that one of the options in the New ATL Object dialog was a check box enabling support for **ISupportErrorInfo**. Although we did not select this option at that time, in general you probably will for your own projects. We are now going to add **ISupportErrorInfo** to the existing **Stopwatch** project, thereby demonstrating what code the wizard adds if you select this option from the start.

To begin, add **ISupportErrorInfo** to the list of classes from which **CStopwatch** is derived. As you saw in the previous chapter, if you add a new interface, you must also insert it into the COM MAP so that when a client calls **QueryInterface( )** to request **ISupportErrorInfo**, the requested interface is returned. You also need to declare the **InterfaceSupportsErrorInfo( )**

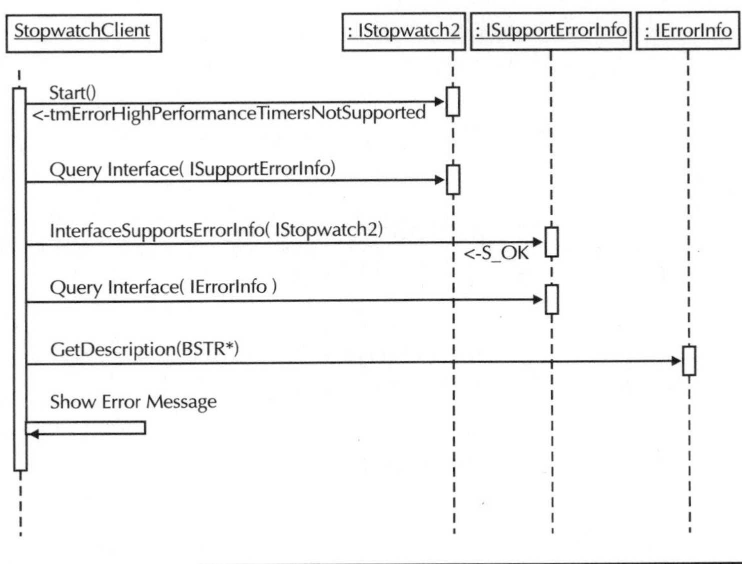

A use case view of rich error handling
Figure 9-2.

9

function within your class. You need to override this method because not only is it a pure virtual function in **ISupportErrorInfo** but also you have to identify which interfaces will support **IErrorInfo**. The code below indicates the necessary changes to **Stopwatch.h**.

```
////////////////////////////////////////////////////////////////////////
// CStopwatch
class ATL_NO_VTABLE CStopwatch :
  public CComObjectRootEx<CComSingleThreadModel>,
  public CComCoClass<CStopwatch, &CLSID_Stopwatch>,
  public IStopwatch,
  public ISupportErrorInfo,
  public IDispatchImpl<IStopwatch2, &IID_IStopwatch2,
    &LIBID_TIMERSLib, tmLibraryVersionMajor,
    tmLibraryVersionMinor>
{
...
BEGIN_COM_MAP(CStopwatch)
  COM_INTERFACE_ENTRY(IStopwatch)
  COM_INTERFACE_ENTRY(IStopwatch2)
  COM_INTERFACE_ENTRY(ISupportErrorInfo)
  COM_INTERFACE_ENTRY(IDispatch)
END_COM_MAP()

// ISupportsErrorInfo
      STDMETHOD(InterfaceSupportsErrorInfo)(REFIID riid);

...
}
```

Since in the above code we added the declaration for **InterfaceSupportsErrorInfo( )**, we also need to add the implementation to **Stopwatch.cpp** as shown below:

```
...
////////////////////////////////////////////////////////////////////////
// CStopwatch
STDMETHODIMP CStopwatch::InterfaceSupportsErrorInfo(REFIID riid)
{
  static const IID* arr[] =
  {
    &IID_IStopwatch,
```

```
    &IID_IStopwatch2,
  };
  for (int i=0; i < sizeof(arr) / sizeof(arr[0]); i++)
  {
    if (InlineIsEqualGUID(*arr[i],riid))
      return S_OK;
  }
  return S_FALSE;
}

HRESULT CStopwatch::FinalConstruct()
...
```

By default, if you select the **ISupportErrorInfo** option, the ATL wizard will add the above code for you. However, each time you add a new interface, you must be sure to update the **arr** array with the new interface (assuming of course that it supports **IErrorInfo**). If you fail to do this, the call to **ISupportErrorInfo** will return **S_FALSE**, and rich error handling will not be enabled.

IErrorInfo is implemented automatically by ATL.

You will notice that we have explicitly added support for **ISupportErrorInfo**, but we did not explicitly do this for **IErrorInfo**. The reason for this is that the ATL code has already implemented this for us. Therefore, if you were to call **QueryInterface( )** and request a pointer to the **IErrorInfo** interface, the call would return successfully.

At this point, we have gone through the process of adding all the necessary declarations to indicate to the client that we support **IErrorInfo**, but we are not actually using the rich error handling mechanism—we are not populating the **IErrorInfo** data. We need to therefore change **Start( )** and **ElapsedTime( )**, the two functions that return custom errors, so that they supply the required rich error handling information.

ATL has made the setting of these values relatively easy. All you need to do is call the **Error( )** method on **CComCoClass**, one of the classes from which **CStopwatch** is derived. The prototype for the simplest version of **CComCoClass::Error( )** is shown below:

static HRESULT Error(LPCOLESTR *target*, const IID& *iid* = GUID_NULL,
HRESULT *result* = 0);

However, **Error( )** is overloaded, so there are also versions that take resource IDs rather than strings and other versions that allow you to pass the help context ID and the help filename.

Before using the **Error( )** function in the stopwatch code, it is worthwhile to briefly discuss what the function does under the covers. It turns out that in order to set the error info, we need to use the **ICreateErrorInfo** interface, whose declaration is found in **oaidl.idl** and is shown below.

```
interface ICreateErrorInfo: IUnknown
{
    typedef [unique] ICreateErrorInfo * LPCREATEERRORINFO;
    HRESULT SetGUID( [in] REFGUID rguid );
    HRESULT SetSource( [in] LPOLESTR szSource );
    HRESULT SetDescription( [in] LPOLESTR szDescription );
    HRESULT SetHelpFile( [in] LPOLESTR szHelpFile );
    HRESULT SetHelpContext( [in] DWORD dwHelpContext );
}
```

You will notice that the information simply mirrors **IErrorInfo**, providing methods for setting the error information rather than retrieving it. Therefore, **CComCoClass::Error( )** calls **QueryInterface( )** to retrieve a pointer to **ICreateErrorInfo**, and then it calls each of its methods and sets the rich error handling information. Another point to mention about **CComCoClass::Error( )** is that it includes an assertion that checks that your **HRESULT** code is between 0x200 and 0xffff, a requirement we detailed in the previous section.

Although we have not yet discussed the details of multiple threads, you can probably guess that if multiple threads were accessing the object simultaneously, it would be possible for one thread to use the error information of a different thread. To avoid this problem, ATL automatically assigns a different error object to each thread.

Let's now make the last edit to the **Stopwatch** object so as to support rich error handling. A complete listing of the final **Stopwatch.cpp** file is shown below:

```
// Stopwatch.cpp : Implementation of CStopwatch
#include "stdafx.h"
#include "Timers.h"
#include "Stopwatch.h"

#include <mmsystem.h> // Multimedia timers

/////////////////////////////////////////////////////////////////////////////
// CStopwatch
STDMETHODIMP CStopwatch::InterfaceSupportsErrorInfo(REFIID riid)
{
  static const IID* arr[] =
```

```
  {
    &IID_IStopwatch,
    &IID_IStopwatch2,
  };
  for (int i=0; i < sizeof(arr) / sizeof(arr[0]); i++)
  {
    if (InlineIsEqualGUID(*arr[i],riid))
      return S_OK;
  }
  return S_FALSE;
}

HRESULT CStopwatch::FinalConstruct()
{
  // Set the type library version numbers
#ifdef _DEBUG
  HRESULT hr;
  CComPtr<ITypeLib> pTypeLib;
  hr = AtlModuleLoadTypeLib(&_Module, 0, &(CComBSTR)NULL, &pTypeLib);
  TLIBATTR* ptla;
  hr = pTypeLib->GetLibAttr(&ptla);
  ATLASSERT(_tih.m_wMajor == ptla->wMajorVerNum);
  ATLASSERT(_tih.m_wMinor == ptla->wMinorVerNum);
#endif

  // Save the frequency of the performance counters
  QueryPerformanceFrequency ((LARGE_INTEGER*) &m_nFrequency);
  CComDispatchDriver
  Start();
  ElapsedTime( &m_nOverhead );

  // Initialize the remaining member variables
  m_nStartTime.QuadPart = 0;

  return S_OK;
}


STDMETHODIMP CStopwatch::Start()
{
  if ( QueryPerformanceCounter( (LARGE_INTEGER*) &m_nStartTime) )
    return S_OK;
  else
  {
    Error("The hardware does not support the high "
      "performance counters", GUID_NULL,
      tmErrorHighPerformanceTimersNotSupported);
```

9

```
    return tmErrorHighPerformanceTimersNotSupported;
  }
}

STDMETHODIMP CStopwatch::ElapsedTime(float *Time)
{
  HRESULT hr;
  LARGE_INTEGER nStopTime;

  // Set the stop time immediately so that a minimum
  // amount of timer code is executed between the start
  // and stop times
  if ( !QueryPerformanceCounter( (LARGE_INTEGER*) &nStopTime ) )
  {
    Error("The hardware does not support the high "
      "performance counters", GUID_NULL,
      tmErrorHighPerformanceTimersNotSupported);
    return tmErrorHighPerformanceTimersNotSupported;
  }
  else if (m_nStartTime.QuadPart == 0)
  {
    hr = tmErrorStartNotCalled;
    Error("Start needs to be called before ElapsedTime.",
      GUID_NULL, tmErrorStartNotCalled);
  }
  else
  {
    *Time = (float) (nStopTime.QuadPart - m_nStartTime.QuadPart);
    *Time = (*Time / m_nFrequency.QuadPart);
    hr = S_OK;
  }

  return hr;
}

STDMETHODIMP CStopwatch::get_Overhead(float *pOverhead)
{
  *pOverhead = m_nOverhead;
  return S_OK;
}

STDMETHODIMP CStopwatch::put_Overhead(float OverheadValue)
{
  m_nOverhead = OverheadValue;
```

```
  return S_OK;
}
```

The edits are relatively simple. Simply call **CComCoClass::Error( )**, specifying the error description text along with the **HRESULT** value. In the **Error( )** call, the same **helpstring** text that accompanied the error enumeration values declared in the IDL is used for the error description text. (The In-Depth box provides one way you can retrieve the error text from the enumeration **helpstring** dynamically at runtime.) As you can see, once you add the **ISupportErrorInfo** interface support, providing rich error handling information is simply a one-line call to **Error( )**.

If for some reason you don't have access to the **CComCoClass::Error( )**, you can also use the **AtlReportError( )** function, which achieves the same result.

IN DEPTH

Retrieving the Error Message from the Type Library

One advantage of defining your error codes inside an enumeration within your IDL is that you are able to provide help strings that accompany the enumeration values. This allows developers to view explanations of each enumeration rather than just viewing the values. Because the help strings have already been provided, you simply return these strings when the error occurs, rather than writing an entirely new string.

One way to do this is to retrieve the error string from the type library using the **ITypeLib** and **ITypeInfo** interfaces. Both of these interfaces are supported by default in an ATL component. Below is a listing of the code that retrieves the type library interfaces and then calls into them in order to get the helpstring attributes for the error enumeration values.

```
#define SET_ERROR_INFO(hr) SetErrorInfo(hr, L#hr)

HRESULT SetErrorInfo(HRESULT hr, WCHAR* ErrorName)
{
  HRESULT hresult;
  CComPtr<ITypeLib> pTypeLib;
```

IN DEPTH

CONTINUED

```
  CComPtr<ITypeInfo> pTypeInfo;
  USHORT NumberOfIds = 1;
  MEMBERID Id;
  unsigned long lHashVal = 0;

  CComBSTR name(ErrorName);
  CComBSTR error_message;

  hresult = AtlModuleLoadTypeLib(
    &_Module, 0, &(CComBSTR)NULL, &pTypeLib);
  if (SUCCEEDED(hresult))
  {
    hresult = pTypeLib->FindName(name,
      0, &pTypeInfo, &Id, &NumberOfIds);
  }
  if(SUCCEEDED(hresult) && (Id != MEMBERID_NIL ) )
  {
    hresult = pTypeInfo->GetDocumentation(
      Id, NULL, &error_message, NULL, NULL);
  }
  if(SUCCEEDED(hresult))
  {
    AtlReportError(__uuidof(Stopwatch), error_message,
      IID_IStopwatch,
      hr );
  }
  return hresult;
}
```

To begin, pointers to the **ITypeLib** and **ITypeInfo** interfaces are declared using the **CComPtr** template. This template serves a purpose similar to the **_com_ptr_t** template discussed in Chapter 5. **CComPtr**, however, is designed to be used inside ATL, as it does not throw any exceptions. Next, the type library is retrieved from the module using **AtlModuleLoadTypeLib( )**. Assuming this call completes successfully, the **ITypeLib**::**FindName( )** function is called. This searches for the item in the type library whose name matches **name**. The key item returned from **ITypeLib**::**FindName( )** is the **ITypeInfo** interface pointer. This pointer is used to retrieve the **helpstring** via a call to

IN DEPTH
CONTINUED

ITypeInfo::GetDocumentation( ). Once the help string has been retrieved, it is used as the error message text in a call to **AtlReportError( )**.

Rather than using the **SetErrorInfo( )** function directly, you should use the **SET_ERROR_INFO( )** macro. The reason for this is that the **ITypeLib** and **ITypeInfo** interfaces are looking for the strings that appear in the type library, not the values. By using the **SET_ERROR_INFO** macro, you automatically convert a value into its string equivalent using the macro # syntax. This way, the name of the enumerator and the string value of the name will always match. The **SET_ERROR_INFO( )** macro is illustrated by the **ElapsedTime( )** function shown here:

```
STDMETHODIMP CStopwatch::ElapsedTime(float *Time)
{
  HRESULT hr;
  LARGE_INTEGER nStopTime;

  // Set the stop time immediately so that a minimum
  // amount of timer code is executed between the start
  // and stop times
  if ( !QueryPerformanceCounter( (LARGE_INTEGER*) &nStopTime ) )
  {
    // Report error using SET_ERROR_INFO macro
    SET_ERROR_INFO(tmErrorHighPerformanceTimersNotSupported);
    return tmErrorHighPerformanceTimersNotSupported;
  }
  else if (m_nStartTime.QuadPart == 0)
  {
    // Report error using SET_ERROR_INFO macro
    SET_ERROR_INFO(tmErrorStartNotCalled);
    hr = tmErrorStartNotCalled;
  }
  else
  {
    *Time = (float) (nStopTime.QuadPart -
           m_nStartTime.QuadPart);

    *Time = (*Time / m_nFrequency.QuadPart);
```

IN DEPTH
CONTINUED

```
    hr = S_OK;
  }

  return hr;
}
```

In this code listing, the **SET_ERROR_INFO( )** macro is used rather than a call to **CComCoClass::Error( )**.

Retrieving the help string from the type library is useful not only in a COM server but also in a client. Retrieving the help string allows the client to retrieve the error message corresponding to an error enumeration value even if the COM server does not support rich error handling.

Reading in the type library has other uses besides error handling. For example, you could write a small program that could read through a type library and output an HTML file that documents an interface, or even write a program that could read the type library of any component and display what methods and properties are supported so as to allow a user to call them dynamically.

Using Rich Error Handling at the Client

Now that we have updated the **Stopwatch** component to provide rich error handling information, we need to update the client to use this functionality. If you look back at Figure 9-2, you will see that from the client perspective, retrieving the error can be quite an involved process. Fortunately, however, **#import** simplifies the required code significantly. Below is a listing of the necessary updates for the **StopwatchClient.cpp** file:

```
int main(int argc, char* argv[])
{
  int n_return = 0;
  CoInitialize( NULL );
  try
  {
    IStopwatchPtr pStopwatch(__uuidof(Stopwatch));
```

```
#ifdef CREATE_RUNTIME_ERROR
    // ERROR!!!!
    // Intentionally introduce an error to test the
    // error handling mechanism
    pStopwatch->ElapsedTime();
#endif

    UseStopwatch(pStopwatch);
  }
  catch(_com_error e)
  {
    std::cout << "ERROR(" << e.Error() << "):  ";
    if( e.Description().length() > 0)
      std::cout << (char*)e.Description() << std::endl;
    else
      std::cout << e.ErrorMessage() << std::endl;
    n_return = 1;
  }

  CoUninitialize();
  return n_return;
}
```

In the code above you will notice a **#ifdef** directive around the call to **ElapsedTime( )**. This is for testing the error handling mechanism. If you define **CREATE_RUNTIME_ERROR**, the **Stopwatch** component will report an error, and the rich error handling mechanism will kick in and display the error text reported by the **Stopwatch** component.

One thing to remember is that **ErrorMessage( )** and **Description( )** return different data types. The former returns a **TCHAR*** and the latter an **_bstr_t**. Forgetting this detail is a common source of errors. This is why in the **catch** code above, **e.Description( )** is cast to a **char***, while **e.ErrorMessage( )** is not. Since **std::cout** does not support wide characters, all strings must be converted to **char*** before being output. If you wish to output a wide character string using the standard library, use **std::wout** instead.

_com_error

Let's now look a little more closely at **_com_error**, a topic that we introduced in Chapter 5. **_com_error** is defined inside **comdef.h**. As far as the class members go, **_com_error** is essentially a wrapper of **IErrorInfo** with some additional functionality added for good measure. Table 9-3 shows the most commonly used class members in **_com_error**.

Class Member	Description
_com_error(HRESULT *hr*, IErrorInfo **pErrorInfo* = NULL) throw( ); _com_error(const _com_error &*error*) throw( );	There are two constructors. The first takes a pointer to an **IErrorInfo** interface along with the **HRESULT**, and the second takes another **_com_error**.
HRESULT Error( ) const throw( );	**Error( )** returns the **HRESULT** corresponding to the error.
_bstr_t Description( ) const throw ( );	**Description( )** returns the error message stored in **IErrorInfo::GetDescription( )**.
_bstr_t Source( ) const throw( );	The program ID of the object that caused the error. Corresponds with **IErrorInfo::GetSource( )**.
DWORD HelpContext( ) const throw( );	The help context ID stored in **IErrorInfo::GetHelpContext( )**.
_bstr_t HelpFile( ) const throw( );	The help filename returned by **IErrorInfo::GetHelpFile( )**.
const TCHAR * ErrorMessage( ) const throw( );	**ErrorMessage( )** retrieves the system error message corresponding to a standard **HRESULT**. **ErrorMessage( )** calls the API function **FormatMessage( )** to retrieve the system text for the **HRESULT** value. If the **HRESULT** is not a standard value, but rather a custom error returned by the component, then the returned string is "Unknown error <hresult>," where the <hresult> is in hexadecimal form.
IErrorInfo * ErrorInfo( ) const throw( );	**ErrorInfo( )** returns the **IErrorInfo** pointer that contains the latest error.

Most Commonly Used **_com_error** Class Members
Table 9-3.

Looking at the **_com_error** class may cause you to wonder why you would not simply use the **IErrorInfo** interface. There is a lot of duplication between the two, but the addition of the **ErrorMessage( )** function alone makes **_com_error** well worth using. The amount of code that has to be written to call the API function **FormatMessage( )** is not something you will want to repeat too often. The real power of **_com_error**, however, comes when it is used in conjunction with **_com_raise_error** and **_com_raise_errorex**.

Debugging Your ATL Code

Before we end the chapter, let's look at some mechanisms provided for debugging your code.

Writing Messages to the Debug Windows

Writing a trace message out to the debug window involves using the **AtlTrace( )** function. **AtlTrace( )** uses a **printf** style of writing strings to the debug window. Therefore, it takes a variable number of arguments, the first of which is the format string. The prototype for **AtlTrace( )** is shown here:

void _cdecl AtlTrace(LPCTSTR *format*, ...);

There is also a macro version of **AtlTrace( )**, which is **ATLTRACE( )**. Do not let the macro version deceive you into thinking that **AtlTrace( )** still produces tracing when in a release build—it does not. The difference is that in a release compile **ATLTRACE( )** becomes **(void) 0**, which is essentially nothing. This is more efficient (although not noticeably) than the **AtlTrace( )** version, which continues to have code execute, but the code does nothing. Thus, you should use the macro version, **ATLTRACE( )**, in release builds because it does nothing more efficiently than **AtlTrace( )**! Below is an example that writes out the error message to the debug window: 9

```
#include <atlbase.h>
...
  catch(_com_error e)
  {
    ATLTRACE(_T("ERROR(%d):  "), e.Error());
    std::cout << "ERROR(" << e.Error() << "):  ";
    //if( e.Description().length() > 0)
    {
      std::cout << (char*)e.Description() << std::endl;
      ATLTRACE(_T("%s\n"), (TCHAR*)e.Description());
    }
    //else
    {
      ATLTRACE(_T("%s\n"), e.ErrorMessage());
      std::cout << e.ErrorMessage() << std::endl;
```

```
    }
    n_return = 1;
  }
...
```

Since the above code is found in the client and the client does not have access to ATL, you will have to include **atlbase.h** in order to use the above trace functionality.

There is also the **ATLTRACE2( )** macro, which has the added advantage of message levels and categories. In other words, **ATLTRACE( )** always writes out the debug information; whereas with **ATLTRACE2( )**, you can change a global flag for either the category or the level, and you can immediately change what ends up getting written to the debug windows.

ATLTRACE2( ) is declared like this:

ATLTRACE2(DWORD *what*, UINT *priority*, LPCSTR *format*, ...)

The first parameter, *what*, determines what will be traced. This parameter can be one or more of various predefined constants, such as **atlTraceGeneral**, **atlTraceCOM**, and **atlTraceRefcount**. The *priority* is the priority you place on displaying the message. The lower the number, the higher the priority.

Whether or not a trace message is written depends on what categories you define and what trace level you set. The first of these is done using the **ATL_TRACE_CATEGORY** macro. For example, if you want both the general and COM categories of macros to appear, you would use

```
ATL_TRACE_CATEGORY atlTraceGeneral | atlTraceCOM
```

To use the second method to filter your messages, you would use **ATL_TRACE_LEVEL**. For example, if you wish to display only messages that are at a level 2 or less, you would use

```
ATL_TRACE_LEVEL 2
```

Items that are less critical, for example, will use the **ATLTRACE2( )** macro with level 4 so that they will not be displayed when the programmer is not interested in that level of detail.

Verifying All Is Well Using ATLASSERT( )

Another useful function is the **ATLASSERT( )** macro.

ATLASSERT(*expr*)

ATLASSERT( ) causes a program assertion using **_CrtDbgReport( )** whenever the *expr* value is false. The assertion fires inside only a debug build since in a release build it simply compiles to **(void) 0**. Therefore, **ATLASSERT( )** is used to identify programming errors during development only.

Debugging QueryInterface( ) and Reference Counting

Not only is the preceding tracing mechanism useful for debugging your own code, but Microsoft has added some built-in tracing for the reference counting code within ATL. Since it is quite common for a reference counting issue to occur, Microsoft has added a built-in mechanism for watching the reference counting calls and calls to **QueryInterface( )** within your server.

There is a **#define** constant that turns on reference counting trace messages. The name of the constant is **_ATL_DEBUG_INTERFACES**, and if you declare it inside **stdafx.h**, prior to including **atlcom.h**, then trace messages will be output indicating the current reference count and whether it is being incremented or decremented, as shown in Figure 9-3. (Note that you must define **_ATL_DEBUG_INTERFACES** before **atlcom.h**, or it will have no effect.)

Here is the code:

```
...
#define _ATL_APARTMENT_THREADED

#define _ATL_DEBUG_INTERFACES

#include <atlbase.h>
//You may derive a class from CComModule and use
// it if you want to override something, but do
// not change the name of _Module
extern CComModule _Module;
#include <atlcom.h>
...
```

One other constant, **_ATL_DEBUG_QI**, does not provide the same level of detail but simply lists which interfaces are being requested. Both of these debugging facilities can be great tools when you are having reference counting problems or when you want to know which interfaces are being queried for in your client. Programmers often turn on these tools by default because they are not included in released versions.

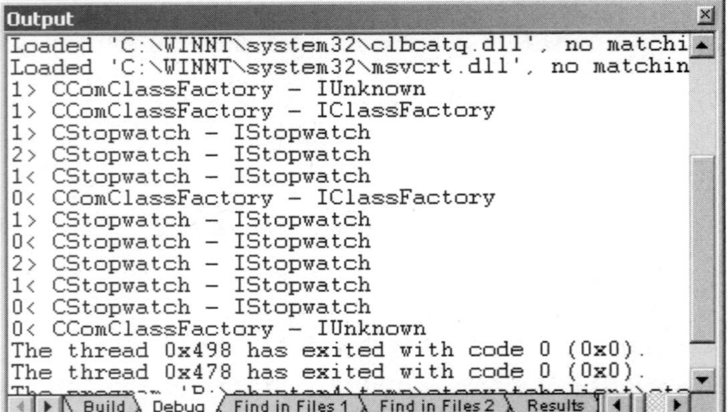

Reference counting trace messages
Figure 9-3.

Running Both a Client and a Server in the Debugger

Depending on the type of development you are doing, you will often find that you are writing both a COM client and a COM server. For example, you will often create both a client and a server for testing purposes. Given this need, you will find it useful to step through the code in both a server and a client, switching from one to the next as your program executes.

To do this you should use the following steps:

1. Add both the client and the server to the same workspace. (From the Project menu, select Insert Project Into Workspace.)
2. Compile both projects using the debug configurations.
3. Set the server as the active project. (Right-click on the project and select Set as Active Project.)
4. Place break points in the code of either the server or the client.
5. Run the project. At this point you will see a dialog asking for the executable filename.
6. Enter the full path to the debug version of the client application.

Once you have done this, your code will halt on the specified break points, and you will be able to step into each piece of code.

Another way to debug both the client and the server at the same time is to enter the path to the Visual Studio IDE in step 5. This will launch a second instance of Visual Studio from which you can load the client project and run it. A similar method can be especially useful if you are trying to debug a Visual Basic client along with a C++ server. In this last case, you would enter the path to the Visual Basic IDE in step 5. Lastly, to debug an executable server, run the server inside the debugger first, and then launch the client application from inside another instance of Visual Studio.

CHAPTER 10

Events

In the preceding nine chapters, we have focused on how a client calls a server. What we have not covered, however, is how a server initiates a call to a client. In this chapter we will examine the mechanism that makes this possible: the event.

To understand why events are important, imagine that you want to create a countdown timer component that notifies the client when a specified time has elapsed. To do this, the timer component must be able to call back to the client when the specified amount of time has passed. Using the techniques discussed so far, there is no way for such a callback to occur. COM events are the mechanism that allow this to take place.

An Event Overview

A server communicates with a client by generating an event. But this raises a fundamental question: How does the client know that an event has been generated? As was briefly suggested in Chapter 3, the crudest method is for the client to poll the server repeatedly, each time asking if the event has occurred yet. Although appropriate in some circumstances, the disadvantages of polling are considerable. First, polling is extremely inefficient, especially when the events occur relatively rarely. To poll a server continually for an event that occurs only a few times a day results in a significant waste in processing power and, if such polling takes place over the network, unnecessary round-trip calls. Second, the accuracy in detecting the event is dependent on the frequency with which the polling takes place. In other words, how quickly the client can respond to a server event is dependent on how often the client polls the server to ask whether the event has occurred yet.

A server notifies a client by firing an event.

An alternative to polling is for the server to notify the client when the event occurs. In this manner, once the server detects the event, it can immediately call into the client directly without waiting for the client to initiate a call to the server first. This is the method used by COM. It works like this: When the server has something to tell the client, the server calls (through an interface) a method inside the client. In the language of COM, when such a call is made, the server is said to have *fired* an event.

As far as COM is concerned, there is no inherent difference between the way a server communicates with a client and the way a client communicates with a server. The only requirement is that both the server and the client support an interface. In fact, the distinction between the client and the server becomes blurred. Which part of the system is considered the client and which is considered the server depends on who is calling whom. When the client is calling the server, as we have seen in the book so far, it is easy to distinguish which is which. When the server begins to call back into the client for the purposes of event notification, however, the server essentially becomes a client to the client (which has become a server). Thus, both components must be capable of being either a client or a server.

An event source is a component that generates events.

An event listener is a component that waits for events to occur.

Rather than talking about clients and servers, we need to introduce new terminology for purposes of understanding events. The first term is *event source*. An event source is a COM component that is reporting events back to other components. These "other components" are known as *event sinks*, or *listeners*, because they are waiting to be notified of the events that the server is reporting. Notice that both the event source and the event listener are COM components, hence the ambiguity between which component is the server and which is the client.

Returning to the countdown example, a simple countdown timer (the source component) would supply a "register" method that the client, or listener, calls to notify the countdown object that the listener should be called when the countdown time has elapsed. This method will include a parameter by which the listener passes a pointer to itself, for the countdown component to call back on. For COM, this register method is usually called **Advise( )**. The server would also have a method, **Interval( )** for example, on which the listener could call to set the length of the countdown. After calling **Interval( )** and returning, the listener would wait for notification from the countdown component on when the time has expired. Figure 10-1 shows this simple process. Eventually, when the listener no longer needed notification from the source, it would call **Unadvise( )** to disconnect from the source component.

There are at least two requirements for such an event notification to work using the COM framework. First, the listener needs to support a COM interface that the source component knows about in order for the source component to be able to call into the client. Second, the server needs to have, or be able to obtain, a pointer to the client (or clients) interface, without which there would be nothing to call into.

The source interface is supported by the client (listener) in order for the server (event source) to call back to the client.

The distinguishing characteristic from any of the scenarios we have considered in previous chapters is that now both the client *and* the server support an interface. This is necessary because in order for the client to receive an event notification it needs to receive a call from the server. This could even be a call that is made out of process and across a network. Since COM allows for location independence when going from the client to the server, the same requirement exists when going in the reverse—from the

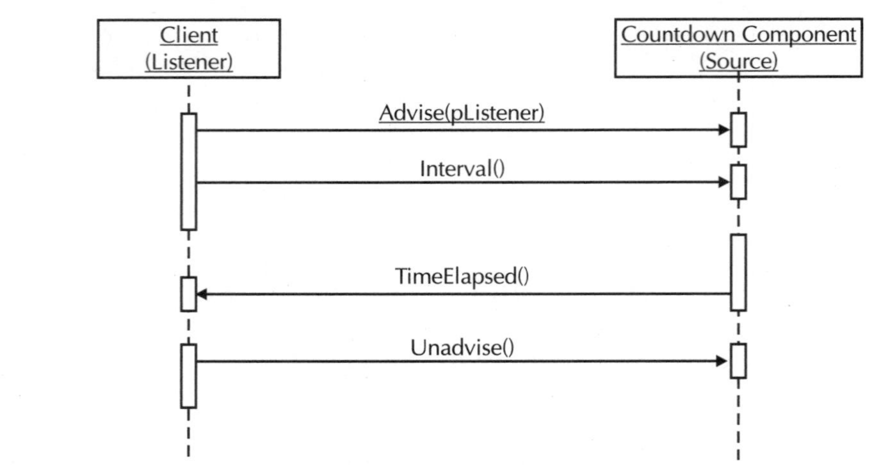

The interaction between a listener and its event source

Figure 10-1.

The source interface is usually defined by the source component (the server) rather than by the client that actually implements the interface.

source (server) back to the listener (client). Otherwise, the server would not have true location independence.

The client, therefore, needs to support a COM interface for the server to call back on. The interesting thing about this interface is that it is generally defined by the source component, even though it is the listener that is required to actually implement the interface. In other words, the component server contains the interface definition the client will support. This is known as the *source interface*.

Connection Points

Although the mechanism just described presents an overview of the COM event notification system, it is a bit more complicated when a component actually implements it. Consider, for example, the fact that a component could support many event interfaces. Furthermore, when calling the **Advise( )** method, how does the server distinguish between two different listener interfaces so that it disconnects the correct one when **Unadvise( )** is called?

Since the mechanism for connecting to an event server is essentially generic, Microsoft has engineered a standard set of interfaces for the purpose. This set of interfaces is known as *connection points*. Let's now take a look at the connection point process. To do this we will return to the countdown example and look at the interaction between the client and the server component in a little more detail. Figure 10-2 provides an overview of the process.

Before we look at each of the five steps indicated on the diagram, notice the two connection point interfaces. **IConnectionPoint** is the interface on which a client registers its desire to receive events. In other words, it supports the **Advise( )** and **Unadvise( )** methods. The second interface, **IConnectionPointContainer**, is responsible for keeping a list of all the **IConnectionPoint** interfaces supported by the source component. A source component can fire notifications to multiple sets of different source interfaces, and **IConnectionPointContainer** holds the master list for each of these. Let's now take a look at the process.

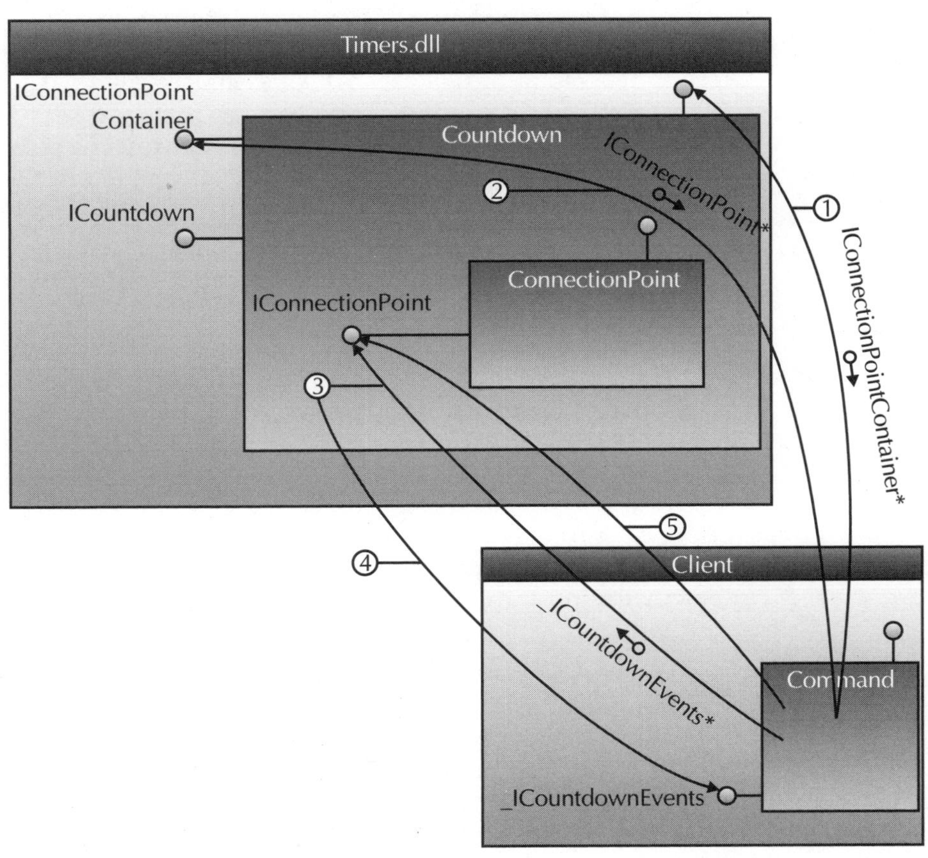

Connection points interaction diagram
Figure 10-2.

The steps for establishing the connection are as follows:

1. The client calls **QueryInterface( )** on the server component and requests the **IConnectionPointContainer** interface.
2. Using the **IConnectionPointContainer** interface, the client calls **FindConnectionPoint( )**, passing in the interface ID for **_ICountdownEvents**, which is the source interface on which it wants to receive event notification.
3. Using the **IConnectionPoint** interface, the listener calls **Advise( )**. This call establishes the connection so that when an event occurs within the **Countdown** component, it will notify the listener.

   You will notice in Figure 10-2 that the **IConnectionPoint** interface appears as an embedded component within the **Countdown** component. This is not a typical COM object, in the sense that there is no CLSID associated with it. Since **IConnectionPoint** is not an interface that can be retrieved via a call to **QueryInterface( )** on the **Countdown** component, and because there is essentially a separate reference count on the **IConnectionPoint**, it is a separate component with a unique COM identity. As we shall see later in the chapter, ATL's implementation hides the details of the separate object implementation.
4. Once the listener has called **Advise( )** and passed a pointer to its sink interface, the source component can call into the sink interface whenever notification is required.
5. Once a listener no longer wants to receive notification (such as when it is shutting down), it should call **Unadvise( )** on the **IConnectionPoint** interface to cancel the notification subscription.

The Connection Point Interfaces

Of the two connection point interfaces, **IConnectionPoint** is the easiest to understand the need for and also probably the one client programmers will interact with most. A listing of its class members is shown in Table 10-1.

The functions that are most important for us are **Advise( )** and **Unadvise( )**. As we saw in the overview, these are used to register with an event source that you want to receive event notification and then cancel this registration once you no longer need it. You will notice that the **Advise( )** method returns a *cookie*, via the *pdwCookie* parameter, back to the client. The purpose of the cookie is to provide an identifier to the listener's collection so that when it calls **Unadvise( )**, the server is able to identify which connection the listener wishes to disconnect.

Class Member	Description
HRESULT Advise(IUnknown **pUnkSink*, DWORD **pdwCookie*);	Registers the listener component with the client so that it is notified of the events particular to the source interface associated with the **IConnectionPoint** instance. *pUnkSink* is a pointer to the client interface that the source component will call back on. *pdwCookie* is a unique identifier that the client will use to disconnect from the component.
Unadvise(DWORD *dwCookie*);	Allows the listener to notify the source component that it is no longer interested in being notified of events on the interface associated with the **IConnectionPoint** instance.
HRESULT GetConnectionInterface(IID **pIID*);	Returns the GUID corresponding to the event interface that is supported by the **IConnectionPoint** interface instance.
EnumConnections(IEnumConnections ***ppConEnum*);	Provides an interface through which a client can iterate each of the connected objects.
HRESULT GetConnectionPointContainer(IConnectionPointContainer ***ppCont*);	Returns the **IConnectionPointContainer** that is responsible for managing the set of all connection points available on the component.

IConnection-Point Class Members
Table 10-1.

The first parameter on the **Advise( )** method points to an **IUnknown** interface. This will be the callback interface that the source component will use to call back to the client. Before the callback is made, the server will have to call **QueryInterface( )** in order to retrieve the **IDispatch** interface or the source interface supported by the listener.

The **GetConnectionInterface( )** method allows a client to find out which event interface this connection point is associated with. The

EnumConnections( ) function is actually more useful to the server than it is to the client because it provides quick access to each of the listener interface instances to call back on.

The last method, **GetConnectionPointContainer( )**, returns a pointer to the **IConnectionPointContainer** interface. The key to understanding why **IConnectionPointContainer** is necessary is to realize that each component can have more than one event interface. Consider, for example, a database table object: You could have one event interface that fires when the table definition changes, such as when adding a new column, and another event interface for when the data within the table changes. Supporting all the various table change events via two interfaces breaks up the events into categories: data definition events (the table definition; columns, indexes, etc.) versus data modification events (adding, deleting, or updating records within the table).

Supporting multiple interfaces can be a performance asset, too, because it allows the client to listen to a smaller set of all the events that an object may fire. If a component has one large event interface, listeners will receive calls on every method, even if the event is not of interest. If, however, the interface is broken down into several smaller interfaces, a listener will be able to decrease the number of calls it receives from the server for events in which it is not interested.

Although connection points allow it, there is one drawback to supporting multiple event interfaces. Visual Basic is able to receive notifications only from the default event interface. In other words, event notification from components with multiple event interfaces is not fully supported by Visual Basic.

The **IConnectionPointContainer** keeps a list of the set of **IConnectionPoint** interfaces supported by the source component. Usually, the **IConnectionPoint** interface is not supported directly off of a component. In other words, usually you cannot successfully request an **IConnectionPoint** interface directly from a component object. Instead, you must request the **IConnectionPointContainer** interface and then use this interface to find the **IConnectionPoint** interface associated with the source interface you wish to receive notification from. Table 10-2 shows each of the **IConnectionPointContainer** class members.

Given all the complexity surrounding connection points, you may think that there is a lot of work to be done to support them. Although this is true, with ATL, Microsoft has essentially done most of this work for us. Let's see how it

Class Member	Description
HRESULT EnumConnectionPoints(IEnumConnectionPoints **ppConPEnum*);	Returns a collection of each of the event interfaces supported by the component.
HRESULT FindConnectionPoint(REFIID *riid*, IConnectionPoint **ppConP*);	Given the GUID of the event interface to receive notification on, a listener can use **FindConnectionPoint( )** to retrieve the associated **IConnectionPoint**.

IConnection-PointContainer Class Members
Table 10-2.

all fits together by first creating a server with connection points, and then creating a client that monitors the connection points.

Creating a COM Server That Supports Events

In this section we are going to add a new component to the **Timers** project. Until now, the **Timers.dll** had only one component, **Stopwatch**. Rather than a timer that counts time up, the new component we are about to add will count time down—that is, it will be a countdown timer.

Interface Design

The **Countdown** component will have a dual interface in addition to a source interface for its listeners to support. The dual interface, **ICountdown**, will be used to specify the interval and start the **Countdown** timer. The default method on **ICountdown** will be the **Interval** property that will set the timer to begin counting down from the specified interval value. Once the interval property is set, the component will immediately begin counting down. Setting the **Interval** property to zero will stop the countdown and reset it. In addition, **ICountdown** will support a read-only property called **TimeRemaining**, which the client can call to find out how much time is left before the countdown expires. Finally, the default interface will support an **IterationCount** property that the client can use to set how many times the countdown should run. For example, the **Interval** could be set to 60,000 milliseconds and the **IterationCount** to 5, in which case the countdown component will fire an event every minute for five minutes.

The interface declaration is shown here:

```
[
  object,
  uuid(6764B148-93BE-40C1-B2BA-81650C57E33E),
  dual,
  oleautomation,
  helpstring("ICountdown Interface"),
  pointer_default(unique)
]
interface ICountdown : IDispatch
{
  [propget, id(DISPID_VALUE),
    helpstring("The time period of the countdown in milliseconds.\
    When set to 0 the countdown is inactive.")]
    HRESULT Interval([out, retval] long *pInterval);
  [propput, id(DISPID_VALUE),
    helpstring("The time period of the countdown in milliseconds.\
    When set to 0 the countdown is inactive.")]
    HRESULT Interval([in] long Interval);
  [propget, id(1), helpstring("The amount of time \
    (in milliseconds) remaining before interval has elapsed.")]
    HRESULT TimeRemaining([out, retval] long *pTimeRemaining);
  [propget, id(2), helpstring("The number of times for the \
    countdown to repeat. The default, -1, signifies repeat \
    continuously.")]
    HRESULT IterationCount(
      [out, retval] long *pRemainingIterations);
  [propput, id(2), helpstring("The number of times for the \
    countdown to repeat. The default, -1, signifies repeat \
    continuously.")]
    HRESULT IterationCount([in]
      long NumberOfTimesToRepeatCountdown);
};
```

The use of **DISPID_VALUE** identifies the **Interval** property as the default property on the interface.

The second new interface to be added to the **Timers.idl** file is the source interface. As we have already discussed, this is not an interface that the source component, **Countdown**, implements. It is, however, still defined in the source component's IDL file because the source component knows best what events it can notify listeners about. The interface definition is shown here:

```
enum TmICountdownEventsDispatchId
{
  tmICountdownEventsDispatchIdOnTimeElapsed = 1
};
[
  uuid(95C0B4CE-A39B-463A-BE4B-06137333BD8E),
  helpstring("_ICountdownEvents Interface")
]
dispinterface _ICountdownEvents
{
  properties:
  methods:
  [id(tmICountdownEventsDispatchIdOnTimeElapsed),
    helpstring("This event fires when the countdown interval has \
      elapsed. RemainingIterations identifies how many more times\
      the countdown will fire.")]
    HRESULT OnTimeElapsed([in] long RemainingIterations);
};
```

There are two things noteworthy about this interface definition. First is the fact that an enumeration is defined for each of the dispatch IDs. We shall see later when we write the client how this is used. It is not a requirement but rather a convenience to clients when this is done because it prevents the client from having to define the enumeration or use hard-coded dispatch IDs for an interface that the server defines.

A dispinterface is an interface that supports each of the **IDispatch** methods but does not have an additional interface derived from it that can be called via direct vtable calls.

The second noteworthy item is that the interface uses the **dispinterface** IDL keyword for defining the interface rather than the **interface** keyword we have used throughout the book so far. **dispinterface** defines an **IDispatch** interface that is not a dual interface. In other words, it does not support a custom interface derived from **IDispatch**. This is known as a *dispinterface.*

Back in the stopwatch example, we could call **QueryInterface( )** and successfully request both the **IDispatch** and the **IStopwatch2** interfaces. **IStopwatch2** was derived from **IDispatch**. In contrast, dispinterfaces successfully return only the **IDispatch** interface, not the custom interface derived from **IDispatch** (because there is no custom interface derived from **IDispatch** in the dispinterface declaration case). To call into a dispinterface, you must use **Invoke( )** rather than the direct vtable call because there is no direct vtable to call except for the one on the dispatch interface.

As we discussed in the previous chapter, **IDispatch** is significantly less efficient than a dual interface, so why did ATL generate code with the **dispinterface** rather than a dual interface? There are three significant reasons. First, scripting languages cannot support anything but dispinterfaces, so they cannot be expected to implement a dual interface. (Remember, the client is the one that actually implements the interface, not the server.)

Second, if the client is a COM object itself, it probably already has a dual interface defined as its default interface. Having a client support two dual interfaces is difficult at best for C++ clients and not supported for Visual Basic clients; therefore, it is not usually a valid option. If you try this, you will find that the Visual Basic client will not even compile when you use the **WithEvents** syntax to define a variable that has a dual interface.

Last, using a dispinterface removes from a client the burden to implement all the methods on an interface. For example, if there were five methods on a dual interface, the client would have to implement all five, even if it was really interested in only one of the events fired. If a client, however, provides access only to the **IDispatch** interface, then it needs to support only the methods on the **IDispatch** interface. All calls from the source component to the listener will be made via **IDispatch::Invoke( )**. If the listener receives an **Invoke( )** call for a method with which it is not concerned, it can simply return **DISP_E_MEMBERNOTFOUND** to indicate that the method is not supported. Again, in contrast, if the vtable method was used and the method was not declared, at best the application would crash!

Let's take a quick look at the **_ICountdownEvents** interface. The name is prefixed with an underscore. This is because development environments such as Visual Basic treat such interfaces as hidden. The one method or *event* defined on this source interface is the **OnTimeElapsed( )** event. Once the interval of time has expired, the **Countdown** component will fire an event on its source interface, using the **OnTimeElapsed( )** method, to notify the client that the specified time interval has elapsed.

It is not enough to simply define the interface; you also need to attach it to the CoClass that will support the interface. This is done as part of the **Countdown** component declaration, as shown below:

```
[
  uuid(8D2B73A4-441E-49CA-B36B-D6F748C236D4),
  version(1.0),
```

```
    helpstring("Countdown Component 1.0")
  ]
  coclass Countdown
  {
    [default] interface ICountdown;
    [default, source] dispinterface _ICountdownEvents;
  };
```

Notice the use of both the **default** and **source** attributes in the **_ICountdownEvents** declaration. **source** is critical because it specifies the interface that the client should support if it wishes to receive events. **default** is used because multiple source interfaces could be supported and the **default** keyword identifies which one is the default. This is key for Visual Basic clients because they can listen to only one interface—the default interface. Many clients read the type library looking for this attribute in order to identify which source interface to implement.

Now that you have a good idea what the interfaces will look like, let's go ahead and build the **Countdown** component.

Adding the Countdown Component and Defining Its Interfaces

As described in Chapter 3, add a new ATL object to the **Timers** project. For the short name of the component, enter **Countdown**. On the Attributes tab, check the Support ISupportErrorInfo and Support Connection Points options. Leave the defaults for the remaining options.

After adding the component, from the Class View tab on the workspace window, select the **ICountdown** interface, and then right-click to add a property. The property should be called **Interval**, and the data type should be **long**. After adding the property, change the dispatch ID to **DISPID_VALUE** to make this the default property. Follow the same procedure to add the remaining properties described in the preceding section, "Interface Design."

Following the same procedure, add a method to the **_ICountdownEvent** interface. The method name should be **OnTimeElapsed** with a **helpstring** of "This event fires when the countdown interval has elapsed."

While you are editing the **Timers.idl** file, update the **MAJORVERSION** value to 3 along with the library **helpstring** to "Timers 3.0 Type Library." While changing the IDL file version, you should also update the DLL version in the resource file as we described in the previous chapter.

A full listing of the new IDL file is shown below with changes highlighted.

```
// Timers.idl : IDL source for Timers.dll
//

// This file will be processed by the MIDL tool to
// produce the type library (Timers.tlb) and marshalling code.

import "oaidl.idl";
import "ocidl.idl";

#include <winerror.h>
#define MAKE_HRESULT_ERROR(nError) \
    MAKE_HRESULT(SEVERITY_ERROR, FACILITY_ITF, nError)

  typedef [uuid(39FB3AB1-DE17-4a10-A3DB-95236C055135),
    helpstring("Possible error return codes")]
    enum TmError
  {
    [helpstring("The hardware does not support the high \
      performance counters")]
      tmErrorHighPerformanceTimersNotSupported =
        MAKE_HRESULT_ERROR(0xffff),
    [helpstring("Start needs to be called before ElapsedTime.")]
      tmErrorStartNotCalled,
    [helpstring("The interval value cannot be negative.")]
      tmErrorInvalidIntervalValue,
    // Other error codes go here
  } TmError;

  [
    object,
    uuid(EEBF6D1E-8EF1-4acf-9E5F-4D95E01D698A),
    oleautomation,
    helpstring("IStopwatch Interface"),
    pointer_default(unique)
  ]
  interface IStopwatch : IUnknown
  {
    [helpstring("Starts the timer")]
      HRESULT Start();
    [helpstring("Returns the number of seconds that have \
      passed since Start was called")]
      HRESULT ElapsedTime([out, retval] float* Time);
    [propget, helpstring("Returns/sets the overhead time \
      using the timer.")]
      HRESULT Overhead([out, retval] float *pOverhead);
    [propput, helpstring("Returns/sets the overhead time \
      using the timer.")]
```

```
    HRESULT Overhead([in] float Overhead);
};

[
  object,
  dual,
  oleautomation,
  uuid(C04E9202-BAFA-45e2-9F07-942D7CF76361),
  helpstring("IStopwatch2 Interface"),
  pointer_default(unique)
]
interface IStopwatch2 : IDispatch
{
  [id(1), helpstring("Starts the timer")]
    HRESULT Start();
  [id(DISPID_VALUE), helpstring("Returns the number of \
    seconds that have passed since Start was called.")]
    HRESULT ElapsedTime([out, retval] float* Time);
  [id(2), propget, helpstring("Returns/sets the overhead \
    time using the timer. The value is in Seconds.")]
    HRESULT Overhead([out, retval] float *pOverhead);
  [id(2),propput, helpstring("Returns/sets the overhead \
    time using the timer. The value is in Seconds.")]
    HRESULT Overhead([in] float Overhead);
};

[
  object,
  uuid(6764B148-93BE-40C1-B2BA-81650C57E33E),
  dual,
  oleautomation,
  helpstring("ICountdown Interface"),
  pointer_default(unique)
]
interface ICountdown : IDispatch
{
  [propget, id(DISPID_VALUE),
    helpstring("The time period of the countdown in \
    milliseconds. When set to 0 the countdown is inactive.")]
    HRESULT Interval([out, retval] long *pInterval);
  [propput, id(DISPID_VALUE),
    helpstring("The time period of the countdown in \
    milliseconds. When set to 0 the countdown is inactive.")]
    HRESULT Interval([in] long Interval);
  [propget, id(1), helpstring("The amount of time \
    (in milliseconds) remaining before interval has elapsed.")]
    HRESULT TimeRemaining([out, retval] long *pTimeRemaining);
  [propget, id(2), helpstring("The number of times for the \
    countdown to repeat. The default, -1, signifies \
    repeat continuously.")]
```

10

```
        HRESULT IterationCount([out, retval] long *pRemainingIterations);
      [propput, id(2), helpstring("The number of times for the \
        countdown to repeat. The default, -1, signifies repeat \
        continuously.")]
        HRESULT IterationCount([in] long NumberOfTimesToRepeatCountdown);
  };

#define MAJORVERSION 3
#define MINORVERSION 0
#define VERSION MAJORVERSION.MINORVERSION
enum TmLibraryVersion
{
  tmLibraryVersionMajor = MAJORVERSION,
  tmLibraryVersionMinor = MINORVERSION
};

[
  uuid(D7EBA784-2BF1-11D3-A48B-0000861C844E),
  version(VERSION),
  helpstring("Timers 3.0 Type Library")
]
library TIMERSLib
{

  importlib("stdole32.tlb");
  importlib("stdole2.tlb");

  enum TmLibraryVersion;
  enum TmError;

  enum TmICountdownEventsDispatchId
  {
    tmICountdownEventsDispatchIdOnTimeElapsed = 1
  };
  [
    uuid(95C0B4CE-A39B-463A-BE4B-06137333BD8E),
    helpstring("_ICountdownEvents Interface")
  ]
  dispinterface _ICountdownEvents
  {
    properties:
    methods:
    [id(tmICountdownEventsDispatchIdOnTimeElapsed),
      helpstring("This event fires when the countdown \
      interval has elapsed. RemainingIterations identifies \
      how many more times the countdown will fire.")]
      HRESULT OnTimeElapsed([in] long RemainingIterations);
  };
```

```
  [
    uuid(8D2B73A4-441E-49CA-B36B-D6F748C236D4),
    version(1.0),
    helpstring("Countdown Component")
  ]
  coclass Countdown
  {
    [default] interface ICountdown;
    [default, source] dispinterface _ICountdownEvents;
  };

  [
    uuid(83DC3C46-1259-4f95-A2D1-CD11A8819E2E),
    version(2.0),
    helpstring("Stopwatch Component")
  ]
  coclass Stopwatch
  {
    [default] interface IStopwatch2;
    interface IStopwatch;
  };

};
```

Another change to note is the addition of the **TmLibraryVersion** enumeration to the library. You will see why this is important when we write the listener for **Countdown**.

As you saw in the previous chapter, the **IDispatchImpl** template needs to be updated with the type library version numbers, so let's edit it now. Edit the **Countdown.h** file and add the additional version parameters as shown below:


```
// Countdown.h : Declaration of the CCountdown

#ifndef __COUNTDOWN_H_
#define __COUNTDOWN_H_

#include "resource.h"       // main symbols

const short SECONDS2MILLISECONDS = 1000;

#include <map>
using namespace std;

#include "stopwatch.h"
#include "TimersCP.h"
```

```
class CCountdown;
typedef map<UINT, CCountdown*> MAP_TIMERS;

/////////////////////////////////////////////////////////////////////////////
// CCountdown
class ATL_NO_VTABLE CCountdown :
  public CComObjectRootEx<CComSingleThreadModel>,
  public CComCoClass<CCountdown, &CLSID_Countdown>,
  public ISupportErrorInfo,
  public IConnectionPointContainerImpl<CCountdown>,
  public IDispatchImpl<ICountdown, &IID_ICountdown,
    &LIBID_TIMERSLib, tmLibraryVersionMajor,
    tmLibraryVersionMinor>,
{
public:

  CCountdown():
    m_nTimerID(0),
    m_nInterval(0),
    m_nIterationCount(-1)
  {
  }
  ~CCountdown()
  {
    StopCountdown();
  }


DECLARE_REGISTRY_RESOURCEID(IDR_COUNTDOWN)

DECLARE_PROTECT_FINAL_CONSTRUCT()

BEGIN_COM_MAP(CCountdown)
  COM_INTERFACE_ENTRY(ICountdown)
  COM_INTERFACE_ENTRY(IDispatch)
  COM_INTERFACE_ENTRY(ISupportErrorInfo)
  COM_INTERFACE_ENTRY(IConnectionPointContainer)
END_COM_MAP()

BEGIN_CONNECTION_POINT_MAP(CCountdown)
 END_CONNECTION_POINT_MAP()

// ISupportsErrorInfo
  STDMETHOD(InterfaceSupportsErrorInfo)(REFIID riid);

// ICountdown interface members
public:
  STDMETHOD(get_IterationCount)(
    /*[out, retval]*/ long *pRemainingIterations);
```

```
  STDMETHOD(put_IterationCount)(
    /*[in]*/ long NumberOfTimesToRepeatCountdown);
  STDMETHOD(get_TimeRemaining)(
    /*[out, retval]*/ long *pTimeRemaining);
  STDMETHOD(get_Interval)(/*[out, retval]*/ long *pInterval);
  STDMETHOD(put_Interval)(/*[in]*/ long Interval);

// Helper functions
public:
  // Perform class initialization
  virtual HRESULT FinalConstruct();

protected:
  // Starts the Windows timer
  long StartCountdown();

  // The function for the windows timer to call back to.
  static void __stdcall TimerCallback(
    HWND hwnd,      // handle of window for timer messages
    UINT uMsg,      // WM_TIMER message
    UINT idEvent,   // timer identifier
    DWORD dwTime    // current system time
    );

  // Handles the callback "event"
  void CCountdown::OnTimeElapsed();

  // Stops any active timers
  HRESULT StopCountdown();

  // Member variables:

  // Counts the remaining number of times
  // to fire the countdown.
  long m_nIterationCount;

  // Used to calculate the remaining time
  // before firing the TimeElapsed event.
  CComObject<CStopwatch>* m_Stopwatch;

  // The id of the running timer associated with
  // the Countdown object instance
  UINT m_nTimerID;

  // The interval for how long the countdown
  // will take.
  unsigned long m_nInterval;

  // This is a list of all timer ids where each timer id is
```

```
    // associated with a specific Countdown object
    static MAP_TIMERS s_Timers;

};

#endif //__COUNTDOWN_H_
```

You will notice that several other edits have been made as well. First, the constructor was changed to initialize a few member variables. A destructor was also added to reset any active timers before the object is destroyed.

Next, four additional helper functions have been added, one of which is a static function. The first function, **StopCountdown( )**, is used to turn off the countdown timer so that it no longer fires. There is also a **StartCountdown( )** function, which, as you might guess, starts the countdown. **StartCountdown( )** calls the Windows API function **SetTimer( )** and requests that a callback be set up for a specific time. **SetTimer( )** passes the address of **TimerCallback( )**. This is the callback function used by Windows to notify your program that the interval time has passed.

Finally, several member variables are provided. **m_nIterationCount** keeps track of the number of times the **Countdown** object still needs to fire. **m_Stopwatch** is used to return the value for **ICountdown**'s **TimeRemaining** property. You will notice that **Stopwatch** is declared as a **CComObject<CStopwatch>**. It would also have been possible to use one of the ATL component wrapper classes such as **CComPtr**, but by using the **CComObject** template instead, we can directly access the component without invoking the overhead of **CoCreateInstance( )**.

m_nTimerID keeps track of the timer ID associated with the **SetTimer( )** API function call, and **m_nInterval** saves the interval value. **s_Timers** keeps a map of all the instantiated **Countdown** objects so that when a timer fires, the corresponding **Countdown** object can be retrieved. This last variable is static because the Windows API function **SetTimer( )** callback function must be static, and as a static function it cannot access nonstatic member variables. Instead, the callback uses the **s_Timers** map to look up the corresponding **Countdown** component instance. **s_Timers** is defined as a **MAP_TIMERS**, which is an STL map that uses the timer's ID as an index and stores pointers to **Countdown** components for the data. **MAP_TIMERS** is defined at the top of the file.

Also note that since **s_Timers** is static, you will need to declare it externally from the class, too. This is done with one line of code at the top of the **Countdown.cpp** file, as follows:

```
MAP_TIMERS CCountdown::s_Timers;
```

The **s_Timers** static variable is currently not protected against simultaneous access by two threads. Potentially this could be a problem, and we will look at how to prevent simultaneous access in Chapter 13.

Implementing the ICountdown Interface

The next step is to implement the functionality of the **Countdown** component. This code is all part of **Countdown.cpp**. Let's investigate each function one by one.

We have already covered the first method, **InterfaceSupportsErrorInfo( )**, in Chapter 9. It indicates which interfaces support rich error handling.

```
STDMETHODIMP CCountdown::InterfaceSupportsErrorInfo(REFIID riid)
{
  static const IID* arr[] =
  {
    &IID_ICountdown
  };
  for (int i=0; i < sizeof(arr) / sizeof(arr[0]); i++)
  {
    if (InlineIsEqualGUID(*arr[i],riid))
      return S_OK;
  }
  return S_FALSE;
}
```


Next comes **FinalConstruct( )** in which a **Stopwatch** component is created. The purpose of this component is to support the **TimeRemaining** property. The **Stopwatch** object is instantiated now, however, so as not to impact performance later.

```
HRESULT CCountdown::FinalConstruct()
{

  // Initialize the remaining member variables
```

```
  m_Stopwatch->CreateInstance(&m_Stopwatch);

  return S_OK;
}
```

The next set of functions all relate to starting and stopping the Windows API timer and receiving notifications. Each of them is shown here:

```
// Sets up a timer
long CCountdown::StartCountdown()
{

  ATLASSERT(m_nInterval > 0);

  StopCountdown();

  // Set the timer.
  m_nTimerID = ::SetTimer(0,      // handle of main window
    0,                            // timer identifier
    (long) m_nInterval,           // interval (milliseconds)
    CCountdown::TimerCallback);   // timer callback function

  m_Stopwatch->Start();

  ATLTRACE2(atlTraceGeneral, 4, _T("The TimerID value after calling
            SetTimer is %d\n"),
    m_nTimerID );

  // Insert the id
  CCountdown::s_Timers.insert(
    MAP_TIMERS::value_type(m_nTimerID, this));

  return m_nTimerID;

}


// The function which the SetTimer() API calls
// back to when the time has elapsed.
/*static*/ void __stdcall CCountdown::TimerCallback(
  HWND hwnd,      // handle of window for timer messages
  UINT uMsg,      // WM_TIMER message
  UINT idTimer,   // timer identifier
  DWORD dwTime    // current system time
  )
{

  //  Search the map for the timer that fired.
  MAP_TIMERS::iterator it;
  ATLTRACE2(atlTraceGeneral, 4, _T("TimerProc called with idTimer = %d\n"),
```

```
idTimer );
  it = CCountdown::s_Timers.find(idTimer);
  ATLASSERT( it != s_Timers.end() );

  // Notify the countdown component
  // that the timer has elapsed.
  it->second->OnTimeElapsed();
}


// Respond to the elapsed timer "event"
void CCountdown::OnTimeElapsed()
{
  float elapsed_time=0;

  // Time how long it takes to process the event
  m_Stopwatch->Start();

  // Drop the IterationCount unless it is negative
  // in which case the IterationCount is not used.
  if(m_nIterationCount > 0)
    m_nIterationCount--;
  // Stop the countdown if it is zero.
  if(m_nIterationCount == 0)
    StopCountdown();

  Fire_OnTimeElapsed(m_nIterationCount);

  // If the time to process the event was greater than the interval,
  // then restart the interval at its full time. Any intervals which
  // have elapsed during the processing of the event are effectively
  // ignored and not published to the client.
  if(m_nIterationCount!=0)
  {
    m_Stopwatch->ElapsedTime(&elapsed_time);
    if(elapsed_time*SECONDS2MILLISECONDS - m_nInterval > 0)
    {
      put_Interval(m_nInterval);
    }
    // Restart the stopwatch for get_RemainingTime() function
    m_Stopwatch->Start();
  }
}

// Stops the timer identified by m_nTimerID
HRESULT CCountdown::StopCountdown()
{
  long nKillTimer = 0;


  if ( m_nTimerID != 0 )
```

```
  {

    // TODO: Raise an error if this fails.
    nKillTimer = KillTimer(
      0,            // handle to window that installed timer
      m_nTimerID    // timer identifier
      );
  }

  if (nKillTimer > 0)
  {
      // Successful
      s_Timers.erase(m_nTimerID);
      m_nTimerID = 0;
      return S_OK;
  }
  else
    return HRESULT_FROM_WIN32(GetLastError());
}
```

The first function, **CCountdown::StartCountdown( )**, makes the call to the **::SetTimer( )** Windows API function. This starts the clock ticking. The last parameter on the **::SetTimer( )** call is a pointer to the **CCountdown::TimerCallback( )** function, which the API function timer will call back into when the time expires. (Technically, this is handled via a **WM_TIMER** message, but the effect is the same.) Immediately after starting the timer, the stopwatch is also started so that we know how much time has expired since the timer started. The **::SetTimer( )** API call returns a timer ID, which, in addition to being stored into **m_nTimerID**, is also used as an index into the **s_Timers** map.

Next the stopwatch is started. This marks the point at which the countdown started so that later we can determine how long it has been running and how much time remains. The last function call in **CCountdown::StartCountdown( )** is to add an entry for the **Countdown** object to the **s_Timers** map so that it can be retrieved later. The timer ID value returned from **::SetTimer( )** supplies the index into the map.

Once the countdown has started, the **CCountdown** object waits for a callback into the **CCountdown::TimerCallback( )** function. Upon callback, the first item on the agenda is to retrieve the **CCountdown** object corresponding to the timer ID parameter in the callback function. This is done using the STL **map::find( )** function. Once the **CCountdown** object has been located, it is notified that the timer has elapsed using the **OnTimeElapsed( )** function.

The **OnTimeElapsed( )** function does the real work of handling the timer callback. First of all, it starts the stopwatch again. We will use the stopwatch to calculate how long the client takes to process the event—a calculation we will use toward the end of the function. Next, **OnTimeElapsed( )** evaluates the current **m_nIterationCount**. You will recall that this value determines how many times the timer should fire. Negative values are simply ignored because they indicate that the timer should fire continuously until stopped. Positive values are decremented by one. Once the **m_nIterationCount** reaches 0, the timer is stopped altogether.

The **Fire_OnTimeElapsed( )** call is used to notify the client of the event. We will look at this in further detail later when we implement the connection point portion of the component.

At the end of the function is another check to verify that more timers will be fired. Assuming this to be true, the elapsed time from the start of the event to the end is retrieved from the **Stopwatch** component. This evaluates the time it takes to process the event, including the client time. If the time it takes to process the event is greater than the interval time, all timers that expired during the processing of the event are ignored, and the timer will simply be restarted. The result is that for event processing that takes longer than the **Interval** time, the elapsed time between when the last event processing ended and the next event processing started will always be consistent. For example, if the timer was set to expire every second but the listener took one and a half seconds to process, the time between when the listener finished processing the event and the time that it started processing the next event would still be one second.

The purpose of the next function, **StopCountdown( )**, is to stop the timer callback associated with the **Countdown** component. This is done using the **KillTimer( )** API function, which takes in the timer ID returned from **::SetTimer( )** in order to know which timer to stop. Once the timer has been stopped, it is also removed from the **s_Timers** map.

The remaining functions relate to the various properties supported by the **ICountdown** interface. They are all listed here:

```
////////////////////////////////////////////////////////////////////
// ICountdown Interface Class member implementation
////////////////////////////////////////////////////////////////////
STDMETHODIMP CCountdown::get_Interval(long *pInterval)
{
  *pInterval = m_nInterval;
  return S_OK;
}

STDMETHODIMP CCountdown::put_Interval(long Interval)
```

```
{
  HRESULT hr = S_OK;
  if (Interval < 0)
  {
    // Report error using SET_ERROR_INFO macro
    // as defined in stdafx.h
    SET_ERROR_INFO(tmErrorInvalidIntervalValue,
      __uuidof(Countdown), __uuidof(ICountdown));
    hr = tmErrorInvalidIntervalValue;
  }
  else
  {
    m_nInterval = Interval;
    if (Interval == 0)
    {
      hr = StopCountdown();
    }
    else
    {
      StartCountdown();
    }
  }
  return hr;
}

STDMETHODIMP CCountdown::get_TimeRemaining(long *pTimeRemaining)
{
  HRESULT hr;
  float elapsed_time;
  hr = m_Stopwatch->ElapsedTime(&elapsed_time);
  if(hr == tmErrorStartNotCalled)
    *pTimeRemaining = -1;
  else
    *pTimeRemaining = m_nInterval -
      (elapsed_time*SECONDS2MILLISECONDS);
  return hr;
}

STDMETHODIMP CCountdown::get_IterationCount(
  long *pRemainingIterations)
{
  *pRemainingIterations = m_nIterationCount;
  return S_OK;
}

STDMETHODIMP CCountdown::put_IterationCount(
```

```
  long NumberOfTimesToRepeatCountdown)
{

  HRESULT hr = S_OK;

  m_nIterationCount = NumberOfTimesToRepeatCountdown;

  return hr;
}
```

Each of these functions is self-explanatory based on which property they are implementing. Essentially, they store or return the value requested. In addition, **put_Interval( )** starts or stops the countdown appropriately.

Implementing a Connection Point and Firing Events

All the infrastructure work for the component has now been completed. The only part missing is the actual event notification piece. As we pointed out earlier in the connection point overview, the ATL wizard does most of the necessary work for you when you check the Support Connection Points check box. To begin, let's examine the additional code that was added by the wizard. The first changes involve items in the **Timers.idl** file that we have already looked at earlier in the chapter. In contrast to the **Stopwatch** component, the **Countdown** component added a definition for an event interface, **_ICountdownEvents**. In addition, it declared the interface as the source interface. These changes are shown again here:

```
[
  uuid(95C0B4CE-A39B-463A-BE4B-06137333BD8E),
  helpstring("_ICountdownEvents Interface")
]
dispinterface _ICountdownEvents
{
  properties:
  methods:
};

[
  uuid(8D2B73A4-441E-49CA-B36B-D6F748C236D4),
  version(1.0),
  helpstring("Countdown Component")
]
coclass Countdown
```

```
{
  [default] interface ICountdown;
  [default, source] dispinterface _ICountdownEvents;
};
```

Note that **_ICountdownEvents** had no methods at the start.

The remaining changes occur in the **Countdown.h** file. Notice that **CCountdown** is derived from **IConnectionPointContainerImpl< CCountdown>** in addition to all the other classes. This additional base class provides the implementation for the **IConnectionPointContainer** methods. In order for a client to access the interface, however, you need to update the COM map in **Countdown.h** so that **QueryInterface( )** will successfully return the **IConnectionPointContainer** interface.

```
class ATL_NO_VTABLE CCountdown :
  public CComObjectRootEx<CComSingleThreadModel>,
  public CComCoClass<CCountdown, &CLSID_Countdown>,
  public ISupportErrorInfo,
  public IConnectionPointContainerImpl<CCountdown>,
  public IDispatchImpl<ICountdown, &IID_ICountdown,
    &LIBID_TIMERSLib, tmLibraryVersionMajor,
    tmLibraryVersionMinor>,
  public CProxy_ICountdownEvents< CCountdown >,
  public IProvideClassInfo2Impl<&CLSID_Countdown,
    &DIID__ICountdownEvents, &LIBID_TIMERSLib,
    tmLibraryVersionMajor, tmLibraryVersionMinor>
{
public:
...
BEGIN_COM_MAP(CCountdown)
  COM_INTERFACE_ENTRY(ICountdown)
  COM_INTERFACE_ENTRY(IDispatch)
  COM_INTERFACE_ENTRY(ISupportErrorInfo)
  COM_INTERFACE_ENTRY(IConnectionPointContainer)
END_COM_MAP()

BEGIN_CONNECTION_POINT_MAP(CCountdown)
CONNECTION_POINT_ENTRY(DIID__ICountdownEvents)
END_CONNECTION_POINT_MAP()
...
```

In addition to the **COM_INTERFACE_ENTRY** you will see that a new map has been added. This is the connection point map, and it contains a list of the source interfaces supported by the connection point container. Notice that the GUID passed in the **CONNECTION_POINT_ENTRY** macro is **DIID__ICountdownEvents**, not **IID__ICountdownEvents**. The "D" prefix is used for dispinterfaces.

There is one last item to take care of in order to send event notification to the component listeners. As was mentioned in the previous section, the function that does this is called **Fire_OnTimeElapsed( )**. Nowhere in the code so far, however, has this function been implemented. Furthermore, it involves some complexity because the event interface is a dispatch interface. This means calling **IDispatch::Invoke( )**, which (as you saw in the preceding chapter) can be rather tedious.

Fortunately, Microsoft provides a wizard to help out. This wizard will implement all the source interface methods for us so that we don't have to write any of them. To invoke the wizard, right-click on the **Countdown** component and select the Implement Connection Point menu. This will display the dialog shown in Figure 10-3.

The interfaces shown will be the source interfaces listed within your type library. (Note that you will have to have compiled your program at least once because the dialog requires a type library. In addition, the project type library must be in the target directory, or no interfaces will appear.) Check the **_ICountdownEvents** interface and click the OK button. This will generate a new file called **TimersCP.h**, which will contain the definition and

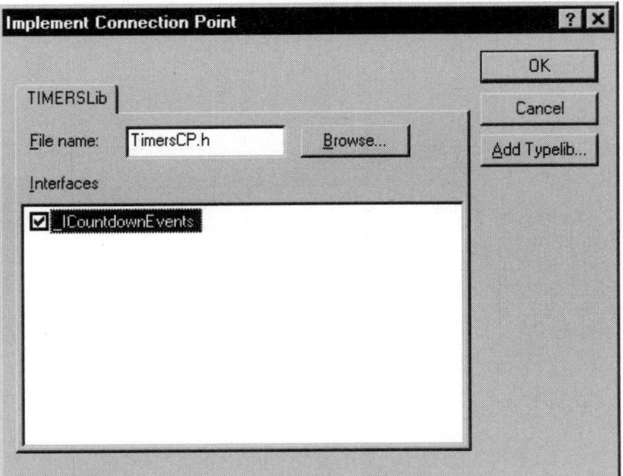

Implement Connection Point dialog

Figure 10-3.

implementation for all the methods supported by the selected source interface. Here is a listing of the generated code:

```
#ifndef _TIMERSCP_H_
#define _TIMERSCP_H_

template <class T>
class CProxy_ICountdownEvents :
  public IConnectionPointImpl<
    T, &DIID__ICountdownEvents, CComDynamicUnkArray>
{
  //Warning this class may be re-created by the wizard.
public:
  HRESULT Fire_OnTimeElapsed(LONG RemainingIterations)
  {
    CComVariant varResult;
    T* pT = static_cast<T*>(this);
    int nConnectionIndex;
    CComVariant* pvars = new CComVariant[1];
    int nConnections = m_vec.GetSize();

    for (nConnectionIndex = 0;
       nConnectionIndex < nConnections; nConnectionIndex++)
    {
      pT->Lock();
      CComPtr<IUnknown> sp = m_vec.GetAt(nConnectionIndex);
      pT->Unlock();
      IDispatch* pDispatch = reinterpret_cast<IDispatch*>(sp.p);
      if (pDispatch != NULL)
      {
        VariantClear(&varResult);
        pvars[0] = RemainingIterations;
        DISPPARAMS disp = { pvars, NULL, 1, 0 };
        pDispatch->Invoke(0x1, IID_NULL,
          LOCALE_USER_DEFAULT, DISPATCH_METHOD,
          &disp, &varResult, NULL, NULL);
      }
    }
    delete[] pvars;
    return varResult.scode;

  }
};
#endif
```

As you can see, the code retrieves **IDispatch** and prepares all required parameters so that they are passed into the **IDispatch** interface correctly. Your only responsibility is to call the **Fire_<Event>** function at the correct time within your implementation code. The added advantage is also that during development the source interface could change, but with the wizard, it is simple to regenerate the notification code.

Another point about the code is that it actually defines a template. Your coclass still needs to be derived from this template. Again, however, you will find that the wizard has stepped in and done this for you, as shown here in **Countdown.h**:

```
#include "TimersCP.h"

class CCountdown;
typedef map<UINT, CCountdown*> MAP_TIMERS;

/////////////////////////////////////////////////////////////////////////////
// CCountdown
class ATL_NO_VTABLE CCountdown :
  public CComObjectRootEx<CComSingleThreadModel>,
  public CComCoClass<CCountdown, &CLSID_Countdown>,
  public ISupportErrorInfo,
  public IConnectionPointContainerImpl<CCountdown>,
  public IDispatchImpl<ICountdown, &IID_ICountdown,
    &LIBID_TIMERSLib, tmLibraryVersionMajor,
    tmLibraryVersionMinor>,
  public CProxy_ICountdownEvents< CCountdown >
{
public:
...
```

10

By the way, if you have added line feeds into the **IDispatchImpl< >** declaration as we have done here, the wizard usually splits the declaration and puts the **CProxy_ICountdownEvent** class in the middle. Simply move it to the end of the class declaration as shown above, and you shouldn't have any more problems.

At this point the project is complete except for one adjustment that needs to be made in each of the release configurations in order to resolve what is probably one of the most infamous linker errors for new ATL programmers. If you try to compile your project as it is, you will receive a linker error LNK2001 with its accompanying message, "unresolved external symbol _main." To provide a little more detail, a second error LNK1120, "unresolved external symbol _main," follows immediately. These are the kind of error messages that at best are most helpful if you have encountered the problem before and already know the solution! If not, Microsoft might as well have left the error text out because it is not very helpful in diagnosing the problem, especially when the cause could be something as unrelated as using STL libraries.

If you receive linker error "LNK2001: unresolved external symbol _main" during a release build of your project, try removing **_ATL_MIN_CRT** from the configuration settings of your project.

The problem is that as part of the optimization process, Microsoft deliberately left out the standard C/C++ runtime library (CRT) of all release configuration options. The result is a 25k reduction in module size. This is great if you are downloading the module over a 28.8KB connection but probably not an issue otherwise. Anyway, the culprit requiring the C/C++ runtime is the STL map. Since we have included this in our code, we also need to include the runtime library. This involves editing the configuration. Choose Project | Settings, and select the configuration you wish to edit. Then on the C/C++ tab, with the category set to General, remove the preprocessor definition **_ATL_MIN_CRT**. Figure 10-4 shows the dialog with highlighting on the text to be deleted.

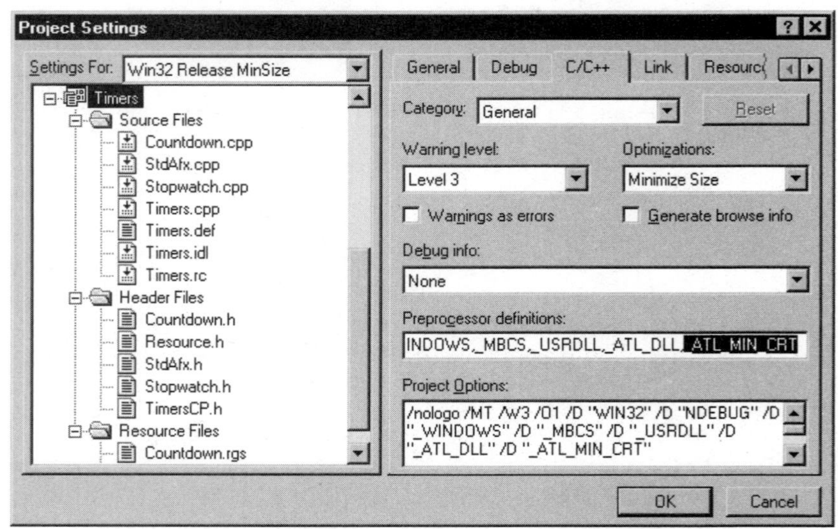

Removing **_ATL_MIN_-CRT** from the settings
Figure 10-4.

After making this configuration change, your project should compile. Unfortunately, however, we have not yet written any code to listen to the events. To do this we will start a new client project that will be an alarm. The trigger for the alarm will be the **Countdown** component.

Implementing IProvideClassInfo2

You can make an additional change to your component that is not required. Making the change, however, will enable components to set up the connection point slightly more efficiently when the listener uses the type library to retrieve the default source interfaces. The change is to support one more interface, **IProvideClassInfo2**. **IProvideClassInfo2** has two methods. The first, **GetClassInfo( )**, returns a pointer to the **ITypeInfo** interface of your component. You will recall from Chapter 9 that this interface can be used to read the type library. The second method, **GetGUID( )**, returns the GUID for the default source interface.

Providing support for the **IProvideClassInfo2** interface means adding one more class from which **CCountdown** is derived. Also, you need to add it to the COM map. The code is shown here:

```
class ATL_NO_VTABLE CCountdown :
  public CComObjectRootEx<CComSingleThreadModel>,
  public CComCoClass<CCountdown, &CLSID_Countdown>,
  public ISupportErrorInfo,
  public IConnectionPointContainerImpl<CCountdown>,
  public IDispatchImpl<ICountdown, &IID_ICountdown,
    &LIBID_TIMERSLib, tmLibraryVersionMajor,
    tmLibraryVersionMinor>,
  public CProxy_ICountdownEvents< CCountdown >,
  public IProvideClassInfo2Impl<&CLSID_Countdown,
    &DIID__ICountdownEvents, &LIBID_TIMERSLib,
    tmLibraryVersionMajor, tmLibraryVersionMinor>
{

...

BEGIN_COM_MAP(CCountdown)
...
  COM_INTERFACE_ENTRY(IProvideClassInfo)
  COM_INTERFACE_ENTRY(IProvideClassInfo2)
END_COM_MAP()
...
```

IN DEPTH

Connection Points Without a Dispinterface

As explained earlier, there are three reasons why you should use a dispinterface rather than a vtable interface when working with connection points. To review: First, scripting languages cannot support anything but dispinterfaces, so they cannot be expected to implement a dual interface. Second, if the client is, itself, a COM object, it probably already has a dual interface defined as its default interface. Having a client support two dual interfaces is difficult at best for C++ clients and not supported for Visual Basic clients. Third, using a dispinterface removes from a client the burden to implement all the methods on an interface. These reasons are sufficiently compelling that most programmers use a dispinterface rather than a vtable interface. However, there is a work-around to the second problem if the first and third issues are not important to you. (In other words, you don't need scripting clients to receive event notifications, and the implementation of all the methods by the client is an insignificant burden.)

The work-around is to define an event interface that is not decorated with the **dual** attribute. Visual Basic will be able to receive events from the interface, and in addition, you will be able to make vtable calls into the client, which will be more efficient. In fact, the wizard will automatically adapt to make calls using the vtable interface rather than using **IDispatch** calls. In following the traditional dispinterface implementation, which has the most universal compatibility, we will not look at the code for doing this specifically, but you can easily see what it looks like by changing the dispinterface to be a normal interface and regenerating the code using the wizard. In addition, although not shown here, it is not unusual for component developers not to use the dispinterface declaration for an event interface. As long as you are willing to accept the two drawbacks, this is certainly a viable option.

Receiving Event Notification from a Component

There are clearly two parts to understanding events. First is the source component part—what does the source component need to do in order to publish events? Second is the listener part—how do you implement the client so that it can receive event notification? Since we covered the first part in the preceding sections, we are now ready to move on to the second part. In this part of the chapter, we are going to create an Alarm program. The user of the program will be able to specify a period of time and a message. Given this information, the alarm will begin counting down until the time has elapsed, at which point it will beep and display the message. The dialog shown in Figure 10-5 shows what the program will look like after the alarm has fired.

In addition, the Alarm program allows you to display help information so you know how to use it. If you specify the /? option as a program argument, a dialog will display with the following text:

```
Starts an alarm.

Alarm.exe [/RegServer || /UnregServer || /?]
Alarm.exe waittime [message]

/RegServer       Registers the component server.
/UnregServer     Unregisters the component servers.
waittime         The time, in milliseconds, before the alarm will
                 fire.  Cannot be negative.
message          The text displayed when the alarm fires.
/?               This help text.
```

The second syntax, with *waittime* and *message,* will be the arguments we are most concerned with. Since our project will not include any components, neither the *RegServer* nor the *UnregServer* arguments will be used because there is nothing to register. The code is left in the project, however, so that you can see what is normally included in an ATL-generated executable by default.

Creating an ATL Executable

Up to this point, we have stayed with a relatively simple console application when demonstrating COM. In this section, we will deviate from this simplicity a little and instead create an ATL executable using the ATL wizard. To do this,

The alarm display after the time has elapsed

Figure 10-5.

follow the same steps as described in Chapter 3. Use "Alarm" for the project name. Instead of choosing the Dynamic Link Library as we did for the **Timers** project, this time, select the Executable (EXE) option.

This ATL wizard will create many of the same files we saw before when creating a DLL. First, there is the **Alarm.cpp** file, which contains the entry point into the program. Since we are now creating an executable, the entry point will be **_tWinMain( )** rather than **DllMain( )**. Next there are the IDL and RGS files, **Alarm.idl** and **Alarm.rgs**, for describing any interfaces and components and how they are to be registered. Since we will not be adding any components that will require registration, these files will not be used. The remaining files, **StdAfx.h**, **StdAfx.cpp**, and **Resource.h**, are very similar to the standard files we saw before and are described in Chapter 3.

A full listing of the **Alarm.cpp** file is shown here:

```
// Alarm.cpp : Implementation of WinMain


// Note: Proxy/Stub Information
//      To build a separate proxy/stub DLL,
//      run nmake -f Alarmps.mk in the project directory.

#include "stdafx.h"
#include "resource.h"
#include <initguid.h>
#include "Alarm.h"

#include "Alarm_i.c"

#include "Display.h"
// time for EXE to be idle before shutting down
const DWORD dwTimeOut = 5000;
// time to wait for threads to finish up
const DWORD dwPause = 1000;

const TCHAR* HELP_TEXT =
  _T("Starts an alarm.\n")
  _T("\n")
  _T("Alarm.exe [/RegServer || /UnregServer || /?]\n")
  _T("Alarm.exe waittime [message]\n")
  _T("\n")
  _T("/RegServer  \t Registers the component server.\n")
  _T("/UnregServer\t Unregisters the component servers.\n")
  _T("waittime    \t The time, in milliseconds, ")
  _T(                "before the alarm will fire.  ")
```

```
  _T(                  "Cannot be negative.\n")
  _T("message      \t The text displayed when the alarm fires.\n")
  _T("/?           \t This help text.\n");
void ShowHelp()
{
  // Display help text;
  MessageBox(NULL, _T(HELP_TEXT), _T("Alarm"), MB_OK);
}

// Passed to CreateThread to monitor the shutdown event
static DWORD WINAPI MonitorProc(void* pv)
{
  CExeModule* p = (CExeModule*)pv;
  p->MonitorShutdown();
  return 0;
}

LONG CExeModule::Unlock()
{
  LONG l = CComModule::Unlock();
  if (l == 0)
  {
      bActivity = true;
      // tell monitor that we transitioned to zero
      SetEvent(hEventShutdown);
  }
  return l;
}

//Monitors the shutdown event
void CExeModule::MonitorShutdown()
{
  while (1)
  {
    WaitForSingleObject(hEventShutdown, INFINITE);
    DWORD dwWait=0;
    do
    {
      bActivity = false;
      dwWait = WaitForSingleObject(hEventShutdown, dwTimeOut);
    } while (dwWait == WAIT_OBJECT_0);
    // timed out
    // if no activity let's really bail
    if (!bActivity && m_nLockCnt == 0)
    {
#if _WIN32_WINNT >= 0x0400 & defined(_ATL_FREE_THREADED)
```

10

```
      CoSuspendClassObjects();
      if (!bActivity && m_nLockCnt == 0)
#endif
          break;
    }
  }
  CloseHandle(hEventShutdown);
  PostThreadMessage(dwThreadID, WM_QUIT, 0, 0);
}

bool CExeModule::StartMonitor()
{
  hEventShutdown = CreateEvent(NULL, false, false, NULL);
  if (hEventShutdown == NULL)
    return false;
  DWORD dwThreadID;
  HANDLE h = CreateThread(NULL, 0,
    MonitorProc, this, 0, &dwThreadID);
  return (h != NULL);
}

CExeModule _Module;

BEGIN_OBJECT_MAP(ObjectMap)
END_OBJECT_MAP()

// Retrieve information about the next parameter
// on the command line.
// The return value points just past the end of the
// next parameter.
// p1 points to the beginning of the parameter but
// could be moved if the parameter is encapsulated
// in quotes.
// length returns the length of the retrieved parameter.
LPCTSTR FindNextParam(LPCTSTR& p1, UINT& length)
{
  LPCTSTR p;
  TCHAR t = _T(' ');
  length = 0;

  if(*p1 == _T('\"'))
  {
    t = _T('\"');
    p1 = CharNext(p1);
  }

  p = p1;
```

```
  while(*p != NULL)
  {
    p = CharNext(p);
    length++;
    if(*p == t)
    {
      break;
    }
  }
  return p;
}

// Returns a pointer which points at the
// next location in p1 after the occurrence
// of the string p2.
LPCTSTR FindOneOf(LPCTSTR p1, LPCTSTR p2)
{
  while (p1 != NULL && *p1 != NULL)
  {
    LPCTSTR p = p2;
    while (p != NULL && *p != NULL)
    {
      if (*p1 == *p)
        return CharNext(p1);
      p = CharNext(p);
    }
    p1 = CharNext(p1);
  }
  return NULL;
}

/////////////////////////////////////////////////////////////////////////////
//
extern "C" int WINAPI _tWinMain(HINSTANCE hInstance,
HINSTANCE /*hPrevInstance*/, LPTSTR lpCmdLine, int /*nShowCmd*/)
{
  // Custom variables
  USES_CONVERSION;
  // The amount of time to put on the alarm
  long wait_time = 0;
  // The message displayed when the alarm fires.
  CComBSTR alarm_message = NULL;
  // The value returned from _tWinMain()
  int nRet = 0;
  // Indicates whether the program is to run fully or whether
```

```
  // to simply handle registration or display the help text.
  BOOL bRun = TRUE;
  UINT i;

  //this line necessary for _ATL_MIN_CRT
  lpCmdLine = GetCommandLine();

#if _WIN32_WINNT >= 0x0400 & defined(_ATL_FREE_THREADED)
  HRESULT hRes = CoInitializeEx(NULL, COINIT_MULTITHREADED);
#else
  HRESULT hRes = CoInitialize(NULL);
#endif
  _ASSERTE(SUCCEEDED(hRes));
  _Module.Init(ObjectMap, hInstance, &LIBID_ALARMLib);
  _Module.dwThreadID = GetCurrentThreadId();

  ///////////////////////////////////////
  // Parse the command line
  TCHAR szTokens[] = _T("-/");

  // Skip past the command name
  LPCTSTR lpszToken = FindNextParam(lpCmdLine, i);

  // Loop through each token
  lpszToken = FindOneOf(lpCmdLine, _T(" "));
  while (lpszToken != NULL)
  {
    // Look for option tokens (tokens that begin with / or -)
    for(i=0; i<(_tcslen(szTokens)); i++)
    {
      if(szTokens[i] == *lpszToken)
        break;
    }
    if( i < (UINT)(lstrlen(szTokens)) )
    {
      // Move past the token identifier (/ or -)
      lpszToken = CharNext(lpszToken);

      // We found an option token but which one?
      if (lstrcmpi(lpszToken, _T("UnregServer"))==0)
      {
        _Module.UpdateRegistryFromResource(IDR_Alarm, FALSE);
        nRet = _Module.UnregisterServer(TRUE);
        bRun = FALSE;
        break;
      }
```

```
  else if (lstrcmpi(lpszToken, _T("RegServer"))==0)
  {
    _Module.UpdateRegistryFromResource(IDR_Alarm, TRUE);
    nRet = _Module.RegisterServer(TRUE);
    bRun = FALSE;
    break;
  }
  else if ( (lstrcmpi(lpszToken, _T("Help"))==0) ||
    (lstrcmpi(lpszToken, _T("?"))==0) )
  {
    ShowHelp();
    bRun = FALSE;
    break;
  }
}
else
{
  // We have a normal parameter (no '-' or  '\"')
  if(wait_time == 0)
  {
    wait_time = _ttol(lpszToken);
    bRun = TRUE;
  }
  else if(alarm_message.Length() == 0)
  {
    LPCSTR p = lpszToken;
    i = 0;
    lpszToken = FindNextParam(p, i);
    SysReAllocStringLen(&alarm_message.m_str, T2OLE(p), i);
  }
  else
  {
    // Error on command line so show help text.
    ShowHelp();
    bRun = FALSE;
  }
}

  // Move to the next parameter/option
  lpszToken = FindOneOf(lpszToken, _T(" "));
}
///////////////////////////////////////


if (bRun)
{
```

```
    // Check for required parameters
    if(wait_time == 0)
      ShowHelp();
    else
    {
      _Module.StartMonitor();
#if _WIN32_WINNT >= 0x0400 & defined(_ATL_FREE_THREADED)
      hRes = _Module.RegisterClassObjects(CLSCTX_LOCAL_SERVER,
        REGCLS_MULTIPLEUSE | REGCLS_SUSPENDED);
      _ASSERTE(SUCCEEDED(hRes));
      hRes = CoResumeClassObjects();
#else
      hRes = _Module.RegisterClassObjects(CLSCTX_LOCAL_SERVER,
        REGCLS_MULTIPLEUSE);
#endif
      _ASSERTE(SUCCEEDED(hRes));

      MSG msg;
      while (GetMessage(&msg, 0, 0, 0))
          DispatchMessage(&msg);

      _Module.RevokeClassObjects();
      Sleep(dwPause); //wait for any threads to finish
    }
  }

  _Module.Term();
  CoUninitialize();
  return nRet;
}
```

We will start examining the file at the execution entry point, **_tWinMain( )**. All C/C++ executables begin with some form of **main( )**. Windows executables generally use **WinMain( )**, but in order to provide compatibility with both Unicode and ANSI compiles, the wizard code uses **_tWinMain( )**, where the "t" indicates the parameters are **TCHAR***s. **_tWinMain( )** supplies the entry point for code execution. Next, a few local variables are defined. The **USES_CONVERSION** macro is used for converting one string type to another, as you learned back in Chapter 6. Following the variable declaration, the command line string is retrieved using **GetCommandLine( )**. As the wizard-generated comment indicates, this is required because of the **_ATL_MIN_CRT**. Next come the calls to **CoInitialize( )** and **CoInitializeEx( )** for initializing the COM subsystem on the main thread. As with the DLL, **_Module** is also initialized, although in the EXE case, the main thread ID is also stored.

Following all the initialization, it is time to parse the command line parameters. Aside from the few **BSTR** API calls, which we discussed in Chapter 6, this code is relatively straightforward C++, so we will not discuss its implementation details here. The purpose of the code is to populate the **wait_time** and **alarm_message** message variables so that they can be used in running the alarm. Any failure to do this correctly will cause the help text to be displayed, via the **ShowHelp( )** function. The /RegServer and /UnregServer arguments are used to register any component supported by the executable. In contrast to a DLL, which requires the use of **regsvr32.exe** or some other executable to make calls into its registration functions, an executable can register itself. This is done using the "/(Un)RegServer" arguments.

Next in the code comes a call to **_Module.StartMonitor( )**. This starts a new thread that is responsible for waiting until there are no more objects instantiated. The code for **StartMonitor( )** along with the thread callback **MonitorProc( )** and the bulk of its implementation, **MonitorShutdown( )**, are all found at the top of **Alarm.cpp**.

The calls to **_Module.RegisterClassObjects( )** and **CoResumeClassObjects( )** are used to instantiate any class factories and register them with the COM subsystem so that, if a call is made to instantiate any of the components supported by the **Alarm.exe** server, it will occur more efficiently.

After registering the components, a Windows message loop is started to process the messages. Once the message loop exits due to a quit message or equivalent, the class factories are unregistered, any module cleanup is carried out, and the program exits. You should be able to compile the program now, although it will not do anything of value.

Adding a Dialog

The next step in creating the **Alarm** component is to add a dialog that will display the alarm message once the **Countdown** expires. Again, we will use the ATL wizards to do this. Right-click on the Alarm project from the Class View pane and select the New ATL Object menu. From the ensuing dialog, select the miscellaneous category, and then select the Dialog Object. After clicking Next, enter **Display** for the Short Name. Leave the default values for the remaining text boxes.

Edit the dialog that is created. Go to the Resource View page in the Workspace window and select the **IDD_DISPLAY** resource item. Delete the OK button and insert a static text control. After adjusting the size and location a little, the dialog should look something like what is shown back in Figure 10-5, although the text will be different. This difference can be ignored since we will set the values for both the static text and the Cancel button using code within the **CDisplay** class.

Declaring the Source Interface Implementation

Here is a listing of **Display.h** with alarm event notifications highlighted:

```
// Display.h : Declaration of the CDisplay

#ifndef __DISPLAY_H_
#define __DISPLAY_H_

//  Exception declaration not yet standardized
#pragma warning(push)
#pragma warning( disable : 4290 )

#import "..\Timers\Timers.dll" no_namespace, named_guids

#include "resource.h"       // main symbols
#include <atlhost.h>

class CDisplay;
const UINT ID_ALARM = 1;

typedef IDispEventImpl<ID_ALARM, CDisplay,
  &__uuidof(_ICountdownEvents),
  &LIBID_TIMERSLib,
  tmLibraryVersionMajor, tmLibraryVersionMinor>
  /* AS */ AlarmCountdownEvents;

/////////////////////////////////////////////////////////////////////
// CDisplay
class CDisplay :
  public CAxDialogImpl<CDisplay>,
  public AlarmCountdownEvents
{
public:
  CDisplay()
```

```
  {
  }

  ~CDisplay()
  {
  }

  enum { IDD = IDD_DISPLAY };

//////////////////////////////////////
// Alarm Sink interface declaration
BEGIN_SINK_MAP(CDisplay)
SINK_ENTRY_EX(ID_ALARM,
  __uuidof(_ICountdownEvents),
  tmICountdownEventsDispatchIdOnTimeElapsed,
  AlarmTimeElapsed)
END_SINK_MAP()


//////////////////////////////////////
// COM Event hookups
public:
  STDMETHOD(AlarmTimeElapsed)(long RemainingIterations);


//////////////////////////////////////
// Windows messages
BEGIN_MSG_MAP(CDisplay)
  MESSAGE_HANDLER(WM_INITDIALOG, OnInitDialog)
  COMMAND_ID_HANDLER(IDCANCEL, OnCancel)
END_MSG_MAP()


  // Dialog initialization
  LRESULT OnInitDialog(UINT uMsg, WPARAM wParam,
    LPARAM lParam, BOOL& bHandled);

  // Cancel button is pushed
  LRESULT OnCancel(WORD wNotifyCode, WORD wID,
    HWND hWndCtl, BOOL& bHandled);


// Final message sent to dialog
void OnFinalMessage(HWND hWnd);
```

```
//////////////////////////////////////
// Helper Functions
  // Shut down the application
  HRESULT ShutdownApplication();

  // Initialize the dialog.
  HRESULT Initialize() throw (_com_error);

  // Display the _com_error to the
  // dialog.
  void ShowError(_com_error e);

  // Set the alarm period.
  HRESULT put_Interval(long NewInterval);

  // Set the alarm message.
  HRESULT put_AlarmMessage(CComBSTR MessageText);


//////////////////////////////////////
// Member Variables
protected:
  // The message displayed when the alarm expires
  CComBSTR m_AlarmMessage;

  // The Countdown component for the alarm
  ICountdownPtr m_alarm;

};

#pragma warning(pop)

#endif //__DISPLAY_H_
```

As explained at the beginning of the chapter, in order for a client to receive event notification, it needs to support the source interface of the component firing the events. We also explained that the source interface was a dispinterface, meaning that its method could be called only via **IDispatch**. Therefore, what we need to do in the **CDisplay** class is support the **IDispatch** interface. Fortunately, Microsoft has provided two main templates for doing this. The first, **IDispEventImpl**, is used to receive the countdown notification for the alarm. In the next section we will consider a second template, **IDispSimpleEventImpl**. Since there are several parameters to the **IDispEventImpl** template, a **typedef** for **AlarmCountdownEvents**, which uses **IDispEventImpl**, is used.

```
template <UINT nID, class T,
  const IID* pdiid = &IID_NULL,
  const GUID* plibid = &GUID_NULL,
  WORD wMajor = 0, WORD wMinor = 0,
  class tihclass = CComTypeInfoHolder>
class ATL_NO_VTABLE IDispEventImpl :
  public IDispEventSimpleImpl<nID, T, pdiid>
{
  ...
}
```

The first parameter, **nID**, is an arbitrary ID you assign to the interface that will be receiving the event. Potentially, you could have multiple components, all using the source interface. Since **IDispEventImpl< >** implements **Advise( )** and **Unadvise( )**, the calls to these functions could be ambiguous if there were multiple source connections for the same interface. Because of the **nID** parameter, you can call the **Advise( )** implemented specifically for the component you want to establish the connection with. Secondly, the **nID** allows you to associate specific callback function names so that, again, if you have multiple notifications for the same source interface, you could have them fire into different functions. Notice that except for the first two parameters, all other parameters have defaults specified. When **IID_NULL** is used for the source interface ID, **IDispEventImpl< >** will automatically query the type library for the default interface and then use that. This is where support on the source component for **IProvideClassInfo2** is useful. Rather than having to search the type library, the **GetGUID( )** function on **IProvideClassInfo2** can return the information directly.

The second parameter, **T**, is the class that will be derived from **IDispEventImpl**. In our case this is **CDisplay**. The next parameter, **pdiid**, is the DIID of the dispinterface into which event notification should fire. The next three parameters are the type library IDs and version numbers. Earlier in the chapter when we listed the **Timer.idl**, we noted that you should add the **TmLibraryVersion** enumeration to the library declaration. Now you can see why this is important. It defines constants that we can then use as parameters into the **IDispEventImpl** template.

Without these enumerations, we would have to hard-code the version numbers. Another point to note is that **LIBID_TIMERSLib** is not defined by default. Instead, in the **#import** statement for **Timers.dll**, you need to include the **named_guids** option so as to declare the Timers type library GUID. The full import statement looks like this:

```
#import "..\Timers\Timers.dll" no_namespace, named_guids
```

The **nID** value we use for **AlarmCountdownEvents** is **ID_ALARM**. This is declared immediately above the **typedef**. If you have lots of IDs, you may wish to enter them as resource IDs.

Following the class declaration are the constructor and destructor functions. In addition, the dialog resource ID for the class is declared in a short enumeration.

The next step in implementing the connection point is to declare each of the source event functions you want the client to be notified of. These are each declared using the SINK map. Each entry into the SINK map corresponds to a specific method on the source interface that you wish to receive a call for. The entries are defined using the **SINK_ENTRY_EX** macro. The first parameter for the macro is the **nID** used as part of the **IDispEventImpl** declaration. The next is the DIID of the source interface. The next parameter is the dispatch ID of the function from which you want notification. Here again we see the usefulness of declaring an enumeration within the source components IDL. Rather than having to hard-code dispatch ID values (which theoretically could change for dispinterfaces), we can instead use the **TmICountdownEventsDispatchId** enumeration value for **tmICountdownEventsDispatchIdOnTimeElapsed**. The last parameter in the **SINK_ENTRY_EX** macro is the function within your class that will be called. Notice that this function name does not have to match the function name of the method on the source interface. In fact, in this case it does not. The source interface name for the event is **OnTimeElapsed**, whereas the function name used here is **AlarmTimeElapsed**. The complete SINK map is shown here:

```
BEGIN_SINK_MAP(CDisplay)
SINK_ENTRY_EX(ID_ALARM,
  __uuidof(_ICountdownEvents),
  tmICountdownEventsDispatchIdOnTimeElapsed,
  AlarmTimeElapsed)
END_SINK_MAP()
```

The last step in setting up the connection point interface within the header file is to declare the **AlarmTimeElapsed( )** function:

```
STDMETHOD(AlarmTimeElapsed)(long RemainingIterations);
```

Notice that this method uses the **STDMETHOD** macro, which resolves to

```
HRESULT __stdcall AlarmTimeElapsed(long RemainingIterations);
```

The use of **__stdcall** is what is important. This is an easy item to forget, and without the specification, the callback will not work, even though your program will compile.

Next in the header file comes the message map and its corresponding message handler functions. Since we deleted the OK button from the dialog, we also need to remove the corresponding **OnOK** entry from the message map along with its declaration. This was added by the wizard when we added the dialog class. By default, the message handler functions are implemented within the class declaration. To keep all the implementations together, these have been moved to the **Display.cpp** file, and only the function declaration should remain. The first function, **OnInitDialog( )**, is called with the **WM_INITDIALOG** message. We use this function to perform all the component initialization, including establishing the connection point. The **OnCancel( )** initiates the shutdown of the application. Although the **OnFinalMessage( )** is not actually handled via the **CDisplay** message map, it fits into the same category. It disconnects the connection points and releases the **Countdown** components.

To factor out some of the functionality, several helper functions have been defined. Each of these is self-explanatory, and we will cover them in more detail when we look at their implementation.

The last items to mention are the two member variables **m_alarm** and **m_AlarmMessage**. The first corresponds to the **Countdown** component, which will fire when the interval time has elapsed. The second contains the message to be displayed when the alarm goes off.

Connecting the Connection Point

Let's now focus on the code required to register for event notification, the receiving of those events, and then the cleanup when event notification is no longer required. To begin with, we need to instantiate and initialize a **CDisplay** object. This is done inside **Alarm.cpp** immediately before entering the message pump, as shown here:

```
// ShowDialog.....
CDisplay display;
display.Create(NULL);
if(alarm_message.Length()!=0)
  display.put_AlarmMessage(alarm_message);
display.put_Interval(wait_time);
display.ShowWindow(SW_SHOWNORMAL);

MSG msg;
while (GetMessage(&msg, 0, 0, 0))
    DispatchMessage(&msg);
```

After declaring the display, **Create( )** is called to create the window. Following this, **put_AlarmMessage( )** is called on the **CDisplay** object to specify the message to be displayed. The **put_AlarmMessage( )** is called only if a message was specified on the command line; otherwise, a default message will be used. Next, the timing period for the alarm is set via a call to **put_Interval( )**. Lastly, **ShowWindow( )** is called to display the dialog.

The call to **CDisplay::Create( )** is the catalyst for getting the event notification mechanism set up. This call causes the **WM_INITDIALOG** message to be sent, which in turn calls the **OnInitDialog( )**, which, after initializing a default message, calls **Initialize( )**. These functions are shown here:

```
LRESULT CDisplay::OnInitDialog(UINT uMsg, WPARAM wParam,
  LPARAM lParam, BOOL& bHandled)
{
  LRESULT n_return = 1;
  if(m_AlarmMessage.Length() == 0)
    m_AlarmMessage.LoadString(IDS_DEFAULTMESSAGE);
  try
  {
    Initialize();
  }
  catch(_com_error e)
  {
    ShowError(e);
    n_return = 0;
  }
```

```
HRESULT CDisplay::Initialize() throw (_com_error)
{
  HRESULT hr;

  try
  {
    if(FAILED(hr = m_alarm.CreateInstance(__uuidof(Countdown))))
      _com_raise_error(hr);

    if(FAILED(hr = AlarmCountdownEvents::DispEventAdvise(m_alarm,
          &__uuidof(_ICountdownEvents))))
      _com_raise_error(hr);

    m_alarm->IterationCount = 1;
    m_update_display->Interval = 100;
  }
  catch(_com_error e)
  {
    throw e;
  }

  return hr;
}
```

Initialize( ) is responsible for instantiating the **Countdown** component pointed to by **m_alarm**. Assuming this is successful, a call to establish the connection is made via **AlarmCountdownEvents::DispEventAdvise( )**. Making the call is relatively simple, but all the complexity associated with connecting to a source component is buried under the covers. This includes querying for the **IConnectionPointContainer** interface, finding the **IConnectionPoint** interface associated with the source interface, and then calling **Advise( )** on the resulting **IConnectionPoint** interface pointer. Fortunately, with ATL, you do not need to perform any of this by hand.

If for some reason an error occurs at any point during this process, **ShowError( )** will be called to display the error in the dialog.

Now that the connection to the source component has been established, we need to handle the event notification when it occurs. This is done in the **AlarmTimeElapsed( )** function shown here:

```
STDMETHODIMP CDisplay::AlarmTimeElapsed(
  long RemainingIterations)
{
```

```
  HRESULT hr = S_OK;
  USES_CONVERSION;
  ATLTRACE(_T("Finished\n"));
  CComBSTR text;

  try
  {
    // Turn off the update
    SetDlgItemText(IDC_TIMEREMAINING, OLE2T(m_AlarmMessage));
    SetDlgItemText(IDCANCEL, _T("Close"));
  }
  catch(_com_error e)
  {
    ShowError(e);
    hr = e.Error();
  }

  SetForegroundWindow(this->m_hWnd);
  MessageBeep(MB_ICONEXCLAMATION);
  SetDlgItemText(IDCANCEL, _T("Close"));

  return hr;
}
```

AlarmTimeElapsed( ) simply beeps and changes the display text to the alarm message.

Any time the dialog is displayed and the user clicks the Cancel button, **OnCancel( )** will be called, which in turn will call **ShutdownApplication( )**. **Shutdown( )** is responsible for calling **PostQuitMessage( )** to initialize the shutdown of the application, as shown here:

```
LRESULT CDisplay::OnCancel(WORD wNotifyCode, WORD wID,
  HWND hWndCtl, BOOL& bHandled)
{
  ShutdownApplication();
  return 0;
}

HRESULT CDisplay::ShutdownApplication()
{
  DestroyWindow();
  PostQuitMessage(0);
```

```
  return S_OK;
}

void CDisplay::OnFinalMessage(HWND hWnd)
{
  m_update_display.DispEventUnadvise();
  AlarmCountdownEvents::DispEventUnadvise(
    m_alarm);

  m_alarm = NULL;
}
```

The result of this message is a call to **OnFinalMessage( )**, which provides an opportunity to remove the event notification and release the components. Since **m_alarm** is a smart pointer, this release is called by setting it to **NULL**.

The only thing remaining is the **put_Interval( )** and **put_AlarmMessage( )** implementation. This is shown here:

```
HRESULT CDisplay::put_AlarmMessage(CComBSTR MessageText)
{
  m_AlarmMessage = MessageText;
  return S_OK;
}

HRESULT CDisplay::put_Interval(long NewInterval)
{
  HRESULT hr = S_OK;
  ATLASSERT(m_alarm!=NULL);
  try
  {
    m_alarm->Interval = NewInterval;
  }
  catch(_com_error e)
  {
    hr = e.Error();
    ShowError(e);
  }
  return hr;
}
```

Since calling **put_Interval( )** directly sets the interval on **m_alarm**, the alarm starts as soon as **put_Interval( )** is called.

Reference Counting and Connection Points

As explained earlier in this book, the key to reference counting is that whenever a new reference to an interface is created, **AddRef( )** must be called, and when the reference is removed, **Release( )** must be called. One of the fascinating things about **IDispEventImpl< >**, however, is that even though it has implementations for both **AddRef( )** and **Release( )**, both implementations do nothing except return one. Here is the code, which can be found in **Atlcom.h**:

```
virtual ULONG STDMETHODCALLTYPE AddRef()
{
  return 1;
}
virtual ULONG STDMETHODCALLTYPE Release()
{
  return 1;
}
```

The obvious question is why don't these functions keep track of any references to themselves? The reason is circular references. Since the client keeps a reference to the source interface, if the source interface also kept a reference to the client, then the reference count on these components would always be greater than zero, even when in reality they were not being referenced by anything else besides themselves. The result would be that unless one of the two participants explicitly called **Release( )** on the other, the components would be forced to stay in memory. If, for example, the **m_alarm** interface pointer were not released until the destructor for **CDisplay** was called, and the destructor for **CDisplay** were not called until its reference count went down to zero, then these components would never be released because each of their reference counts would remain at one. To avoid this problem, the base classes of **IDispEventImpl** do not perform any real reference counting within their implementation of **IUnknown**.

Although the above method provides a simple solution for cases in which the class listening to the event is not a full ATL object, this does not work in the more complex case. When your implementation class is a component whose most derived class is **CComObject** or one of its cousins, the **AddRef( )** and **Release( )** methods on these classes take precedence over the **IDispEventImpl< >** reference counting implementation. **CComObject** overrides the **AddRef( )** and **Release( )** methods supported by **IDispEventImpl< >**. This presents a problem because now there are two conflicting **AddRef( )/Release( )** requirements. In one case these methods must actually do reference counting, and in the second they should not. The result is that a circular reference counting problem can occur.

The solution to the problem that we will consider in our client is to create embedded classes inside **CDisplay** that can be responsible for handling the events or sending notification to **CDisplay**. By placing the event notification code within a second class, the conflict in **AddRef( )/Release( )** functionality no longer occurs. The **CComObject**-derived component will perform reference counting as it should, and the embedded component simply pretends to perform reference counting. Figure 10-6 provides a graphical view of the mechanism.

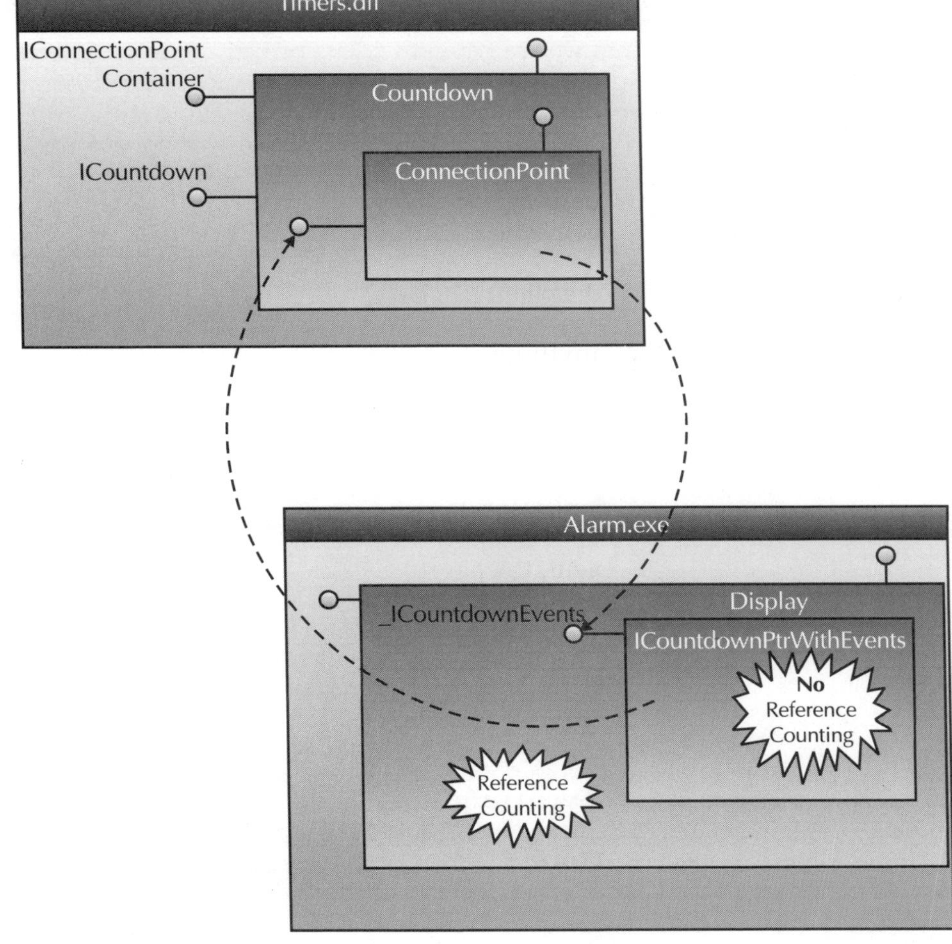

Avoiding the circular reference by using an embedded class without reference counting

Figure 10-6.

To demonstrate how to code the embedded class, we are going to add a second **Countdown** element to the **Alarm**. Rather than simply displaying the message at the end, when the time has elapsed, we will use a second **Countdown** object to notify the **Alarm** every 100 milliseconds, so that the dialog can be updated with the remaining time. Since **CDisplay** is not a real COM object, we could use the same mechanism that we did before, deriving **CDisplay** from a new **IDispEventImpl**, but instead we will use the embedded mechanism to demonstrate how it can be done for those cases in which you may have a full ATL object that is listening to events.

Avoiding Circular Reference Counts with an Embedded Listener Class

In this section we are going to create one more **Countdown** listener. The purpose of this listener is to update the display every 100 milliseconds so that it shows how much time is remaining before the alarm will expire. As we have described above, we are going to create an additional class whose sole responsibility will be listening to the "update display" timer.

Although we could certainly include this new class as an internal class within **CDisplay**, because of the likelihood that other **Countdown** listeners will be created, we will instead define a template for the purpose. The name of the template class is **ICountdownPtrWithEvents** and it like its parent, **ICountdownPtr**, will be a smart pointer class. A listing for the class, which is defined in **CountdownWithEvents.h**, is shown below.

```
#import "timers.dll" no_namespace, named_guids

//////////////////////////////////////
// Update Sink class declaration
#define ICOUNTDOWN_DISP_EVENT_IMPL  \
    IDispEventImpl<I, ICountdownPtrWithEvents, \
    &__uuidof(_ICountdownEvents), \
    &LIBID_TIMERSLib, \
    tmLibraryVersionMajor, tmLibraryVersionMinor>

template <UINT I, class T>
class ICountdownPtrWithEvents :
  public ICOUNTDOWN_DISP_EVENT_IMPL,
  public ICountdownPtr
{
```

```
public:
  ICountdownPtrWithEvents()
  {
  }

  ~ICountdownPtrWithEvents()
  {
  }

// Overriding these as private prevents an inadvertent
// call from being made.  Instead, explicit calls to
// RealAddRef() and RealRelease() should be used.
private:
  virtual ULONG STDMETHODCALLTYPE AddRef()
  {
    return ICOUNTDOWN_DISP_EVENT_IMPL::AddRef();
  }
  virtual ULONG STDMETHODCALLTYPE Release()
  {
    return ICOUNTDOWN_DISP_EVENT_IMPL::AddRef();
  }

public:
  // Normally, AddRef( ) and Release() for this
  // class are fake because it is to be used
  // as a callback interface only.  However,
  // if real reference counting is required on
  // the ICountdown interface then use the methods
  // below.
  virtual ULONG STDMETHODCALLTYPE RealAddRef()
  {
    ICountdownPtr::AddRef();
    return 1;
  }
  virtual ULONG STDMETHODCALLTYPE RealRelease()
  {
    ICountdownPtr::Release();
    return 1;
  }


public:
  BEGIN_SINK_MAP(ICountdownPtrWithEvents)
    SINK_ENTRY_EX(I,
```

```
        __uuidof(_ICountdownEvents),
        tmICountdownEventsDispatchIdOnTimeElapsed,
        OnTimeElapsed)
    END_SINK_MAP()


    STDMETHOD(OnTimeElapsed)(long RemainingIterations)
    {
      ATLASSERT(m_pDisplay != NULL);
      return m_pDisplay->OnTimeElapsed(this, RemainingIterations);
    };

    // Override DispEventAdvise to prevent a call
    // without initializing m_pDisplay.
  private:
    HRESULT DispEventAdvise( IUnknown* pUnk )
    {
      ATLASSERT(false)
    };

  public:
    // Overload DispEventAdvise to simplify the call
      HRESULT DispEventAdvise(T* pDisplay)
    {
      HRESULT hr;
      m_pDisplay = pDisplay;
      IUnknownPtr pUnk;
      hr = QueryInterface(__uuidof(IUnknown), &pUnk);
      if (SUCCEEDED(hr))
      {
        hr = ICOUNTDOWN_DISP_EVENT_IMPL::DispEventAdvise(pUnk);
      }
      return hr;
    }

    // Override DispEventUnadvise so as to simplify
    // the call later on.
    HRESULT DispEventUnadvise()
    {
      HRESULT hr;
      m_pDisplay = NULL;
      IUnknownPtr pUnk;
      hr = QueryInterface(__uuidof(IUnknown), &pUnk);
      if (SUCCEEDED(hr))
```

```
    {
      hr = ICOUNTDOWN_DISP_EVENT_IMPL::DispEventUnadvise(pUnk);
    }
    return hr;
  }

  ICountdownPtr& operator=(int null)
  {
    return ICountdownPtr::operator=(null);
  }

private:
  T* m_pDisplay;

};
```

The **ICountdownPtrWithEvents** class is derived from two other classes. The first is **IDispEventImpl**, which we have already examined. The second, **ICountdownPtr**, is the **Countdown** timer's smart pointer from the **#import** of **Timers.dll** or **Timers.tlb**. The addition of **ICountdownPtr** is not a requirement but is helpful because it handles things like instantiation, and, since the default interface (**ICountdown**) is required in order to start the **Countdown** anyway, it is helpful to simply combine them into one class.

In spite of the fact that one of the key advantages to the **ICountdownPtr** is that it automatically handles reference counting, as a source interface, this is not something we want to use. This fact explains why the **AddRef( )** and **Release( )** functions have been overridden and the overriding functions direct the reference counting calls to the **IDispEventImpl** implementations rather than the **ICountdownPtr** implementations. That way, when the event source calls into the **_ICountdownEvents** interface implemented by **ICountdownPtrWithEvents**, fake reference counting will take place and the circular reference problem will be avoided. For the times when you do need to perform "real" reference counting, **RealAddRef( )** and **RealRelease( )** have been added.

The **ICountdownPtrWithEvents** class is a template with two parameters—the ID of the component you will be listening to and the name of the class that will contain it; this containing class is **CDisplay**. The purpose of adding the ID as a template parameter is that it enables you to supply multiple listener functions on the **CDisplay**. Thus, for times when you are monitoring multiple **Countdown** components, you can have different functions listening to different instances of the **Countdown** and performing different actions.

Because the **ICountdownPtrWithEvents** class takes the ID parameter, you can effectively overload the function call from the listener class into your main class, **CDisplay**. Not only do you have the option of having multiple functions on **CDisplay**—each one responsible for a different **Countdown** component ID and each one performing a different action—you can also just have one function that monitors multiple components. This prevents you from having to write a separate set of functions to listen to each **Countdown** instance, providing a different ID for each instance. To do this, you would specify the same ID for multiple member variables (or even an array of member variables). Distinguishing which **Countdown** component is reporting an event is then based on the pointer passed into the callback.

Let's take a look at some of the **CDisplay**-to-**ICountdownPtrWithEvents** communication specifically to see how this works. Inside the **ICountdownPtrWithEvents** class we have the **OnTimeElapsed( )** member function. It is this function's responsibility to dispatch all calls to the appropriate container class and function as shown below.

```
STDMETHOD(OnTimeElapsed)(long RemainingIterations)
{
  ATLASSERT(m_pDisplay != NULL);
  return m_pDisplay->OnTimeElapsed(this, RemainingIterations);
};
```

Notice the passing of the **this** pointer. This allows the called function to identify which component is calling, even if the same **Countdown** ID was used, such as in an array. Below is the corresponding declaration in **CDisplay** that will be called.

```
////////////////////////////////////
// COM Event hookups
public:
  STDMETHOD(AlarmTimeElapsed)(long RemainingIterations);
  HRESULT OnTimeElapsed(
    ICountdownPtrWithEvents<ID_UPDATE_COUNTDOWN, CDisplay>* const update,
    long RemainingIterations);
```

The function declaration shown is for the **Countdown** component with the ID of **ID_UPDATE_COUNTDOWN**. This function is then used by the **m_update_display** member variable.

```
  // The Countdown component used to update
  // the display with the remaining time.
  ICountdownPtrWithEvents<
    ID_UPDATE_COUNTDOWN, CDisplay> m_update_display;
```

Since we have only one listener declared using **ICountdownPtrWithEvents**, it is a bit of overkill to use a template to provide the functionality shown. However, if you were to have this one class listening to multiple **Countdown** components, the template would be extremely useful. Without it you would have to define the **ICountdownPtrWithEvents** multiple times, each with a different name. Also, as already mentioned, you do not have to use different IDs if you wish the same code to be executed for a set of source components. For example, a second **ICountdownPtrWithEvents<ID_UPDATE_COUNTDOWN, CDisplay>** variable could be declared, in which case **CDisplay::OnTimeElapsed( )** would receive the notification from both. Again, to distinguish between the **m_update_display** variable and the new variable you would check the **ICountdownPtrWithEvents<ID_UPDATE_COUNTDOWN, CDisplay>** variable that is passed in. (This is the first parameter in the **OnTimeElapsed( )** function shown above.)

Interestingly enough, the current version of Visual Basic does not support this capability. In Visual Basic you must define a variable (not even an array) for every source component you wish to listen to. The result is that the maximum number of listeners needs to be defined at compile time and cannot dynamically increase above the maximum at runtime.

The **DispEventAdvise( )** and **DispEventUnadvise( )** methods on **IDispEventSimpleImpl** are overloaded, first to ensure that **m_pDisplay** gets set and second to simplify the call by retrieving the **IUnknown** pointer.

To finish the example, let's take a look at the final **Display.cpp** file:

```
// Display.cpp : Implementation of CDisplay
#include "stdafx.h"
#include "Display.h"

//  Exception declaration not yet standardized
#pragma warning(push)
#pragma warning( disable : 4290 )

/////////////////////////////////////////////////////////////////////
// CDisplay

/////////////////////////////////////////////////////////////////////
// Windows Events
LRESULT CDisplay::OnInitDialog(UINT uMsg, WPARAM wParam,
  LPARAM lParam, BOOL& bHandled)
{
  LRESULT n_return = 1;
  if(m_AlarmMessage.Length() == 0)
    m_AlarmMessage.LoadString(IDS_DEFAULTMESSAGE);
  try
```

```
  {
    Initialize();
  }
  catch(_com_error e)
  {
    ShowError(e);
    n_return = 0;
  }


  return n_return;  // Let the system set the focus
}

LRESULT CDisplay::OnCancel(WORD wNotifyCode, WORD wID,
  HWND hWndCtl, BOOL& bHandled)
{
  ShutdownApplication();
  return 0;
}

void CDisplay::OnFinalMessage(HWND hWnd)
{
  m_update_display.DispEventUnadvise();
  AlarmCountdownEvents::DispEventUnadvise(
    m_alarm);
  m_update_display = NULL;
  m_alarm = NULL;
}

////////////////////////////////////////////////////////////////////
// COM Events

// Called by the source Countdown component, m_alarm,
// when the timer expires.
STDMETHODIMP CDisplay::AlarmTimeElapsed(
  long RemainingIterations)
{

  HRESULT hr = S_OK;
  USES_CONVERSION;
  ATLTRACE(_T("Finished\n"));
  CComBSTR text;

  try
  {
    // Turn off the update
    m_update_display->Interval = 0;
    SetDlgItemText(IDC_TIMEREMAINING, OLE2T(m_AlarmMessage));
    SetDlgItemText(IDCANCEL, _T("Close"));
  }
  catch(_com_error e)
```

```
  {
    ShowError(e);
    hr = e.Error();
  }

  SetForegroundWindow(this->m_hWnd);
  MessageBeep(MB_ICONEXCLAMATION);
  SetDlgItemText(IDCANCEL, _T("Close"));

  return hr;
}

HRESULT CDisplay::OnTimeElapsed(
  ICountdownPtrWithEvents<ID_UPDATE_COUNTDOWN, CDisplay>* update,
  long RemainingIterations)
{
  HRESULT hr;
  USES_CONVERSION;
  CComVariant time_remaining;
  CComBSTR bstr_text;
  const TCHAR* label_text;

  try
  {
    time_remaining = (_variant_t)m_alarm->TimeRemaining;
    if(time_remaining.lVal == (long)-1)
      bstr_text = _T("Alarm not set!");
    else
    {
      hr = time_remaining.ChangeType(VT_BSTR);
      ATLASSERT(SUCCEEDED(hr));
      bstr_text = time_remaining.bstrVal;
      bstr_text += L" Milliseconds Remaining on Alarm";
    }
    label_text = OLE2T(bstr_text);

    SetDlgItemText(IDC_TIMEREMAINING, label_text);
  }
  catch(_com_error e)
  {
    ShowError(e);
  }
  return S_OK;
}


/////////////////////////////////////////////////////////////////////
// Helper Functions
void CDisplay::ShowError(_com_error e)
{
```

```
    USES_CONVERSION;
    CComBSTR bstr;
    TCHAR* full_error_message;
    PVOID p_args[2];
    HRESULT error_number;
    TCHAR* error_description;


    if( e.Description().length() > 0)
    {
      bstr += (TCHAR*)e.Description();
    }
    else
      bstr += e.ErrorMessage();

    error_number = e.Error();
    error_description = OLE2T(bstr);

    p_args[0] = &error_description;
    p_args[1] = &error_number;

    FormatMessage(
      FORMAT_MESSAGE_ALLOCATE_BUFFER |
      FORMAT_MESSAGE_FROM_STRING ,
      _T("Error(%2!d!):  %1!s!"),
      NULL,
      MAKELANGID(LANG_NEUTRAL, SUBLANG_DEFAULT), // Default language
      (LPTSTR) &full_error_message,
      0, (va_list*)  &p_args );

    ATLTRACE(_T("%s\n"), (TCHAR*)full_error_message);
    SetDlgItemText(IDC_TIMEREMAINING, (TCHAR*)full_error_message);

    LocalFree( full_error_message );
  }

  HRESULT CDisplay::Initialize() throw (_com_error)
  {
    HRESULT hr;

    try
    {
      if(FAILED(hr = m_alarm.CreateInstance(__uuidof(Countdown))))
        _com_raise_error(hr);

      if(FAILED(hr =
          m_update_display.CreateInstance(__uuidof(Countdown))))
        _com_raise_error(hr);
      if SUCCEEDED(hr = m_update_display.DispEventAdvise(this))
        hr = AlarmCountdownEvents::DispEventAdvise(m_alarm,
```

```
            &__uuidof(_ICountdownEvents));

        if(FAILED(hr))
          _com_raise_error(hr);

        m_alarm->IterationCount = 1;
        m_update_display->Interval = 100;
      }
      catch(_com_error e)
      {
        throw e;
      }

      return hr;
    }

    HRESULT CDisplay::put_AlarmMessage(CComBSTR MessageText)
    {
      m_AlarmMessage = MessageText;
      return S_OK;
    }

    HRESULT CDisplay::put_Interval(long NewInterval)
    {
      HRESULT hr = S_OK;
      ATLASSERT(m_alarm!=NULL);
      try
      {
        m_alarm->Interval = NewInterval;
      }
      catch(_com_error e)
      {
        hr = e.Error();
        ShowError(e);
      }
      return hr;
    }

    HRESULT CDisplay::ShutdownApplication()
    {
      DestroyWindow();
      PostQuitMessage(0);
      return S_OK;
    }

    #pragma warning(pop)
```

The connection point setup essentially mirrors that used for the **m_alarm** variable.

The implementation of **CDisplay::OnTimeElapsed( )** retrieves the remaining time from the **Countdown** component pointed to by **m_alarm** and displays the result within the dialog.

By the way, since the callback implementation can be somewhat complex, it may be helpful for you to consider distributing a template such as the **ICountdownPtrWithEvents** template along with your component. One additional comment: consider using the **CComPtr** or **CComPtrQI** classes in place of the **ICountdownPtr** classes in your inheritance tree for **ICountdownPtrWithEvents**.

IDispEventImpl and IDispEventSimpleImpl

There are a few more details about **IDispEventImpl** and its base class that are worth discussing. First, the implementation of **IDispEventImpl< >** provides for a unique COM identity to the source component. In other words, rather than returning a pointer to **CDisplay**'s vtable, a different COM object is created specifically for the purpose of event notification. The interesting thing about its implementation is that **QueryInterface( )** will support interfaces on the main component—in this case, **CDisplay**. Second, **IDispEventImpl** requires that you have the type library information at compile time. It then uses this information at runtime when connecting to the component source. This introduces a small inefficiency that could be avoided with some slightly more complex programming. The solution is to use the **IDispEventSimpleImpl< >** template from which **IDispEventImpl< >** is derived. Using **IDispEventSimpleImpl< >** requires that you use the **_ATL_FUNC_INFO** structure. This is required for describing each of the functions on which the listener wants to receive notification. The **_ATL_FUNC_INFO** structure is defined within **Atlcom.h** as follows:

```
struct _ATL_FUNC_INFO
{
  CALLCONV cc;
  VARTYPE vtReturn;
  SHORT nParams;
  VARTYPE pVarTypes[_ATL_MAX_VARTYPES];
};
```

The **cc** field indicates the calling convention. This should be **CC_STDCALL**. The next element, **vtReturn**, declares the return value from the function call. Typically, there is no return value from an event call, so **VT_EMPTY** should be used. The next element is the count of the number of elements in the **pVarTypes** array, which is used to pass an array of the parameter types to the listener. As with **IDispEventImpl**< >, **IDispEventSimpleImpl**< > also has a SINK map. The difference with **IDispEventSimpleImpl**< >, however, is that each entry is added using the **SINK_ENTRY_INFO** macro because you need to include the **_ATL_FUNC_INFO** structure associated with the event in the map.

This completes a rather in-depth analysis of connection points. In spite of the inherent complexity of connection points, they are not very difficult to implement on either the client or the server, thanks to the ATL classes and wizards.

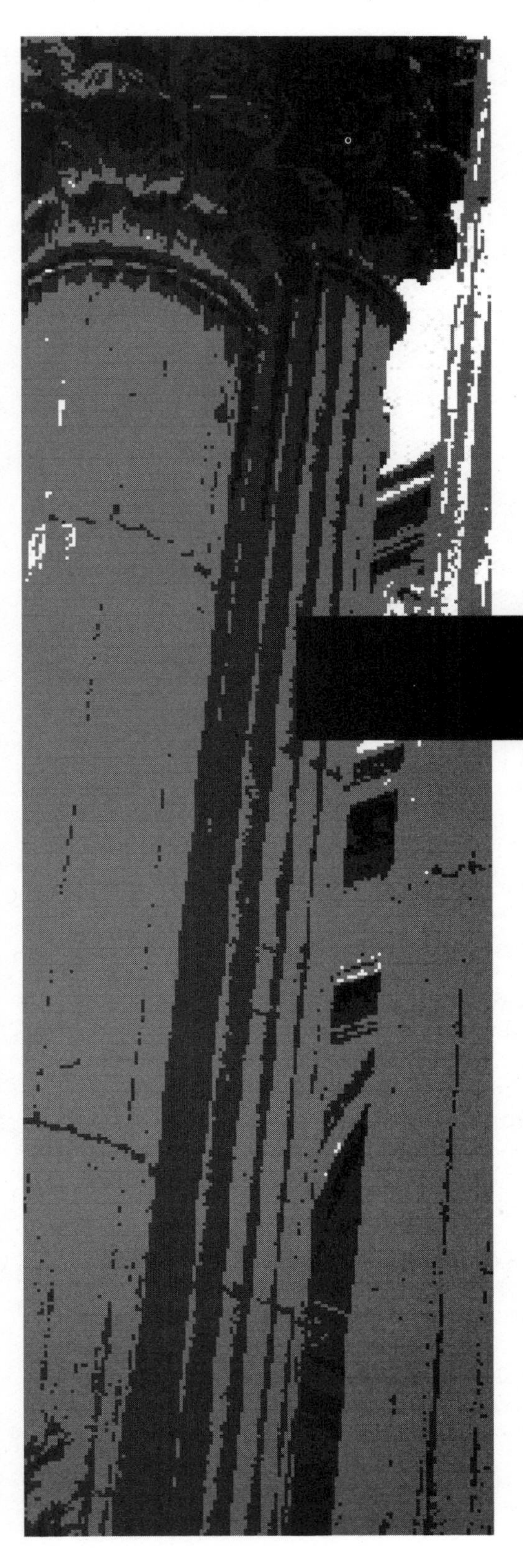

CHAPTER 11

ActiveX

Before moving on to more advanced COM topics, we will pause for a moment to examine one of the most common uses of COM: ActiveX. ActiveX is a technology based on COM. It was initially created to extend the COM functionality to the Internet, but it can be used by any application. Although ActiveX comprises all interobject communication based on COM, most people associate ActiveX with ActiveX *controls*, which are the focus of this chapter.

ActiveX Controls

A control is a graphical user interface (GUI) item that allows a user to interact with a Windows program. Windows comes with a set of standard controls (such as pushbuttons, edit boxes, drop-down boxes, etc.) that are fine for basic data entry and toolbars. However, for more sophisticated user interfaces, a custom control is required.

The first custom controls available in Windows were Visual Basic Extension (VBX) controls. VBX controls were DLLs with specific entry points, and they were designed to work with Visual Basic forms. When OLE was introduced, VBX controls were replaced with the COM-based OLE Custom Controls (OCX). These had much better C++ support, as well as all the other COM benefits such as type libraries and menu and toolbar merging. However, all this functionality came at a price. The OCX control specification listed all the COM interfaces that OCX containers expected. If any of these were not present, the container could refuse to embed your control. This meant that you had to implement interfaces you didn't need, just to keep the container happy, which bloated your code unnecessarily. In the Internet world, where controls are sent to users over potentially slow connections, this was unacceptable. Therefore, a new standard was made—the ActiveX control. An ActiveX control is an OCX control, but all of the interfaces are optional. This means a control can be very lightweight. Controls that have no user interface at all (for example, ActiveX Data Objects) need not implement any of the UI interfaces. Controls used for calculations that don't store any data need not implement the persistence interfaces, and so on.

An ActiveX control is essentially an OCX control, but all of the interfaces are optional.

Developing an ActiveX Control

In Chapter 2 we developed a stopwatch using raw C++, implementing the interfaces "manually." In Chapter 3 we introduced ATL and used it to take the drudgery out of implementing the interfaces. In this chapter we will use ATL to develop an ActiveX control. We are going to take the **Stopwatch** object created in Chapter 3 and put a "skin" around it—in other words, we are going to create a graphical user interface (GUI) for it. We will cover

- Creating an empty ATL project and using the wizard to add features
- Identifying the interfaces needed by an ActiveX control
- Reusing code through aggregation
- Getting the container to save and restore permanent data (*persistence*)
- Adding a property page dialog
- Creating controls dynamically at runtime

The stopwatch control's user interface will show the current elapsed time and will provide a button to reset the timer. The programmatic interface will provide access to the same functionality: It will export the current elapsed time as a property and provide a method to reset the timer.

Creating an Empty ATL Project

To create the stopwatch control, start with an empty ATL project as you did in Chapter 3. Enter **Stopwatch** in the Project name field. In the Step 1 of 1 dialog, select the server type Dynamic Link Library (DLL). After clicking Finish and then OK, you will have an empty project.

Adding a Control Template

ATL is extremely versatile and allows for the creation of many types of projects. In order to make this project into an ActiveX control, you need to add a control template using the wizard. As we have done in previous chapters, return to the Class View tab, click the right mouse button over "Stopwatch classes," and select New ATL Object from the context menu. The ATL Object wizard will appear.

As you have already seen, the Object wizard is a code-generation wizard that will insert source code into your C++ project based on the category and object you choose. Here is a brief overview of the categories and the types of objects available. The categories are listed in the left pane of the ATL Object wizard.

The first category is the Object category.

- **Simple object**: This is what we used in Chapter 3 to make the **Stopwatch** component. It inserts the code for a basic COM object with a custom dual interface.

- **Add-in object**: This object is used to change the characteristics of the Visual Studio development environment.
- **Internet Explorer object**: This adds all the COM interfaces for controlling IE. You would use this type of object if you were writing a Browser Helper Object (BHO), for example. A BHO is loaded automatically by IE and uses IE's user interface, so you don't need one in your DLL.
- **ActiveX server component**: This helps you extend IIS by writing COM servers to act as middleware between your code and ASP pages (similar to Enterprise Java Beans and JSP). These components are sometimes referred to as *ISAPI plug-ins*.
- **MMC snap-in**: In order to eliminate the clutter of control panel applets, and to centralize the UI for all control panel–type applications, Microsoft introduced the MMC (Microsoft Management Console). It has the standard "tree view on the left, properties page on the right" user interface. Instead of control panel applets, the MMC takes *snap-ins,* which are just COM DLLs with specific known interfaces. You can use the MMC SnapIn object to create a skin for your existing application and port the functionality over.
- **MS Transaction Server object**: This provides all the interfaces needed by MTS to make a complete transaction object. We will discuss this further in Chapter 14, but Windows 2000 no longer requires much of the functionality that this wizard includes. Unless you require Windows NT 4.0 support, this selection will not be used.
- **Component registrar object**: This object inserts code that gives you complete control over how the components in your DLL are registered. Of course, this applies only to DLLs that comprise more than one component! If you do not implement this class yourself, ATL will automatically register all components in your DLL via **DllRegisterServer** and will unregister them when **DllUnRegisterServer** is called.

A lite ActiveX control includes only the interfaces required by Internet Explorer.

Under the Controls category, you can add as many controls to your project as you like. (Each one will have a separate GUID and ProgId, so they can be instantiated separately.) For all but the Property Page there is a "full" and a "lite" version of the control. The only difference is that the lite version includes only interfaces that are used by Internet Explorer. So if the only target for your control is a Web page displayed in IE, use the lite version.

- **Full (lite) control**: This is a basic ActiveX control. You can paint directly into the client area of the control (as we will in this example), or you can insert a child dialog to host child controls. You can create windowed or windowless controls (controls that do or do not have an **HWND**). Windowless controls can still get Windows messages (they are forwarded by the container). Use this control if you don't want any child controls, or if none of your child controls are ActiveX controls (in other words, they are all Windows controls).
- **Composite (lite) control**: The composite control is an ActiveX control container, so it can host other ActiveX controls. The Dialog object can host only standard Windows controls, not ActiveX controls, so you will need a composite control if you are planning on having child ActiveX controls.
- **HTML (lite) control**: The HTML control is like the composite control in that it is embeddable and it hosts an ActiveX control, but it hosts a specific ActiveX control: the Microsoft Web Browser control. This is the same control that is used by Internet Explorer, the Active Desktop, the file system Explorer, and so on. The wizard creates code that gives you access to the **IWebBrowser2** pointer, so you have complete access to the document object model, the navigation operations, and so on.
- **Property page**: The property page object inserts the code for a custom property page. You do not need to add a property page for stock properties; ATL handles that automatically. We will add a custom property page later in this chapter.

Next, the Miscellaneous category is a catch-all category for objects that don't fit into the other categories. Currently, the only object defined in Miscellaneous is this:

- **Dialog**: This is very similar to adding a dialog object in MFC. ATL adds the appropriate dialog resource to your RC file and adds stub code for the creation, message routing, and so on, of the dialog. Child controls are added to the dialog using the resource editor.

The two objects in the Data Access category are used to generate COM objects for use with OLEDB. The OLEDB architecture is designed around *consumers* and *providers* of data.

- **Provider**: This object adds the interfaces necessary for an OLEDB provider. A provider supplies data.

- **Consumer**: This adds template code that allows an object to consume data from an OLEDB provider.

We want to add a full control template, so click on Controls in the left list box and select Full Control from the right list box. Then click Next to proceed.

Enter **StopwatchControl** for the short name and leave the defaults. Once the names are filled in, we can proceed to the Attributes tab. (This was also discussed in detail in Chapter 3.) The defaults are adequate here, so let's proceed to the Miscellaneous tab, shown in Figure 11-1. These options allow you to further customize the code generated by the ATL Object wizard.

The View Status options are used by containers (through the **IView-StatusEx** interface) to determine how the control should be drawn. (Refer to the OLE documentation on the **VIEWSTATUS** enumeration.) An opaque control is one that is not transparent. In other words, the control promises to take care of painting its entire client area. This is the behavior of most controls; so select Opaque unless you have a good reason to see the content of the container "under" the control. Checking Solid Background optimizes the drawing by allowing a quick rectangular fill with a solid color instead of creating a patterned brush.

The Miscellaneous tab

Figure 11-1.

Use the "Add control based on" combo box if you want to create an ActiveX control based on one of the standard Windows controls, but with your own custom behavior. The wizard will add some boilerplate code (principally a **CContainedWindow** class and some message handlers) for that particular control; then you can add your custom code.

The Misc Status fields are some of the fields available in the **OLEMISC** enumeration, which is returned through the **IOleObject** interface. "Invisible at runtime" creates an invisible control. Invisible controls are useful as calculating engines, or gateways to a database. They can be added to a form using a standard GUI builder (such as VB or Microsoft Access) in design mode and will not display when actually running. "Acts like button" is a hint to containers that this control should be treated as a button to enable this as a default button (the one that gets "pressed" as the user presses ENTER or the SPACEBAR). "Acts like label" is for control containers that understand labels (such as MS Access). These containers often allow mnemonic keys (a letter preceded by an ampersand) in the label, which allows the user to set the focus to the next control in the tab order. The "acts like" bits are only hints to the container; they can be ignored.

The last group of controls appears in the Other fields. Normalize DC is used to indicate that you want ATL to "normalize" the DC in its **OnDrawAdvanced( )** method before calling your **OnDraw( )**. If you don't normalize, the control will get the raw DC from the container, which could be in any mapping mode and could have the window and/or viewport origins shifted away from (0,0). By normalizing, you can be sure the mode is **MM_TEXT** and the origin is where you would expect it to be. The normalized DC is passed in to your drawing code via the **ATL_DRAWINFO** parameter of **OnDraw( )**. **OnDrawAdvanced( )** sets the DC back to the way it was before returning.

Windowed Only forces ATL to create a window for all containers, even ones that support windowless controls. If you don't need an **HWND**, leave this unchecked, and your control will be even lighter for containers that support windowless controls. You can still receive and handle Windows messages, even if you do not have an **HWND**. The container passes these messages to the control via the **IOleInPlaceObjectWindowless** interface. ATL wraps that call and simply calls your handler macros exactly as it would for windowed controls. Insertable adds a special registry key that marks the control as available in the Insert Object dialog of most containers. This allows users to insert your control using a GUI. Mark this control as insertable by checking the box, and move on to the Stock Properties tab.

On the Stock Properties tab you'll find a large number of properties that are supported automatically by ATL through the **CStockPropImpl** class. Any stock properties you select here will cause the wizard to add the appropriate **PROP_MAP** macros, as well as the appropriate entries in the IDL file to export the get and put operations. For this example, select Background Color, and then press the ≥ key to move it to the right-hand list box (see Figure 11-2). This allows the user to set the background color programmatically or through the properties dialog (which we will add later). Note that this is the only place that ATL provides wizard support for adding stock properties; so you should make sure you select all of the stock properties you are going to need in your control here, or else you will have to add them "manually" yourself. This is not difficult, but the wizard automatically assigns the correct dispatch IDs, which saves you from having to research the one corresponding to your stock property.

Now click OK. The wizard will add the **StopwatchControl** object.

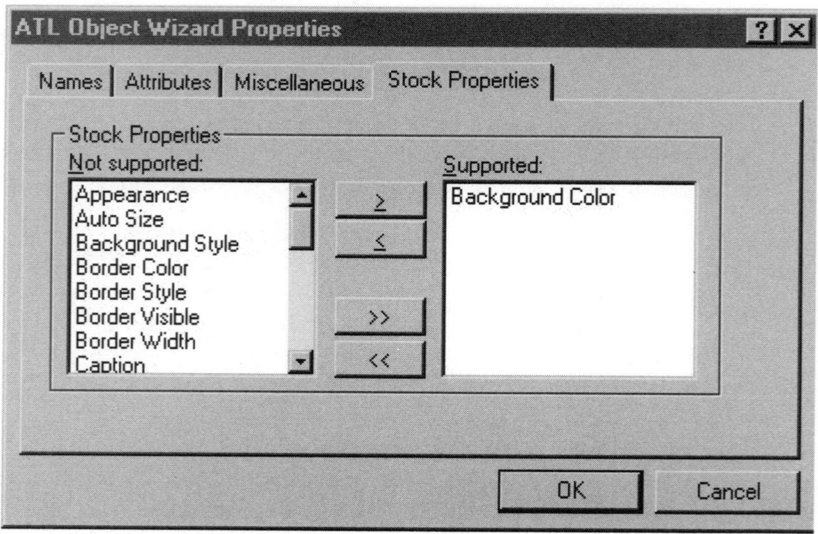

The Stock Properties tab
Figure 11-2.

The StopwatchControl Object

The wizard has just added three files to our project (**StopwatchControl.h**, **StopwatchControl.cpp**, and **StopwatchControl.rgs**) and has modified the IDL file somewhat. Let's examine these in detail.

The RGS File

The RGS file is very similar to the one generated in Chapter 3, with some additional keys marking this as a control, and as insertable. It is shown here:

```
HKCR
{
  Stopwatch.StopwatchControl.1 = s 'StopwatchControl Class'
  {
    CLSID = s '{897704DC-0B8D-437A-B2DE-D2251515BE14}'
    'Insertable'
  }
  Stopwatch.StopwatchControl = s 'StopwatchControl Class'
  {
    CLSID = s '{897704DC-0B8D-437A-B2DE-D2251515BE14}'
    CurVer = s 'Stopwatch.StopwatchControl.1'
  }
  NoRemove CLSID
  {
    ForceRemove {897704DC-0B8D-437A-B2DE-D2251515BE14} \
      = s 'StopwatchControl Class'
    {
      ProgID = s 'Stopwatch.StopwatchControl.1'
      VersionIndependentProgID = s 'Stopwatch.StopwatchControl'
      ForceRemove 'Programmable'
      InprocServer32 = s '%MODULE%'
      {
        val ThreadingModel = s 'Apartment'
      }
      ForceRemove 'Control'
      ForceRemove 'Insertable'
      ForceRemove 'ToolboxBitmap32' = s '%MODULE%, 101'
      'MiscStatus' = s '0'
      {
          '1' = s '131473'
      }
      'TypeLib' = s '{EE676989-F2F9-4167-BB9F-5F507B3BCC86}'
```

```
        'Version' = s '1.0'
      }
    }
  }
```

The ATL shorthand takes a little getting used to, but you will find that these RGS scripts are very powerful. (Refer to the ATL documentation for a more detailed explanation.) You can, of course, add any registry settings, not just the ones generated by the wizard. The keys are added whenever your **DllRegisterServer( )** function is called. **DllRegisterServer( )** is called by most component installers and also by the Visual C++ IDE whenever you do a build. It is also called by the **RegSvr32.exe** program. Note that the keys are not removed by **DllUnregisterServer( )** unless you mark them with the **ForceRemove** keyword. This gives you the option of preserving registry settings between installations. The RGS source file is compiled by the resource compiler into a binary object, which is linked to your control's resources.

Note the **ToolboxBitmap32** value. This enables you to specify the resource ID of the bitmap that will appear within a toolbox button bar in various development environments. By default, the wizard specifies one for you.

The IDL File

IDL files were discussed in detail in Chapter 4, so we will go over the items briefly here. Below, you can see that the wizard created a dual interface (which, as you know, means that methods can be called generically through **IDispatch**, or directly by containers with specific knowledge of the interface). So far our interface has only two methods, those to put and get the background color property. We will add more later.

```
[
  object,
  uuid(CBD2DA34-B182-4396-B2BD-D8D11B827CE7),
  dual,
  helpstring("IStopwatchControl Interface"),
  pointer_default(unique)
]
interface IStopwatchControl : IDispatch
{
  [propput, id(DISPID_BACKCOLOR)]
    HRESULT BackColor([in]OLE_COLOR clr);
  [propget, id(DISPID_BACKCOLOR)]
    HRESULT BackColor([out,retval]OLE_COLOR* pclr);
};
```

The StopwatchControl Files

The wizard put all the code into the **StopwatchControl.h** file. A great deal of functionality is represented in this one file, which is listed below:

```
// StopwatchControl.h : Declaration of the CStopwatchControl

#ifndef __STOPWATCHCONTROL_H_
#define __STOPWATCHCONTROL_H_

#include "resource.h"       // main symbols
#include <atlctl.h>


/////////////////////////////////////////////////////////////////
// CStopwatchControl
class ATL_NO_VTABLE CStopwatchControl :
  public CComObjectRootEx<CComSingleThreadModel>,
  public CStockPropImpl<CStopwatchControl, IStopwatchControl,
&IID_IStopwatchControl, &LIBID_STOPWATCHLib>,
  public CComControl<CStopwatchControl>,
  public IPersistStreamInitImpl<CStopwatchControl>,
  public IOleControlImpl<CStopwatchControl>,
  public IOleObjectImpl<CStopwatchControl>,
  public IOleInPlaceActiveObjectImpl<CStopwatchControl>,
  public IViewObjectExImpl<CStopwatchControl>,
  public IOleInPlaceObjectWindowlessImpl<CStopwatchControl>,
  public IPersistStorageImpl<CStopwatchControl>,
  public ISpecifyPropertyPagesImpl<CStopwatchControl>,
  public IQuickActivateImpl<CStopwatchControl>,
  public IDataObjectImpl<CStopwatchControl>,
  public IProvideClassInfo2Impl<&CLSID_StopwatchControl, NULL,
&LIBID_STOPWATCHLib>,
  public CComCoClass<CStopwatchControl, &CLSID_StopwatchControl>
{
public:
  CStopwatchControl()
  {
  }

DECLARE_REGISTRY_RESOURCEID(IDR_STOPWATCHCONTROL)

DECLARE_PROTECT_FINAL_CONSTRUCT()

BEGIN_COM_MAP(CStopwatchControl)
  COM_INTERFACE_ENTRY(IStopwatchControl)
  COM_INTERFACE_ENTRY(IDispatch)
```

```
    COM_INTERFACE_ENTRY(IViewObjectEx)
    COM_INTERFACE_ENTRY(IViewObject2)
    COM_INTERFACE_ENTRY(IViewObject)
    COM_INTERFACE_ENTRY(IOleInPlaceObjectWindowless)
    COM_INTERFACE_ENTRY(IOleInPlaceObject)
    COM_INTERFACE_ENTRY2(IOleWindow, IOleInPlaceObjectWindowless)
    COM_INTERFACE_ENTRY(IOleInPlaceActiveObject)
    COM_INTERFACE_ENTRY(IOleControl)
    COM_INTERFACE_ENTRY(IOleObject)
    COM_INTERFACE_ENTRY(IPersistStreamInit)
    COM_INTERFACE_ENTRY2(IPersist, IPersistStreamInit)
    COM_INTERFACE_ENTRY(ISpecifyPropertyPages)
    COM_INTERFACE_ENTRY(IQuickActivate)
    COM_INTERFACE_ENTRY(IPersistStorage)
    COM_INTERFACE_ENTRY(IDataObject)
    COM_INTERFACE_ENTRY(IProvideClassInfo)
    COM_INTERFACE_ENTRY(IProvideClassInfo2)
  END_COM_MAP()

  BEGIN_PROP_MAP(CStopwatchControl)
    PROP_DATA_ENTRY("_cx", m_sizeExtent.cx, VT_UI4)
    PROP_DATA_ENTRY("_cy", m_sizeExtent.cy, VT_UI4)
    PROP_ENTRY("BackColor", DISPID_BACKCOLOR, CLSID_StockColorPage)
    // Example entries
    // PROP_ENTRY("Property Description", dispid, clsid)
    // PROP_PAGE(CLSID_StockColorPage)
  END_PROP_MAP()

  BEGIN_MSG_MAP(CStopwatchControl)
    CHAIN_MSG_MAP(CComControl<CStopwatchControl>)
    DEFAULT_REFLECTION_HANDLER()
  END_MSG_MAP()
  // Handler prototypes:
  //  LRESULT MessageHandler(UINT uMsg,
  //    WPARAM wParam, LPARAM lParam, BOOL& bHandled);
  //  LRESULT CommandHandler(WORD wNotifyCode,
  //    WORD wID, HWND hWndCtl, BOOL& bHandled);
  //  LRESULT NotifyHandler(int idCtrl, LPNMHDR pnmh, BOOL& bHandled);



  // IViewObjectEx
    DECLARE_VIEW_STATUS(VIEWSTATUS_SOLIDBKGND | VIEWSTATUS_OPAQUE)

  // IStopwatchControl
```

```
public:

  HRESULT OnDraw(ATL_DRAWINFO& di)
  {
    RECT& rc = *(RECT*)di.prcBounds;
    Rectangle(di.hdcDraw, rc.left, rc.top, rc.right, rc.bottom);

    SetTextAlign(di.hdcDraw, TA_CENTER|TA_BASELINE);
    LPCTSTR pszText = _T("ATL 3.0 : StopwatchControl");
    TextOut(di.hdcDraw,
      (rc.left + rc.right) / 2,
      (rc.top + rc.bottom) / 2,
      pszText,
      lstrlen(pszText));

    return S_OK;
  }
  OLE_COLOR m_clrBackColor;
};

#endif //__STOPWATCHCONTROL_H_
```

Listed within this file you will find the following items:

- The default implementations for COM services and all interfaces using multiple inheritance
- The COM MAP macros to support **QueryInterface( )**
- The PROP MAP macros to support properties (including dummy prototypes should you wish to add your own properties)
- The MSG MAP macros to handle Windows messages (also including dummy prototypes)
- Default drawing code
- Member variables

Default Implementations and COM Interfaces As you saw in earlier chapters, ATL makes use of multiple inheritance in C++ to provide default implementations for the interfaces and to provide base functionality. The important thing to remember is that you can always override any of the methods to provide your own implementation when necessary. You will also note that there is not a one-for-one relationship between the implementation classes and the interfaces exported through the COM MAP. As we noted with the **Timers** project, this is because some ATL implementation classes cover more than one OLE interface. (For example, the **IViewObjectExImpl** class handles the **IViewObjectEx**, **IViewObject2**, and **IViewObject** interfaces.) Table 11-1 summarizes the implementation classes for the Stopwatch object:

Class Name (Interfaces)	Description
CComObjectRootEx (IStopwatchControl, IDispatch)	This class provides the default functionality for a COM object such as ours. It works with the COM MAP macros to provide the functions needed by all COM objects, namely **QueryInterface( )**, **AddRef( )**, and **Release( )**.
CStockPropImpl	This class works with the PROP MAP macros to provide complete support for all stock properties. The get and put methods exported through the IDL file are mapped via the macros to member functions, which end up setting or returning the value of the corresponding member variable. In our case we set only one stock property, Background Color; the member variable **m_clrBackColor** will be set and supplied automatically.
CComControl	This is the base class for all ATL ActiveX controls. It derives from **CWindowImpl**, so it has all of the **CWindow** methods that wrap the Win32 window functions. (This is similar to the **CWnd** class in MFC.) It also derives from **CCom-ControlBase**, so it has methods that help interact with a container. A very good sample on the Microsoft Web site, called the **CIRC** sample, demonstrates the methods of this class. There is a lot of functionality within this class, and you will find it helpful to browse the source code, which can be found in **AtlCtl.h**.

Default Implementation Classes for the Stopwatch-Control Object
Table 11-1.

Class Name (Interfaces)	Description
IDataObjectImpl (IDataObject)	This class provides the support for the **IDataObject** interface. **IDataObject** is the interface through which the control can support Uniform Data Transfer, either from the clipboard or via drag and drop.
IOleControlImpl (IOleControl)	The **IOleControl** interface provides containers with information about this control and allows a container to send us shortcut keys as well as to inform us that we should shut down or reenable our UI. Many containers use the presence of this interface as their main clue that this is an ActiveX control.
IOleObjectImpl (IOleObject)	This is arguably the most important interface. It is the primary means by which an embedded COM object communicates with its container. When the container creates and embeds the control, it will call **SetClientSite( )** on its **IOleObject** interface to give the control the **IOleClientSite** pointer. This is the basis for a two-way communication between the container and the control. The control can then register for notification of events from the container by finding connection points in the container and calling **Advise( )** on that connection point.
IOleInPlaceActiveObjectImpl (IOleInPlaceObject, IOleInPlaceActiveObject)	An *in place* object is one that activates within the client area of the container (as opposed to an *out of place* object that opens up in its own frame window outside of the container). The ATL implementation class handles all the communication within the container. The main effect for us is that when the user resizes the border (using grab handles in the UI), ATL will call through to our **OnDraw( )** function so we can repaint the clock and button.

Default Implementation Classes for the Stopwatch-Control Object *(continued)*

Table 11-1.

Class Name (Interfaces)	Description
IOleInPlaceObjectWindowless-Impl (IOleInPlaceObjectWindowless)	This interface extends **IOleInPlaceObject** and allows for windowless controls, which are more lightweight than controls that have an **HWND**. It allows the control to receive Windows messages and also drop notification without the creation of a window object. Windowless controls are simply allocated space inside the container's client area, and they are allowed to draw inside that space. Since there is no window and thus no Window *proc*, the container calls the method **OnWindowMessage( )** to forward the message to the control. The ATL macros will actually map incoming messages to your message handlers regardless of whether they came in from **OnWindowMessage( )** or through a traditional message pump; so all of this is actually transparent to our control.
IPersistStorageImpl, IPersistStreamInitImpl (IPersist, IPersistStorage, IPersistStreamInit)	These classes provide the basic support for persistence, or saving and loading data to and from disk files or other media. Since we implement **IPersist**, the container knows that the Stopwatch control can participate in persistence. The interface **IPersistStorage** is used by most containers to tell an embedded control to Load or Save its data. It will pass a pointer to the **IStorage** of the disk file, and we can simply load or save the data from there. ATL automatically takes care of loading and saving the stock properties, so we only have to persist our custom data. You will see how to do that a bit later.

Default Implementation Classes for the Stopwatch-Control Object *(continued)*

Table 11-1.

Class Name (Interfaces)	Description
IProvideClassInfo2Impl (IProvideClassInfo, IProvideClassInfo2)	The presence of this interface tells the outside world that we can provide class information dynamically at runtime. ATL will automatically return a pointer to our type information whenever a container calls on this interface.
IQuickActivateImpl (IQuickActivate)	The **IQuickActivate** protocol was introduced to reduce the amount of handshaking between containers and controls. If the container supports quick activation, it can send the control its vital pointers (client site, advise sink, etc.) and some basic stock properties, all in one call. Then on the return trip our control can send back View Status and event information. This speeds up the initialization process dramatically. ATL takes care of mapping all the pointers and sending back all the data, so our control functions the same way whether or not the container supports quick activation.
ISpecifyPropertyPagesImpl (ISpecifyPropertyPages)	The **ISpecifyPropertyPages** interface tells the container that we have a property page dialog available. If the container allows it, the user can select a menu option or button to access the properties page. Since we selected a stock property (Background Color), ATL will provide a property page that allows the user to change the background color. We will add our own custom property later.
IViewObjectExImpl (IViewObject, IViewObject2, IViewObjectEx)	The **IViewObject** interface identifies us to the container as a *viewable object*—in other words, one with a user interface. This allows the container to call **Draw( )** (which ATL maps to our **OnDraw( )** method) whenever it must repaint the user interface. The extended interface **IViewObjectEx** supports nonrectangular controls.

Default Implementation Classes for the Stopwatch-Control Object *(continued)*

Table 11-1.

The COM MAP Macros As you have already learned, the COM MAP provides a list of the interfaces that can be returned to an outside caller through **QueryInterface( )**. Since the **StopwatchControl** class derives through multiple inheritance from the ATL implementation classes, **QueryInterface( )** can basically return the correct **static_cast** of the *this* pointer.

Later in the chapter we will add a **COM_INTERFACE_ENTRY_AGGREGATE** entry to our COM MAP to automatically handle aggregation. We will use this macro to aggregate the **Stopwatch** component. Don't worry if you don't yet know what is meant by the term *aggregation*; we will be explaining this, too.

The PROP MAP Macros As we saw in earlier chapters, the COM MAP macros are used by ATL to list the interfaces that should be exported to the outside world. Similarly, the PROP MAP macros are used to identify the properties (both stock and custom) that are exposed by this control. The PROP MAP is used for the following functions:

- **To provide containers with a mechanism for persisting the property values**: The PROP MAP macros are used by various ATL implementation classes to give containers access to properties for the purpose of persistence. Persistence of data means that the values are stored on some permanent storage (such as a disk file) to be recalled later. This is very important for control properties because users get quite upset if they customize a control to their liking, just to find that it has reverted to the default behavior the next time they run it. There are two main ways of persisting data in ActiveX: streaming it to a disk file and using a property bag. Both of these will be discussed later in this chapter. The important point is that by adding your properties to the PROP MAP, you get persistence virtually for free.
- **To allow users to access or change the properties graphically by using a property page**: External objects can access the properties via the dual interface, but it is also essential to provide users with a GUI so they can change the properties graphically. The PROP MAP macros allow you to specify the property page through which a property can be changed.

Other than the **BEGIN** and **END** macros, there are four PROP MAP macros:

- **PROP_DATA_ENTRY**: This macro identifies properties that are to be persisted but do not have an associated property page. You will notice that the wizard inserted code to persist the dimensions of the control using this macro.
- **PROP_ENTRY**: This is the main macro for adding stock and custom properties to the PROP MAP. It allows you to specify a text name for the property (used by property bags), the DISPID of the property's get and/or put methods in the dual interface, and the CLSID of the property page to display for this property. If you have more than one property on your property page, you specify the same CLSID in all the macros for that page; the page will appear only once in the properties dialog.
- **PROP_ENTRY_EX**: This is just like **PROP_ENTRY**, but you can specify a different dual interface if you want to use one other than the default interface for this class.
- **PROP_PAGE**: This allows a property page to be added to the properties dialog but does not specify any variables for persistence.

Later in this chapter we will add a custom property with a custom property page. We will use the **PROP_ENTRY** macro to add it to the PROP MAP for automatic persistence and inclusion in the properties dialog.

The MSG MAP Macros The MSG MAP provides for the routing of Windows messages to our handler methods. For controls with an **HWND**, the messages come in through the traditional Windows message pump. For windowless controls, the container forwards the message to the control via the **OnWindowMessage( )** member of the control's **IOleInPlaceObject-Windowless** interface. ATL transparently handles these two situations and calls the same handlers either way.

There are three basic types of macros for handling messages: the *notify* handler (for **WM_NOTIFY** messages), the *command* handler (for **WM_COMMAND** messages), and the *message* handler for all others. The wizard adds MSG MAP macros for us automatically when we add message handlers, as we shall see the following.

For those readers familiar with MFC, there are a few differences in how ATL handles message mapping. The most obvious one is that (other than for **WM_COMMAND** and **WM_NOTIFY**) ATL does not crack the **WPARAM** or **LPARAM** parameters for you, so you have to crack them yourself. This is fairly straightforward; just look up the documentation for that particular "WM_" message. You should also look at the return code for the message, and send that back as the **LRESULT** return value for the handler.

The big difference between MFC and ATL, though, is in how the messages are routed from one handler to another. ATL uses the concept of a chain of handlers. It starts by looking in your class for a handler. If it can't find one, it looks up the chain until it does find a handler. The chain of handlers is defined by the **CHAIN_MSG_MAP** macros, which can specify any of the base classes for your object, any contained classes, and/or any other class in your project. Once a handler is found, it is offered the chance to handle the message. If it accepts, it can just return from the method normally. If it does not want to handle the message (in other words, it just wants to peek), it must set the **bHandled** parameter to false. This will instruct ATL to keep searching the chain of handlers.

In addition to the **CHAIN_MSG_MAP** macro, you will notice that the ATL Object wizard added a **DEFAULT_REFLECTION_HANDLER** macro. This inserts code to handle messages that are reflected back to the control from the parent (the container). If you don't handle a reflected message, the **DEFAULT_REFLECTION_HANDLER** will dutifully pass it to **DefWindowProc( )**, which will, in effect, throw it away.

The Default Drawing Code ATL inserts an **OnDraw( )** method that simply writes the text "ATL 3.0 : StopwatchControl" in the middle of the client area. We will change this to something more meaningful later. The important thing to note is that it is passed an **ATL_DRAWINFO** structure. Since it is not documented in the online help, here is the structure from the header file:

```
struct ATL_DRAWINFO
{
  UINT cbSize;          // Set to sizeof (struct ATL_DRAWINFO)
  DWORD dwDrawAspect; // Drawing aspect - typically DVASPECT_CONTENT
  LONG lindex;          // Commonly -1, which specifies all of the data
  DVTARGETDEVICE* ptd; // Render the object for this target device
  HDC hicTargetDev;    // Information context for the target device
  HDC hdcDraw;          // Draw on this device context
  LPCRECTL prcBounds; // Draw within this rectangle
  LPCRECTL prcWBounds; // Window extent and origin when rendering a
                        // metafile
```

```
  BOOL bOptimize;    // Can control use drawing optimizations?
  BOOL bZoomed;      // Object extent differs from drawing rectangle?
  BOOL bRectInHimetric; // Rectangle in HiMetric?
  SIZEL ZoomNum;     // Rectangle size: X zoom = ZoomNum.cx/ZoomDen.cx
  SIZEL ZoomDen;     // Extent size: Y zoom = ZoomNum.cy/ZoomDen.cy
};
```

- **dwDrawAspect**: This value from the **DVASPECT** enumeration specifies how to render the view. If the control is being minimized, it contains **DVASPECT_ICON**. If the control is being printed, it contains **DVASPECT_DOCPRINT**; this is often interesting since we can change the rendering to make it more suitable for printed output. **DVASPECT_THUMBNAIL** is sent by some (but not too many) containers when the user requests a thumbnail view. Thumbnails are defined as 120-by-120-pixel, 16-color DIBs (device independent bitmaps). For normal rendering, **DVASPECT_CONTENT** is received, so just draw normally.
- **ptd**: This pointer to a **DVTARGETDEVICE** structure gives you detailed information about the device driver. It is unlikely that you would ever need such detailed information unless you were doing some device-dependent rendering.
- **hicTargetDev**: This is an information context for the device. For most devices, this will return the same information as **hdcDraw**.
- **hdcDraw**: This is the device context onto which we must draw. If you elected to normalize the DC in the Object wizard (as we did in this example), ATL will get a DC from the container and do some preprocessing on it before sending it down to our **OnDraw( )**. So either a normalized or raw DC will be supplied in **hdcDraw**. You can then use standard Win32 GDI functions to draw into the DC.
- **prcBounds**: This is the bounding rectangle (in client coordinates). You must never draw outside of these bounds.
- **bOptimize**: This tells us whether we can use drawing optimizations. Whenever you select GDI objects into a DC, it is your duty to restore the previous instance of that object before returning to the calling program. Some containers, however, allow optimized drawing, in which child controls do not have to restore the previously selected objects. The container will restore the state after it finishes calling all of the child controls. Remember that if you do leave an object selected into a DC, you cannot destroy that object, so make sure the object survives the scope of **OnDraw( )** (make it into an instance variable of the class and

destroy it in the destructor). If you normalized the DC, this flag will always be on, since ATL restores the container's DC before it returns anyway.

- **Zooming**: Some containers allow zooming (in or out). This means that the object extent is larger (zooming in) or smaller (zooming out) than the current drawing rectangle. The **bZoomed** flag will be on if zooming is occurring. You can then compute the zoom factor in each direction (cx and cy), as shown above, using the **ZoomNum** and **ZoomDen** sizes.

The Stock Member Variables ATL automatically adds member variables for all stock properties. These are automatically set by the macros through the persistence interface, the property page interface, and the *put* function on our **IDispatch** interface. Conversely, they are supplied automatically to the *get* function, the property page, and the persistence interface. You may notice that these member variables are put under the **public** scope. You cannot change this to **protected** or **private** because some of the default implementation classes access them by name and are not declared as friends.

Compiling and Debugging the Stopwatch Control

We now have a default ATL control. It doesn't do much, but we'll fix that. Since we will need to remove the **_ATL_MIN_CRT** within the C++ compile settings for release builds anyway, this may be a good time to do it, even before you compile for the first time. Following this adjustment, compile this default control by selecting Build Stopwatch.dll from the Build menu (or by pressing F7 if you have the standard key mapping). This will create a Debug build, which is fine for now.

To test the control, start the debugger by pressing F5 or by selecting Build | Start Debug | Go. Since this is a DLL, the IDE will prompt you for an executable to launch. Click the little arrow to the right of the edit box, and select ActiveX Control Test Container (see Figure 11-3). Then click OK. You will receive a warning that the test container itself does not contain debugging information; this is fine. To avoid getting this message every time you launch the debugger, check the "Do not prompt in the future" option; then click OK. You will now be inside the test container.

The test container is an excellent application for testing an ActiveX control. It can exercise all the drawing functions, it can call all of the stock and custom properties and methods, and it can test persistence as well. And since it was loaded through the debugger, you can set breakpoints in your code and/or respond to exceptions and asserts.

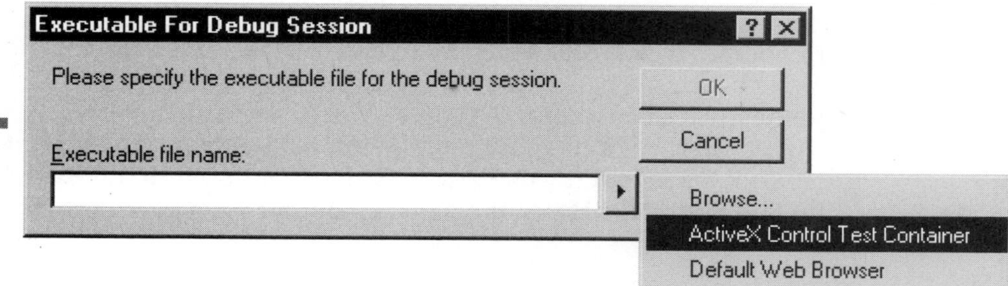

Specifying the ActiveX test container to the debugger

Figure 11-3.

To load the control, select Edit | Insert New Control, or click the toolbar button that has a little arrow pointing to a hand grabbing a button (the tooltip says "New Control"). You will then see the Insert Control dialog (see Figure 11-4). Scroll down until you see the StopwatchControl Class entry (or type **st** to quickly jump down the list), and click OK. You will now see the control inside the test container.

The first thing you will notice is that the control has grab handles around it. If you resize the control, the text stays centered, since our **OnDraw( )** method is called, and we keep adjusting the text position.

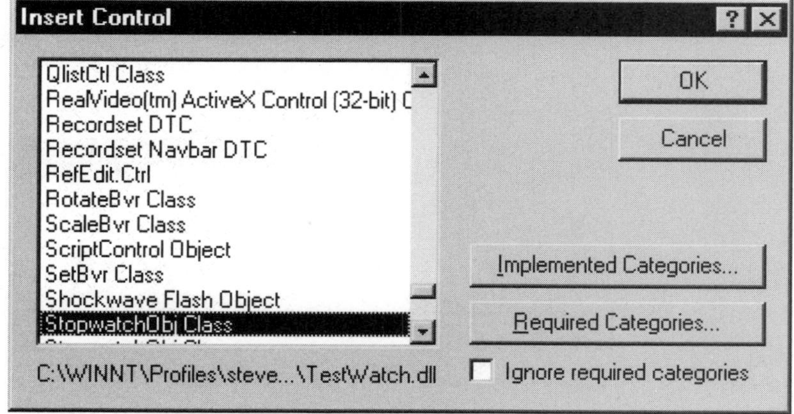

The Insert Control dialog

Figure 11-4.

Let's examine the default property page that was supplied by ATL. Click the Properties button (two over from Insert Control), or select Edit | Properties. The properties dialog has two tabs (see Figure 11-5): Color and Extended. Go ahead and change the background color to any value and click OK. Nothing appears to happen, since we haven't implemented any code to take action when the background color has changed. But internally, thanks to PROP MAP, the control has stored the new background color in our **m_clrBackColor** member variable. How can you tell? You can ask it via the custom interface.

To invoke methods on the custom interface, use the Invoke Methods option of the Control menu (or click the Invoke Methods button on the toolbar, which is next to the Insert Control button). You will see the Invoke Methods dialog (Figure 11-6). We have only two methods at the moment, to get and put the value of the background color. These are methods on our dual interface, **IStopwatchControl**. Since the **CStopwatchControl** class is derived from **CStockPropImpl**, ATL has provided an implementation for the **get_BackColor( )** and **put_BackColor( )** methods, which get and set the **m_clrBackColor** member variable. In the Method Name box, select

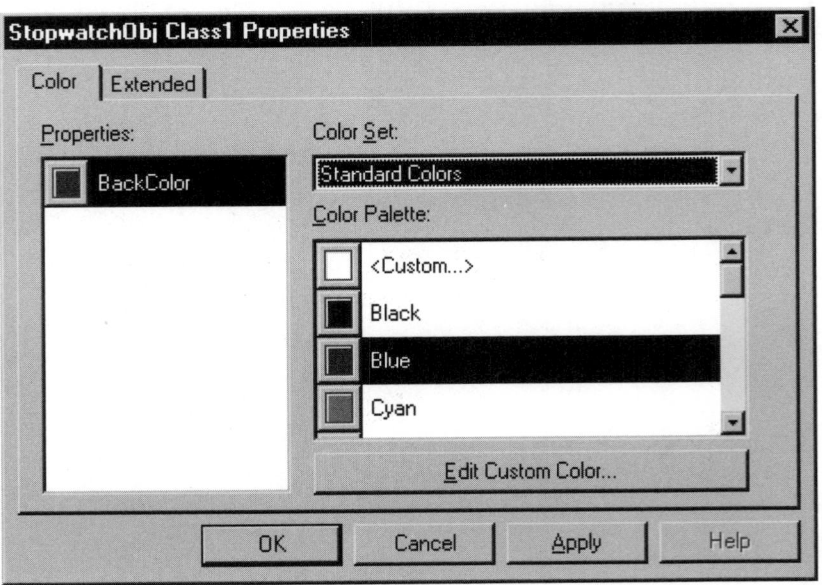

The properties dialog

Figure 11-5.

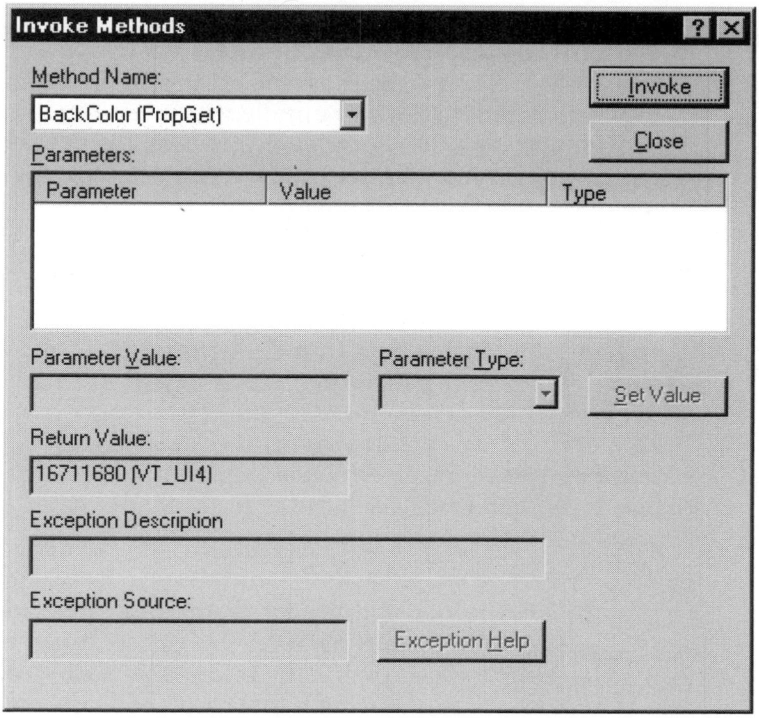

The Invoke Methods dialog

Figure 11-6.

BackColor (ProgGet), and then click Invoke. The Return Value field will be filled in with the decimal value of the color you chose in the properties dialog along with the type, which is a 4-byte unsigned integer (VT_UI4). For example, if you chose blue, it is 0x00FF0000, or 16711680 decimal. (In OLE color, the color values are specified as 00BBGGRR instead of RGB.)

Now we can make our control more interesting. Close the Invoke Methods dialog and exit the test container. (You don't need to save anything.)

Adding Functionality to the Default Control

Before you can turn the control into a stopwatch, you need to add custom functionality. The first thing we will do is aggregate the **Stopwatch** component from Chapter 3. Aggregation is COM's way of allowing one COM object to contain another COM object, much as a C++ object can contain

Aggregation allows one COM object to contain another.

another C++ object. The contained COM object is known as the inner object, and the containing object is the outer object. By using aggregation, the outer object (in our case **StopwatchControl**) can export the interface(s) of the inner object (**Stopwatch**) as well as its own. In this way the container for the control has only one component to deal with, but it can call on the functionality of either component. In fact, the container does not even realize it is dealing with multiple COM components.

After aggregating the **Stopwatch** component, we then add the user interface: drawing code to display the time, a button to reset the time, and a property page for setting stock and custom properties.

Aggregating the Stopwatch Component

When we built the **Stopwatch** component in Chapter 3, we used the ATL Object wizard, and on the Attributes tab we chose "yes" to aggregation, which means that the **Stopwatch** component is "aggregable." This means that it can be aggregated by an outer component. When acting as an inner object, an aggregable component basically delegates all **IUnknown** functions to the outer object. The outer object takes responsibility for handing out interface pointers.

In pure COM, responsibilities are required from both the inner and outer objects in order to get aggregation to work. Fortunately, ATL takes care of all the details of aggregation via the base class **CComObjectRootEx** and COM MAP macros. So aggregating the **Stopwatch** component is quite simple. Add the following code to the **StopwatchControl.h** file:

```
#import "timers.dll" raw_interfaces_only, no_namespace, named_guids
```

We looked at **#import** in detail in Chapter 5, but notice the use of the **raw_interfaces_only** attribute here. This instructs the compiler to extract only the raw interfaces and named GUIDs from the type library rather than the smart pointer type interfaces. Of course, the compiler must be able to find the **timers.dll** file; so you can move it to a place on the PATH, copy it into the current project directory, use a fully qualified path instead of just "timers.dll," or add the timers directory to the "executables" directory for the IDE under Tools | Options | Directories.

We will need to hold a pointer to the inner object; so at the very end of the source file add a protected member section with an **IUnknown** member variable as follows:

```
protected:
 CComPtr<IUnknown> m_spIUnkStopwatch;
```

We need to create an instance of the **Stopwatch** component when the **StopwatchControl** component is instantiated, and release it when it is no longer needed. This is the duty of an outer object. To do this, add the indicated lines right after the constructor:

```
DECLARE_GET_CONTROLLING_UNKNOWN()
HRESULT FinalConstruct()
{
  return CoCreateInstance( CLSID_Stopwatch, GetControllingUnknown(),
    CLSCTX_ALL, IID_IUnknown, (void**)&m_spIUnkStopwatch);
}

void FinalRelease()
{
  m_spIUnkStopwatch.Release();
}
```

The first thing added was the **DECLARE_GET_CONTROLLING_-UNKNOWN( )** macro. This inserts some code to allow us to call **GetControllingUnknown( )**. This is done, as you can see, in the **FinalConstruct( )** method. Then, an instance of the **Stopwatch** is created by calling **CoCreateInstance( )**. Notice we only asked for **IID_IUnknown**. We really want an **IID_IStopwatch** interface so we can call its methods. The laws of aggregation, however, dictate that the only interface that the inner object can return on creation is **IUnknown**. So we will query through this pointer to obtain an **IStopwatch**. When the interface is released, **FinalRelease( )** will be called, so the pointer is released at that time.

The last step is to add the interface to our COM MAP, since we want the outside world to be able to query the component and get an **IStopwatch** pointer. To do that, add the following macro to the COM MAP:


```
COM_INTERFACE_ENTRY_AGGREGATE( IID_IStopwatch, m_spIUnkStopwatch.p )
```

This macro inserts the code that will return the correct pointer to the caller. Make sure you use the "p" member of **m_spIUnkStopwatch**, and not **m_spIUnkStopwatch** itself, or ATL will return the wrong pointer.

That's it! We now have included all the functionality of **Stopwatch** into our control.

Add a Timer

To display the current time, the **StopwatchControl** must update the time every second. To do this we are essentially going to duplicate the connection point functionality described in the previous chapter. Specifically, we are going to use connection points in order to monitor a **Countdown** component. Because the **StopwatchControl** is a component, be sure to implement the callback using a different class. In this case we will use the **ICountdownPtrWithEvents** class from the previous chapter.

With this template, the only thing left to do to receive the countdown notification is to hook it up. A listing of the relevant changes is shown below. Please note that for clarity, no **try/catch** blocks have been used throughout the code in the chapter. If you need production code, you will have to add these or convert the **_com_ptr_t** smart pointers to **CComQIPtr**-based pointers instead.

```
#include "resource.h"       // main symbols
#include <atlctl.h>

#include "CountdownWithEvents.h"
...
class ATL_NO_VTABLE CStopwatchControl :
...
{
...
  HRESULT FinalConstruct()
  {
    HRESULT hr;

    // Instantiate the Stopwatch component
    hr =  CoCreateInstance( CLSID_Stopwatch,
        GetControllingUnknown(), CLSCTX_ALL,
        IID_IUnknown, reinterpret_cast<void**>(&m_spIUnkStopwatch));

    // Instantiate the countdown component
    if(SUCCEEDED(hr))
      hr = m_ptrUpdateDisplay.CreateInstance(
        __uuidof(Countdown));

    return hr;
  }

  void FinalRelease()
  {
    m_ptrUpdateDisplay.RealRelease();
    m_spIUnkStopwatch.Release();
  }
...
 //////////////////////////////////////////////
```

```
// Member Variables
/////////////////////////////////////////
...
protected:
...
  ICountdownPtrWithEvents<ID_UPDATE_DISPLAY, CStopwatchControl>
    m_ptrUpdateDisplay;
...
/////////////////////////////////////////
// COM Event Callback functions for
// the Countdown component
/////////////////////////////////////////
  HRESULT OnTimeElapsed(
    ICountdownPtrWithEvents<ID_UPDATE_DISPLAY, CStopwatchControl>
    *const ,
    long RemainingIterations)
  {
    if( m_spAdviseSink )
        m_spAdviseSink->OnViewChange( DVASPECT_CONTENT, -1 );
    Invalidate();
    return 0;
  }
...
  LRESULT OnCreate(UINT uMsg, WPARAM wParam,
    LPARAM lParam, BOOL& bHandled)
  {
    // Register to receive countdown notifications
    m_ptrUpdateDisplay.DispEventAdvise(this);
    // Start the countdown so it updates
    // the display every second.
    m_ptrUpdateDisplay->Interval = 1000;
    ...
    return 0;
  }

  LRESULT OnDestroy(UINT uMsg, WPARAM wParam,
    LPARAM lParam, BOOL& bHandled)
  {
    m_ptrUpdateDisplay.DispEventUnadvise();
    return 0;
  }
  ...
};

#endif //__STOPWATCHCONTROL_H_
```

Let's examine this code. First, the **Countdown** component is created using the **CreateInstance( )** call implemented in **ICountdownPtr** (from which **ICountdownPtrWithEvents** is derived).

Inside **FinalRelease( )**, **RealRelease( )** is called to release the **Countdown** component. It is not necessary to explicitly call this function since the destructor on **ICountdownPtr** will do this automatically, but for clarity the code is placed here anyway.

After declaring **m_ ptrUpdateDisplay**, the **OnTimeElapsed( )** callback function is implemented. This function informs the container that the view has changed. The container will then call back to us and have us repaint. Notifying the container is done through the **IAdviseSink** interface pointer that is passed from the container and stored in a member variable of the **IViewObjectExImpl** class. Not all containers support this, however, so make sure to check for a **NULL** pointer. If the value is **NULL**, then just invalidate the control's client area. This will force the **OnDraw( )** method to be called.

The last part of hooking up the **Countdown** is to call **DispEventAdvise( )** to register for event notification and **DispEventUnadvise( )** to unregister. Notice also that following the **DispEventAdvise( )** call we set the interval for when the **Countdown** should fire.

Change the Drawing Code

Finally, the drawing code is changed. First, the client area is filled with the indicated background color. (Note: This should be done in a **WM_ERASEBKGND** message handler if you are writing a real control, but we'll do it in the **OnDraw( )** for simplicity.) Next, we call on the **IStopwatch** interface to return the time that has elapsed since the last reset and build a text string in the format HH:MM:SS. We then use our ATL-supplied code to draw the text in the center of the rectangle, as follows:

```
//////////////////////////////////////////
// Windows Message Handling Functions
//////////////////////////////////////////
public:
  HRESULT OnDraw(ATL_DRAWINFO& di)
  {
    // get our bounding rectangle
    RECT& rc = *(RECT*)di.prcBounds;

    // Set the background color
```

```
    COLORREF color;
    ::OleTranslateColor( m_clrBackColor, NULL, &color );
    HBRUSH hBrush = ::CreateSolidBrush( color );
    ::FillRect( di.hdcDraw, &rc, hBrush );
    ::DeleteObject( hBrush ); // need to release the brush handle

    // call on the IStopwatch object to return
    // the elapsed time in seconds
    float fElapsedTime = 0.0;
    IStopwatchPtr ptrStopwatch( m_spIUnkStopwatch );
    fElapsedTime = ptrStopwatch->ElapsedTime();
    char szText[100];
    long lElapsedTime = (long)fElapsedTime;
    long lHours =  lElapsedTime / 3600;
     lElapsedTime -=  lHours * 3600;
    long lMinutes = lElapsedTime / 60;
    long lSeconds = lElapsedTime % 60;
    wsprintf( szText, "%02d:%02d:%02d",
    lHours, lMinutes, lSeconds );

    // draw the text in the center of the rectangle
    SetTextAlign(di.hdcDraw, TA_CENTER|TA_BASELINE);
    SetBkColor(di.hdcDraw, color );
    TextOut(di.hdcDraw,
      (rc.left + rc.right) / 2,
      (rc.top + rc.bottom) / 2,
      szText,
      lstrlen(szText));

    return S_OK;
  }
```

The only trick here is that the background color is stored as an **OLE_COLOR** and not a **COLORREF**. So we call **OleTranslateColor( )** to do the translating for us. We also have to set the text background color, or the time would draw on a white background. 11

Testing the New Build

Add the control to the test container as you did before. You should see the elapsed time ticking away. Go into the properties page and change the background color. When you click Apply or OK, the background color will change.

Persistence

Persistence is the feature that handles the storage and retrieval of properties.

Now that you have changed the background color to one that you like, it would be a nuisance if you had to change it every time you used the control. Fortunately, you don't have to do that, since the stopwatch control implements **IPersist**, and since ATL takes care of storing the stock properties for us. In the language of COM, this is called *persistence*. From the Control menu select Save To Storage. You will be prompted for a filename. Enter any name and click Save. The test container will save the control to a file; then it will show you that file using the DOC file viewer. (A DOC file is the old name for a file that uses OLE structured storage.) Since the DOC file is in a binary format, it isn't very interesting to look at, so just close the viewer. Back in the test container move the Stopwatch control over to the right with the mouse. Use the properties pane to change the background color to some other color. From the Edit menu select Insert Control From Storage, and select the file you just saved. A new instance of the control will be added, but with the "old" background color, which was persisted in the file. Close the test container, and we will add more features to our control.

Adding a Button

Through the **IStopwatchControl** custom interface, users can change or retrieve the background color, and they can query or reset the timer through the **IStopwatch** interface. The background color can also be set graphically using the properties pane, but currently there is no way of resetting the timer through the GUI. So we will add a Reset button.

To Dialog or Not to Dialog?

There are two ways in which we could add our button. We could use a new feature of ATL 3 and add a dialog box (very similar to the MFC **CDialog** class), and then host the dialog box within our control window. This would be the natural way if we had a lot of child controls to manage. However, since we are adding only one button, we can get away with just creating and hosting it "manually," without adding a dialog resource.

Adding a Command ID

Even though we are creating the button itself programmatically, it still needs to have a unique ID associated with it. That way, when the user clicks the Reset button, we will be notified with a **WM_COMMAND** message. To do this, select View | Resource Symbols. Click the New button, and you will see the New Symbol dialog (see Figure 11-7). For the name, enter **ID_RESET**, and keep the value suggested by the dialog. Click OK to close the New Symbol dialog, and then close the Resource Symbols dialog. The same procedure could be used for **ID_UPDATE_DISPLAY** in place of the **#define** we used earlier in the chapter.

Coding the Button

Now we are ready to add our button. In the **StopwatchControl.h** file, add two new member variables to our protected section, as follows:

```
CWindow      m_btnReset;
SIZE         m_sizeReset;
```

This declares the button as an instance of **CWindow**. We need to create the button in our **OnCreate( )** handler. We will also cache the button size in **m_sizeReset**, since we will need it from time to time. A complete listing

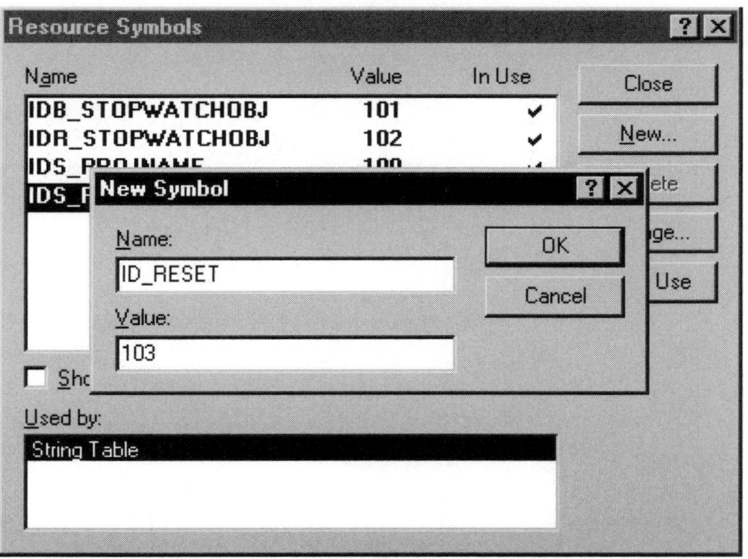

The New Symbol dialog

Figure 11-7.

of the **OnCreate( )** function is shown below with the relevant changes highlighted.

```
LRESULT OnCreate(UINT uMsg, WPARAM wParam,
  LPARAM lParam, BOOL& bHandled)
{
  // Register to receive countdown notifications
  m_ptrUpdateDisplay.DispEventAdvise(this);
  // Start the countdown so it updates
  // the display every second.
  m_ptrUpdateDisplay->Interval = 1000;

  // Start the stopwatch
  IStopwatchPtr ptrStopwatch( m_spIUnkStopwatch );
  ptrStopwatch->Start();

  TCHAR* szReset = RESET_BUTTON_TEXT;

  HDC dc = GetDC();
  ::GetTextExtentPoint32( dc, szReset,
    strlen( szReset ), & m_sizeReset);
  ReleaseDC( dc );

  RECT rect = { 0,0, m_sizeReset.cx+=4 , m_sizeReset.cy+=2 };
  m_btnReset.Create( "BUTTON", m_hWnd, rect, szReset,
       WS_CHILD | BS_PUSHBUTTON | BS_TEXT, 0, ID_RESET );


  return 0;
}
```

First, we need to find out how wide (and high) to make the button to accommodate the Reset button text. We call **GetTextExtentPoint32( )** to do this. We are actually calling this with the control's DC, not the button's DC, which is technically not correct, but this way we can do the create in one call. To do this properly you should create the button with a temporary size, and then get the button's DC and call **GetTextExtentPoint32( )** on it.

Once we have the size, we create a rect (adding some pixels to the width and height for a border) and call **Create( )** on the **CWindow** object. We use the preregistered window class name of BUTTON, and pass in the control's window handle as the parent, its location and dimensions (the button is temporarily positioned at 0,0 but will be moved shortly), the caption text, the window styles, no extended window styles, and the command ID. Notice we did not specify **WS_VISIBLE** as one of the styles. That is because we have not yet positioned our button.

Positioning the Button

Nowadays users are accustomed to free-form dialogs that adjust their controls when the border is resized. In Java, layout manager classes do all that automatically. We don't have that luxury, so we have to redo our layout manually. When the user resizes a control, the container will send us a **WM_SIZE** message. Add a message handler for **WM_SIZE** using the same technique used for the other messages. Then enter the indicated code in the handler body:

```
LRESULT OnSize(UINT uMsg, WPARAM wParam,
  LPARAM lParam, BOOL& bHandled)
{
  if( m_btnReset.IsWindow() )
  {
    WORD wWidth = LOWORD( lParam );
    WORD wHeight = HIWORD( lParam );
    // center the button at the bottom of the control
    long lLeft = (wWidth-m_sizeReset.cx)/2;
    long lTop = wHeight-m_sizeReset.cy-5;
    m_btnReset.SetWindowPos( NULL,
      lLeft, lTop, 0,0, SWP_NOSIZE | SWP_SHOWWINDOW );
  }

  return 0;
}
```

m_btnReset.IsWindow( ) is checked to verify that the button window has been created before the **ON_SIZE** message arrives. ATL doesn't have the same message crackers as MFC, so we have to extract the new size from the **LPARAM** of the message. We compute the new left and top coordinates for the button, and then call **SetWindowPos( )** to move the window and make it visible at the same time.

Adding a Handler for the Button

All we need to do now is add a message handler for the button. When the button is clicked, the control will receive a **WM_COMMAND** message with an ID of **ID_RESET**. There is no wizard to help with this one, so in the MSG MAP, just before the **END_MSG_MAP** macro, insert the following line:

```
COMMAND_ID_HANDLER( ID_RESET, OnReset )
```

This will cause our **OnReset( )** member function to be called whenever an **ID_RESET** command message is received. To add **OnReset( )**, find the **CommandHandler( )** line, which is a commented out prototype supplied by the ATL code generator. Copy that line to the clipboard, scroll down to the end of the class (just after **OnSize( )** is fine), and paste the line there. Remove the two slashes and the trailing semicolon (since we will be filling in the body right here in the header file). Change the method name from **CommandHandler( )** to **OnReset( )**, and you are left with the following:

```
LRESULT OnReset(WORD wNotifyCode, WORD wID, HWND hWndCtl, BOOL& bHandled)
```

Calling **Start( )** on our **Stopwatch** component resets the timer, so that's what we want to do when the Reset button is clicked. Add the following code as the body for **OnReset( )** function:

```
{
  CComQIPtr<IStopwatch, &IID_IStopwatch>
    spStopWatch( m_spIUnkStopwatch );
  spStopWatch->Start();
  return 0;
}
```

Testing

Start the debugger and thus the test container. Insert the control, and you should see the Reset button. Use the grab handles to resize the control, and the button will move. Notice that if you make the window very small, the button will obliterate the text. You can fix this by handling **WM_GETMINMAXINFO** so that the user cannot make the window too small.

Adding a Custom Property Page

Adding a custom property page with ATL is quite simple; in fact the wizard does most of the work. But before we add a custom property page, we need to add a custom property. Let's give the user the option of displaying the elapsed time in seconds only, or in hours, minutes, seconds as it is now.

Add the Property to the Code

Create a new member variable after the other protected members, as follows:

```
bool m_bSecondsOnly;
```

Also add an initializer to the constructor to set this property initially to false (in other words, not seconds only):

```
CStopwatchControl()
      : m_lTimer( 0 ),
      m_bSecondsOnly( false )
{
}
```

Now we need to change the drawing code to capitalize on the new **m_bSecondsOnly** flag. Substitute this code for the appropriate existing code in **OnDraw( )**:

```
HRESULT OnDraw(ATL_DRAWINFO& di)
{
  // get our bounding rectangle
  RECT& rc = *(RECT*)di.prcBounds;

  // Set the background color
  COLORREF color;
  ::OleTranslateColor( m_clrBackColor, NULL, &color );
  HBRUSH hBrush = ::CreateSolidBrush( color );
  ::FillRect( di.hdcDraw, &rc, hBrush );
  ::DeleteObject( hBrush ); // need to release the brush handle

  // call on the IStopwatch object to return
  // the elapsed time in seconds
  float fElapsedTime = 0.0;
  IStopwatchPtr ptrStopwatch( m_spIUnkStopwatch );
  fElapsedTime = ptrStopwatch->ElapsedTime();
  char szText[100];
  long lElapsedTime = (long)fElapsedTime;
  if( m_bSecondsOnly )
    wsprintf( szText, "%d", lElapsedTime );
  else
  {
    long lHours =  lElapsedTime / 3600;
    lElapsedTime -=  lHours * 3600;
    long lMinutes = lElapsedTime / 60;
    long lSeconds = lElapsedTime % 60;
    wsprintf( szText, "%02d:%02d:%02d",
      lHours, lMinutes, lSeconds );
  }
```

11

```
  // draw the text in the center of the rectangle
  SetTextAlign(di.hdcDraw, TA_CENTER|TA_BASELINE);
  TextOut(di.hdcDraw,
    (rc.left + rc.right) / 2,
    (rc.top + rc.bottom) / 2,
    szText,
    lstrlen(szText));

  return S_OK;
}
```

Add the Property to the Interface

Not only do we make the property available to our internal code, we also need to expose it via the **IStopwatchControl** interface. You can add the property using the Add Property wizard. (In the Class View, click the right mouse button over the **IStopwatchControl** interface, and select Add Property from the context menu.) For the Property Type select **VARIANT_BOOL**, and for the name type select SecondsOnly.

```
  [
    object,
    uuid(B45BFC92-2972-4829-9A0B-AE4EAE2916C1),
    dual,
    helpstring("IStopwatchControl Interface"),
    pointer_default(unique)
  ]
  interface IStopwatchControl : IDispatch
  {
      [propput, id(DISPID_BACKCOLOR)]
    HRESULT BackColor([in]OLE_COLOR clr);
      [propget, id(DISPID_BACKCOLOR)]

    HRESULT BackColor([out,retval]OLE_COLOR* pclr);
    [propget, id(1), helpstring("property SecondsOnly")]
      HRESULT SecondsOnly([out, retval] VARIANT_BOOL *pVal);
    [propput, id(1), helpstring("property SecondsOnly")]
      HRESULT SecondsOnly([in] VARIANT_BOOL newVal);
};
```

As is shown above, the wizard will add the get and put methods to the IDL file. It will also add the corresponding get and put methods into our **CStopwatchControl** class. Let's edit the implementation code for these by adding the following text inside **StopwatchControl.cpp**:

```
STDMETHODIMP CStopwatchControl::get_SecondsOnly(VARIANT_BOOL *pVal)
{
  *pVal = m_bSecondsOnly ? VARIANT_TRUE : VARIANT_FALSE;

  return S_OK;
}

STDMETHODIMP CStopwatchControl::put_SecondsOnly(VARIANT_BOOL newVal)
{
  m_bSecondsOnly = newVal ? true : false;

  return S_OK;
}
```

As mentioned in Chapter 7, notice that we automatically convert the value to a valid **VARIANT_BOOL** value just in case a client simply passed a different value for true.

Since the timers will be ticking away every second, we do not worry about updating the display—this will happen soon enough.

Creating a Custom Property Page

Now that you have created a custom property, you can add a custom property page so that the users can change it with the UI. To add a property page, use the ATL Object wizard (the same one we used to add the control template earlier). From the Class View, click the right mouse button over Stopwatch classes; then select New ATL Object from the context menu. Select Controls from the left list box, then select Property Page from the palette on the right, and then click Next.

On the Names tab, enter **StopwatchProp** as the short name, and all the other fields will fill in. The Interface field is grayed out because property pages don't use a custom interface.

Accept the default attributes, and skip to the Strings tab (see Figure 11-8). The title will appear on the tab, so keep it as short as possible. You can use the ampersand (&) to denote a shortcut key if you like. Under Title, enter **&Display** and under Doc String, **Display Options**. Click OK to continue.

The wizard will add a new implementation and header file for your property page, a new registry script file (RGS), and a new dialog template. In the

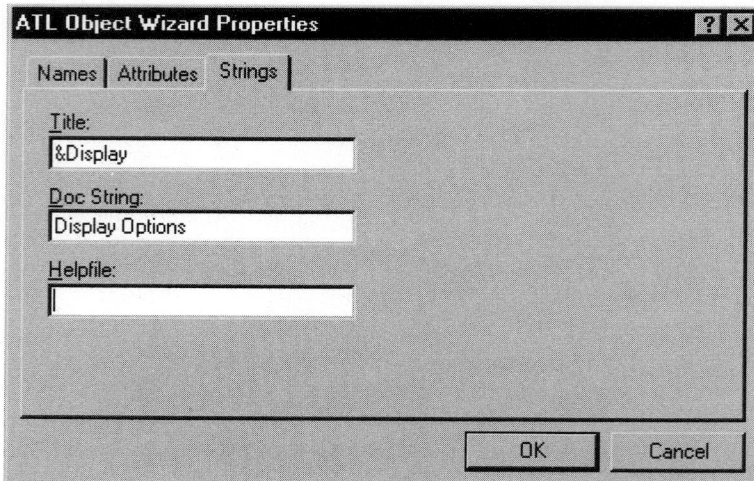

The Strings tab
Figure 11-8.

StopwatchProp.h header file, you will see that the property page exports the COM interface, **IPropertyPage**.

```
////////////////////////////////////////////////////////////////////
// CStopwatchProp
class ATL_NO_VTABLE CStopwatchProp :
  public CComObjectRootEx<CComSingleThreadModel>,
  public CComCoClass<CStopwatchProp, &CLSID_StopwatchProp>,
  public IPropertyPageImpl<CStopwatchProp>,
  public CDialogImpl<CStopwatchProp>
{
public:
...
BEGIN_COM_MAP(CStopwatchProp)
  COM_INTERFACE_ENTRY(IPropertyPage)
END_COM_MAP()
...
}
```

IPropertyPage is the interface through which the properties dialog (which is a Property Page Site) accesses our new page. It is exposed to the container via the **StopwatchControl**'s support of the **ISpecifyPropertyPages** interface, which was inserted into **StopwatchControl.h** when we first ran the ATL Object wizard to create the control.

```
///////////////////////////////////////////////////////////////////////
// CStopwatchControl
class ATL_NO_VTABLE CStopwatchControl :
  ...
  public ISpecifyPropertyPagesImpl<CStopwatchControl>,
  ...
{
public:
  ...
BEGIN_COM_MAP(CStopwatchControl)
  ...
  COM_INTERFACE_ENTRY(ISpecifyPropertyPages)
  ...
END_COM_MAP()
```

After adding the property page, the wizard will open the resource editor and take you to the dialog template so you can add your fields. Delete the dummy label that says to add your controls here, and add a check box control by dragging it over from the control palette. Press ALT+ENTER to open the properties dialog. Change the ID to **IDC_SECONDSONLY** and the text to **Seconds Only** (see Figure 11-9). Now go to the Styles tab and check Tri-state. We will discuss why we need this later. Close the dialog window.

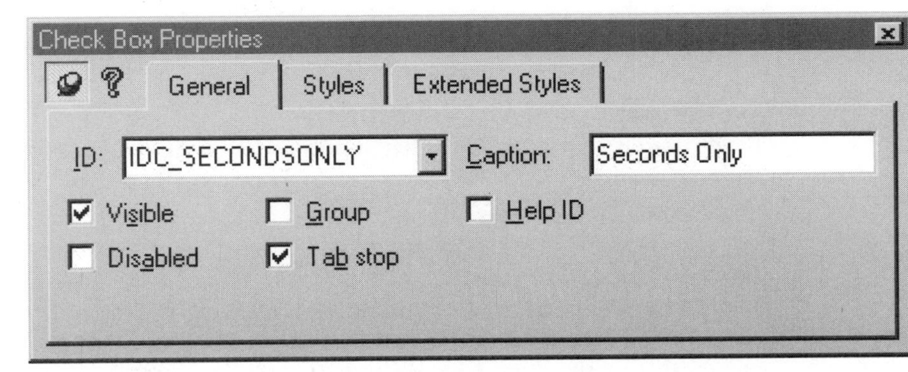

Check box properties
Figure 11-9.

Handling Apply

Once the user changes the value and clicks Apply, we need to take some action. This is done in the **Apply( )** method of our new **CStopwatchProp** class. Within the implementation for this function, you will see that the wizard added a **for** loop and some commented-out code. The reason the **for** loop has been inserted is because some containers allow the user to set the properties for multiple controls at one time. A list of the **IDispatch** interfaces for each of the controls is kept in the **m_ppUnk** member variables. (This list is set by the container through our **IPropertyPage** interface.) Looping through these pointers, you can query for the **IStopwatchControl** custom interface, and then set the value using the put method. First, you need to include the **StopwatchControl.h** header file, so at the top of the **StopwatchProp.h** file add this:

```
#include "StopwatchControl.h"   // our header file
```

Now go back to the **Apply( )** method and insert the highlighted text:

```
STDMETHOD(Apply)(void)
{
  BOOL b = (BOOL) IsDlgButtonChecked( IDC_SECONDSONLY );
  for (UINT i = 0; i < m_nObjects; i++)
  {
    CComQIPtr<IStopwatchControl> spStopwatch( m_ppUnk[i] );
    spStopwatch->put_SecondsOnly( b );
  }
  m_bDirty = FALSE;
  return S_OK;
}
```

Notice the use of the **CComQIPtr** template. This is an ATL class that is used to wrap your class. It automatically handles **QueryInterface( )** calls for you in a manner similar to the one **_com_ptr_t** provided by the **#import** directive.

Setting the Dirty Flag

The **CStopwatchProp** class's **m_bDirty** flag is used to enable or disable the Apply button. (When dirty, the Apply button is enabled.) When the user clicks on the check box, you need to turn the dirty flag on so that the Apply button can be enabled. To do this, go to the Class View and right-click on the **CStopwatchProp** class. Select Add Windows Message Handler from the context menu. In the "Class or object to handle" list box, you will see

IDC_SECONDSONLY. Select this, and the left list box will change to show the only two messages that can be handled for this control—clicked and double-clicked. Select **BN_CLICKED** and click Add and then Edit (you can accept the suggested method name). When you get to the method body, change the TODO line to the following, which will enable the Apply button.

```
LRESULT OnClickedSecondsonly(WORD wNotifyCode,
  WORD wID, HWND hWndCtl, BOOL& bHandled)
{
  SetDirty( TRUE );
  return 0;
}
```

Setting the Initial Values

When the property page is first displayed, we want the controls (in our case the Seconds Only flag) to display the current state. MFC users take this for granted, since they have the Data Exchange macros. In ATL you have to handle the **WM_INITDIALOG** message and set the control values "manually." Fortunately, **CWindow** provides the **SetDlgItemText( )**, **SetDlgItemInt( )**, and **CheckDlgButton( )** methods. The tricky part is not setting the values in the UI, but determining what value to set. As we saw in the Apply button, the property page can be servicing multiple controls. Each control could have a different value for the property you are about to set. It's really up to you how you want to handle situations like that. For check boxes like ours, it is traditional to use a tri-state box. If all of the controls have the value turned off, the check box is empty; if they are all on, the box is checked; and if there are some on and some off, the box is set to an indeterminate state.

Add a handler for **WM_INITDIALOG** by right-clicking on the **CStopwatchProp** entry in the Class View tree and selecting Add Windows Message Handler. Then replace the TODO line with the following:


```
LRESULT OnInitDialog(UINT uMsg,
  WPARAM wParam, LPARAM lParam, BOOL& bHandled)
{

  UINT uiState = BST_INDETERMINATE;
  for (UINT i = 0; i < m_nObjects; i++)
  {
    BOOL b;
    CComQIPtr<IStopwatchControl> spStopwatch( m_ppUnk[i] );
    spStopwatch->get_SecondsOnly( &b );
```

```
        // first time?
        if( i == 0 )
          uiState = b ? BST_CHECKED : BST_UNCHECKED;

        // not first time
        else if( (b && uiState == BST_CHECKED) ||
             (!b && uiState == BST_UNCHECKED) )
          continue;

        // mix of states
        else
        {
          uiState = BST_INDETERMINATE;
          break;
        }
      }

      CheckDlgButton( IDC_SECONDSONLY, uiState );

      return 0;
    }
  };
```

Edit boxes are a little more difficult. Some control containers (such as Microsoft Access) hide edit controls when there is a mixture of values. Some (such as Microsoft Word and the Visual Studio IDE) leave the edit box blank, using blank to mean "no change" and any other value to mean "change all values to this one."

Adding the Property Page to the Control

The final step is to add a PROP MAP macro that will add our new property page to the properties dialog of our control. Add the following to the PROP MAP just after the entry for BackColor inside **StopwatchControl.h**:

```
BEGIN_PROP_MAP(CStopwatchControl)
  PROP_DATA_ENTRY("_cx", m_sizeExtent.cx, VT_UI4)
  PROP_DATA_ENTRY("_cy", m_sizeExtent.cy, VT_UI4)
  PROP_ENTRY("BackColor", DISPID_BACKCOLOR,
    CLSID_StockColorPage)
  PROP_ENTRY("SecondsOnly", 1, CLSID_StopwatchProp)
  // Example entries
  // PROP_ENTRY("Property Description", dispid, clsid)
  // PROP_PAGE(CLSID_StockColorPage)
END_PROP_MAP()
```

The first parameter is a text description that is used to persist the property, and the second number is the DISPID assigned to this property. If you examine the **Stopwatch.idl** file, you will see that the **SecondsOnly** property has an ID of 1. The third parameter is the CLSID of our property page, which you can find at the top of the **StopwatchProp.h** file. Note that if you have multiple properties on one property page, you need multiple **PROP_ENTRY** macros for them; but they, of course, will all specify the same CLSID for the property page.

Testing the Property Page

Build the **Stopwatch.dll**, and fire up the debugger. Insert a **Stopwatch** control, and you will see the time displayed in HH:MM:SS. Now show the property page dialog by selecting Edit | Properties, or by clicking the Properties toolbar button. You will then see properties dialog with the Display tab (see Figure 11-10). Check Seconds Only and click Apply. You will see that the display changes to seconds only. Click OK on the properties page and show it again. This time when you return to the Display tab, the check box is checked, showing that we are, in fact, displaying seconds only.

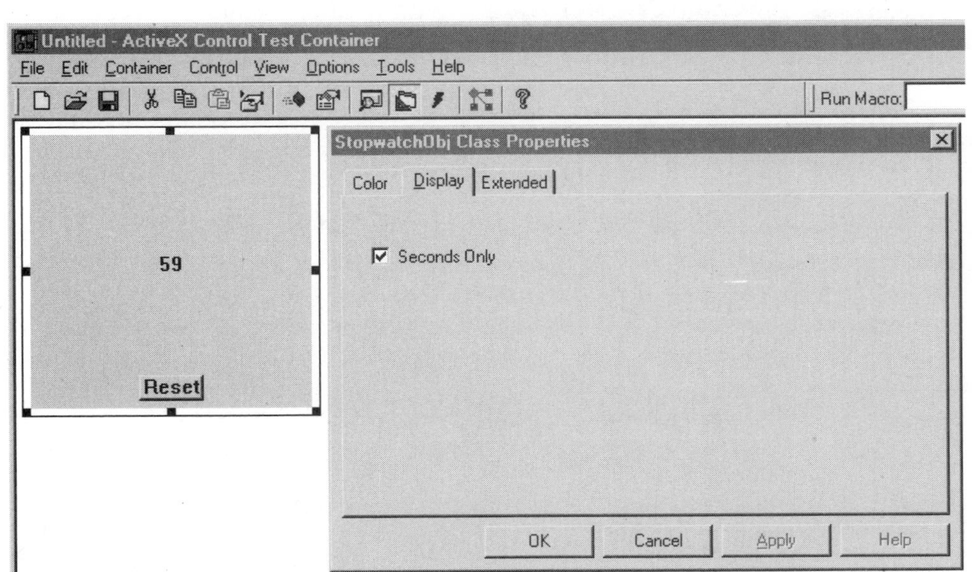

Figure 11-10. The Display tab

Now to put it all together. Save this control to a storage using the Save to Storage option of the Control menu. Go back to the property page, uncheck Seconds Only, and click OK. We now display HH:MM:SS again. Move the control off to the right and select Edit | Insert Control From Storage. It will display the time in seconds only, since that is how it was persisted. Use the mouse to swipe both controls at once (you should see grab handles on both controls when you let go of the mouse). Now show the properties page. If you go to the Display tab, you will see that the check box is in the indeterminate state. If you set or clear the check box and click Apply, both controls will have the same state.

Persistence and Property Bags

A property bag allows a container to load and store a property by name.

So far, we have been saving properties to a disk file using OLE structured storage. Many containers use storages (for example, MS Word). But some containers (such as Visual Basic and Internet Explorer) use a more modern way to store properties—the *property bag*. The property bag allows the container to attach a text name to the property and, thus, load and store it by name. Although these containers will degrade gracefully and will use structured storage if that's all you support, you can easily add property bag support to the stopwatch control by adding the ATL **IPersistPropertyBagImpl** to the list of base classes and **IPersist-PropertyBag** to the COM MAP.

```
/////////////////////////////////////////////////////////////////////////////
// CStopwatchControl
class ATL_NO_VTABLE CStopwatchControl :
  ...
  public IPersistPropertyBagImpl<CStopwatchControl>,
  ...
{
public:
  ...
BEGIN_COM_MAP(CStopwatchControl)
  ...
  COM_INTERFACE_ENTRY(IPersistPropertyBag)
  ...
END_COM_MAP()
```

That's all you have to do! ATL does the rest. You can try this out in the test container by selecting Save to Property Bag from the Control menu. Instead of saving it to a file, as before, the test container will put up a GUI that shows you the properties in your bag.

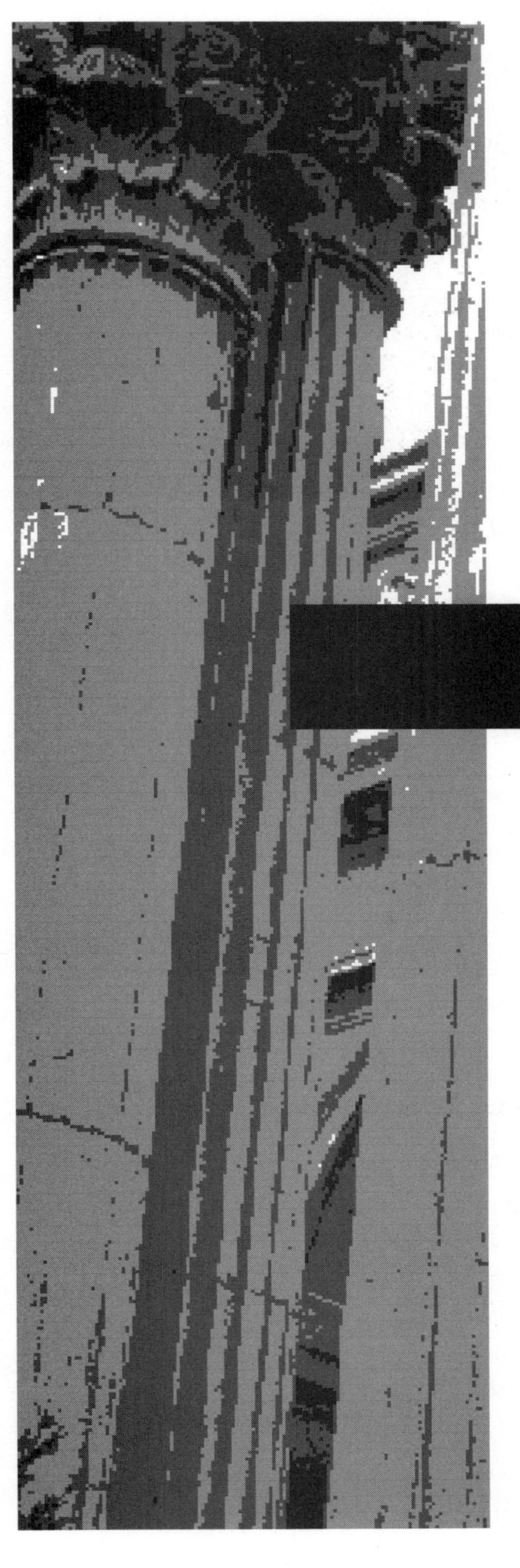

CHAPTER 12

DCOM

When you first consider what advantages can be leveraged by choosing COM, you are most likely to be attracted by its ability to allow binary modules to communicate regardless of the language in which those modules were written. This, of course, is a large part of why COM exists in the first place, and as you have seen, it opens up tremendous opportunities for both large and small projects. However, early in Chapter 1 we mentioned location transparency as being another key feature included in the COM technology. Location transparency is enabled by Distributed COM (DCOM) and enables a client to call a server running on a remote machine. With location transparency, neither the client nor the server requires any knowledge of where the other is located. When instantiating a COM component, for example, the client simply calls **CoCreateInstance( )**, and depending on how the component was configured, that component might be instantiated on a computer across the network or even over the Internet. This is arguably one of the most impressive features of the COM technology. It lets you distribute an application across multiple computers without writing a single additional line of code. Of course, you need to have followed all the COM requirements and designed your application so that a distributed approach makes sense; but assuming this, you are all set.

In this chapter, we begin by explaining how to configure a component that will be instantiated on a remote machine. As you will see, this is a configuration mechanism and does not require any special API calls. Next, we look at some of the ways to write the client instantiation code so that rather than being dependent on the server component's configuration, the client can specify within the code where it wants the server component to be instantiated. After that we tackle the most difficult part of DCOM—security. We look at how to set up security so that a client can receive callbacks and event notifications from the server. Finally, we look at how DCOM works by examining marshalling.

Configuring the DCOM Default Settings for All Applications

You can configure your application to use DCOM with **DCOMCnfg.exe.**

Before you configure your application, register it with an AppID.

The easiest way to enable DCOM is to use the DCOM configuration utility, **DCOMCnfg.exe**, which is located within the system32 directory. If you run it, you will see that it opens with a list of each of the COM-enabled applications on your computer, as shown in Figure 12-1. Each application displayed in the list has a corresponding application GUID or *AppID*. The AppID enables you to configure various COM settings so that when the application runs, the COM subsystem can determine the context of how the applications will run. It is important to note that configuration takes place at the application level, not the individual component level. Therefore, configuration changes made with

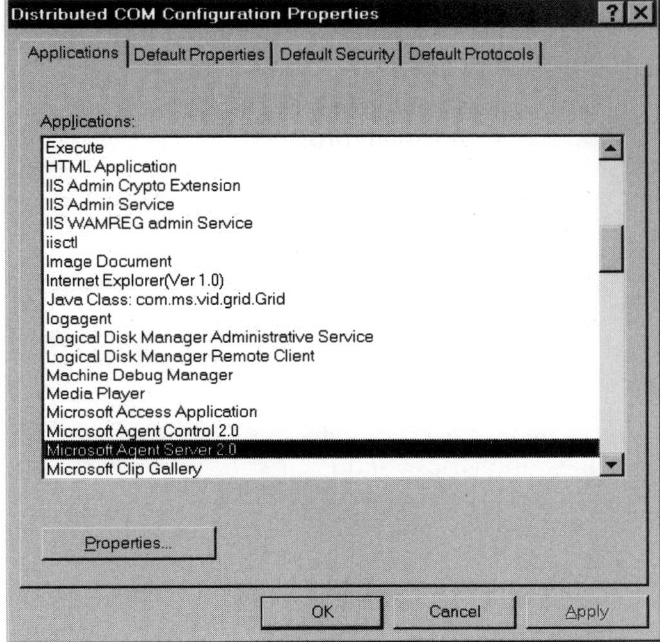

The Distributed COM Configuration program

Figure 12-1.

DCOMCnfg.exe will be for all components within the module supplying the application ID.

Since **DCOMCnfg.exe** works with an application-supplied AppID, you are required to enter an AppID for your component if you want it to be configurable with **DCOMCnfg.exe**. Executables generated with the ATL Object Wizard automatically register their AppID, which is specified in the **<ProjectName>.rgs** file. The AppID is put into the registry under HKEY_CLASSES_ROOT/AppID. Within this folder, a key corresponding to the application's GUID is stored for the executable. The default value for this key is set to the application name, which then appears in the Applications tab of **DCOMCnfg.exe**. Below is a listing of the **Alarm.rgs** file, which is included in the Alarm project in Chapter 10.


```
HKCR
{
  NoRemove AppID
  {
    {BA621077-5AC3-475D-9291-FA3922D370C8} = s 'Alarm'
```

```
      'Alarm.EXE'
      {
        val AppID = s {BA621077-5AC3-475D-9291-FA3922D370C8}
      }
    }
}
```

Next, we take a look at the various settings that can be configured inside **DCOMCnfg.exe**. We start by looking at the default tabs that configure the properties for all applications. We recommend that you do not change any of the default settings unless you are increasing the security level. Instead, if you want to provide DCOM services, change the settings for a particular application rather than for all applications. Often you do not know exactly what an application can be programmed to do, so rather than making all applications available by lowering the security settings on the default tabs, pick the individual applications you want to configure and change those. We will examine how to do this shortly. First, however, let's take a look at each of the default tabs within **DCOMCnfg.exe**.

Default Properties

The Default Properties tab, shown in Figure 12-2, allows you to enable three features: Distributed COM, COM Internet Services, and additional security. Each is described in the following sections.

Enable Distributed COM on This Computer

You must enable the Distributed COM setting in order to use DCOM.

The first check box on the Default Properties tab turns DCOM on and off. If this box is not checked, you will not be able to perform any DCOM operations, whether calling COM servers running on other machines or receiving calls from other machines to a COM server running on the local machine. The check box serves as the main switch for all DCOM operations.

Enable COM Internet Services on This Computer

The second check box allows DCOM to work over the Internet, possibly even through a firewall. Essentially, this option enables COM to listen on port 80, which is the default port for all HTTP traffic. Normally, TCP/IP port allocations for DCOM are dynamically allocated. Furthermore, they are dynamically allocated on ports that are usually blocked by a firewall. Configuring COM to use COM Internet Services (CIS) will enable all registered applications to run DCOM via port 80, which is generally open to allow HTTP traffic (Web traffic) through.

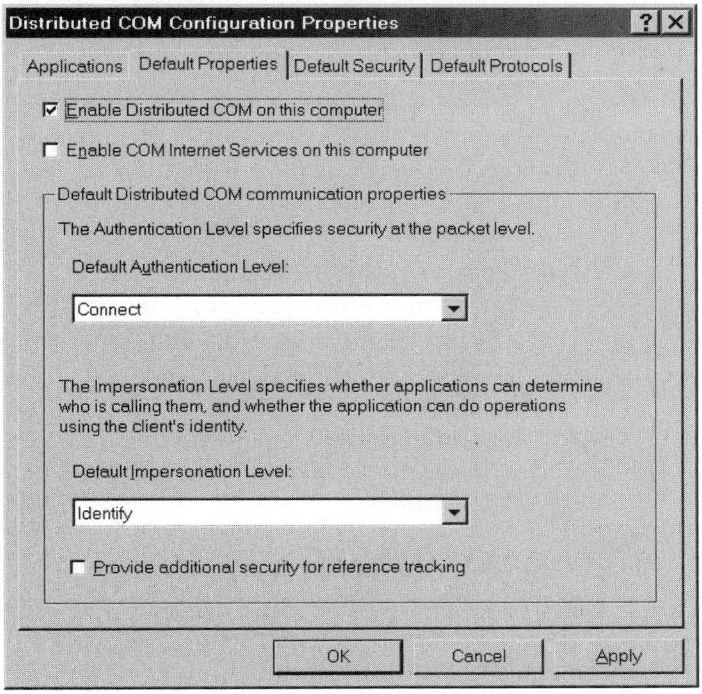

The Default Properties tab
Figure 12-2.

CIS does not change the COM protocol to be HTTP, so if the firewall allows only HTTP traffic to pass through, DCOM will not work. However, assuming that the firewall simply opens or blocks particular ports, this will work. Of course, in this case, being able to perform a particular operation does not mean that you should. If not configured correctly, this option could open a security hole into your network, so use this option judiciously.

Default Authentication Level

In the drop-down box under Default Authentication Level, you define the level of checking that will take place to verify the caller's identity. Following are the settings. Note that these settings are listed from lowest to highest authentication level, not in the order in which they appear in the drop-down.

- **None**: No authentication takes place.

- **Connect**: Authentication will take place only at the time of the initial connection to the server. Following this check, no additional checks will be made.
- **Call**: At the beginning of each call, DCOM checks the authentication, verifying that the client is who it says it is.
- **Packet**: All data that is sent is checked to make sure that it came from the client it claims to have come from—the client who initially made the connection.
- **Packet Integrity**: With this setting, the server not only verifies that the client is who it says it is, but the server also analyzes each data packet to verify that it has not been tampered with while traveling from the client to the server.
- **Packet Privacy**: All of the authentication checks found in Call, Packet, and Packet Integrity are performed; in addition, all packets are encrypted so that they cannot be read with a packet sniffer (at least not unless they are decrypted first).
- **Default**: This is operating system dependent. On NT 4.0 it resolves to Connect, and on Windows 2000 it uses a security negotiation algorithm that takes into consideration the client authentication level.

Default Impersonation Level

The settings in the Default Impersonation Level drop-down determines whether the server module being called can identify who is calling it and whether the server can perform operations, pretending it has the identity of the client. The following settings are available:

- **Anonymous**: Not supported—this is automatically upgraded to Identity.
- **Identity**: With this setting, the server is able to determine who the client is, but it cannot impersonate the client and perform actions on the client's behalf. In other words, the server cannot pretend to be the client when it performs various actions that require security checks.
- **Impersonate**: The server can impersonate the client and perform actions on behalf of the client's identity, as long as the actions occur on the same computer on which the server is running. The client's identity cannot be passed to another machine such that the other machine could also use the client's identity.
- **Delegate**: With this setting, the server can perform actions using the client's identity, and it can pass its identity to other servers, enabling them to perform actions on behalf of the client's identity as well.

Provide Additional Security for Reference Tracking

The last check box on the Default Properties tab configures whether calls to **AddRef( )** and **Release( )** will be secure. Checking this box will ensure that rogue clients cannot maliciously increment or decrement a reference count. Selecting this will incur a slight performance cost because verification calls will need to be made back to the client for every **AddRef( )** and **Release( )** call.

Default Security

The Default Security tab, shown in Figure 12-3, allows you to specify which users can access, launch, and configure the server.

Default Access Permissions

The first setting allows you to configure the permissions for which users can call various components in a server. By default, no users are given access permission. As already suggested, it is probably a good idea to leave this setting as is. Instead, you should configure access permissions for the individual applications, as we shall examine shortly.

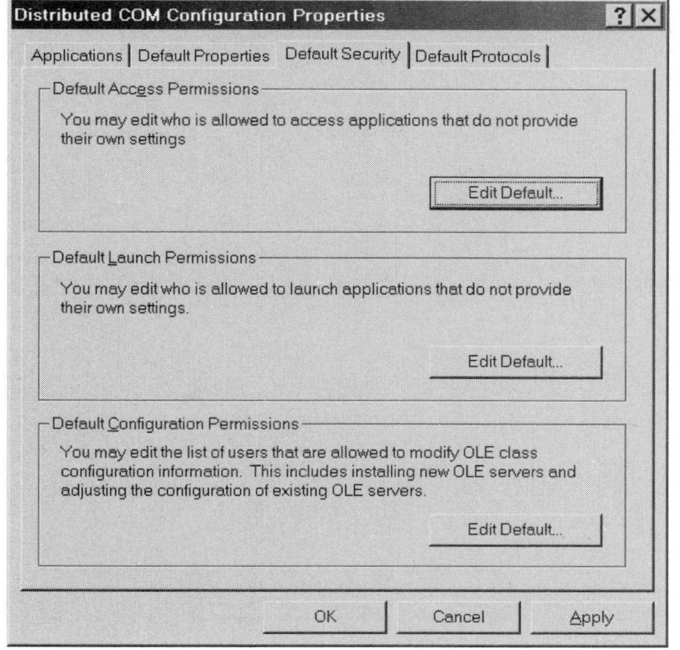

The Default Security tab in **DCOMCnfg.exe**

Figure 12-3.

Default Launch Permissions

The second part of the Default Security tab identifies which users can initially start the application. DCOM (at least on Windows NT platforms) does not require that the application be manually started before a call can be made. The first user to request a component within the application will also start the application, as long as that user has been granted launch permission.

Default Configuration Permissions

Finally, the Default Configuration Permissions setting determines which users are allowed to change the DCOM configuration settings.

Default Protocols

The Default Protocols tab, shown in Figure 12-4, is used to configure the allowable protocols over which DCOM can run.

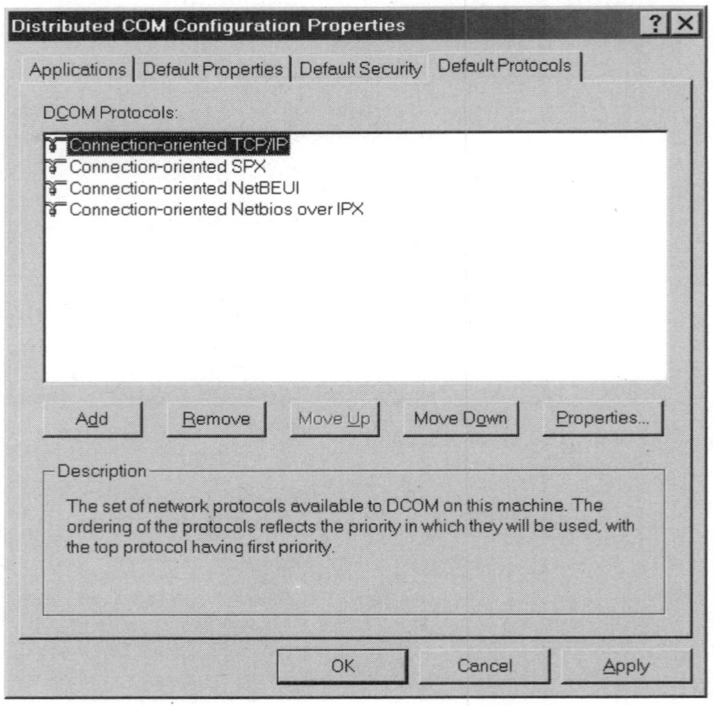

The Default Protocols tab
Figure 12-4.

Configuring a Particular Application for DCOM

Now we will look at how to configure an individual application for DCOM. Specifically, we will make some changes to the MS Agent Server application so that we can have the **Merlin.exe** program from Chapter 5 use DCOM, thereby displaying the Microsoft Agent character on a remote computer. You will recall that this program activated one of the Microsoft Agent characters and then had it display in a bubble above its head (and say out loud) a specified message.

Note that to truly do DCOM, you will need two computers, although you could use one computer as both the server and the client. In this example, our client computer is named Buttercup and a remote server computer is named Wesley.

Configuring the Client Computer

On the client, Buttercup, start **DCOMCnfg.exe** and search through the applications until you come to Microsoft Agent Server. (Note that you can type the name, and the program will search for the application for you as you type.)

General Tab

Now click the Properties button, and the dialog box shown in Figure 12-5 will appear. The General tab allows you to configure the authentication level for the application. The options here match the Authentication Level options on the Default Properties tab we looked at in Figure 12-2. A setting of Default results in the default authentication level specified for all applications, as described previously. When you are deciding what kind of authentication is required, think about where an application will be deployed (over the Internet, on a LAN, etc.) and whether the data that is being sent needs to be encrypted. For example, if you are going to be sending passwords or other private information, you may want to configure a higher authentication level than you would for other kinds of data.

Location Tab

The key DCOM setting on the client computer is found on the Location tab, shown in Figure 12-6. The "Run application on the following computer" option allows you to configure the client so that when **CoCreateInstance( )** is called, rather than invoking the COM server on the local machine, it

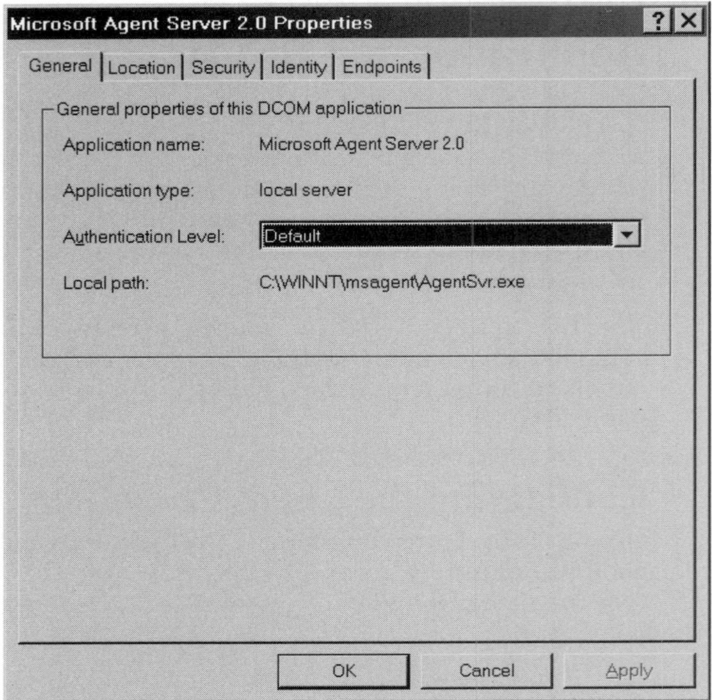

The General tab inside **DCOMCnfg.exe**

Figure 12-5.

will instead be started on the remote machine identified in the text box. In our case, because we are configuring the Microsoft Agent Server, when the Merlin application (from Chapter 5) executes, rather than displaying the Microsoft Agent character locally, the character will appear on the server machine, Wesley.

The "Run application on the computer where the data is located" option is for OLE automation documents that have associated data.

The remaining setting, "Run application on this computer," is the default setting, and it allows the server to run on the local machine. Note that if none of these check boxes is enabled, when **CoCreateInstance( )** is called, a "Class not registered" error will occur and the call will fail. Therefore, you could disable COM for a particular application by unchecking each option on this tab.

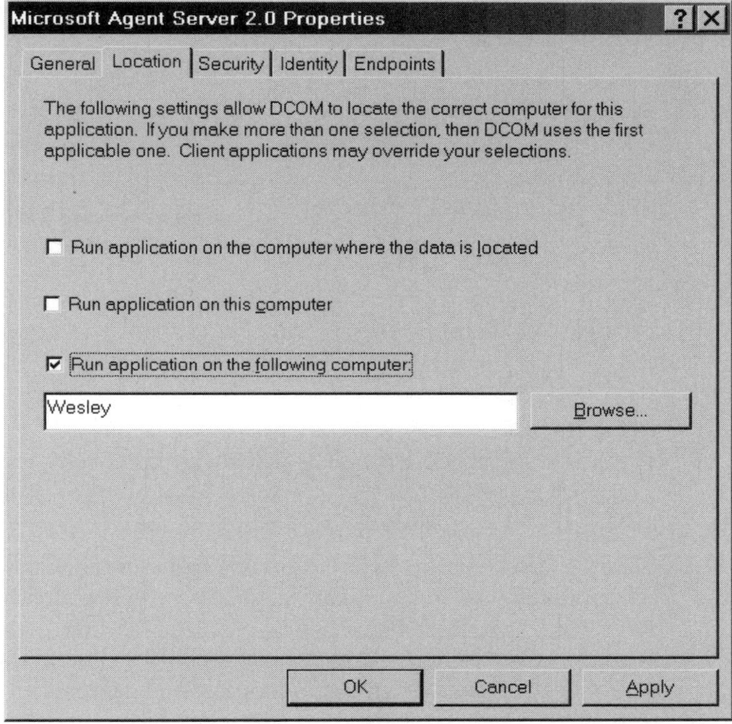

The Location tab inside **DCOMCnfg. exe**

Figure 12-6.

In our example, you do not want to have both "Run application on this computer" and "Run application on the following computer" checked because the first option will take precedence, and we will not be able to see the remote execution.

Simply specifying the "Run application on the following computer" will not be sufficient to allow the application to run remotely. The server computer must be configured to allow remote activation as well. Let's take a look at how to do this now.

Configuring the Server Computer

Now that we have configured the client so that a call to instantiate the Microsoft Agent will be forwarded to the remote computer, it is time to configure the remote computer to allow the call. On the remote computer this time, run **DCOMCnfg.exe** and open the properties for Microsoft Agent Server.

Security Tab

Select the Security tab. This tab looks identical to the Default Security tab identified earlier, and it serves the same function except that rather than configuring security for all applications, it configures security for the Microsoft Agent Server application only. Edit the access permissions, and add System, Interactive User, and Network to the list of users. Note that System is always required when you are doing DCOM. We also add Interactive User because this is the Identity under which we will configure the server to run, as we shall see next.

Identity Tab

The Identity tab configures the security context under which an application is to run. As shown in Figure 12-7, the available options are "The interactive user," "The launching user," and "This user."

"The interactive user" specifies that the application will run as though it were executed by the user currently logged onto the server computer. Therefore, if any user interface (or sound) is to be displayed, it will be seen by the currently logged-on user. Because in our case the Microsoft Agent Server is displayed as speaking some text interactively, we want to select this option. This is also a good choice when you are debugging because it allows you to interact with the running application, appropriately addressing any dialog boxes that may appear. However, unless you specifically need to be visible to the logged-on user, you should avoid this choice for a production application because the application will not start unless a user is logged on. In other words, in a dedicated server scenario, it is not normal that a user will be logged onto the machine, so "interactive user" should not be used for production.

The next choice is "The launching user." With this selection the server will launch under the security context of the user who instantiated the server component from the client computer. Usually this is the user who launched the client application, but not always, because the security context can be programmatically changed. The advantage of using this option is that the security context for the server application will be set automatically so that the only actions that can be performed are those that the client user has permission to perform. The disadvantage of this option is that every client user will launch a new instance of the application, each with its own security

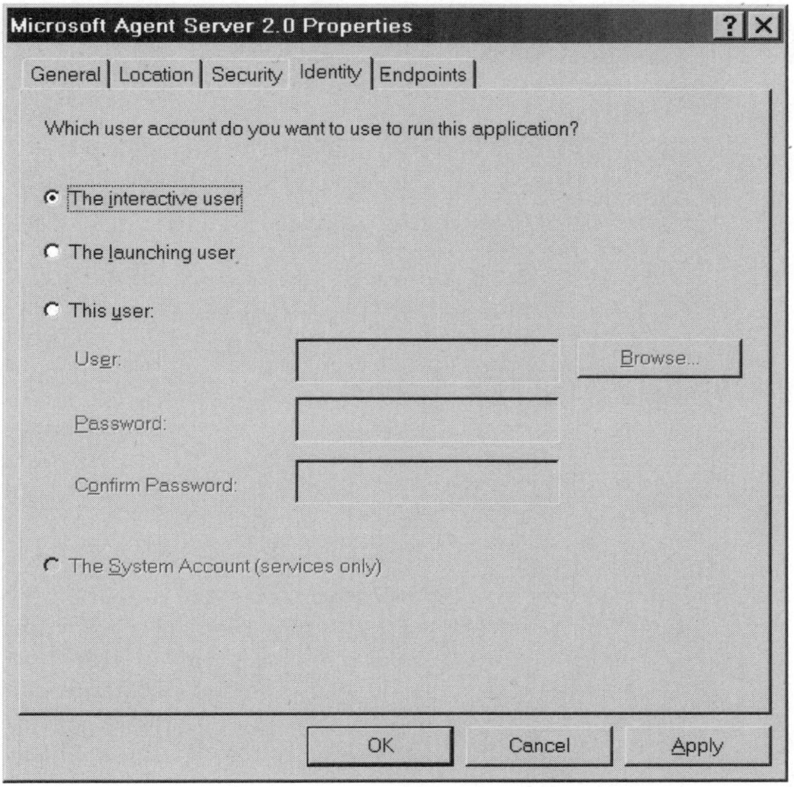

Microsoft Agent Server 2.0 Properties

General | Location | Security | Identity | Endpoints

Which user account do you want to use to run this application?

- (•) The interactive user
- ( ) The launching user
- ( ) This user:
  - User:
  - Password:
  - Confirm Password:
  - Browse...
- ( ) The System Account (services only)

OK | Cancel | Apply

The Identity tab of **DCOMCnfg.exe**

Figure 12-7.

context. This significantly reduces the server application's scalability. In general, you would not want to start a new process for every user that connects.

The "This user" option allows you to configure the server to run under the security context of the specified user. This is generally the best option for production systems. It does not require that a user be logged on to the server computer, and it scales well because a new application is not started each time the client invokes the server. The disadvantage is that the security context is the same for all users. This, however, can be changed programmatically in the server code if you wish different client users to have different security clearances. We will discuss how to do this when we examine the security API later in the chapter.

The last option on the Identity tab, "The System Account (services only)," is available only if the server application is running as a service. The result is that the server runs under the context of the system account. We do not recommend choosing this option, as the system account generally has the security access settings of an administrator or higher. If the service can be manipulated to perform any malicious actions, you will introduce a significant security hole into your system.

Endpoints Tab

The last tab is the Endpoints tab. This tab allows you to override the default protocols configured on the Default Protocols tab discussed earlier.

Running the Client

Before we can run the **Merlin.exe** sample from Chapter 5, one more registry change needs to be made. This change is required due to a problem with Microsoft Agent Server 2.0 that causes it to return a "critical error" when called over DCOM. The work-around is to add the registry key HKEY_LOCAL_MACHINE\SOFTWARE\Microsoft\Microsoft Agent\UseStandardMarshaling.

After adding this key, you should be able to launch the **Merlin.exe** application written in Chapter 5. From the server computer, you will see the Microsoft Agent Server character appear and hear the spoken text specified on the command line. (Refer to the end of Chapter 5 for a refresher on the Merlin application.) After testing the sample as described, be sure to change the Location tab on the client computer back to "Run application on this computer."

Using DCOM Programmatically

The ability to configure a component to use DCOM is a nice feature. Many times, however, a client program may need to decide where to invoke the server component at runtime. In addition, the client program may want to change the security context under which the server runs rather than having it run under the context of the user who launched the client application, as it would by default. Even in our sample program, **Merlin.exe**, it would be useful to be able to specify on the command line where the Microsoft Agent Server will be invoked. This way, you could send messages to remote machines based on the command line setting, rather than having to configure DCOM each time. In this part of the chapter, we will look at changing the Merlin code to programmatically invoke Microsoft Agent Server on a machine specified on the command line and under the security context of a user also specified on the command line. The key API function for doing this is **CoCreateInstanceEx( )**.

CoCreateInstanceEx( )

The **CoCreateInstanceEx( )** COM API function is used to instantiate components on remote computers programmatically. The function is declared as follows:

```
HRESULT CoCreateInstanceEx(REFCLSID rclsid,
                          IUnknown *pOuterUnknown,
                          DWORD dwClsCtx,
                          COSERVERINFO *pServerInfo,
                          ULONG nMultiQI,
                          MULTI_QI *pMultiQI);
```

The first three parameters are exactly the same as those parameters used in **CoCreateInstance( )**, described in Chapter 2. To review, the first, *rclsid*, is used as in **CoCreateInstance( )**, to identify the GUID of the component to be instantiated. The next parameter, *pOuterUnknown*, is used for aggregation, as we described in Chapter 11. It points to the outer component that will aggregate the component being instantiated. Next comes the *dwClsCtx* parameter, which identifies the type of activation that is requested of the server component. You can continue to use **CLSCTX_ALL** for this parameter, but if you want to force the use of DCOM, you will want to use **CLSCTX_REMOTE_SERVER**.

Each of the remaining parameters is described in the following sections.

COSERVERINFO

The next parameter is *pServerInfo*, which is a pointer to the **COSERVERINFO** structure. This structure identifies the remote machine on which the server component is to be instantiated, the user who will be launching and accessing the component, and the authentication and impersonation level. In other words, the **COSERVERINFO** structure essentially contains all the settings that can be specified using **DCOMCnfg.exe**. If a value of **NULL** is used for this parameter, the default settings found in **DCOMCnfg.exe** will be used. The **COSERVERINFO** structure is declared as follows.

```
typedef struct _COSERVERINFO
{
  DWORD dwReserved1;
  LPWSTR pwszName;
  COAUTHINFO  *pAuthInfo;
  DWORD dwReserved2;
} COSERVERINFO;
```

The first and last of these data members are not currently used. Instead, they are reserved for future use. The value specified, however, must be 0 for both of these items. The second data member, **pwszName**, is key, as it identifies on which machine the component will be instantiated. Notice that this is a pointer to a wide character string. Any machine naming convention can be used as long as it is compatible with the network protocol that will be used. By default, any UNC name will work. For example, you can use the full DNS computer name, humperdink.michaelis.net, or the IP address 38.193.190.254. In addition, the non-fully qualified name HUMPERDINK or \\HUMPERDINK can be used.

COAUTHINFO

The third data member in **COSERVERINFO**, **pAuthInfo**, is a pointer to the **COAUTHINFO** structure. **pAuthInfo** identifies the authentication level, and embedded within it is the identity of the user who is to instantiate the component. **COAUTHINFO** is declared as follows:

```
typedef struct _COAUTHINFO
{
  DWORD dwAuthnSvc;
  DWORD dwAuthzSvc;
  LPWSTR pwszServerPrincName;
  DWORD dwAuthnLevel;
  DWORD dwImpersonationLevel;
  COAUTHIDENTITY *pAuthIdentityData;
  DWORD dwCapabilities;
} COAUTHINFO;
```

The first item, **dwAuthnSvc**, identifies the service that will provide authentication to the client user's identity. On Windows NT 4.0, the only authentication service supported is **RPC_C_AUTHN_WINNT**, and we recommend that you use this setting.

dwAuthzSvc specifies the service that will provide authorization. This service is responsible for granting or denying the user access permission.

In general, you will want to use **RPC_C_AUTHZ_NONE** with Windows NT–based platforms.

pwszServerPrincName indicates the principal name to be used. In general, this value should be **NULL** because the value for **dwAuthnLevel** is **RPC_C_AUTHN_WINNT**.

The next item, **dwImpersonationLevel**, corresponds to the impersonation level we saw on the Default Properties tab earlier in the chapter. The only available option is **RPC_C_IMP_LEVEL_IMPERSONATE**. Before we look at the structure of the **pAuthIdentityData** item, let's quickly look at the **dwCapabilities** variable. This is supposed to allow further options for the proxy, but at this time only one value is valid, and that is **EOAC_NONE**.

COAUTHIDENTITY

Buried inside the **COAUTHINFO** structure is the option to specify the client identity under which the server will be called. Essentially, this structure is used to set the username, password, and domain under which the call to the server will be made. The structure is shown below:

```
typedef struct _COAUTHIDENTITY
{
  USHORT *User;
  ULONG UserLength;
  USHORT *Domain;
  ULONG DomainLength;
  USHORT *Password;
  ULONG PasswordLength;
  ULONG Flags;
} COAUTHIDENTITY;
```

As you can see, the structure is fairly simple. The user, password, and domain strings are each specified as a string pointer, with the character length for each item also required. Because the structure allows for either Unicode or ANSI strings, you need to identify which was used within the **Flags** member variable. **SEC_WINNT_AUTH_IDENTITY_ANSI** indicates the strings are ANSI, and **SEC_WINNT_AUTH_IDENTITY_UNICODE** indicates they are Unicode.

MULTI_QI

The last parameter to **CoCreateInstanceEx( )** is a pointer to an array of the **MULTI_QI** structure, *pMultiQI*. This structure is used in conjunction with the *nMultiQI* parameter. *pMultiQI* is used to return a set of interface pointers requested by the client, and *nMultiQI* indicates how many items are in the array. It may seem strange that more than one interface pointer can be returned, but this is done for efficiency. Rather than calling **QueryInterface( )** across the network multiple times, the *pMultiQI* parameter allows you to query for multiple interfaces all at once and have them all returned in one call. The structure of **MULTI_QI**, therefore, consists of the parameters required for calling **QueryInterface( )**. The structure is as follows:

```
typedef struct _MULTI_QI
{
  const IID* pIID;
  IUnknown* pItf;
  HRESULT hr;
} MULTI_QI;
```

pIID is the interface ID requested. **pItf** is the returned interface pointer, and **hr** is the **HRESULT** returned when the server calls **QueryInterface( )** on the instantiated object. Note that it is important to check the **hr** value even if the returned **HRESULT** from **CoCreateInstanceEx( )** is successful. The object may have been instantiated properly, but one of the interfaces in the **MULTI_QI** array may not have been retrieved successfully.

A DCOM Client Sample

To see **CoCreateInstanceEx( )** at work, let's convert the **Merlin.exe** sample from Chapter 5 to use DCOM programmatically. The code is provided below with the required changes highlighted. (Additional changes from raw interfaces to smart pointer interfaces were also made, but because these are secondary to the DCOM changes, they are not highlighted.)

```
// Merlin.cpp : Defines the entry point for the console application.
//

#define _WIN32_DCOM  // Needed in order to call CoInitializeEx()

#include <windows.h>
#include <iostream>
#include <TCHAR.H>

// Import the Microsoft Agent Control
#import "c:\winnt\msagent\agentsvr.exe" no_namespace
```

```
//  Exception declaration not yet standardized
#pragma warning(push)
#pragma warning( disable : 4290 )

const long PAUSE_AFTER_SPEAKING = 20000;
const BSTR DEFAULT_SPEECH =
  L"This is a test of the Emergency Broadcast System!!";

HRESULT CreateAgent( IAgentExPtr& ptrAgent,
  _bstr_t Machine,
  COAUTHIDENTITY AuthorId);

void SayIt(IAgentExPtr ptrAgent, _bstr_t message_text)
  throw (_com_error);

int main(int argc, char* argv[])
{

  HRESULT hr;
  int n_return = 0;

  try
  {
    int arg_count = 1;
    _bstr_t machine = L"";
    COAUTHIDENTITY author_id;
    _bstr_t message_text;
    IAgentExPtr ptrAgent;

    // Initialize COM
    hr = CoInitializeEx(NULL, COINIT_APARTMENTTHREADED);
    if( FAILED( hr ))
      _com_issue_error(hr);

    // Initialize COAUTHIDENTITY
    ZeroMemory( &author_id, sizeof(author_id) );
    author_id.Flags = SEC_WINNT_AUTH_IDENTITY_ANSI;

    // Figure out what to say
    if (argc > arg_count)
    {
      // The user specified the message text on the command line
      message_text = argv[arg_count];
    }
    else
    {
      message_text = DEFAULT_SPEECH;
    }

    // Check to see if a machine name was specified
    arg_count++;
```

```
    if (argc > arg_count)
    {
      machine = argv[arg_count];
    }

    // Check to see if a user name was specified
    arg_count++;
    if (argc > arg_count)
    {
      author_id.User =
        reinterpret_cast<unsigned short*>(argv[arg_count]);
      author_id.UserLength = strlen(argv[arg_count]);
    }

    // Check to see if a password was specified
    arg_count++;
    if (argc > arg_count)
    {
      author_id.Password =
        reinterpret_cast<unsigned short*>(argv[arg_count]);
      author_id.PasswordLength = strlen(argv[arg_count]);
    }

    // Check to see if a domain was specified
    arg_count++;
    if (argc > arg_count)
    {
      author_id.Domain =
        reinterpret_cast<unsigned short*>(argv[arg_count]);
      author_id.DomainLength = strlen(argv[arg_count]);
    }
    hr = CreateAgent(ptrAgent, machine, author_id);
    if( FAILED( hr ))
    {
      std::cout << "CreageAgent failed on machine = '" <<
        (char*)machine << "'." << std::endl;
      _com_issue_error(hr);
    }
    SayIt(ptrAgent, message_text);
    //ptrAgent.Release();
  }
  catch(_com_error e)
  {
    std::cout << "ERROR(" << e.Error() << "):  ";
    if( e.Description().length() > 0)
      std::cout << (char*)e.Description() << std::endl;

    std::cout << e.ErrorMessage() << std::endl;
    n_return = 1;
  }
```

```
  // Uninitialize COM
  CoUninitialize();

  return n_return;

}


HRESULT CreateAgent( IAgentExPtr& ptrAgent,
  _bstr_t Machine,
  COAUTHIDENTITY AuthorId)
{
  HRESULT hr;

  // CoCreateInstanceEx structures
  COAUTHINFO author_info;
  COSERVERINFO server_info;
  MULTI_QI mqi[1];

  if ( Machine.length == 0 )
  {
    hr = ptrAgent.CreateInstance(__uuidof(AgentServer));
    if( FAILED(hr) )
      _com_issue_error(hr);
  }
  else
  {

    // Initialize COAUTHINFO
    ZeroMemory( &author_info, sizeof(author_info) );
    author_info.dwAuthnSvc = RPC_C_AUTHN_WINNT;
    author_info.dwAuthzSvc = RPC_C_AUTHZ_NONE;
    author_info.dwImpersonationLevel = RPC_C_IMP_LEVEL_IMPERSONATE;
    author_info.dwCapabilities = EOAC_NONE;
    author_info.pAuthIdentityData  = &AuthorId;

    ZeroMemory( &server_info, sizeof(server_info) );
    server_info.pwszName = Machine;
    server_info.pAuthInfo = &author_info;

    ZeroMemory( mqi, sizeof(mqi) );
    mqi[0].pIID = &__uuidof(IAgentEx);
    mqi[0].pItf = static_cast<IUnknown*>(ptrAgent);

    hr = CoCreateInstanceEx( __uuidof(AgentServer),
      NULL, CLSCTX_REMOTE_SERVER,
      &server_info, 1, mqi);
  }

  if ( FAILED(hr) )
  {
```

```
    // The CreateFailed
  }
  else if( FAILED(mqi[0].hr) )
  {
    // QueryInterface failed
    hr = mqi[0].hr;
    ptrAgent = NULL;
  }
  else
    // Attach to the returned interface
    ptrAgent.Attach( reinterpret_cast<IAgentEx*> (mqi[0].pItf) );

  return hr;
}


void SayIt(IAgentExPtr ptrAgent, _bstr_t message_text)
{

    HRESULT hr = E_FAIL;

    IAgentCharacterExPtr pCharacter;
    IDispatchPtr ptr_idisp_character;
    VARIANT var;
    VariantInit(&var);
    long nCharacterId;
    long nRequestId;

    // Load the character and retrieve it.
    ptrAgent->Load(var, &nCharacterId, &nRequestId);
    VariantClear(&var);
    ptrAgent->GetCharacter(nCharacterId, &ptr_idisp_character);
    pCharacter = ptr_idisp_character;
    ptr_idisp_character.Release();

    pCharacter->Show(false, &nRequestId);
    pCharacter->Speak( message_text, L"", &nRequestId );
    Sleep(PAUSE_AFTER_SPEAKING);
    pCharacter->Hide(1L, &nRequestId);
    pCharacter.Release();
    ptrAgent->Unload(nCharacterId);

}

#pragma warning(pop)
```

Note that in order for this to work you will still need to add the registry key HKEY_LOCAL_MACHINE\SOFTWARE\Microsoft\Microsoft Agent\UseStandardMarshaling, or you will receive a critical error. (Included with the download code from the Osborne Web site is a REG file that will

update the registry correctly for you.) Also note that the earlier changes described in the section "Configuring the Server Computer" are still needed because they provide the appropriate permissions on the Microsoft Agent Server so that it can be instantiated over DCOM.

To run the application, use the following command line syntax:

```
Merlin.exe ["MessageText" [MachineName [UserName [Password [ Domain] ] ] ] ]
```

For example, to have Merlin say "Cheese" on a remote computer named "Wesley" using the username "Michaelis" and Password "Elisabeth," you will have a command line as follows:

```
Merlin.exe "Cheese!" Wesley Michaelis Elisabeth
```

IN DEPTH

DCOM with a DLL Server

In the preceding sample, we used an executable as the server. This works fine because the executable is able to host its own components. This, however, is not the case with a DLL server. A DLL cannot instantiate itself. Instead it must be configured with a surrogate process to host it. The surrogate process is usually Microsoft's **dllhost.exe**, although in theory you could write your own host. To configure the surrogate process, add the HKEY_CLASSES_ROOT\AppID\<AppId> key for your application, adding a string named "llSurrogate" whose value is "c:\winnt\system32\dllhost.exe." If you prefer not to edit the registry directly, this setting can be configured using **OLEView.exe**. Select the component you want to configure, and then on the Implementation tab, check the Use Surrogate Process check box and specify the path to the process that will host your DLL, as shown in Figure 12-8.

Note that in Figure 12-8, Microsoft Agent Control is a different COM server from Microsoft Agent Server. They both support very similar functionality, but their interfaces are different.

IN DEPTH
CONTINUED

Those of you who have some experience with COM may find it strange that this topic is described within an In-Depth box rather than a section of the chapter. However, with the advent of Component Services, DLLs are much more likely to run within the context of COM+, where they can be configured, rather than to be configured using **DCOMCnfg.exe**.

OleView.exe can also be useful for troubleshooting purposes.

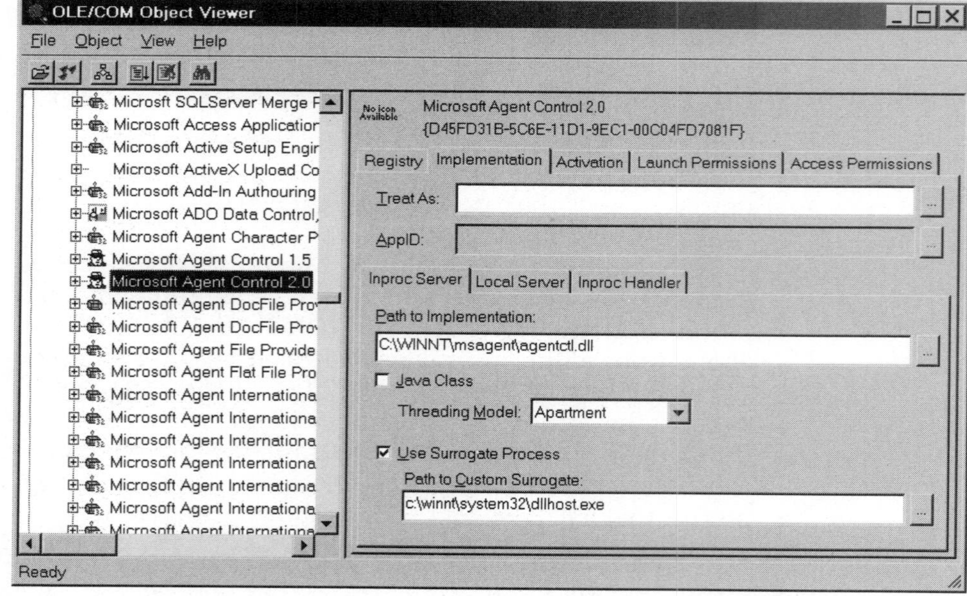

Figure 12-8. Specifying the surrogate process for a DLL using **OLEView.exe**

Troubleshooting DCOM

In spite of the location-transparency goal of DCOM, it is amazing how many problems can occur that prevent DCOM from working. The majority of these are security related, but there are other reasons, too. You may be lucky and have your DCOM system work on the first try, but, if experience is an indicator, this is extremely unlikely. Here are a few suggestions for how to get things up and running after your first attempt fails to work.

1. Get Things Working Locally

Often the problems you may experience are not DCOM related at all but are attributed to registration or incorrect parameter values or even a programming bug. The first thing to do, therefore, when troubleshooting a problem, is to get your program working locally. Get it working on one computer before moving to multiple computers.

Even when working locally, use **CoCreateInstanceEx( )** rather than **CoCreateInstance( )**, and specify the **COSERVERINFO** and **COAUTHINFO** just as you would if you were going across multiple machines. For the machine name, specify the local machine's name. If you are using **DCOMCnfg.exe** to configure your component for remote activation, continue to use the "Run applications on the following computer" option, and for the computer name, specify the local machine name.

This is a good time to get **OleView.exe** involved as well. After locating your component within **OleView.exe**, right-click on it and select the Create Instance menu item. If that works, select the Create Instance On menu item and specify the local machine name.

Before you try true DCOM calls between two computers, get things working locally on both machines, not just the client or just the server machine. Follow the procedures outlined earlier on both machines instead. Sometimes you may have registered the server correctly on the client machine but incorrectly on the server machine; so even though it works locally on the client, it still will not work on the remote machine. Therefore, test locally on both machines.

2. Be Sure the Remote Machine Is Available

The next step is to verify that the network is functioning correctly. The quickest check is to perform a **PING**. This will verify that there is

PING verifies that there is a connection between the client and server computers.

a connection between the client computer and the server. From the command line, enter

PING <server machine>

For the server machine, first try the IP address to verify that the connection is up. Next, try using the computer name just as you would for the **pwszName** of the **COSERVERINFO** in your **CoCreateInstanceEx( )** call. This will verify that the name is being resolved to an IP address. (It is assumed that a TCP/IP network is being used here, so you may need to translate to other network protocols.) **PING** is not guaranteed to work because some network administrators may prevent it—especially through a firewall—but, in general, **PING** can be a very useful tool.

A related technique is simply to access the remote machine via a network browse. Check to see if you can view any of the shared directories of the remote computer. One caveat: Some security settings will prevent this, which is why you will probably first want to get things working without security.

3. Lower the Security Settings as Much as Possible

There is probably no greater reason for DCOM failure than incompatible security settings. Therefore, whenever possible, you should remove as much of the security settings as possible. For many network administrators, this is scary advice, but when it comes to troubleshooting DCOM, it can really help. Remove all security restrictions, and then get everything working. After you have successfully configured things without security, it is time to increase the security level—but not before. Probably the easiest way to do this is to log in as an administrator on both the client and the server machines, and then have the server run under the identity of the interactive user. Also be sure to add administrators to the list of users with access and launch permissions on the server. As noted earlier, this is probably not how you want to leave the server configured, but it is a good way to start. Later in the chapter we look at how to remove security programmatically, and you may want to consider using this within a debug build.

4. Try the Real Thing

It is now time to try doing some real DCOM. If things are still not working, try using **OleView.exe** again, but this time specify the remote machine.

Interpreting Error Results

It would be nice if failed **HRESULT**s always returned a pinpoint error message that enabled you to know exactly where to go to fix the problem. Unfortunately, this is not the case. An **E_ACCESSDENIED** error, for example, could be attributed to a DCOM issue, but it could also be caused by the server component performing some action that the security context under which it is running does not allow. For example, the server may read or write a file or registry value for which it doesn't have access. This has nothing to do with DCOM, but nonetheless, it will usually manifest itself as a failed **HRESULT**.

Below are a few of the most common errors and some of the most likely things to check out if you receive one of them.

E_ACCESSDENIED—You don't have the security to do that.

This is a generic security error encountered whether using DCOM or not. This makes it difficult to diagnose. As already suggested, remove as many of the security settings as possible, and see if the problem is reproduced. If you are in a debugging environment, also try to remove the body of a method, and see if the error still occurs. That way you can diagnose whether it is a COM problem or an issue with the specific code inside the function that is being executed.

RPC_S_SERVER_UNAVAILABLE—Who are you talking to?

Unfortunately, this message is generic to most RPC errors, so pinpointing the problem can be difficult. Surprisingly, this error message is often due to not being able to find the computer on which you want to instantiate the server component. This is a good time to use step 2 of the troubleshooting routine to verify that the connection to the server computer is working. Other possibilities are that DCOM on the server machine has been disabled (Default Properties page within **DCOMCnfg.exe**).

REGDB_E_CLASSNOTREG—I have no record of such a COM server even existing.

12

The problem here is that the server or proxy is not registered correctly. Again, in this scenario you want to verify that everything is working locally first. Also, in **DCOMCnfg.exe** on the server computer, verify that one of the location check boxes is checked. Try using **OleView.exe** to instantiate the component.

COM Security API Functions

Several API functions allow you to configure the security of either the server or the client and to determine the security context of both. In this section we will examine **CoInitializeSecurity( )**, **CoImpersonateClient( )** and its counterpart **CoRevertToSelf( )**, and **CoQuerySecurityBlanket( )**.

Configuring Security Permissions Using CoInitializeSecurity( )

You learned in Chapter 10 that in order for the server (the event source) to report events back to a client (the listener), the listener essentially becomes a COM server to the event source. For this to work, the client needs to configure its security settings similarly to how we configure security for the server. One way to do this is for the client to register its own AppID, which enables you to configure the application using **DCOMCnfg.exe**, as we described earlier. A second way is to configure the security at runtime. This way, the client can be sure to have sufficient security clearance such that it can receive a callback from the server.

This is just one example of why you would want to configure the security programmatically. There are obvious other reasons for performing the same configuration on the server. For example, you may want to override any settings made using **DCOMCnfg.exe** and instead specify the security requirements at runtime based on what you know are the requirements of the code within the COM server. Sometimes, allowing someone to change the security requirements with **DCOMCnfg.exe** is a bad thing because he or she may not realize the minimum settings the server requires.

The key API function for setting up the security is **CoInitializeSecurity( )**, which is declared as follows:

```
HRESULT CoInitializeSecurity(PSECURITY_DESCRIPTOR pSecDesc,
                             LONG AuthCount,
                             SOLE_AUTHENTICATION_SERVICE *AuthService,
                             void *NotUsed1, DWORD dwAuthLevel,
                             DWORD dwImperLevel,
                             SOLE_AUTHENTICATION_LIST *pAuthList,
                             DWORD dwFlags, void *NotUsed2);
```

pSecDesc is a pointer to an object that specifies an access permission. There are three types of such objects: a security descriptor, an AppID, and an **IAccessControl** object. *pSecDesc* can also be **NULL**, which disables access control altogether.

The *AuthCount* parameter specifies the number of services specified by *AuthService*. *AuthService* is a pointer to an array of **SOLE_AUTHENTICATION_SERVICE** structures. The **SOLE_AUTHENTICATION_SERVICE** structure is defined like this:

```
typedef struct tagSOLE_AUTHENTICATION_SERVICE {
  DWORD dwAuthnSvc; // RPC_C_AUTHN... service
  DWORD dwAuthzSvc; // RPC_C_AUTHZ... service
  OLECHAR *oPrincipleName; // principle name or NULL
  HRESULT hr; // result
} SOLE_AUTHENTICATION_SERVICE;
```

If no **SOLE_AUTHENTICATION_SERVICE** objects are used, pass **NULL** in *AuthService*.

NotUsed1 and *NotUsed2* are not used and should be set to **NULL**.

dwAuthLevel determines the authentication level. It must be one of the **RPC_C_AUTHN_LEVEL...** identifiers.

dwImperLevel determines the impersonation level as it applies to proxies. It, too, must be one of the **RPC_C_AUTHN_LEVEL...** identifiers.

For Windows 2000, the *pAuthList* parameter is a pointer to a **SOLE_AUTHENTICATION_LIST** structure, which is defined like this:

```
typedef struct tagSOLE_AUTHENTICATION_LIST {
  DWORD cAuthInfo; // number of authentication objects
  SOLE_AUTHENTICATION_INFO *aAuthInfo; // pointer to objects
}; SOLE_AUTHENTICATION_LIST;
```


The **SOLE_AUTHENTICATION_INFO** structure is defined like this:

```
typedef struct tagSOLE_AUTHENTICATION_INFO {
  DWORD dwAuthnSvc; // RPC_C_AUTHN... service
  DWORD dwAuthzSvc; // RPC_C_AUTHZ... service
  void *pAuthInfo   // authentication-specific info
}; SOLE_AUTHENTICATION_INFO;
```

For Windows NT 4, *pAuthList* must be **NULL**.

The *dwFlags* parameter specifies the various capabilities of the COM object. To specify no additional capabilities, pass **EOAC_NONE** for this parameter.

CoInitializeSecurity( ) is a sophisticated function, especially because of the fact that each operating system release provides more options. To maintain backward compatibility, however, stick to using the NT 4.0 options, which all work on Windows 2000 as well.

At times you will want to turn off all security settings. For example, if your client application does not have any publicly creatable objects (objects that can be instantiated via a **CoCreateInstance[Ex]( )** call), the easiest way to make sure the server will be able to call back into the client is to turn off all security. In addition, when trying to identify security problems that may prevent a component from successfully being instantiated, it is often helpful to turn off all security in an effort to identify whether security is causing the problem in the first place. The code to turn off all security using **CoInitializeSecurity( )** is shown below:

```
HRESULT hr;
hr = CoInitializeSecurity( NULL, -1, NULL, NULL
  RPC_C_AUTHN_LEVEL_CALL, RPC_C_IMP_LEVEL_IMPERSONATE,
  NULL, EOAC_NONE, NULL);
```

Note that this setting does not work for specifying the launch permissions. On the client, this doesn't make sense since it will be launched by the user. On the server, the configuration is just as nonsensical because in order for the **CoInitializeSecurity( )** function to be called, the program would have to be running already.

Impersonating the Client Identity: CoImpersonateClient( )

The Identity tab inside the **DCOMCnfg.exe** application allows you to specify the security context under which the server process will run. Earlier, when we discussed the settings available on this tab, we suggested that usually you will want to select "This user" and then specify the user under which the process will run. The advantage of doing this is that each client that instantiates a component within the server will not start a new instance of the process. This is important when the process is an NT service. The disadvantage of this choice is that, by default, the security context will always be that of the user specified in **DCOMCnfg.exe**. This means that you cannot restrict specific actions based on the caller's identity. To avoid this problem, you can use the **CoImpersonateClient( )** API function. This will change the security identity for the currently running thread, for the duration of the current client call, to be that of the client. You can switch the context back to the process security identity using the **CoRevertToSelf( )** API function. However, if you don't call this before the COM function call exits, the security setting will automatically revert on its own.

There is one important restriction to the **CoImpersonateClient( )** call. The authentication level must be at a minimum of **RPC_C_AUTHN_LEVEL_-CONNECT**. Therefore, you may want to call **CoInitializeSecurity( )** prior to calling **CoImpersonateClient( )** on a particular thread.

You can also check the authentication level (among other things) beforehand by using the **CoQuerySecurityBlanket( )** API function.

One last thing: Do not use **CoImpersonateClient( )** during component construction—for example, inside **FinalConstruct( )**—because the caller is essentially unknown at the time a component is being instantiated.

Determining the Security Settings with CoQueryClientBlanket( )

To determine the identity of the security context for the current thread, either before or after calling **CoImpersonateClient( )**, you will want to use the **CoQueryClientBlanket( )** API function. This is declared as follows:

```
HRESULT CoQueryClientBlanket(DWORD *pAuthenticationService,
                DWORD *pAuthorizationService,
                OLECHAR **pServerPrincipalName,
                DWORD *pAuthenticationLevel,
                DWORD *pNotUsed,
                RPC_AUTHZ_HANDLE *pPrivilegeInformation,
                DWORD **pCapabilities);
```


For the most part, the parameters' names indicate what they are for: *pAuthenticationService* is the authentication service, *pAuthorizationService* is the authorization service, and *pAuthenticationLevel* indicates the authentication level. Surprisingly, *pNotUsed* is not used. However, be careful because this parameter appears as *pImpLevel* when using IntelliSense, so it can mislead you into thinking that it is the impersonation level.

The not-so-obvious *pServerPrincipalName* returns information about the caller's identity. This is great if you need to access a resource using the identity of a specific client or to write information about the caller's identity to a log file. *pPrivilegeInformation* returns a handle to the privilege information. The format of this structure is dependent on the authentication service being used.

As with **CoImpersonateClient( )**, the results returned from **CoQueryClientBlanket( )** are not valid during component instantiation.

Marshalling

Now that we have finished looking at all the practical parts of DCOM and how to get it to work, it is time to examine some of the theory behind how it all works. Specifically, we are going to look at marshalling.

Marshalling is the process of preparing and transmitting data across a COM boundary.

Marshalling is the mechanism for transmitting data across process and network boundaries. The purpose of marshalling is to allow data to pass from one process into another, even across a network. (Marshalling is also required to pass interfaces from one COM apartment [or context] into another, but we will postpone this discussion until the next chapter, when we look at threading models in detail.)

In the context of DCOM, marshalling involves placing the data into a data packet that can be sent across to the server computer. Once the packet arrives at its destination, it is unmarshalled and sent to the COM server.

Proxies and Stubs

The proxy invisibly intercepts the call to the server. It then takes the parameters and marshals them into packets to be sent across the COM boundary to the stub.

A key requirement in the entire process of marshalling is that it is invisible to both the client and the server that marshalling is taking place. As shown in Figure 12-9, in order for the process to work transparently for both the client and the server, two additional items, the *proxy* and the *stub*, are involved in the process.

The proxy is responsible for appearing to the client as if it is actually the server. As far as the client is concerned, it has a pointer to the server's interface. In reality, however, the client has a pointer to something that looks like a server, feels like a server, but in reality, is simply a façade. Instead, it is the proxy-provided interface pointer. The proxy is responsible for actually performing the marshalling of the data. It knows how to take each of the

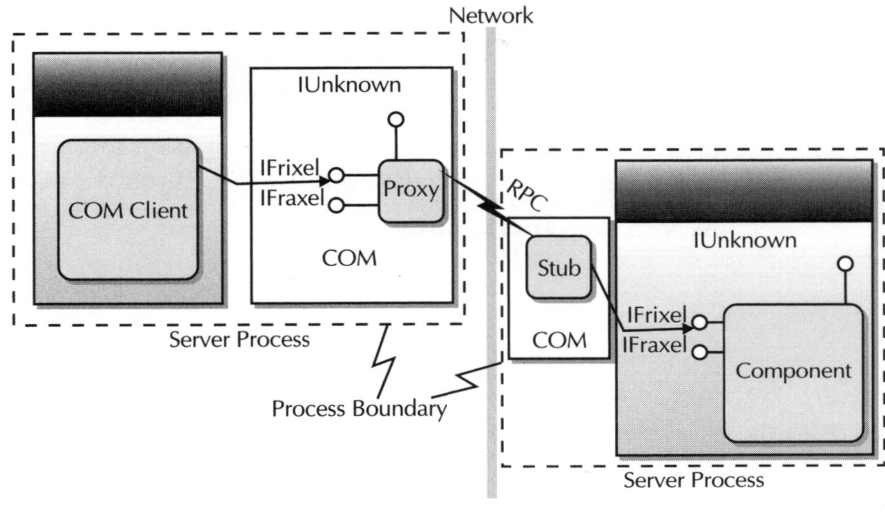

Marshalling data from the client to the server

Figure 12-9.

parameters that the client sends it and to pass them across to the stub. The stub, on the other hand, looks exactly like the client to the server...but it isn't either. The stub unmarshals the data coming from the proxy and sends it into the COM server exactly as the client would if it were doing it directly. The result is location transparency to both the client and the server. Neither the client nor the server knows where the other is located; they simply make and receive the calls, and the proxy and stub take care of the details.

A stub is used to translate calls from the proxy into the server so the server does not need to know the details of the client's location when returning data. The proxy interacts with the stub as though it were the client.

The next question we need to tackle is this: How do the proxy and stub intercept the call to the server? The answer is that the COM subsystem takes care of the details. When a client calls **CoCreateInstance( )**, the COM subsystem checks to see where the server is to be located. If it is located across a COM boundary (in the DCOM case, on a different computer), then the COM subsystem will instantiate the server on the remote machine and pass back to the client a pointer to the server's proxy rather than a pointer to the server's interface directly. Given this method, the client will make calls into the proxy as though it were calling the server; the proxy will then convert the call appropriately and direct it to the server. From the server's perspective, it looks like it is directly interacting with the client as well.

Even for experienced programmers, the concept of "hydrating" data into a pipe and sending it across the network to then be accessed from a different computer sounds like a difficult operation unless they have specifically programmed in that area before. (*Hydrate* is slang for marshalling data back and forth between a server and a client.) Since this is exactly what marshalling does, you may be tempted to think that DCOM is difficult to implement and therefore avoid it altogether. In reality, it is not too hard, but it can be tedious programming. Fortunately, Microsoft has invested a significant effort in this area so that only in rare circumstances do you actually need to write any marshalling code. Now let's consider three different kinds of marshalling.

"Hydrate" is slang for marshalling data.

Custom Marshalling

There are in fact three different kinds of marshalling. The most difficult of these, *custom marshalling*, requires that you write the specific code for passing your data across the process/network boundary. This is usually required only for exceptional performance requirements or for unique kinds of data for which such custom marshalling would be more efficient.

Type Library Marshalling

At the other end of the "difficulty scale" is type library marshalling. This is the most common type of marshalling and essentially requires no additional code work on the part of the server programmer. The MIDL compiler generates the type library, and this is all that is needed for type library marshalling. There is one data requirement if you want to use type library marshalling: You can support only interfaces that use the standard oleautomation interfaces we discussed back in Chapter 5. To ensure this, you should decorate all nondual interfaces with the **oleautomation** attribute. It is not required for dual interfaces because the **oleautomation** attribute is built in for these interfaces.

Type library marshalling is implemented for you by **oleaut32.dll**, which uses its **IDispatch** marshaller. Since you are restricted to the oleautomation data types (those supported by **IDispatch**), the **oleaut32.dll** already knows how to marshal each of the data types you use. Therefore, it can be invoked to handle all marshalling between the client and the server.

For configuration, you will need to distribute the type library and register it on each client machine. This is automatically done for you if your project is built using the ATL wizard and you distribute the server module to the client machine. However, if you wish to avoid installing the server module on the client machine, you can simply register the type library. To do this, you could call the **RegisterTypeLib( )** API function. However, to do this you are required to have a pointer to the **ITypeLib** interface. Instead, you can use **LoadTypeLibEx( )** with the **REGKIND_REGISTER** option, which will do all you need in one call. **LoadTypeLibEx( )** is defined as follows:

```
HRESULT LoadTypeLibEx(LPOLESTR FileName,
                      REGKIND TypeOfRegistration,
                      ITypeLib **ppTypeLibrary);
```

Here, *FileName* specifies the name of the type library. *TypeOfRegistration* determines how the library is registered. Normally, you will want to specify **REGKIND_REGISTER** so that the library is registered. You can write a small utility to do this, but several such programs are also available on the Internet. They can be downloaded for free and include such features as file associations. On return, the object pointed to by *ppTypeLibrary* contains an indirect pointer to the type library interface, **ITypeLib**.

For the majority of circumstances, you will find that type library marshalling is all you need to use.

The MIDL-Generated Proxy/Stub

The last kind of marshalling involves code that is automatically generated for you by the MIDL compiler. The MIDL compiler creates two proxy source code files, **<project>_p.c** and **dlldata.c**. Furthermore, the ATL wizard creates the **<project>_ps.mk** and **<project>_ps.def** files. Using these files, and the **<project>_i.c**, you can compile a standard marshaller.

To generate the proxy/stub DLL, use **nmake.exe**. For example:

```
"NMAKE.exe <project>ps.mk"
```

Note that you need to have run the ...**vc98\bin\VCVARS32.BAT** file in order to have the appropriate environment settings prior to running **nmake.exe**. The result will be a custom proxy DLL that you will be required to register on the client as follows:

```
Regsvr32.exe <project>ps.dll
```

Note that you are required to create this DLL only if your interfaces are not oleautomation compatible.

DCOM Summary

Seemingly, DCOM would involve a tremendous amount of work on the part of the developer. However, because location transparency was a feature designed into COM from the beginning, there is not much more work necessary to use DCOM. The most difficult part of DCOM is not the coding but configuring the security (either programmatically or using **DCOMCnfg.exe**). In the next chapter you are going to learn a bit more about marshalling as you see that marshalling does not just occur when crossing process or machine boundaries. It takes place across apartment and even context boundaries.

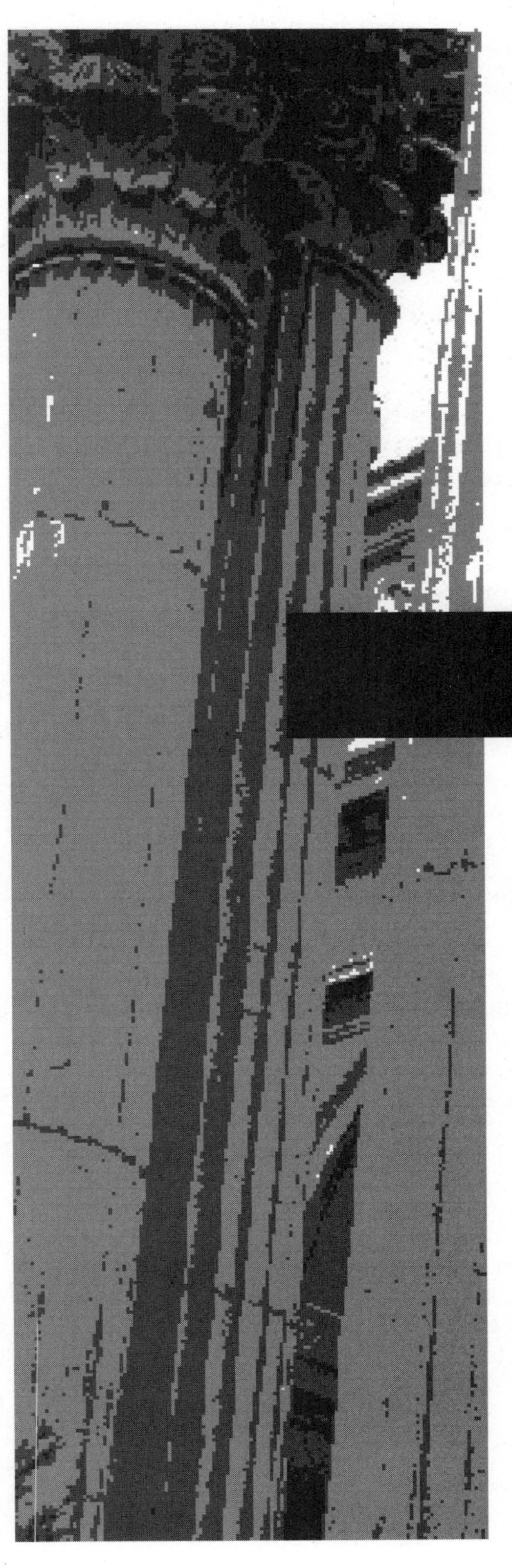

CHAPTER 13

Threading

For many programmers, COM threading is viewed with some trepidation. Fortunately, much of what you can achieve with COM can be done with little regard for threading. In fact, if you stick with apartment threaded objects, there is little about threading that you need to be concerned with. Of course, as your projects become more sophisticated, there will come a point at which you must deal with threading, concurrency, and asynchronicity.

To understand COM threading, you must first understand why various threading models exist at all and why the rules surrounding COM are so important. Since one of the main purposes of COM is to allow binary objects to communicate and be shared amongst each other, sooner or later the question of synchronization is bound to arise. What happens when two different threads try to access the same object instance of code or memory at the same time? What happens, for example, if a component performs a check on a member variable before incrementing it as follows:

```
if( m_Count <= 4 )
  m_Count++;
```

The problem with code like this is that if two different threads access the same component code simultaneously, there is potential for **m_Count** (a member variable) to increase above 4, because, while one thread may have completed checking that the value is 4, the other may be in the process of actually incrementing it. The net result is that they both increment the value—a situation surely not intended by the programmer. This is known as a *race condition*.

To prevent race conditions from occurring, it is necessary to use mutexes and semaphores, which prevent simultaneous access. It is not so difficult to simply add a mutex before and after a call, but thread synchronization becomes more complicated when trying to ensure that deadlocks don't occur. Even if you are able to handle all these issues with ease, the next complicated part comes in testing your components. It takes some rather rigorous stress testing to reveal where you may have introduced a deadlock or missed a particular synchronization check.

In order to simplify programming and allow component developers to focus on the primary logic of their program, Microsoft introduced some automatic thread synchronization. There are various levels of synchronization depending on how your component is configured and how much you want Microsoft's automatic synchronization to take effect. The basic mechanism for thread synchronization is found in the *apartment*.

An apartment is a logical thread context in which a COM object runs.

A COM apartment refers to the logical thread context within which COM objects run. Essentially, the type of apartment in which your component runs defines the level of synchronization that you want COM to perform for you. There is a one-to-many relationship between apartments and COM objects. Each apartment can have multiple objects within it, but a COM object runs in exactly one apartment. In other words, a particular component instance cannot span multiple apartments. In order for COM to know in which apartments a component can run, the component is configured with a *threading model*. The threading model defines which apartments a particular component is compatible with.

A threading model determines the type of apartments in which an object can run.

Let's review the various threading models via an analogy. Except for the last model, which is supported only on Windows 2000, each of these models was first introduced in Chapter 3. And from there you will recall that you are presented with the choice of which one to select when you run the New ATL Object wizard.

A Threading Model Analogy

Consider a computer manufacturer, Fraxel Computer, which is responsible for—you guessed it—making computers. Fraxel Computer has several different plants. Each Fraxel plant is divided into various workgroups. Within each workgroup is a set of stations. Some types of stations take care of assembling the computer. Another type is used for running a full test cycle on each computer. In addition, a packing station packs the computer into a box. A diagram of such a facility is shown in Figure 13-1. There are two additional station types that are not pictured. One type is the loading dock, and the other is the supply station.

In the analogy, an entire factory corresponds to a process. Each workgroup corresponds to a COM apartment. The workers within an apartment are each different threads. Each station represents a component instance.

Let's consider each of the threading models in light of this analogy.

Single Threading Model

The first approach to threading that we will examine is the single threading model. All stations that belong to the single threading model share one worker to do all the work of those stations, as shown in Figure 13-2. There may be other work areas that have different models within the factory, but all stations that belong to the single threading model are all part of the same work area, and they are assigned exactly one worker for the entire area.

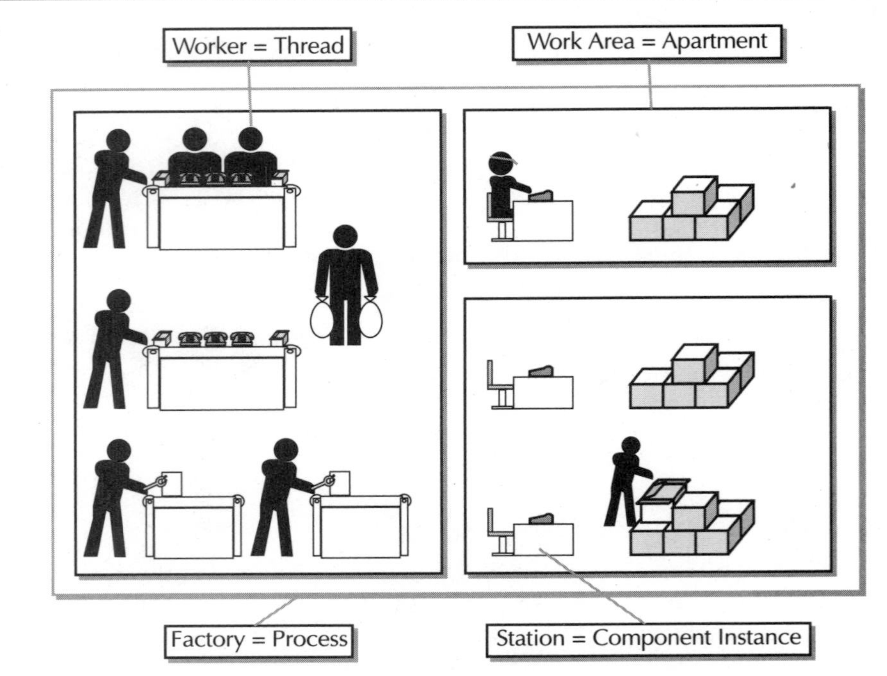

Fraxel Computer's manufacturing facility
Figure 13-1.

When additional threads require work to be done by a single threaded component, they end up requesting that the work be performed by the main thread of the process; they do not actually perform the work themselves.

Furthermore, although not depicted in Figure 13-2, there could be multiple types of stations, which are assigned to the single threading model workgroup, which means they, too, will be sharing the same worker.

At no point can there be more than one worker in the workgroup area using any of the stations. In fact, only the area's assigned worker can access the stations directly.

Therefore, if additional workers come along and want to have work done at a station assigned to this group, they need to send a request to the workgroup's worker, who will then perform the work and pass the completed work to the original workers. The workers who are waiting outside do not actually perform any operations on the stations within. They simply request that the operations be performed and then wait around until the work completes.

In the single threaded COM model, a similar principle occurs. All components marked for the single threading model can run on only one

A single threaded workgroup
Figure 13-2.

thread. Furthermore, it is not just any thread, but it must be what is known as the *main* thread, the one that first called **CoInitialize( )** or **CoInitializeEx(NULL, COINIT_APARTMENTTHREADED)** within the process. (You may remember from Chapter 5 that these two calls are equivalent because **CoInitialize( )** simply calls **CoInitializeEx(NULL, COINIT_APARTMENTTHREADED).**) If no thread within the process has yet called **CoInitialize( )** (because the caller used **COINIT_MULTITHREADED** instead), COM will effectively call **CoInitialize( )** for you on a new thread, which all single-thread-modeled components will then use. The result is that to use any component marked as being in the single threading model, you have to wait until the main thread is no longer busy doing any work.

Just as the inefficiencies of the single threaded manufacturing facility are glaring, the same holds true for the single threaded type of component. In fact, the only advantage is that you are guaranteed that any data within the component, including any static data (or even any global data if there are no other types of components within the module), will be synchronized so that there will be no need to prevent access to the static data by two different threads at the same time. This small advantage has an expensive performance price, however, when you consider that to enable protection for static and global data is not particularly difficult. Essentially, the single threading model exists for historical purposes, and it is rare that you would ever need to create a component that requires this model.

The ThreadingModel value under a component's InprocServer32 key in the registry defines what type of threading model a component belongs to.

In order to declare the threading model of a particular component, a registry value needs to be added to the InprocServer32 key (for in-process servers) already defined for the component. The name of the value is *ThreadingModel*.

If the ThreadingModel is not entered into the registry, a component will default to the single threading model. The single threading model can also be specified explicitly by entering the value "Single" for the ThreadingModel setting.

The ThreadingModel for an in-process component that is to run in the single threading model is either blank or set to "Single".

For out-of-process servers (executables), the threading model is determined by the **CoInitialize[Ex]( )** call directly. Since an executable will not need to call **CoCreateInstance( )** for objects within its module, an executable essentially defines the threading model of a component by whichever thread the component is instantiated on. In the case of the single threaded object, calling **CoInitialize( )** (or **OleInitialize( )**) for the first time will essentially establish the main thread on which the single threading model component can then be instantiated.

Single Threading Model at a Glance

- Objects always run in the process' main thread.
- ThreadingModel setting in the registry is left blank.
- Inefficient and should generally be avoided.
- Threads outside the main apartment cannot run any code belonging to objects within this apartment. Instead they request that the work be performed by the main thread.

Apartment Threading Model

In an apartment threading model, each workgroup is still limited to one worker per area. The distinction from the single threading model, however, is that stations marked as apartment threaded can be placed in any area, not just the main area. It is still the rule that workers outside the area cannot perform work on stations living within the work area.

Since the main workgroup defined by the single threaded model allows only one worker inside that apartment, stations that are apartment threaded can also be placed inside the main workgroup, as shown in Figure 13-3.

You will notice that the packing station (shown by the boxes) can be placed in any workgroup limited to one worker. The key for the apartment threading model is that stations can be placed only in workgroups that are restricted to one worker.

Each workgroup in the factory corresponds with an apartment in the COM world. In contrast to the single threading model, the apartment threading model can capitalize on additional threads that are created. Each apartment

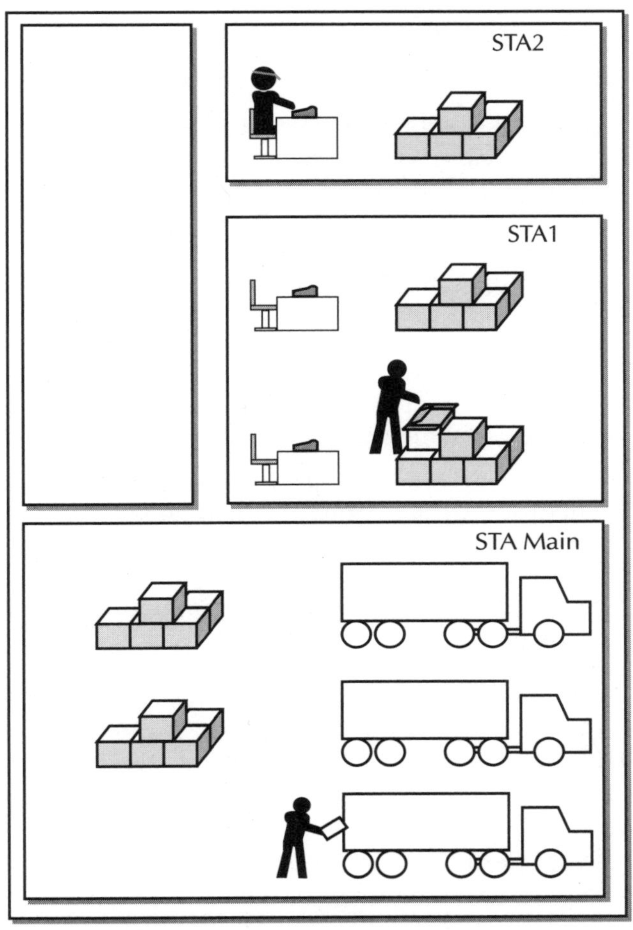

Apartment threading model workgroups
Figure 13-3.

can have at most one thread running within it. The apartments are therefore called *Single Threaded Apartments* or STAs.

Be careful not to confuse this with the single threading model, which we discussed in the previous section. The single threading model has objects that can run within only one STA—the main STA.

In-process apartment threaded components have a threading model setting of "Apartment".

The thread inside each STA must be initialized with a **CoInitializeEx(NULL, COINIT_APARTMENTTHREADED)** call (either explicitly via the client or implicitly by COM when an object within an incompatible threading model instantiates the component). The **CoInitializeEx( )** call on the thread creates the apartment within which each component that is instantiated on the thread will run. In order for a component outside a particular STA to achieve work on an object within the same STA, it must request that the lone worker thread within the STA perform the work. Outside threads cannot execute code within the STA.

At first, the distinction between the apartment threaded model and the single threaded model may seem subtle. The performance improvement can be significant, however. Components belonging to the apartment model have a strong advantage over single threading model objects because they can capitalize on any additional threads on which they may be instantiated. In the single threading model there is no advantage to a client creating additional threads for working with the single threaded objects because access to these objects will always be serialized to the main thread. In contrast, apartment threaded objects can be instantiated on additional threads; so two objects instantiated on two different threads (in other words, within two different apartments) will be able to run concurrently.

Apartment threaded objects continue to offer a significant level of synchronization because all member variables on a particular component instance are still protected via the apartment mechanism. This is due to the fact that only one thread (the lone thread running in the apartment) can execute code on a particular component instance at a time. The only time you need to worry about synchronization, therefore, is when you access static or global variables. These will have to be protected with appropriate blocking mechanisms. This makes the apartment threading model one of the most useful of all the models. It allows you to capitalize on COM's synchronization to a large degree without sacrificing performance. Unless you have specific performance needs, this is generally a safe choice.

Apartment Threading Model at a Glance

- Only one thread can access an STA object at a time.
- The ThreadingModel setting in the registry is "Apartment".

- Provides a good balance between performance and synchronization.
- Be sure to synchronize access to global and static data.
- Member variables for STA components do not need to be synchronized.
- Threads outside the STA cannot run any code belonging to objects within this apartment. Instead, they request the work be performed by the STA's lone thread.

Free Threading Model

Stations that are tagged for the free threading model hold one thing in common with the single threading model. They are restricted to one area within the entire factory. They are radically different, however, because that one area can have multiple workers active within it at the same time. Workers outside the area still have to request work to be performed (rather than doing it themselves), but there are multiple workers within the area that could perform the requested work, as shown in Figure 13-4. In addition, some workers can be dedicated to specific tasks. For example, some workers could be responsible only for unpacking boxes whenever they arrive and placing their contents on a conveyer.

Notice that no stations marked as free threaded can be located in workgroups other than the one free threaded workgroup (MTA).

Although free threaded stations might seem quite efficient, this is not necessarily the case (assuming each worker has the same level of politeness as a thread). First, a significant amount of work is required to make sure that resources within each station are not used simultaneously. It would be bad, for example, if one worker entered a purchase order number using the same keyboard that a second user was simultaneously using to enter a different purchase order. Furthermore, in order for work to happen within a different work area, workers must send a message to the other area requesting the work, rather than simply performing the work themselves, because they cannot leave their work area. This could end up being less efficient if most of the stations that the worker required were located within different workgroups.

There is only one MTA per process.

In the COM world, the workgroup designated for free threaded components is known as the *Multi-Threaded Apartment* or MTA. There is only one such apartment per process, and components designated as free threaded cannot run in any other apartment besides this one. In the other models we have examined thus far, there is a one-to-one correlation between apartments and threads. With a Multi-Threaded Apartment this is no longer the case. The number of threads that can participate in the MTA is limited by resources, not by COM threading rules.

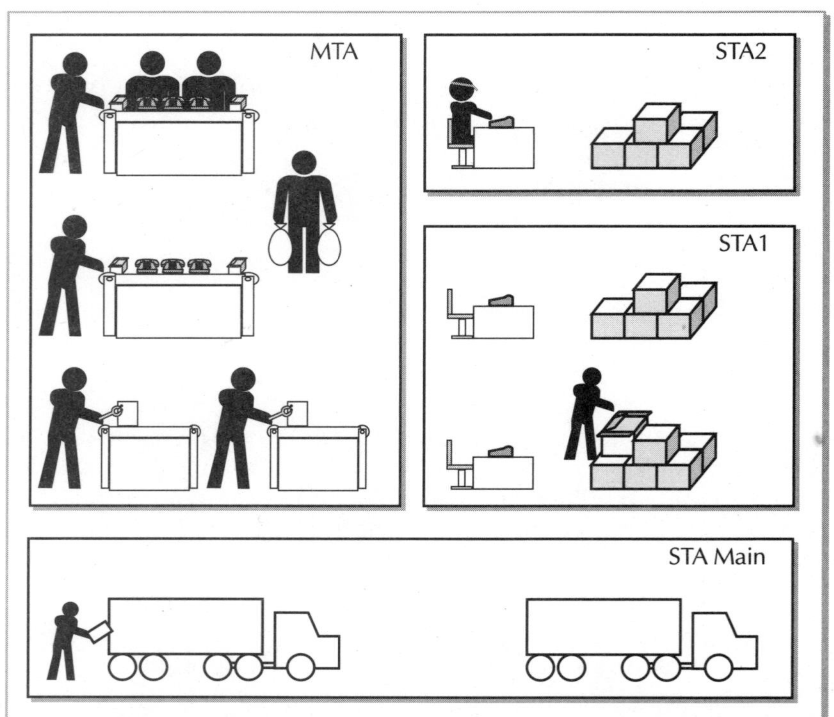

A free threading model workgroup
Figure 13-4.

In order for a thread to participate in the MTA, it must call **CoInitialize-(NULL, COINIT_MULTI-THREADED).**

In general, if you wish to create a worker thread that is to have direct access to your component, you will want to designate your component as free threaded. Threads that are designated to participate in an MTA must each call **CoInitialize(NULL, COINIT_MULTITHREADED)**. Note, however, that calling **CoInitialize(NULL, COINIT_MULTITHREADED)** does not always create a new apartment since there can only be one MTA per process. Assuming one already exists, subsequent calls will assign the thread, which made the call, to participate in the one and only MTA rather than creating a new STA.

As with the factory floor, free threading does not necessarily imply better performance. If you have one free threaded object that is repeatedly accessing components running in a different apartment, or vice versa, then each call to the other component's apartment will have to endure marshalling. As we have already learned with the other models, threads in one apartment cannot directly call components in another apartment. Instead they have to request that the other apartment's thread perform the work and pass back the results. This is significantly slower than the component performing the work directly. If, for example, the free threaded component could instead be instantiated in the other apartment, then it could make the calls directly. However, this would mean that the free threaded component could not have a worker thread that accessed it directly.

The obvious solution is to have the other components be free threaded. That way, they can participate in the MTA, and marshalling will not have to take place between calls. Unfortunately, the use of the word "free" within the free threading model applies to the runtime execution; it does not apply when it comes to developing the component. As was hinted at in the analogy, as soon as you have a free threaded component, you are immediately removed from any synchronization benefits that the previous models offered. Free threaded components must take care of all synchronization. Therefore, you need to protect all member variables and other shared resources. (For those unfamiliar with threading, you do not need to protect local function variables because each time a thread enters the function those new local variables are allocated.) This can add a significant development effort, which is why the other models exist in the first place.

Components designated for the free threading model must handle all synchronization to their shared resources.

In order to designate an in-process component as free threaded, the ThreadingModel registry entry should be set to "Free".

Free Threading Model at a Glance

- There is only one MTA per process.
- Free threaded components must be careful to protect access to all shared resources.
- In order to have a worker thread that can directly access your component, you must use the free threading model.
- Threads outside the MTA cannot run any code belonging to objects within this apartment. Instead, they request the work be performed by one of the MTA's threads.

Threading Model Both

As the name implies, the threading model "both" is a combination of the apartment model and the free threading model. In-process components designated as "both" can execute within the context of either the MTA or any STA (or the thread neutral apartment, to be discussed shortly). Let's briefly return to the analogy.

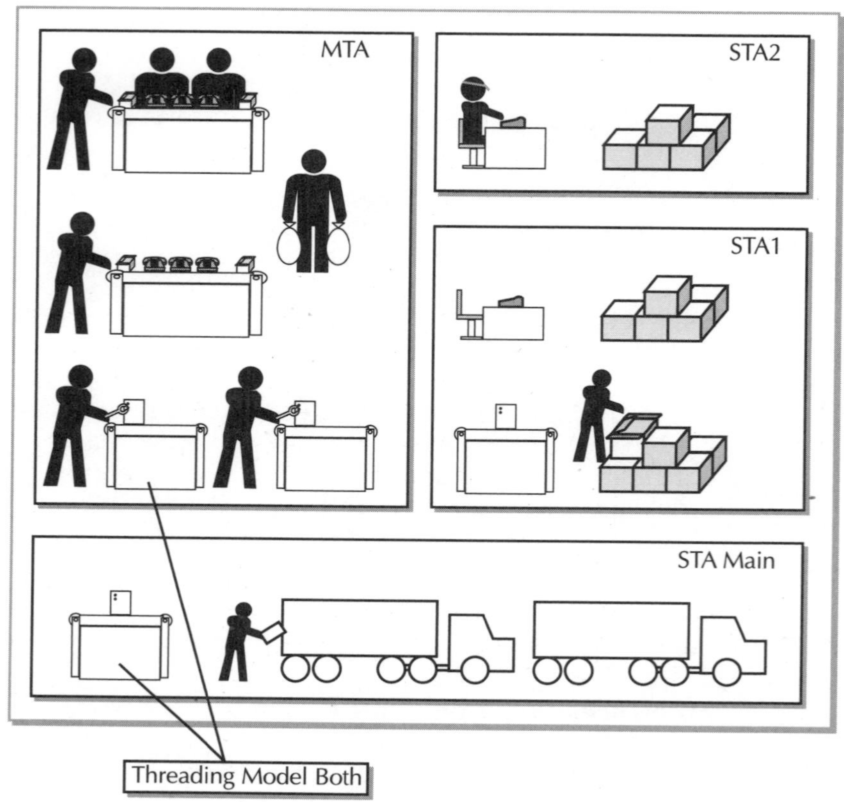

Stations with threading model both can run in both the MTA or any STA
Figure 13-5.

As shown in Figure 13-5, stations designated for "both" can participate in whichever workgroup they are first used from. In other words, the station can be used inside any workgroup, but once it has been placed in that workgroup it cannot be moved to another workgroup. The advantage over free threaded objects is that workers who use these objects do not have to call out to workers in other workgroups to perform the work. Instead, if a station is located within a worker's workgroup, the worker can use the station directly.

Components with threading model both still have the significant drawback of having to synchronize access to their shared resources for the times when they may be located within an MTA. However, they offer the advantage that if they are located within an STA, the STA's thread can access them directly without having to cross an apartment boundary and wait for another thread to actually perform the required task. The result is that both-designated components do not have to endure cross-apartment calls nearly as often as they would if they were free threaded.

A both threaded component belongs to whichever apartment created it. The apartment that creates the component will create it within its own apartment. If an MTA creates it, the component will reside within that apartment. If an STA component creates it, then it will end up in the same STA. In addition, if created by a thread neutral component (to be discussed shortly), the both component will belong to the thread neutral apartment. This last point may seem a little confusing since the component is marked as "both." This is an historical mismatch because when the both model was first introduced there were only two types of apartments.

Components with threading model both cannot create worker threads that can access the component's interface directly because this would violate the ability for the component to run in an STA.

Unfortunately, the big advantage of a free threaded component—the ability to create worker threads within the apartment—no longer applies. Since a both component may be located within an STA, it cannot create a worker thread that accesses its interfaces directly. The result would be two threads running within the same STA, thereby defeating the synchronization mechanism of the entire model.

Since threading model "both" does not introduce any new kinds of apartments, there are no new calls to **CoInitializeEx( )**.

To designate an in-process component as participating in threading model "both," the ThreadingModel registry entry must be set to "Both".

Threading Model Both at a Glance

- Developers must protect concurrent access to shared resources.
- Since these components are located within the apartment that created them, they do not have to endure as many cross-apartment calls as they would if they were free threaded only.
- Cannot easily have any worker threads. (See "Working with Worker Threads" later on.)
- Threads outside the component's apartment cannot run any code within the component's apartment. Instead they request that the work be performed by one of the component apartment's threads.

Thread Neutral Model

All the threading models we have seen so far incur a significant overhead when they try to access components that reside within a different apartment. The issue is that a call outside an apartment requires marshalling. For example, if object A running inside apartment X tried to access object B running inside apartment Y, COM would have to step in to provide *thread switching* in order to allow the call to work. Thread switching enables calls from one apartment into another without breaking the integrity of the apartment model into which the call is made. The details of thread switching are described later, but for now understand that it can be an expensive operation, and it occurs automatically for you as part of the marshalling that takes place when you call from one apartment into another.

A Thread Neutral Apartment does not have any threads of its own.

In response to this problem, Windows 2000 introduced the concept of a *thread neutral component*. Along with the new type of model, a new kind of apartment resulted as well. Unlike all the apartments we have seen so far, the Thread Neutral Apartment (TNA) does not have any threads of its own. Instead, it allows the threads running in other apartments to access its components directly, without incurring the cost of thread switching.

Let's return to the analogy once again, as shown in Figure 13-6.

The thread neutral model places stations within a workgroup on the shop floor that any worker can access no matter which apartment type the worker belongs to. For example, in Figure 13-6 the worker who is assigned to the main workgroup can leave that area and go to the thread neutral workgroup to pick up supplies.

The apartment associated with thread neutral objects is the Thread Neutral Apartment. As with the MTA, there can be only one TNA per process. The significant advantage of the TNA is that objects outside the TNA will not have to endure a thread switch, but instead they can access an object almost directly. This provides a significant performance enhancement. Essentially, no longer are threads confined to run code only within their apartment; instead components marked as thread neutral indicate to their clients that they can be directly accessed by any thread within the process. Thread neutral components behave almost like internal C++ classes when it comes to threading.

Because a thread neutral component has no thread of its own, it will not be able to have a message loop. This restricts it from being used with any user interface components because without a message loop it will not be able to respond to any Windows messages.

The Thread Neutral Apartment

Figure 13-6.

Even without a thread of its own, a component running in a TNA is still responsible for providing all its own synchronization. The reason is that there is no protection against two threads from different apartments accessing the TNA concurrently. By default, no synchronization is supplied for components set to thread neutral. Therefore, you are responsible for handling all concurrency issues and protecting all member as well as static and global variables, just as you would if your component were free threaded and running in an MTA.

In spite of all the caveats with configuring a component for thread neutral, if none of these is too restrictive, then thread neutral should be the threading model of choice. This is certainly the preferable configuration for components that will reside within Component Services (discussed in Chapter 14). The reason for this is that a TNA component allows for the least amount of interference from the COM subsystem.

Threading Model Neutral at a Glance

- Supported only under Windows 2000 and up.
- Has no threads of its own.
- Can be accessed directly from threads running in other apartments.
- Does not have a Windows message loop.
- Cannot be used for components that have a user interface.
- Is the preference for components running inside Component Services.

The Free Threaded Marshaller

In addition to each of the threading model options that are presented when running the New ATL Object wizard, there is also a check box for whether your component will support the Free Threaded Marshaller. The Free Threaded Marshaller does not introduce a new type of threading model, or even a new type of apartment. Instead, it changes the way a component can be called across apartments. Essentially, the Free Threaded Marshaller changes an object so that when it is called it behaves as though it were "apartment neutral." Although a component may be configured to belong to one particular model or another, if a component supports the Free Threaded Marshaller, it will be called from any apartment as though it were running directly inside the caller's apartment. No marshalling (thread switching or otherwise) will occur. Note that supporting the Free Threaded Marshaller is an additional option to whichever threading model a component may have. For example, a component can be tagged for threading model both and still support (or not support) the Free Threaded Marshaller.

Although using the Free Threaded Marshaller may seem like it avoids the performance drawback to the various threading models, using it can end up breaking the entire threading mechanism that COM sets up for you. The problem is that the Free Threaded Marshaller essentially avoids any marshalling. While this may seem like a good thing, marshalling is an important part of the COM infrastructure. In regard to threading and synchronization, overriding any marshalling may be appropriate for components that are synchronized (free, both, and neutral threaded objects). This would be a bad idea, however, for single and apartment threaded objects because without the marshalling code, there will be nothing to prevent a second thread from entering an STA, thereby breaking the entire mechanism. Therefore, if the Free Threaded Marshaller is used at all, it should be used only with components that have been programmed for concurrency. However, even with these components you should not use the Free Threaded Marshaller unless you are sure you know what you are doing. The Free Threaded Marshaller does not handle any thread switching, and it doesn't marshal any of the COM parameters. Therefore, the Free Threaded Marshaller cannot hold on to any parameters that it may be passed without marshalling them each manually.

Let's consider an example. If object A is an apartment modeled component, then only one thread, the STA thread, is allowed to run any of its code. If object A calls object B, which is configured as supporting the Free Threaded Marshaller and is running in a different apartment, then object A's thread will call directly into object B without any thread switching occurring. This would be similar to what would happen if object B were configured as thread neutral. The problem, however, occurs when object A passes a pointer to one of its interfaces into object B, and then object B saves this pointer. By saving the pointer, object B will have a direct pointer to object A, and if any thread other than the one running in object A's apartment accesses object B and uses A's saved interface pointer, two threads will end up running within object A. *Not good!* Therefore, an important restriction of the Free Threaded Marshaller is that free threaded objects should not save pointers to other objects. There is a work-around to this restriction: you could choose to manually program the marshalling of the interfaces—both those you pass in and those you pass out. However, the ease with which you could make an error here tends to outweigh the benefits.

You may be tempted to think that the Thread Neutral Apartment supersedes the Free Threaded Marshaller, making the latter obsolete. This, however, is not the case. The Free Threaded Marshaller removes the interception of any marshalling code that may be invoked to call a component. The thread neutral component still requires marshalling when it is called, but it avoids the thread switching that may occur during marshalling. To emphasize this point, it would be legitimate to configure a component as both thread neutral and supporting the Free Threaded Marshaller.

IN DEPTH

Setting the Synchronization Attribute via Component Services

Our discussion of the various threading models has placed considerable emphasis on which threading models require you to write synchronization code. It turns out that Windows 2000 offers some assistance in this area if you run a component within Component Services. Although we will not discuss this until Chapter 14, it is worthwhile to point out now that Component Services offers the option of configuring the synchronization requirements so that you do not need to manually program thread synchronization into your component. Using this setting, even MTA components can avoid having to write synchronization code and instead allow the COM+ services of Windows 2000 to intercept calls and provide appropriate blocking. This option is available only on Windows 2000, however, and it does not replace the existing threading models. Each of the threading models still has various advantages and disadvantages as pointed out. At a minimum, allowing COM+ to take care of threading for you will remove the level of control over when synchronization occurs because Windows 2000 will lock the entire component as it would for an STA component. Furthermore, being required to run within Component Services eliminates all executable servers, since only DLLs can be configured within Component Services. The result is that if you can live with these restrictions, you should specify the threading model for your component as thread neutral (again assuming no user interface, as discussed previously). Then have it run within Component Services, and you will not be required to manually provide thread synchronization. Instead, you can configure the synchronization setting with Component Services to provide synchronization for you.

Marshalling Across Apartments

With a fundamental understanding of each of the apartments and the components that run within them, it is time to tackle the topic of marshalling across apartments. In the previous chapter, we introduced the topic of marshalling and how it is used to transmit data from one computer to another, thereby enabling location transparency. It turns out that marshalling is not only required when crossing machine boundaries, or even simply when calling from one process to another. In fact, marshalling is required whenever you cross apartment boundaries. Furthermore, it comes into play when you cross context boundaries. (Context will be covered at length within Chapter 14.) Marshalling is not restricted to the packaging of data. In addition, marshalling takes care of synchronization, enforcing the rules of each apartment within which an object runs.

In order for an object within one apartment to run code that resides on an object within another apartment, the first object needs to post a message to the second apartment's thread. Therefore, except for the thread neutral objects, which do not have any thread of their own, all apartments need to have message loops that process messages. Without this mechanism, threads would access each component directly, thereby breaking the threading rules assigned to that apartment and forcing programmers to write all their own synchronization code regardless of the threading model selected.

Consider this example: If **ObjectA**, which resides in apartment X, wants to call a function on **ObjectB**, which resides in apartment Y, then **ObjectA**'s thread will need to post a message to **ObjectB**'s thread. When **ObjectB**'s thread encounters the message, it will perform the work and pass back the results to **ObjectA**'s thread, which is waiting for the task to complete. (See Figure 13-7.)

Interceptors—Proxies and Stubs

In the previous section we saw that components are not allowed simply to call into another's apartment; otherwise, the threading model would be broken. Instead, messages need to be sent to components that participate in different apartments. The problem, however, is that for this to work the caller would have to know the threading model of the server. The result would be that every time a component called a server, special code would have to be written depending on the threading model of the server. This, of course, would break the transparency that is key to the COM system. Furthermore, some threading models, such as the thread neutral model, do not require message loops, so the introduction of a new apartment model would break all existing clients.

Communication happens via Windows message posts
Figure 13-7.

Not only is there no way to find out the threading model of the server, but there is no reason for the client to know. Rather than accessing a component directly, the client will instead access an *interceptor* that will trap any cross-boundary call, convert it into the appropriate kind of call for the

An interceptor, or proxy, traps a call across a boundary, converting it into a call compatible with the server.

server, and then send the call on. Upon completion, the call will be sent back to the client. The interceptor is responsible for converting all calls appropriately and sending them on to the server. The interceptor knows the threading model of the server and will appropriately post a message when required or make a direct call into the component if the component is appropriately tagged for synchronization support. The result is that the client does not need to know anything about the server's threading model or even where the server is located. It simply makes the call and expects the interceptor to take care of the details. The interceptor is a proxy similar to the kinds of proxies we looked at in Chapter 12. In fact, the terms can be used interchangeably. The only difference here is that the interceptor is less involved in trying to convert data so that it can be sent over the wire than it is with ensuring that appropriate COM boundaries are enforced.

The mechanism for invoking the interceptor is exactly the same as it was in Chapter 12. When a client calls **CoCreateInstance( )**, the COM subsystem checks to see whether the server component is compatible with the client. If it isn't—for example, if it requires an apartment different from the one the caller uses—then it will instantiate the server within the correct apartment and pass back to the client a pointer to the server's proxy rather than a pointer to the server's interface directly. Given this method, the client will make calls into the interceptor as though it were calling the server; the interceptor will then convert the call appropriately and direct it to the server.

As is fairly obvious at this point, cross-apartment calls essentially need to be marshalled. Marshalling not only takes care of appropriately accessing a COM server's apartment, but it must transform the data, too. For example, when passing an interface from one component to another within the same apartment, a direct interface pointer can be passed. However, when crossing a boundary, the interceptor's pointer needs to be passed so that when the server accesses the interface, all calls will be appropriately translated for the interface's apartment. This is why using the Free Threaded Marshaller is so dangerous; the step of marshalling the interface needs to be manually put in place or the direct interface pointer is passed across apartment boundaries.

Working with Worker Threads

For the most part, you can count on the COM subsystem to perform the required marshalling for you automatically. However, there are times when you may want to access an interface from a thread different than the one you are currently using—for example, if you create a worker thread that will need access to an interface on a component that has already been instantiated. In these cases, you will have to marshal the interface in order to pass it to a different thread. There are several methods for doing this.

Using the Interface Marshalling API Across Apartment Boundaries

The first method is to use **CoMarshalInterThreadInterfaceInStream( )** and **CoGetInterfaceAndReleaseStream( )**. These are specifically designed to marshal interfaces between two threads that are each running in different apartments. The first function hydrates the interface into a stream. (Recall that "hydrates" is a slang term often used when discussing marshalling. It illustrates the concept of placing the interface into a pipe to be sent across to the server.) Upon arriving at its destination—in this case the new thread—**CoGetInterfaceAndRelease- Stream( )** removes the interface pointer from the stream object and provides an appropriate proxy for the new thread to call into. Each of these COM API functions is declared as follows:

```
HRESULT CoMarshalInterThreadInterfaceInStream(
                REFIID riid,
                LPUNKNOWN pUnknown,
                LPSTREAM *ppIStream);
```

Here, *riid* is the IID of the interface being marshalled, *pUnknown* is a pointer to the interface to be marshalled, and *ppIStream* is a pass-by-reference pointer to the resulting **IStream** into which the interface is marshalled.

```
HRESULT CoGetInterfaceAndReleaseStream(
                LPSTREAM pIStream,
                REFIID riid,
                LPVOID *pIUnknown);
```

The parameters for **CoGetInterfaceAndReleaseStream( )** essentially mirror those used in **CoMarshalInterThreadInterfaceInStream( )**. Here, *pIStream* is the pointer to the **IStream** interface into which the interface was marshalled, *riid* is the type of interface that was marshalled, and *pIUnknown* is a pass-by-reference pointer to the resulting interface. Below is an example of the entire process:

```
DWORD __stdcall CreateThreadCallback( void* pStream );

void main()
{
```

```
  IMyInterface pInterface;
  LPSTREAM p_stream = NULL;
  DWORD threadid;

  CoInitialize(NULL);
   ...

  CoMarshalInterThreadInterfaceInStream(
    __uuidof(IMyInterface),
    pInterface, &p_stream);

  ::CreateThread( NULL, 0,
      CreateThreadCallback,
      static_cast<void*>(p_ stream),
      0, &threadid);

   ...
  pInterface->Release( )
}

DWORD __stdcall CreateThreadCallback( void* pStream )
{

  CoInitialize(NULL);

  IMyInterface pInterface;
  CoGetInterfaceAndReleaseStream(
    static_cast<LPSTREAM>(pStream),
    __uuidof(IMyInterface),
    reinterpret_cast<void**>(&pInterface) );

   ...
  pInterface->Release();
}
```

Note the calls on the new thread to **CoInitialize[Ex]( )**. All threads must make this API function call, and a worker thread is no exception. Without this call, the **CoGetInterfaceAndReleaseStream( )** function will fail.

Before we leave this example, consider the case when the calling thread and the newly created thread both initialize the apartment to **COINIT_MULTITHREADED**. In this case, both threads will end up running in the same MTA, which means that no apartment boundary will be crossed. Therefore, no marshalling needs to be performed between the first and second threads.

There are two other API functions, **CoUnmarshalInterface( )** and **CoMarshalInterface( )**, which are actually more generic than **CoMarshalInterThreadInterfaceInStream( )** and **CoGetInterfaceAndReleaseStream( )** because they can handle marshalling interfaces across processes and machine boundaries. However, unless you are writing your own custom marshalling code (something we wouldn't recommend), you seldom need to use these and instead can rely on the previously named functions.

Marshalling Using the Global Interface Table

One problem with the API method described above is that the returned stream can be used only once. That is, you cannot call **CoGetInterfaceAndReleaseStream( )** multiple times on the same stream. If this is a problem, you will need to use the global interface table (GIT) to store a reference to your interface. In spite of its name, the GIT is processwide only and cannot be used across process boundaries. The GIT is a COM object itself—however, there is only one instance of the GIT per process. Even if you attempt to create the GIT twice, it will still return the same object.

To use the GIT, you need to call **CoCreateInstance( )** using the CLSID of the GIT, which is **CLSID_StdGlobalInterfaceTable**. The call will look something like this:

```
CoCreateInstance(CLSID_StdGlobalInterfaceTable,
  NULL,  CLSCTX_INPROC_SERVER,
  IID_IGlobalInterfaceTable,
  reinterpret_cast<void**>(&g_pGlobalInterfaceTable) );
```

In this call, **g_pGlobalInterfaceTable** is a global pointer to the **IGlobalInterfaceTable** interface. It is not actually required that you keep the global pointer since you could call **CoCreateInstance( )** again from the other apartment. This, however, will return the same instance of the GIT because there is only one per process. The additional call, therefore, is not required, and instead the **IGlobalInterfaceTable** can be accessed globally.

Once you have the GIT, you can register and unregister any interfaces that you want to be available across all apartments within the process by using the **RegisterInterfaceInGlobal( )** and **RevokeInterfaceFromGlobal( )** member functions. **RegisterInterfaceInGlobal( )** returns an ID, known as a *cookie*, which you can then use to retrieve the registered interface by calling **GetInterfaceFromGlobal( )**. The following code demonstrates using the GIT to pass interfaces across apartment boundaries:

```
IGlobalInterfaceTable* g_pGIT;
DWORD __stdcall CreateThreadCallback ( void* ppv );
...

void main()
{
  CoInitialize(NULL);
  IMyInterface* pIMyinterface;
  HANDLE thread_handle;
  DWORD cookie;

  ...

  CoCreateInstance( CLSID_StdGlobalInterfaceTable,
    NULL, CLSCTX_INPROC_SERVER,
    __uuidof(IGlobalInterfaceTable),
    reinterpret_cast<void**>(&g_pGIT));

  g_pGIT->RegisterInterfaceInGlobal(
    static_cast<IUnknown*>(pIMyinterface),
    __uuidof(IMyInterface), &cookie);

  thread_handle = CreateThread(
    NULL, 0, CallObjectNoMarshalling,
    &cookie, 0, &thread_id);

...

  WaitForSingleObject(thread_handle, INFINITE);
  hr = g_pGIT->RevokeInterfaceFromGlobal(cookie);
  g_pGIT->Release();
```

Don't forget to release the GIT global variable once all threads have finished using it.

Worker Threads for STA Components

Although both of the above methods will work, there may be times when you want to have a component with a worker thread, but you still want to rely on COM to handle all thread synchronization for you. In other words, you want to create an STA component that supports a worker thread. This is an attempt to have your cake and eat it too, but in actual fact this can be achieved relatively easily by hooking into the message loop of the component. In fact, since you are using the message loop, you do not even need to marshal your interface pointer across to the worker thread.

Essentially, the procedure is to pass the window handle of your component to the worker thread. Then, in order for the worker thread to report events back to the main component, use the **PostMessage( )** API function.

Clearly the above method can be achieved using the standard synchronization mechanisms already discussed. However, it is sometimes simpler to use the message loop than to implement the complexity of the marshalling API or the global interface table.

Worker Threads Inside In-Process DLLs

In general, do not place worker threads inside DLLs

In general, it is advised that you do not place worker threads inside COM DLLs. This is good advice. The problem is the risk that the DLL will be unloaded before the worker threads have all exited. If this happens, the memory allocated to variables that are declared on the stack inside the thread will all be lost. This is a documented side effect of using threads that do not exit properly or even of using those that are terminated using the **TerminateThread( )** API function. The obvious work-around to the above dilemma is to use an executable rather than a DLL whenever you require worker threads.

Unfortunately, using an executable is not always an option. For example, if you want your component to support transactions by running inside Component Services, your component will have to be a DLL (unless you manually enlist in a transaction). If you encounter a scenario such as this, when an executable is not a viable option, the rule is that all threads must exit before the last component within your DLL is destroyed.

If you must have worker threads inside a DLL, make sure that all threads will exit cleanly before the last component is destroyed.

To make sure all threads exit, add a **FinalRelease( )** function to your component. **FinalRelease( )** is always called immediately before the destructor of a component class. Inside **FinalRelease( )**, take appropriate measures to shut down the thread, and then use the API functions **WaitForSingleObject( )** or **WaitForMultipleObjects( )** on the worker threads' handles in order to wait until the threads exit. Unfortunately, the "appropriate measures" part of the equation depends on what the thread is doing. For example, if the thread is reading from a file, you could close the file handle so that the read failed. Inside your thread, therefore, you would simply have to check for the appropriate failure on the read file and then exit when that occurred. The important point to realize here is you must place appropriate measures within your worker thread code to allow for the thread to exit gracefully when the last component goes out of scope. If you cannot do this, then do not create the worker thread within a DLL in the first place.

Synchronization with ATL

Throughout the chapter we have mentioned that several threading models require you to implement your own thread synchronization to prevent race conditions. Several Win32 API functions provide the necessary mutexes and semaphores needed to synchronize access to your object. They include, but are not limited to, **WaitForSingleObject[Ex]( )**, **WaitForMultipleObjects( )**, **EnterCriticalSection( )**, and **Leave-CriticalSection( )**. In addition, check out the interlocked functions that allow you to modify shared resources in a protected fashion. These include **InterlockedIncrement( )** and **InterlockedDecrement( )**, which are used by COM to increment and decrement the reference counts for objects that could potentially run within an MTA.

ATL has been carefully designed so the minimum amount of synchronization code is added to your component based on the threading model that the component supports. Notice that in the declaration of both the **Stopwatch** and the **Countdown** components, the parameter passed to the **CComObjectRootEx< >** template (from which both **CStopwatch** and **CCountdown** are derived) is **CComSingleThreadModel**.

```
class ATL_NO_VTABLE CCountdown :
  public CComObjectRootEx<CComSingleThreadModel>,
  public CComCoClass<CCountdown, &CLSID_Countdown>,
...
```

CComSingleThreadModel has both an **Increment** and a **Decrement** function, which are used for incrementing and decrementing the reference count on the component. However, since both of these components are apartment model components, they will never have more than one thread accessing them at the same time. Therefore, the code within the **Increment** and **Decrement** functions simply uses the non-thread-safe C++ increment and decrement operators. (By the way, notice that although the **CComSingleThreadModel** class is named "Single Thread Model," it is appropriate for apartment threaded components as well. The "Single" part of the name refers to the number of threads that could potentially be supported by the class.)

If you change your component to one of the models that requires synchronization (free, both, or thread neutral), you must be sure to change the **CComObjectRootEx< >** parameter to use **CComMultiThreadModel** rather than **CComSingleThreadModel**. Instead of using the non-thread-safe C++ increment and decrement operators, **CComMultiThreadModel** uses the **InterlockedIncrement( )** and **InterlockedDecrement( )** API functions. In addition to changing the above template parameter, also edit the **stdafx.h** file so that this line

```
#define _ATL_APARTMENT_THREADED
```

reads instead

```
#define _ATL_FREE_THREADED
```

In fact, you can change the level of synchronization supported by your component based on this **#define** by using **CComObjectThreadModel** for the **CComObjectRootEx< >** parameter. This will automatically use **CComSingleThreadModel** if **_ATL_APARTMENT_THREADED** is defined, or it will use **CComMultiThreadModel** otherwise. Your class declaration will then end up looking as follows:

```
class ATL_NO_VTABLE CCountdown :
  public CComObjectRootEx<CComObjectThreadModel>,
  public CComCoClass<CCountdown, &CLSID_Countdown>,
...
```

The result will be that if you define **_ATL_APARTMENT_THREADED**, your class will be derived from **CComSingleThreadModel**; otherwise, it will be derived from **CComMultiThreadModel**.

ATL provides some additional synchronization classes that you can use for synchronizing your component rather than using the Win32 API directly. The two classes that you will use are **CComCriticalSection** and **CComAutoCriticalSection**. Both of these classes are designed to aid in protecting critical sections within your code. They can be used to protect shared resources, for example. So, what is the difference, you ask? First, **CComAutoCriticalSection** initializes the critical section for you within its constructor. This allows you simply to call **Lock( )** to start the critical section rather than having to call **Init( )** and then **Lock( )** as you would for the **CComCriticalSection**. More important, the destructor for **CComAutoCriticalSection** automatically releases the lock within its destructor. Therefore, you are guaranteed that the lock will be released even if you forget to call **Unlock( )** explicitly. Consider the following example, which uses **CComAutoCriticalSection** to protect the call to **insert()** on the static **s_Timers** map that we used within the **CCountdown** class in Chapter 10.

```
long CCountdown::StartCountdown()
{
  CComAutoCriticalSection critical_section;

  ATLASSERT(m_nInterval > 0);

  StopCountdown();

  // Set the timer.
  m_nTimerID = ::SetTimer(0,          // handle of main window
    0,                                // timer identifier
    (long) m_nInterval,               // interval (milliseconds)
    CCountdown::TimerCallback);       // timer callback function

  m_Stopwatch->Start();

  // Insert the id into the map
  critical_section.Lock();
  CCountdown::s_Timers.insert(
    MAP_TIMERS::value_type(m_nTimerID, this));

  return m_nTimerID;

}
```

Notice that **Unlock( )** is not called explicitly since it will be called in the destructor.

Unfortunately, the code shown here is not sufficient for protecting the **s_Timers** resource, as it is accessed from the **StopCountdown( )** and **TimerCallback( )** functions as well. Therefore, to sufficiently protect this resource, it will be necessary to declare a static variable of type **CComAutoCriticalSection**, as shown below:

```
////////////////////////////////////////////////////////////////////
// CCountdown
class ATL_NO_VTABLE CCountdown :
   ...
{
  ...
  // Critical section for protecting s_Timers
  static CComAutoCriticalSection s_TimersCriticalSection;
};
```

Although **CComCriticalSection** could also be used, this would require a one-time call to **TimersCriticalSection.Init( )**. Because **CComAutoCriticalSection** has this call built in, it is preferable in this case. Highlighted below are the additional code changes necessary to protect the **s_Timers** resource.

```
MAP_TIMERS CCountdown::s_Timers;
CComAutoCriticalSection CCountdown::s_TimersCriticalSection;

//////////////////////////////////////////////////////////////////////
// CCountdown
...
// Sets up a timer
long CCountdown::StartCountdown()
{

  ATLASSERT(m_nInterval > 0);

  StopCountdown();

  // Set the timer.
  m_nTimerID = ::SetTimer(0,      // handle of main window
    0,                            // timer identifier
    (long) m_nInterval,           // interval (milliseconds)
    CCountdown::TimerCallback);   // timer callback function

  m_Stopwatch->Start();

  // Insert the id into the map
  s_TimersCriticalSection.Lock();
  CCountdown::s_Timers.insert(
    MAP_TIMERS::value_type(m_nTimerID, this));
  s_TimersCriticalSection.Unlock();

  return m_nTimerID;

}

// The function which the SetTimer() API calls
// back to when the time has elapsed.
/*static*/ void __stdcall CCountdown::TimerCallback(
  HWND hwnd,      // handle of window for timer messages
  UINT uMsg,      // WM_TIMER message
  UINT idTimer,   // timer identifier
  DWORD dwTime    // current system time
  )
```

```
{

  //  Search the map for the timer that fired.
  MAP_TIMERS::iterator it;
  s_TimersCriticalSection.Lock();
  it = CCountdown::s_Timers.find(idTimer);
  s_TimersCriticalSection.Unlock();
  ATLASSERT( it != s_Timers.end() );

  // Notify the countdown component
  // that the timer has elapsed.
  it->second->OnTimeElapsed();
}

...

// Stops the timer identified by m_nTimerID
HRESULT CCountdown::StopCountdown()
{
  long nKillTimer = 0;


  if ( m_nTimerID != 0 )
  {

    // TODO: Raise an error if this fails.
    nKillTimer = KillTimer(
      0,            // handle to window that installed timer
      m_nTimerID    // timer identifier
      );
  }

  if (nKillTimer > 0)
  {
      // Successful
      s_TimersCriticalSection.Lock();
      s_Timers.erase(m_nTimerID);
      s_TimersCriticalSection.Unlock();
      m_nTimerID = 0;
      return S_OK;
  }
  else
    return HRESULT_FROM_WIN32(GetLastError());
}

...
```

The preceding code above allows only one call into **s_Timers** at a time. Technically, it would be sufficient to allow concurrent calls to **s_Timers.find( )** as long as **s_Timers.insert( )** and **s_Timers.erase( )** maintained exclusive access. For simplicity's sake, however, exclusive access is given whether writing or reading the **s_Timers** map.

Asynchronous COM Calls

Before we close the chapter, let's briefly consider some new functionality available only in Windows 2000 that helps automate the process of making an asynchronous COM call. In the past, an asynchronous COM call was made manually, through the creation of a new thread that makes a normal synchronous COM call without disrupting the currently running thread. Obviously, this involves some of the thread marshalling API functions that we have already covered in this chapter and can involve a lot of work for the programmer. With Windows 2000, there is a better way. Windows 2000 has support for the IDL **async_uuid** attribute, which, when added to an interface definition, will notify the MIDL compiler to generate proxy/stub code for the standard marshaller. The code automatically allows for an asynchronous call, without any additional work by the component developer. Even the client code that will be using the asynchronous interface is relatively simple.

Defining the Asynchronous Interface Inside the Component Server

To demonstrate an asynchronous COM call, we will use the example of a **WebPageCache** component. We will not actually implement any Web page caching, but, conceptually, it provides a good example of an action that might take some time. The **WebPageCache** component will have one method, **GetPage( )**, which will first check its cache to see whether the specified page already exists locally; if not, it will go out to the Internet to retrieve it. To create the server sample, open a new ATL project called "WebPageCacheSvr" and select an executable, not a DLL, for the project type.

As we detailed in the introduction to this topic, one important restriction that you should be aware of when creating an asynchronous interface is that calls into the interface must invoke the standard marshaller proxy. Therefore, any asynchronous calls must cross an apartment boundary in order to work. The easiest way to force this to happen is to implement the server component within an executable. Then all calls will be across a process boundary, thereby fulfilling the cross-apartment requirement. Implementing the component

The standard marshaller must be invoked in order to intercept an asynchronous call and provide the asynchronous functionality.

within a DLL is more difficult because you have to create the new apartment yourself, or the server would have to do it for you. Since marshalling must occur, your component cannot aggregate the free threaded marshaller or the proxy will never be invoked.

Now add a new ATL object called **WebPageCache**. All default attributes will suffice except one. Any asynchronous interface cannot also be a dual interface. Therefore, you will need to select Custom rather than Dual for the type of interface. On the **WebPageCache** component, we will provide one method, as shown in the interface description below:

```
[
  object,
  uuid(88B8C6EF-7038-472F-A86A-178FF4260942),
  helpstring("IWebPageCache Interface"),
  pointer_default(unique)
]
interface IWebPageCache : IUnknown
{
   [helpstring("Retrieve a web page from the internet")]
     HRESULT GetPage([in] BSTR URL, [out] BSTR* HTMLText);
};
```

The implementation of the method doesn't actually retrieve a Web page but instead pops up a message box that will stop the method from exiting until the Okay button has been clicked. The code for the method is shown below:

```
STDMETHODIMP CWebPageCache::GetPage(BSTR URL, BSTR *HTMLText)
{
  MessageBox(NULL, _T("Click Okay to complete the call!"),
    _T("Inside GetPage()"), 0);
  return S_OK;
}
```

The call to **MessageBox( )** provides an easy way for controlling when the component server method will terminate. This completes the creation of a synchronous component server—nothing different from what we have done in all other samples so far.

13

Now let's add the two lines of code that will add asynchronous support. The two-line code change is made to the **WebPageCacheSvr.idl** file, and a listing is provided:

```
import "oaidl.idl";
import "ocidl.idl";
  [
    object,
    uuid(88B8C6EF-7038-472F-A86A-178FF4260942),
    async_uuid(E129C8D4-FE20-4852-AC63-3E4A2990AF55),
    helpstring("IWebPageCache Interface"),
    pointer_default(unique)
  ]
  interface IWebPageCache : IUnknown
  {
    [helpstring("Retrieve a web page from the internet")]
      HRESULT GetPage([in] BSTR URL, [out] BSTR* HTMLText);
  };

[
  uuid(F437EF34-B538-401F-AF34-02789BC5F283),
  version(1.0),
  helpstring("WebPageCacheSvr 1.0 Type Library")
]
library WEBPAGECACHESVRLib
{
  importlib("stdole32.tlb");
  importlib("stdole2.tlb");

  interface AsyncIWebPageCache;

  [
    uuid(BED97240-A787-4080-8711-5B7898527FAD),
    helpstring("WebPageCache Class")
  ]
  coclass WebPageCache
  {
    [default] interface IWebPageCache;
  };
};
```

As you can see, there really isn't much to providing the functionality. First, we add the **async_uuid** attribute to the **IWebPageCache** interface. Second, we declare the **AsyncIWebPageCache** so that it appears within the type library. The last step is not required if you instead choose to distribute the header files along with your component, but including it makes the interface available to Visual Basic and Java clients as well.

Based on the addition of the **async_uuid** attribute, the MIDL compiler will automatically create a second interface, **AsyncIWebPageCache**, in addition to the normal interface. The second interface will be defined as follows:

```
[
  uuid(E129C8D4-FE20-4852-AC63-3E4A2990AF55),
]
interface AsyncIWebPageCache : IUnknown
{
  [helpstring("Retrieve a web page from the internet")]
    HRESULT Begin_GetPage([in] BSTR URL);
  [helpstring("Retrieve a web page from the internet")]
    HRESULT Finish_GetPage([out] BSTR* HTMLText);
};
```

Notice how this interface is very similar to the **IWebPageCache** interface except that the **GetPage( )** method has been split into two methods. The first method is prefixed with "Begin_", and it contains only the **[in]** parameters. The second method is prefixed with "Finish_", and it contains only the **[out]** parameters. If there were any **[in][out]** parameters in the original interface, they would have been added to both methods.

This completes the server component creation, but there is one last step in the process and that is to create the standard marshaller. Before compiling, using **nmake.exe** as described in the previous chapter, open the proxy/stub make script, **WebPageCacheSvrps.mk**. You will notice that by default, the file was generated with **D_WIN32_WINNT** set to 0x0400. Since the **async_uuid** attribute is supported only on Windows 2000 platforms, you will need to change this to 0x0500, as shown below:

```
.c.obj:
  cl /c /Ox /DWIN32 /D_WIN32_WINNT=0x0500 /DREGISTER_PROXY_DLL \
    $<
```

Once this is complete, you can compile the standard marshaller. (As outlined in the previous chapter, you will execute the command "nmake.exe WebPageCacheSvrps.mk".) Upon compiling the marshaller, you also have to register it, which, as you have already learned, is done using **regsvr32.exe**. If you will be changing and compiling the server often, you may wish to add these last two steps, building and registering the standard marshaller, to the post-build steps within the settings of your project.

Calling Asynchronously

As you saw above, changing the component server so that it supports asynchronous COM calls did not require any special threading code but merely involved the addition of an attribute to the interface definition. Calling asynchronously into the component from the client is only slightly more complicated. A listing of the significant client code is shown below. Note that, for the sake of clarity, error handling has not been included in the listing. However, the files that can be downloaded from the Osborne Web site do include error handling.

```
...
#import "..\WebPageCacheSvr\WebPageCacheSvr.exe" \
  no_namespace, named_guids, raw_interfaces_only

int main(int argc, char* argv[])
{

  CoInitialize( NULL );

  HRESULT hr;
  IWebPageCache* p_web_page_cache = NULL;
  ICallFactory* p_call_factory = NULL;
  AsyncIWebPageCache* p_async_web_page_cached = NULL;
  ISynchronize* p_isynchronize = NULL;

  bstr_t s_URL = L"http://www.osborne.com";
  bstr_t s_HTML_text;

  // *** 1 *** Create the component object
  CoCreateInstance(__uuidof(WebPageCache),
    NULL, CLSCTX_ALL, __uuidof(IWebPageCache),
    reinterpret_cast<void**>(&p_web_page_cache) );

  // *** 2 *** Retrieve the ICallFactory Interface
  p_web_page_cache->QueryInterface (IID_ICallFactory,
    reinterpret_cast<void**>(&p_call_factory) );

  // *** 3 *** Retrieve the asynchronous interface
  p_call_factory->CreateCall(__uuidof(AsyncIWebPageCache),
    NULL, __uuidof(AsyncIWebPageCache),
    reinterpret_cast<IUnknown**>(&p_async_web_page_cached));

  // *** 4 *** Retrieve the ISynchronize interface in order
```

```
  // to check the status of the asynchronous call.
  p_async_web_page_cached->QueryInterface(
    uuidof(ISynchronize),
    reinterpret_cast<void**>(&p_isynchronize) );

  // *** 5 *** Start the asynchronous call
  cout << "Before calling GetPage() asynchronously." << endl;
  hr = p_async_web_page_cached->Begin_GetPage(s_URL);


  // *** 6 *** Optionally wait for call to complete
  while(p_isynchronize->Wait(0, 1000) == RPC_S_CALLPENDING)
  {
    // Do something after each check for completion;
    ...
  }

  // *** 7 *** Finish the call
  hr = p_async_web_page_cached->Finish_GetPage((BSTR*)&s_HTML_text);

  // Release interfaces
  ...
  CoUninitialize();
  return 0;
}
```

Let's take a step-by-step look at what needs to take place in order to make the asynchronous call.

1. Instantiate the component object you want to call into as you would normally.
2. Using the interface returned from instantiating the component, call **QueryInterface( )** and request the **ICallFactory** interface. The **ICallFactory** interface is not actually supported by your component object directly. Rather, it is supported by the proxy/stub. The way this is achieved is that the standard marshaller aggregates the server component. This, of course, raises another restriction for the technology: Asynchronous components must be aggregable. (Aggregation was covered in Chapter 11.)
3. From the **ICallFactory** interface, you need to create a call object. This is done via a call to **ICallFactory**'s **CreateCall( )** function, which is declared inside **objidl.h** as shown on the following page.

```
virtual HRESULT STDMETHODCALLTYPE CreateCall(
  /* [in] */ REFIID riid,
  /* [in] */ IUnknown __RPC_FAR *pCtrlUnk,
  /* [in] */ REFIID riid2,
  /* [iid_is][out] */ IUnknown __RPC_FAR *__RPC_FAR *ppv) = 0;
```

riid is the ID of the asynchronous interface. In our example this is **__uuidof(AsyncIWebPageCache)**. Next comes an **IUnknown** interface for purposes of aggregation. Although we didn't use it here, this parameter is important if you want to make asynchronous calls and then receive a callback notification once the method has completed. We will discuss how to do this a little later. **riid2** is the IID of the interface you want to call into. In most cases, this will probably be the **IID_ISynchronize** or the asynchronous interface identified by **riid**. The one important exception is when you want to receive notification concerning completion of the function call. In these cases, you will undoubtedly want to request the **IUnknown** interface because this is the only time you will be able to retrieve it. Without the **IUnknown** interface, you will have difficulty retrieving the inner object's **ISynchronize** interface, which you will need. The last item, **ppv**, will point to the specified interface.

4. In this step we retrieve the **ISynchronize** interface. This is entirely optional, but once performed, you will be able to check on the status of your asynchronous call as shown in step 6. Before we get there, however, we need to start the asynchronous call.
5. To start the asynchronous call we call the "Begin" version of the function we wish to access. This will initiate the call to the component server and return immediately.
6. In this step we call **ISynchronize::Wait( )**. This function will wait for the asynchronous call to finish. The amount of time to wait can be adjusted using the second parameter in the function call, which allows you to specify the number of milliseconds to wait for the call to complete. A value of 0 for this parameter will return immediately, and a value of **INFINITE** will wait indefinitely until the function completes. In the code above we poll the server intermittently. You may be leery of using a polling method like this, but it does not involve a round-trip call all the way to the server component (which could be expensive if DCOM was involved). Instead, the call simply goes to the proxy and returns relatively quickly.

7. The last step is to call the "Finish" method. This function completes the call and returns the **[out]** parameters. If the call had not yet completed, the Finish method would block until the method call to the server completed. Therefore, calling the Finish function immediately after the Begin function would result in a synchronous call similar to what would have happened on the synchronous interface.

As you can see, there is quite a bit more to making an asynchronous COM call than there is to identifying an interface as asynchronous. However, the process is relatively simple, especially when you consider what it would take to write all this functionality from scratch.

If after calling **ISynchronize::Wait( )** you discover that the call still hasn't returned, Windows 2000 also provides the ability to cancel a COM call. To do this, query for the **ICancelMethodCalls** interface from the call object (using **QueryInterface( )** on **ISynchronize** or **AsyncIWebPageCache**, for example). Assuming this is successful, calling **ICancelMethodCalls::Cancel( )** will cancel the asynchronous call. After canceling the call you should still call the Finish method, but all parameters in the Finish method are garbage and should be discarded. The **HRESULT** returned after calling the Finish method will be 0x8007071A (–2147023078), which, as of this writing, did not have a corresponding **#define** value. Below is a code snippet canceling an asynchronous call:

```
const HRESULT CALL_CANCELED = 0x8007071A;
...
p_async_web_page_cached->Begin_GetPage(s_URL);

// Wait for call to complete
while(p_synchronize->Wait(0, 1) == RPC_S_CALLPENDING)
{
  if (MessageBox(NULL, "Do you wish to cancel the call?",
      "WebPageCacheClient", MB_YESNO) == IDYES)
  {
    hr = p_async_web_page_cached->QueryInterface(
      __uuidof(ICancelMethodCalls),
      reinterpret_cast<void**>(&p_cancel_method_calls));
    if(SUCCEEDED(hr))
      p_cancel_method_calls->Cancel(0);
  }
}
```

```
hr = p_async_web_page_cached->Finish_GetPage(
  (BSTR*)&s_HTML_text);
if( hr = CALL_CANCELED )
{
  hr= S_OK;
  SysFreeString(s_HTML_text);
}
```

Asynchronous Method Completion Notification

As we already pointed out above, although the **ISynchronize::Wait( )** call is efficient, because it involves only a call into the proxy, it is still a polling solution that may not always be the ideal approach. To overcome this, you can aggregate the call object retrieved from **CreateCall( )**. The outer object (whose **IUnknown** interface you will specify for the **pCtrlUnk** parameter of **CreateCall( )**) will need to support the **ISynchronize** interface. Then when **QueryInterface( )** is called on this outer object, the call will simply be forwarded to the inner object's **QueryInterface( )** unless the requested interface ID is **IID_Synchronize**, in which case a pointer to the outer object's **ISynchronize** interface would be returned. What is so important about the **ISynchronize** interface? As we saw above, the **ISynchronize** interface is used to check on the status of an asynchronous call. In addition, this interface has a **Signal( )** method, which when called, signifies that the asynchronous call has completed. Therefore, by aggregating the asynchronous call, you can identify when the call has completed via a notification mechanism rather than via a polling mechanism. Note that even though **ISynchronize** is implemented by the outer component, all **ISynchronize** calls within the implementation should be forwarded to the inner object's version of **ISynchronize**.

Sometimes this will provide a significant advantage over the simpler polling method shown above. The key for the notification method to work is to provide the **IUnknown** of a component that supports the **ISynchronize** interface. Since you are aggregating the call object (the object retrieved in this **CreateCall( )** function), when a call comes into **QueryInterface( )**, the component that is passed for the **pCtrlUnk** parameter will check that the call completed.

Implementing Asynchronous COM Servers

Before we end this discussion on asynchronous interfaces, let's briefly touch on asynchronous server components. Although not obvious at first, there are times when the server may want to implement an interface asynchronously, even if the client did not make an asynchronous call. This prevents the situation that can occur with regular COM calls in which a calling thread that enters into a component is blocked, waiting for the method to complete. For example, if the thread is normally responsible for servicing the Windows message pump, it will be blocked for the duration of the call.

Again, consider the **WebPageCache** component described previously. When a client requests a URL that has already been cached, the server component can simply return the requested file immediately. However, if the requested URL is not cached and, furthermore, if it takes a long time to retrieve it, then the server would want to create another thread, which can retrieve the requested URL separately and then continue to service the message pump. Although not a difficult operation, there is little point to each programmer reengineering the same functionality. Therefore, Microsoft defined a formal approach.

First, create your component exactly as you would normally and as we described earlier when we implemented the **WebPageCache** component. As before, add the **async_uuid** attribute to the interface that you want to support asynchronous calls. This is exactly what you would do if you were simply counting on the standard marshaller to handle the asynchronous client call for you.

The next step is to add support for the **ICallFactory** interface to your component. Since there is only one method on this interface, **CreateCall( )**, that is all you need to implement. Inside the implementation, you need to pass back a call object. In order to do this, you will need to create it.

The three interfaces that the call object requires are **ISynchronize**, **ICancelMethodCall**, and the asynchronous interface (for example, **AsyncIWebPageCache**). The first of these interfaces, **ISynchronize**, would probably involve the most work if it were not for the fact that Microsoft has created a **ManualResetEvent** component (with class ID **CLSID_ManualResetEvent**) that can implement all the functionality for you. All you need to do is aggregate it. This, too, is only a couple lines of code. First, declare a member variable of type **IUnknown***. (You could use the **CComPtr** template for this if you want to avoid having to call **Release( )** in the called object's final **Release( )** method.) Next, inside your COM MAP, instead of specifying that your component support the **ISynchronize** interface using the **COM_INTERFACE_ENTRY**, you will want to use the **COM_INTERFACE_ENTRY_AUTOAGGREGATE** macro because it will automatically aggregate the **ManualResetEvent** component for you.

Next you need to implement the asynchronous interface (**AsyncIWebPageCache**). This will involve the most coding on your part. For each of the Begin methods on the asynchronous interface, you want to start a new thread (or retrieve a thread from a thread pool using the **QueueUserWorkItem( )** API function). Also note that prior to these functions exiting, you must store all the necessary parameters that were passed in so that they can be made available to the new thread. In order to notify the stub that you have completed the Begin function, call **Signal( )** on the **ISynchronize** interface that you aggregated.

This new thread will actually perform the operation that the function requires. By requesting that this thread, rather than the calling thread, perform the work, you will be able to exit the Begin function without blocking while waiting for the operation to complete. Inside the new thread, do the work that the function call requires. As before, in order to notify the standard marshaller that you have completed the work, you need to call **ISynchronize::Signal( )**. This will cause the standard marshaller to call the Finish method, from which you will populate all the outgoing parameters with the newly acquired data. Make sure that if the Finish method is called early, you block until the worker thread has completed.

Although we have only scratched the surface of asynchronous COM calls, this is a topic that many of you will want to explore in depth on your own. In the next chapter, you will learn about queued components, which provide another method for implementing an asynchronous server using COM+.

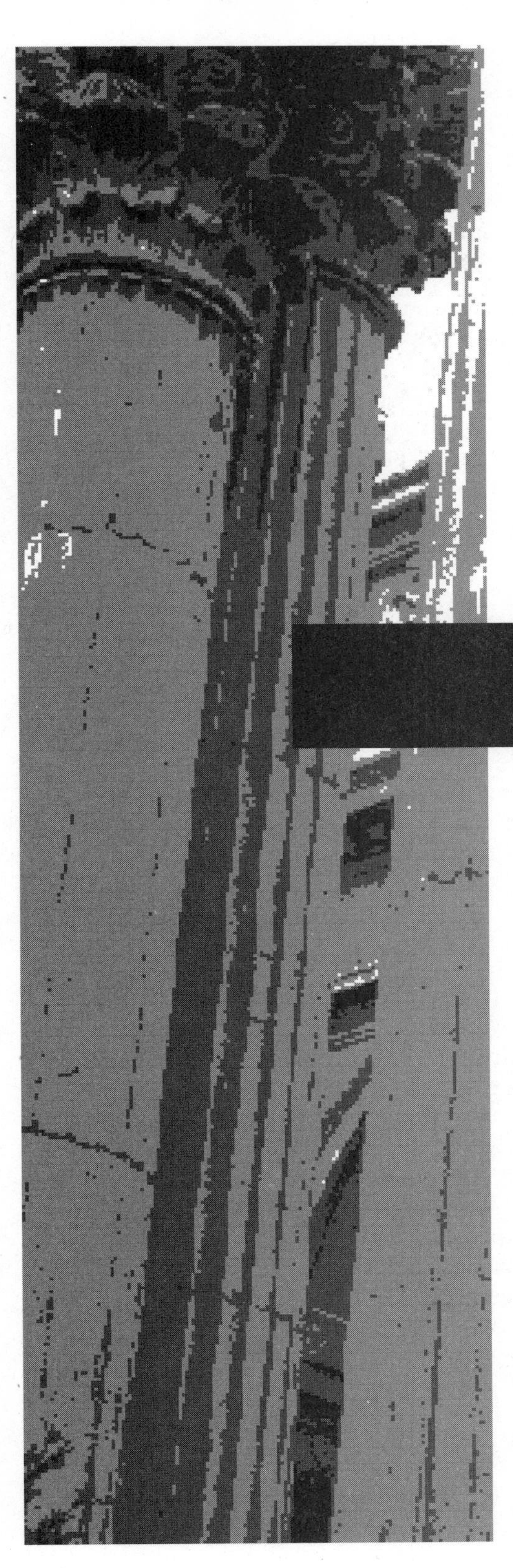

CHAPTER 14

The COM+ Evolution

As explained at the beginning of this book, COM+ is built upon the foundation of COM. The preceding 13 chapters have examined that foundation at length. It is now time to move on to the "+" part of COM+.

COM+ is an evolution, not a revolution. All of the COM features, techniques, and concepts described in the foregoing chapters apply to COM+. COM+ simply expands the set of problems that the COM technology can handle effectively. In this and the following chapter we will look at those aspects of COM+ that are unique to COM+. We will begin by offering the following simple definition for COM+:

> COM+ is the unification of COM with Microsoft Transaction Server plus several new services.

In the course of this chapter you will discover the rather large implications contained within this short definition.

Our discussion of COM+ is divided into two chapters. This chapter provides a detailed discussion of what COM+ is and how it works, along with an in-depth review of each of the services it provides. For the most part, this chapter focuses on the theory surrounding COM+ rather than the practical "how-to's" of building and configuring COM+ applications. In the next chapter, we will focus on the practical, showing how to build a COM+ application that incorporates most of the COM+ features discussed in this chapter.

Why COM+?

Given the impressive power of COM, it is only natural to ask why more features were required. The answer lies in the changing nature of the computing environment. You have already seen that with DCOM, COM applications can be distributed across multiple computers, sharing each other's component resources in order to achieve the work demanded by a particular system. With the advent of the Web, however, applications are often not contained within one organization. It has become increasingly likely that applications are global, spanning multiple enterprises, sites, and countries. Such applications are designed to interact with a myriad of other systems in order to accomplish the work that business-to-business (B2B) transactions require. Furthermore, given the ease with which systems can be broadcast to consumers using the Web, these computer systems now incorporate direct business-to-consumer (B2C) interactions and consumer-to-consumer (C2C) traffic. Also, often users need to work in a disconnected environment—when the networks are down or the users are on the road, for example. In these situations, users can continue to

Enterprise+ systems cross the organization boundary to include business-to-business (B2B) applications and beyond.

work with the application, even though they are not currently connected. We will call these expansive, disconnected, and seemingly unbounded systems *Enterprise+ systems*, and in the next two chapters we will discuss how COM+ works to enable developers to create such systems.

It is with the introduction of Windows 2000 that COM moves to become COM+. COM+ is the combination of a set of services that began with the release of Microsoft Transaction Server and the ability either to commit or revoke a set of component actions so that either all changes were successful or all changes failed. In addition, Microsoft Transaction Server was designed to provide the scalability required to build systems that could not only support hundreds of users, but if built correctly, could support the thousands of simultaneous users that Enterprise+ systems require.

COM+ provides the ability to build scalable distributed systems that can span the globe and support thousands of simultaneous users.

Building on this initial effort, COM+ provides the ability to move from desktop and relatively small DCOM applications to large, enterprise-wide systems that can potentially be scaled to support more users by simply adding more hardware. It provides the infrastructure for multitier distributed applications, including Web-based solutions. In short, COM+ provides the ability to build scalable distributed systems that can span the globe and support large numbers of simultaneous users.

Of course, COM+ puts even more responsibility on the programmer. Expertise in building such extensive systems requires not only good interface design techniques (also required for small systems), but also careful thought on how the system is divided into its modules so that they can be deployed in a manner that can capitalize on the new architecture.

Introducing COM+ Services and Terminology

COM+ provides an integrated set of services that is used to build and support the scalable and distributed COM–based systems described above. Generally speaking, if you are not interested in building application components that will be shared by more than one user on more than one machine, you will not need COM+ services. However, in this day and age, the single-user system is becoming increasingly rare. Fortunately, with the arrival of Windows 2000 and COM+, shared systems have become significantly easier to build. COM+ provides a set of application services that components can use to support functionality that otherwise would not be available unless explicitly coded. Writing your own infrastructure for this functionality is both hard work and typically not where you will be adding value to the application. Here, we will review the services that COM+ provides and introduce several COM+-related terms.

Component Services

Component Services allows you to manage COM+ components.

The central "station" from which all the COM+ features can first be viewed is known as Component Services. Component Services is a Microsoft Management Console snap-in through which COM components can be configured for the various settings and services they require. The Microsoft Management Console (MMC) is a common framework that application vendors can use to host their configuration screens so that consumers can then configure applications using the same familiar user interface common to all the MMC supporting applications. The specific screens and functionality that one vendor provides are packaged into a snap-in that will then be hosted within the MMC. To launch the Component Services snap-in, from the Start menu, browse to the Programs | Administrative Tools group and select the Component Services icon. This will launch the screen shown in Figure 14-1.

The Component Services snap-in (henceforth simply referred to as Component Services) provides the ability to configure COM+ applications and the

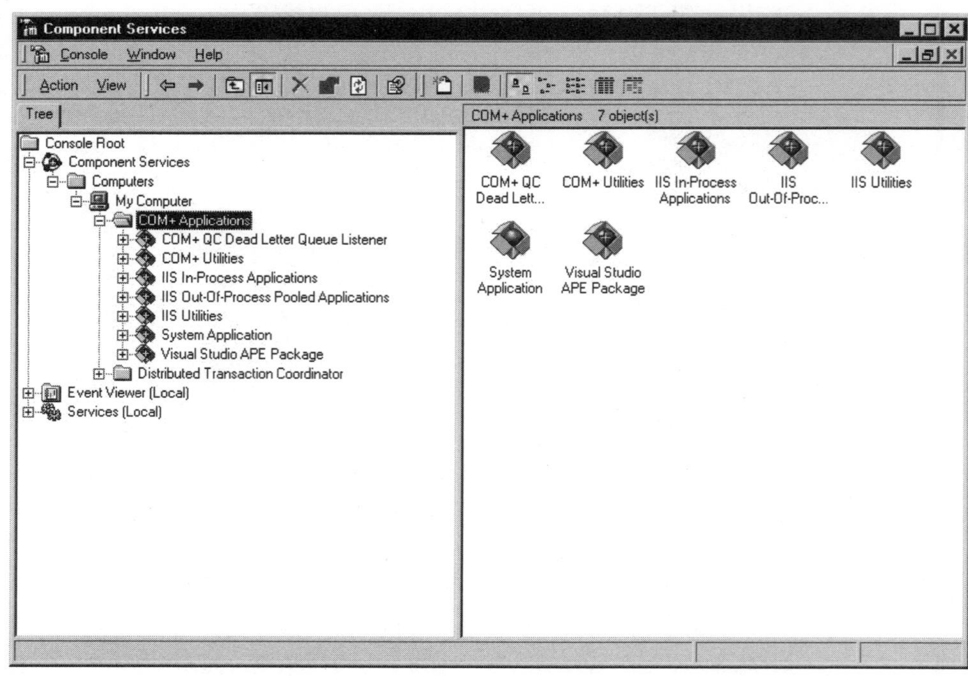

Component Services default view with COM+ Applications opened

Figure 14-1.

components that make up these applications. COM+ applications are not executables created explicitly using a development tool and programming language. Rather, they are declared within Component Services and provide a logical grouping for components that make up an application. Once each of these components has been added, Component Services supplies the user interface for designating the services in which a component will enlist. The specified settings will determine the attributes of the *context* in which the component will execute at runtime.

COM+ Services

Given all the abstract discussion of "services," it is time that we establish exactly what these services are. The following is a list of the COM+ services: contexts, transactions, compensating resource managers, queued components, event services, object pooling, just-in-time activation, role-based security, and the Shared Property Manager. Let's briefly define each of these.

- *Context* is the logical execution environment that surrounds a set of components in much the same way that an apartment defines the threading environment. In fact, "context" and "apartment" are related. An apartment surrounds a set of one or more contexts. Which context a particular component runs in depends on the various configuration settings it is assigned.
- *Transaction* defines a unit of work that is to be completed in its entirety or failed in its entirety. The important characteristic of a transaction is that it is discrete. There may be several different tasks that go into a transaction, but in order for any one of those tasks to be completed successfully, they all have to be completed successfully. And if any of the tasks fail, all the tasks will fail. Component Services allows you to configure the type of transaction support that a component requires.
- *Compensating resource managers* provide the framework for creating modules that can participate within transactions and that can be used to persist or not persist information based on the outcome of a particular transaction.
- *Queued components* allow a set of method calls on a particular interface to be made asynchronously, even when the server is disconnected from the client. Perhaps more important, queued components provide a mechanism for COM calls to be made to a server that is disconnected from the client. With queued components, method calls from the client

to the server are made, but rather than the call taking effect immediately, it is recorded. Later on, the recorded method calls can be played back (executed) even after the client that initially made the calls has shut down.

- *Event services* provide the ability to implement a loose binding mechanism between two components. The mechanism establishes a central resource to which both event publishers and event subscribers can register in order to communicate. Component Services provides the user interface for the registration to be recorded.
- *Object pooling* minimizes the startup cost involved with instantiating a component. Once all clients have completed working with a component, and they have each released their reference counts on that component, COM+ places the instantiated component into a logical *pool* of components. Therefore, rather than releasing the component in its entirety, COM+ maintains an uninitialized but still instantiated version of the component in memory so that later on, when another client requests a component of the same type, COM+ will provide one of the pooled component instances.
- *Just-in-time (JIT) activation* is similar to object pooling in that it relates to an instantiated object's lifetime. With JIT activation, COM+ will postpone actual object creation until a method is called on an object. Furthermore, COM+ may deactivate the object after the method call even if the client still holds a reference to the object. If the client calls another method, COM+ will reactivate the object. It is therefore possible for a client to hold on to a proxied interface even if the underlying object supporting the interface is not actively participating with the client. JIT activation can be turned on or off from inside Component Services, but it is required for transaction support. JIT activation can also further benefit from object pooling. Deactivated objects are returned to the pool rather than being unloaded, and an object can be claimed from the pool when it is reactivated.
- *Role-based security* enables you to configure the security for a particular component down to the interface or even method call level without writing any specific code. The available security settings in Component Services are similar to those provided by **DComcnfg.exe** except that they can be configured down to the call level rather than simply the application level.
- The *Shared Property Manager* enables the synchronized (protected) sharing of data between components within the same process. Although not

directly configured within Component Services, this is closely related to how components are registered within Component Services.

This list provides an overview of the functionality that COM+ provides. We will look at each of these in more detail as we progress through the chapter.

Configured Components

The characteristic common to most of the above services is that nearly all of them can be *configured*. Used in the COM+ sense, the term "configure" does not relate to the ability to tweak a particular setting from inside Component Services, however. Rather, it relates to a component's capacity to enlist the COM+-provided features without having to code the entire infrastructure that these features require.

The ability to set (whether programmatically or via Component Services) the various configuration settings is not in itself what makes COM+ so powerful. Rather, the key point is that with COM+ you no longer have to implement all the plumbing that the above features would require. Instead, this functionality is delegated to COM+, and you simply exploit it as needed. COM+, therefore, provides the ability to "configure" the characteristics for how a component will work without having to implement the infrastructure that the configuration designates. Components that are to enlist these COM+ features are registered within Component Services, at which point they are called *configured components*.

The key advantage of configured components is that they can enlist in the services provided by COM+ rather than having to manually implement all the features that a configuration specifies.

For example, rather than coding large portions of code to handle transactions, you simply designate your components as requiring transaction support and then call the one or two API functions to enlist this support. This is extremely powerful and makes Enterprise+ systems significantly easier to build.

Overview of How COM+ Works

COM+'s technique for providing its services is to intercept calls into a component from a client application. This should be familiar to you because it is the same mechanism that was used for implementing DCOM and again for marshalling calls across different threading models, as we discussed in the previous chapter. When a client requests that a configured component be activated, COM+ will check the COM+ Registration Database (RegDB) to determine the configuration settings that have been assigned to the component. Based on the settings, COM+ will find or create an appropriate context in which to run the component. The context will then wrap around the component in order to intercept all calls coming to and going from the

An interceptor is a lightweight proxy.

component's interfaces over the interception boundary. Next COM+ will activate the component and, finally, return a reference to the proxy it created back to the client. This proxy object that COM+ creates is commonly referred to as the *interceptor*, and the only difference between it and the one discussed in previous chapters is that it is usually much lighter, having significantly less impact on performance.

COM+ never returns a direct reference to an activated component's interface to a nonconfigured client (a client that is not also running inside Component Services). Instead, COM+ always returns a reference to the interceptor, which acts on behalf of your object for the client. A diagram of this process is shown in Figure 14-2.

The technique of interception allows a COM client to connect to a COM server without needing to know or care about the server's use of COM+ services or, in fact, how the services themselves are configured. This is consistent with the COM goal of location transparency. A server responds to client requests in the same way it would if it were running outside of COM+. The server does not

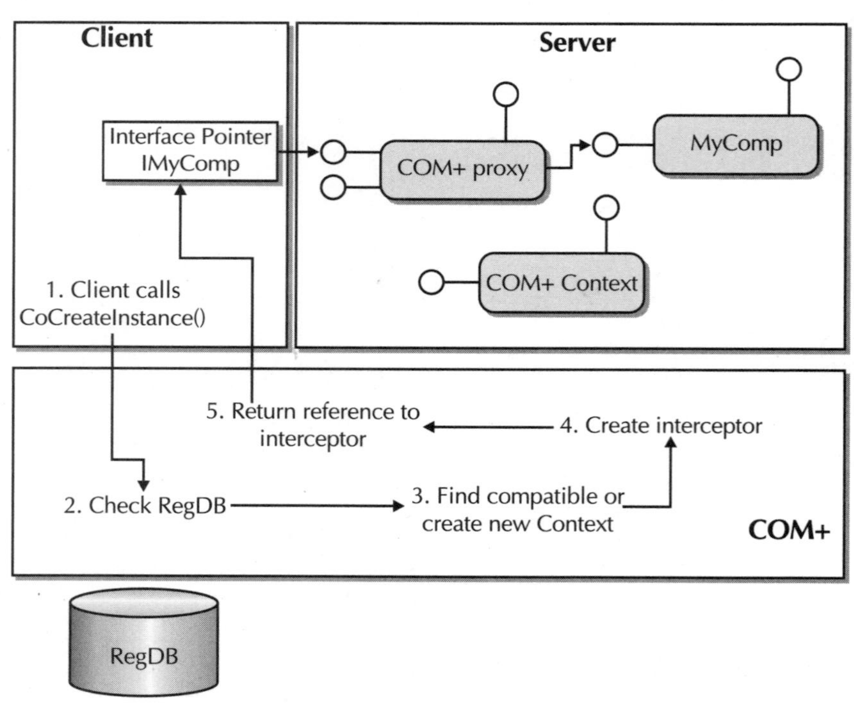

Overview of COM+ interception

Figure 14-2.

need to know that it is running inside COM+ either, and in fact, server components can take advantage of many COM+ services without the need for any extra code. Instead, COM+ intercepts client calls, and then, at a minimum, adds an object context. The object context then implements the services assigned to a component based on the component's configuration inside Component Services as well as the specific attributes requested by your server component programmatically. This approach greatly reduces the amount of code that a server component requires in order to take advantage of COM+ features.

The services provided by COM+ can be programmed or configured using various defined attributes, and because the services indicated by these attributes are implemented by COM+, your server component does not need to be aware of many of them in order to take advantage of them. In contrast, when a component is configured in MTS, the server registry settings for the component are adjusted (some use the term "hacked") so that the MTS infrastructure is called instead of the original component. In COM+, this is no longer required since all calls to **CoCreateInstance( )** will consult the COM+ Registration Database (RegDB) in order to determine whether the component being created is configured. If it is, COM+ will intercept the call to create the component using an interceptor. The interceptor will then be responsible for activating the server object for the client and passing back a reference to the proxy in place of a direct interface on the component. This is true even when the component runs in the same process as the client.

The mechanism by which COM+ is implemented is through an interception layer placed between the client and server whenever the client and the server are within different contexts.

So, the basic concept is client, server, with COM+ in the middle. This is a helpful mental picture to have as we discuss more COM+ details throughout this chapter and the next.

Once the interceptor is established, COM+ can provide advanced services without the server component's direct involvement, and components can declare rather than program their service requirements. The pre- and postprocessing of each client's call to the server object's interfaces then provide the ability for COM+ to add service-level functionality.

Object Context Details

As we discussed above, the configured environment within which an object runs is called a context. An object will run in at most one object context; however, multiple objects can run in the same context if their configured attributes are deemed compatible by COM+.

COM+ requires that all calls to and from objects across contexts be marshalled via proxies. For this reason, raw object references should never be passed outside of a context. You need to be especially wary of this when multiple components are implemented within the same module. As we learned in the previous chapter, **CoMarshalInterface( )** and **CoUnmarshalInterface( )** are used to pass interfaces across COM boundaries, and context boundaries are no exception. The API will appropriately create and destroy compatible proxies when passing object references. As with all calls across COM boundaries, marshalling is automatically invoked for you for situations in which the interfaces are passed as parameters. You have to enlist the help of the marshalling API or the global interface table, however, for global interface pointers that are internally (within your code) crossing a COM boundary. This is very similar to the process used to cross apartment boundaries, except now the boundaries are much more subtle. Before, you could explicitly see when you were crossing apartment boundaries because usually you manually created the threads that defined the additional apartments. With COM+ the lines are not nearly as well defined. Furthermore, they could change based on the configuration assigned to individual components within Component Services. Therefore, you always need to call the appropriate marshalling mechanism when calling from one component into another. Do not make direct internal C++ calls from one C++ component implementation to a different component's implementation without invoking the marshalling code.

You may be tempted to think that context is simply a logical distinction. This is not the case, however. Context is both logical and physical, and there are specific context interfaces that can be accessed once your object has been created and activated. The attributes of the context are based on the declared attributes for the component as well as those demanded by the object. COM+ uses context attributes to group similar objects and to keep separate those that are not context compatible. COM+ will create a new object in one of three places: inside the context of its caller, inside a brand new context, or inside the default context for a different apartment.

- COM+ will create a new object in the context of its caller if COM+ determines that the caller's context is compatible or if the new object is created from a nonconfigured component with no COM+ requirements (not dropped into Component Services).
- COM+ proxies call across contexts. When a caller lives in one context and a called object lives in another, a new proxy is created to handle the incompatible attributes. Some of the context properties will flow through to the second context. COM+ takes care of setting the attributes correctly and performs the required context proxy work between the two objects. A critical example of this concerns the transaction attribute discussed later in the chapter.

- If COM+ determines that there is an existing compatible context, it will place the object in that context. Again, COM+ will proxy calls across the contexts.

A context is generally created and associated with an object at **CoCreateInstance( )** time, but an object context will not be created if COM+ can find an existing compatible context. Instead, the new object will be created in that context.

Concurrency and Activity

Before we move on to discussing the particular features that COM+ offers, one more term needs to be defined. The term is *activity*, and it relates to the grouping of contexts that share the same concurrency characteristics. You will recall from the previous chapter that concurrency was built into COM via the apartment model. The apartment model grouped sets of one or more threads, and, at least prior to the Windows 2000 introduction of the Thread Neutral Apartment (TNA), threads were restricted to execute within their assigned apartment. The result was that components that were not manually programmed for synchronization could instead be "configured" to run within an apartment in which COM ensures they are protected.

When a component runs inside COM+, this concurrency model becomes more controlled and directed. No longer is concurrency protection restricted to the boundaries of apartments; rather the concurrency model enables us to wrap groups of contexts (and thereby the objects running within those contexts) that are not necessarily within the same apartment. In fact, the concurrency grouping can span not only an apartment, but also processes and computer boundaries, as shown in Figure 14-3. The concurrency grouping is known as an *activity*, and, as we shall see shortly, it plays a key role in the ability for COM+ to provide transaction support.

Essentially, the activity boundary provides protection so that no components outside the activity can interact with components inside an activity. This is crucial for transaction support, but it also provides a more granular level of synchronization without incurring the cost of providing manual synchronization using the various synchronization API functions. Let's take an in-depth look at COM+ transactions to see why the activity boundary is crucial.

COM+ Transactions

To understand the functionality provided by each COM+ service, it is helpful to understand the problem that the service is designed to address. In this

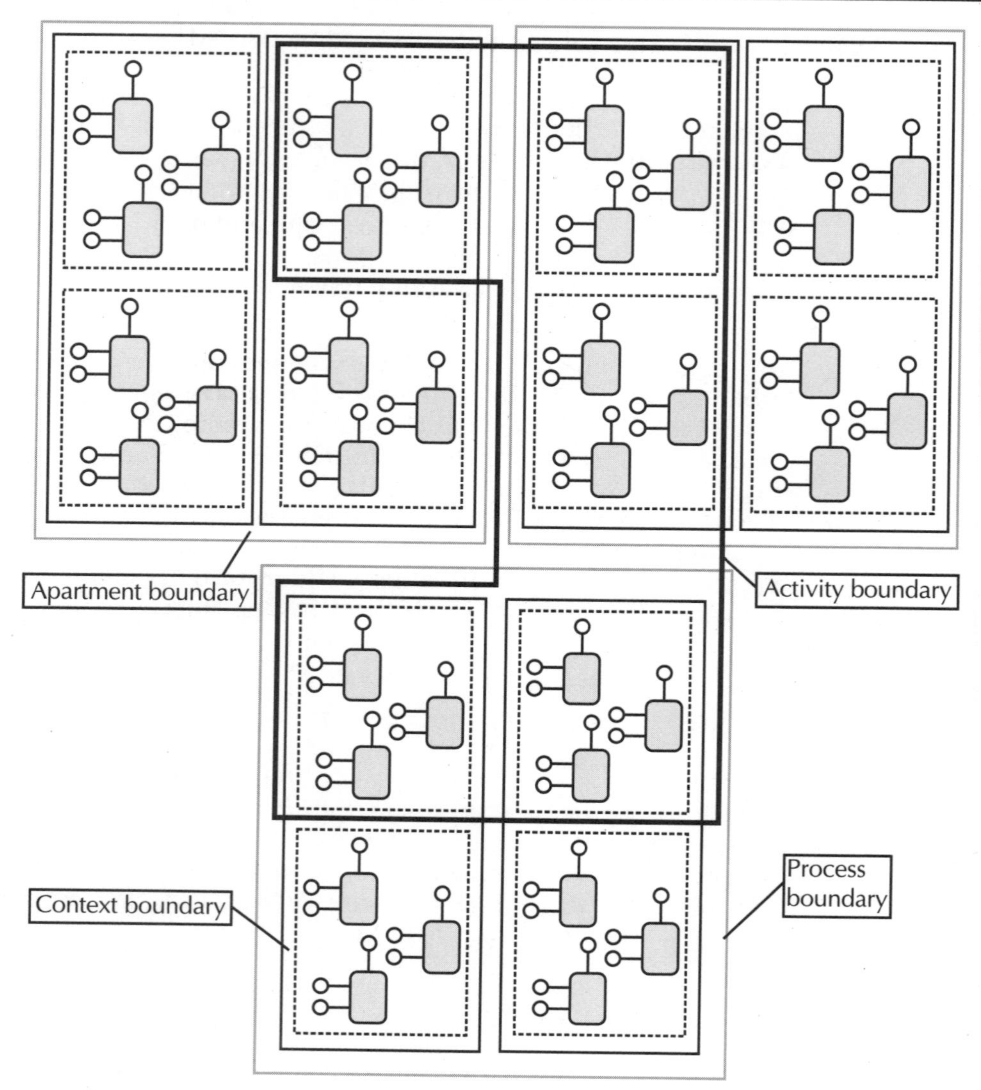

An activity spanning both apartment and process boundaries

Figure 14-3.

section and the ones following, we will look at each of the COM+ services by first understanding the problem and then delving into the details regarding how these services work to solve the problem. Probably the key feature in the

COM+ services is the ability to support transactions. It is with this in mind that we begin our discussion by looking at COM+ transactions.

Data Consistency

The problem of data consistency relates to how the set of actions that make up a discrete transaction must be executed or failed as one discrete unit rather than some actions being successful and other actions not. The data stored within Enterprise+ applications can be extremely complicated, with numerous business rules defining how one data-defined entity within the system relates to another data-defined entity.

Consider the following scenario: A customer order has line items. Each line item is a product in the vendor's product catalog. If a customer submits an order for multiple line items, we want to be sure that the *entire* order can be created successfully. This can be done in a couple of different ways. The first is carefully checking the availability of each product before submitting the order. Unfortunately, even in this case you could have trouble. For example, another order could be placed between the time you check inventory and the time the order is stored, or the product could be deleted from the catalog just after you check its availability. Using transactions is the other way. This connects an availability or validity check with the actual creation of the order that requires inventory of the product. It protects (locks) all resources involved in the transaction, preventing deletions or outside updates of any kind, and makes sure that the entire transaction happens in an all-or-nothing mode.

A COM+ transaction is either completed or failed in its entirety.

Classic database programming includes the concept of beginning a transaction (SQL BEGIN statement), doing some work, and then either committing the transaction if everything is okay (SQL COMMIT statement) or rolling back the transaction if not (SQL ROLLBACK statement). COM+ transactions extend this concept to COM components. COM+ transactions are the mechanism used to maintain this data consistency, forcing transactions to be either completed or failed in entirety regardless of the various kinds of system failures.

It is worth noting that the concept of transaction support outside a database environment is not new to the Microsoft platform. Transaction support from Microsoft started with the Viper project in 1992. The Viper project first delivered the Distributed Transaction Coordinator for Microsoft SQL Server. Later, transaction support was delivered in Microsoft Transaction Server (or MTS) 1.0 in 1996 and MTS 2.0 in 1998. COM+ can be viewed as

"MTS 3.0" and represents the integration of Microsoft Transaction Server directly into the COM subsystem.

ACID stands for atomic, consistent, isolated, and durable.

Transactions are single units of work and are said to have ACID properties. ACID stands for *atomic*, *consistent*, *isolated*, and *durable*. Every COM transaction has these properties. Atomic means that a single transaction is considered a single unit of work, even though it will typically combine the work of multiple components. Consistent means that either the transaction happens (commits) or it doesn't (aborts). If the transaction commits, all actions prescribed by the transaction will be performed. If the transaction aborts, the system will be in the same state it was prior to the transaction and will not be left in any interim state. Isolated means that the transaction will act as if it is the only action being performed on the system, even if other transactions are being executed concurrently. Transactions will be protected from each other in that no other transaction will affect the outcome of an in-process transaction. Durable means that when the transaction commits, the state of the system is guaranteed to have changed correctly, even if the system fails and restarts in the middle of a transaction.

Invoking Transaction Support

Given the robustness of the COM+ transaction support, you might be tempted to think that there is a lot of work involved to participate in the transaction mechanism. In fact, for the most part, transaction support is an invisible mechanism that surrounds a component and with which the component requires very little interaction. COM+ will create transactions automatically, and therefore a component does not need to explicitly create a transaction. Instead, a component is required to do its work and then vote in the outcome of the transaction, approving the transaction if it believes everything is fine or aborting the transaction if it encountered a problem. In fact, the component can participate in the voting process automatically via a method's returned **HRESULT**. This automatic voting occurs if the "Auto-done" property is configured for the component. Using "Auto-done," if the component returns **S_OK**, the transaction vote will be a yea, and otherwise it will be a nay.

The voting process is simple, but definitely not "majority rules": a single vote against the transaction aborts it (a single call to **IContextState::SetMyTransactionVote(FALSE)** or a single call to **IObjectContext::SetAbort( )**, as we shall see in the next chapter). In other words, all components with a transaction must consent (either explicitly or via the "Auto-done" property) to a transaction being completed. If any component rejects the transaction completion, the entire process will be rolled back to the state prior to the start of the transaction.

Since COM+ creates the transactions, and all the server components do is vote, COM+ can combine multiple server components into a single transaction without their explicit cooperation or knowledge. Individual components are concerned only with doing their work and voting. COM+ takes care of coordinating the component's efforts with others into a single transaction.

Transaction Flow

Concurrency management is the mechanism by which simultaneous access to the set of components enrolled in a transaction is protected.

An important part to achieving the ACID goals is maintaining and protecting a system's state while in the process of committing a transaction. This in turn requires *concurrency management*. Concurrency management is the mechanism by which simultaneous access to the set of components enrolled in a transaction is protected, so that external objects that are not participating in the transaction do not change the state of these components. As we saw in the previous section, the logical boundary that concurrency management invokes is known as an activity. COM+ cannot allow your transacted object state to change unless all objects participating in the transaction are going to change, and no object outside of the transaction should be able to access or change a transacted object's state while it is participating in a transaction.

Having to manually program concurrency management can be rather difficult, and testing to see that sufficient protection has been provided is also a complex operation. Fortunately, COM+ steps in to take care of synchronization for you. It is the responsibility of COM+ to serialize access to objects participating in transactions, and it does this by implementing locks in the interception layer (yet another good reason for this layer to exist). Clients do not need to care about serializing their access; they just call their objects. Based on the transaction and synchronization attributes set for your component, when a client makes a method call to an object, COM+ will try to obtain a process level lock on the object, and if it can, it will allow the call to proceed. If it can't, the call will be blocked until the lock is available. The "blanket" that the lock places on the set of objects involved in a transaction is called an activity. This process of object locking is called *activity-based synchronization*. Because transactions require synchronization, they are automatically placed within an activity. Furthermore, as we stated in the previous section, activity-based synchronization works well for locking not only in a single process, but also across process and system boundaries.

As components are created that participate in transactions, a logical chain of objects is created. The first component created in this chain is called the transaction's *root object*. Objects chained together create a *transaction stream*. All of the objects involved in a single transaction stream make up a single serialized activity.

A chain of transaction objects is called a transaction stream.

In Microsoft Transaction Server (MTS—the previous implementation of context and transaction services), the only way to chain components together in a transaction stream was through explicit calls to **IObjectContext::CreateInstance( )**. Under COM+, transaction flow is automatic and built in for every configured component. Therefore, this syntax is no longer required, and a configured component can chain together a transaction without doing any explicit coding.

Table 14-1 shows the four available settings for how a component can be configured. The listing uses the custom IDL attributes that can be assigned to

Custom Transaction IDL	Description
TRANSACTION_REQUIRED	Indicates that this component requires a transaction to run. If the component is not currently in a transaction, COM+ will start a new transaction.
TRANSACTION_SUPPORTED	Indicates that the component will run in a transaction, but it does not require one.
TRANSACTION_NOT_SUPPORTED	Indicates that the component will not run in a transaction. If the component is called from within a transaction's activity, COM+ will create the component in a context running outside of the current activity.
TRANSACTION_REQUIRES_NEW	Indicates that the component requires a new transaction. If the component is called from within a transaction, COM+ will start a new transaction activity for this component. Use this setting if you want to ensure that this component's transaction is unaffected by the success or failure of others.

IDL Keywords Used for Specifying Transaction Requirements
Table 14-1.

components in order to specify the component's transaction requirement at design time. Each of these custom IDL attributes is defined in **mtxattr.h**.

These attributes match the Transactions tab of the component's properties dialog available from Component Services. Even though Component Services allows the transaction attributes to be configured by a systems administrator, you as the server component writer are most familiar with the specific requirements of your component. If you know that your component will require transactions, then it should be marked as such in the interface definition of the component. Leaving it up to an administrator configuring a system might be desired in some cases, but it can also be dangerous to the consistency of the resources that your component is accessing.

Let's now consider how the various transaction attributes affect the way the component works in regard to transaction participation. Figure 14-4 illustrates three components, A, B, and C, which are all created within a single transaction stream. The client creates A, A creates B, and B creates C. Since their transaction attributes are compatible, they make up a single transaction stream. When the three components complete their work and vote yea for the transaction, they will be unloaded or deactivated. When A is unloaded or deactivated, the transaction will be committed.

A single transaction stream exists in at most one activity. Multiple transaction streams, however, can also exist in a single activity. This will occur when a nonroot object is called within an existing transaction stream and the object is marked as Requires New. Alternatively, multiple transaction streams can occur when an interim component is marked as Not Supported and it invokes another component that is marked as Required or Requires New. When either of these scenarios occurs, the two transaction streams are

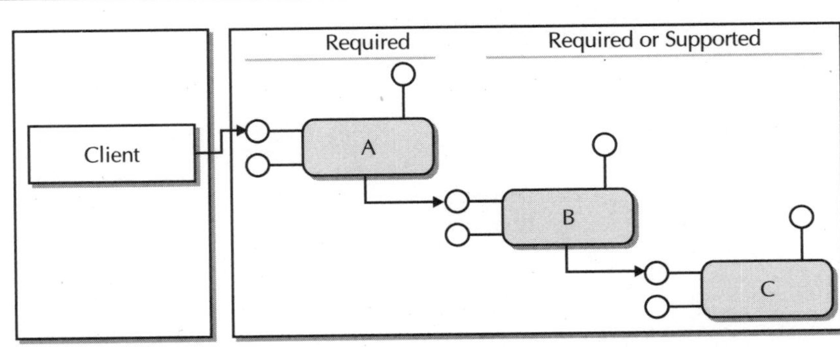

Simple transaction stream
Figure 14-4.

isolated from each other. The Requires New component has insisted that its work must be done independently of all others.

Consider the transaction diagram shown in Figure 14-5. In this scenario, object B creates object C, which is marked as Requires New. This causes a second, isolated transaction stream to be created. In this scenario, when C and D are done with their work, their transaction will be committed or aborted with complete disregard to the current state of the transaction started with A.

An important point to emphasize is that a transaction is active until the root object deactivates. When the root object deactivates, the Distributed Transaction Coordinator (DTC) will attempt to commit the transaction. All objects that participated in the transaction are destroyed, and all locks obtained for the transaction are released. Any cached information that was saved is subject to change, so it should be flushed in order to start fresh with the next transaction. Any information changed or accessed outside of a transaction should be considered suspect. In this manner, transactions are used to ensure consistent state information.

As a result, components that support transactions should be stateless across transacted method calls. That is, they themselves should not maintain a client state beyond the scope of a single method call. The significant data in them will be destroyed when the transaction is completed. Do not imply from this statement that state dependencies are bad or that COM+ components that maintain a state cannot be written. State-dependent components do need to be carefully designed and carefully deployed in order to protect system consistency, scalability, and durability. Remember that your transacted components are built to manage state. However, these components themselves should obtain a state and update a state only within the context of a transaction and never outside of it.

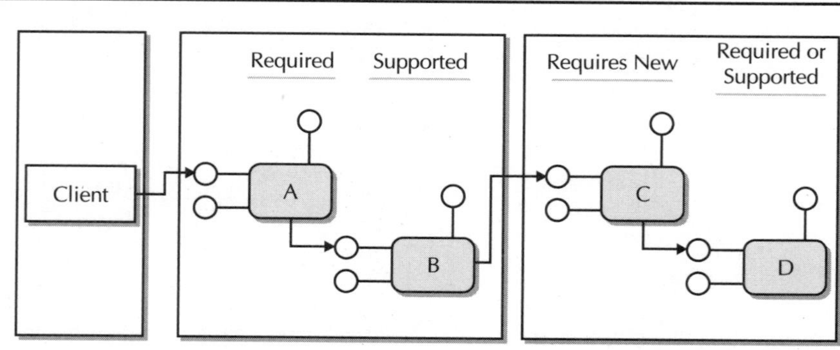

Independent transaction streams
Figure 14-5.

Resource Managers and Resource Dispensers

Resource managers are responsible for maintaining the durable state of transactions for a given resource.

Resource dispensers maintain nonpersisted pools of connections to the resources provided by a resource manager.

For work to be aborted or committed as a unit, transactions require the coordinated use of *resource managers* and *resource dispensers*. Resource managers are responsible for maintaining the durable state of transactions for a given resource such as a database or a queue. The Microsoft SQL Server OLEDB driver is an example of a resource manager that is used to store persistent state data associated with a transaction. A purchase order, for example, can contain a lot of data such as customer details, order details, and line item details. SQL Server can be used to safely persist this in an efficient and reliable manner. Resource dispensers are used to maintain nonpersisted pools of connections to the resources provided by a resource manager. Microsoft SQL Server also supports resource pooling.

Resource managers are enlisted in the transaction via Microsoft's Distributed Transaction Coordinator services, or DTC. The DTC coordinates transaction commitments among multiple types of resource managers. COM+ will automatically enlist resource managers when a component uses a managed resource from within a transaction. Resource managers will obtain resource locks to protect access to the resources for the duration of the transaction. When the component's work has been completed, COM+ will call the DTC's "Begin Transaction" method for you from the interception layer.

The transaction streams avoid deadlocking if the components are designed correctly and the transaction stream is not broken. You will need to be careful when mixing transactional components with nontransactional components, especially if the nontransactional components share resources with the transacted component. This, however, is generally not a good idea and should be avoided if at all possible.

DTC implements the two-phase commit protocol required for distributed transactions. The basics of two-phase commit are as follows: The first phase is the voting phase. Each resource manager is polled to see if it is okay with the transaction. The second phase is the commit phase. If each of the resource managers involved indicates that it is okay with the transaction, the DTC will notify the resource managers to commit their transactions in the second phase. If any of the managers returns not okay (vote for an abort) during the first phase, the second phase will notify all of the managers to abort their transactions. Note that the objects themselves vote, with **SetAbort( )** or **SetComplete( )** calls, before the DTC two-phase commit process. Microsoft DTC, through the proper cooperation of the resource managers, ensures that this process is durable enough to survive the various forms of application or system crashes.

As we indicated above, resource managers are responsible for durable persistence of the state of a transaction. Resource dispensers are used to maintain nonpersisted pools of connections to the resources provided by a resource manager. Through pooling, connections to resource managers can be maintained by the pool instead of being re-created every time a connection is needed. This is especially important when using transactions for a couple of reasons:

- Connections to resources are typically expensive in terms of system resources and the time it takes to create a connection to the resource. If you've connected to a database before, you will understand this.
- To achieve scalability, supporting many clients, connections to resources should be obtained at the last possible moment and given up as soon as they are no longer needed. Without a dispenser to pool the connections, the developer is going to be faced with the difficult decision of whether to sacrifice speed for safety and scalability. A major benefit of COM+ is to eliminate the need to ask the question in the first place.

Examples of resource managers provided by Microsoft Windows 2000 include ODBC and OLEDB drivers for SQL Server and Microsoft Message Queue. The DTC also interoperates with the X/Open Distributed Transaction Processing group's transaction processing protocol so that any XA-compliant resource can also be managed by COM+. COM+-compliant resource managers are available from third parties as well.

Resource managers provide automatic enlistment in transactions. This means that you don't have to do any code to get the transaction functionality. Simply access the resources from within a configured component, and you will get transaction support. If you find that you need to provide finer control over a transaction or would like to enlist a transaction on your own, you can gain access to the transaction interface for the current context through **IObjectContextInfo::GetTransactionInfo( )**. The DTC provides the **ITransaction** interface method **ITransaction::Commit( )**, which enlists resource managers to get the work done on the transaction.

As we stated previously, the DTC implements two phases: The first phase is the voting phase, and the second phase is used to notify participating resource managers to commit (yea vote) or abort (nay vote). The **ITransaction** interface and DTC are a part of the "transaction goo" and are needed only in special circumstances. These circumstances include developing a resource manager or manually enlisting nonconfigured components in transactions. If, for example, you have a set of components that you don't have source to, you can manually enlist these components, call them to do work for you, and then call **ITransaction::Commit( )** on your own to combine their work into a single transaction. Another significant example is a server executable that requires transaction support but is not easily broken into in-process DLLs that can be configured for COM+. Preferably, you will not need to do this, and instead you can provide DLLs that can be configured within COM+, thereby avoiding the extra work.

Another important point regarding the DTC's commit phase is that the objects that participate in transactions do not directly participate in the ultimate outcome of the transaction. They do work and vote. That's it. In contrast, resource managers are required to do all of the dirty work of getting the transaction stored. If you need to actively participate in the outcome of the transaction, you must write your own resource manager. A brief glance at the interfaces required to do this will have you muttering, "Ugh. Can I do this another way?"—with Windows 2000, the answer is yes. This is what a Compensating Resource Manager, or CRM, will let you do.

Compensating Resource Managers (CRMs)

The Compensating Resource Manager allows your components to participate fully in the DTC's two-phase commit.

The Compensating Resource Manager, or CRM, is an additional service that COM+ provides to allow your components to participate fully in the DTC's two-phase commit without requiring you to build a complete resource manager of your own. In effect, what you are implementing when you implement a CRM is a lightweight resource manager. The CRM infrastructure provides the needed plumbing and interfaces required for durability and voting participation. Some examples of where a CRM is appropriate include providing transacted access to files for read, write, or delete or transacted access to other nontransacted resources such as the Windows registry.

Implementing a CRM requires that you create two types of components, CRM workers and CRM compensators, that will call a COM+ interface provided by the CRM clerk. The CRM worker performs the required work of the transaction. It calls the **ICrmLogControl** interface of the CRM clerk to record a durable log of the work and to indicate which component is the CRM compensator for this worker. The CRM compensator stores the work of the transaction and must be able to recover in the event of catastrophic failure midstream in the transaction. The CRM compensator implements the **ICrmCompensator** interface, which is called by the CRM infrastructure during the DTC's two-phase commit.

Before you say, "That looks easy!" you will need to keep a few things in mind as you build a CRM. If the transaction fails midstream, the same log entry could be reprocessed on recovery. In fact, if something in the current transaction is causing the system to crash, say, by accessing a faulty hard disk, the same log record could be processed many times. Therefore, CRM compensators must be idempotent. *Idempotent* essentially means "same power." No matter how many times the CRM compensator is called with a given log record, it must record the result as if the log entry was processed only once. So, if the compensator is responsible for entering a journal entry in a text file, the compensator must insure that the log entry is written once and not the number of times the compensator is called. This clearly indicates that the log entry created by the worker must give the compensator enough information to work with, and the compensator must be written with a bit of care.

CRMs do not automatically provide concurrent access to their own resources and therefore must ensure serialized and protected access to resources they are writing to. In other words, the CRM programmer must manually put in place locks on any shared resources. Existing resource managers provide this as part of their infrastructure. A CRM must provide that part of the infrastructure for whatever resource it is writing to. It is entirely conceivable that multiple workers and compensators are active at the same time servicing other transactions.

Writing Disconnected Applications with Queued Components

Queued components allow a system to function even though disconnected from the network.

The next COM+ service we will examine is *queued components*. Consider a computer system in which the users of the system are not always connected to the network, and yet they still have to be able to work with the system, performing many of the same operations as if they were connected. The disconnection may be due to a network or server failure, or it may be one of the identified scenarios that the system was designed to run under. Disconnected systems are what queued components were designed for.

Consider the example of a hospital computer system that is used to monitor a patient's vital signs along with other patient information such as name, insurance, allergies, and dietary needs. All the information is stored on a central database server where it can be backed up or retrieved at a later stage. Now imagine that same system on an ambulance speeding toward the hospital but continually recording the same information exactly as it would inside the hospital, even though there is no network connection of any kind between the ambulance and the hospital. Furthermore, even if the network within the hospital went down, each workstation alongside each bed would

continue to function as though nothing had happened. The key feature about a system like this is that it can continue to function regardless of whether the server is available or not. When it comes to recording a patient's vital signs, whether the central system is up or not becomes irrelevant—the patient's blood pressure was taken and needs to be recorded, and so it is. Later on, when the system becomes available, all the information can automatically be sent to the server, where it can be processed.

Queued components allow a system to continue to function even when disconnected from the network. In the case of the ambulance, even though the computer is entirely disconnected from the central server at the hospital, the ambulance application records the information exactly like the application at the hospital. In fact, the two systems are identical, and the disconnected state is buried under the covers of COM.

Without queued components, probably the most obvious way to create a disconnected system would be to record all the information into a file that can then be uploaded to the central system. For example, as each patient's blood pressure reading is taken, a new line could be written to a flat file recording the time and the vital data. The drawback to this is that you need to map all the data into a storage mechanism. Furthermore, on the server side, not only do you have to write code to retrieve the data, but you also need to write the code that will then manipulate the data.

Queued components are significantly more powerful than this, however. Rather than recording just the data, queued components record the method and function calls made to a component along with all their parameters. Therefore, in addition to the data, which is buried within the parameters, queued components also invisibly store the logic for how to process the data. Furthermore, this is done under the covers of COM; so from the client application's point of view, it behaves exactly as it would if it were connected. The client application simply makes method calls and has no knowledge of what happens under the covers of the component whose methods the client is calling. This eliminates the need to write a batch system to import all that data and then process it accordingly. It allows multiple systems to use the same queued components to do different things, in a different order, without having to worry about some special disconnected state-handling code or custom file format that must be created and then read.

With queued components, the system is designed as a COM system built up of various COM components almost exactly as it would be if designed to be constantly connected. The **Monitor** component could have a method on it called **BloodPressure( )** that could be called from a graphical application or recorded automatically by a blood pressure cuff on the patient's arm. Each time the cuff took a reading, its drivers would call the **BloodPressure( )** method and pass in a reading. If the central system was available, the monitor component would then process that call. On the other hand, if the central system was down, COM+ services would instead record the fact that the **BloodPressure( )** method was called, and later, when the system became available, the COM+ services would play back each method call and execute it.

This paradigm of being able to build disconnected systems without having to implement any of the disconnected infrastructure, but rather focusing on the business logic that will add genuine value to your applications, is extremely powerful. In spite of all this power, the way you program to utilize this functionality is exactly like making a normal COM call. As with all COM+ services, queued component functionality is configured, not programmed. To configure a component as queued, the component is added to Component Services and the queued flag is set. The result is a queued component that can be called even when the client doesn't have access to the machine that contains the component.

From the client, if you want to instantiate the component as queued, you would specify the queue moniker when calling **CoCreateInstance( )**. The result is that all the method calls to the component will be recorded for later playback, rather than executed immediately. The queue moniker tells COM+ services that rather than instantiating the component, the interceptor should instantiate a recorder-type object. The recorder object then records each call made to the component. At a later time, the COM+ application, within which the component is configured, will be started, and then all the recorded calls will be executed in order.

There is one restriction, which so far we have avoided discussing. This is not a restriction in the power of queued components themselves but rather a restriction placed upon them by the laws of science. The restriction is that interfaces that are designated as queued cannot return any data to the caller. Why not? Because when the client calls a component, the code within the component does not necessarily execute immediately, so it is not possible to return any data. The only information returned is the **HRESULT** indicating whether or not the method was successfully recorded. The **HRESULT** doesn't even indicate whether the method call was successful—how could it? The method call hasn't even run yet. In order to enforce this restriction, all interfaces designated as queued are allowed to have only **[in]** parameters. Neither **[out]** nor **[in, out]** parameters are allowed. This means that if you want to utilize queued functionality, you will have to design your interfaces so they conform to this restriction, or it will not be possible to configure them as being queued within Component Services.

One other point about queued components that deserves mention now is that their functionality uses Microsoft Message Queue. So in order to utilize them, you must have Microsoft Message Queue services installed on the computer.

The Publish and Subscribe Event Service

In Chapter 10 we took an in-depth look at connection points and how they are used to enable a client application to receive notification from a server rather than polling the server to find out when an event occurred. In that same chapter we learned that the event source is the component that is sending notifications to clients. At the other end, the event listener is responsible for receiving the event notification via the implementation of the event source interface, which the event source can call into.

The COM+ event service is designed to achieve similar functionality but in a more loosely coupled way. To begin, an event class is added to Component Services. This event class is not actually a real component in that it does not contain any implementation code; rather, it is only a type library that declares a component and the interface supported by the component. (Even though only the library is required, a self-registering DLL must be supplied because when registering the event class within Component Services, calls into the registration functions of the DLL are made.) The type library provides the connection specification between both the publisher and the subscriber. It is important to realize that although a CLSID is associated with the component, there is no such actual component. In order to publish an event, the publisher (either an executable or a DLL) will make a call to **CoCreateInstance[Ex]( )** and specify the class ID of the type library declared component. The call to **CoCreateInstance[Ex]( )** will then search RegDB for all the components that are configured to subscribe to the declared component and redirect all calls into these subscribing components. The only programming requirement of the subscribed components is that they implement the interfaces that the declared component supports. If multiple interfaces are supported, the subscriber needs to implement only the interfaces on which it wants to receive events.

To understand this a little better, let's return to the example of the hospital/ambulance system described earlier. Consider that upon arriving at the hospital several departmental computer systems need to be notified that a new patient has arrived. The room where the patient will be staying needs to be assigned and then prepared. Food service needs to be notified so it can prepare food for the new patient. Nurses and doctors need to be assigned and their schedules adjusted to include the new patient.

To implement this system, first the event class needs to be created. We will call this event class **PatientArrival**, and it will support the **IPatientArrival** interface. A type library will be created that declares the interface and the associated component. Remember, no C++ CoClass code will be required, only the IDL code that the MIDL compiler uses to generate the TLB file. To register the type library within Component Services, the TLB is combined into a self-registering DLL. Next, a Web page is created that instantiates the **PatientArrival** component and calls its **Arrived( )** method.

The next step is to create each of the subscribers that will listen for the event. The **MenuPlanning** component, for example, needs to be changed to implement the **IPatientArrival** interface. That completes all the coding. The last step is simply to install the system by configuring the **MenuPlanning** and **PatientArrival** components within Component Services.

As with queued components, the one restriction to the event services is that all methods on the publish/subscribe interfaces must have only **[in]** parameters. This is due to the fact that there may be multiple subscribers, and they can't all be returning data or the publisher would have to implement special code to handle the returns.

Another point to consider when designing your system is that the method call that publishes a particular event does not return to the publisher until all subscribers have finished processing the event. If this presents a performance problem, you may wish to combine the event services functionality with queued components so that the calls are asynchronous.

Controlling Object Lifetime to Increase Scalability

In order for Enterprise+ systems to support vast numbers of users, they need to efficiently manage resources. One of the primary resources within COM+ is the instantiated components themselves. Two COM+ services that aid in this regard are object pooling and just-in-time activation.

Object Pooling

It is an expensive operation to instantiate a component only to destroy it a few seconds later when a transaction is completed or the component is no longer needed. To compensate for this inefficiency, COM+ uses *object pooling*.

Object pooling keeps a set of running object instances in memory for quick access by clients.

Object pooling keeps a set of running object instances in memory for quick access by clients. This minimizes the startup time required to open and initialize required resources. Object pooling works best when heavy object initialization is required and the work that the object performs is relatively lightweight.

For object pooling to work, a new type of object state needs to be introduced. This state is known as *activation*, and it indicates whether an object is activated or deactivated. Now, when a client requests an object, rather than re-creating the object, COM+ simply retrieves an existing object from the pool and initializes it before returning the object-requested interface to the client.

Object pooling in COM+ is automatic and configurable, but it does place some basic requirements on components before they can be pooled. Poolable components must be run within a Thread Neutral or a Multi-Threaded Apartment. Also, they must be aggregable and manually enlist in transactions if a connection to a resource will be held across object activations.

Just-In-Time (JIT) Activation

The lack of scalability due to a client maintaining references that it seldom uses is the basic problem that JIT activation is designed to address. Transactions grab resources and lock them. While this is a good thing for consistency, it's a bad thing for system throughput. Clients like to create objects and hold on to references. While that's convenient for the client (and there's nothing your server component can do to prevent it), holding on to references limits the number of active clients that can be supported.

In spite of the inefficiency of component instantiation, sometimes having an instantiated component that holds on to expensive resources is not a good idea either. If a client maintains a reference count to such a component but rarely calls it, significant system resources could be wasted. It is this second problem that JIT activation is designed to address.

With JIT activation, your object can be released (possibly back to the object pool if so configured) even if a client still holds a reference to your interface! Remember that the client is holding a reference to an object manufactured by COM+ and not the interface pointer directly provided by your object. Therefore, COM+ can decide to deactivate or destroy your object even if the client continues to maintain a reference to it. If the client makes another call to your object after it has been deactivated, COM+ will reactivate your object before any method is invoked. Again, this is all due to the interception layer introduced by COM+. With JIT activation, COM+ can postpone calling on your object until it is absolutely necessary.

Objects are automatically configured for JIT activation if they are configured as Transaction Required. In this scenario, calling **IObjectContext::SetComplete( )** signals to COM+ that your object can be released from memory or be recycled if object pooling is enabled.

JIT activation eliminates the need for the client to worry about holding object references unnecessarily long. In fact, the client should feel free to create an object reference at startup, use this reference occasionally, and free the reference only when the client exits. The server component does not need to worry too much about this either. COM+ services will take care of allocating and freeing resources as needed. To prevent COM+ from destroying the object between invocations, it needs to support pooling. This requires the support for the **IObjectControl** interface. This will combine object pooling with JIT activation and enable the component for maximum lifetime efficiency.

The IObectControl Interface

For your component to support object pooling or JIT activation, the component should implement the **IObjectControl** interface. This is required if you want COM+ to be able to direct the object to initialize itself when prompted and then to release any resources when it is no longer active. This functionality is so important that transactional components that are pooled must implement **IObjectControl** so that they can monitor the state of the resources they hold and indicate when they can or can't be reused.

In the object pooling scenario, it is the responsibility of **Activate( )** to insure that a recycled object is properly refreshed.

IObjectControl includes an **Activate( )** method that is called whenever an object instance is activated and a **Deactivate( )** method that is called just prior to returning an object to the pool. **Activate( )** should be used to insure that an object coming from the pool is properly initialized, and **Deactivate( )** should be used to insure that appropriate cleanup and releasing of resources can occur prior to returning the object to the pool.

The **IObjectControl** interface also defines a **CanBePooled( )** method. This method can be used to tell COM+ to destroy an object instead of pooling it. This is appropriate when a condition occurs during the execution of the object that will prevent it from being correctly pooled in the future. If an object returns false from a **CanBePooled( )**, a vote of Abort will be assigned any existing transaction. This is consistent with the rule that transactional components must support **IObjectControl**. A list of the **IObjectControl** interface members is shown in Table 14-2.

IObjectControl Interface Members	Description
HRESULT Activate( );	Called by COM+ when it activates your component. This is the first point at which you can legitimately access the Context object.
BOOL CanBePooled( );	Indicates to COM+ whether this object can be recycled or returned to the object pool This is called just prior to returning the object to the pool. If the object cannot be recycled, FALSE is returned.
void Deactivate( );	Called by COM+ to deactivate a component prior to returning it to the object pool.

IObjectControl Interface Member Functions
Table 14-2.

IObjectControl provides one of your component's primary points of access to COM+. The **Activate( )** method is called after an object is created but before COM+ allows any methods to be called on the object. This allows COM+ to postpone the actual activation of your object and thereby conserve server resources until they are actually needed; hence the term "just-in-time activation." **Activate( )** is also used if your object instance is being claimed from the object pool. If pooling is enabled for your object, the **Activate( )** method needs to be designed so that it can handle both brand-new instances and recycled instances being reclaimed from the pool.

The Shared Property Manager (SPM)

The Shared Property Manager is a COM+ service used to manage component data across transaction boundaries.

The Shared Property Manager (or SPM) is a COM+ service used to manage component data across transaction boundaries. Shared properties are created, used, and destroyed within process boundaries and cannot be shared across process boundaries. The SPM is considered a managed resource and implements concurrency control for its properties. That is, if an object is accessing a property, the SPM will not allow other objects access to that property until it has been released.

As we discussed earlier, objects involved in a transaction are destroyed once the transaction has been committed. If the object used or updated data that is expensive to reobtain, it can store that data inside the COM+ Shared Property Manager where it can be safely accessed either by a new instance of this object or by a related object that requires the same data.

Since the shared properties cannot be accessed across process boundaries, it is recommended that all components that use a common set of properties be configured into the same COM+ application. In fact, ideally, properties should be shared only from within the same server module since it is very easy for a user to mistakenly configure separate modules into separate applications.

The Shared Property Manager implements a simple two-level grouping hierarchy for the properties. Your object defines and creates the groups as well as the properties that will belong to a group, as shown in the following illustration.

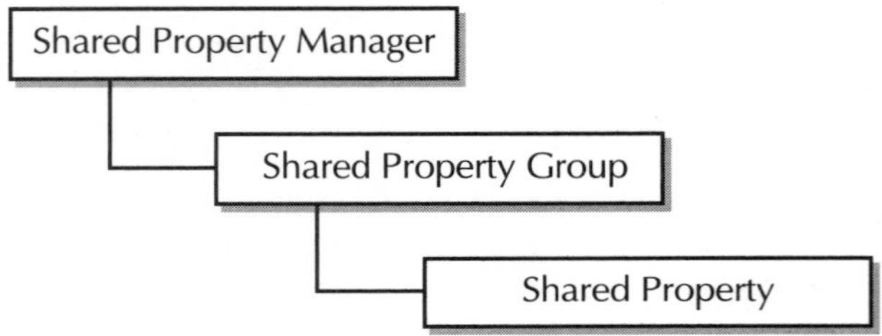

When you create the property group, you determine its isolation mode and its release mode (or when the group will be destroyed). Using the isolation mode, you can protect access to a property for an entire method call (isolation mode set to LockMethod) or simply the duration of gets and puts on the properties of the group (isolation mode set to LockGetSet). With release mode, you can control the lifetime of the property group, keeping properties active until all references to the properties have been released (release mode set to Standard) or until the application exits (release mode set to Process).

Role-Based Security

Role-based security adds roles to the existing COM security services.

COM+ adds role-based security to the existing COM security services. With role-based security, roles are defined, users are given roles, and access to functionality is determined by whether users have been assigned the given role required for the function they are accessing.

With role-based security you can

- Grant access to the entire application to users who possess a given role.
- Grant access by role to specific components within an application.
- Grant access by role to specific interfaces within a component.
- Grant access by role to specific methods on an interface within a component.

In summary, COM+ lets you configure role-based security at the component, interface, and method level. This provides for a very high degree of control over security without doing any programming. But if you insist this isn't enough, even finer-grained control over security using roles is possible through programming. For example, let's say you have a journal component and you want to allow only certain users to write entries in the journal. These users will be given the "Journal Writer" role, and "Journal Writer" will be configured for the **IJournal** interface on the **JournalComp** component. Let's also say that you have a special "Diagnostic" role that enables additional component diagnostics in your component. Only some "Journal Writers" will be given the "Diagnostic" role. This situation cannot be configured and must be explicitly programmed.

The Stage Is Set

As mentioned at the start of this chapter, COM+ is an evolution, not a revolution. However, within that evolution are found many exciting new features. The net effect of these features can be summed up like this: The design of COM+ allows you to start simple and grow your application as dictated by user requirements. Extra transactional logic and complexity can be added if and when you need it or if you have specific user requirements that call for it. In the final analysis, COM+ enables you, the programmer, to concentrate on the business logic instead of the details of building a distributed, transacted infrastructure.

Now that the theoretical stage has been set for COM+, the next chapter shows you how to apply it.

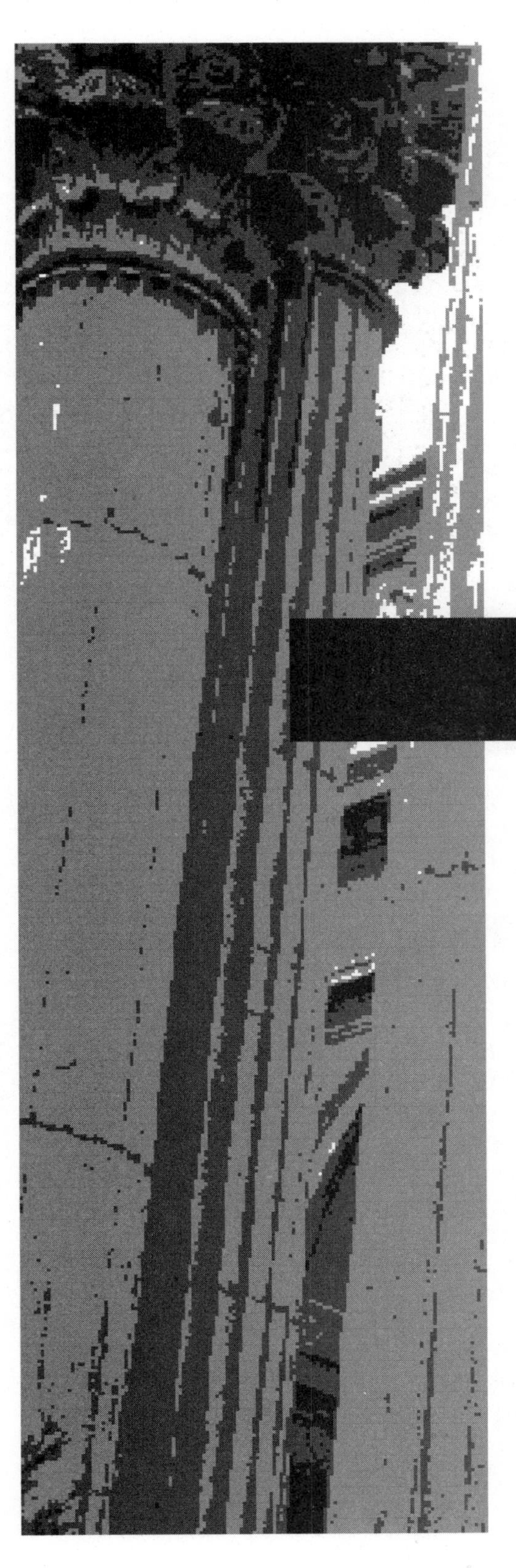

CHAPTER 15

Building a COM+ System

In the previous chapter, we discussed COM+ from a theoretical level, focusing on the various services that COM+ offers and how COM+ is able to provide those services to existing components with relatively little recoding, if any. In this chapter we are going to focus on the details of actually building a COM+ system from start to finish. We will look at each of the Component Services screens and then build a simple Enterprise+ application. Remember, COM+ services are available only inside Windows 2000. Because of the relative newness of this technology, however, you will also require the most recent platform SDK (Software Development Kit) in order to build several of the components within this chapter. If you subscribe to the Microsoft Developer Network (MSDN), you will have this SDK on CD. It is also available free to any developer from the MSDN Web site: http://msdn.microsoft.com/developer/sdk. Therefore, before proceeding, you should make sure that the most recent COM include and library files are installed from the latest Windows Platform SDK.

Sample Scenario

To begin our discussion we need to look first at the overall design of the system. We will be building a hotel reservation system that will accept reservations from around the world for all participating hotels. Customers will telephone to make their reservation, and the telephone operators will type the information into a C++ client application. The client application begs to be written with a Web front end so that customers can make their reservations directly, but to demonstrate the C++ view of things, we will provide a C++ executable instead. You could add Web functionality with relative ease once the system is complete, as you would need to change only the front-end portion of the system. This feature is part of what makes COM so powerful.

The client application is called **HotelReservation.exe**, and the user interface for this is shown in Figure 15-1. This is the only part of the system that is not running within Component Services. To use the system, the operator enters the reservation information and clicks the Reservation button. This in turn publishes an event to the COM+ event services. Subscribers to the event—specifically, the **ReservationSystem** and the **ReservationBilling** system—will pick up the event and perform various actions in response. The **ReservationSystem** component, for example, will call the **ReservationTransfer** component. To help you understand where code is executing, message boxes will be displayed from within each of the components, indicating that they processed the event. Note that displaying message boxes inside COM+ components is not a good idea for production

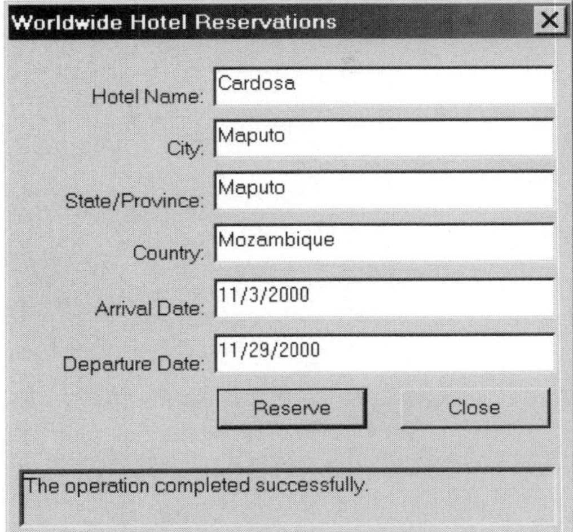

Our application's user interface

Figure 15-1.

systems because generally there is no one there to dismiss them, even in the unlikely event that the systems are configured to run under the identity of interactive user so that the dialogs will be seen. We make an exception to this rule to provide a simple mechanism for demonstrating where code is executing.

We will begin with an overview of the entire COM+ system. At first the system architecture, shown in Figure 15-2, appears rather complex, but there is actually very little code required. Most of the work in creating the system will be at the configuration level, configuring each of the components within Component Services. Each component within the system demonstrates one or more portions of the COM+ services. Each server module and the components it supports is described in the following.

HotelReservation.exe

This module doesn't implement any interfaces; rather, it is a publisher that initiates calls into the entire system. This module demonstrates how to call into the publish/subscribe event mechanism; although in reality, this is almost the same as the call would be without COM+, so there is very little to learn. As you will see, the details concerning much of the functionality in COM+ relate mostly to configuration rather than coding.

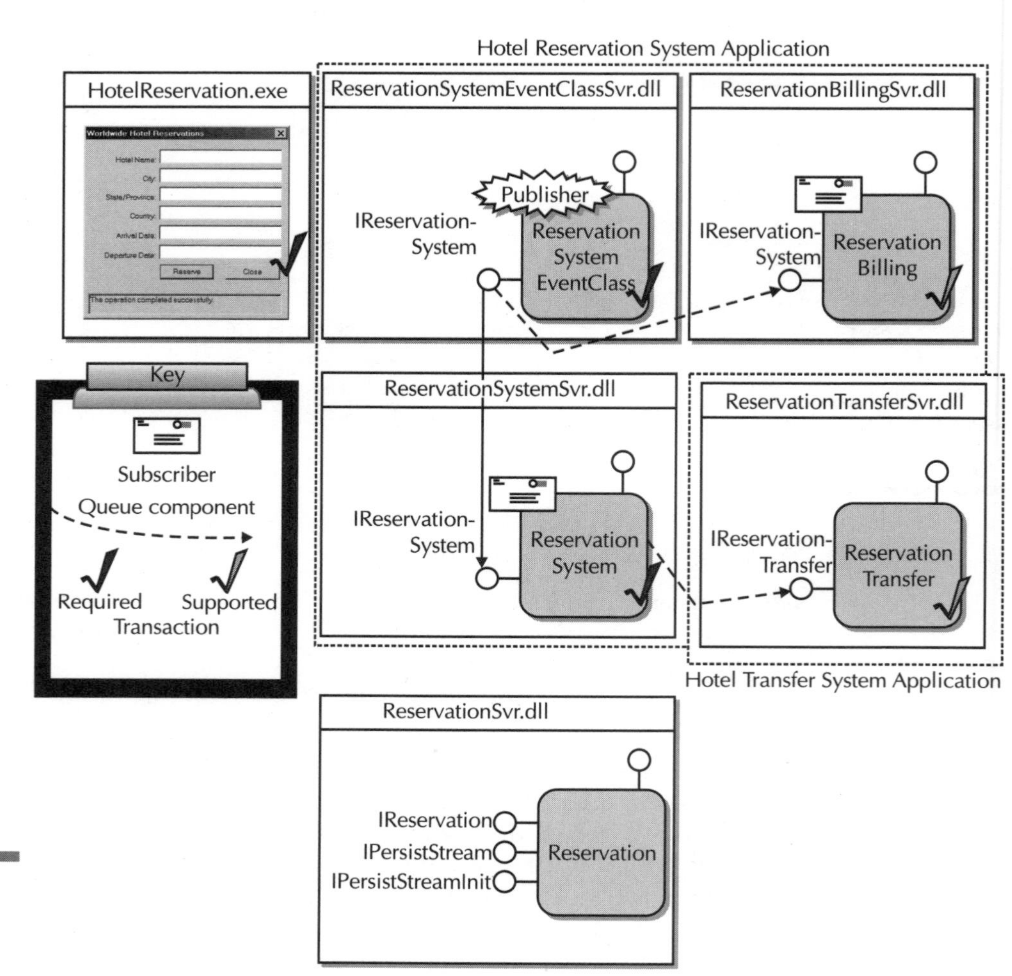

Figure 15-2. The hotel reservation system architecture

ReservationSystemEventClassSvr.dll

This module contains the **ReservationSystemEventClass** component. The component doesn't provide any implementation, but it is required in order to provide the link between a publisher and a subscriber. This component is required for registration purposes only, and it will never actually be instantiated. In building and configuring this component, we will look at how to set up the publish/subscribe mechanism.

Included in the server module is the definition of the **IReservationSystem** interface, which will be the published event interface to which other components can subscribe to receive COM+ event notifications.

ReservationSystemSvr.dll

Once we have finished setting up the publish/subscribe event services, it is time to take a look at configuring a component that actually subscribes to the system. **ReservationSystemSvr** demonstrates how to do this.

This module provides the bulk of the functionality in the system. If the Hotel Reservation System were a real system, this is where data would be persisted into a database. The component implemented in this module is **ReservationSystem**, and it supports the **IReservationSystem** interface, which gets called via the COM+ subscription mechanism.

This component makes a connection to the **ReservationTransfer** component, which is a queued component, so it will receive calls asynchronously.

ReservationTransferSvr.dll

This module implements the **ReservationTransfer** component. The purpose of this component in a real application would be to perform B2B operations with the hotel at which the reservation was made. For example, it would pass the reservation information to the hotel so that the room would actually be reserved for the customer.

This component implements the **IReservationTransfer** interface, which is a queueable interface. The result is that when placed inside component services, this interface will be marked as queued and the component will become a queued component, called asynchronously by the **ReservationSystem** component. The advantage of being queued is that it can be called when disconnected, so even if the link between the system and the hotel is down, the call will be recorded and then executed later when the link is restored.

ReservationBillingSvr.dll

The **ReservationBillingSvr.dll** module is used to simulate the billing portion of the system. This module implements the **ReservationBilling** component, which has the responsibility of billing the customer or hotel at which the customer makes a reservation. Like the **ReservationSystem** component, the **ReservationBilling** component is a subscriber to the

ReservationSystemEventClass. What distinguishes this subscription, however, is that it is also a queued component. Therefore, it will be called asynchronously, and the client—in this case **HotelReservation.exe**—will not have to wait while it performs any billing operations, such as calling into a credit card system.

ReservationSvr.dll

The last component within the system is the **Reservation** component. This component stores information about reservations, such as the hotel name, city, and country. Because the component will be passed as a parameter to queued components, it is required that the component will work inside MSMQ. Therefore, the component supports the **IPersistStream** interface.

Creating a Component That Can Be Persisted

The first step in building the Hotel Reservation System is to create a component that can store the information associated with a reservation—the **Reservation** component. To create the component, start a new ATL project named "ReservationSvr" and select DLL in step 1 of the wizard. Next add a component to the project called "Reservation." The default names and attributes do not need to be altered.

Change the **IReservation** interface to include the properties listed in the **ReservationSvr.idl** file below:

```
import "oaidl.idl";
import "ocidl.idl";

  typedef [uuid(80C2F7E0-43B4-4b0f-8FC8-6DB77373C49E),
    helpstring("Dispatch IDs for the IReservation interface")]
    enum RsIReservationDispatchId
  {
    rsIReservationDispatchIdHotelName = 1,
    rsIReservationDispatchIdCity,
    rsIReservationDispatchIdStateProvince,
    rsIReservationDispatchIdCountry,
    rsIReservationDispatchIdArrivalDate,
    rsIReservationDispatchIdDepartureDate,
    rsIReservationDispatchIdSummary,
  } RsIReservationDispatchId;

  [
    object,
```

```
  uuid(51F160C1-BE51-48F5-B496-29E87962C497),
  dual,
  oleautomation,
  helpstring("IReservation Interface"),
  pointer_default(unique)
]
interface IReservation : IDispatch
{
  [propget, id(rsIReservationDispatchIdHotelName),
    helpstring("The name of the hotel")]
    HRESULT HotelName([out, retval] BSTR *pHotelName);
  [propput, id(rsIReservationDispatchIdHotelName),
    helpstring("The name of the hotel")]
    HRESULT HotelName([in] BSTR HotelName);

  [propget, id(rsIReservationDispatchIdCity),
    helpstring("The city in which the hotel is located")]
    HRESULT City([out, retval] BSTR *pCity);
  [propput, id(rsIReservationDispatchIdCity),
    helpstring("The city in which the hotel is located")]
    HRESULT City([in] BSTR City);

  [propget, id(rsIReservationDispatchIdStateProvince),
    helpstring("The state in which the hotel is located")]
    HRESULT StateProvince([out, retval] BSTR *pStateProvince);
  [propput, id(rsIReservationDispatchIdStateProvince),
    helpstring("The state in which the hotel is located")]
    HRESULT StateProvince([in] BSTR StateProvince);

  [propget, id(rsIReservationDispatchIdCountry),
    helpstring("The country in which the hotel is located")]
    HRESULT Country([out, retval] BSTR *pCountry);
  [propput, id(rsIReservationDispatchIdCountry),
    helpstring("The country in which the hotel is located")]
    HRESULT Country([in] BSTR Country);

  [propget, id(rsIReservationDispatchIdArrivalDate),
    helpstring("The date the guest will arrive at the hotel")]
    HRESULT ArrivalDate([out, retval] BSTR *pArrivalDate);
  [propput, id(rsIReservationDispatchIdArrivalDate),
    helpstring("The date the guest will arrive at the hotel")]
    HRESULT ArrivalDate([in] BSTR ArrivalDate);

  [propget, id(rsIReservationDispatchIdDepartureDate),
    helpstring("The date the guest will leave the hotel")]
```

```
      HRESULT DepartureDate([out, retval] BSTR *pDepartureDate);
    [propput, id(rsIReservationDispatchIdDepartureDate),
      helpstring("The date the guest will leave the hotel")]
      HRESULT DepartureDate([in] BSTR DepartureDate);

    [propget, id(rsIReservationDispatchIdSummary),
      helpstring("Retrieves a summary of the reservation details")]
      HRESULT Summary([out, retval] BSTR *pSummary);

  };

[
  uuid(35D41D98-6292-4E97-9D76-D844271C95D1),
  version(1.0),
  helpstring("ReservationSvr 1.0 Type Library")
]
library RESERVATIONSVRLib
{
  importlib("stdole32.tlb");
  importlib("stdole2.tlb");

  [
    uuid(B8EDD5E0-0BA2-4C16-B30D-DA6EA5679E49),
    helpstring("Reservation Class")
  ]
  coclass Reservation
  {
    [default] interface IReservation;
  };

};
```

To implement the properties, we will use a macro. So, rather than using the wizard to add each property, simply type in the information (assuming you haven't downloaded the files, that is). Note also the addition of the dispatch ID enumeration. We will use this shortly as part of the persistence code.

The decision to use macros for the implementation is based on the fact that each property is essentially generic. A listing of the **Reservation.h** file is provided below:

```
// Reservation.h : Declaration of the CReservation

#ifndef __RESERVATION_H_
#define __RESERVATION_H_
```

```
#include "resource.h"       // main symbols

#define PROPERTY_IMPL(PropertyName)                        \
  CComBSTR m_##PropertyName;                               \
  STDMETHODIMP get_##PropertyName(                         \
    BSTR *p##PropertyName)                                 \
  {                                                        \
    m_##PropertyName.CopyTo( p##PropertyName ) ;           \
    return S_OK;                                           \
  }                                                        \
  STDMETHODIMP put_##PropertyName(                         \
    BSTR PropertyName)                                     \
  {                                                        \
      m_##PropertyName = ##PropertyName;                   \
      return S_OK;                                         \
  }


/////////////////////////////////////////////////////////////////////////////
// CReservation
class ATL_NO_VTABLE CReservation :
  public CComObjectRootEx<CComSingleThreadModel>,
  public CComCoClass<CReservation, &CLSID_Reservation>,
  public IDispatchImpl<IReservation, &IID_IReservation,
    &LIBID_RESERVATIONSVRLib>,
  public IPersistStreamInitImpl<CReservation>
{
public:
  CReservation()
  {
  }
  ~CReservation()
  {
  }

DECLARE_REGISTRY_RESOURCEID(IDR_RESERVATION)

DECLARE_PROTECT_FINAL_CONSTRUCT()

BEGIN_COM_MAP(CReservation)
  COM_INTERFACE_ENTRY(IReservation)
  COM_INTERFACE_ENTRY(IPersistStreamInit)
  COM_INTERFACE_ENTRY2(IPersistStream, IPersistStreamInit)
  COM_INTERFACE_ENTRY(IDispatch)
```

15

```
  END_COM_MAP()

  BEGIN_PROP_MAP(CReservation)
    PROP_ENTRY( "HotelName", rsIReservationDispatchIdHotelName,
      __uuidof(Reservation) )
    PROP_ENTRY( "City", rsIReservationDispatchIdCity,
      __uuidof(Reservation) )
    PROP_ENTRY( "StateProvince", rsIReservationDispatchIdStateProvince,
      __uuidof(Reservation) )
    PROP_ENTRY( "Country", rsIReservationDispatchIdCountry,
      __uuidof(Reservation) )
    PROP_ENTRY( "ArrivalDate", rsIReservationDispatchIdArrivalDate,
      __uuidof(Reservation) )
    PROP_ENTRY( "DepartureDate", rsIReservationDispatchIdDepartureDate,
      __uuidof(Reservation) )
  END_PROP_MAP()

  // IReservation
  public:
    PROPERTY_IMPL(HotelName)
    PROPERTY_IMPL(City)
    PROPERTY_IMPL(StateProvince)
    PROPERTY_IMPL(Country)
    PROPERTY_IMPL(ArrivalDate)
    PROPERTY_IMPL(DepartureDate)
    STDMETHODIMP get_Summary(/*[out, retval]*/ BSTR* pSummary)
    {
      USES_CONVERSION;
      CComBSTR summary;
      summary+=L"Reservation Summary Details:";
      (summary+=L"\n  Hotel Name:      ") += m_HotelName;
      (summary+=L"\n  City:            ") += m_City;
      (summary+=L"\n  StateProvince:   ") += m_StateProvince;
      (summary+=L"\n  Country:         ") += m_Country;
      (summary+=L"\n  ArrivalDate:     ") += m_ArrivalDate;
      (summary+=L"\n  DepartureDate:   ") += m_DepartureDate;

      *pSummary = summary.Detach();
      return S_OK;
    }

  // Required for IPersistStreamInit
  VARIANT_BOOL m_bRequiresSave;
};

#endif //__RESERVATION_H_
```

Included in the macro is a member variable that will store the data string associated with each property. Since all the implementation code is provided within the header file, the **Reservation.cpp** file can be removed from the project.

There is one distinguishing characteristic about this component's implementation that requires discussion. Notice that in addition to each of the implemented properties, the **IPersistStreamInitImpl** class has been added to the list of classes from which **CReservation** is derived. In order for a component to be placed into a message with MSMQ, it requires implementation of the **IPersistStream**. To provide this functionality the component is derived from **IPersistStreamInitImpl**, which implements **IPersistStreamInit**. **IPersistStreamInit** contains all the methods on **IPersistStream** in addition to an **InitNew( )** method. In other words, **IPersistStreamInit** is a superset of the functions in **IPersistStream**. At this point it may be somewhat surprising that MSMQ is required. However, as you will see later in the chapter, MSMQ is used by COM+ to implement queued components, and in the hotel reservation sample, the **Reservation** component will be passed as a parameter to queued components.

To complete the **IPersistStreamInitImpl** implementation, we must indicate what needs to be persisted. This is done using the PROPERTY MAP and the **PROP_ ENTRY** macro. The **PROP_ENTRY** macro uses dispatch IDs to access the properties and methods to be persisted. This is where we use the dispatch ID enumeration declared inside the IDL. **PROP_DATA_ENTRY** could potentially be a preferable macro, as it does not require the use of the dispatch interface; however, as of ATL 3.0, this macro does not support **BSTR**s for some reason. Also note that **IPersistStreamInitImpl** requires that you declare an **m_bRequiresSave** Boolean variable.

One last change is an update to the COM MAP to indicate the newly supported interfaces. First, **IPersistStreamInit** is added. Next, the **COM_INTERFACE_ENTRY2** macro is used. This indicates that the **IPersistStream** macro is also supported because it is a subset of the **IPersistStreamInit** functionality. This completes the **Reservation** component. To test it, we must create the **HotelReservation.exe** client.

Building the HotelReservation.exe Client

The key program that starts on our system is the **HotelReservation.exe** application. This application is used by telephone operators to enter reservation information for customers. To build the application, start a new ATL project with the name "HotelReservation." Select executable for the application type. After creating the project, use the ATL Object Wizard to add a dialog to the project (available from the miscellaneous category). For the dialog name, use "ReservationForm," and click the OK button. Edit the dialog resource, **IDD_RESERVATIONFORM**, and add the edit and label controls, as shown in Figure 15-1. Each of the edit controls should be assigned ID names as follows: **IDC_HOTELNAME**, **IDC_CITY**, **IDC_STATE_PROVINCE**, **IDC_COUNTRY**, **IDC_ARRIVALDATE**, and **IDC_DEPARTUREDATE**. In addition, the button IDs should be changed to **IDRESERVE** and **IDCLOSE**. The status bar at the bottom of the dialog should be given the ID **IDC_STATUS**. A listing of the **ReservationForm.h** file is shown below:

```
// ReservationForm.h : Declaration of the CReservationForm

#ifndef __RESERVATIONFORM_H_
#define __RESERVATIONFORM_H_

#include "resource.h"       // main symbols
#include <atlhost.h>

#import "..\ReservationSvr\ReservationSvr.dll" no_namespace \
  raw_interfaces_only, raw_native_types

/////////////////////////////////////////////////////////////////////////////
// CReservationForm
class CReservationForm :
  public CAxDialogImpl<CReservationForm>
{
public:
  CReservationForm()
  {
  }

  ~CReservationForm()
  {
  }

  enum { IDD = IDD_RESERVATIONFORM };

BEGIN_MSG_MAP(CReservationForm)
  MESSAGE_HANDLER(WM_INITDIALOG, OnInitDialog)
  COMMAND_ID_HANDLER(IDRESERVE, OnReserve)
  COMMAND_ID_HANDLER(IDCLOSE, OnClose)
END_MSG_MAP()

////////////////////////
```

```
// Windows Messages
  LRESULT OnInitDialog(UINT uMsg,
    WPARAM wParam, LPARAM lParam, BOOL& bHandled);
  LRESULT OnReserve(WORD wNotifyCode,
    WORD wID, HWND hWndCtl, BOOL& bHandled);
  LRESULT OnClose(WORD wNotifyCode,
    WORD wID, HWND hWndCtl, BOOL& bHandled);

//////////////////////////
// Helper Functions
  // Show the current status of the system.
  void ShowStatus(HRESULT hr);

};

#endif //__RESERVATIONFORM_H_
```

The required changes are highlighted in bold. Notice the **#import** of the **ReservationSvr.dll** at the top of the file. This uses the **no_namespace**, **raw_interfaces_only**, and **raw_native_types** attributes. The last two parameters are so that only the raw versions of the interfaces are imported. Because this client is an ATL client, we can use the ATL smart pointer **CComPtr** rather than the **_com_ptr_t** versions that are provided by default when **raw_interfaces_only** and **raw_native_types** are not used.

The implementation of the **CReservationForm is found in ReservationForm.cpp**, and it, too, requires little explanation.

```
// ReservationForm.cpp : Implementation of CReservationForm
#include "stdafx.h"
#include "ReservationForm.h"

/////////////////////////////////////////////////////////////////////
// CReservationForm
void CReservationForm::ShowStatus(HRESULT hr)
{
  BOOL success;
  _com_error status(hr);

  success = SetDlgItemText(IDC_STATUS, status.ErrorMessage());

  ATLASSERT(success);

}
```

```
//////////////////////////////////////////////////////////////////////
// Windows Messages
LRESULT CReservationForm::OnInitDialog(
  UINT uMsg, WPARAM wParam, LPARAM lParam, BOOL& bHandled)
{
  HRESULT hr = S_OK;

  ShowStatus(hr);
  return 1;  // Let the system set the focus
}

LRESULT CReservationForm::OnReserve(WORD wNotifyCode,
  WORD wID, HWND hWndCtl, BOOL& bHandled)
{
  USES_CONVERSION;
  HRESULT hr = S_OK;
  CComBSTR property = L"";
  CComPtr<IReservation> reservation;
  hr = reservation.CoCreateInstance(__uuidof(Reservation));

  ATLTRACE(_T("Reserve Hotel at: \n"));
  if(SUCCEEDED(hr))
  {
    GetDlgItemText(IDC_HOTELNAME, property.m_str);
    ATLTRACE(_T("  Hotel Name = %s\n"), OLE2T(property));
    hr = reservation->put_HotelName(property.Detach());
  }

  if(SUCCEEDED(hr))
  {
    GetDlgItemText(IDC_CITY, property.m_str);
    ATLTRACE(_T("  City = %s\n"), OLE2T(property));
    hr = reservation->put_City(property.Detach());
  }

  if(SUCCEEDED(hr))
  {
    GetDlgItemText(IDC_STATE_PROVINCE, property.m_str);
    ATLTRACE(_T("  State\\Province = %s\n"), OLE2T(property));
    hr = reservation->put_StateProvince(property.Detach());
  }

  if(SUCCEEDED(hr))
  {
    GetDlgItemText(IDC_COUNTRY, property.m_str);
    ATLTRACE(_T("  Country = %s\n"), OLE2T(property));
```

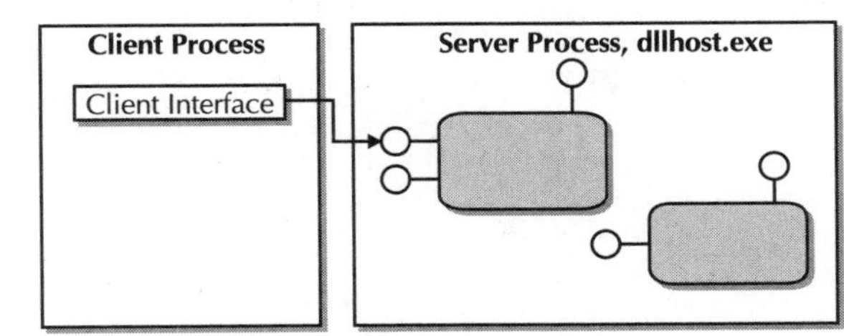

Application configured as a server
Figure 15-3.

Library Applications

COM+ library applications are activated in the client's process.

Library applications are activated in the client's process. This provides a significant performance advantage to the application over server applications while providing access to most COM+ services. Since a library application's client must be running on the same machine as its components, a library application does not support remote access. Library applications also do not support COM+ queued components or connection pooling. User security settings for library applications also do not apply since the security will be determined by the security context of the client application. Role-based security can still be used, however.

Components configured in a library application can be activated from a server application. Use this deployment model if you will have multiple server applications that will be using the same set of components. Instead of configuring the components multiple times in all of the different server applications, simply create one library application and configure the components once. As you can see from Figure 15-4, **dllhost.exe** is not invoked for a library application.

Creating a COM+ Application

Now that you understand the various types of COM+ applications, it is time to look at how to create them. There are currently two options for performing this operation: use the Component Services application, or program for the COM+ administration interfaces. We will concentrate on configuring the component with Component Services, which essentially wraps the administration interfaces. If you're doing extensive work with configured components, you may find that a configuration script accessing the administrative interfaces will make your work more efficient.

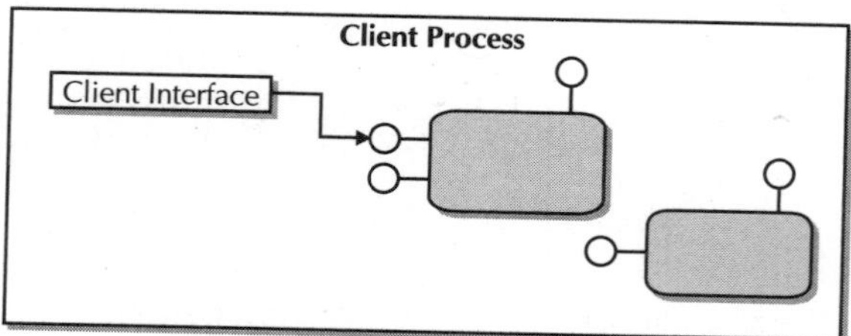

Application configured as a library
Figure 15-4.

To begin, first open Component Services (Start | Settings | Control Panel | Administrative Tools | Component Services). Next browse into the Component Services, expanding Computers, My Computer, and finally, COM+ Applications. You will notice that several COM+ applications have been created for you by Windows 2000, including support for IIS (Internet Information Services, the Microsoft Internet server application), assuming it has been installed. Any other applications that you have installed that use COM+ or MTS will also be listed here.

To create a new application, select the COM+ Applications node. Next, right-click on this same node and select New | Application, as shown in Figure 15-5. New Application can also be accessed from the Action | Application | New menu. This will start the COM Application Install Wizard.

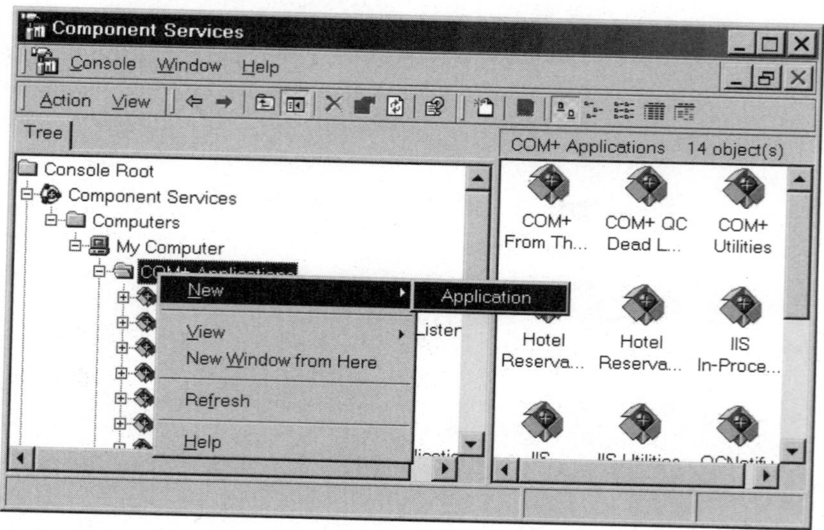

Creating a new COM+ application
Figure 15-5.

After you're greeted with the wizard's welcome screen (Install Wizard, step 1), you will be prompted either to install a prebuilt application or create an empty application, as shown in Figure 15-6.

Select "Create an empty application." You would use the "Install pre-built application(s)" option if you had an existing application installation package that was already created by exporting an existing configuration from Component Services. At this point you will be prompted for the name of the new applications along with the activation type. For the name of the application, enter **Hotel Reservation System**, and verify that the "Server application" option is selected, as shown in Figure 15-7. The majority of components will be configured in this server application, and they will access such services as queued components and object pooling, which are not available from a library application, as already mentioned.

The next dialog (Figure 15-8) enables you to configure the security settings under which your application will run. Select "Interactive user – the current logged on user" for now, as this will aid in debugging and interacting with the application just as it does when configuring a component for DCOM. By default, your server components will have access to resources based on this configuration setting. If the provided account does not have the appropriate privilege to utilize a resource, access by the application's components will be

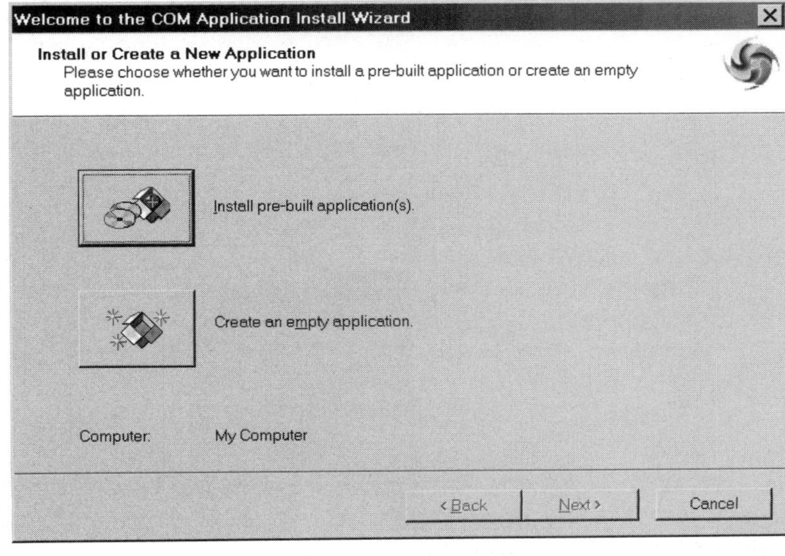

COM Application Install Wizard, step 2—Install or Create a New Application

Figure 15-6.

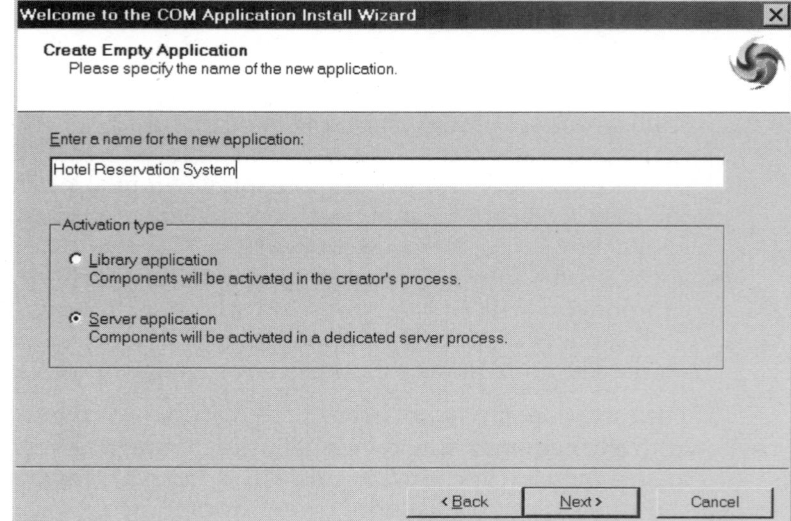

COM Application Wizard, step 3—Create Empty Application
Figure 15-7.

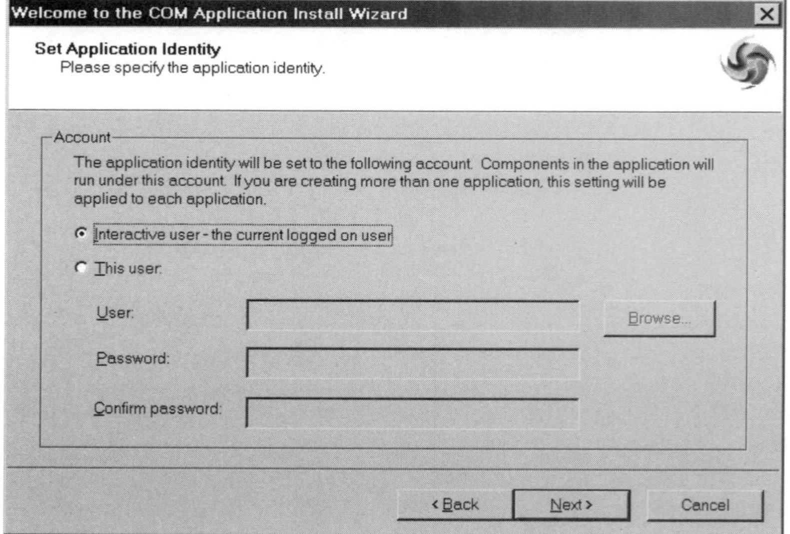

COM Application Install Wizard, step 4—Set Application Identity
Figure 15-8.

denied. If you select "Interactive user," and no user is currently signed on to the system, the component will not be allowed to run. Or if there is an interactive user and the component starts and the user signs off, the application will promptly end as well. Therefore, a setting of "Interactive user" is practical only for debugging and initial testing of new configurations.

At this point the wizard is finished. You can inspect its handiwork by browsing to the application in Component Services and selecting the properties context menu.

Configuring a COM+ Application

The properties dialog (displayed by right-clicking on the newly created applications and selecting properties) exposes the attributes that you or the system administrator can configure. Some of these attributes can be configured and will function independently of the component. However, some of them will require coordination of the component itself and therefore should always be dictated by you, the component developer. Six different application property tabs are available: General, Security, Activation, Identity, Queuing, and Advanced. Each of these is discussed below.

Application Properties, General Tab

In addition to the application name configured when we ran the wizard, in the General tab, you will see a Description field and an Application ID GUID (Figure 15-9). The GUID was generated by the Component Services New Application Wizard and is important when configuring for debugging, which is described later in the chapter.

Application Properties, Security Tab

The Security tab (Figure 15-10) allows an administrator to configure security for your application. Note that in addition to these settings, you can make explicit security checks via the **IObjectContext::IsCallerInRole( )** method, which we will cover later in the chapter. This technique should be required only if the default security configuration is not sufficient.

If "Enforce access checks for this application" is checked, COM+ will check the security of the caller, based on the current configuration. During normal development and debugging it can be useful to disable security checks, as was the case when configuring DCOM.

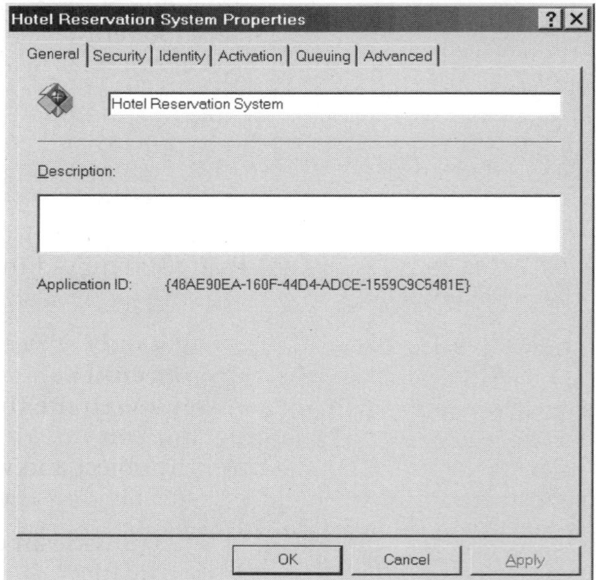

Application properties, General tab

Figure 15-9.

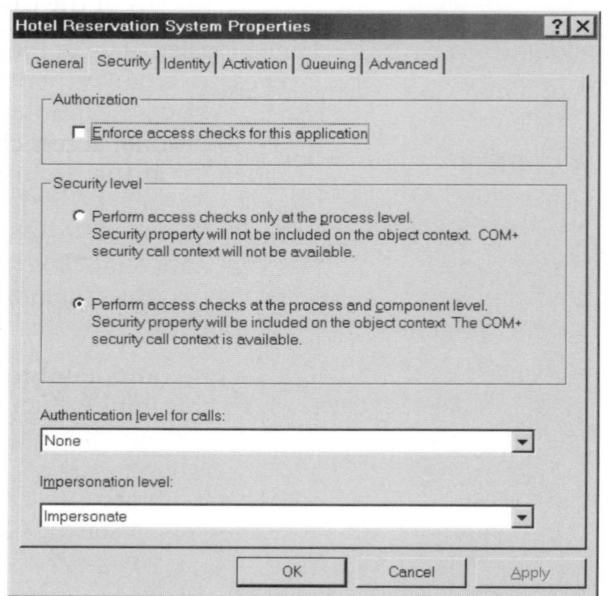

Application properties, Security tab

Figure 15-10.

The security level determines whether security will be done only at the process level or for each component. If "Perform access checks only at the process level" is selected, all component-level security is disabled and call security context information will not be provided. If process-level security is sufficient, select this option.

If "Perform access checks at the process and component level" is selected, access checking will be done for each method call. In addition, security information will be included in the object context and call context, and an appropriate or new object context may be chosen based on security attributes. Note that this setting is required to implement security checking for library applications since library applications run in their caller's process.

Let's say you wanted to insure that only authorized callers were allowed to write journal entries using a **Journal** component if, for example, the log included some traffic data for a Web site that earned users points in a marketing bonus awards program. You wouldn't want an unauthorized call because someone may discover the object and write a spoofing component to give himself unearned points. This kind of security can be easily configured.

The remaining settings on this tab provide an exact match to those already discussed in Chapter 12. "Authentication level for calls" allows you to configure the level of security required. Make sure that you understand your security requirements, because higher authentication levels increase the overhead on each call. The levels determine how frequently and in exactly what manner the security credentials of the caller will be checked.

A setting of None allows any caller that is otherwise authenticated to access the application's components without authentication. A setting of Connect authenticates the caller for every connection to a component, but after the connection is made, no additional access checks will be made. A setting of Call will authenticate the user at the beginning of each call. A setting of Packet will authenticate each packet that is required to make the call. The Packet Integrity setting authenticates each packet and validates the packet data to insure that it has not changed. The Packet Privacy setting authenticates and encrypts the packets, including the data as well as the sender's security identification.

Impersonation allows the server component to assume the client's security identity. The degree to which this impersonation takes place is determined by the "Impersonation level" setting. This determines what kind of access the server will provide to the resources it uses. Impersonation level applies only to server applications since library applications automatically assume the identity of the hosting process. A setting of Anonymous is not fully supported but is intended to indicate that the server can impersonate the client identity but will not use any additional security details of the client. The server application will not be able to gain access to protected resources for which additional client security details are required. The Identity setting allows the server application to impersonate the client for purposes of access checks and therefore grants the server access to local protected resources that the client has rights to access. A setting of Impersonate provides similar access to Identity but allows only the server to access resources using the client's access on the client machine or resources local to the server machine. The Delegate setting allows the impersonation to take place for any local or remote resource.

Application Properties, Activation and Identity Tabs

The Activation and Identity tabs display the values selected while using the wizard and allow you to change them. The tabs match the wizard screens, so refer to Figure 15-7 and Figure 15-8 to view the corresponding screens.

Application Properties, Queuing Tab

The Queuing tab is used to configure an application for queued components. Since library applications do not support queued components, all controls on this tab will be disabled. As shown in Figure 15-11,there are two check boxes. The first check box, Queued, designates that the applications can contain queued components. Therefore, components within the application can be instantiated using the queue moniker. The second check box, Listen, indicates that the queued component can be processed immediately. The result is that as soon as a queued component message is written to MSMQ , the COM+ application will begin processing the message. If Listen is not checked, the message will remain in the queue until the application is reconfigured with this item checked and the application is restarted.

For this application, select both the Queued and Listen check boxes.

Application Properties, Advanced Tab

On the Advanced tab, shown in Figure 15-12, Server Process Shutdown gives the administrator some control over how the application will shut down when all object references for the application are released. "Leave running when idle" keeps the server component running and ready for use even when no clients are accessing the component. This decreases the startup time required for future method calls into the component. The trade-off is that server resources will never be freed. "Minutes until idle shutdown" is similar to leaving the application running but allows you to

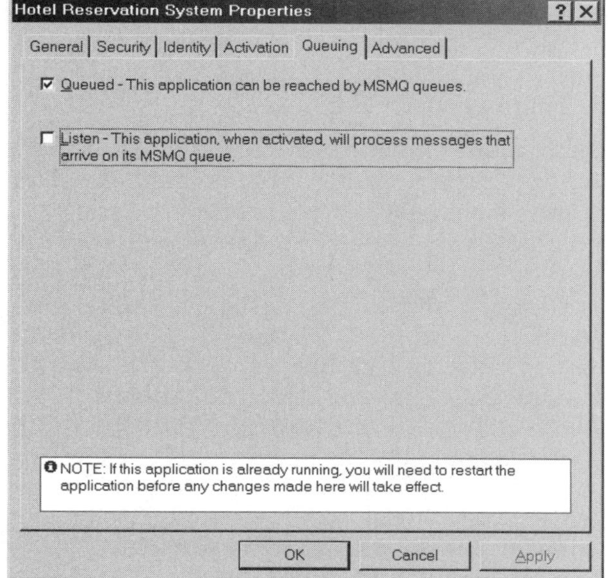

Figure 15-11. Application properties, Queuing tab

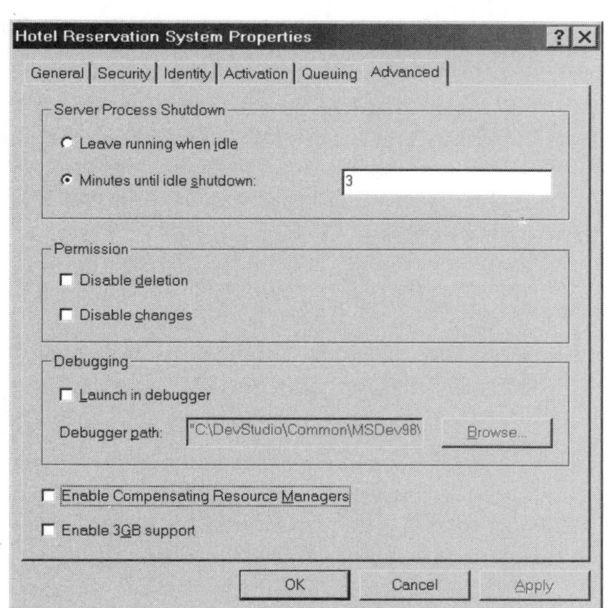

Figure 15-12. Application properties, Advanced tab

specify a number of minutes. This assumes that once a method call is made, additional method calls will be made soon after, and that if not, it is better to free up the server resources for other purposes. Select "Leave running when idle" for debugging purposes, because it ensures that the application does not unload unexpectedly.

Permission settings control access to configuration changes. "Disable deletion" prevents unauthorized or accidental removal of the configured application. "Disable changes" prevents unauthorized or accidental changes to the configured application. To observe the effect of the "Disable changes" setting, select it and then click the OK button. Now reopen the properties dialog and observe that all except the permission options are disabled. To reenable them, uncheck the check box. Obviously, this doesn't provide much of a security mechanism, but it reduces the chance that an administrator would modify your application's settings inadvertently because of the extra steps involved to make any changes. Although this provides weak security, we highly recommend using this setting, especially if you're writing an install script. The ability to allow even an administrator to configure your system without knowledge of the system opens up a significant possibility for error, and this setting can discourage this.

The Debugging area provides server-side debugging options. "Launch in debugger" will launch the configured debugger when a client first activates the server application. Additional debugging options and approaches are described in detail later in the chapter.

The "Enable Compensating Resource Managers" setting tells COM+ to call the Compensating Resource Manager (CRM) components for this application. A CRM implements CRM Worker and Compensator objects. COM+ will call the Compensator during the commit phase of transactions for this application if this option is enabled. CRMs were covered in the previous chapter.

Last, "Enable 3GB support" allows the component to access the extended memory services of Windows 2000.

This completes a look at the various application options. Each setting is fairly simple on its own, but using the wrong setting can result in some hard-to-find errors because they can sometimes seem unrelated to the application's settings.

The next items that require configuration are the components that will be placed inside the application. Before you can do this, you will have to create the component. The remaining portion of the chapter will focus on creating COM+ components and then configuring them with Component Services.

Utilizing the COM+ Event Services

The first service that we will cover in depth is the event service. You will recall from the previous chapter that this service enables the loose coupling of event publishers and event subscribers. In this section we will build and configure the publish and subscribe mechanism for the **ReservationSystem** component.

Creating the Event Class

The key component that connects the publisher with the subscriber is the *event class*. The event class defines the set of interfaces to which a publisher can report events and a subscriber can register to monitor those same events. The key to writing an event class is, first, the declaration of the component within the type library, including the interfaces that it will support. Second, the module must implement the self-registration functions that Component Services can call into when registering the component.

To create the server module, start a new project with the name **ReservationSystemEventClassSvr**. The module should be a DLL without any of the other wizard options selected. Now add a new component to the module using the ATL Object Wizard. Name the component **ReservationSystemEventClass**. Because this class will never be instantiated, most of the attributes for this component can be ignored. However, the interface supported by this component will be "IReservationSystem" rather than the default, "IReservationSystemEventClass," so modify that on the names tab before clicking OK.

Because this component will never be instantiated, it does not actually require any implementation code. However, to use ATL's registration mechanism, it still requires an implementation class. A listing of the **ReservationSystemEventClass.h** file is shown in the following listing:

```
// ReservationSystemEventClass.h :
// Declaration of the CReservationSystemEventClass

#ifndef __RESERVATIONSYSTEMEVENTCLASS_H_
#define __RESERVATIONSYSTEMEVENTCLASS_H_

#include "resource.h"       // main symbols
```

```
////////////////////////////////////////////////////////////////////////////
// CReservationSystemEventClass
class ATL_NO_VTABLE CReservationSystemEventClass :
  public CComObjectRootEx<CComMultiThreadModel>,
  public CComCoClass<CReservationSystemEventClass,
    &CLSID_ReservationSystemEventClass>
// REM  public IDispatchImpl<IReservationSystem,
// REM    &IID_IReservationSystem,
// REM    &LIBID_RESERVATIONSYSTEMEVENTCLASSSVRLib>,
{
public:
     CReservationSystemEventClass()
  {
  }

DECLARE_REGISTRY_RESOURCEID(IDR_RESERVATIONSYSTEMEVENTCLASS)

// REM DECLARE_PROTECT_FINAL_CONSTRUCT()

BEGIN_COM_MAP(CReservationSystemEventClass)
// REM    COM_INTERFACE_ENTRY(IReservationSystem)
// REM    COM_INTERFACE_ENTRY(IDispatch)
END_COM_MAP()

};

#endif //__RESERVATIONSYSTEMEVENTCLASS_H_
```

Note that rather than having to add code to the class, code has instead been commented out (using // REM) because it is no longer needed.

Because there are no member functions within the class, the **ReservationSystemEventClass.cpp** file can be removed from the project.

In our sample, only one method—**Reserve( )**—is required on the interface. The **Reserve( )** method, however, passes an **IReservation** interface, defined inside **ReservationSvr.idl**, as a parameter. Therefore, this will require you to import the **ReservationSvr.idl** file into the **ReservationSystemEvent-ClassSvr.idl** file. Although the full path to the file could be provided, two other files, **ReservationSvr.h** and **ReservationSvr.tlb**, are also required, so it is easier to add the **ReservationSvr** directory to the include path of the project. Open the settings for the project and set the "Additional include directories" edit box to **..\ReservationSvr** on both the C++ and MIDL tabs. For the C++ tab, you will need to select Preprocessor in the category drop-down to view this option.

Once you have changed the include paths, you are ready to import the **ReservationSvr.idl** file and add the **Reserve( )** method to the interface. A listing of the changes to **ReservationSystemEventClassSvr.idl** are highlighted below:

```
import "oaidl.idl";
import "ocidl.idl";
import "ReservationSvr.idl";

  [
    object,
    uuid(3B6314D4-456D-4977-BE08-742A795B8A28),
    dual,
    helpstring("IReservationSystem Interface"),
    pointer_default(unique)
  ]
  interface IReservationSystem : IDispatch
{
    [id(1), helpstring("Create the reservation in the system.")]
      HRESULT Reserve([in] IReservation* reservation);
  };


[
  uuid(83F6FE0D-5CF6-4F2C-8E1C-8303D97D7850),
  version(1.0),
  helpstring("ReservationSystemEventClassSvr 1.0 Type Library")
]
library RESERVATIONSYSTEMEVENTCLASSSVRLib
{
  importlib("stdole32.tlb");
  importlib("stdole2.tlb");

  interface IReservation;

  [
    uuid(15FE644E-D07B-4040-A98B-B6C1F2FDB6C7),
          helpstring("ReservationSystemEventClass Class")
  ]
     coclass ReservationSystemEventClass
  {
          [default] interface IReservationSystem;
  };

};
```

Note that the inclusion of the **IReservation** declaration in the **library** statement is entirely optional. It makes the interface available to clients of the **ReservationSystemEventClass** without having to import **ReservationSvr.dll** in addition to **ReservationSystemEvent-ClassSvr.dll**. If a client includes both, using the **#import** statement and then an accompanying **exclude("IReservation")** will be required.

At this point, the component is complete and can be compiled. The next step is to configure it within Component Services.

Adding a Component to Component Services

Now that we have created the event class, it is time to add it to Component Services. To do this, return to the Hotel Reservation System application node created in the last section and drill down to the Components node. Select either Action | New | Component, or right-click and select New | Component. This will bring up the COM Component Install Wizard.

Click Next to get past the welcome screen. You'll see the Import or Install a Component screen. As is clear from Figure 15-13, this screen presents three options for installing a component.

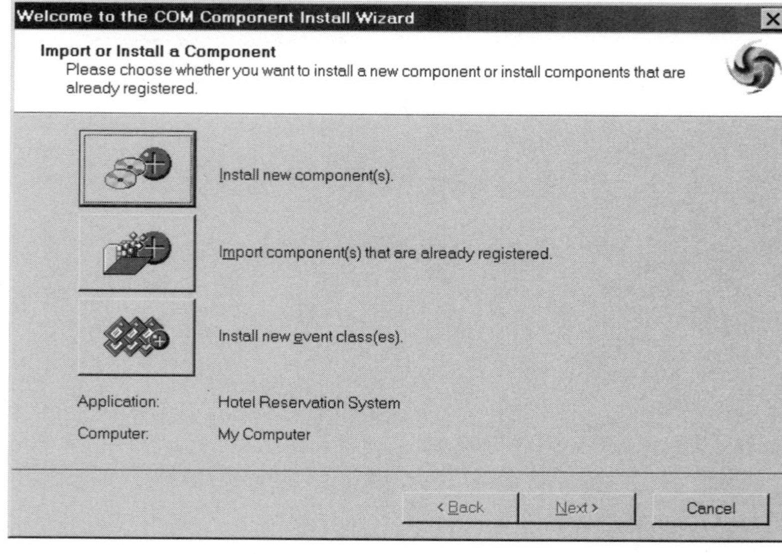

Component Install Wizard—Import or Install a Component

Figure 15-13.

Since we are in the process of installing the event class, "Install new event class(es)" is obviously the option you want to select. But before moving on, let's consider the other options. "Install new component(s)" is probably the most common choice for a developer. Selecting this option allows you to insert a component into COM+ so that it can run within the COM+ environment and capitalize on the various facilities that COM+ provides. The middle option, "Import component(s) that are already registered," allows you to select a component from the list of COM components already installed on the machine. In contrast, the previous two options will cause a file open dialog to appear, which will enable you to browse for the module that contains the event class or component that you wish to install. After selecting the module or the previously registered component, you will be presented with the Files to Install dialog shown in Figure 15-14.

Using the Add button, you can insert additional components along with those already selected. To complete the wizard, click Next and then Finish.

Configuring an Event Class Inside Component Services

Now that we have added the event class to Component Services, we need to configure the specific settings. Let's look at two of the property tabs. The

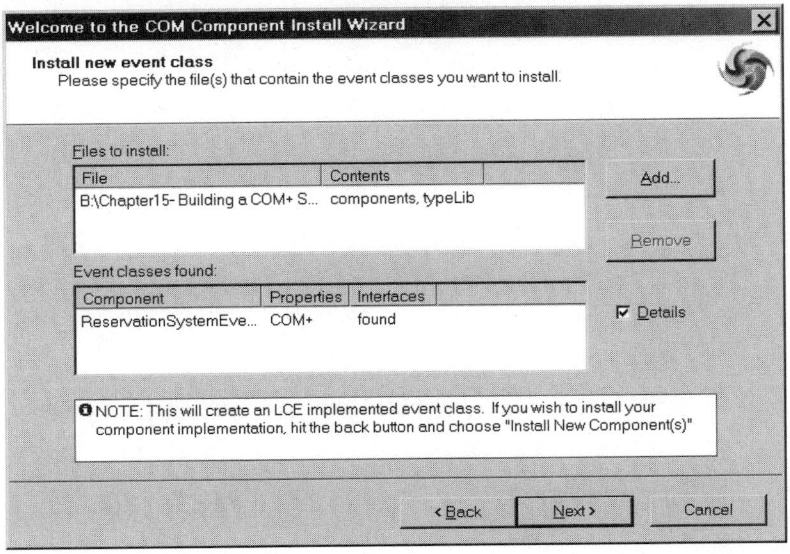

Component Install Wizard—Files to Install
Figure 15-14.

first tab is the General tab shown in Figure 15-15. As with the application properties, the General tab for the component properties provides a text box where you can enter a description of the component.

The tab that we are most interested in with regard to the event class is the Advanced tab, shown in Figure 15-16. "Queuing exception class" is the means for handling MSMQ problems when queued components are involved. We will defer our discussion of this until later in the chapter. The remaining settings, "Fire in parallel," "Allow in-process subscribers," and "Publisher ID," are specific to the event class configuration, however.

"Fire in parallel" allows multiple subscribers to be called simultaneously rather than synchronously. With this setting selected, the second subscriber will not necessarily have to wait for the first subscriber to complete before the second subscriber is invoked. This can provide some performance improvements, but it should not be selected if the order in which subscribers process messages is significant. This is not a requirement in our system, so you may check this setting.

"Allow in-process subscribers" is an obvious choice if you have control over all the subscribers and you are not concerned that some will misbehave if they are allowed to run within the same process space. If, however, this is

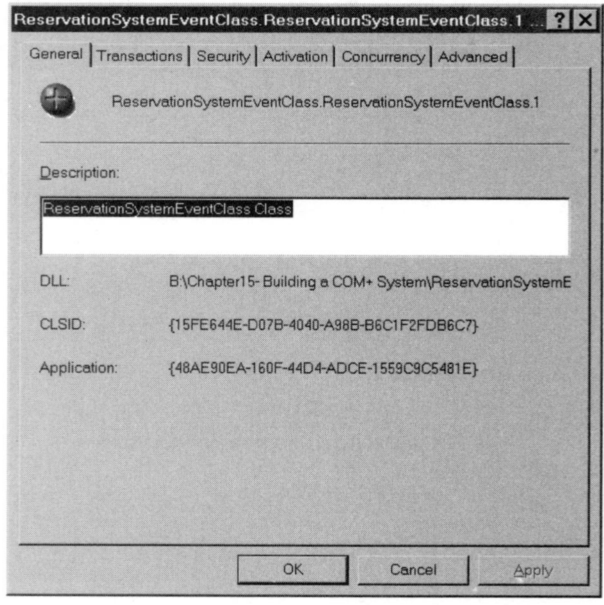

Component properties, General tab
Figure 15-15.

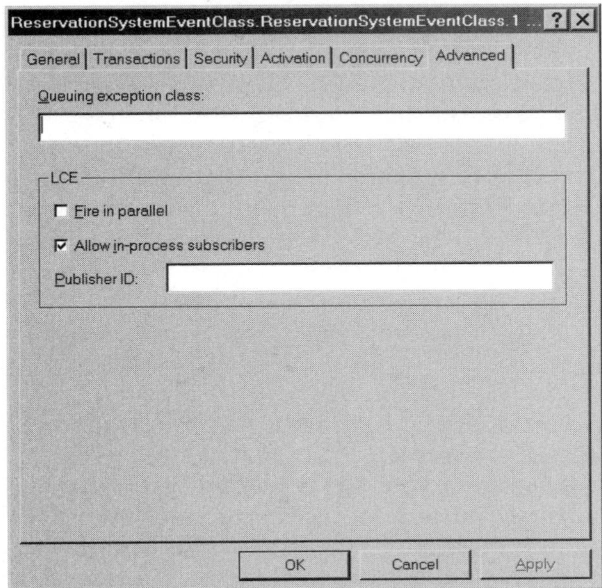

Component properties, Advanced tab

Figure 15-16.

not the situation, you would not want this selected, thereby forcing the subscriber to be instantiated within its own process space. Note that this setting is applicable only to library applications because server applications run within their own process space anyway.

The last setting, Publisher ID, is a way to identify the publisher within the subscriber screens.

This completes the event class configuration. Now we need to move on to creating and configuring a subscriber. We will discuss the remaining property tabs as we install the other components.

Creating an Event Subscriber

Now that we have finished setting up the event class, it is time to create a subscriber that will monitor the events. The requirement of a subscriber is that it implements the interfaces of the event class component. In the **ReservationSystemEventClass** component, this interface is limited to the **IReservationSystem** interface. Therefore, all we need to do in order to build a subscribing component is to create a component that implements the **IReservationSystem** interface. Let's do this now.

Create a new ATL DLL and specify **ReservationSystemSvr** for the project name. Next, add an ATL object with the name **ReservationSystem**. On the attributes page, select the ISupportErrorInfo check box and change the threading model to Free. This will cause the component to have protected reference counting via the **CComObjectRootEx<CComMultiThreadModel>** class. It is not actually important whether you choose Free or Both, as the threading model of choice for COM+ components is Neutral. Open **ReservationSytem.rgs** and change the threading model entry to Neutral, as shown below:

```
{
  val ThreadingModel = s 'Neutral'
}
```

The next step is to import the **IReservationSystem** interface from the **ReservationSystemEventClassSvr.dll**. To do this, add an **importlib** statement to your **ReservationSystemSvr.idl** file. While you are editing the IDL file, you should delete the previous **IReservationSystem** interface definition that was created by the wizard. Note that it would have been perfectly acceptable to define the **IReservationSystem** interface inside the **ReservationSystemSvr.dll** rather than the **ReservationSystemEvent-ClassSvr.dll**. We chose to do it this way to reflect the order in which the components were created.

A listing of the final **ReservationSystemSvr.idl** file follows:

```
import "oaidl.idl";
import "ocidl.idl";

[
  uuid(A9F935EA-E1D8-4877-99D2-79F2077D32E9),
  version(1.0),
     helpstring("ReservationSystemSvr 1.0 Type Library")
]
library RESERVATIONSYSTEMSvrLib
{
  importlib("stdole32.tlb");
  importlib("stdole2.tlb");
  importlib("..\ReservationSystemEventClassSvr\" \
      "ReservationSystemEventClassSvr.tlb");

  [
    uuid(39EC8E2C-87BB-4B5A-A6BB-3E4A12F706B8),
    helpstring("ReservationSystem Class")
```

```
  ]
  coclass ReservationSystem
  {
    [default] interface IReservationSystem;
  };
};
```

Now we need to write the implementation code for the **Reserve( )** method on the **IReservationSystem** interface. Add the function implementation to the **ReservationSystem.h** header file as shown here:

```
// IReservationSystem
public:
  STDMETHODIMP Reserve(/*[in]*/ IReservation* reservation)
  {
    USES_CONVERSION;
    HRESULT hr;
    CComBSTR message;
    CComBSTR titlebar;

    titlebar.LoadString(IDS_PROJNAME);
    hr = reservation->get_Summary(&message.m_str);
    if(SUCCEEDED(hr))
    MessageBox(NULL, OLE2T(message),
      OLE2T(titlebar), 0);
    else
    {
      _com_error err(hr);
      MessageBox(NULL, err.ErrorMessage(),
        OLE2T(titlebar), 0);
    }
    return S_OK;
  }
```

As with most of the implementation code in this system, we will display a message box that will identify what code is executing when the system is running. In this case the title bar will display "Reservation System," and the message identifies the reservation being made.

At the same time, you will need to declare the **IReservation** and **IReservationSystem** interfaces within the C++ code. Previously they were added to the library portion of the IDL, but this does not cause the MIDL compiler to add them to the **ReservationSystemSvr.h** header file.

To include these declarations, **#import** the **ReservationSystemEvent ClassSvr.dll** in the ReservationSystem.h header file as shown below. Note that you will have to add the DLL location folder unless you move it into the path.

```
#import "ReservationSystemEventClassSvr.dll" \
  no_namespace, raw_interfaces_only, raw_native_types, named_guids
```

This completes the code for the subscriber. Now we need to configure this newly created component.

Configuring the Subscriber Inside Component Services

In order for a subscriber to monitor COM+ events, it needs to be configured. As before, we will use Component Services to do this rather than writing any scripting code. As you did with the event class, open Component Services and browse to the Hotel Reservation System application; then drill down to the Components node. Now right-click and select New | Component. As before, you should see the welcome screen, and then you will be prompted for whether you want to import or install the component. This time, select "Install new component(s)," and at the ensuing file dialog, browse for the **ReservationSystemSvr.dll** file. After selecting it, click Next and Finish to complete the wizard. The component will have been inserted within the Hotel Reservation System application. Any clients of the component would still be able to instantiate it as they would if the component were registered using **Regsvr32.dll**.

Now that the component has been inserted, it is time to configure which publishers it will subscribe to. You will notice that two folders are listed as child nodes to the newly added ReservationSystemSvr.ReservationSystem.1 component node. The first is titled "Interfaces," and it lists each interface that the type library indicated were supported. In this case, only **IReservationSystem** is listed.

Below the Interfaces node is the Subscriptions node, which contains a list of all the event class components to which the **ReservationSystem** subscribes. Since we have not yet added any, the list is blank. To add a subscription, right-click on the Subscriptions node and select New | Subscription. After the welcome, you will be prompted with a list of the interfaces that the **ReservationSystem** component supports. The screen is shown in Figure 15-17.

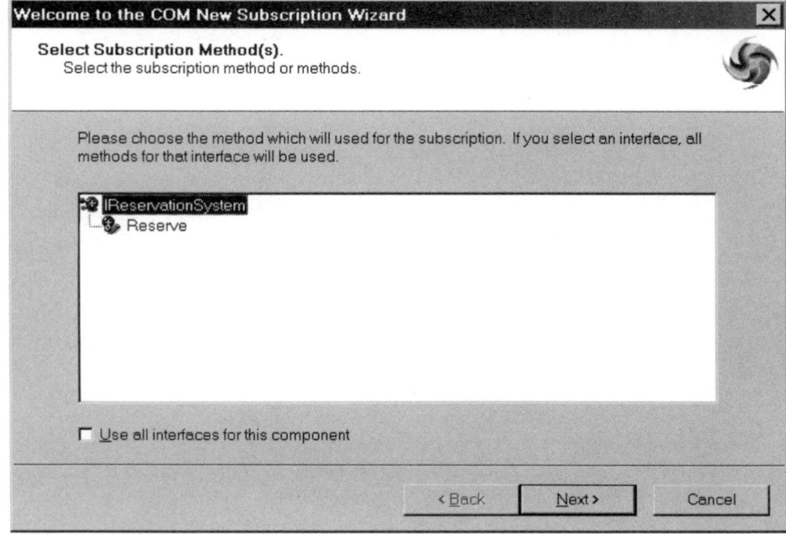

Subscription Wizard—subscription method or interface selection

Figure 15-17.

Notice that listed below each interface is each of the methods on the interface (in this case there is only one, but there could be more). This indicates the flexibility in what the subscriber can select to monitor. Rather than being forced to monitor the entire interface, you can choose to monitor individual methods. Furthermore, although we will not discuss the details in this book, you can use filter interfaces to monitor only certain methods depending on the parameters passed. This provides the capacity to pinpoint the subscription mechanism so as not to process more events than necessary. For our example, select **IReservationSystem** (although this isn't really necessary since our interface supports only one method). After you click Next, Component Services will browse through its catalogs and find all the components that are publishing the selected interfaces. Since there is only one, ReservationSystemSvr.ReservationSystemEventClass.1, that will be the only one that appears in the ensuing list, which is shown in Figure 15-18. Select this sole component and click Next.

The last screen of the wizard, not including the thank-you dialog, allows you to enter the name of the subscription and also to enable the subscription immediately (see Figure 15-19). Enter **ReservationSystem Subscriber** for the name and check the check box to immediately enable the subscription.

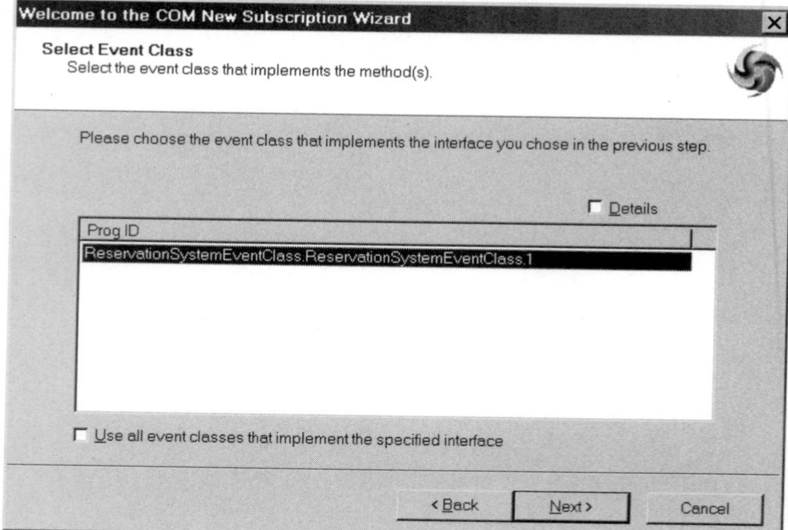

Susbcription Wizard—publisher selection

Figure 15-18.

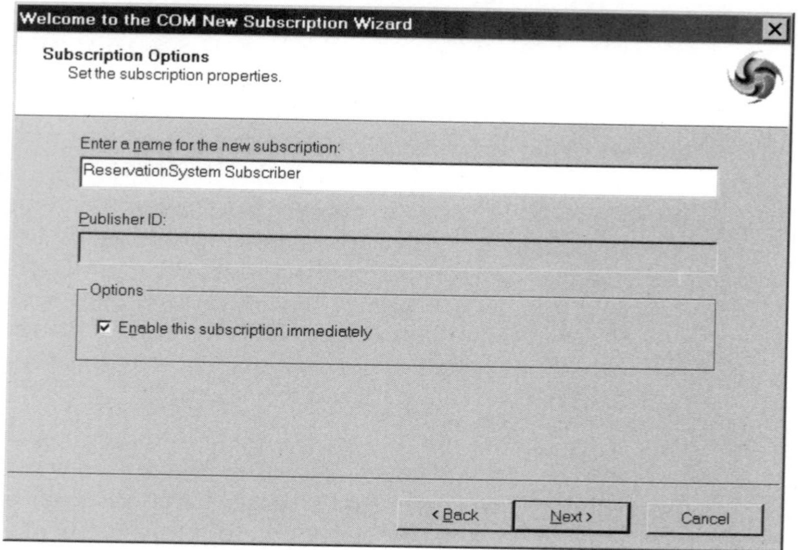

Subscription Wizard—properties

Figure 15-19.

Not selecting the check box will register the subscription but not activate it. To activate it, open the properties screen on the newly created subscription and select the Enabled check box on the Options tab, as shown in Figure 15-20.

We will discuss the Queued property later in the chapter. Also available on this page is the "Server name" text box. This allows you to configure the subscription to monitor an event class that is running on a different machine. The "Filter criteria" property allows you to limit the subscription to parameters with certain values only.

This completes the creation and configuration of the subscriber. All that remains is to publish the events that the subscriber is now monitoring. To do this we will modify the **HotelReservation.exe** client so that rather than storing only the reservation properties in the **Reservation** component, it will send the **Reservation** component to the **ReservationSystem** to be processed.

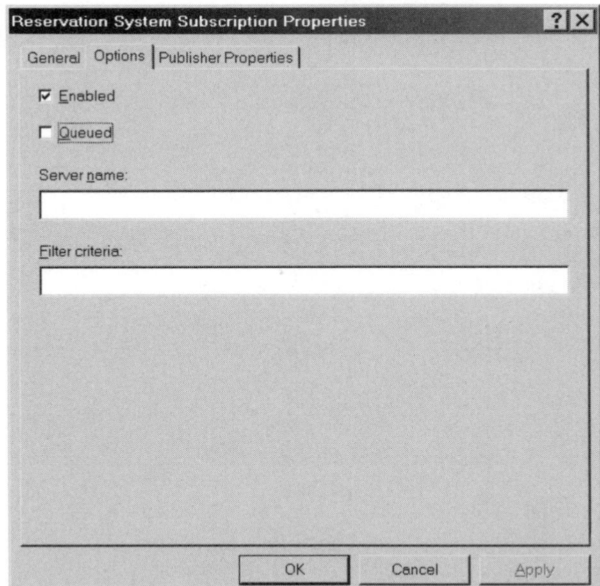

Reservation System Subscriber Properties dialog, Options tab
Figure 15-20.

Publishing Events to the Subscribers

The procedure for publishing events to the event service is quite simple: you "instantiate" the event class, just as you would if the component was a normal component registered with **Regsvr32.dll**. The reason that "instantiate" is placed in quotes is that although from the client perspective instantiation is exactly what you will do (using **CoCreateInstance[Ex]( )**, etc.), on the server side things may happen a little differently. The call to **CoCreateInstance[Ex]( )** will be intercepted by COM+, which will then find the event class component within **RegDB**. Once located, COM+ will search through **RegDB** for all the subscribing components, instantiate them, and call into them rather than the event class that the client directed. In this manner, the number of subscribers and the details of which subscribers to instantiate and call are completely invisible to the client program. COM+ takes care of everything for you. Let's now make the modifications to **HotelReservation.exe** so as to publish the events. Open the **HotelReservation** project if it is not already open, and edit the **ReservationForm.h** file as highlighted below:

```
#import "..\ReservationSvr\ReservationSvr.dll" no_namespace \
  raw_interfaces_only, raw_native_types
...
LRESULT CReservationForm::OnReserve(WORD wNotifyCode, WORD wID, HWND hWndCtl, BOOL& bHandled)
{
  USES_CONVERSION;
  HRESULT hr = S_OK;
  CComBSTR property = L"";
  CComPtr<IReservation> reservation;
  CComPtr<IReservationSystem> reservation_system;

  hr = reservation_system.CoCreateInstance(
    __uuidof(ReservationSystemEventClass));

  hr = reservation.CoCreateInstance(__uuidof(Reservation));

  ATLTRACE(_T("Reserve Hotel at: \n"));

  // Set each Reservation object property here
  ...

  // Publish the reservation so that it
  // gets recorded into the Reservation System.
```

```
    if(SUCCEEDED(hr))  {
      hr = reservation_system->Reserve(reservation);
    }

    if(reservation!=NULL)
      reservation.Release();

    ShowStatus(hr);

    return 0;
}
```

As you can see, there is very little to the entire publication mechanism. The only real difference at the client is that the CLSID of the event class is used rather than the CLSID of the **ReservationSystem** component itself. At this point you can run the **HotelReservation.exe** program, and after clicking the Reserve button, you should see the message box displayed from the **Reserve( )** method inside the **ReservationSystem** component.

Queued Components

The features of the COM+ events publish/subscribe mechanism are powerful because of the ability to allow multiple components to publish to the same event class and then multiple subscribers to respond to those events through configuration alone. You will notice, however, that when the message box from the **ReservationSystem::Reserve( )** method is displayed, the client is blocked, waiting for its subscribers to complete. The call to the subscriber mechanism is synchronous, therefore.

COM+, however, offers another service known as *queued components*, as we discussed in the previous chapter. Queued components provide the ability to make asynchronous calls to a component.

Perhaps more important, because queued components use MSMQ, they can make asynchronous COM calls to a component that may not even be available at the time the calls are made. In other words, the client or server could be disconnected from the network when the calls were made or, perhaps, the server is down. The use of MSMQ by queued components clearly establishes that you must have MSMQ installed on the machine if you wish to use the queued component functionality. In this discussion we will focus on queued components through two examples.

Creating a Queueable Component

In the first example we will build a new **ReservationTransfer** component. The role of this component within the Hotel Reservation System will be to transfer the reservation record to the participating hotels via the Internet or some other relatively "unreliable" connection. This component will demonstrate the queued component features of operating in a disconnected environment. Even if the Internet connection were down for a time, the queued component method calls would still be recorded so that when the connection was restored, the calls could be processed.

A queueable component must have at least one **[in]***-only interface.*

One thing to note as you read each of the following steps is that there is essentially nothing distinguishable about creating a queueable component from creating any other kind of component, as long as your component has at least one **[in]**-only interface. (An **[in]**-only interface is one that only has functions with **[in]** parameters. No **[out]** or **[in,out]** parameters are allowed.) In fact, any existing COM component that supports an **[in]**-only interface could be configured inside Component Services as a queued component, and therefore, the component is considered a queueable component. The distinction between a *queueable* and a *queued* component is that any component that supports an **[in]**-only interface is considered queueable. However, not until the component is placed within Component Services, and the **[in]**-only interface has been configured as queued, does the component become a queued component.

We will begin by creating the **ReservationTransfer** component. To do this, create a new ATL DLL with the project name ReservationTransferSvr. Next insert a new ATL object called ReservationTransfer. As before, select the threading model to be Free to eliminate any thread affinity, as required by COM+ events. After creating the component, change the threading model to Neutral inside the **ReservationTransfer.rgs** file.

Next, using the ATL wizard, add a Transfer method, **Confirm( )**, to the **IReservationTransfer** interface. The method should have one parameter, an **[in]** parameter of type **IReservation***. To have access to the **IReservation** interface, however, you will need to add the **ReservationSvr** folder to your project settings and import the **ReservationSvr.idl** file, as was described for the **ReservationSystemEventClassSvr** project earlier in the chapter. A listing of the **ReservationTransferSvr.idl** file is shown below:

```
// ReservationTransferSvr.idl : IDL source for ReservationTransferSvr.dll
//
```

```
// This file will be processed by the MIDL tool to
// produce the type library (ReservationTransferSvr.tlb)
// and marshalling code.

import "oaidl.idl";
import "ocidl.idl";
import "ReservationSvr.idl";


  [
    object,
    uuid(90952478-A0FC-4FB9-8B50-2A7F563FB6A6),
    dual,
    helpstring("IReservationTransfer Interface"),
    pointer_default(unique),
  ]
  interface IReservationTransfer : IDispatch
  {
    [id(1), helpstring("method Confirm")]
      HRESULT Confirm([in] IReservation* reservation);
  };

[
  uuid(1100CFAF-0614-4390-89D2-7EFCD6203D10),
  version(1.0),
  helpstring("ReservationTransferSvr 1.0 Type Library")
]
library RESERVATIONTRANSFERSVRLib
{
  importlib("stdole32.tlb");
  importlib("stdole2.tlb");

  interface IReservation;

  [
    uuid(62CADF2F-0EB3-4E2C-9498-F134AEE58DD4),
    helpstring("ReservationTransfer Class")
  ]
  coclass ReservationTransfer
  {
    [default] interface IReservationTransfer;
  };
};
```

For the **CReservationTransfer::Confirm( )** method implementation, simply add a message box as shown in the **ReservationTransfer.cpp** file listed below:

```
// ReservationTransfer.cpp : Implementation of CReservationTransfer

#include "stdafx.h"
#include "ReservationTransferSvr.h"
#include "ReservationTransfer.h"

//////////////////////////////////////////////////////////////////////
// CReservationTransfer


STDMETHODIMP CReservationTransfer::Confirm(
  IReservation *reservation)
{
  USES_CONVERSION;
  HRESULT hr;
  CComBSTR message;
  CComBSTR titlebar;

  titlebar.LoadString(IDS_PROJNAME);
  hr = reservation->get_Summary(&message.m_str);

  if(SUCCEEDED(hr))
  {
    MessageBox(NULL, OLE2T(message),
      OLE2T(titlebar), 0);
  }

  ATLASSERT(SUCCEEDED(hr));

  return S_OK;
}
```

At this point you may compile the component, although one more optional change can be made. This last change helps when configuring a queued component within Component Services; but as already pointed out, if you have existing components without this additional attribute, they can still be configured as queued components. The optional step is to include the COM+ custom attribute macro, **QUEUEABLE**, into the interface header. The result is that when adding the component to Component Services, the queued setting for the interface will be configured automatically, so you won't have to perform the step manually. A listing of the new interface definition is shown below:

```
#include "mtxattr.h"

[
  object,
  uuid(90952478-A0FC-4FB9-8B50-2A7F563FB6A6),
  dual,
  helpstring("IReservationTransfer Interface"),
  pointer_default(unique),
  QUEUEABLE
]
interface IReservationTransfer : IDispatch
{
  [id(1), helpstring("method Confirm")]
    HRESULT Confirm([in] IReservation* reservation);
};
```

Notice that in order for the **QUEUEABLE** attribute to be defined, you will need to **#include** the header file **mtxattr.h**. This file also contains the other COM+ custom attribute macros used for transaction support, as we shall see in the section "COM+ Transactions," later in the chapter.

Configuring a Component to Be a Queued Component

Now that we have created a component, we need to add it to Component Services so that it becomes a queued component. To demonstrate the disconnected functionality, we will want to place this component into a second COM+ application. To start out, however, we will demonstrate the disconnected mode using one computer. Later in the chapter, in the section "Deploying an Application," we will go into the details of how to set up the system for distributed operation. Therefore, alongside the Hotel Reservation System, create a new application called **Hotel Reservation Transfer**. After creating the application, open the properties dialog and check the Queued check box on the Queuing tab. Messages will not be processed until you set the Listen option, but we will delay this setting until after messages have been queued to demonstrate the disconnected functionality.

Setting the Queued check box will create a number of queues within MSMQ. You can view these queues by opening the Computer Management MMC snap-in and browsing to the Services and Applications node and to the Message Queuing node. From there, you will notice four folders. The two we are interested in are titled "Public Queues" and "Private Queues." If you open these folders, you should be able to see a number of queues related to your COM+ application. In the Public Queues folder, there should be a queue named after your queued COM+ application—in this case, "Hotel Reservation Transfer." In the Private Queues folder, you will find six queues related to the application. The names of the first five are prefixed by the application name, followed by an underscore and then a number from 0 to 4, as shown in Figure 15-21. These queues are known as the *retry queues*.

The reason for the multiple private queues has to do with the queued components exception mechanism. If there is a problem processing a recorded message, the message is moved from one queue to the next until it reaches the application's final resting queue, the *dead queue*, which is the queue beginning with the application name and ending with "_deadqueue."

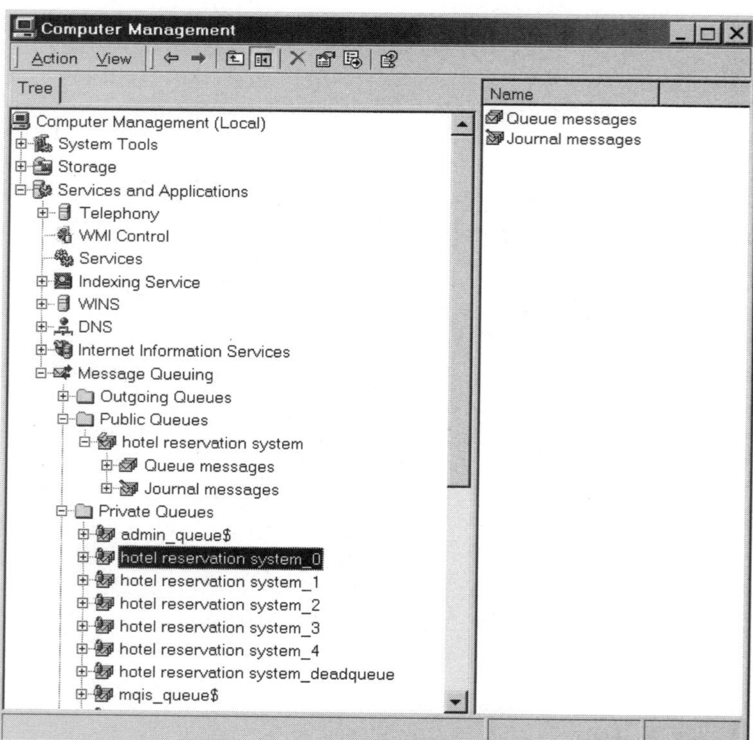

Browsing the queued application's message queues
Figure 15-21.

The queuing exception class, which we mentioned while examining the dialog in Figure 15-16, is called into action immediately before the message reaches the dead queue. Following the final attempt to process a message from the final retry queue, the COM+ queued player (the component that processes the queued component messages) will call into the queued exception class and inform it that the message is to be moved to its final resting queue. This allows the queue exception component to respond to the fact that the message processing failed.

The component responsible for moving the messages from one queue to the next is called the *mover*. Although there are five retry queues, this does not mean that attempts to process the message will occur only five times. Rather, while in each retry queue, three attempts will be made to process the message before moving it to the next queue. The attempts will be made at various intervals (the length is determined by which queue the message is located in).

Before we leave the queue discussion, you should be aware that deleting or renaming a queued application does not clean up the application's queues. This will have to be performed manually.

Let's now return to the Component Services and add the **Reservation-Transfer** component to the application. The procedure for doing this is to add the **ReservationTransferSvr.dll** module to the Hotel Reservation Transfer application exactly as we added the **ReservationSystemSvr** module. Next, browse to the **IReservationTransfer** interface on the newly added component and open the properties dialog to the Queuing tab, as shown in Figure 15-22.

Notice that the Queued setting is checked. This is due to the **QUEUEABLE** attribute that we added to the **IReservationTransfer** interface while creating the component. If we had not added this attribute, the setting would not be checked, but you could check it manually instead. (This would be required for a Visual Basic component, for example.) If the interface were not queueable, due to the existence of **[out]** parameters, the setting would be disabled. Component Services reads through the type library to figure out whether an interface is compatible.

This completes the entire configuration. At this point we have a queued component. Now we need to look at how to instantiate it.

Instantiating and Calling into a Queued Component

Now that we have created and configured a queued component, we are ready to change the client so that it can access the new component. In the Hotel Reservation System, the initiation of the transfer will be requested by the

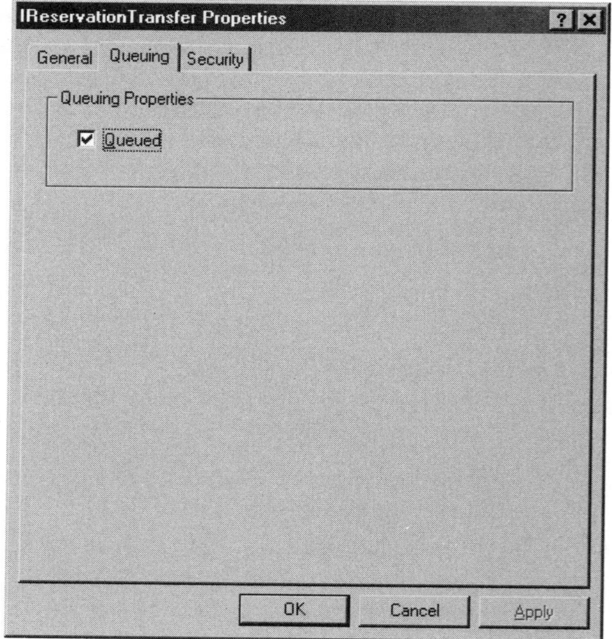

Interface properties, Queuing tab
Figure 15-22.

ReservationSystem component. Therefore, the **ReservationSystem** component will be the client to the **ReservationTransfer** component. Open the **ReservationSystem** component so that you can modify the code.

To instantiate a queued component so that the method calls will be recorded rather than immediately executed on the component, you need to use the **CoGetObject( )** API function along with the queue and new monikers, as shown in the following code snippet:

```
IReservationTransfer* p_reservation_transfer;
hr = CoGetObject(
  L"queue:/new:ReservationTransferSvr.ReservationTransfer",
  NULL, __uuidof(IReservationTransfer),
  reinterpret_cast<void**>(&p_reservation_transfer));
```

Without the queue moniker (queue:) and with only the new moniker (new:), the component would be instantiated synchronously, and no messages would be sent to the queue.

Amazingly, this completes the discussion of instantiation; the queue moniker is all that is required. However, there are a few more items to mention in regard to the instantiation if you want to provide some custom queue specifications. You can provide various parameters as part of the queue moniker, as shown in the example below:

```
IReservationTransfer* p_reservation_transfer;
hr = CoGetObject(
  L"queue:ComputerName=Ignorance, Label=\"Reservation Transfer\""
  L"/new:ReservationTransferSvr.ReservationTransfer",
  NULL, __uuidof(IReservationTransfer),
  reinterpret_cast<void**>(&p_reservation_transfer));
```

In this example, the component is assigned to the queue running on the computer named Ignorance, and the message is given the label "Reservation Transfer." Other queue moniker parameters that you may find helpful are **QueueName**, **PathName**, **FormatName**, **Journal**, **Priority**, and **Trace**. Check the documentation for a full description of each of these parameters and more.

The procedure for actually recording the methods that are to be executed on the component is no different from calling a component instantiated using **CoCreateInstance[Ex]( )**. Below is a listing of the new Reserve method inside **ReservationSystem.h**:

```
// IReservationSystem
public:
  STDMETHODIMP Reserve(/*[in]*/ IReservation* reservation)
  {
    USES_CONVERSION;
    HRESULT hr;
    CComPtr<IReservationTransfer> ptr_reservation_transfer = NULL;
    CComBSTR message;
    CComBSTR titlebar;

    titlebar.LoadString(IDS_PROJNAME);
    hr = reservation->get_Summary(&message.m_str);

    if(SUCCEEDED(hr))
    {
      hr = CoGetObject(L"queue:"
        L"ComputerName=Rambler,"
        L"Label=\"Reservation Transfer\""
        L"/new:ReservationTransferSvr.ReservationTransfer",
        NULL, __uuidof(IReservationTransfer),
```

```
        reinterpret_cast<void**>(&ptr_reservation_transfer));
        if(SUCCEEDED(hr))
          hr = ptr_reservation_transfer->Confirm(reservation);

        if(ptr_reservation_transfer!=NULL)
          ptr_reservation_transfer.Release();
    }

    if(SUCCEEDED(hr))
        MessageBox(NULL, OLE2T(message),
        OLE2T(titlebar), 0);
    else
    {
      _com_error err(hr);
      MessageBox(NULL, err.ErrorMessage(),
        OLE2T(titlebar), 0);
    }

    return hr;

  }
```

Note that the **IReservationTransfer** component interface is explicitly released. The methods and properties will not be queued until the interface is entirely released, so it is released explicitly here to expedite that operation.

There is one more change required in order to use the **ReservationTransfer** component, and that is to **#import** the server module. Here is the **#import** statement:

```
#import "..\ReservationTransferSvr\ReservationTransferSvr.dll" \
  no_namespace, raw_interfaces_only, \
  raw_native_types, exclude("IReservation")
```

The **exclude("IReservation")** attribute is included because the **IReservation** interface is already included in the project by the **ReservationSystemEvent-ClassSvr.dll** module, as we discussed earlier.

One last change to consider is changing the **_WIN32_NT** definition inside **stdafx.h** to be 0x0500 rather than 0x0400 because only Windows 2000 can make queued component calls.

At this point, the **ReservationSystem** component is complete and can be recompiled. If the Hotel Reservation System application is running, you may need to shut it down to free up the **ReservationSystemSvr.dll** file for write access. To do this, right-click on the application within Component Services and select Shutdown.

Now the system is ready for testing. However, we need to consider one additional requirement that we have already coded, but up until this point, have not used. The requirement is necessary because the **IReservation** interface is passed as a parameter in the **Confirm( )** method on the **IReservationTransfer** interface. To send a message using MSMQ, the MSMQ system needs to be able to package the message. At its destination, the package can be opened and processed. As with DCOM, this is known as marshalling. The added complexity with MSMQ marshalling, however, is the requirement to persist a message beyond the time that it is instantiated. For simple data types, such as **BSTR**s and oleautomation-compatible numbers, no additional code is required. However, unless a programmer identifies the persistable parts within a component, the marshaller has no way of knowing how to persist a component or even whether it is possible to do so. To provide the assistance the marshaller needs, component developers must support the **IPersistStream** interface if they want to be able to send the component inside an MSMQ message. Fortunately, we already did this in the "Creating a Component That Can Be Persisted" section earlier in the chapter, so no additional effort is required.

To test the newly created component, run the **HotelReservation.exe** application, and after entering hotel information, click the Reserve button. This will publish an event to the **ReservationSystem**, which will then call the **ReservationTransfer** queued component. At this point you might expect the message box inside the **ReservationTransfer** component to be displayed, but this will not happen until you set the Listener setting and start the application. Instead, you will see only the message box from inside the **ReservationSystem**, as before. Click the Reserve button a few more times just for fun, and then select the Close button to shut down the client application.

At this point, the method calls to the **ReservationTransfer** component have all been recorded and queued. Even though the Hotel Reservation Transfer application is disconnected (shut down), the method calls to the **ReservationTransfer** component all executed successfully. The next step is to start the Hotel Reservation Transfer application listening. In Component Services, open the properties dialog and set the Listen check box on the application properties Queuing tab. After closing the dialog, restart the application. (Right-click on the application and click Start.) Now you will see a message box for each time you clicked the Reserve button. Even though the **HotelReservation.exe** application that caused the events is no longer running, COM still queues the method calls correctly. More importantly, even though the Hotel Reservation Transfer application was shut down (in other words, disconnected), when the **ReservationTransfer** component was called, the method calls to it were still successful due to COM's ability to queue the calls using MSMQ.

Disconnected, Asynchronous Subscribers via Queued Events

In the second example of queued components, we will create a second COM+ events subscriber called **ReservationBilling**. As we have outlined already, one drawback to the COM+ event services mechanism is that the client is blocked while all the subscribers are instantiated and the methods on those subscribers are called. The result is a noticeable delay at the client—even in our example with one subscriber. If you consider that the number of subscribers could potentially take a significant amount of time to process the events, (along with the fact that some subscribers may display message boxes that block all further event processing for example), the ability to make calls to these components asynchronously could be quite important. In order to demonstrate a way to reduce this delay, we will show how to configure a queued subscriber. Later on, we will also use this component to demonstrate transactions.

The **ReservationBilling** component will monitor the **ReservationSystem-EventClass** just as the **ReservationSystem** did. Although this component could potentially also be configured on another machine and thereby could demonstrate the features of a disconnected call, the main purpose of this demonstration is to provide a work-around to the synchronicity of COM+ events. To create the **ReservationBilling** component, follow the same procedures outlined for the **ReservationSystem**. The only difference is the implementation of the **Reserve( )** method. Rather than using the function implementation of the **CReservationSystem::Reserve( )** method and using it for the **ReservationBilling** component, take the function body from the **CReservationTransfer::Reserve( )** function. Don't forget to **#import** the **ReservationSystemEventClass.dll** file. After compiling, the component will be complete.

Before proceeding to configure the new component, verify that the application you are adding the component to (in this case, the Hotel Reservation System) is set to be accessed via MSMQ. To do this, open the Queuing tab on the application properties dialog, and verify that the Queued check box is checked (see Figure 15-11). At the same time, check the Listen check box so that immediately upon arrival, the recorded method calls will be executed.

Alternatively, you could leave the Listen box unchecked, in which case the messages wouldn't be processed until later, when it was checked. Note that changing the Listen setting requires that you restart the application.

Now we are ready to add the **ReservationBilling** component. To do this, follow the instructions for adding the **ReservationSystem** component. Once the component has been inserted, however, and the subscription is activated, two more settings need to be adjusted. The first we already encountered when we configured the **ReservationTransfer** queued component. This setting is the Queued setting on the interface properties Queuing tab. The second setting appears on the Options tab of the subscription property dialog shown in Figure 15-20. The setting we are interested in is the Queued setting. This causes the component's subscription to be queued and thereby called asynchronously rather than synchronously.

To test the newly created subscription, rerun the **HotelReservation.exe** application. After clicking the Reserve button, notice the message box that is displayed by the **ReservationBilling** component. Rather than immediately clicking the OK button on this dialog, however, leave the dialog open and click the Reserve button a few more times. As you can see, in contrast to the **ReservationSystem** dialog that blocks the **HotelReservation.exe** application, the **ReservationBilling** component executes asynchronously.

Next, we will examine how the **ReservationBilling** and **Reservation-Transfer** components all participate in a transaction so that none of them will execute unless the entire transaction is successful.

COM+ Transactions

Murphy's Law has a way of striking at such conspicuous times in computing environments as to truly defy reasonable logic. You would think that systems built upon 1's and 0's would be more reliable. Furthermore, most enterprise-plus systems these days will need to run 24x7 (pronounced "24 by 7," meaning 24 hours a day and 7 days a week). This 24x7 requirement increases the opportunity for "bad stuff" to happen. System operators can turn off systems, hard drives can fill up or crash, and data integrity must be maintained through these kinds of catastrophic events. COM+, and specifically COM+ transactions, provide the required infrastructure to help you recover from these types of events while maintaining the consistency and correctness of the system's information.

COM+ transactions help maintain the consistency and correctness of a system's data.

Let us now consider the transaction implications of the system we have built so far and why transactions within this system are so crucial. Consider, for example, the possibility that after the **ReservationSystem** had called the **ReservationTransfer** component, and after the **ReservationBilling** method calls had been recorded, the **ReservationSystem** made a validation check on the data, which indicated that the reservation information was invalid. The question that presents itself is how can the **ReservationTransfer** and **ReservationBilling** calls be aborted? Clearly, the answer is to wrap the entire operation inside a transaction. That way, if either of the calls to **ReservationTransfer** and **ReservationBilling** failed to get recorded successfully, or the **ReservationSystem** component encountered a problem, the transaction would be backed out and the system state would return to the condition prior to the start of the transaction.

One of the key capabilities of a component that supports transactions is that it does not need to be aware of the other components or resource managers that are involved in the transaction. In our example, the **ReservationSystem** component has no knowledge that the **ReservationBilling** component is also participating in the transaction. All the **ReservationSystem** component needs to do is abort the transaction if a failure occurs. COM+ will take care of notifying the resource managers that the transaction was aborted and, therefore, they should not commit their changes.

Even though we will not be writing any resource managers in this chapter, we will still be able to observe how resource managers participate because the queued component recorder uses MSMQ, and MSMQ is a resource manager. Therefore, once we have finished configuring the **ReservationSystem** component, we will be able to witness how it aborts a transaction and, thereby, rolls back the MSMQ messages that would otherwise have been sent to the **ReservationTransfer** and **ReservationBilling** components.

Let's consider now what it would take to change the **ReservationSystem** component so that it is able to abort a transaction, even though it does not know anything about the other participants in the transaction.

Creating a Component That Supports Transactions

Rather than creating a brand-new component with transaction support, we will simply change the **ReservationSystem** component. However, the changes indicated below would be the same as those required for a new component.

At this time it is worthwhile pointing out that in spite of the fact that the Visual Studio Wizard provides two locations for generating transaction support for MTS, and the fact that MTS support is compatible with Windows 2000, you do *not* necessarily want to select the Support MTS check box when creating a new server module. Furthermore, unless also targeting Windows NT 4.0, you should not use the MTS Component Wizard when adding a component to your project. In the first case, COM+ transaction support is built directly into the Windows 2000 operating system, and we do not need the extra libraries that are MTS specific if we target Windows 2000. Second, while the MTS Component Wizard will generate a component that can be configured to run in COM+, it assumes the single threading model, which prevents object pooling and inserts an MTS-specific header file (**mtx.h**). As we have already shown with each of the components developed in this chapter, Threading Model Neutral is the preferred model to use for COM+-configured components.

A brief review of what the support for the MTS setting does to the project along with a detailed explanation of what is generated using the MTS Component Wizard are discussed in the "Building an MTS-Compatible Application Using the ATL COM AppWizard" section later in this chapter.

Auto-complete is the mechanism by which a transaction vote is based upon the **HRESULT** *return value.*

Another item to consider before we make any code changes is that a component can be configured to vote in a transaction without any additional coding on the part of the component developer. Instead, a transaction vote can be made based on the **HRESULT** returned from a method call. This mechanism is known as *auto-complete*, and we will examine how to specify the auto-complete flag in the "Configuring a Component for Transaction Support" section. Although the auto-complete functionality works, developers should be careful in choosing to rely on this capability, as it is too easy for even an administrator to inadvertently change the transaction setting, thereby removing the transaction capability. To be sure the code is executing within a transaction, add the few transaction lines outlined in the following two code listings. If the code is not executing within a transaction, exit the function with an error.

The first change we will make to the **ReservationSystem** component is within the type library definition inside **ReservationSystemSvr.idl**. The changes are highlighted here:

```
// ReservationSystemSvr.idl : IDL source
// for ReservationSystemSvr.dll
//

// This file will be processed by the MIDL tool to
// produce the type library (ReservationSystemSvr.tlb)
// and marshalling code.

import "oaidl.idl";
import "ocidl.idl";
```

```
#include <mtxattr.h>

#include <winerror.h>
#define MAKE_HRESULT_ERROR(nError) \
    MAKE_HRESULT(SEVERITY_ERROR, FACILITY_ITF, nError)

  typedef [uuid(39FB3AB1-DE17-4a10-A3DB-95236C055135),
    helpstring("Custom error return codes")]
    enum ReservationSystemError
  {
    [helpstring("The reservation dates were invalid.")]
      rsReservationDatesWereInvalid = MAKE_HRESULT_ERROR(0xffff),
    // Other error codes go here
  } ReservationSystemError;


[
  uuid(A9F935EA-E1D8-4877-99D2-79F2077D32E9),
  version(1.0),
     helpstring("ReservationSystemSvr 1.0 Type Library")
]
library RESERVATIONSYSTEMLib
{
  importlib("stdole32.tlb");
  importlib("stdole2.tlb");
  importlib("..\ReservationSystemEventClassSvr\" \
    "ReservationSystemEventClassSvr.tlb");

  [
    uuid(39EC8E2C-87BB-4B5A-A6BB-3E4A12F706B8),
    helpstring("ReservationSystem Class"),
    TRANSACTION_REQUIRED
  ]
  coclass ReservationSystem
  {
    [default] interface IReservationSystem;
  };
};
```

Notice that included in the listing is an enumeration for custom error handling, as we discussed in Chapter 9. We will use this as part of the validation code.

More important, notice the use of the custom macro **TRANSACTION_ REQUIRED** in the **ReservationSystem** CoClass header as it relates to transactions specifically. In a similar fashion to the **QUEUEABLE** attribute macro we used earlier, the **TRANSACTION_ REQUIRED** macro declares that the component requires transactions so that when inserted into Component Services, the Required setting for the transaction will automatically be configured. Contrast the fact that the **QUEUEABLE** attribute decorates interfaces, whereas the **TRANSACTION_REQUIRED** attribute goes on the CoClass. As before, the **mtxattr.h** file is again **#included**.

Add the following code to the implementation of **Reserve( )** within the **ReservationSystem.h** file:

```
// IReservationSystem
public:
  STDMETHODIMP Reserve(/*[in]*/ IReservation* reservation)
  {
    USES_CONVERSION;
    HRESULT hr;
    CComPtr<IReservationTransfer> ptr_reservation_transfer = NULL;
    CComBSTR message;
    CComBSTR titlebar;

    CComPtr<IContextState> context_state = NULL;

    // Get our object context
    hr = CoGetObjectContext(IID_IObjectContext,
      reinterpret_cast<void**>(&context_state) );
    // Should be null anyway but set explicitly because
    // we count on it later on.
    if (FAILED(hr))
      context_state = NULL;

    titlebar.LoadString(IDS_PROJNAME);
    if(SUCCEEDED(hr))
      hr = reservation->get_Summary(&message.m_str);

    if(SUCCEEDED(hr))
    {
      hr = CoGetObject(L"queue:"
        L"ComputerName=Rambler,"
        L"Label=\"Reservation Transfer\""
        L"/new:ReservationTransferSvr.ReservationTransfer",
        NULL, __uuidof(IReservationTransfer),
        reinterpret_cast<void**>(&ptr_reservation_transfer));
        if(SUCCEEDED(hr))
          hr = ptr_reservation_transfer->Confirm(reservation);

        if(ptr_reservation_transfer!=NULL)
```

```
        ptr_reservation_transfer.Release();
    }

    ATLASSERT(SUCCEEDED(hr));

    if(SUCCEEDED(hr))
    {
      CComBSTR bstr_date;
      CComVariant var_arrival_date;
      CComVariant var_departure_date;

      reservation->get_ArrivalDate(&bstr_date);
      var_arrival_date = bstr_date;
      reservation->get_DepartureDate(&bstr_date);
      var_departure_date = bstr_date;

      hr = var_arrival_date.ChangeType(VT_DATE);

      if(SUCCEEDED(hr))
        hr = var_departure_date.ChangeType(VT_DATE);

      if( FAILED(hr)
        || (var_departure_date.date<var_arrival_date.date) )
      {
        hr = rsReservationDatesWereInvalid;
      }
    }

// Commit or Abort the transaction
    if (context_state!=NULL)
    {
      if(SUCCEEDED(hr) )
      {
        hr = context_state->SetMyTransactionVote(TxCommit);
      }
      else
        // Don't reset hr as we want to report the
        // first error even if Abort failed.
        context_state->SetMyTransactionVote(TxAbort);
    }

    if(SUCCEEDED(hr))
      MessageBox(NULL, OLE2T(message),
        OLE2T(titlebar), 0);
    else
```

```
    {
      if(hr = rsReservationDatesWereInvalid)
        MessageBox(NULL, _T("The reservation dates were invalid."),
          OLE2T(titlebar), 0);
      else
      {
        _com_error err(hr);
        MessageBox(NULL, err.ErrorMessage(),
          OLE2T(titlebar), 0);
      }
    }

    return hr;

  }
```

In the code above, access to the object context is obtained through a call to **CoGetObjectContext( )**. Because it is required that the component support transactions and be run within Component Services, the inability to successfully retrieve the **IContextState** interface results in an error. After calling the **ReservationTransfer** component, **Reserve( )** performs some validation on the reservation dates. If the departure date is before the arrival date, then **Reserve( )** sets the **HRESULT** to rsReservationDatesWereInvalid and aborts the transaction. Any other failed **HRESULT** will also cause a transaction abort. If, however, no errors occur, the transaction is explicitly committed.

To define the required interfaces for COM+ services, including those used above, the following line has been added to the **ReservationSystem.h** header file:

```
#include <comsvcs.h>
```

This completes the **ReservationSystem** component for the moment. Next we will discuss how **ReservationSystem** participates in the transaction using **ObjectContext**.

Participating in a Transaction Using the ObjectContext Interfaces

To participate in the transaction voting mechanism, you need to retrieve the **ObjectContext**, which provides access to the COM+ services. To do this within Windows 2000, you call **CoGetObjectContext( )**. Assuming that the

ObjectContext was retrieved successfully in the **Reserve( )** function, the method votes with the **SetMyTransactionVote(TxCommit)** statement if no error occurred within the method, and with **SetMy-TransactionVote(TxAbort)** if one did occur. That's all there is to participating in the transaction.

It turns out that three interfaces are used for working with object context. **CoGetObjectContext( )** allows you to select which one to retrieve by specifying the IID of the requested interface. If your component is targeting Windows 2000 only, you can use the **IObjectContextInfo** and **IContextState** interfaces. These interfaces, which are refactored from the Windows NT 4.0–compatible **IObjectContext** interface, provide more explicit object context information and state control. The declaration for **CoGetObjectContext( )** is shown below.

```
WINOLEAPI CoGetObjectContext( REFIID riid, LPVOID **ppv);
```

The **riid** parameter identifies the interface ID, and **ppv** is used to retrieve the pointer to that interface. Let's now briefly consider the three interfaces that can be requested. Note that although it is not shown in any listing here, the downloadable code includes a **ContextHelper** class that is used for dumping out the transaction context. This is useful as a tool if you are adjusting transaction settings and you want to see the effect this has on a component's context. Later in the chapter we will use the object constructor string to specify the filename for this class.

IObjectContextInfo

The **IObjectContextInfo** interface shown in Table 15-1 represents specific context information of the refactored **IObjectContext** interface. Therefore, it is essentially a read-only interface that can be used for such things as transaction verification.

Member Function	Description
BOOL IsInTransaction( );	Returns TRUE if the object is currently running in a transaction.
HRESULT GetTransaction(IUnknown *ppTrans*);	Retrieves a pointer to the ITransaction interface for the active transaction. Note that this is required only if the component is doing manual transaction enlistment and management.

IObjectContext-Info Interface Members
Table 15-1.

IObjectContext-Info Interface Members *(continued)*
Table 15-1.

Member Function	Description
HRESULT GetTransactionId(GUID **pguid*);	Retrieves the GUID of the active transaction.
HRESULT GetActivityId(GUID **pguid*);	Retrieves the GUID of the current activity.
HRESULT GetContextId(GUID **pguid*);	Retrieves the GUID of the context object.

Not only can it retrieve information about the transaction, but using the **GetTransaction( )** function enables you to retrieve the **ITransaction** interface.

IContextState

The **IContextState** interface represents the refactored state information of **IObjectContext**. **IContextState** allows the transaction and done bits to be set independently. With **IObjectContext**, you set both of these bits at the same time through **SetComplete( )**, **SetAbort( )**, **EnableCommit( )**, and **EnableAbort( )**. **IContextState** also provides methods to retrieve the current transaction and done states, as shown in Table 15-2.

IContextState Interface Members
Table 15-2.

Member Function	Description
HRESULT SetDeactivateOnReturn(VARIANT_BOOL *bDeactivate*);	Sets the done bit to VARIANT_TRUE or VARIANT_FALSE. If set to VARIANT_TRUE, the object will deactivate when it returns from the current method call.
HRESULT GetDeactivateOnReturn(VARIANT_BOOL **pbDeactivate*);	Retrieves the current state of the done bit.
HRESULT SetMyTransactionVote(TransactionVote *txVote*);	Sets the transaction's consistency bit to 0 (txCommit) or 1 (txAbort). The bit is inspected only when the object returns from the current method call. It can be set multiple times from within the same method call.
HRESULT GetMyTransactionVote(TransactionVote **ptxVote*);	Retrieves the transaction's current consistency bit state.

IObjectContext

Table 15-3 shows the interface for **IObjectContext** returned by the older **GetObjectContext( )** API function. As already mentioned, **CoGetObjectContext( )** can also retrieve this interface, although there is little need for it to do so.

Member Function	Description
HRESULT CreateInstance(REFCLSID *clsid*, REFIID *iid*, LPVOID FAR **ppvObj*);	Creates an object that will inherit this object's context. The context is valid only if the object being created is a COM+ configured component.
HRESULT DisableCommit( );	Prevents the current transaction from committing and leaves the object instance running beyond the current method. The object can vote to commit the transaction later.
HRESULT EnableCommit( );	Enables the commitment of the current transaction and leaves the object instance running until a **SetComplete( )** or **SetAbort( )** call.
BOOL IsCallerInRole(BSTR *bstrRole* BOOL* *pflagInRole*);	Determines whether the object's direct caller is in the specified role. Be sure that security is enabled with **IsSecurityEnabled( )** before calling this method.
HRESULT IsInTransaction( );	Indicates whether the object is in a transaction. This can be used to fail a method call if a transaction is required, or to otherwise redirect flow based on the existence of a transaction.
BOOL IsSecurityEnabled( );	Returns TRUE when role-based security is enabled for the component.
HRESULT SetAbort( );	Declares that the current transaction should be aborted. The object will be deactivated after returning from the method call.

IObjectContext Interface Members
Table 15-3.

IObjectContext Interface Members *(continued)*
Table 15-3.

Member Function	Description
HRESULT SetComplete( );	Declares that the current transaction should be committed. The object will be deactivated after returning from the method call.

In addition, the **IObjectContextActivity** interface is available, which provides access to the GUID of the current activity. Note that this interface was introduced in MTS, and the same information is available from the **IObjectContextInfo** interface **GetActivityId( )** method.

Interestingly enough, in addition to a component's context, there also exists a *call context*. The call context relates to the circumstances surrounding a specific COM method call, not just the context with which the component has been configured. A component will also have a call context set up for each method call on its objects. This context may be different from the object context and is available through **CoGetCallContext( )**.

Configuring a Component for Transaction Support

We are now ready to reconfigure the **ReservationSystem** component within Component Services. To do this, open the Transactions tab from the **ReservationSystemSvr.ReservationSystem.1**'s properties dialog (see Figure 15-23).

The Transactions tab allows you to configure the transaction settings from the services menu. The transaction settings, first mentioned in the previous chapter, are all available from this tab. In addition, a component's transaction attribute can be set to Disabled, which tells COM+ to ignore the transaction attribute when determining the context in which to place the component's objects. This will override any transaction setting that the component has. The dialog in Figure 15-23 shows the default when the component is not marked for transactions. If the component is marked for transactions, this default will change appropriately. Note that this is a default. An administrator can still come in and change this setting! Be sure that if your component requires transactions, it explicitly checks for them and does something reasonable if they do not exist, such as generate an error indicating that transaction support is required.

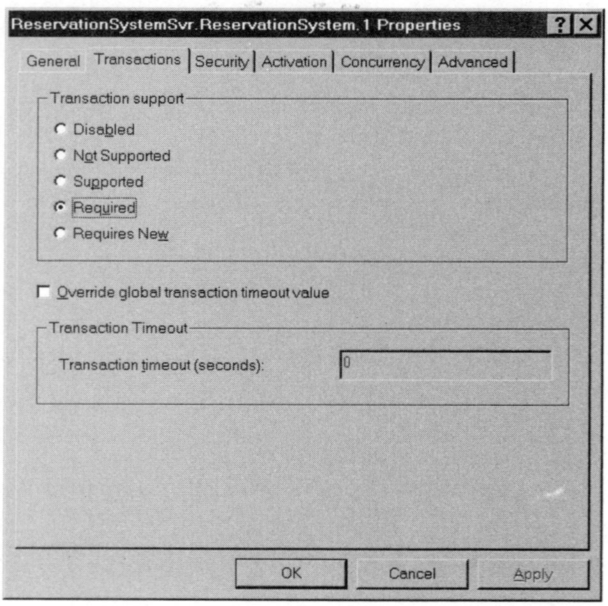

Component properties dialog, Transactions tab
Figure 15-23.

As you can see, there are five possible transaction settings. If we had re-added the **ReservationSystem** component, its setting would automatically have been set to Required because of the **TRANSACTION_REQUIRED** macro added during development. You can also configure the default transaction timeout. The default transaction timeout is 60 seconds. Extending this can be handy when debugging live transactions. This setting is available only if you have a transaction support setting of Required or Requires New, because you cannot dictate the timeout of other components when you don't require a transaction yourself.

Table 15-4 lists the five transaction support options. This list is a superset of the options provided in Table 14-1.

The reason Required was selected for the **ReservationSystem** component was clearly because it is aware of transaction context and even votes in it. Furthermore, it requires a transaction because it does access a transaction-managed resource. The transaction-managed resource accessed by the **ReservationSystem** component is MSMQ, via the queued component **ReservationTransfer**.

Transaction Setting	Description
Disabled	Simulates the setting of a component that is not configured within Component Services. Components with this setting should not write to any managed resources and should not make any calls to components that manage resources.
Not Supported	Indicates that the component will not run in a transaction. If the component is called from within a transaction's activity, COM+ will create the component in a context running outside of the current activity. This setting is generally the default unless the interface definition declares otherwise.
Supported	Indicates that the component will run in a transaction, but it does not require one.
Required	Indicates that this component requires a transaction to run. If the component is not currently in a transaction, COM+ will start a new transaction.
Requires New	Indicates that the component requires a new transaction. If the component is called from within a transaction, COM+ will start a new transaction activity for this component. Use this setting if you want to insure that this component's transaction is unaffected by the success or failure of others.

Available Transaction Settings
Table 15-4.

We have not completed configuring the system yet, but it would be well worth running it at this point anyway. Notice that if you enter a departure date that's prior to the arrival date, the **ReservationSystem** reports an error. Nonetheless, both the **ReservationTransfer** and the **ReservationBilling** components display dialogs. Clearly, the transactions are not being aborted as you would expect. If an error occurs, neither of these other two dialogs should be displayed because the queued message should be deleted.

The problem relates to incompatible transaction settings that result in multiple contexts that are not all wrapped by the same transaction activity. If you look at the transaction settings for the **ReservationSystemEvent Class**, **ReservationBilling**, and **ReservationTransfer** components, you will notice that by default all their transaction settings were set to Not Supported. The result is that none of these components is wrapped within a transaction, and instead, they all execute independently, as shown in Figure 15-24.

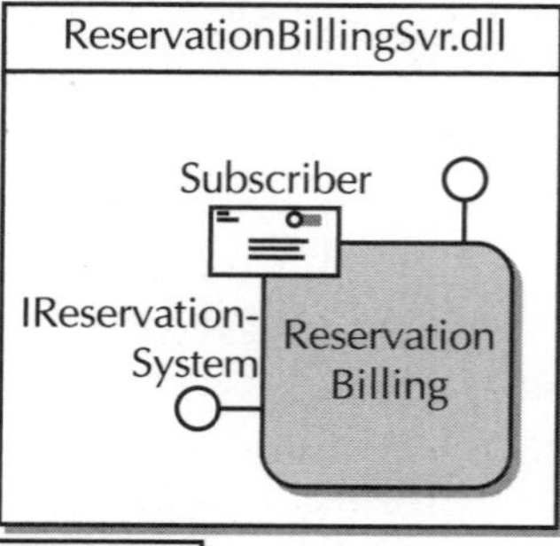

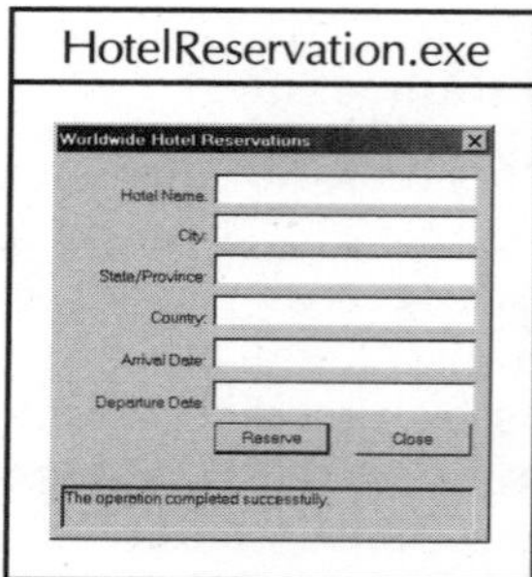

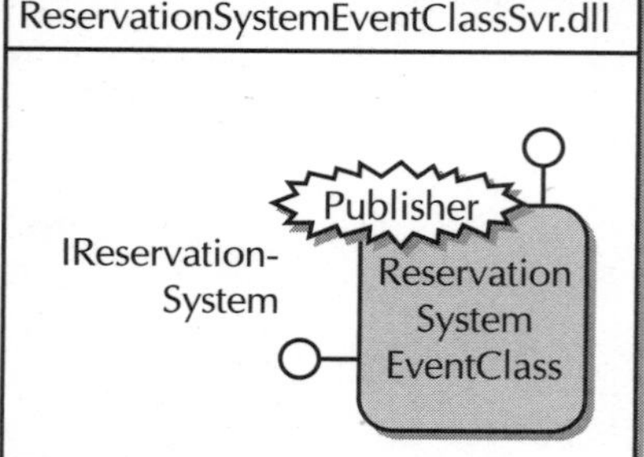

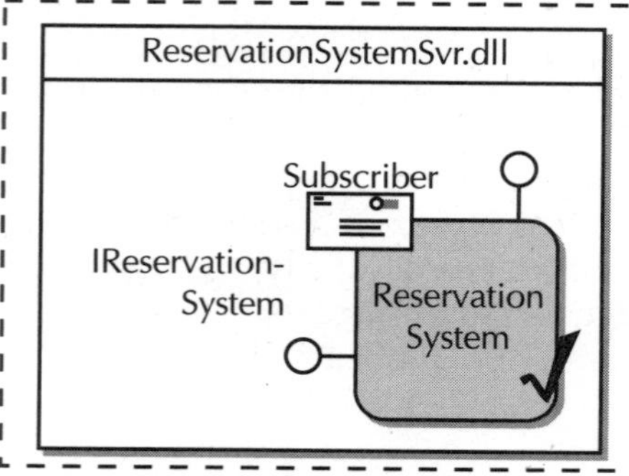

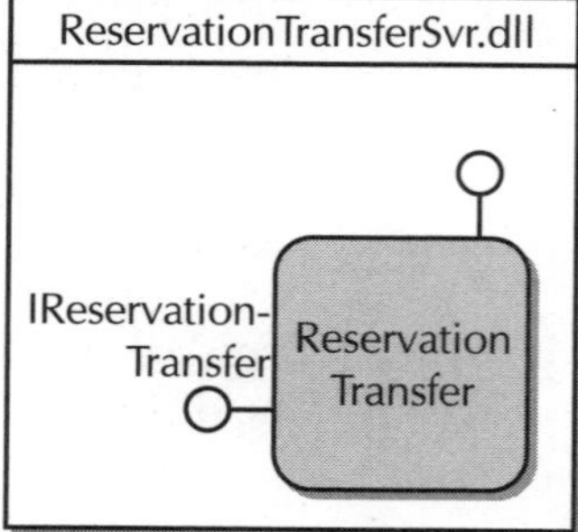

Transaction-only wrapping Reservation System

Figure 15-24.

First of all, the transaction isn't created until the event class calls into the **ReservationSystem**. Therefore, the **ReservationBilling** component is never wrapped into the same transaction. Second, even though a transaction has been created by the time the **ReservationTransfer** component is involved, since this component is not configured to support transactions, the transaction doesn't "bother" to flow to it either.

To fix the problem, the transaction needs to be started earlier. Because the **ReservationSystemEventClass** is to be accessing transaction-managed resources, its transaction setting needs to be configured as Required. In fact, since at development time it is unknown what subscribers will connect to an event class, it is recommended that the **TRANSACTION_REQUIRED** setting be added to the CoClass definition; so by default it is configured as Required. Furthermore, in order for the transaction to flow to both the **ReservationBilling** and the **ReservationTransfer** components, these components need to be configured as Supported. It should be noted that because these components are queued, it is not possible for them to abort a transaction. However, it is possible that the recorder could fail and abort the transaction. Technically, in fact, it is not these components but their "recorder" that is being marked as transaction supported. As with the **ReservationSystemEventClass**, if you know up front that a component is to be queued, it is advisable to mark the component as **TRANSACTION_-SUPPORTED** within the IDL to specify the default when the component is installed. If you test the system now, you will notice that when invalid dates are specified, both the **ReservationBilling** and **ReservationTransfer** components fail to execute because the transaction is aborted. A diagram of the transaction activity is shown in Figure 15-25.

As mentioned, the downloadable sample code includes a class, **ContextHelper**, that writes context properties to a journal file. You can use Component Services to configure the component in various ways and see the impact on the context information displayed in the created journal file. For example, change the transaction attributes to Supported for each of the components, and notice how no transaction even gets created. Next, change the **ReservationSystemEventClass** settings back to Required, and a transaction will be created that ends up wrapping all components. Setting **ReservationSystem** to Requires New will cause a new independent transaction to be created for the ReservationSystem object. This last setting would make sense if you want the **ReservationSystem** and **Reservation-Transfer** components to execute regardless of the success of any other components involved in the call. A diagram of this last setting is shown in Figure 15-26.

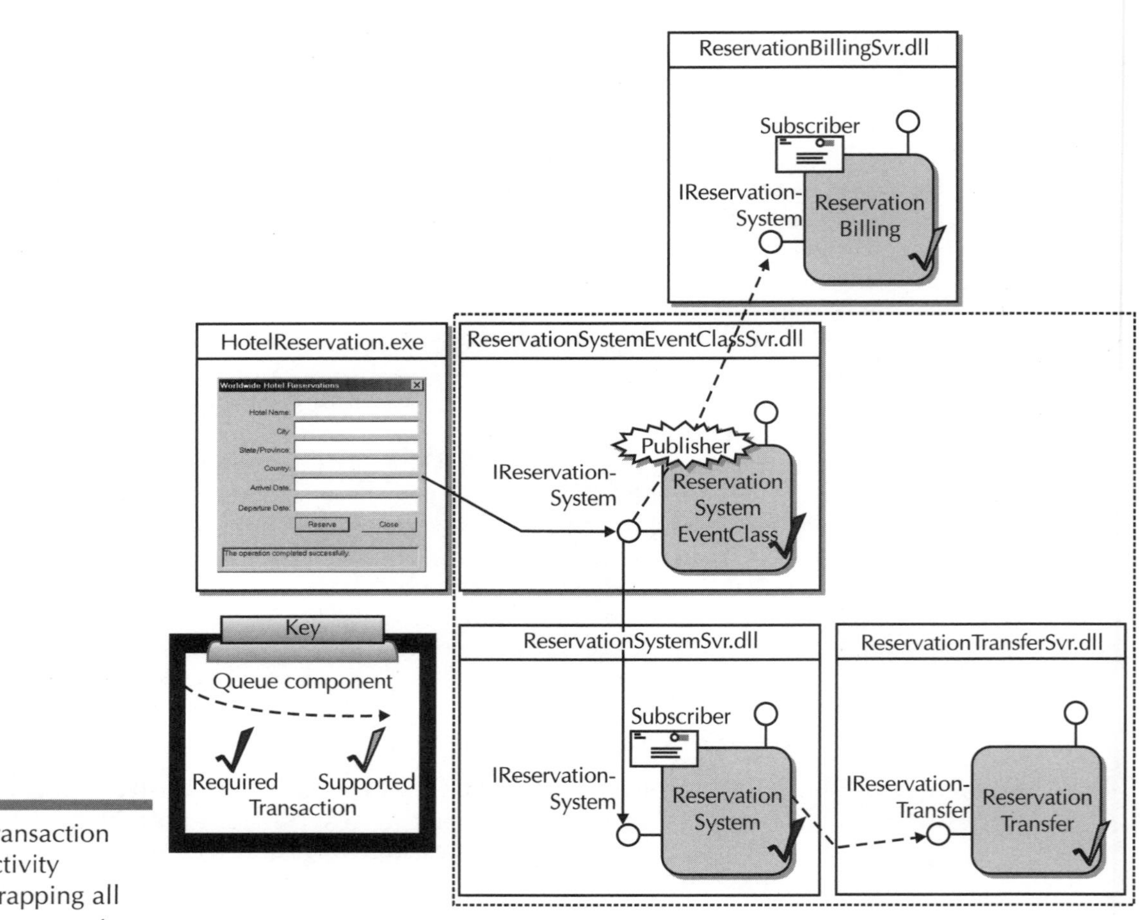

Transaction activity wrapping all components

Figure 15-25.

Before we leave the topic of configuring transactions, let's review how to set the returned **HRESULT** to be the mechanism used for committing or aborting a transaction. This is known as *auto-complete*. Inside Component Services, if you browse all the way down the tree to an individual method and open the properties dialog for that method, you will see the properties dialog, similar to the one shown in Figure 15-27.

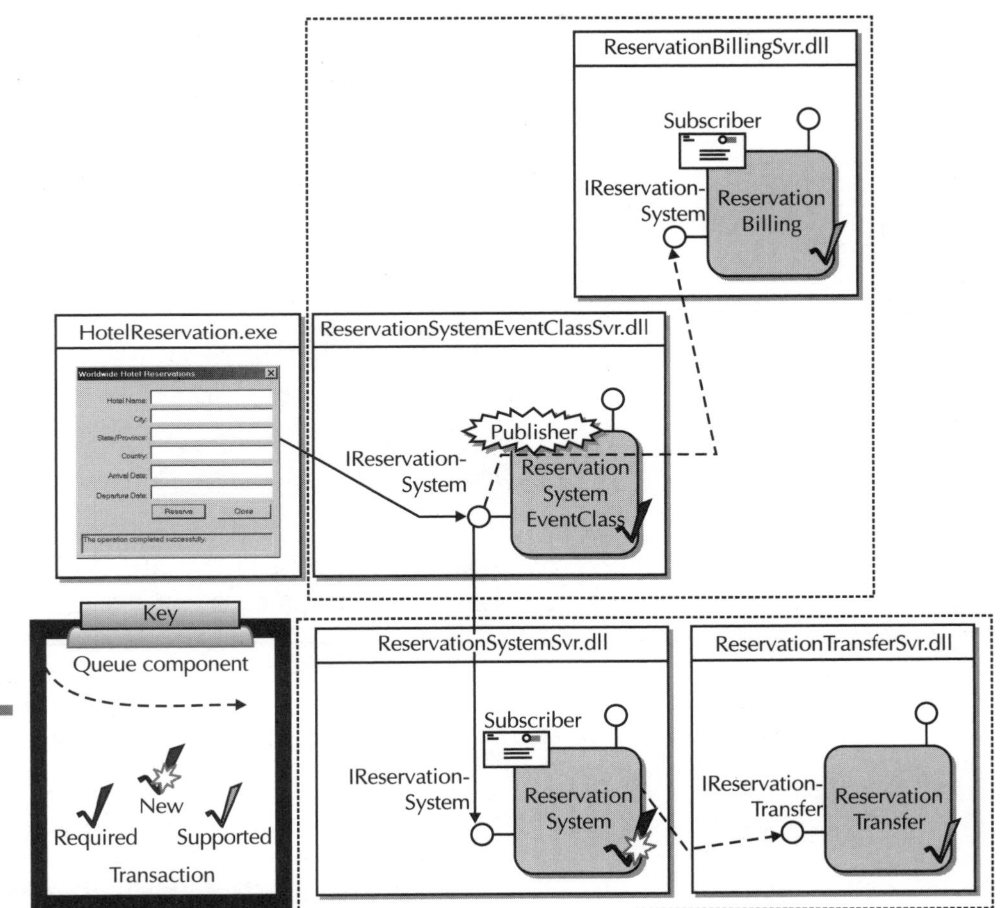

Figure 15-26. Changing the Reservation System component transaction setting to Requires New

On the General tab, you will notice the check box for "Automatically deactivate this object when this method returns." In spite of the cryptic text, this option will cause the component to deactivate after the function call completes, and if transaction support is configured for the component, the returned **HRESULT** will dictate whether the transaction is aborted or committed.

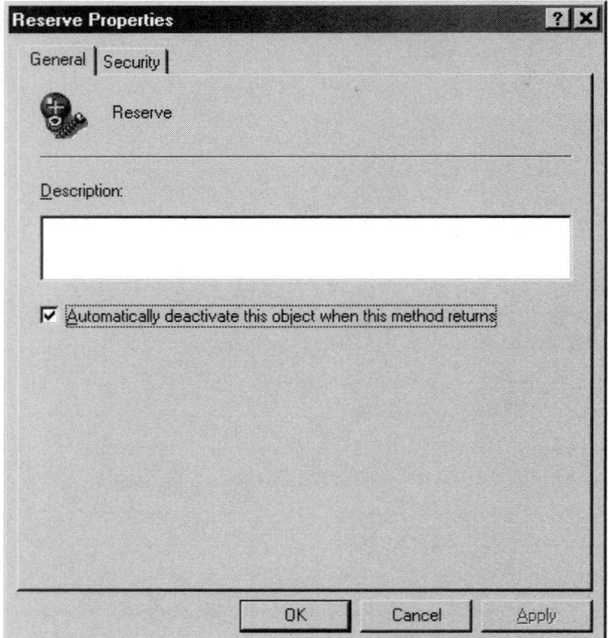

Properties dialog for the **Reserve** method
Figure 15-27.

Programmatically Enlisting an Executable in a Transaction

Before we leave the discussion of transactions, it is worth briefly mentioning how to include an executable in a transaction. As you will notice from the transaction figures in the previous section, the transaction context always fails to wrap the client. Therefore, if the client called into a COM+-configured component and separately accessed a managed resource on its own, the two would run within separate transactions. However, a client can programmatically enlist itself into a transaction so that all operations fail or succeed together, as shown in Figure 15-28.

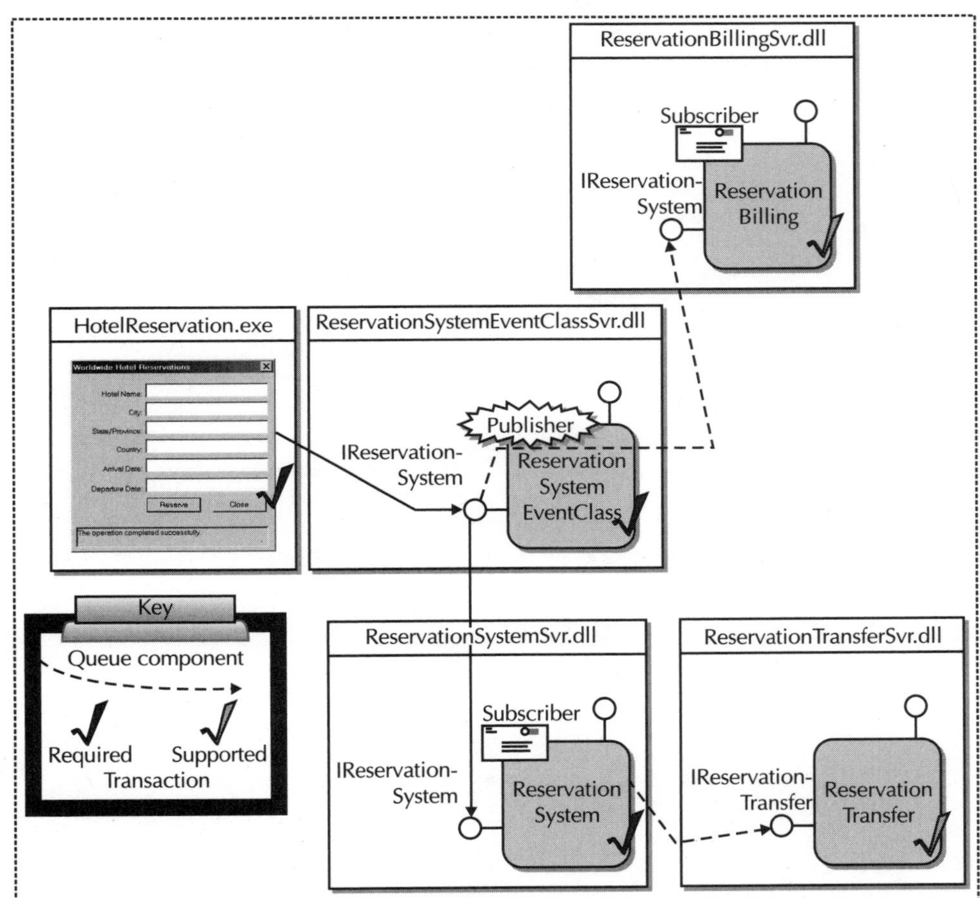

A client executable included within the transaction

Figure 15-28.

Let's add this support to the **HotelReservation.exe** application. Open the **ReservationForm.cpp** file and edit the **OnReserve( )** function as shown below:

```
LRESULT CReservationForm::OnReserve(WORD wNotifyCode,
  WORD wID, HWND hWndCtl, BOOL& bHandled)
{
  USES_CONVERSION;
  HRESULT hr = S_OK;
  CComBSTR property = L"";
  CComPtr<IReservation> reservation;
  CComPtr<ITransactionContextEx> transaction_context;
  CComPtr<IReservationSystem> reservation_system;

  hr = transaction_context.CoCreateInstance(
    CLSID_TransactionContextEx);

  if(SUCCEEDED(hr))
    hr = transaction_context->CreateInstance(
      __uuidof(ReservationSystemEventClass),
      __uuidof(IReservationSystem),
      reinterpret_cast<void**>(&reservation_system.p));

  if(FAILED(hr))
    hr = reservation_system.CoCreateInstance(
      __uuidof(ReservationSystemEventClass));

  // Since the reservation component does not support
  // transactions, it is not required that it be
  // created using the transaction context.
  if(SUCCEEDED(hr))
    hr = reservation.CoCreateInstance(__uuidof(Reservation));

  ATLTRACE(_T("Reserve Hotel at: \n"));

  if(SUCCEEDED(hr))
  {
    GetDlgItemText(IDC_HOTELNAME, property.m_str);
    ATLTRACE(_T("  Hotel Name = %s\n"), OLE2T(property));
    hr = reservation->put_HotelName(property.Detach());
  }

  ...
  if(SUCCEEDED(hr))
  {
```

```
    hr = reservation_system->Reserve(reservation);
  }

  if(reservation!=NULL)
    reservation.Release();

  if(transaction_context != NULL)
  {
    if(SUCCEEDED(hr))
      transaction_context->Commit();
    else
      transaction_context->Abort();
    transaction_context.Release();
  }


  ShowStatus(hr);

  return 0;
}
```

As you can see, the process is rather simple. First, you instantiate a transaction context object and request the **ITransactionContextEx** interface. Then, using this interface, you instantiate any components that you want to be included within the same transaction by using the **CreateInstance( )** call. In this case, should this fail, you instantiate the component normally so that the client will run on Windows 9X platforms as well. (Note that the **TransactionContext** component will work on both NT 4.0 and Windows 2000.) Lastly, at the end of the function call, you commit or abort the transaction depending on whether or not an error occurred.

Configuring Component Activation

As we already outlined in the previous chapter, configuring a component within COM+ introduces an interception layer, which, although slight, will reduce performance over a direct in-process call. Once you've configured the component in COM+, you will notice that the startup time for the server application is noticeably slower than the other two configuration options (nonconfigured and library). Remember that COM+ is looking up the component in the catalog and starting a new application to host the component. Subsequent requests while the server application is active return much faster. Several configuration settings can be applied to your component to further reduce its instantiation time. This is done through the reuse of a component instance. These settings, and a few more, are all available from the Activation tab in the component properties dialog shown in Figure 15-29.

Let's now consider each of these settings, many of which will require some small code changes in order to take full advantage of them.

Object Pooling

There is one drawback to the Hotel Reservation System that could be quite significant in some circumstances. You will notice that while the message box is displayed, the **HotelReservation.exe** application is frozen, waiting for the **Reserve( )** method call to return. Clearly, the call from the publisher to the subscribers is a synchronous call that causes the publisher to wait for each subscriber to be instantiated, and then for each method call to complete on each subscriber, before the published event returns control to the publisher. If you placed a message box into a final construct method on the **ReservationSystem** component, you would notice that every time **Reserve( )** is called, the message box is displayed. In other words, every method call reinstantiates the subscriber, runs the method, and then shuts down the component. Let's consider a possible improvement.

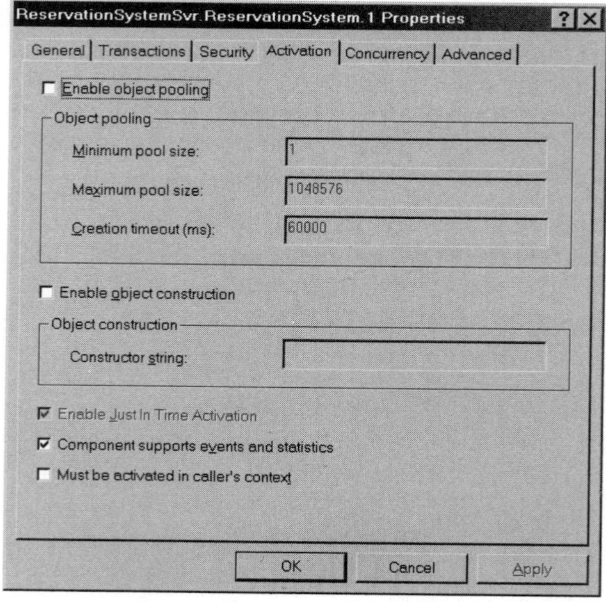

Component properties, Activation tab

Figure 15-29.

Given that instantiation is an expensive operation, one obvious solution to consider is the reduction of the number of times that a subscriber needs to be instantiated. The method for achieving this is object pooling, which, as we discussed in the previous chapter, maintains a pool of instantiated objects, which are then released into action whenever an instantiation request is made. That way, the request to instantiate the component is eliminated, and instead an instantiated component is provided.

Configuring Object Pooling

To enable object pooling, open the **ReservationSystem** component properties dialog and select the Activation tab (shown in Figure 15-29). At the top of the Activation tab you will notice an "Enable object pooling" check box. If you check this, COM+ will *enable* **ReservationSystem** objects to be placed into an object pool, and the "Object pooling" group of text boxes will become enabled. (Note that whether or not object pooling will actually be enabled depends on the support of an additional interface, as we shall see shortly.) These three text boxes provide some operating parameters for how object pooling should function. The first option, "Minimum pool size," indicates what the minimum number of components should be within the pool at any given point in time, even if no client is accessing them. For example, if you were confident that at least 100 clients would be running the majority of the time but that for short periods the client count would drop below this, you may want to set this value to 100. That way, even when demand did not require more instances, the objects could be "kept warm" waiting for the next client to activate them. This will reduce the startup time of the COM+ application, because when the application starts, that number of components will be instantiated, even though they have not yet been called. However, once running, instantiation time could be significantly faster depending on the resources consumed by the component.

Setting the minimum number of objects in the pool is an important feature if you want to reduce instantiation time and you know the usual quantity of components that should be available at all times. On the other hand, there may be times when there are so many requests to instantiate a component, and the resources allocated for that component are so substantial, that it is necessary to limit the number of objects that can be placed in the pool and instantiated by clients. This limit is configured with the "Maximum pool size" text box. There will never be more than the maximum number of components instantiated, either active or inactive, at a time. If a client requests a component, and the maximum pool size has already been reached, the request will be delayed until the next component becomes available. In order for this delay not to exceed a maximum time period, the last text box, "Creation timeout(ms)," is provided. Changing this value will therefore change the amount of time a client is delayed while waiting for the component to instantiate. If the maximum time is exceeded, an **E_TIMEOUT HRESULT** error value will be returned to the caller.

Implementing IObjectControl

As demonstrated above, configuring a component for object pooling is as simple as flipping a configuration switch on the component. This could introduce a potential problem, however. Earlier we mentioned that if you displayed a message box within the **FinalConstruct( )** method of the **ReservationSystem** component, you could explicitly observe the calls to instantiate the component. After configuring the component for object pooling, you would notice that each time **Reserve( )** is called, the message box within the **FinalConstruct( )** method is no longer called. This, of course, is what we were trying to achieve. However, this could also potentially introduce a bug. What would happen, for example, if the **FinalConstruct( )** code included some critical initialization code that assigned a unique ID each time the component was instantiated or opened a file with a unique filename? Because the **FinalConstruct( )** method is no longer being called, a bug could potentially be introduced by the variance in behavior.

Potentially more damaging and more prevalent, consider the behavior of a component that was not initially written as a subscriber. If a property for the component was set to value A, it would be expected that during a follow-up call the property would remain as A. However, if the component were configured as a subscriber, then the property would be reset without object pooling and remain without object pooling. Object pooling, therefore, would change the runtime behavior. Furthermore, if object pooling was enabled and a new component was instantiated from the pool, this component could be initialized with the data from the previous activation.

To avoid all this, object pooling involves a little more than a configuration switch. In addition, your component needs to support the **IObjectControl** interface. This interface can be used to notify the client when it is going into and out of the object pool. More specifically, as the object pooling configuration may be off, this allows you to be notified when the object becomes activated and deactivated.

This solution involves adding support for the **IObjectControl** interface to the **ReservationSystem** component. If we had used the MTS wizard to create our component, it would have added an implementation of **IObjectControl** to our component. Fortunately, there is very little work required to implement anyway, so we will implement it by hand. The changes are highlighted below:

```
#include <comsvcs.h>
...
//////////////////////////////////////////////////////////////////////////
// CReservationSystem
class ATL_NO_VTABLE CReservationSystem :
  public CComObjectRootEx<CComMultiThreadModel>,
  public CComCoClass<CReservationSystem, &CLSID_ReservationSystem>,
  public IDispatchImpl<IReservationSystem,
    &IID_IReservationSystem, &LIBID_RESERVATIONSYSTEMLib>,
  public IObjectControl
{
...
BEGIN_COM_MAP(CReservationSystem)
    COM_INTERFACE_ENTRY(IReservationSystem)
    COM_INTERFACE_ENTRY(IDispatch)
    COM_INTERFACE_ENTRY(IObjectControl)
END_COM_MAP()
...

// IObjectControl
  STDMETHOD(Activate)()
  {
    return S_OK;
  }
  STDMETHOD_(VOID, Deactivate)()
  {
    return;
  }
  STDMETHOD_(BOOL, CanBePooled)()
  {
    return TRUE;
  }
};
```

Let's briefly review the methods. As we introduced in the previous chapter, object pooling adds a new type of status to the component. When configured for object pooling, a component can be activated or deactivated depending on whether it is actively executing and performing work or instead, waiting idly in the pool until called upon. The **Activate( )** and **Deactivate( )**

methods on the component are called when the object transitions from inactive to active and then active to inactive, respectively. Therefore, any initialization code that needs to run every time the component makes one of these transitions will need to be moved from **FinalConstruct( )**, for example, to **Activate( )**. Since our **ReservationSystem** component doesn't require any such code, the default implementation code can be left in place.

The last method, **CanBePooled( )**, is set to return **TRUE**, indicating that the **ReservationSystem** component can be pooled. An interesting thing to note about this setting is that it does not disable the "Enable object pooling" check box on the Activation tab of the component's properties. To do this would require that the component be instantiated during configuration time, which may not be appropriate in all cases. Therefore, although the component can be configured for object pooling, if the **CanBePooled( )** method returns **FALSE**, object pooling will not occur, just as if there was not support for **IObjectControl** in the first place.

Object pooling requires that components are aggregable and do not have thread affinity.

Two other important criteria are required for object pooling to be successful. First, components are not allowed to have any *thread affinity*—meaning they cannot be bound to one thread over another. Therefore, components that support object pooling cannot support the Apartment Threading Model because this restricts an instantiated component to one particular thread and can drastically inhibit performance. Second, components must be aggregable due to the workings of the interception mechanism.

Just-in-Time Activation

Let's consider another possible performance improvement directed at ensuring that objects don't remain in an active state longer than necessary. Returning to the Hotel Reservation System, imagine that the **Reservation-Transfer** component maintained an active link across the Internet in order to send reservations across to participating hotels. Furthermore, consider that this link had a limited bandwidth so it was undesirable to have too many active links at once. Last, consider that rather than the **ReservationSystem** component calling the **ReservationTransfer** component, it is called by a different client that maintains a reference count on the **Reservation-Transfer** component, forcing it to stay around in memory, hogging the link, until the client application shuts down.

To combat this type of problem, Microsoft included Just-in-Time (JIT) activation in the COM+ services. As you may have noticed, JIT is automatically configured for those components that are set to support or require transactions. The result is that each time a transaction is completed, each of these components is deactivated either by returning it to the object pool if object pooling is enabled, or by uninstantiating it. The important point about this mechanism is that it occurs whether or not the client releases all pointers to the component's interfaces. Therefore, a client could have a pointer to a component that is no longer instantiated. Fortunately, in reality this is a pointer to the interceptor, and when the client calls back into the interface, the interceptor will reactivate the component so that the call will be successful. What it will not do, however, is restore the object's state.

There are several potential solutions to this dilemma. First, it is advised that components written to avoid this problem be stateless. In fact, although not always appropriate, it is usually beneficial that all components written for COM+ applications be stateless. This means that data should not be maintained inside the component across method invocations or groups of method invocations. In other words, each method or set of methods should initialize the component at the beginning of the call and uninitialize the component
at the end of the call. It should not be expected that data specific to one client's method invocation would be consistent with the same client's next method invocation. Practically speaking, therefore, don't write components that rely on the state of the component during one call (or group of calls) to be the same during the next call (or group of calls).

Another possibility could be used in addition or in place of the stateless component composition. This, of course, involves support for the **IObjectControl** interface, just as with object pooling. With this interface, you can perform any initialization during the activation call and uninitialize during the deactivate call. It is during these two calls, for example, that the **ReservationTransfer** component would activate and deactivate its link so as to consume this valuable resource for the minimum amount of time.

One more important point to consider is to extend or shorten the activation context beyond the transaction boundary. This can be achieved using the **IContextState**'s **SetDeactivateOnReturn( )** function. This function takes a Boolean parameter that enables you to prevent the deactivation, sending false, or else force the deactivation even before a transaction commits (by sending true). Code demonstrating the latter is shown for the **Reservation-System** component's **Reserve( )** function below:

```
hr = CoGetObjectContext(IID_IObjectContext,
  reinterpret_cast<void**>(&context_state) );
if (FAILED(hr))
  context_state = NULL;
else
{
  hr = context_state->SetDeactivateOnReturn(VARIANT_TRUE);
}
```

In our system, this doesn't much change what occurs since the transaction doesn't last significantly beyond the **Reserve( )** method completion. However, if another component were to call the **Reserve( )** method and wait before calling completed, the **SetDeactivateOnReturn(VARIANT_TRUE)** method would allow the **ReservationSystem** component to be deactivated even before the transaction was committed.

Utilizing the Construction String Inside Your Component

The next setting that appears on the Activation tab in Figure 15-29 is the "Enable object construction" check box. One subtle frustration that many new COM programmers experience is the inability to specify any construction parameters when instantiating a component. **CoCreateInstance[Ex]( )** and **CoGetObject( )**, the most typical ways for instantiating a component, have a fixed set of parameters, and neither provides the ability to pass data into the constructor. With the advent of Windows 2000 and COM+, this capacity has been added to a limited degree. The "Constructor string" text box on the Activation tab allows you to insert a text string that can then be accessed from inside the component.

To access the string from inside the component, you need to add support for the **IObjectConstruct** interface. This interface supports one method that takes an **IDispatch** parameter that can be queried for the **IObjectConstructString** interface. Given this interface, calling **get_ConstructString( )** will retrieve the constructor string. To demonstrate this, we will add support to the **ReservationSystem** component that will allow us to configure a context log filename to which context information can be dumped if the filename is provided.

Below is a code listing of the implementation:

```
// IObjectConstruct
STDMETHODIMP CReservationSystem::construct_string(
  IDispatch * pCtorObj)
{
  //  construct_string method is called by COM+
  //  if so configured in Component Services.
  //  Component Properties, Activation tab, Object
  //  constructor settings.

  HRESULT hr;
  CComPtr<IObjectConstructString> object_construct_string;
```

```
  BSTR construct_string;

  // first get the IObjectConstructString interface from the
  // constructor object
  hr = pCtorObj->QueryInterface(IID_IObjectConstructString,
    reinterpret_cast<void**>(&object_construct_string) );
  if (SUCCEEDED(hr))
  {
    // Then get the constructor string and
    //  set it to the log filename
    hr = object_construct_string->get_ConstructString(
      &construct_string);

    if (SUCCEEDED(hr))
    {
      m_LogFileName = construct_string;
    }
  }

  return hr;
}
```

If for some reason the above code isn't called, be sure to set any variables you use to a default. It will not be called if your component is not configured in Component Services or if it is configured and the user doesn't enable the object constructor string on the component properties Activation tab.

For this to compile, you will obviously also need to add the function declaration to the **CReservationSystem** header file along with the **m_LogFileName**, which is a **CComBSTR**. In addition, make the usual changes for supporting a new interface, updating the class hierarchy and the COM MAP with references to the new interface.

```
// CReservationSystem
class ATL_NO_VTABLE CReservationSystem :
  public CComObjectRootEx<CComMultiThreadModel>,
  public CComCoClass<CReservationSystem, &CLSID_ReservationSystem>,
  public ISupportErrorInfo,
  public IDispatchImpl<IReservationSystem,
    &IID_IReservationSystem, &LIBID_RESERVATIONSYSTEMLib>,
  public IObjectControl,
  public IObjectConstruct
{
  ...
```

```
BEGIN_COM_MAP(CReservationSystem)
  COM_INTERFACE_ENTRY(IReservationSystem)
  COM_INTERFACE_ENTRY(IDispatch)
  COM_INTERFACE_ENTRY(ISupportErrorInfo)
  COM_INTERFACE_ENTRY(IObjectControl)
  COM_INTERFACE_ENTRY(IObjectConstruct)
END_COM_MAP()
  ...
  CComBSTR m_LogFileName;
```

Additional Activation Settings

There are two remaining settings on the Activation tab. The first, "Component supports events and statistics," enables COM+ to record object statistics. Component Services itself will watch for these events and update its display when this feature is enabled. You can then view the status of the application, for example, by selecting the component's node within your COM+ applications and then right-clicking on the same node and going to View | Statistics View. It is useful to view these, especially if you want to see how many objects are currently active versus how many are pooled, as shown in Figure 15-30.

In addition, events and statistics from an application can be monitored by system- and transaction-monitoring applications. When this is not enabled, events and statistics are not available. The best approach is to leave this enabled during development and testing and then to disable it when an

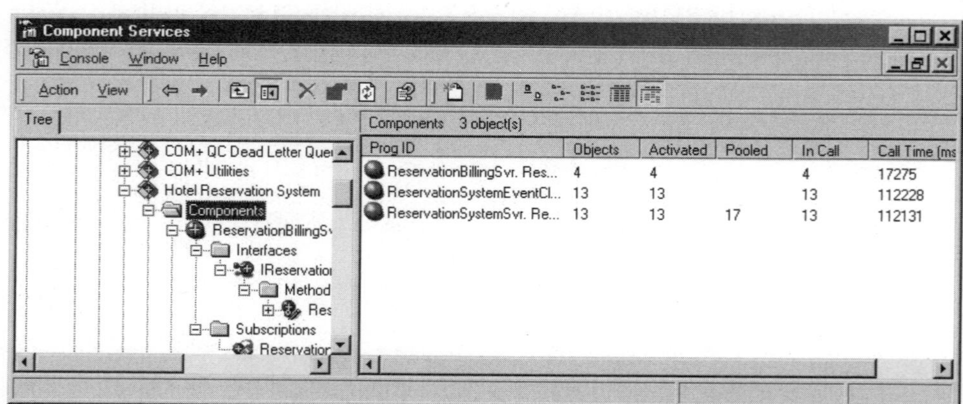

Application status

Figure 15-30.

application is in production and no monitoring is being done. If performance issues arise, this can be enabled so that monitoring applications can be used to diagnose the issues.

The last setting on the Activation tab, "Must be activated in the caller's context," is one more performance enhancement. This setting essentially insists that the component be placed within the caller's context, and if for some reason this was not possible, the component instantiation call should fail. Be careful choosing this selection, as it is very easy for someone to later change either the caller or the component's configuration to create an incompatible context.

Role-Based Security

One topic that we have not discussed in this chapter so far is security. Basic security is described briefly here to cover the differences between COM+ role-based security and those settings available within DCOM, which we discussed in Chapter 12.

COM+ adds role-based security.

COM+ adds role-based security to the existing COM security services. With role-based security, roles are defined, users are given roles, and access to functionality is determined by whether or not users have been assigned the given role required for the function they are accessing.

A user's role determines access rights.

COM+ lets you configure role-based security at the component, interface, and method levels. This provides for a high degree of control over security without doing any programming. Role-based security can also be taken a step farther programmatically. With role-based security, you can

- Grant all users who possess a given role access to the entire application
- Grant access by role to specific components within an application
- Grant access by role to specific interfaces within a component
- Grant access by role to specific methods on an interface within a component

And once again, this can all be accomplished without any additional programming. But if this isn't enough, even finer grained control over security using roles is possible.

Let's say you want to allow only certain users to use the Hotel Reservation System. These users will be given the "Hotel Reserver" role, which will be configured for the **IReservationSystem** interface on the **ReservationSystem** component. Let's also say that you have a special "Expensive Hotel

Reserver" role that enables certain users to reserve some of the more exclusive hotels. The first role, "Hotel Reserver," can be configured directly from Component Services. The second role, "Expensive Hotel Reserver," can be programmed only into the **ReservationSystem** component, as it requires an explicit check of which hotels to include in the "exclusive" category.

Configuring Roles and Role-Based Security

First we need to configure the roles that we have defined and add user accounts to these roles. Then the roles are assigned to the functions. Roles are application specific and are therefore configured under the application. Navigate through Component Services to Roles, which appears directly under Components for a given application. Either right-click on Roles and select New Role, or select Action | New Role when Roles is selected. This will display the dialog shown in Figure 15-31.

Create a "Hotel Reserver" and "Expensive Hotel Reserver" role. Once you've created these roles, you can then assign user accounts to them. Note that you can assign individual users or user groups to the role.

Next, navigate to Component, open the component properties dialog, and select the Security tab, shown in Figure 15-32.

The two roles that have been defined will be displayed in the list. You assign a role by selecting it in the list. Select the "Hotel Reserver" role.

Finally, you need to turn on access checks for the application. This can be performed from the Security tab of the application dialog (see Figure 15-10). Now that the roles have been configured, they can be accessed programmatically through two different interfaces. The preferred method is through the **ISecurityCallContext** interface, and the other is using the **IObjectContext** interface. A component gets the **ISecurityCallContext** interface by calling **CoGetCallContext( )**.

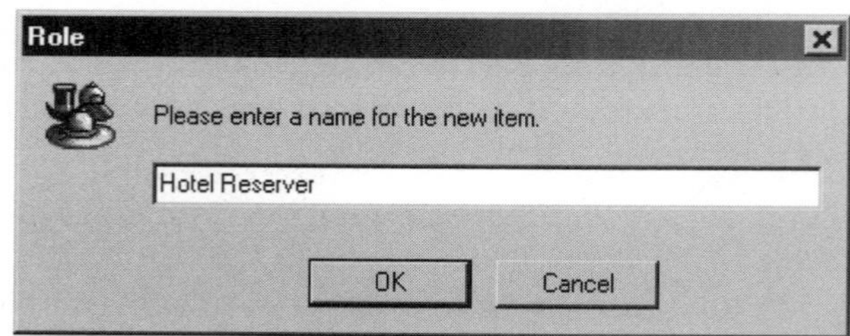

Creating a new role with Component Services

Figure 15-31.

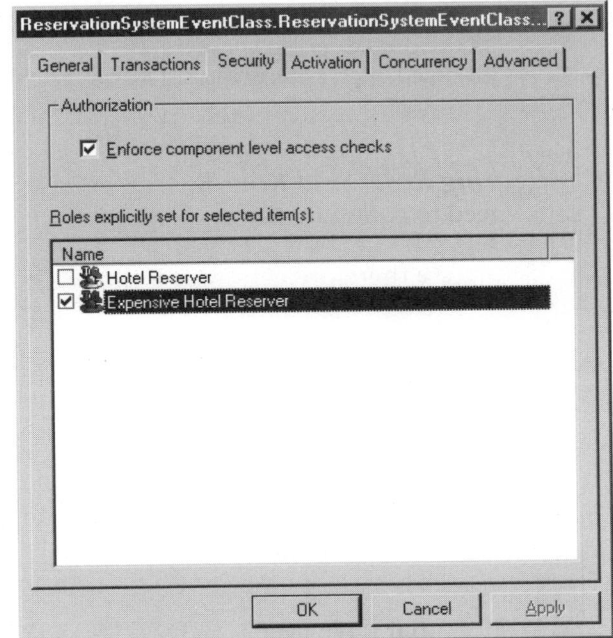

Assigning a role to a component

Figure 15-32.

The sample code includes a private method called **CheckSecurity( )**, which wraps the role-based security calls. This is shown below:

```
BOOL CReservationSystem::CheckSecurity()
{
  HRESULT hr;
  CComPtr<ISecurityCallContext> security_context = 0;
  VARIANT_BOOL b_security_is_enabled;
  CComBSTR sRole;
  VARIANT_BOOL bCallerIsInRole = false;

  hr = CoGetCallContext(IID_ISecurityCallContext, (void**)&security_context);
  if (security_context != 0) {
    hr = security_context->IsSecurityEnabled(&b_security_is_enabled);
    if (SUCCEEDED(hr) && b_security_is_enabled) {
      sRole = L"Expensive Hotel Reserver";
      hr = security_context->IsCallerInRole(sRole, &bCallerIsInRole);
    }
  }

  return bCallerIsInRole;
}
```

The **CheckSecurity( )** method explicitly checks for the "Expensive Hotel Reserver" role and returns TRUE if it is present and FALSE if security is not enabled or the user does not possess this role. In our system, a hotel beginning with *E* will be considered exclusive, as shown here:

```
// Check security
if(SUCCEEDED(hr))
{
  CComBSTR hotel_name;

  hr = reservation->get_HotelName(&hotel_name.m_str);
  if(SUCCEEDED(hr))
  {
    if((hotel_name[0] == L'E') && (!CheckSecurity())
      hr = ERROR_INVALID_ACCESS;
  }
```

Note that the code above makes a call to **IsSecurityEnabled( )** before checking to see whether the caller is in the specified role. This is because **IsCallerInRole( )** will return TRUE when role-based security is not enabled.

Debugging Server Components

There are a few different approaches to debugging server components. Regardless of approach, you should work out as many of the logic bugs using standard testing and debugging before deploying the component in COM+. For those features that require COM+, deploy as a library application in a test host prior to deploying as a server application (assuming no object pooling or queued component functionality, of course). Any of these configuration options can be debugged using the methods outlined in Chapter 9. For those issues that are COM+-application specific, runtime debugging is also possible and is explained in further detail below.

Debugging a Server Component Configured as a Library Application

When the application is configured as a library application (in the application properties Activation tab, the Activation type selected is Library application), the components will run in the client's process. In this case, to configure the test client executable, from Visual Studio choose Project | Settings, and on the Debug panel, select "Executable for debug session." Debugging in this scenario is not much different from debugging in a normal scenario. You will notice, however, that COM+ interception can and will get between your test client and server component.

Remember that **Activate( )** is not called until a method is invoked, rather than when the object is created. Since neither JIT nor object pooling is available to a library application, **Deactivate( )** will be called only after all active references are removed.

Configured as Server Application/Debugging from the Active Workspace

You have two choices for invoking runtime debugging if the application is configured as a server application (from the application properties Activation tab, the Activation type is Server application). In this case, COM+ uses **dllhost.exe** to host the components. Therefore, the "Executable for the debug session" setting in Visual Studio should be set to **dllhost.exe**, which is located in the Windows System32 directory. One additional parameter required when using **dllhost.exe** is the application GUID. This is specified as parameter /ProcessID to dllhost. So, when debugging a configured server application, your debug settings should look something like those depicted in Figure 15-33.

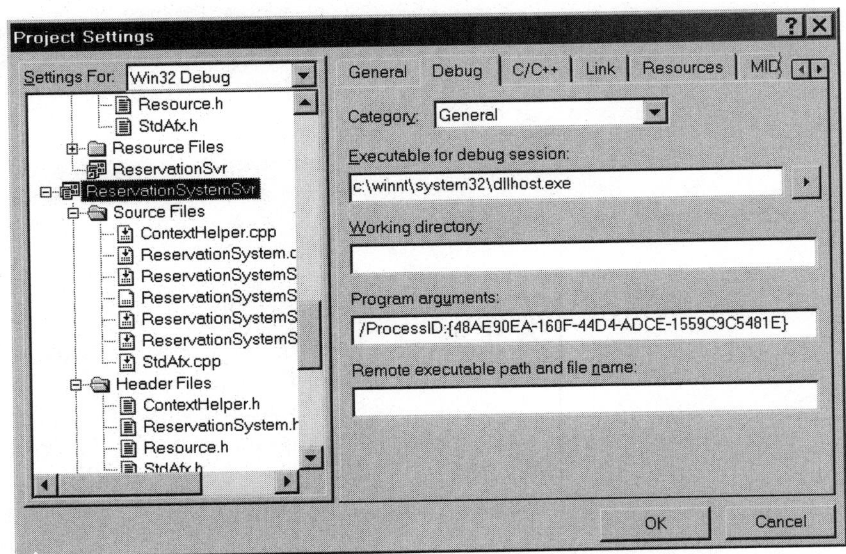

Project settings for debugging a server application

Figure 15-33.

The easy way to configure the /ProcessID is by navigating to the Advanced tab (Figure 15-12) of the application properties; then temporarily set "Launch in debugger," and copy the /ProcessID string and paste it into the "Program arguments" text box on the Debug panel. While you are there, you may want to select the "Leave running while idle" option if it is not already selected. If you don't, COM+ may shut down the process unexpectedly because no one is using it. When you execute the debugger, COM+ **dllhost.exe** will fire up.

An alternative is to use the "Launch in debugger" setting (Figure 15-12) for its intended purpose (as opposed to a handy paste buffer for /ProcessID, as indicated above). In this case, any client creating an instance of your server will fire up the debugger. These are both fine approaches if you just need to debug the server. If you are debugging both client and server, you can step into the server calls directly from the client. When you do, COM+ will fire up an instance of the default debugger even if "Launch in debugger" is not set.

If you are debugging transactions, you may need to adjust the default transaction timeout. If the timeout is exceeded, COM+ will terminate the transaction and thereby could abort your debugging session early.

Deploying an Application

Once you've built and tested your system on a local machine, you will want to test it across the network. This, of course, will be the real test for your queued components. Perhaps more importantly, you will need to deploy the application to client machines and deploy this application to other test and production servers. Using Component Services, you can easily generate either a server or client deployment package.

In the first step, right-click on your application and select Export. This will display the wizard shown in Figure 15-34, which presents the option of exporting an application proxy or the entire server application.

Application Proxies

Selecting "Application proxy" generates a Windows Installer package (an MSI file) that can be installed on client machines. Application proxies include all registration and component proxy information required to access a configured server application. Even the machine name of the server that the application proxy was exported from will be included in the package. This provides an automated DCOM configuration mechanism.

At the client you will be able to use the Windows Installer package to install the proxy on all client machines. However, if the client is being deployed to a Windows NT or Windows 98 machine, an updated Windows Installer must

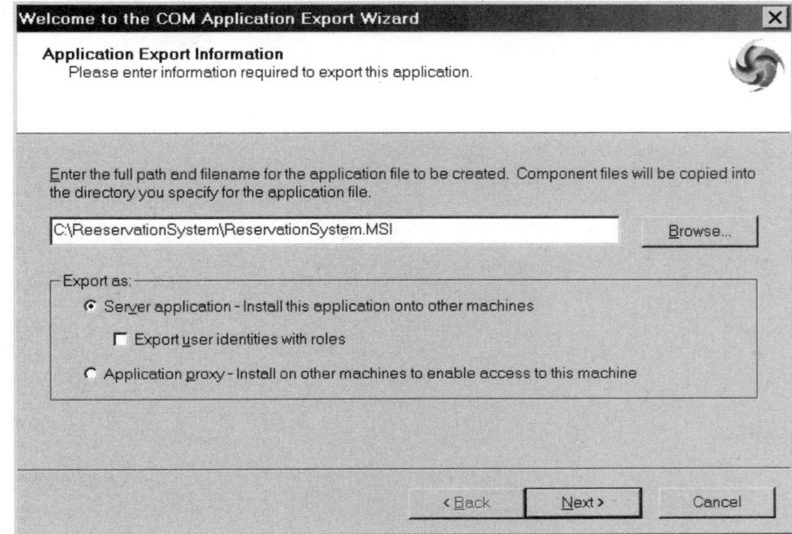

The Application Export Wizard
Figure 15-34.

first be present. New client code is not required in order to access the components on a remote server. The clients used to access the component on a single machine will work from a client once the installation is run using the server name included in the proxy. If you need to change your application to use a different server, you can right-click on the client properties and navigate to the Activation tab, where you will be provided with the opportunity to change the server name, as shown in Figure 15-35.

Note that this dialog is available only on Windows 2000 machines. All other options will be disabled. If you are installing to Windows NT, 98, or 95, all of the application details are placed into the registry along with all the other required registry settings. For these operating systems, if the configured server changes, the registry can be adjusted, or a new installation package can be generated and installed at the clients.

Note that you have a few options to consider when deploying your component to a client machine. You can deploy only the TLB and use OLE Automation type marshalling, or the proxy/stub DLL and use standard proxy/stub marshalling, just as you would with straight DCOM. Be sure to manually include all additionally required DLLs in the MSI package. For example, in the Hotel Reservation System, the **ReservationSvr.dll** file was never included in

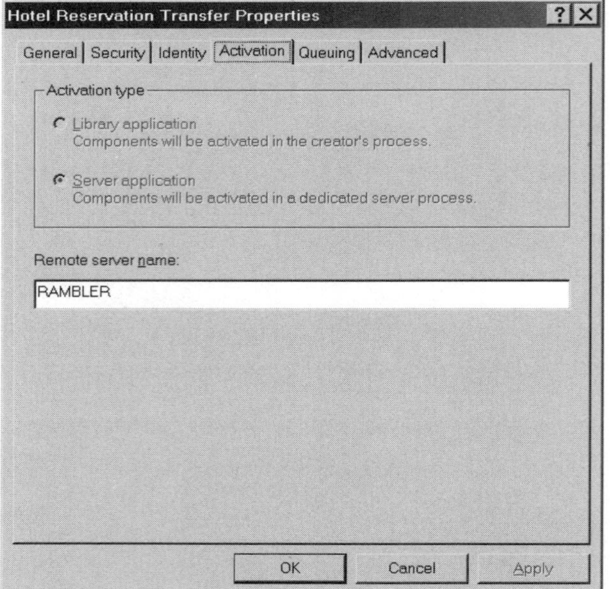

Application proxy properties, Activation tab

Figure 15-35.

Component Services, so it will not be added to the MSI file. Since the installation package generated by Component Services can be edited using any editor that is compatible with Windows Installer (including one from the platform SDK), the manual step is required only for generating the setup, not for actual deployment on all the clients.

Server Applications

A selection of "Server application" from the dialog in Figure 15-34 generates a Windows Installer package that can be used to deploy the application to other servers. The server application package will include all configured components and configuration settings. The server application package generated is compatible only with Windows 2000/COM+.

With either the server application or application proxy packages, only the configured components or proxies for the configured components are included in the installation package. So, just as with the client, you will need to include **ReservationSvr.dll** manually in your deployment package. Note that included in the download code are the MSI files for each application and proxy discussed in this chapter.

Building an MTS-Compatible Application Using the ATL COM AppWizard

In the sections above, we have detailed building a COM+-specific application. This is fine if your component will be targeting only Windows 2000. If, however, you also need your component to run on Windows NT 4.0, you will need to create components that are compatible with MTS (Microsoft Transaction Server). MTS-compatible components will run on Windows 2000, but they cannot take advantage of many new features in Windows 2000 COM+ Services, such as queued components, and they will not be able to access any of the updated interfaces, such as **IContextState** and **IObjectContextInfo**.

To build an MTS-compatible ATL component application, use the ATL wizard and check the MTS compatibility check box "Support MTS," as shown in Figure 15-36.

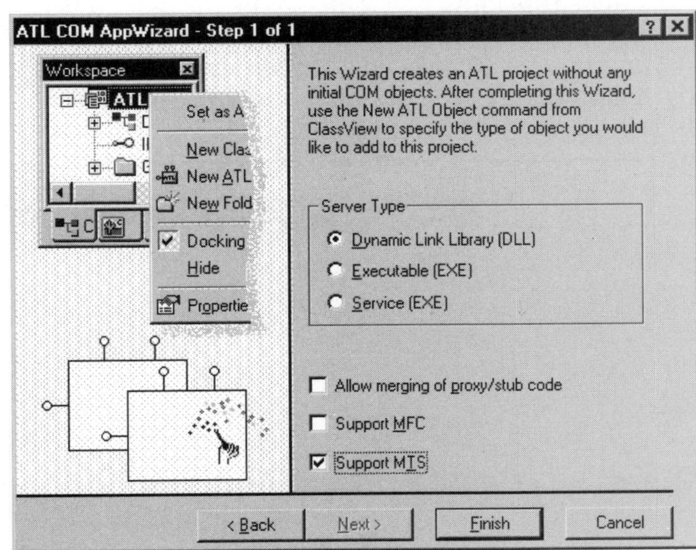

The ATL COM AppWizard generating a project with MTS support

Figure 15-36.

This adds the MTS libraries to the various build lines:

```
# ADD LINK32 kernel32.lib user32.lib gdi32.lib winspool.lib
comdlg32.lib advapi32.lib shell32.lib ole32.lib oleaut32.lib
uuid.lib odbc32.lib odbccp32.lib mtx.lib mtxguid.lib delayimp.lib
/nologo /subsystem:windows /dll /debug /machine:I386
/pdbtype:sept /delayload:mtxex.dll
```

Also, it adds a /MD to the proxy/stub in order to generate a multithreaded proxy-stub.

To create an MTS-compatible component, you use the ATL Object Wizard and select "MS Transaction Server Component." An MTS tab is then available. Let's review the settings on the MTS tab, shown in Figure 15-37.

We've seen the Interface setting of Dual or Custom in previous chapters. Dual interfaces are recommended by default. If "Support IObjectControl" is checked, the wizard will generate a default implementation of the COM+ **IObjectControl** interface. If "Support IObjectControl" is not checked, there is nothing that makes this component different from a standard COM component generated by the ATL wizard.

Notice that the wizard does not support the selection of a threading model. Single threading is assumed to be the default because this is the setting most often used by transactional components. If this isn't changed in the generated source code, COM+ object pooling will be prevented. This isn't an issue for MTS because object pooling support is not built in.

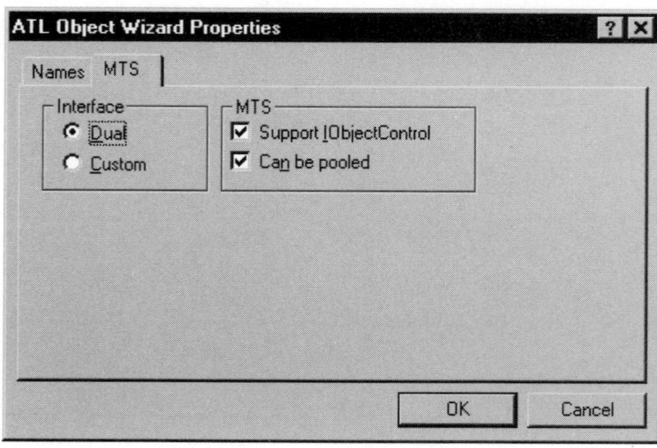

The ATL Object Wizard properties dialog, MTS tab
Figure 15-37.

The wizard-generated code for **ReservationSystem.h** is listed below:

```
// ReservationSystem.h : Declaration of the CReservationSystem

#ifndef __RESERVATIONSYSTEM_H_
#define __RESERVATIONSYSTEM_H_

#include "resource.h"       // main symbols
#include <mtx.h>

/////////////////////////////////////////////////////////////////////////////
// CReservationSystem
class ATL_NO_VTABLE CReservationSystem :
  public CComObjectRootEx<CComSingleThreadModel>,
  public CComCoClass<CReservationSystem, &CLSID_ReservationSystem>,
  public IObjectControl,
  public IDispatchImpl<IReservationSystem, &IID_IReservationSystem,
    &LIBID_SAMPLEWITHMTSLib>
{
public:
  CReservationSystem()
  {
  }

DECLARE_REGISTRY_RESOURCEID(IDR_RESERVATIONSYSTEM)

DECLARE_PROTECT_FINAL_CONSTRUCT()

DECLARE_NOT_AGGREGATABLE(CReservationSystem)

BEGIN_COM_MAP(CReservationSystem)
  COM_INTERFACE_ENTRY(IReservationSystem)
  COM_INTERFACE_ENTRY(IObjectControl)
  COM_INTERFACE_ENTRY(IDispatch)
END_COM_MAP()

// IObjectControl
public:
  STDMETHOD(Activate)();
  STDMETHOD_(BOOL, CanBePooled)();
  STDMETHOD_(void, Deactivate)();

  CComPtr<IObjectContext> m_spObjectContext;

// IReservationSystem
```

```
public:
};

#endif //__RESERVATIONSYSTEM_H_
```

Here is the code generated for the CoClass:

```
// ReservationSystem.cpp : Implementation of CReservationSystem
#include "stdafx.h"
#include "AReservationSystem.h"
#include "ReservationSystem.h"

///////////////////////////////////////////////////////////////////////////
// CReservationSystem

HRESULT CReservationSystem::Activate()
{
  HRESULT hr = GetObjectContext(&m_spObjectContext);
  if (SUCCEEDED(hr))
    return S_OK;
  return hr;
}

BOOL CReservationSystem::CanBePooled()
{
  return TRUE;
}

void CReservationSystem::Deactivate()
{
  m_spObjectContext.Release();
}
```

You can now build the sample and run it. Since you selected the Support MTS option when you ran the application wizard, you will be given a build instruction to "Execute mtxrereg.exe before using MTS components in MTS." Again, this is a legacy of MTS and is not required when running the component under COM+.

For the **ReservationSystem** component above, you could easily convert at least the transaction portion of the application to be MTS compatible. To do this, change the transaction code to use the **IObjectContext** interface rather than its Windows 2000 replacements, **IContextState** and **IObjectContextInfo**. Also, because **CoGetObjectContext( )** is not supported on NT 4.0, you will need to convert it to use the compatible version **GetObjectContext( )**, which is declared as follows:

```
HRESULT GetObjectContext (
  IObjectContext** ppObjectContext
);
```

As is obvious from the above listing, and in contrast to **CoGetObjectContext( )**, **GetObjectContext( )** doesn't even give you a choice as to which interface to return.

The resulting **Reserve( )** function code would look as follows:

```
// IReservationSystem
public:
  STDMETHODIMP Reserve(/*[in]*/ IReservation* reservation)
  {
    USES_CONVERSION;
    HRESULT hr;
    CComPtr<IReservationTransfer> ptr_reservation_transfer = NULL;
    CComBSTR message;
    CComBSTR titlebar;

#if W2K_ONLY
    CComPtr<IContextState> context_state = NULL;
#else
    CComPtr<IObjectContext> object_context = NULL;
#endif

    // Get our object context
#if W2K_ONLY
    hr = CoGetObjectContext(IID_IObjectContext,
      reinterpret_cast<void**>(&context_state) );
    // Should be null anyway but set explicitly because
    // we count on it later on.
    if (FAILED(hr))
      context_state = NULL;
    else
    {
      hr = context_state->SetDeactivateOnReturn(VARIANT_TRUE);
    }
#else
    hr = GetObjectContext(&object_context);
    // Should be null anyway but set explicitly because
```

```
    // we count on it later on.
    if (FAILED(hr))
      object_context = NULL;
#endif

    // In order to enable none COM+/MTS hosted execution
    // ignore the inability to not acquire the context
    // or the inability to handle JIT.
    hr = S_OK;

    titlebar.LoadString(IDS_PROJNAME);
    hr = reservation->get_Summary(&message.m_str);

    if(SUCCEEDED(hr))
    {
      hr = CoGetObject(L"queue:"
        L"ComputerName=Rambler,"
        L"Label=\"Reservation Transfer\""
        L"/new:ReservationTransferSvr.ReservationTransfer",
        NULL, __uuidof(IReservationTransfer),
        reinterpret_cast<void**>(&ptr_reservation_transfer));
        if(SUCCEEDED(hr))
          hr = ptr_reservation_transfer->Confirm(reservation);

        if(ptr_reservation_transfer!=NULL)
          ptr_reservation_transfer.Release();
#if !W2K_ONLY
        // Reset hr as it is not required that queued
        // components be supported.
        hr = S_OK;
#endif
    }


    ATLASSERT(SUCCEEDED(hr));

    if(SUCCEEDED(hr))
    {
      CComBSTR bstr_date;
      CComVariant var_arrival_date;
      CComVariant var_departure_date;

      reservation->get_ArrivalDate(&bstr_date);
      var_arrival_date = bstr_date;
      reservation->get_DepartureDate(&bstr_date);
```

```
        var_departure_date = bstr_date;

        hr = var_arrival_date.ChangeType(VT_DATE);

        if(SUCCEEDED(hr))
          hr = var_departure_date.ChangeType(VT_DATE);

        if( FAILED(hr)
          || (var_departure_date.date<var_arrival_date.date) )
        {
          hr = rsReservationDatesWereInvalid;
        }
      }

// Commit or Abort the transaction
#if W2K_ONLY
      if (context_state!=NULL)
      {
        if(SUCCEEDED(hr) )
        {
          hr = context_state->SetMyTransactionVote(TxCommit);
        }
        else
          // Don't reset hr as we want to report the
          // first error even if Abort failed.
          hr = context_state->SetMyTransactionVote(TxAbort);
      }
#else
      if (object_context!=NULL)
      {
        if(SUCCEEDED(hr) )
        {
          hr = object_context->SetComplete();
        }
        else
          // Don't reset hr as we want to report the
          // first error even if Abort failed.
          object_context->SetAbort();
      }
#endif

      if(SUCCEEDED(hr))
        MessageBox(NULL, OLE2T(message),
          OLE2T(titlebar), 0);
      else
```

```
  {
    if(hr = rsReservationDatesWereInvalid)
      MessageBox(NULL, _T("The reservation dates were invalid."),
        OLE2T(titlebar), 0);
    else
    {
      _com_error err(hr);
      MessageBox(NULL, err.ErrorMessage(),
        OLE2T(titlebar), 0);
    }
  }

  return hr;

}
```

Because **IObjectContext** is fully supported in Windows 2000, using **IObjectContext** may even be preferable to using the newer Windows 2000–only interfaces in general. How long such compatibility will last into future operating systems is, of course, somewhat suspect, and if you require other Windows 2000 services, you might as well use the newer versions. In the code above, you could convert the queued components call to a **CoCreateInstance( )**, in which case you would utilize the component but without the queued functionality, rather than simply ignoring the fact that the **ReservationTransfer** component is called. Of course, without Windows 2000 support, you will also have to change the **HotelReservation.exe** application to use the CLSID of the **ReservationSystem** rather than the **ReservationSystemEventClass**, as COM+ event services are not supported under Windows NT 4.0.

You will also have to add **mtx.lib mtxguid.lib delayimp.lib /delayload:mtxex.dll** as outlined above when describing the various wizard changes (in the **ReservationSystemSvr.dll**, **Rpcrt4.lib** was used in place of **mtxguid.lib** in order to access some API for the ContextHelper class). Note that these library additions cause a linker warning when they are not used; so when you change the **_WIN32_WINNT #define** to 0x0500, this linker error will occur.

```
#define STRICT
#ifndef _WIN32_WINNT
#define _WIN32_WINNT 0x0400
#endif
```

```
#define _ATL_APARTMENT_THREADED

#define W2K_ONLY _WIN32_WINNT >= 0x0500

#include <atlbase.h>
```

Above is the **W2K_ONLY** macro definition within **stdafx.h**. Now, to switch from Windows 2000–only to NT 4.0–compatible code, simply change **_WIN32_WINNT** from 0x0500 back to 0x0400 in **stdafx.h**.

One final note about using alternative operating systems with COM+: Clearly, none of the COM+ functionality can be achieved directly on any operating system except Windows 2000 or later. For example, you cannot install an event class without Windows 2000. However, much of the Windows 2000 functionality can be achieved using DCOM. For example, the client application **HotelReservation.exe** could easily be run from Windows 95 with DCOM installed. You could then configure the Windows 95 machine to instantiate the event class installed on a remote Windows 2000 machine and achieve full publish/subscribe functionality, with the only drawback being the DCOM time delay and network dependency. Even transaction support could be achieved via DCOM calls to a Windows 2000 machine hosting the transaction-enabled components.

Final Thoughts

You have come a long way since Chapter 1. As you have seen, COM+ offers the programmer remarkable power. If you have read and worked through the examples in the preceding chapters, you are ready to take control of that power. Like many things, programming is best learned by doing, and a good way to reinforce what you have learned is to write several of your own COM+ components, experimenting with different features and approaches. Although COM+ is a challenging environment, it is worth whatever effort it takes to master it.

As the art of programming continues to evolve, you can expect COM+-based solutions to increase. COM+ offers a resilient, reliable way to construct programs that utilize component methodology. Because of the location transparency that is inherently built into COM+, programming solutions can be easily adapted for nearly any computing and networking environment. Because of its support for queued components, transactions, role-based security, and so on, COM+ is integral to enterprise computing. Is COM+ in nearly every programmer's future? The answer is a resounding Yes!

Index

Symbols

A

B

D

G

H

I

J

K

L

M

O

T